ROBERT PAYNE

THE RISE AND FALL OF STALIN

UNABRIDGED

D1387309

PAN BOOKS LTD : LONDON

First published in UK 1966 by W. H. Allen & Co.

This edition published 1968 by Pan Books Ltd.,
33 Tothill Street, London, S.W.1

330 02146 X

Printed in Great Britain by
Richard Clay (The Chaucer Press) Ltd., Bungay, Suffolk

ACKNOWLEDGEMENT

Thanks are due to the following for permission to reproduce photographs:

Margaret Bourke-White, *Time-Life*
Wide World Photos
Hoover Institution on War, Revolution and Peace,
  Stanford University
The U.S. Army
The Imperial War Museum
Pictorial Parade

CONTENTS

THE RISE AND FALL
OF STALIN

INTRODUCTION

> *As they carried him out of the mausoleum,*
> *there came through the chinks of the coffin*
> *a small breath of steam.*
> *But the man inside remained silent –*
> *threateningly silent,*
> *Sullenly clenching his fists,*
> *those embalmed fists,*
> *While he pressed himself against the chinks,*
> *pretending to be dead . . .*

SO THE RUSSIAN POET Evgeny Yevtushenko described the strange scene when the body of Stalin was removed from the Lenin mausoleum on the Red Square in Moscow one winter's day in 1961. Only a few hours before Stalin had been lying under a sheet of crystal, a reddish light shining on his wrinkled face, with banners around him, near the body of Lenin. The son of an obscure cobbler, he had become during the last years of his life the most powerful man on earth. No emperor had ever enjoyed the power he possessed. He had taken the world by the throat, and forced it to do his will. He was one of the world-shakers, and when he died in 1953 it was thought proper that his remains should be exhibited as an object of reverence and worship in the Lenin mausoleum, the holy of holies of the Soviet empire. Now he was being removed to a burial place reserved for lesser heroes of the revolution.

When Stalin's body was removed from the mausoleum, obscure and long-forgotten rites of expiation were being invoked. A dead god was being transformed into a dead man, a dead emperor was being dethroned, a dead criminal was being executed. The ritual murder of a dead murderer was being performed, as it might have been performed among ancient Scythian tribesmen. But far more than a ritual murder was at stake. The Supreme Soviet and the Central Committee, which decreed the punishment now being inflicted on the corpse of Stalin, were attempting to absolve themselves from responsibility for his crimes. They were saying: 'We are not responsible, we are casting him away, he is not one of us! He committed such terrible crimes that we will have none of him.' For nearly thirty years Stalin had ruled tyrannically over Russia. History, too, was being consigned to oblivion.

There were many besides Yevtushenko who believed that nothing was changed by the act of removing Stalin to a burial place a hundred yards from the Lenin mausoleum. He was still alive, his influence was still spreading over Russia. His fists were clenched, he was watching everything that happened through the chinks of the coffin and he was only pretending to be dead.

In the following pages I have attempted to draw a portrait of the living Stalin, who pretends to be dead. I wanted to see him as he was, face to face, when he was in command of Russia's destiny, and to learn what became of him after his death, and how he died his many deaths. I especially wanted to see him going about his daily affairs, sustaining himself, as men do, on his hopes and ambitions, his pleasures and affections. There was a time when his name inspired the utmost fear, the utmost reverence; he was adored as men have rarely been adored, and cursed as they have rarely been cursed. Few men in history have begun so obscurely and risen to such heights of power and eminence. By what accidents, what innate talents did he achieve his high position? I wanted to know why he behaved as he did, and how he succeeded in dominating a vast and virile country for nearly thirty years.

In the nature of things a life of Stalin is not for those with weak nerves. Terror, naked and unadorned, was his accomplice; the terrors of the day and night stalked through his life. There were no treacheries or cruelties he was incapable of performing, no vows or promises he was incapable of breaking. There was something terrifyingly mechanical in his murders, so that he comes at last to resemble the harrowing machine in Franz Kafka's story 'In the Penal Colony', which inscribed on the body of the condemned man a labyrinth of mysterious lines pricked out with needles. When an explorer came upon the machine, he asked for an explanation of the inscriptions written in blood. 'It's no calligraphy for schoolchildren,' said the officer. 'It needs to be studied closely.'

So with Stalin. What he wrote on the living body of Russia was no calligraphy for schoolchildren, and needs to be studied closely. We need to know how he rose to power, and what he did with his power, and what wounds he left, and whether they can be healed. We need to know, too, how he bent his accomplices to his will, and why he visited so much punishment on his own people, and why he went to such pains to create his own legend. Was he an isolated phenomenon, or a portent of worse things to come? Who were his ancestors, and who became his heirs? They are questions of some importance, since over large areas of the world his influence can still be felt.

How it could have happened that a man of Stalin's intellectual attainments could have ruled over so many people for so long a time, and murdered so many people, and caused so much harm and havoc in the world, may never be wholly explained. Here and there we shall find dark areas in his life where we cannot penetrate. Shadows fall over him; he vanishes; out of the darkness comes a voice pleading for pity. When we see him again he is the genial storekeeper puffing calmly on his pipe, wondering what all the fuss was about. Yet there were times when he seems to have known he was evil, a curse on an unhappy land.

Though he liked to enshroud himself in mystery, and enjoyed all the arts of silence, nevertheless he was continually revealing himself. We know what he was doing through most of his mature life. There exists a precise chronology of his actions, which is as interesting for its deliberate omissions and inaccuracies as for its repeated claims of having performed great and daring acts at critical moments of Russian history. He wrote much about himself, and especially enjoyed rewriting the books he commissioned others to write for him. His style is readily recognizable. He will insert a paragraph here and there or rewrite a whole chapter to suit his imaginary portrait of himself. So we find in books ostensibly written by Barbusse, Yaroslavsky and Beria long passages of authentic autobiography. Like all dictators he took a deep pleasure in reviewing his life.

We have his early poems, his speeches, articles and proclamations, the testimonies of those who served him and of those who suffered at his hands, together with the reminiscences of innumerable diplomats, correspondents and party officials. We have an abundance of films and photographs, and there exists a generous collection of tape recordings of his speeches. Only a handful of his letters have been published, but he did not express himself well in letters and it is unlikely that he maintained a large correspondence. Lenin kept voluminous notebooks, and his preliminary sketches for articles and speeches occasionally survive, permitting us to catch his thought on the wing. We have nothing like this from the pen of Stalin. Lenin enjoyed writing, and his collected works amount to fifty fat volumes in small type. The collected works of Stalin, who wrote with some difficulty, amount to thirteen thin volumes in large type. Though he was constantly revising and distorting his own writings, he gives a clear image of himself and the distortions follow an established pattern. He never learned to hide himself, though he spent a good deal of his life making the attempt.

Like Lenin he was a man of astonishing energy and determination, but he had none of Lenin's gift for brilliant improvisation and never knew when to stop. Lenin was supremely indifferent to popular fame; for Stalin fame was the spur, and all his energies were subordinated to the creation and embellishment of his legend. He lived long enough to believe the fictions he had invented about himself, even those which were demonstrably untrue; and having a distaste for the truth and a love of falsehood he came inevitably to live in a no man's land where truth and falsehood became meaningless terms. Lenin attracted men by his charm, by his enthusiasm and by his towering intellectual attainments. Stalin had neither charm, nor enthusiasm, nor any real intellectual pretensions. His gifts were of a minor order. Lenin called him *grub*, meaning that he was coarse, but that was to underestimate his talents. Stalin raised coarseness to the pitch of genius.

Throughout his life everyone underestimated him, until it was too late. Wolf-like, he would prowl in the shadows, a ghostly shape seen in the distance. People became accustomed to his ghostly presence, and they were surprised when he came in for the kill.

He belongs to a new species – the mass-murderer, who kills without compunction and without enjoyment. He murdered by habit or out of laziness, often without thought, because murder often solved problems which could be solved with more difficulty by hard thinking. He was so ruthless in his betrayals and so adept at murder that he came to resemble a force of nature rather than a human being; and he had no more pity than a hurricane. For nearly thirty years this hurricane swept over Russia, crushing everything in its path. He came to power when the revolution was exhausted and betrayed, and then destroyed it. Out of its ruins he built a monument to himself.

It is an enduring monument, and we would be foolish if we thought his death had put an end to it. He is one of those who are always returning from the dead. His ghost, his energy, remains. His successors have denied him, but they speak with his authentic voice, imitate his gestures and console themselves for his absence by embarking on the same crimes. There was a time not long ago when they called themselves his faithful comrades-in-arms. Even now they cannot escape from his domination.

So I have studied Stalin as a man, but with the knowledge that he does not fit into any of the ordinary patterns of human behaviour. He was larger than life and almost as large as death. The convulsions he inflicted on his country had little to do with Marxist theory, of which he was surprisingly ignorant; they arose from his incredible criminality, his fatal nihilism and habitual ruthlessness, which placed him outside the context of humanity. This small, brooding, pock-marked man with a crooked arm, black teeth and yellow eyes, was the greatest tyrant of his time, and perhaps of all time.

THE KNIGHT IN THE LEOPARD SKIN

It is hard to deal with the heart of man; it is mad alike in grief and joy; it is always wounded, the passing world is never whole for him. He can only trust the world who is his own foe.

—RUSTHAVELI, in his epic poem,
The Knight in the Leopard Skin

THE KNIGHT IN THE LEOPARD SKIN

OVER THE LAND of Georgia between the Black Sea and the Caspian the winds blow clean, and the vines and wheat grow in abundance, and there are few days in the year when there is no sunshine. The air shimmers with the whiteness of the snows of the High Caucasus, and all of Georgia lies on the southern slopes of those fiercely cragged mountains. The rivers flow east and west, swiftly flashing, cutting deep gorges into the reddish-yellow earth. The rains come in late spring, the autumns are mild, the winters sunlit. On the plains the shepherds and drovers guard their herds, and orchards flower by the rivers, and in the high mountains the ibexes with huge and heavy horns decorate the skyline. It is a smiling land, very fertile, worked by an industrious and pleasure-loving people. The ancient Greeks called it Colchis, the land of the Golden Fleece.

In Georgia everything seems to have been devised to give men pleasure. The shapes of the mountains and of the terraced plains and of the tumultuous rivers have a pleasing luxuriance. Imagine southern Spain with the Alps behind it, and you have Georgia. It is not quite paradise, for sometimes inexplicable savage winds rise in the gorges and hurtle along the rivers, destroying everything in their path, and sometimes, too, the leopards descend from the mountains to raid the sheepfolds. In the lowlands there are red vipers.

The mind of a people is coloured by its surroundings, and the Georgians are temperamentally akin to their romantic landscape. They are a dark-eyed people, small and well-built, with the melancholy, exuberance and violence characteristic of people who live in subtropical lands. They delight in gestures, in drinking, in singing and in dressing up. Traditionally, they make better warriors than statesmen, better poets than scholars. They are fond of gallantry, and regard the Russians in much the same way as the Austrians regard Prussians: too sober, too mechanical to be really alive. They have an intensity which disturbs the Russians, and a gaiety which is altogether foreign to the Russian nature. They are quick to take offence, and lavish in their friendships. They are deeply aware of their ancient traditions.

The kingdom of Colchis struck its own silver coins, traded with Persia and Greece and formed an alliance with Corinth. Its wealth came from its wheat, which may have been the Golden Fleece of the ancient legends. When Byzantium became the capital of the Roman Empire, Georgia became Christian with its own church, its own patriarchs and its own saints. Christianity indeed gave unity to a people who were continually being invaded, for a land so rich inevitably became a prey to conquerors. The Sassanian Persians came in the sixth century, the Arabs in the seventh, the Seljuk Turks in the eleventh. Each in turn ravaged the country, but the Arabs were the most merciless. Then under Queen Tamara in the twelfth century the tide turned, and the Georgians themselves became conquerors, occupying Armenia and the northern Caucasus, and extending their rule over large areas of Persia. A magnificent civilization came to birth during the Queen's reign.

From all over the Middle East philosophers and artists flocked to her court. There was a great revival of learning, as Greek, Arab and Persian works were translated into the Georgian tongue. A munificent treasury permitted the building of innumerable churches elaborately decorated with frescoes and mosaics. For thirty years Georgia seemed to be the centre of the earth.

The queen was intelligent, beautiful, high-spirited and very feminine. The court poets flattered her, and among the most disarming of these poets was Shotha Rusthaveli, who dedicated to her his epic poem *The Knight in the Leopard Skin* written between AD 1198 and 1207. The poem begins with the coming to the throne of a legendary Arabian princess, evidently modelled on Queen Tamara, 'whose munificence was like a snowstorm whirling down from the sky'. Her eyes, says the poet, shone like suns and her black eyelashes pierced the heart. Veiled in gossamer silks, and robed in ermine, she appeared as an incarnation of merciless beauty.

But it was not so much for the sake of the visionary queen that generations of Georgians read that immensely long epic. They read it chiefly because it celebrated an extraordinary hero called Tariel, the knight in the leopard skin, who combined in himself so many warring virtues and vices that he was like a man torn asunder by his own strangeness. Tariel is the knight of the woeful countenance, stronger than a lion, weaker than a woman. He is by turns gentle, affectionate, callous, passionate, ingeniously treacherous, long-suffering, murderously cruel. When we see him first, he is weeping tears of blood for the sake of the long-lost Princess Nesthan-Daredjan, who has been made captive by the demons and imprisoned in the mysterious fortress of Kadjethi. Then he vanishes, and the knight Avthandil goes in search of him, only to find that he is one of those who leave no traces on the earth. He vanished as mysteriously as he appeared.

Tariel is the spirit of evil, of brooding vengeance, of easy conquests, of a pride so ferocious that it is always close to destroying him. He can kill a lion with his bare hands and slice a man in two with a single stroke of his whip. There is something primitive about him, and at the same time he possesses an air of excessive refinement. After many years of wandering, Avthandil met him by the purest chance in a dark forest, and came to know him as well as any man can come to know another. Avthandril says of him: 'Longing slays him, and lack of the sight of his gravedigger.'

In love with longing and in love with death, Tariel pursues his adventures, weeps, dreams of Nesthan-Daredjan, slaughters singlehandedly any army which strays across his path, and calls upon God to witness that no hero has ever suffered so deeply. Death-defying, he belongs to death. He descends from Prometheus, the Titan chained to the Caucasian rock, the spirit of freedom channelled into a relentless will, as vast as the mountain peak on which he dwells.

Greek mythology, Persian legends, Byzantine epics, ancient folklore all went into the composition of that portrait. Rusthaveli writes in a classic tradition and borrows from whatever source pleases him, but what emerges is a living portrait of a man haunted by demons and driving himself to the uttermost. He is the first of the purely romantic heroes. Six hundred years before the Byronic hero emerged in England, he had already come to birth in Georgia.

Once when he was asked why he was weeping, Tariel answered: 'I weep because I am thinking of my destroyer.' If he could, he would twist God's neck and bring down the heavens in ruins, because there must be some punishment reserved for the God who threatened him and kept him so far from his beloved. Soviet critics have observed with some satisfaction that Christ is never mentioned in the poem, and that when Tariel addresses himself to God, he is addressing himself to the God of warriors. But *The Knight in the Leo-*

pard Skin is not wholly pagan. His nobility and generosity and the sweet temper which sometimes succeeds in blunting his implacable desire for revenge have Christian sources. It is because he is half-pagan and half-Christian that he belongs to no man's land and feels that every hand is against him.

The minds and spirits of Georgians are steeped in knowledge of Tariel. For them, even today, Tariel represents the national genius in its purest form, so that there is scarcely a Georgian whose imagination has not in some way been profoundly affected by the image of the hero clothed in a leopard skin and riding his black horse in the teeth of the world's tempests. For them, there is something immensely satisfying in the portrait of the restless hero who fears no one on earth and finds cause for melancholy even in his own fearlessness.

Even in translation *The Knight in the Leopard Skin* is a work of quite astonishing magnificence. No other work by Rusthaveli has come down to us, and little enough is known about him. He appeared during the brief cultural renaissance which flourished in the reign of Queen Tamara. There is a legend that he became treasurer of her court, fell hopelessly in love with the Queen, and when his suit was rejected, he abandoned his high position, and became a monk in Jerusalem. In AD 1221 the Mongols invaded Georgia and sacked the cities. The cultural renaissance of Georgia came to an end as suddenly as it had begun.

From the beginning the Georgians were aware that Rusthaveli had created a masterpiece. He was another Homer, and they regarded him with bemused awe and veneration. Seven cities claimed to be his birthplace. Like Homer, he gave shape and form to the national ethos. Consciously or unconsciously, the Georgians follow in the footsteps of Tariel.

From Tariel's soliloquies, and from some of the sayings of those he encountered, it is possible to compose a kind of romantic catechism:

My heart was born in the embers of a glowing furnace. My path has been cut off, and I am caught in a snare.

The world always does evil. The sparks from its anvil burn me with eternal fires.

To whom God gives a young cypress, from him He withdraws the spear, though at first He lacerates the heart with it. He will grant us His mercy, He will thunder it from heaven, He will turn our sorrow into joy.

I forsook the haunts of men; the retreats of goats and deer seemed a fitting abode for me; I roamed and trod the plains below and the hills above.

I am sundered from life, and death has become shy of me.

To cure me seemed hard even to Him who created me – therefore I roamed wild in the fields.

Of all the foes the most hateful is the friend-foe.

Woe, O passing world, in falsehood thou art like Satan, none can know thee well, where thy treachery is.

The wise know the world, therefore they despise it: to them it is contemptible.

It is hard to deal with the heart of man; it is mad alike in grief and joy; it is always wounded, the passing world is never whole for him. He can only trust the world who is his own foe.

He can only trust the world who is his own foe ... So speaks Tariel, Prince of India, to the Arabian knight Avthandil, and both, of course, are Georgians aware of the desperate feuds and invasions which raged for centuries in Georgia, the families divided, at the mercy of conflicting loyalties. The theme of the epic is treachery. The knight of the woeful countenance, feeling himself assailed by treachery on all sides, abandons the world and wreaks his vengeance on the traitors. Yet, at the very end, when he comes to grips with the traitors, they seem to exist only in his imagination, and the least convincing verses in the poem describe how Tariel stormed the fortress of the treacherous demons who had carried off his beloved Nesthan-Daredjan.

When at last he discovers that almost inaccessible fortress, the demons fall like ninepins. He kills ten thousand of them singlehandedly, wading through mountains of corpses, splintered armour and sword blades. He enters the fortress with his face concealed in his helmet, a dark and mysterious figure, more like a shadow than a man, and he discards the helmet only when he catches sight of Nesthan-Daredjan. The lovers hurl themselves into one another's arms and weep for joy. The epic ends with the marriage of Tariel and Nesthan-Daredjan and the swearing of eternal brotherhood between Tariel, Avthandil and Phridon, the King of the Seas, who helped to conquer the fortress. As sovereigns, they rule the world peacefully between them. Then, says the poet, 'they poured down mercy like snow on all alike, they enriched orphans and widows and the poor did not beg, they terrified evildoers, the lambs did not suck from strange ewes, within their dominions the goat and the wolf fed together.'

The poem ends with the dream of paradise, and we are far removed from the brooding and savage Tariel who had brought the dream about.

Stalin read *The Knight in the Leopard Skin* both in his boyhood and when he was a student at Tiflis, as we know from his friend Kapanadze, who claims to have lent him a copy of the book, but even if he had not read the poem, he would have been unable to escape its influence. Tariel was in the air men breathed, in the blood flowing through their veins, in the shapes of the mountains, in the colours of the Georgian earth. Tariel was unescapable, and one could no more escape from him than one could escape from oneself.

For most Georgians Tariel exists as a figure of romance, penetrating their lives and thoughts. They remember his audacity and wilfulness, his reckless courage in the service of his beloved, his careless generosity and self-sacrificing devotion, forgetting the other side of the coin. There were two Tariels, one merciful, the other vengeful, and they were both contained in the same person. What is singular in Stalin is how closely he came to resemble the dark Tariel, brooding, vengeful, contemptuous of human life, dreaming of world conquest. He, too, could have said: 'I am sundered from life, and death has become shy of me.' The merciless Tariel finds his latter-day exemplar in Stalin, who also fought against demons – the demons who walk in the sunlight and the even more dangerous demons who take up their abode in the imagination.

This is not to say that Stalin modelled himself on Tariel, but there were elements of Tariel in him. He became the dark Tariel of the interminable feuds, treacheries and devastations, who thought nothing of slicing a man in two with a whip if he got in the way, forgetting the bright Tariel who lived only to free the princess from her dungeon and who wept inconsolably because he could not reach out to her. There was no nobility in him, no kindness, no gentleness. While he resembles the dark Tariel, he also resembles the typical Georgian *abrek*, the outlaw turned highwayman, who lives in the mountains and makes a living by raiding the peaceful villagers at night, killing them in their beds and vanishing in the dawn. Sometimes, too, these *abreks* would attack Tsarist convoys. In the popular imagination they were endowed with superhuman courage and extraordinary daring, and they were always represented as being completely merciless.

In that restless country there were always outlaws. History and geography conspired to make them inevitable; and they became more prominent and more powerful after the Russian conquest. So many tribes went to form Georgia, so many peoples were at one another's throats, that it would have been marvellous beyond belief if there had not been a hard core of lawlessness. In a speech delivered in 1918 Stalin spoke of the variety of peoples in his homeland. He mentioned the Russians, Georgians, Armenians, Azerbaijanis, Tatars, Turks, Lezghians, Ingushes, Ossets, Chechens, Abkhazians, Greeks and Kumyks, adding that this was only the beginning. At one time or another all these people had been conquerors, and when the conquerors were themselves conquered, they left small enclaves in the valleys of Georgia. Until recently there were villages within ten miles of one another which spoke languages so completely different that they had no means of communication. Georgia is a place where all the conquerors have come to grief.

In Georgia Stalin spent the first twenty years of his life. His habits of thought, his manners, his tastes, his rough humour were essentially those of a Georgian *abrek*, and he liked to surround himself with Georgian advisers, so that the Russians came ruthfully to the conclusion that having been conquered by the Bolsheviks, they had seen the Bolsheviks conquered by Georgians. To the end of his life Stalin spoke Russian with a marked Georgian accent. It was so heavy an accent that many who heard him found him almost incomprehensible.

He wrote his early romantic poems in Georgian, and when he wrote his harsh laws, they, too, had a Georgian look about them, as though they had been written by an *abrek* turned feudal prince reigning over an obscure village in the Georgian highlands. He possessed, too, the characteristic Georgian belief in the necessity to acquiesce to the feudal order; and he established his own court and his own feudal order with clearly marked ranks and divisions. When he ordered poets to write odes comparing him to the sun, and when he gave himself portentous titles and honours, he was not necessarily the victim of megalomania. Feudal princes in Georgia, ruling over a few square miles of territory, had done the same, and he was merely following in their tradition. Within the hard, mechanical communist, there was always the dark Tariel dreaming his ruinous dreams.

We cannot understand Stalin unless we see him in his Georgian setting. He was, above all, the child of that beautiful and ravaged land.

THE CHILDHOOD OF JOSEPH DJUGASHVILI

'ALL HAPPY FAMILIES resemble one another,' wrote Tolstoy, 'but all unhappy families are unhappy in their own special way.'

The family of Joseph Vissarionovich Djugashvili was unhappy in its own special way. The boy's father was a drunkard, a spendthrift, a man who possessed a violent temper, with no feeling for his wife or his son; he beat them unmercifully. He was a cobbler by trade, with a small shop in an obscure street on the outskirts of Gori. The boy's mother was a quiet, withdrawn, deeply religious woman, beautiful in her youth, who found her chief pleasure in attending church services and in contributing out of her sparse earnings to the upkeep of the priests. She earned money by performing menial tasks in the houses of the rich, laundering, baking bread and running errands. She was also an occasional seamstress, and one of the boy's childhood friends, who was not unsympathetic to him, remembered that she sometimes earned a living by cutting, sewing and laundering underwear. She was a proud woman and kept her sufferings to herself.

Of Vissarion Ivanovich Djugashvili and his origins almost nothing is known except that he was born to a peasant family in the village of Didi-Lilo, in the hill country a few miles from Gori. It is a tiny village lying in the general direction of Tiflis. The American photographer Margaret Bourke-White, who visited the village in 1932, found thirty or forty peasants with wide foreheads, deep-set eyes and strong Asiatic features all answering to the name of Djugashvili. They pointed to a primitive hut consisting of a square hole cut into the earth, roofed with a few wooden beams, with only a chink for the smoke to come out, and claimed that this was the birthplace of Stalin. When she returned nine years later she learned that there was rivalry between the citizens of Didi-Lilo and Gori, for both claimed the honour of being the authentic birthplace. Since the earlier claim was made for Didi-Lilo, it would seem likely that he was born there. Stalin himself claimed that he was born in Gori.

In Gori so many races had mingled that the bloodlines were confused. At various times it had been conquered by

Ossets, Imeretians and Persians. Armenians and Jews had settled there. The town, founded in the eleventh century, was famous for its sweet-scented apples and plump vines, but in the nineteenth century it owed its importance chiefly to its cotton fields and the fact that it was the last stop before Tiflis on the Transcaucasian railroad. Tiflis was thirty miles away to the east.

Of the origins of Stalin's mother, born Ekaterina Georgievna Geladze, nothing is known except that she is said to have been the daughter of a peasant serf from the village of Gambareuli.

When Ekaterina Geladze married Vissarion Djugashvili in 1874, she was a girl of seventeen and her husband was twenty-two. The first three children are said to have died in childbirth, Joseph, born on December 21st, 1879, being the only child to grow to maturity. Vissarion died when the boy was in his eleventh year, and Ekaterina survived her husband by nearly fifty years. She was a small, fragile, indomitable woman, who remained deeply religious throughout her life and always wore a black nun-like costume. Except for a single brief visit to Moscow, she never left her native Georgia. Her last years were spent in two rooms set aside for her in the Governor's Palace at Tiflis, and there at the age of eighty-one she died in 1938. She was buried according to the rites of the Orthodox Church in the Cemetery of King David at Tiflis.

The family of Lenin was a happy one. They belonged to the gentry and were accustomed to moderate comforts, with nurses, servants and coachmen to do their bidding. They spent their long summer holidays on their country estate, played the piano, spoke French, German, Swedish and Russian at table, and rather self-consciously enjoyed an air of quiet cultivation. They received the latest magazines from Moscow and eagerly discussed the latest ideas. Wearying of ideas, they would play croquet in the garden or gather fruit in the orchard. It was not unlike the families in Chekhov's plays.

The family of Stalin might have come out of Gorky's play *The Lower Depths*. It was brutally unhappy. They lived in grinding poverty, constantly in debt. Sometimes the neighbours would have pity on the struggling seamstress and her undernourished son; and their pity may have done more harm to Joseph than the beatings he received from his father. Sometimes poverty drove Ekaterina close to madness, and we hear of her wandering through the streets with her hair dishevelled, crying, praying, singing and muttering to herself. From a very early age the boy knew what it was to live a)ne in the world.

When he was very young, they settled in Gori in a house tl 't was another hovel. It was about fifteen feet square, with a oor of crude brick. There was an earth-walled cellar and a mall loft. In the dimly lit kitchen there was a stove, an i ι stovepipe, a small table, three or four wooden stools, a c an covered with a straw mat. There was no sanitation. I ring the day light came through a shutterless window, at 1 ht there was the yellow flame of a kerosene lamp. A small am trickled down a sloping alleyway outside. The smell ι brick, fetid water and damp earth hung over the hovel.

Today this hovel is protected from the elements by a glass and metal canopy resting on marble pillars, and there is a fading notice which says in Georgian and Russian: 'Great Stalin, leader of the workers of the world, was born and lived here 1879–1893.' The canopy was built at the orders of Lavrenty Beria in 1937, at a time when it was still obligatory to call Stalin 'great'. Today few visitors come to the shrine. Dust gathers on the floor, the walls are beginning to crumble, and soon the pathetic hovel will become a ruin, suffering the fate reserved for the shrines of gods who are no longer wanted by mankind. The nearby Stalin Museum has already been converted into a Museum of the Revolution, with only a few faded photographs on the walls demonstrating that he played some not unimportant role in his country's history.

It is worth while to look carefully at this hovel, for it is not at all what it seems to be. In its misery and poverty it looks commonplace enough, like a shed put up at the bottom of a garden and then forgotten. This obscure shack in an obscure street of shacks became a battlefield in a war between a boy and his father, and there is scarcely anyone on earth who has not in some way been affected by that war.

There are no photographs of Stalin's father, and we can only guess at his appearance from a brief description left by Joseph Iremashvili, the friend of Stalin's youth. He describes the father as a heavy-set, imposing man, with thick black eyebrows and a black bristling moustache, who wore the conventional dress of a Georgian – a long, knee-length *tchoka*, blue trousers thrust into knee boots and a fur cap. This is all he could remember – the three heavy black lines etched on a dark face – and it is almost enough. The two boys were of the same age, and it could not be expected of them that they could remember in any detail the face of a man who died when they were ten years old.

Perhaps this was all Stalin remembered, for he had every reason to forget. According to Iremashvili, who knew the family well and was constantly in and out of the house, the father beat the son vengefully, remorselessly, with a kind of brooding, deliberate passion, without pleasure and without any sense of guilt or wrongdoing, for no other purpose than to provide himself with some excitement in an otherwise empty and purposeless existence. The result was inevitable. The boy learned to hate. Most of all he hated his father, but gradually this hatred expanded until it included all other fathers, all other men.

'I never saw him crying,' Iremashvili relates, and the statement has the ring of authenticity. The boy became hardened by his beatings, and became in the end terrifyingly indifferent to cruelty. His face and body were covered with bruises, but he was determined not to surrender. Somehow he would survive his father, but in order to survive it was necessary to become as brutal as his father. He was too puny to hit back, but he could provide himself with a brutal protective armour of indifference and scorn. 'Those undeserved and fearful beatings,' says Iremashvili, 'made the boy as hard and heartless as his father.'

There were few consolations. The little street on which he lived was called the Sobornaya, or Church Street, and there was a church about a hundred yards away. Here he sang in the choir when he was a schoolboy, and the liturgies so deeply affected him that their rhythms and phrasing appeared in his own writings long after he learned to celebrate another religion altogether. In the Greek Orthodox church the altar lies hidden behind the iconostasis; much of the chanting takes place behind this mysterious barrier separating the priests from the worshippers. God is infinitely remote, all powerful, unyielding in His demand to be perpetually adored, and in many subtle ways this God influenced and coloured his thoughts when many years later he set in motion the long and complicated processes of self-deification.

Church was a consolation, for no one beat him in church, no one scorned him or had pity on him. As a choirboy he walked in processions, sang hymns, wore brilliant vestments, and being close to the priests, he was closer to the source of the mystery. His earliest ambition was to be a priest; and his mother looked forward to the time when she would be blessed by her son.

His greatest consolation however was his mother, who worked herself to the bone to provide for him and who lived for him. We are told that she liked bright colours, always had a clean tablecloth on the table, and enjoyed wearing the colourful costume with the long floating veil and rainbow-coloured skirts, which Georgian women wore on feast days and holidays. She was still young when she had trouble with her eyesight, from working at her sewing machine by the light of a kerosene lamp; and she began to wear spectacles. Her love for her son was an intense and possessive love, and she was the only person he loved.

He was seven when he suffered an attack of smallpox, which left disfiguring scars that remained to the end of his life. It must have been a serious attack, for the scars were large and numerous, with the result that when he came to power thousands of photographs of him had to be carefully doctored.

An even more distressing affliction occurred when he was about ten. He only once spoke about it, and then only briefly when he was explaining why, when he was in exile in Siberia during the First World War, he was not called up for military service. He told the story to Anna Alliluieva, his sister-in-law, who published it in her memoirs:

> The left arm of Stalin was badly bent at the elbow. The injury occurred during his childhood. An infection set in, and since there was no one to give it treatment, blood-poisoning followed. Stalin was close to death.
> 'I don't know what saved me,' he told us. 'Either it was due to my healthy organism or to the ointments smeared on it by the village quack, but I got my health back again.'
> The vestiges of that injury remain to the present day.

Anna Alliluieva is a trustworthy witness, all the more so because her memoirs, published in 1946, were banned shortly afterwards on the grounds that she had written too familiarly about Stalin. In fact, she wrote with a kind of distant and troubled affection without familiarity of any kind, and the book was banned because she had simply told the truth.

As a result of the injury Stalin's left arm was some three inches shorter than the right, and he never had complete muscular control of his left hand. At various times he wore a brace to support the elbow; the outline of the brace can be seen in several photographs. A distinguished orthopaedic surgeon has suggested on the basis of Alliluieva's account and a number of photographs that Stalin suffered 'a compound fracture with resultant osteomyelitis and a subsequent hand deformity secondary to disturbance of growth of the arm, the hand deformity being produced by a Volkman's contracture subsequent to improper treatment of the fracture'.

Such a diagnosis is, of course, largely speculative. The medical records of Stalin have never been published, and it is unlikely that they will be published for some years to come. What is certain is that the left arm was warped, lacked the strength of the right arm, and caused him pain and discomfort throughout his life. The awkward shoulder brace was a constant reminder that he suffered from an incurable deformity, and he had only to look at his left hand, which never opened properly, to remember that he was not like other men. He went to considerable trouble to conceal his deformity, which could only be successfully hidden when he was wearing a heavy greatcoat with unusually long sleeves. The crooked arm probably had a profound effect on his emerging character.

There is no clue as to how the injury occurred. It seems likely to have happened as a result of one of the ferocious beatings he received from his father.

There exists a photograph of him taken when he was twelve or thirteen while attending the church school at Gori. It is one of those conventional photographs taken at the end of the school year, with the two teachers sitting in the middle and the pupils clustered round them. One of the teachers is a pleasant open-faced monk in a long flowing gown, while the other with a sterner caste of features wears the ceremonial evening dress which in those days was the customary uniform of executioners and schoolteachers. The pupils look neat and alert, their hair close-cropped or smoothly slicked down. Joseph is seen standing on the top row, his right hand resting on the shoulder of the bearded monk, and although the left hand is invisible there is the characteristic thick bunching of cloth at the left shoulder. We shall see the same bunching in photographs taken more than fifty years later.

Joseph stands out because he is shorter than the other pupils in the top row. The photograph is faded, but the expression on the face can be made out, and it is clear that he is thrusting himself forward. One shoulder is higher than the other, the chin juts out, he has an air of defiance. There is something ungainly and uncomfortable about his posture; he is not at ease.

Iremashvili, who was genuinely fond of him when they were both young, has left a description of him at this time which tallies remarkably with the photograph. He writes: 'He was a scrawny sinewy boy with a long face full of freckles and innumerable pockmarks. His head was somewhat bent back so that his strongly marked nose rose brusquely in the air. The look from his dark-brown Georgian eyes was bold, lively, not one to inspire confidence. His walk with his long, narrow legs had something childlike about it, and this was partly the result of his peculiar way of swinging his long arms and bony, thickly veined hands.'

At first, according to Iremashvili, the boy was cordially disliked in the church school, which he entered in the summer of 1890. There was something strange and forbidding in his manner. He was proud, and showed his pride by rarely speaking, and then always curtly. Generally he stood apart from the games played in the school yard, but once, when invited to fight by Iremashvili, he proved to be an unexpectedly good boxer and wrestler. He gave Iremashvili such a blow in the chest that he was thrown down, and for a while they wrestled in the grass. Although he was small, he was unusually strong, and succeeded in planting his foot on Iremashvili's chest in the posture of triumph common among victorious boys. 'Afterwards we shook hands and kissed.'

It was the beginning of a long friendship. On holidays and sometimes in the afternoons they would wander together in the surrounding countryside. Their favourite haunts were the nearby hills and especially the cone-shaped hill of Gori-Djvari with its ruined yellow-walled citadel and small church said to have been founded by Queen Tamara, or else they went to the abandoned catacomb city of Uplis Tsikhe, meaning 'God's fortress'. These catacombs, carved by unknown hands, honeycombed a cliff which was about an hour's drive from Gori. Gori-Djvari was especially romantic with its fierce battlements and crumbling towers. In their youthful imaginations all legends, all fairy tales began in that ghostly fortress. So Iremashvili tells us, and we can well believe that a medieval castle can fill a child's imagination with the wildest dreams.

The hill was a jungle of oak trees, and they would climb up the steep slope hand in hand, dreaming their lives away, inventing stories about the princes who once ruled from the castle and held the country in fee.

Ghosts lurked in the castle, and there were people in Gori who spoke of having seen the ghosts with their naked eyes. Once people had come from all over Georgia to worship at the shrine of St George, whose relics were kept in the church in a silver reliquary. Queen Tamara once held court there, and Shotha Rusthaveli had recited his poems from the battlements. From the castle gates knights rode down on caparisoned horses, with banners flying, to make war against the infidels. These are not small matters to a child who dreams of a mysterious time when he too will be worthy of knighthood. It was perhaps in unconscious memory of Gori-Djvari that Stalin wrote in one of his first political articles that the party must be 'a fortress, whose gates are opened only to those who are worthy'.

To be worthy, in the eyes of a Georgian schoolboy, was to be a heroic figure like Tariel or his later descendants, the *abreks* of the Caucasus. Dreaming of knights and robber chieftains children can go happily mad; and these heroic tales left an indelible mark on the boy's character.

Joseph was about thirteen when he discovered one of the best of the novels about the *abreks*. It was called *Nunu*, and was written by Alexander Kasbeki (1848–1893) about an *abrek* called Koba and his adventures with his friend Iago, the lover of the beautiful sixteen-year-old Nunu. Koba has all the virtues of the Knight in the Leopard Skin. He is loyal, merciless, chaste, and vengeful. There is nothing he will not do for his friend, but it must be admitted that he fails lamentably to protect Nunu from the designs of a singularly unpleasant police spy called Girgola. The story should be told briefly, for it was to have an incalculable effect on Joseph.

Nunu is the daughter of a poor itinerant musician. Girgola is determined to possess her, and when he is rejected for Iago, the handsome and penniless son of a landowner who has come down in the world, he plots a diabolic revenge. The *abreks* have come down from the mountains and raided a caravan. Girgola informs the local police chief that Iago took part in the raid. Iago is arrested, beaten and tortured, and Nunu is compelled to marry Girgola's half-mad brother; sooner or later Girgola will have Nunu for himself.

Koba learns of Iago's arrest, breaks into the prison and releases him. They take to the mountains and join the shepherds. They can do little to help Nunu, who is raped by Girgola. When she refuses to submit to him further she is flung into a fortress, where she attempts to kill herself. At last Koba and Iago discover where she is, they raid the fortress, kill three guards, and escape with Nunu. But Nunu enjoys her freedom only for a little while. Captured by Girgola, she is reduced to slavery again.

The two *abreks* join the army of the Caucasian chieftain Shamil, and in an engagement with a Cossack patrol kill five Cossacks and run off with their horses. They take the horses to a village inn, thinking they are among friends, but the innkeeper makes contact with the Russians and offers to surrender Koba and Iago. Girgola hears the innkeeper talking with the Russian colonel, for he is in the next room. The inn is surrounded by Cossacks, who set it on fire in the hope of forcing Koba and Iago to surrender. Iago is killed. Koba escapes, vowing vengeance.

Girgola believes that Koba vanished in the flames. He decides to inflict exemplary punishment on Nunu by killing her father at night. When she awakes, she sees her father lying dead beside her, and begs the police to find the murderer. The police arrest her for patricide. She is taken to Vladikavkaz, placed on trial, and sentenced to hard labour in Siberia. Holding a crucifix in her hands, she dies of a broken heart.

Girgola has triumphed, for he has defeated Nunu. On the following day he is travelling in a troika with a local official when a shot rings out from the woods. The official falls dead, and Girgola is mortally wounded. A voice calls from the woods: 'It is I, Koba! You are paying for the life of Iago!' Girgola survives for a few more hours – long enough to confess to the priest that he murdered Nunu's father. His last words are a prayer for help, as he calls upon Nunu and her father to save him.

Nunu is a strange story, not particularly well-written, but possessing the haunting quality which sometimes enters stories where absolute evil and absolute good confront one another. The beautiful, dark, slim-waisted Nunu confronts the bestial

Girgola with the calm of innocence. She is helpless before his rages, and her very helplessness brings about her ruin. Koba enters the story too late to save her. We never see him clearly, and he is never described. He plays on the *bandura*, sings about the heroic deeds of the past, hates the Russians and cheerfully joins forces with Shamil, the enemy of the Tsar. But it is Girgola who is the most memorable figure in the novel; and Stalin, who took the name of Koba from the story, ended by playing the role of Girgola, the police spy, who brought ruin on the family of Nunu.

Koba, of course, was simply Tariel brought up to date. Instead of making war on the mysterious and far-off demon-guarded fortress of Kadjethi, he makes war on the prisons and fortresses of Russian invaders. He is more modest than Tariel who slew ten thousand demons in a morning, but he is the equal of fifty Russians. Sometimes Tariel appears to be no more than a power of nature, a strange shivering in the sky. No one had ever seen him except with the eyes of the imagination, but every rough mountaineer with a gun under his arm resembled Koba in appearance, though he might lack Koba's ferocious daring.

Joseph modelled himself on Koba, dreamed about him, invented new stories about him, and never tired of speaking about him, in exactly the same way as an American child will dream about Superman. It was a form of madness common among Georgian children, thousands of them dreaming the same dreams. Iremashvili has described what happened after Joseph read the novel *Nunu*:

> Koba, the hero of Kasbeki's novel *Nunu*, became his dream image, his divinity, the meaning of his life. He set his heart on becoming a second Koba, as famous a fighter and hero as the first. He wanted to recreate the image of Koba in himself. From this time onward he called himself Koba, and permitted no one to address him by any other name. His face shone with pride and joy when we called him Koba. Soso preserved this name for many years, and it became his first pseudonym when he began to write and carry out propaganda work for the Social Democratic party.

Iremashvili is not our only authority for the statement that the boy deliberately modelled himself on Koba. Other young students remembered his peculiar addiction to the

name, which Stalin was to use in a multitude of forms –
Koba, Ko, K. St, K. Kato, K – until it was buried altogether
under the weight of the final pseudonym. To this day in
Georgia he is known as Koba-Stalin.

It is not surprising that a schoolboy should fall in love
with a character in a novel and attempt to model himself on
the character. What is surprising is that he should have been
so persistent, so determined to recreate the image of Koba
in himself. Of all the influences which shaped him the image
of Koba, the ferociously daring bandit, was probably the
strongest.

He would have had no difficulty in finding the book. By
all accounts he was an omnivorous reader, who went through
the school library like a cat devouring milk. 'He was a serious
and persistent scholar,' wrote his school friend Gogokhiya.
'After his schoolwork he usually hurried home, and he was
always seen poring over a book.' Perhaps he was making up
for lost time, for there is a curious annotation by Yaroslavsky,
his official biographer, that 'at the age of seven he began to
study the alphabet and within a year he was able to read,
both in Georgian and Russian'. It is an odd statement, because Georgian children do not usually wait until they are
seven before they learn the alphabet. One might deduce that
in his early years he was somewhat retarded, did not go to
school, and did not learn to read until he was recovering from
smallpox. By the age of eleven or twelve reading became his
whole life.

The statement by Yaroslavsky is intended to demonstrate
his brilliance before the brilliance manifested itself: it is one
of the diseases of the official hagiographers that they are not
content to leave well enough alone. The check is continually
being antedated, and the most implausible stories are related
as though they were fact. We hear of Stalin riding on another
schoolboy's back and shouting: *'Ya stal!* – I am steel!' Yaroslavsky will have us believe that he was already a Marxist
before he left the school at Gori at the age of fourteen and a
half, and that before this age he had proved to his own
satisfaction the non-existence of God. At the age of thirteen,
according to an anecdote related by his schoolboy friend
Glurdjidze, he was saying: 'They are deceiving us. There is
no God.' Yaroslavsky relates the anecdote at some length:

I began to speak of God. Joseph heard me out, and

after a moment's silence he said: 'You know, they are deceiving us. There is no God —'

I was astonished by these words. I had never heard anything like it before.

'How can you say such things, Soso?' I exclaimed.

'I'll lend you a book to read,' he replied. 'It will show you that the world and all living things are quite different from anything you can imagine, and all this talk about God is sheer nonsense.'

'What book is it?' I asked.

'Darwin,' he said. 'You must read it.'

The anecdote strains credulity. A gifted boy might have read Darwin; he could hardly have extracted from it a proof of the non-existence of God. Disbelief came later when he was a seminarian in the theological college at Tiflis, probably at the age of sixteen, a not unusual age for a boy to express scepticism. There was in fact very little that was unusual about Joseph Djugashvili as a schoolboy: there were no intimations of greatness, no signs of the superhuman powers which the hagiographers see in him. There were thousands of gifted boys who acted in very much the same way: were conceited and introverted in the same way, and read books, and were gifted and quick at their lessons. They said of him that he was curt in his speech and given to fits of laziness, but these were not unusual characteristics. What was unusual in him was the sense of bitter frustration which comes to all children who are bullied by their fathers. For the ferociously brutal father he substituted the brutal *abrek,* whose ferocity was expressed in more romantic ways, and who had only to shout a single word from the mountain top and a hundred men would emerge from their hiding places and accompany him on glorious battles against the Tsar.

So he withdrew into a private world where all things were possible: one day he too would become an *abrek* and shout the word from the mountain top.

But that day was far in the future; there were more urgent problems to be attended to. There were only four grades in the church school at Gori, and in the summer of 1894 Joseph had received all the schooling that Gori could give him. If he was not at the top of his class, he was very close to it, and he received a certificate of merit. He was liked by the monks in charge of the school, and with their help he was offered a scholarship at the Tiflis Theological Seminary, where everything would be free. His uniform, his shoes, his lodging and meals, and his textbooks, all these would be given to him by the beneficent monks who would train him to become a priest of the Orthodox Church. His mother prayed that he would become a great dignitary of the Church, and this seems to have been his ambition when he set out for Tiflis.

He spent his summer vacation roaming the countryside, reading every book he could put his hand on, and singing in the church. Then in the autumn of 1894, with a cotton satchel over his arm, he took the train to Tiflis.

SEMINARIAN AND POET

THE THEOLOGICAL SEMINARY OF Tiflis was a grey four storey building looking out on Pushkin Square in the centre of the city. It was a dark and gloomy place, more like a spiritual barracks than a college. The windows were barred, the seminarians lived under strict discipline, the draughty corridors echoed with the footsteps of boys marching to class in orderly processions. In such a place a boy might learn to turn his back on the world and devote himself to the study of God, or he might become a rebel against the Church. The Theological Seminary was a breeding ground for rebellion.

As early as 1873 it became known that seditious books and pamphlets were being smuggled into the seminary: Renan's *Vie de Jésus*, Victor Hugo's *Napoléon le Petit*, and Chernyshevsky's *What Is To Be Done?* were intercepted by the police, and the students found in possession of these books were punished. Darwin, Buckle, Mill and other liberal freethinkers of the nineteenth century continued to be read secretly by the seminarians. There was no university in Georgia, and the Theological Seminary inevitably attracted boys who would otherwise have attended a university. They fought for knowledge, and since the monks failed to provide it, they took it wherever it could be found.

The boys who came to the college from all over Georgia were fiercely nationalistic, feeling with some reason that the Church and the autocracy were in an unholy alliance to stamp out national feeling. In 1885, six years after the birth of

Joseph Djugashvili, a seminarian called Sylvester Djibladze publicly rebuked the rector of the college for casting a slur on Georgian nationalism. He left his place among the student benches, marched up to the platform, and struck the rector, Pavel Chudetsky, a resounding blow on the face. The seminarians cheered. Sylvester Djibladze was arrested, placed on trial, and sentenced to three years' detention in a military prison. The consequences could have been foreseen: he became a revolutionary.

The rector was a Russian, who had neither understanding nor sympathy for the aspirations of the Georgian people, and he continued to proclaim the glories of the autocracy to students who would have preferred him to recite the histories of Georgian national heroes. He was a stubborn authoritarian, vindictive, cruel, and relentless in his determination to punish rebellion. In June 1886 he was shot to death by Joseph Laghiashvili, the son of a Georgian priest, who had been expelled from the seminary. Laghiashvili was hanged, and became a national hero. At his trial some evidence was produced that he was a member of a conspiratorial organization headed by Sylvester Djibladze, who was still in prison. But the evidence was inconclusive, and it was generally agreed by the officials that the seminarians were infected by a disease common throughout Georgia: a morbid hatred of the authoritarian regime. The seminary was closed in the vain hope that the disease would die a natural death.

The seminary opened again the following year, but the disease still flourished. The students demanded to be taught in Georgian; they demanded the dismissal of the more rabid Russian teachers, and they demanded the establishment of a chair of Georgian literature. All these demands were refused. In December 1893 they came out on strike. Eighty-seven of the strikers were expelled, and once more the seminary was closed. Among those who were expelled were Lado Ketskhoveli, who some years later was to become the first martyr of the Georgian Social Democratic movement when he was shot in his cell in Tiflis by an exasperated prison guard, and Mikha Tskhakaya, who became one of Lenin's most intimate friends, accompanying him to Russia in the sealed train in 1917.

When Joseph Djugashvili entered the seminary in September 1894 it was still seething with rebellion. The discipline, always strict, had become stricter. There was no chair of

Georgian literature, and the teachers continued to speak in Russian, and no Georgian books except the Bible and a few homiletic texts were permitted in the seminary library.

Iremashvili, who entered the seminary at the same time, has left a sombre account of life within its walls:

> Life at the school was sad and monotonous. Day and night we were locked within barrack walls, and felt like prisoners forced to sit out a long term of imprisonment though we were guiltless of any crimes. The atmosphere was dull and oppressive. There was scarcely any expression of youthful joy, hemmed in as we were by rooms and corridors which cut us off from the outside world. When, as happened from time to time, we gave expression to our youthful temperaments, we were quickly suppressed by the monks and monitors. The Tsarist inspectorate of schools forbade us the reading of Georgian literature and newspapers. They feared that if we read the classical writers of our homeland – Prince Ilya Chavchavadze, Akaki Tseretelli, Vasha Pshavela, Alexander Kasbeki, Nikoloz Baratashvilii and others – we would become inspired with ideas of our country's freedom and independence, and our young souls would be infected with the new teachings of socialism. Even the few literary works that lay authorities allowed us to read were forbidden by the church authorities, because we were future priests. Dostoyevsky, Tolstoy, Turgenev and many others remained forbidden to us.

The sullen students were held to an exacting and rigid regimen. They awoke in the early hours of the morning, attended services, took a light breakfast, studied, prayed, studied, prayed, took a light lunch, studied, prayed again, and were let out in the afternoons between three and five, usually to take carefully guarded walks through the city; then there was roll call, and more prayers, and a glass of tea at eight o'clock, before they began their homework. At ten o'clock they were sent to their dormitories, and the lights went out.

On Sundays there were interminable services in church. Years later Iremashvili would remember the gloom that descended on him in church when he saw the sun pouring through the windows while his feet grew numb from standing on the same stone slab for hours. 'Even the most pious would have unlearned to pray under the influence of those interminable services,' he wrote. 'We concealed our thoughts from the attentive monks behind pious countenances.' Sometimes, according to Glurdjidze, who also left the church school at Gori to attend the seminary, they were able to read surreptitiously during services by hiding their books under the pews, but the punishments were severe if they were found out.

Although the official historians claim that Joseph was rebellious from the beginning, eagerly disseminating revolutionary Marxism from the moment he entered the seminary, he appears to have been a submissive and attentive pupil during the first year. His report card has survived: he received 5, the top mark for conduct. He was excellent in liturgy, fair in Russian composition, and better than average in Scripture and Church Slavonic. The report card also adds that he was absent fourteen times, which probably meant that he was ill. Iremashvili speaks of the many students who died of tuberculosis while at the seminary. Joseph suffered from a racking cough, and there were times when he would look so ill and cough so loudly while reading late at night that he would be asked to put out the candle. 'Many times,' says Iremashvili, 'I put out his candle myself.'

We have a good idea of what the boy looked like when he entered the seminary. A photograph shows him in uniform, hair neatly combed, the expression grave, the lips pursed primly. What is chiefly remarkable is that there is nothing remarkable; he might be any seminarian. It was such a photograph as one sees in pious cottages, where the sons have gone out to be priests. Seeing it, you would think he was a candidate for the priesthood who would remain a priest for the rest of his life.

He was working hard, devoting himself especially to civic history and logic; he had no particular gift for theological studies, though he worked at them well enough to get passing marks. During that first year in the seminary his chief interest was poetry, and he seems to have been writing verses all the years he was in the college. Only a few of his verses have been preserved. Some four or five are known to have been published, and some twenty more may one day be resurrected from the literary journals and magazines of the period.

The poems are notable for their intense nationalistic feeling expressed in fervent lyrics. They are not the poems of a young revolutionary, but of someone devoted to his country at a time of national resurgence. The first poem was published in the magazine *Iveria,* then edited by Prince Ilya Chavchavadze, on January 14th, 1895, shortly after his fifteenth birthday:

დილა.

გარის გაეფურჩქნა კოკორი,
გადახვეოდა იასა.
ზამბახსაც გალეიძებოდა
და თავს უხრიდა ნიავსა.

*

ტოროლა მაღლა ღრუბლებში
წკრიალ-წკრიალით გალობდა.
ბულბულიც გახარებული
ნაზის ხმით ამას ამბობდა~

*

აყვავდი, ტურფა ქვეყანავ,
ილხინე ივერთ მხარეო,
და შენც, ქართველო სწავლითა
სამშობლო გაახარეო.

MORNING

The rose opens her petals,
And embraces the violet.
The lily too has awakened.
They bend their heads to the zephyrs.

The lark climbs high in the sky
And sings his ringing song:
The nightingale with subtle voice
Sings softly on:

'Flourish, O adorable country,
Rejoice, O land of Iveria,
And you also, O learned men of Georgia,
May you bring joy and happiness to the country!'

For some reason the poet chose to sign his work: J. G--shishvili. It was the first of his many pseudonyms.

The poem is remarkable for its fervent Georgian nationalism, and for this reason was sometimes included in books of Georgian poetry, where it would usually appear anonymously. It is an accomplished little poem, all the more remarkable because it was written by a boy. The appeal to the learned men of Georgia reflects the prevalent belief that salvation for Georgians lay in education. Education, according to Prince Ilya Chavchavadze, was the key to independence. In the original the poem has a quiet, effortless quality.

The second poem, which appeared in *Iveria* on October

11th, 1895, reflects a more romantic preoccupation. It is more personal, and more dramatic. Stalin, although astonishingly secretive about his poems, seems to have had some fondness for it, for he permitted four lines to appear under his own name in a collection of Georgian poetry translated into Russian in 1939. These were in fact the only four lines which he permitted the Russians to read during his lifetime, and perhaps inevitably the translation was not altogether accurate. Here is the poem in Georgian as it appeared on the front page of *Iveria*:

TO THE MOON

Move on, O tireless one—
Never bowing your head,
Disperse the misty clouds,
Great is the providence of the Almighty.
   Smile tenderly upon the world
   Which lies outspread beneath you;
   Sing a lullaby to Mkhinvari,*
   Which hangs from the sky.
Know well that those who once
Fell to the oppressors
Shall rise again and soar,
Winged with hope, above the holy
     mountain.†
And as in former days,
O beauty, you shone among the clouds,
So now let your rays play in splendor
In the blue sky.
   I shall rip open my shirt
   And bare my breast to the moon,
   And with outstretched hands
   Worship her who showers her light
     on the world.

მთვარეს

იარე დაუღალავად—
თავი ნუ ჩაგიქინდია,
გამფანტე ნისლი ღრუბლების,
უფლის განგება დიდია.
ნაზად შესცინე ქვეყანას
შენ ქეხ-ქვეშ გადაშლილს;
მყინვარს დამღერი ნანინა,
ზეციდამ გადმოკიდულს.
იცოდე, რომ ერთხელ
ხრის დაცემული, ჩაგრული
კვლავ-აღმართივის მთას წმლდას,
იმედით აღტაცებული.
ჩემ, ტურფავ, წინანდებურად
ღრუბლებში გიკაშკაშე,
ლურჯ კამარაზე სამამე
სხივები შეგათამაშე.
მკი გადავიხსნი საკინძეს
და მკერდს მოგიშვერ მთვარეს,
ხელ-განპყრობილი თაყვანს-გცემ
ჩეუქრად შუქ-მომფინარეს!

————

* Mkhinvari is the Georgian name for Mount Kazbek in the Central Caucasus. It was on this peak that Zeus chained Prometheus in punishment for stealing fire from heaven.

† The sacred mountain, in this context, could be Mount Kazbek, but a Georgian would normally think of Mamadavitismta, St David's Mountain overlooking Tiflis. The oppressed would then be those who died in the Metekh fortress, the Tsarist jail in Tiflis. On the mountain there is the famous cemetery where many Georgian heroes were buried.

Such is the longest of Stalin's poems to survive, and there is perhaps some significance in the fact that he signed it with his own name: Soselo, a diminutive form of Soso, itself the short form of Yosip, or Joseph. It is a poem which a boy would write with considerable enjoyment, delighting in romantic attitudes, steeped in romantic languor until, in the very last verse, he lays the trap and shows himself to be a man of heroic impulse so much in love with the moon that he must strip himself in adoration of the moonlight. The sight of Stalin moonstruck at the age of fifteen is an odd one, but there is no denying the fervour of his happy lunacy. He pours out his romantic yearnings without reserve, gaily and joyfully. The verse on those who fell to the oppressors, by which he means the martyrs of Georgian nationalism, involves a wonderfully effective romantic conceit, for he sees them rising from their graves and soaring above the moonlit mountain peaks. It was this verse which appeared in a Russian translation in 1939, changed a little, but still recognizably conveying a deeply religious feeling:

> *And know that he who fell like ashes on the earth,*
> *Who long ago became enslaved,*
> *Will rise again higher than the great mountains,*
> *Winged with bright hope.*

The ashes were added, the holy mountain became great mountains, hope acquires an adjective, but no great harm is done. The translation by Alexander Kancheli could not have been published without Stalin's approval. Only these four lines were published. To this day there are few Russians who know that Stalin once wrote a poem in which he rounded out his first verse with the words: 'Great is the providence of the Almighty.'

These early verses are important, because they show how his mind was working. None of his school essays survive. We know what he was reading, but there are large areas of his mind which remain impenetrable. Yet in these poems he is making no effort to conceal his emotions, and he shows clearly that he was capable of genuine religious feeling and possessed a romantic attachment to the oppressed, following a centuries-old Georgian poetic tradition. Already there is evidence of a small but real poetic talent.

The third poem appeared in *Iveria* on October 29th, 1895, on the anniversary of the death of the Georgian poet Prince

Rapiel Eristavi. The most famous of Eristavi's poems was entitled *A Suppliant to a Judge* and described the humiliations of a Mingrelian peasant, one of the many who came out in open revolt in 1857, were arrested, and brought to trial. The prince was one of the many Georgian nobles who took up the cause of the peasants, whom he celebrated in poem after poem; and what is chiefly remarkable about his poetry is the prevailing note of melancholy. If tears could kill, he would have killed off the entire Tsarist bureaucracy and army. Most of his poems were laments over the suffering inflicted on the peasants. Here, for example, is a characteristic poem of a peasant bewailing his fate:

SESIA'S THOUGHTS

Dust am I, to dust I cling;
A rustic born, my life is one
Eternal strife and endless toil,
And endless woe ... till life is gone.
I plough, I sow, I labour on,
With muscles strained, in sun and rain.
I scarce can live on what I earn,
And tired and hungry I remain.
The owner of the land torments me;
Even the tiny ant's my foe.
For townsfolk, priests and native country
In bloodlike sweat I plough and sow ...
How long, O God, this endless grind,
This life of sorrow and of toil?
Alas! I fear that death alone
Will bring me rest within this soil!

The young Stalin's poem to the prince's memory was a deliberate and rather self-conscious attempt to celebrate him as the poet of an overwhelming sympathy for the people. There is genuine feeling in the poem, and at the same time there can be detected a note of self-congratulation, as he demonstrates his youthful powers.

The early poems of Stalin deserve study, but it would be dangerous to deduce from them anything more than that he possessed a modest but genuine talent. There is no doubt that the talent was genuine. What is in doubt is whether it would have progressed beyond the stage of youthful poetic excitement. He was writing in an established tradition, and had

TO R. ERISTAVI

When you heard the lamentations of the
    peasants,
You came with tears in your eyes
To offer up your grief to the heavens,
For you sacrificed yourself for the nation.

როს მწირომელ გლეხთა ვაებით
საბრალო აცრემლებული
ზეცას შეჰკვნესდი, მგოსანო,
ერისთვის თავდადებული.

When you heard the people were living
    well,
You were agreeably enchanted,
And played sweetly on your harp
A music that seemed to fall from the
    heavens.

როს ერის კეთილ დღეობით
საამოდ აღტაცებული
სიმთ აჟღერებდი ტკბილ ხმაზედ,
ვით ზეცით მოვლინებული.

When you sang to the motherland,
You expressed a passionate desire,
And you played for her on your harp
The ravishing music of your heart.

როს დაჰგალობდი სამშობლოს
ის იყო შენი ტრფიალი
მისთვის გაჰკვროდა შენს ჩანგსა
გულის წარმტაცი წკრიალი.

So now, O poet, the Georgian people
Have prepared for you a heavenly
    monument,
And all the toil and sorrows of the past
Are crowned in the present age.

მაშინ, მგოსანო, ქართველი
თურმე ციურ ძეგლ გიგებდა
და წარსულელ შრომას, ვაებას
აწმყოთი გიგირგვინებდა.

obviously read widely. He is a self-conscious poet, and knows
exactly what he is doing at every moment. Only once is there a
hint of the mature poet, who might have developed. Quite
suddenly and unexpectedly in *To the Moon*, we see the martyrs rising high above the holy mountain, transformed in a
moment of glory into the shining of the night sky. At that
moment we are made aware very briefly of visionary power;
and never, so far as we know, did he write in that vein
again. He knew what he was doing when he permitted these
lines to be translated into Russian.

    There is youthful sympathy and excitement in these poems,
but little social awareness. They are not the poems of a
rebel, but of a boy in a state of half-delirious exaltation. The
rebel was to appear later, during his last years at the theological seminary.

    In 1893 – the year when Joseph Djugashvili entered the

theological seminary – Noah Jordania founded the first Social Democratic, or Marxist, party in Georgia under the name of *Messame Dasy*, meaning 'the Third Estate'. Noah Jordania was twenty-three years old. He was a former student of the Tiflis Theological Seminary, a rather precise, slow-moving, deliberate man, who became a Social Democrat as a result of study rather than of revolutionary ardour. Inevitably he became a Menshevik. Just as inevitably – for he was a fervent nationalist and inspired great confidence – he became the first president of the first Georgian Republic in 1918, a post he retained until Stalin ordered the invasion of Georgia by the Red Army in 1921, when he escaped to France.

Noah Jordania was the founding father of Social Democracy in Georgia, the first Georgian to embrace the cause of Marxism. This fact is faced squarely in the opening pages of Lavrenty Beria's curious compilation called *Stalin's Early Writings and Activities*, where it is accepted as one of those unpleasant truths which cannot be avoided. The name Messame Dasy did not appear until the following year, being heard for the first time in a speech delivered by Georgy Tseretelli at the funeral of his friend Ignatius Ninoshvili. The funeral provided the occasion for a general statement of Social Democratic aims, and years later Noah Jordania was to reflect ruefully that the history of Social Democracy was largely the history of deaths, funerals and graves.

Messame Dasy was not a conspiratorial organization. As Beria observed quite accurately, it propagated Marxist doctrines openly in the liberal press and derived from bourgeois and nationalistic ideas already current. 'They admired the capitalist system, expecting it would regenerate the Georgian people,' wrote Beria, 'and they never raised the question of waging a revolutionary struggle against capitalism and of overthrowing the bourgeoisie.' The questions never arose because Georgia was still largely feudal, owned by innumerable Georgian princes in alliance with the autocracy.

While Messame Dasy showed little interest in bringing about a revolutionary upheaval, it was nevertheless the breeding ground for a whole generation of Georgian revolutionaries. Mikha Tskhakaya, Philipp Makharadze, Alexander Tsulukidze, Lado Ketskhoveli, Isidor Ramishvili, and many others whom we shall meet in these pages, became members of it. Beria tells us that the young Stalin became a member of the group in 1897, adding characteristically that 'with the coming of Stalin a new, revolutionary element entered into the life of the group'.

It is doubtful whether Stalin had the least effect on the group. He was one of the many students of the theological seminary who sympathized with its aims, which could be described as the establishment of an independent Georgia in a form which would only be arrived at after slow and patient study. Members of the Messame Dasy regarded themselves as social scientists. Their motto was 'Scientific inquiry into the new trends'. Marxist dogmatism had not yet reared its head.

Nor was there any reason to believe that Stalin was reading Marx while at college. We hear of a handwritten copy of *Capital* circulating secretly among the students, who had paid for it out of their pocket money. The existence of this secret, handwritten copy was revealed for the first time by Stalin in 1938. Shortly afterwards there appeared paintings and drawings showing Stalin expounding the text to a group of worshipful admirers. Soon the youthful expounder of Marxism was included among the legends of Stalin.

A short list of the books he read in the theological seminary can be compiled from the recollections of his fellow seminarians, and produces few surprises. He was reading what all the other students in Russia were reading. He read Darwin's *Descent of Man*, Charles Lyell's *Antiquity of Man*, Camille Flammarion's popular accounts of astronomy, Ludwig Feuerbach's *Essence of Christianity*, Victor Hugo's *Toilers of the Sea* and *Ninety-three*, some of Balzac's novels, Thackeray's *Vanity Fair*, Erckmann-Chatrian's *Story of a Peasant*, Buckle's *History of Civilization in England*, Letourneau's *Literary Evolution of the Nations*, Spinoza's *Ethics*, brief lives of Copernicus and Galileo, and Mendeleyev's *Chemistry*, which for some reason deeply impressed him. He read widely in the Russian classical authors of the nineteenth century: a good deal of Tolstoy, Gogol and Chekhov; and he appears to have had a particular fondness for the satirist Saltykov-Shchedrin. He also read *Kvali* (The Furrow), which was the weekly magazine of the Messame Dasy, and its monthly companion *Moambeh* (The Herald), both published legally and available on the news-stands.

Some of these books were banned by the college authorities, and like many other students he got into trouble for reading them. The conduct book of the theological seminary has survived, with the entries recording his infractions of discipline. An entry for November 1896 reads:

> It seems that Djugashvili has a ticket to the cheap library, from which he borrows books. Today I confiscated Victor Hugo's *Toilers of the Sea,* in which I found the aforesaid library ticket.
>
> S. MURAKHOVSKY, Asst Supervisor
FATHER HERMOGENES, Supervisor

> *Proposed Action*: He is to be confined to the punishment cell for a prolonged period. I have already warned him once about an unsanctioned book, Victor Hugo's *Ninety-three.*

A few months later he was again placed in a punishment cell for reading books displeasing to the authorities. The entry was made in March 1897:

> At 11 pm I took away from Joseph Djugashvili Letourneau's *Literary Evolution of the Nations*, which he has borrowed from the cheap library. The library ticket was found in the book. Djugashvili was found reading the aforesaid book on the chapel stairs. This is the thirteenth time this student has been discovered reading books borrowed from the cheap library. I handed over the book to the Father Supervisor.
>
> S. MURAKHOVSKY, Asst Supervisor

These infractions of discipline cannot have been very serious if the authorities gave him altogether thirteen separate warnings without expelling him. Other seminarians were suffering the same punishment, and it became a point of honour to acquire a certain number of demerits for reading unauthorized books. In their memoirs the seminarians sometimes speak of the difficulty of acquiring books, but in fact there were at least four bookshops in Tiflis at the time and the difficulty would seem to have been in raising the money to pay for them or to take them out on loan. There was a cheap bookshop on Kirochnaya Street, a stone's throw away from the seminary, with a small lending library attached. Gutsa Parkadze, one of Joseph's close friends, suggested in his memoirs that it was a waste of time for the college supervisors to censor their reading, 'because no one suspected how much political dynamite we extracted from the most ordinary books'. It was a revealing remark. In those days a Georgian student would find an abundance of political dynamite in a simple history of Russia.

In 1898 Joseph Djugashvili was no longer the proud, idealistic youth who wrote the poems that were printed in *Iveria*. He was already a man, for like all Georgians he matured early. He was weary of the supervisions of the monks, restless, bitter, alienated, dreaming only of the day when he could escape from the seminary. He had long ago discovered that he lacked the temperament of a priest. He seems to have stayed on because he enjoyed singing in the choir, because he was fond of some of the students, and because the certificate of graduation from the seminary would provide him with a teaching position and therefore a small but steady income. At the same time he was growing increasingly despondent as he compared the extent of his ambitions with the provincial realities of Tiflis. Koba, the great *condottiere*, was a small, underfed, seedy student of theology consumed with a vast hatred for autocracy and nearly everyone around him.

Again and again Iremashvili refers to that ferocious hatred which would express itself in biting sarcasm and invective. He would get into a rage if another student assumed the leading role in a discussion; he, and he alone, knew the proper answers and was in possession of the proper tablets of the law. He expected and demanded assent on all the views he put forward; anyone who took an opposite point of view would be bludgeoned into silence. Already he was demonstrating an authoritarian temper. He was also becoming violently ambitious. 'Ambition,' says Iremashvili, 'made him into an atheist.'

He appears to have decided upon a revolutionary career in the spring of 1898 after some secret meetings with railroad workers. With one or two other seminarians he would slip out of the seminary at night and make his way to a workman's house on the surrounding hills. Iremashvili remembered the first time they ever attended one of these meetings:

One evening Koba and I stole secretly out of the seminary and made our way to Mount Mtatsminda and a small house leaning against the side of a cliff, owned by a worker on the Tiflis railroad. Soon other seminarians who shared our views came and joined us. Here, too, we met a Social Democratic labour organization of railroad workers.

At this first meeting, or perhaps a little later, a former political prisoner who had escaped from Siberia made a picturesque appearance. His name was Ormozadze; he wore a black blouse with a red scarf; and he was every inch the revolutionary, capable of talking for hours without a single gesture about the sufferings he had witnessed in Siberia. He told stories of men being flogged to death by their guards; these terrible stories kept his audience of workingmen and seminarians on the edge of their seats. He was a thin, pale-faced, fiery man with deep-sunken blue eyes, and to most of those who listened to him he was the incarnation of all the revolutionaries who had ever been sent to Siberia.

Ormozadze made a deep impression on Iremashvili, who called him 'the martyr of our faith in the coming brotherhood of men and nations'. He was a good speaker who could some-how give to words like 'brotherhood', 'justice' and 'freedom' a resonance derived from his long Siberian exile. When the young seminarians asked him what they should do with their lives, Ormozadze told them to work for brotherhood with the labouring classes. Soon there was a small handful of seminarians actively engaged in working with railroad workers. There was nothing particularly unusual in this, for the Narodniki in the eighties had gone out among the labourers and peasants, teaching them to read and write, and explaining to them their rights under the law, and the tradition still continued. In later years Stalin would call them 'revolutionary Marxist circles', as though they were fully formed conspiratorial organizations, but they were in fact little more than small study circles where the teachers learned more than the pupils.

In *Stalin's Early Writings and Activities* we are given a surprisingly complete account of eight separate Social Democratic circles which Stalin is supposed to have 'conducted' between 1896 and 1898. The names of most of the students are given. The first two circles consisted entirely of seminarians, and it is only with the establishment of the third circle in 1898 that we come upon the names of workers. Joseph Iremashvili is included among the names of the members of the first circle, which would appear to have been nothing more than a small discussion group. There were two Russian circles, attended by workmen who did not speak Georgian, and in addition there were circles attended by workers from a boot factory and from two tobacco factories. Stalin claims to have 'led' these circles in 1898, and they are referred to as 'Stalin's circles'. It is not explained how he could have conducted so many circles while attending classes all day long at the seminary.

Nevertheless the year 1898 marks the inclusion of Stalin in the ranks of revolutionary workers. He seems to have spent the summer vacations in the working-class district of Tiflis, busily engaged in propaganda activities, and when he returned to the seminary in September he lost all interest in his studies. He had been a better than average pupil during his early years; now there was a calamitous falling off of marks. 'It so happened that Koba, who was convinced of the uselessness of any earnest studies, gradually became the worst pupil in the seminary,' writes Iremashvili. 'He would answer the reproaches of his teachers with poisonous and disdainful laughter.'

Previously the authorities had found fault with him for reading forbidden books, a crime he shared with many other seminarians. Now they accused him of deliberate insubordination and of reading forbidden books aloud to other students. The conduct book for September 29th, 1898, has the following entry:

At 9 pm a group of students gathered in the dining-hall around Joseph Djugashvili, who read them books not sanctioned by the seminary authorities, in view of which the students were searched.

What punishment was meted out is unknown; presumably the students were confined to the punishment cells. On December 16th, 1898, there is a more ominous entry:

In the course of a search of students of the fifth class made by members of the board of supervision, Joseph Djugashvili tried several times to enter into an argument with them, expressing dissatisfaction with the repeated searches of students and declaring that such searches were never made in other seminaries. Djugashvili is genuinely disrespectful and rude towards persons in authority and systematically refuses to bow to one of the masters (S. A.

Murakhovsky), as the latter has repeatedly complained to the board of supervision.

A. RZHAVENSKY, *Asst Supervisor*

Proposed Action: He is to be reprimanded and confined to the punishment cell for five hours on the orders of the Rector, Father Dmitry.

Yaroslavsky tells the perfectly credible story that when the Rector entered his dormitory after one of these searches, Joseph paid no attention to him and went on reading. 'Don't you see who is standing before you?' the Rector asked. Joseph rose to his feet, rubbing his eyes. 'I don't see anything,' he answered, 'except a black spot before my eyes!'

Joseph's days at the seminary were obviously coming to an end. He was deliberately daring the authorities to expel him, and they, just as deliberately, were refusing to take the last drastic steps. Perhaps they acted out of pity, for the five-year course would end in May 1899 and it would have been senseless to deprive him of his diploma. They permitted him to take the final examinations. When he simply refused to sit for the examinations, they had no alternative but to expel him.

On May 27th, 1899, the ruling body of the seminary met to discuss among other problems what should be done with Joseph Djugashvili. It was decided to expel him unless he could show cause for his absence. Two further days of grace were given to him in the hope that he would be able to justify his absence, and when he failed to do so he was formally expelled on May 29th, 1899. The conduct sheet bore the statement: 'Expelled for not attending examinations, reasons unknown.'

Yaroslavsky, who quotes from the document of expulsion, adds that this was not the real reason. The real reason, he tells us, was the one given by Stalin in one of those interminable questionnaires which were continually being handed out to members of the Communist Party. In 1931 he wrote in a questionnaire: *'Education:* Expelled from a theological seminary for propagating Marxism.'

At various times other explanations have been offered to explain the expulsion. A fellow student called Gogokhia, writing when Joseph was in a position of vast power, said that he was expelled 'at the insistence of the ferocious monk Abazhidze, who guessed why the talented, well-developed Djugashvili with his incredibly rich memory studied only for passing marks and therefore succeeded in obtaining his expulsion from the seminary'. Gogokhia says nothing about the failure to attend the final examination, and implies that Abazhidze knew that Joseph was engaged in revolutionary activity. Beria in *Stalin's Early Writings and Activities* says he was expelled 'for political unreliability'. To Henri Barbusse, Stalin said he was expelled 'for political lack of balance'.

Still another explanation was offered by Stalin's mother, who told an American that he was not expelled; she had herself removed him from the seminary because of his failing health. 'When he entered the seminary he was fifteen years old and one of the strongest boys you ever saw,' she said, 'but then he studied too hard in the seminary and by the time he was nineteen he was so run down that the doctors said he would get tuberculosis. So I took him out of the school. He did not want to go. I took him out. He was my only son.'

It is customary to discount the evidence of Stalin's mother, but it is possible that she was closer to the truth than the others. It should be remembered that he was expelled, according to the seminary authorities, not for anything he did, but for something he did not do – he failed to attend the final examinations during the last week of his five-year course at the seminary. He had nothing to gain by not acquiring a diploma, and much to lose. He had been carrying on revolutionary propaganda by night and attending classes by day; he was at loggerheads with the teaching staff, but he was also at loggerheads with many of the students, who refused to bow to his imperious will and hated him for his arrogance and rudeness; he was in bad health; he was without resources, and had no prospects; and after five years at the seminary he was mortally tired. Confronted by the knowledge that within a few days he would be thrown out into a world he despised, he may have suffered a crisis of the will. A prisoner sentenced to a long period of imprisonment will often have a nervous collapse on the eve of his release, because he cannot face the world which is waiting outside. Something very similar seems to have happened to Joseph. Poverty, illness, overwork, dreams of a revolutionary future in which he would appear as another Koba, all these may have conspired to produce a nervous breakdown. There were to be many other breakdowns. Again and again in the course of his long life we shall see him standing like a man paralysed in all his limbs, silent, withdrawn, incapable of any action, staring straight ahead with a strange look of mingled arrogance and humility as he slowly recovers his forces.

'When he left the seminary,' says Iremashvili, 'he took with him a ferocious and enduring hatred against the college administration, against the bourgeoisie, against everything in the country that embodied Tsarism. He had an overwhelming hatred against all authority.'

THE YOUNG AGITATOR

THE EARLY YEARS of a revolutionary are often shadowy and insubstantial, leaving no record in history except the occasional reports of police officers and the bland photographs which appear in police files. Furtive, silent, strangely incoherent when he permits himself to speak, the young revolutionary usually gives the impression of a man who lives on the margins of existence, hating the world which he feels called upon to remake in his own nebulous image. His adolescence extends into his manhood; he does not know where he is going; uncertainty becomes a way of life. The rage within him – that rage which makes him a revolutionary – feeds triumphantly on his misery.

So it was with Stalin. There are long periods in his early life when he almost disappears from sight, a shadow among shadows. We see him briefly lurking near the railway yards of Tiflis, vanishing for a while to become a book-keeper in the Observatory, agitating in a tobacco factory and the boot and shoe factory where his father once worked, always poor, always restless, leaving so few traces that sometimes we have the feeling he spent most of these years sitting in a dark corner and communing with himself. Of this period there were no writings which can be said to have been indisputably written by him. Such writings as there are, existing in Russian translation from the Georgian, are unsigned editorials in a party newspaper, occasional pamphlets, and a few letters which give the appearance of being heavily edited. After 1896 he wrote no more poems, or if he did they were never printed. His speeches, if he delivered them, went unrecorded, and no one troubled to remember the ideas he expressed in the Marxist study circles which he claimed to have led. Between May 1899 and November 1904 there is a broad gap filled with a few uncertain dates and shadowy assertions that he was the leader of a vast underground movement.

At various times Stalin would refer to this period of his life, but always reluctantly and apparently without any deep interest. For the biographical chronicle which forms the Appendix of the first volume of his *Collected Works* the dates and descriptions of his actions are brief to the point of effrontery. Here, for example, is all he wished to remember about the years 1899 and 1900:

1899

May 29	J. V. Stalin is expelled from the Tiflis Theological Seminary for propagating Marxism.
December 28	J. V. Stalin starts work at the Tiflis Physical Observatory.

1900

April 23	J. V. Stalin addresses a workers' May Day meeting in the region of Salt Lake, on the outskirts of Tiflis.
Summer	J. V. Stalin establishes contact with V. K. Kurnatovsky, a well-known supporter of Lenin's *Iskra*, who had arrived in Tiflis for party work.
August	J. V. Stalin leads a mass strike of the Central Railway Workshops in Tiflis.

Stalin wishes us to believe that at the age of twenty he was already a disciplined revolutionary and strike leader with an important position in Tiflis revolutionary circles, but the role he actually played seems to have been a minor one. These were the years when he was feeling his way, never quite sure which direction to take. He was reading voluminously, catching up with the time lost in the theological seminary, and learning from the young workmen in the railway depots about life in other parts of Russia. The railway workers were traditionally the most revolutionary, and he had a lot to learn from them.

Of the seven-month period between his expulsion from the theological seminary and his job at the Observatory nothing is known. He probably returned to Gori to stay with his mother for a while, for he always returned to her when he was in trouble. Afterwards he seems to have made a casual living in Tiflis as a tutor to rich men's children. The job at the Observatory was poorly paid. According to one of his fellow revolutionaries he was employed to make astronomical observations with the aid of intricate instruments, a task demanding great nervous concentration and patience, but this is to give him credit for more scientific knowledge than he possessed. The police archives listed him as a book-keeper.

The Observatory stood in a pleasant park between the Kura river and the Mikhailovsky Prospect, one of those long roads which cut through the whole northern part of the town. It was next to the military academy and only a few minutes walk from the railroad station. Stalin lived in a small, barely furnished single room on the Mikhailovsky Prospect. Iremashvili, who often visited the room, described it as forbiddingly austere, the chief article of furniture being a table piled high with books and pamphlets, with the works of Plekhanov and Lenin notably prominent. When at home, Stalin was accustomed to wear an old black blouse in the Russian style, and there would be a red scarf round his neck to demonstrate his political leanings. The blouse was usually dirty and his shoes unpolished; and he wore this uniform not so much because he was poor as because these rumpled clothes formed part of his continuing protest against the detested bourgeoisie. He was slovenly, but self-consciously slovenly; and he would not be seen dead in a white collar or a European suit.

His work at the Observatory left his evenings free; it also gave him a useful refuge from too much vigilance by the police. For the first time in his life he was enjoying his privacy. Books were his passion, and he haunted the second-hand bookstores and spent all his spare cash on them. When he was not reading, he would saunter down to the railroad station and talk with the workers in the engine sheds. He was well known to them; his views carried weight; and there were always small groups prepared to listen to his expositions of Marxist theory. At the age of twenty he was by no means a revolutionary leader. Men like Noah Jordania and Sylvester Djibladze carried far more authority and were regarded with far greater respect. In those years Stalin was like a young priest attending to the needs of his first parish, while Jordania and Djibladze superintended the entire episcopal see.

About this time the *mayevka*, the May Day parade, was being introduced in Russia. It was still a tentative affair, with no roots in the country, and no one knew quite what to do with it. Some of the workers decided to hold a secret *mayevka*, not in Tiflis itself, but in the hills outside. So secret was the meeting place that only a handful of workers were told about it. The rest were given instructions to meet in the suburb of Nakhalovka. Then they were to go in small groups to the Monastery of St Antony, where they would be told the next stage of the journey after giving the password. The journey was made in the early hours of the morning. Small lamps gleamed, they spoke only in whispers, there was an air of subdued excitement and expectancy. Sergo Alliluiev, one of the railroadmen who took part in the *mayevka*, was reminded of a pilgrimage: they were like conspirators making their way secretly to some mysterious and holy place.

Towards dawn, having whispered the password to perhaps a dozen pickets, they came to a place in the mountains called Salt Lake. It was Sunday morning, and they could hear the bells of a monastery. There was a light mist on the mountains, but soon the rising sun burned the mist away. Then they unfurled their red banners on which someone had roughly sketched the features of Marx and Engels; the banners were inscribed in Russian, Armenian and Georgian. Later they sang the 'Marseillaise', not in French but in the more formidable and bloodthirsty Russian version. Sergo Alliluiev says that about five hundred workers were present, and many of them had tears in their eyes as they saw the banners cracking in the wind.

After the 'Marseillaise' came the speakers, who addressed the crowd, telling them of the significance of this first *mayevka*, and how it portended the coming revolution. Writing many years later Alliluiev could remember only four speakers – Vano Sturua, Zachar Chodrishvili, Mikho Bochoridze and Stalin. The first three were workmen. Many others spoke, for Alliluiev mentions that they were addressed by revolutionary intellectuals, railroadmen and factory workers. He could not remember what Stalin said; only that he was present and said a few words. It was evidently not a striking speech, and it was memorable only because it was the first time that Stalin spoke in public.

An hour or two later they shouted: 'Long live the first of

May! Down with the autocracy!' Then they descended the mountain and went furtively to their own homes.

Stalin was still the amateur revolutionary, living on the margins of life, enjoying conspiracy for its own sake. Like Conrad's revolutionary 'he walked frail, insignificant, shabby, miserable'. How shabby and miserable we know from those curious broken anecdotes which Stalin thirty years later related to Henri Barbusse, when together they set out to write an authorized biography. Here is Stalin speaking through the lips of Barbusse about those early days when he was still an apprentice revolutionary:

He was penniless. Comrade Ninua and a few others gave him food, in about 1900 in Tiflis, where he held discussions each evening in the eight circles which he directed.

One of the most important supplemental parts of the agitator's work consisted in hiding himself. At Tiflis is shown a house which contained one of the 'illegal hiding places' of the man whose career we are following. With its slim little columns, its covered balcony and its narrow ogival double doors, the house is like a great many other houses in Tiflis, which was the first condition it had to fulfil in view of the use to which it was being put.

He would appear suddenly at meetings, and would sit down without a word and listen until the time came for him to speak. He was always accompanied by two or three comrades, one of whom would keep watch by the door. He would not speak for long. If he took a train journey, he would take endless trouble to throw people off the track.

He was at that secret meeting which was held near the wings of a theatre, so that when the police surrounded the building, they had only to break down a door and mix with the audience with a look of absorbed attention on their faces.

He walked into the huge Popoff library. He asked for a book of Belinsky's, which he had begun to read attentively, all the time keeping an eye on the manoeuvres of one of the assistants, to whom he handed, unseen and unrecognized by anyone, two false passports. They were to secure the escape of two comrades whom the police intended to arrest a little later – a little too late.

So Stalin remembered those years – the small house with

the slender columns, the dark wings of a theatre, the book-shop belonging to a devout monarchist where the clerks acted as revolutionary couriers, and the interminable secret meetings where he waited patiently and spoke only briefly, vanishing into the dark with the two or three comrades who watched over his safety. We never learn what happened to the two false passports or whether the police succeeded in trapping the revolutionaries hiding in the wings of a theatre. What one remembers most is the poverty in the midst of shady conspiracies and the 'narrow ogival double doors,' behind which Stalin spent so much of his time hiding.

There was need to hide, for the conspiracies were real, dangerous and carefully watched by the police. All through the spring and summer the workers were coming out on strike; strikebreakers were brought in; informers found their way into the secret Marxist organizations; there was war between the police and the workers. The revolutionaries however were still feeling their way. Jordania and Djibladze were moderate Marxists, followers of Plekhanov, with no illusions about seizing power by force.

In the summer of 1900 a slight, distinguished-looking man arrived in Tiflis as the personal emissary of Lenin. His name was Victor Kurnatovsky and he was by profession a chemical engineer, having graduated from the Zurich Polytechnical Institute. He was also an experienced revolutionary, having begun his revolutionary activity as a member of the terrorist organization of the Narodnaya Volya. He had spent six years of his life in exile, first in Archangel and then in Minusinsk, where he came to know Lenin, who was exiled in the nearby village of Shushenskoye. They were devoted to one another, and on all essential matters they were in complete agreement. Kurnatovsky was one of the seventeen Social Democrats who signed Lenin's 'A Protest by Russian Social Democrats' against a famous 'Credo' drawn up by Ekaterina Kuskova, who had pleaded for a moderate socialistic programme. Like Lenin he was an activist, who cared less for the programme than for seizing power.

Kurnatovsky's arrival in Tiflis was the signal for a more determined revolutionary policy. In his quiet way he was a capable inciter of unrest. The workers of Tiflis found him generous with carefully considered advice; a testimonial written by men who shared his imprisonment in Tiflis jail, discovered many years later, says: 'All the comrades went to

Kurnatovsky with their disagreements and disputes. His opinions and conclusions were always accepted without objections. Kurnatovsky was a staunch and unyielding revolutionary.' There is no reason to doubt that this testimonial was written, but there is some reason to wonder whether Stalin and Kurnatovsky were ever on close terms. In Beria's *Stalin's Early Writings and Activities*, there can be found the forthright statement that on his arrival in Tiflis Kurnatovsky 'established close contact with Comrade Stalin and became his intimate friend and co-worker'. Stalin was still a comparatively obscure revolutionary. To suggest that he was an intimate friend and a co-worker suggests a degree of prominence he had not yet attained. Such claims belong properly to hagiography, and since they appear frequently in the works supervised and edited by Stalin but infrequently elsewhere, we have a right to be on our guard against them.

Nevertheless Stalin was a practising revolutionary, filled with rage against society and instinctively aware that the slow, cautious approach to socialism desired by Noah Jordania was lacking in excitement. He wanted action – swift action. He looked forward to a rousing *mayevka* the following year, and he seems to have taken some obscure part in the strike of the railroad workers in the late summer. We know nothing about his activities during the winter, but there exists a circumstantial account of a police raid on his apartment in the spring. The account was written by Vasso Berdzenishvili, a former student at the theological seminary. The raid took place on the night of March 21st, 1901, and is notable chiefly because it throws some light on Stalin's conspiratorial habits. When Iremashvili visited Stalin the previous year, Stalin's table was piled high with illegal literature. Now he had learned to be more cautious, and the books and pamphlets were hidden under a brick pile on the banks of the nearby river Kura. Here is Berdzenishvili's account of the raid:

They burst into the room, asked who I was, who else lived in the apartment, and began their search. They first ransacked my room, packed up and sealed certain legal publications of a Marxist trend, drew up a protocol and gave it to me to sign. Then they proceeded to Comrade Stalin's room. They turned everything upside down, poked into every corner, shook out the bedding – but found nothing. Comrade Stalin would always return a book after reading it and never kept it at home. As to illegal pamphlets, we used to keep them concealed under a brick pile on the banks of the Kura River. Comrade Stalin was very cautious in this respect. After searching the second room, they again drew up a protocol, and went away empty-handed.

Earlier in the day the police had already arrested Kurnatovsky and taken him to the Tiflis military prison, effectively removing him from the scene. In the summer of 1903 he was exiled to Yakutsk after spending two years in the Metekh fortress in Tiflis. Thereafter this unhappy man went from prison to prison and from one place of exile to another. For taking part in a protest movement at Yakutsk he was sentenced to twelve years' penal servitude. Amnestied a year later, he joined a group of railroad workers and soldiers returning from Manchuria, and took part in the formation of the short-lived Chita Republic. General Rennenkampf marched on the republic, arrested the leaders, and shot them out of hand. For some reason Kurnatovsky was not shot; instead he was ordered to attend the execution of his friends and then sentenced to exile for life. In 1906 he succeeded in escaping to Japan, made his way to Australia where he worked as a lumberjack, reaching Paris four years later. He lived in a small room in the Boulevard Montparnasse, and sometimes Lenin would visit him. At last, weary of violence, Kurnatovsky became a moderate socialist, and there was the inevitable break with Lenin. Poverty-stricken and forgotten, he died in the autumn of 1912.

Kurnatovsky was one of the unlucky ones, whose names are remembered only in the footnotes of revolutionary histories. He had no gift for revolutionary survival; he had neither Stalin's caution nor Lenin's ferocious determination. Yet he was a true portent of his times, and he perished as Stalin and Lenin might very easily have perished.

Caution indeed was to remain one of the guiding principles of Stalin's life. He had a habit of slipping away when danger appeared. He would help to organize a demonstration, watch the first encounters between the workers and the police, and then vanish. So it was at the first *mayevka* held in Tiflis on April 22nd, 1901.

There was nothing in the least tentative about this *mayevka*. The revolutionaries were determined to make a show of strength, and two thousand demonstrators appeared with their red flags on the Soldatsky market place near the Alexandrovsky Gardens in the centre of the city. There was a prolonged *mêlée*, the police charging with drawn sabres, the Cossacks with their nagaikas. It was the first time Stalin had taken any part in a direct confrontation with the police, and he seems to have hovered on the outskirts, egging the demonstrators on while not himself grappling with the police and the Cossacks. In *Stalin's Early Writings and Activities* Beria states categorically that Stalin 'led' the procession, but the words 'led', 'directed' and 'guided' appear so often in the book that they have the effect of counterfeit coins. All that is certain is that Stalin was present, that he escaped in good time, and fled to Gori.

In this *mayevka* fourteen workers were injured, and some fifty were arrested. No one was killed. The government was still sure of itself and there was as yet no need to set up machine guns to mow down the demonstrators.

Iremashvili, who saw Stalin a few days later in Gori, was puzzled and perturbed by the strange exalted look on Stalin's face, the glint in his eyes. He was not hiding in his mother's house, for the police had been searching for him ever since he had escaped from their net a month earlier. His mother's house was the first place they would go to. He therefore hid out in the houses of friends and in the mountains, and sometimes at night he would slip secretly into Iremashvili's house to talk endlessly about the riot, and how there would be an even better and bloodier *mayevka* the following year. How beautiful it had been, how full of hope for the future! 'Not without alarm,' wrote Iremashvili, 'I realized that he was intoxicated by the blood that flowed during the demonstration.'

It was however only a very little blood. The *mayevka* served its purpose by giving the government full warning that the revolutionaries were on the march, but nearly seventy of the best revolutionary workers were put out of circulation. The news reached Lenin's *Iskra* some weeks later. 'The event that took place on Sunday, April 22nd,' said *Iskra,* 'is of historic import for the entire Caucasus; this day marks the beginning of an open revolutionary movement in the Caucasus.' In its characteristic way *Iskra* was inclined to attach greater importance to the demonstration than was warranted, for hundreds of demonstrations were taking place that spring in Russia. The demonstration's importance in history lies in the fact that here Stalin first saw blood flowing in a street battle.

More than ever he was now the dedicated revolutionary, the outlaw, sleeping by day, moving about secretly at night. From this period begins his use of a variety of revolutionary pseudonyms – David, Bars (meaning Leopard), Gayoz Nizheradze, Besoshvili (meaning son of Beso), Zakhar Gregoryan Melikyants, Ogoness Vartanovich Totomyants, and many others. These disguises were not very effective, for reports from informers continued to reach police headquarters in which his real name was clearly stated. To his friends he remained Koba or Soso, the affectionate form of Joseph.

About this time two of his friends gave him some excellent advice. They pointed out that if he wanted to advance in revolutionary circles it was necessary for him to produce a body of written work or at least a series of inflammatory articles. These two friends were Lado Ketskhoveli and Alexander Tsulukidze. Of the two Ketskhoveli was the closer to Stalin, for he was born in Gori and attended the Tiflis Theological Seminary, being expelled in 1893 after a student riot. Ketskhoveli and Tsulukidze were gifted propagandists, and both died young – Ketskhoveli was shot in his prison cell by Tsarist police in 1903 and Tsulukidze died of tuberculosis two years later.

Though Tsulukidze was the author of a number of Marxist pamphlets and had acquired some celebrity for his interpretation of Marxist doctrine, Ketskhoveli was generally regarded as the coming man, who would inevitably become a powerful revolutionary leader. He was a handsome man, with a thick beard, a curling moustache, and a heavy shock of wavy hair. He was less dogmatic than Tsulukidze, more prone to argument, a fiery speaker, gentle and kind in his relations with people. He encouraged Stalin to write, and when in the autumn of 1901 he was able to borrow enough money to bring out occasional issues of an illegal Marxist magazine, Stalin was invited to become a collaborator. The magazine was called *Brdzola* (The Struggle), and was printed in Baku.

Stalin attached enormous importance to *Brdzola* in his later years, and the reason is plain – his first writings on socialism appeared in it. His articles for the magazine and for its successor *Proletariatis Brdzola* occupy the greater part of the first two hundred pages of his *Collected Works*. Not all the articles he claimed to have written were in fact written by him. He claimed for example the authorship of the leading article in the first number, which is notable for its carefully reasoned and humble approach to the problem of producing a Social Democratic literature. It is lucid, simple, and well argued; and lucidity, simplicity, and straightforward argument were not Stalin's strongest qualities. He had however a gift for poetic rhetoric written in a liturgical style, and throughout his life, sometimes at the most unexpected times, he would give vent to it. In the second number of *Brdzola* there appears a long article called 'The Russian Social Democratic Party and Its Immediate Tasks', which begins with a sober history of the development of the Social Democratic movement in Russia, and suddenly launches into a kind of sustained liturgical chant which is printed as prose but is clearly intended to have an accumulative poetic effect. The poet who had previously written *To the Moon* is now grappling with another kind of poetry altogether – the poetry of incitement. With the sevenfold repetition of the words 'groaning under the yoke', he achieves the effect of a socialist hymn. He wrote:

Groaning under the yoke are the Russian peasants, swollen with interminable hunger, impoverished by the burden of taxes too heavy to be borne, thrown to the mercy of bourgeois tradesmen and 'well-born' landlords.

Groaning under the yoke are the small town-dwellers, minor employees in government and private offices, and the minor officials, in a word, the multitudes of small men belonging to the urban population, whose existence is just as insecure as that of the working class and who have reason enough to be discontented with their social position.

Groaning under the yoke are the lower- and middle-class bourgeoisie who cannot resign themselves to the Tsarist knout and the nagaika, especially those members of the bourgeoisie who are educated, the so-called representatives of the liberal professions (teachers, doctors, lawyers, university and high-school students).

Groaning under the yoke are the oppressed nationalities and religious communities in Russia, including the Poles, who have been driven from their native land and whose most sacred feelings have been outraged, and the Finns, whose rights and liberties, granted to them by history,

have been arrogantly trampled underfoot by the autocracy.
Groaning under the yoke are the eternally persecuted and
humiliated Jews, deprived even of those miserable rights
which are enjoyed by other Russian subjects – the right
to live where they choose, the right to attend school,
the right to be employed in government service, and so
on.
Groaning under the yoke are the Georgians, Armenians
and other nations who can neither learn in their own
schools nor be employed by the state, and who are compelled to submit to the shameful and oppressive policies
of *Russification* which are so zealously pursued by the
autocracy.
Groaning under the yoke are the many millions of members of Russian religious sects who want to believe and
worship according to the dictates of their own conscience
and not according to the wishes of the Orthodox priests.
Groaning under the yoke...

With these words, printed in the double number of *Brdzola*
which appeared in December 1901, Stalin makes his first appearance as a revolutionary writer. The liturgical manner, of
course, derives from the long years of study in the theological
seminary, but the content is Marxist doctrine arranged according to his own private understanding, in an order which is
wholly his own. Significantly he begins with the Russian peasants 'swollen with interminable hunger'. Just as significantly
he ends with a plea for freedom for the Russian religious
sects, by which, as a former seminarian turned atheist, he
meant all those who strenuously opposed the doctrines of the
Orthodox Church.
To those who followed Stalin's subsequent career, fearful
and terrible ironies lurk in this hymn. One by one he enumer-
ates the oppressed and humiliated peoples of the Russian
empire: the Poles, the Finns, the Georgians, the Armenians,
and the Jews, and he was to oppress and humiliate them more
than they were ever oppressed and humiliated by the Tsars.
The shameful and oppressive policies of 'Russification' – Stalin
had printed the word in specially thick type in order to
express his disgust – were to become his own policies. The
lower- and middle-class bourgeoisie, to whom he devotes two
separate and ambiguous litanies, were to suffer the full weight

of his murderous contempt, while the Russian religious sects were to be reduced to silence and legislated out of existence. He was to exact a terrible vengeance from every one of the classes and nationalities who were 'groaning under the yoke'. It is as though at the very beginning of his career as a revolutionary he had already marked out those he would destroy, hating them because they were weak, because they were suffering, and because they were oppressed.

The first writings of men who achieve great prominence are rarely so illuminating. Their ultimate purposes tend to remain obscure and ill-defined; they are hesitant and scarcely know where they are going. Stalin seems to have known where he was going. His poems suggest his thirst for grandeur and for high position, while his first prose hints at an overwhelming contempt. Strangely he was most contemptuous when he spoke of 'the many millions of members of Russian religious sects who want to believe and worship according to the dictates of their own conscience'. As a Marxist he could have no sympathy for them, as an atheist he could only despise them, and he therefore introduced them only to represent his *private* hatred of the Orthodox Church.

So, too, when he speaks of the 'minor officials' and 'the lower- and middle-class bourgeoisie' as 'groaning under the yoke', we recognize that he had no sympathy for them and had long ago declared war on them, for they belonged precisely to the class which the Social Democrats found most despicable.

Strangely, too, he felt no need to introduce the working classes into his litany. Indeed, throughout the article which amounts to some twelve pages, they are barely mentioned. Towards the end he wonders aloud whether they will seize power or whether they will drag their tails, acting merely as 'an auxiliary force of the bourgeoisie', but the argument is not pursued at any length, and seems not to have interested him.

What interested him chiefly, as we might suspect, was the prodigious use that could be made of street demonstrations. For page after page he describes their advantages, the way they attract the attention of the public and create 'the favourable soil where we can audaciously sow the seeds of socialistic ideas and political freedom'. Even the timid will be sucked into the turmoil. They will come out and watch, and they will understand instinctively what the fighting is all about. The police had made it almost impossible for the revolutionaries to distribute illegal literature, but the police could not prevent street demonstrations, and by fighting the demonstrators they only made it more certain that the sympathies of the onlookers would be aroused 'as they hear free voices calling upon them to join the struggle and stirring songs denouncing the existing system and exposing our social evils'.

When he speaks of those who watch but take no part in the demonstrations, Stalin is curiously revealing. He speaks about them at some length, a little too insistently, and once more there is the chanting refrain:

The 'curious onlooker' of today will become the demonstrator tomorrow.

The 'curious onlooker' ceases to be indifferent to the whistling sound of the sabre and the nagaika.

The 'curious onlooker' observes that the demonstrators have assembled in the streets to express their wishes and demands, and the government retaliates with beatings and brutal suppression.

The 'curious onlooker' no longer runs away from the whistling of the nagaika, but instead draws nearer, and the whips can no longer distinguish where the 'curious onlooker' ends and the demonstrator begins.

The whip serves us in good stead, for it hastens the revolutionizing of the 'curious onlooker'.

What Stalin is saying is that the more blood shed by innocent people, the better it is for the revolution. It pleases him, as he says, that the whip will fall indifferently on the backs of the young and the old, of women and children, for the more they suffer and the more they are sucked into the demonstrations the more both the government and the people will be roused to fury, and the more excesses will be committed. The whip, long a weapon of oppression, will be transformed into an instrument for arousing the people.

Stalin was twenty-one when he announced his cruel theory. The sadistic streak, which was so often observed in him, appears in his first published writings.

Not that the theory was wholly original with him. It has a respectable ancestry, and can be found in Tkachev and Nechayev, the revolutionaries of an earlier epoch who demonstrated that morality had no place in a Russian revolution; all weapons, including those which were absolutely immoral, were permitted to the revolutionaries. In their eyes morality was expendable.

Stalin, however, seems to have stumbled upon the idea as the result of personal experience. There is more than a suspicion that he was himself the 'curious onlooker', drunk with thoughts of violence, fascinated by the whistling of the whips and in his imagination glorying in the sight of the whips falling on the backs of women and children. As we have seen, he took little or no part in the *mayevka* in Tiflis in the spring of 1901. Sergo Alliluiev, Stalin's future father-in-law, did take some part in it, and there is not a word about Stalin being present in his autobiography, which was first published in the magazine *Oktyabr* in 1942, at a time when it was convenient to glorify Stalin. He had known Stalin for some time and would have had no difficulty in recognizing him. If he had seen Stalin during the *mêlée*, he would have had every reason to mention it.

In his account of the *mayevka* Sergo Alliluiev mentions Stalin once, not as a leader but as a man who made a particularly crafty suggestion about how the demonstrators could protect themselves. He tells how he was walking towards the Soldatsky market place when he saw a man wearing a warm overcoat and a Caucasian sheepskin hat. It struck him as strange that a man should be wearing such heavy clothes on such a hot day, and then he saw that it was Vano Sturua, a young revolutionary who was a close friend of Stalin. The following conversation took place:

'Are you ill?' I asked him.
Vano raised his hat and smiled at me.
'No, I'm quite well.'
'Then why on earth are you dressed like this?'
'Soso told me to.'
'What has Soso to do with it?'
Vano leaned forward and whispered in my ear.
'You have to understand that I and some others are going to take our places at the head of the group ... Do you understand now? What it means is that we shall receive the first blows of the Cossacks' nagaikas. The coat and the hat will soften the blow. Understand?'
'Yes, I understand.'
'Clever, isn't it?'

Clever it was, but in the light of Stalin's repeated assertions

in *Brdzola* written a few months later that the chief purpose
of a demonstration was to suck in innocent spectators including old men, women and children, his cleverness acquires
an ominous character. Already he had become the inventor
of cunning stratagems. In the spring of 1901 the scale was
paltry – a heavy coat against a whip. Later he would invent far more terrible stratagems to soften imaginary blows.

Already his character was formed. Bold, clever, assertive,
completely unscrupulous, he had all the makings of a revolutionary except for one quality which was rare among the
revolutionaries of his time – he was a coward. We never
see him taking part in strikes or demonstrations where there
is any real danger. He lurks in the background, gives whispered orders, vanishes, and only reappears when the coast is
clear. He is not among those who attack the Bastille with
their bare hands; he is among those who incite the mob from
the side streets, and then slip quietly away.

Among the Social Democrats in Tiflis he was known for his
sharp tongue, his assertiveness, his genuine revolutionary passion. No one doubted that he was a determined enemy of
society, but there were some who wondered whether he was
also the determined enemy of other revolutionaries. He conspired against the state, but he also conspired against the other
Social Democrats. When in November 1901 it was decided
to break away from the Messame Dasy and to form a more
activist party, the revolutionaries met secretly in the working-
class district of Avlabar in Tiflis and elected a nine-man
committee, headed by Sylvester Djibladze, the fiery student
who had once slapped the Rector of the theological seminary.
Relations between Djibladze and Stalin were strained, and
the reason soon became clear. Stalin was angry because
Djibladze had become head of the organization, a position
he wanted for himself.

The first meeting took place on November 11th, and was
followed by another meeting two weeks later. The proposal
had been made that the committee, which consisted entirely
of intellectuals, should be broadened to include workmen.
Stalin protested vehemently, on the strange grounds that the
workmen were not intelligent enough to become members. In
his view, only intellectuals could form the revolutionary elite.
Addressing the workmen who were present, he said: 'All they
do is flatter you! I ask you, are there among the workers
present even one or two of you who are suitable for the

committee? Tell the truth! Place your hands on your hearts!'
The workmen were not particularly impressed by the speech,
and accordingly went on to vote their own representatives on
the committee.

The story is told in Arkomed's *The Workingclass Movement and Social Democracy in Georgia,* published in 1910.
The name of Djugashvili was not mentioned, perhaps because
Arkomed had forgotten it; it was an easy name to forget and
even Lenin sometimes forgot it. Instead, Arkomed refers to
him as 'a young, indiscriminately energetic and wholly intelligent comrade', and there is no reason to doubt that he is
describing Stalin. 'The aforementioned young comrade,' Arkomed continues, 'transferred his activity from Tiflis to Batum,
whence the Tiflis comrades heard about his incorrect behaviour and his hostile and disorganizing agitation against the
Tiflis organization and its workers.'

Stalin was not expelled from the Tiflis organization; he was
simply permitted to leave. Djibladze, who had once liked him
and now cordially detested him, seems to have suggested that
everyone, and especially the workers, would be happy if he
absented himself from Tiflis for a while. A few days later he
slipped out of Tiflis and made his way to the coastal city on
the Black Sea.

THE CONSPIRATOR

AT THE TURN OF THE CENTURY Batum looked like an
overgrown Turkish village. There were still signs in Turkish;
the muezzin sounded from the minarets; there were blue-tiled
fountains in all the palm-shaded streets. Half the population
spoke Turkish, which was not surprising because the town
only fell into Russian hands at the end of the Russo-Turkish
war of 1878. The population was 30,000, and some five thousand workmen were employed in the oil depots along the
sea front. The oil came by railroad from Baku, and from
Batum it was exported to the West.

When Stalin came to Batum, he was confronted with difficulties he never had to face in Tiflis. No one knew him; the
town was so small that it was difficult to hide in; there already

existed a small Social Democratic organization among the workers. This was being led by Nikolay Chkheidze, a heavy-set no-nonsense kind of man, devoted to his principles. Chkheidze was to become the chairman of the Petrograd Soviet after the February revolution in 1917. In the name of the revolution he was to welcome Lenin at the Finland Station, making a little speech in which he warned the Bolshevik leader against divisive tactics and any attempt to sabotage the revolution. He had an intense dislike for conspiratorial activity, and he seems to have recognized at once that Stalin rejoiced in conspiracy for its own sake. Within a few weeks he was sending messages to Tiflis, urging the recall of the young revolutionary, complaining that he was stirring up trouble and was altogether too energetic in preaching armed action to the workmen. He called Stalin 'a disorganizer' and 'a madman'. Many years later Stalin remarked that Chkheidze was fainthearted, and Soviet historians accordingly depicted him as a man who walked languidly among the palm trees, hoping that nothing would happen to disturb his peace.

We have a few brief accounts of Stalin's stay in Batum, not all of them reliable. Writing many years later, workmen remembered, or thought they remembered, fragments of his speeches. 'The work is going too slowly,' he said. 'We need to force the pace of the revolutionary movement, comrades.' Or again: 'Comrades, they have sent me to discuss matters with you. As you know, the workers of Tiflis have been aroused from their sleep and they are engaged in war with their enemies. The workers of Batum are still sleeping peacefully. I advise you to follow the example of the Tiflis workers and to go hand in hand with them against the common enemy.' Or again: 'We need the masses, and only the masses! Without them we shall accomplish nothing!'

Much of the time he was in hiding. At one period he moved into the house of an old Muslim, Khashim Smirba, who lived in an Abkhazian village nearby. From time to time members of the illegal organization would come to the house disguised as women, covering their faces with *chadras*, the long dark veils worn by Caucasian women, and the Muslims in the village would ponder the appearance of these strangers who walked like men but dressed like women. Sometimes they could be seen carrying paper in their hands when they left the house, and so it dawned on the villagers that they were engaged in counterfeiting money. They knew there was a printing press in the house, and surely the only useful service of a printing press in such a remote place was to make counterfeit money. They debated the question at length, and old Khashim Smirba had some difficulty in explaining Stalin's presence to the villagers. Probably the idea of disguising his visitors as women came from Stalin, for it was typical of him. Many years later in St Petersburg he was himself arrested while disguised as a woman, his face heavily painted to hide the pockmarks, his head half hidden in a capacious hood. The policemen arrested him because they noticed he was wearing men's boots.

When Stalin came to power, Khashim Smirba was often asked to relate his memories of the days when Stalin hid in his house. Sometimes he would give free rein to his imagination. He remembered a dream in which he had seen Stalin as a great military figure leading his armies across Georgia, and how the next morning he had hurried to see Stalin and tell him about it.

'Never be afraid,' he said, coming into the room. 'Everything you do will turn out well.'

'How do you know?' Stalin replied.

'I've just had a dream, Soso,' Khashim said. 'What a dream! In my dream I saw you liberating the whole of the Caucasus from Tsarist soldiers, and then it seemed to me that all of us would come to live happily and freely.'

A more likely story relates to Khashim's efforts to make Stalin embrace the Moslem faith.

'You're a good man, Soso,' Khashim said one day in a complaining voice. 'It's a pity you are not a Moslem.'

'What would happen if I became a Moslem?'

'I will tell you. I will choose for you a wife more beautiful than any you ever saw. Now do you want to become a Moslem?'

'Yes,' said Stalin. 'I'll gladly become a Moslem.'

Conversations of this kind may well have taken place in that obscure and primitive village on the outskirts of Batum. It was a good hiding place for a small hand press and a revolutionary busy writing inflammatory manifestoes, chiefly addressed to the workers in the Rothschild and Mantashev factories, who were appallingly overworked and underpaid, and therefore ripe for revolt.

At this late date it is impossible to tell how deeply Stalin was involved in the strikes, riots and demonstrations which broke out in the early part of the year. In his biographical chronicle he claimed to have been the organizer of two strikes, and to have led the demonstration which followed the arrest of thirty-two strikers from the Rothschild plant. The demonstrators, numbering some four hundred, marched on the prison on March 8th to demand the release of the strikers. Receiving no satisfaction, they dispersed and during the night arranged for a general strike and a far more impressive demonstration. The next day all the workers of Batum marched on the offices of the military governor, the real ruler of Batum. They marched in well-formed ranks, and they were unarmed. Two workmen, Khimiryants and Gogoberidze, were selected as spokesmen to demand the release of the strikers. The military governor gave orders for the crowd to disperse, and when it refused, soldiers were ordered to clear the square with rifle butts. The workers lost patience, hurled stones at the soldiers, and there was confused rioting. When it was over fourteen workers had been killed and fifty-four wounded, and some five hundred were under arrest.

The massacre at Batum electrified the country, for though street riots and demonstrations were frequent, the military were under orders to use nothing more lethal than rifle butts and nagaikas to disperse the mobs. An official inquiry was opened. The evidence showed that the workers had come out in an orderly fashion, there were no leaders, and the demonstration was completely spontaneous. The name of Djugashvili was not mentioned during the public inquiry, and in the long and circumstantial account of the affair which was printed in *Iskra* many months later there is no suggestion that the demonstration was led by the local organization of the Social Democratic party.

Stalin's role in the Batum riots remains a mystery. To Henri Barbusse he was to say many years later that he placed himself at the head of the demonstration 'like a target'. Yaroslavsky, writing an official biography of Stalin, describes him as standing 'in the midst of the turbulent sea of workers, personally directing the movement', and quoting an old Batum worker called Darakhvelidze, he tells how Stalin carried a wounded comrade off the scene. The accounts of other workmen who were present, written for a memorial volume published when Stalin was at the height of his power, are equally unconvincing. He seems not to have been present. He had helped to fan the flames with his leaflets and manifestoes, but it is only remotely possible that he was present when the firing broke out.

In his biographical chronicle he claimed that he led a workers' demonstration organized 'in connection with the funeral of the victims'. The word 'led' occurs constantly in the biographical chronicle, and would seem to have a variety of meanings ranging from 'took direct command of' to 'had some remote connection with'. His sole connection with the funeral seems to have been a leaflet he wrote in his characteristic liturgical style, in which he addressed the dead workmen:

All honour to you who have laid down your lives for the truth!

All honour to the breasts that suckled you!

All honour to those whose brows are adorned with the crowns of the martyrs, and who with pale and faltering lips breathed words of struggle in your hour of death!

All honour to your shades that hover over us and whisper in our ears, 'Avenge our blood!'

For another three weeks he remained free, printing his inflammatory leaflets which were sometimes distributed by old Khashim Smirba outside the factory gates, and holding secret meetings in the local Muslim cemetery where for a while the type for the hand press was hidden. For months the police had been searching for him. They caught up with him at last in the apartment of the workman Darakhvelidze. Stalin told Henri Barbusse that he heard the police mounting the stairs, and simply went on smoking a cigarette, saying to a friend who was frightened: 'It's nothing to worry about!' The house was surrounded, and there was no escape.

The confidential police report on the arrest has survived. The first page reads:

Secret

To the Chief of Police of the City of Batum: April 1902

REPORT

I have the honour to inform Your Excellency that last night, at midnight, I gave orders to surround the house of Russadze, where, according to the reports of our agents, a meeting of workers was taking place. In the apartment of Darakhvelidze, a worker in the Mantashev factory, I found the following persons: Joseph Djugashvili, dismissed from the Theological Seminary, of no fixed address, living without a passport in Batum, where he attends the sixth form of the local school for boys...

If this report is accurate – and there seems to be no particular reason to doubt its authenticity – Stalin had returned to school at the age of twenty-two. Presumably he felt no need to complete his education; it was simply that school provided an excellent alibi for a dedicated revolutionary.

For a year and nine months Stalin was to remain a prisoner of the police. His stay in Batum had lasted only four and a half months. He had accomplished little – far less than he was to claim, but considerably more than his enemies were to claim for him. For the first time he had created a small revolutionary movement of his own, numbering perhaps twenty people, of whom he was the acknowledged leader. He had created this movement without the help of the Tiflis organization and in defiance of the local organization. For the first time, too, he enjoyed the use of a secret printing press, seeing his own manifestoes in print shortly after he had written them. Although none of his writings of this period has survived except for the poem on the Batum massacre, it was clearly a time of furious intellectual development. He had extended his range of stratagems, worn many disguises, and learned how to give orders.

Shortly after his arrest he was photographed in profile and in full face. These photographs from the police files survive, and though the one taken in full face is considerably touched up, and gives him something of the appearance of a professional seducer, the photographs taken together form a satisfactory portrait of the man. There is something dashing about him in his European coat with his checkered red-and-white scarf. He has a small, carefully trimmed moustache and the beginnings of a beard. The thick brown hair is piled forward in a fashionable manner and grows thickly over the nape of his neck. He is alert, arrogant, rather pleased with himself. One imagines that Bazarov, the young revolutionary in Turgenev's *Fathers and Sons*, would have looked like that. There is no fat on him, and he is recognizably 'the young, indiscriminately energetic and wholly intelligent comrade' of Arkomed's description.

A police description provided by Colonel of the Gendarmerie Shabelsky, made out on June 17th, two months after his arrest, when he was transferred to a new prison in Kutais, reads: 'Height 2 *arshins*, 4½ *vershocks* [just under 5 feet 4 inches]. Body medium. Age 23. Special features: Second and third toes of the left foot attached. Appearance: Ordinary. Hair: dark brown. Beard and moustaches: Brown. Nose straight and long. Face long, swarthy and pock-marked.' The police noticed the slight deformity of the toes, but over-looked the damaged left arm. This is not particularly strange, because the physical examination of the prisoners was usually conducted cursorily, not by doctors but by the police, who searched them carefully but rarely undressed them.

A curious incident occurred shortly after Stalin's arrest. According to the local police files someone threw two notes out of a window into the prison yard. It was the day when visitors were permitted to see the prisoners, but Stalin was being held incommunicado and throwing these notes out of the window was his sole method of reaching the outside world. Two of these notes were intercepted by the prison guards, and though they were unsigned they had no great difficulty in tracing them to Stalin. The first note asked the finder to get in touch immediately with Joseph Iremashvili in Gori and to tell him: 'Soso Djugashvili has been arrested. Please go at once to his mother and say that if a gendarme should ask her "When did thy son leave Gori", she must answer, "He was here all summer and winter until the fifteenth of March".' The second note was addressed to Elizabedashvili, a teacher, telling him that in spite of reverses the struggle would go on. These notes were immediately taken to Captain of the Gendarmerie Djakeli and orders were sent out for the interrogation of Iremashvili and Elizabedashvili. Iremashvili's lodgings were searched, but he was not arrested; he was living the life of a quiet schoolmaster in Gori and it was obvious that he shared none of Stalin's political leanings. Elizabedashvili, however, was arrested, and it was little comfort to him that he owed his arrest to Stalin's carelessness in throwing a note blindly out of a window.

Some light on this curious incident is thrown by Iremashvili himself. Writing in 1932, more than thirty years after the event, he described how two mysterious visitors came to his home in Gori:

Shortly after May 1st, 1902, two men came to my home

in Gori late at night, demanding entrance by a soft tapping. On their frightened faces could be read the knowledge that they had come on a secret mission.

'We are workmen from the Mantashev petroleum factory at Batum,' they said. 'Koba sends us to you with this note. The police are searching for the leader of the recent bloody *mayevka* which took place there. If the police come to you, you are to say he was in Gori in May. He will rely on your testimony.'

Then they said: 'Koba led the demonstration against the police. The police fired at the demonstrators, who fought back with cobblestones. On both sides there are many dead, and more wounded. The jails in Batum are full.'

I gave the messengers the assurance that I would do as Koba wished.

Now it is obvious that the record in the police files at Batum and the recollections of Iremashvili refer to the same event – not to the *mayevka* at Batum, but to the massacre which took place on March 22nd. Stalin was arrested on April 18th, and the police files record that the notes were found in the courtyard three days later. Iremashvili was therefore wrong about the date, but there is no reason to doubt that the messengers did come to him with the demand that he should swear false testimony.

Who were the messengers? Evidently they were not casual visitors who had picked up the notes in the prison courtyard, but members of Stalin's small organization, who knew what was expected of them. When they said that Stalin led the demonstration against the police, they were saying what Stalin wanted them to say, because he was already indulging in the pleasures of inventing his own legend. But this would have to be conveyed in the greatest secrecy. If Stalin had in fact led the demonstration, he would not have been sentenced to a term of imprisonment but would have been executed for incitement to rebellion and direct responsibility for the deaths of the workmen. Yet the trial showed conclusively that the demonstration arose spontaneously, and there was not the least evidence to suggest that Stalin led it or that he placed himself at the head of the demonstrators 'as a target'. In his indictment he was not accused of leading the demonstration: he was charged merely with being a member of an illegal political party.

When Stalin through his messengers claimed that he played a leading role, he was following a well-known revolutionary tradition. There was classic authority for such inventions. In January 1869 Vera Zasulich received a letter in Nechayev's handwriting, reading: 'They are taking me to the fortress. Do not lose heart, beloved comrades. Continue to have faith in me, and let us hope we meet again.' Nechayev, the first and in some ways the most terrifying of the professional revolutionaries who were visited upon Russia, was conveying that he was about to be locked up in the Peter and Paul fortress, reserved for the most dangerous political prisoners. At the time he wrote the letter he was making his way to the frontier, disguised as a woman. With this message to Vera Zasulich he began the cultivation of his own legend, which was later to reach towering proportions.

The police were concerned to discover whether Stalin had indeed played a leading role in the demonstration, and he was therefore kept in jail until the official inquiry ended in the late spring of the following year. At last on July 9th, 1903, he was sentenced to exile in Siberia for three years. The slow and cumbrous machinery for deporting the prisoners to their place of exile kept grinding away for a few more months, and it was not until the autumn, according to Beria, or late November, according to Yaroslavsky, that he set out on the long journey to the village of Novaya Uda in the *guberniya* of Irkutsk.

For nearly a year and a half he had been in prison, suffering the fate of having to obey higher authority, the fate that was most distasteful to him. Prison in Tsarist Russia in the early years of the century was not unendurable provided the prisoner obeyed a few simple rules. The primitive and overcrowded cells had to be kept clean, prison officers had to be addressed by their titles, and their orders had to be obeyed instantly. No demonstrations were permitted, no unauthorized letters could be received or sent out, and efforts to subvert the guards were brutally punished. Prison life was largely a communal affair, and the prison authorities acted with a mixture of paternalism and barbarism.

What the prison authorities feared most of all were the sudden explosions of anger and frustration which would sometimes sweep from one cell to another until the whole prison was caught up in a storm of shouts, screams, confused singing, the breaking of dishes and furniture. The whole prison would become stir-crazy, and the guards would find themselves infected by the madness, which always seemed to arise suddenly, without warning. If the guards had been sensible, they would simply have kept quiet and let the storm exhaust itself. They were rarely sensible. Instead, they ran from cell to cell, shouting insanely, screaming at the top of their lungs to the prisoners to keep quiet, and adding to the confusion. Sometimes the prisoners would set fire to objects in their cells, and this would produce the greatest panic among the guards, who would fire warning shots in the air and search out the main culprits for exemplary punishment, but since the main culprit was the madness which descends on overcrowded prisons, the punishments fell on the guilty and innocent alike.

While Stalin was in prison, there occurred in the fortress prison of Metekh in Tiflis a famous incident of this kind, and the chief victim was Stalin's friend Lado Ketskhoveli, who had been editing and printing the illegal magazine *Brdzola* in Baku. Arrested in Baku in September 1902, he had been transferred by administrative order to Tiflis, where he was still awaiting trial eleven months later. He was a bad prisoner, always taunting the guards and prison officers, incapable of settling down to prison routine. He was the revolutionary who would never cease being a revolutionary, even in prison. The prison was overcrowded and unbearably hot, and the prisoners were in a mood to provoke their guards. Ketskhoveli led them in singing the 'Marseillaise', and during quieter moments he would stand at the window of his cell and utter inflammatory speeches in his powerful voice, and the prisoners would answer with a wild storm of applause and protest. Sergo Alliluiev was in a nearby cell. He describes in his autobiography how he recognized the danger signals and shouted to Ketskhoveli to be quiet and keep away from the window. Ketskhoveli was still shouting when a shot rang out. Then there was silence, and Ketskhoveli's voice was not heard again.

The killing of prisoners was a rare event in the early years of the century. The prison governor was appalled by the shooting, if only because he realized the consequences, and he went about the prison, going from cell to cell, assuring the prisoners that Ketskhoveli was not dead but wounded, and would shortly recover. Some time later the prisoners learned the truth. At nine-thirty in the morning of August 17th, 1903, he had been shot through the heart, dying instantaneously.

The news must have reached Stalin a few days later through the grapevine. For him it was like the death of a father. No one, not even Kurnatovsky, had had such a profound effect on him. No one else had given him so much encouragement. His first writings appeared in Ketskhoveli's magazine, and there was a sense in which he had deliberately modelled himself on the older man, whose murder in the fortress prison of Metekh he must have regarded as only one more of the intolerable outrages committed by the autocracy.

It is worth while to pause over this murder, for it was to have fearful consequences. For Stalin the murder of Ketskhoveli was not simply the result of a shot fired by an overexcited guard; it was judicial murder, and the autocracy was directly responsible. The Tsar himself, and every official wearing the Tsar's uniform was implicated. Inevitably the murder called for vengeance, and in good time Stalin was to exact vengeance on a scale unprecedented in history. For him the murder of Ketskhoveli was final; it meant that there could be no turning back. In the life of Stalin this murder corresponded to the hanging of Alexander Ulyanov in the life of Lenin.

Years later Stalin told Yenukidze that Ketskhoveli was the finest, most gifted and most energetic revolutionary he had ever known, thus placing him above Lenin, and in the pages of Beria's *Stalin's Early Writings and Activities*, the name of Ketskhoveli is given special prominence. Usually the names of the revolutionaries mentioned in the book are given with the surname prefixed by an initial: so we have V. Tsuladze, S. Mdivani, and so on. But when Stalin, speaking through Beria, mentions Lado Ketskhoveli, he never employs the initial and scarcely ever the surname. Alone among the revolutionaries he is called by his Christian name: Lado.

Unlike Ketskhoveli, Stalin appears to have been a model prisoner. He took no part in the occasional savage outbreaks, reserving his strength for the future. His friend Kalandadze remembered him as a man who carefully organized his life: so many hours for exercise, so many for reading, so many for discussion with his fellow prisoners. Ketskhoveli had encouraged him to study, and now that he had a prison library at his disposal he was reading voluminously, trying to think out the next stage of the revolutionary struggle in Russia. He was not a man who read very deeply or thought very profoundly, and one might expect accordingly that any change in direction would come about as the result of an impulse out-side him.

The change came with the Second Congress of the Russian Social Democratic Party which met in London in August 1903, where Lenin brought about the split between the radical Bolsheviks and the moderate Mensheviks. Lenin was deter-mined to introduce a programme of direct action, including terror, and to elevate the proletariat to the position of nomi-nal leaders of the revolt, while reserving for a small elite of the revolutionary intelligentsia the practical control of the revolution. The programme, though outwardly Marxist, re-vealed the influence of the terrorist Narodnaya Volya of the eighties, and the divergence between the Bolsheviks and the Mensheviks was therefore one which could never be healed. Some weeks later news of the split reached Stalin in prison, and it may have pleased him to realize that he had played the same role in relation to the Messame Dasy as Lenin had played in relation to the Russian Social Democratic Party, for he too, with Ketskhoveli and Tsulukidze and a few others, had broken away from the parent body in favour of a more rigidly conspiratorial programme.

Many years later when the enemies of Stalin were attempting to blacken him by discovering unsavoury incidents in his past, they found a prison officer's report written in 1911 describing him as 'originally a Menshevik, later a Bolshevik'. There was however nothing in his character to suggest that he had lean-ings towards the moderate Menshevik programme. By in-stinct and training he favoured direct action. In Lenin he recognized a man who was amoral and completely ruthless in his choice of instruments in the war against society. The con-spirator in Stalin found a fit object of worship in Lenin, and from this time onward he regarded himself as Lenin's faith-ful follower and comrade-in-arms.

A week after Lenin's death Stalin addressed a memorial meeting at the Kremlin Military Academy. He told the stu-dents he would not deliver a set speech on Lenin, for they had heard so many of these speeches. Instead, he proposed to 'throw some light on Lenin's characteristics as a man and a leader'. Inevitably the speech turned on Stalin's meetings with Lenin, and their effect was to throw more light on Stalin than on Lenin. No doubt this was his intention. He said:

I first became acquainted with Lenin in 1903. True, it was

not a personal acquaintance, but one that came about by correspondence. But it made an indelible impression on me, which has never left me through all the years of my work in the party. I was then in exile in Siberia. My knowledge of the revolutionary activities of Lenin since the end of the nineties, and especially after 1901, after the appearance of *Iskra*, convinced me that in the person of Lenin we had a man of singular attainments. In my eyes at that time he was not simply the leader of the party, he was its actual creator, for he alone understood the inner essence and urgent needs of the party.

When I compared him with the other leaders of the party, it always seemed to me that he stood a whole head above them – Plekhanov, Martov, Axelrod, and the rest – and compared with them he was not simply one of the leaders, but a leader of the highest rank, a mountain eagle, who knew no fear in the struggle and who boldly led the party forward along the unexplored paths of the Russian revolutionary movement.

This impression so deeply touched my heart that I felt impelled to write about it to one of my close friends, then living abroad in exile, demanding his opinion. Some time later, when I was already in exile in Siberia – this was at the end of 1903 – I received an enthusiastic reply from my friend and a simple, profoundly interesting letter from Lenin to whom, as it happened, my friend had shown my letter. This little letter [*pis'metso*] was comparatively short, but it contained a bold and fearless criticism of the practical work of our party and a remarkably clear and precise account of the entire plan of work of the party in the immediate future. Only Lenin could write of the most intricate things so simply and clearly, so concisely and boldy – the sentences were not speech so much as pistol shots.

Stalin went on to say that to his infinite regret he followed the old conspiratorial custom of burning this letter and many other letters received from Lenin.

There is some doubt whether he ever received 'the little letter'. According to his own biographical chronicle, a notoriously inaccurate device, he reached his place of exile on November 27th and escaped thirty-nine days later. A letter from Lenin, then in Geneva where he settled after the Second Congress, would take many weeks to catch up with him; it would go from one group of exiles to another, hidden in the binding of a book or disguised in some other way, and by the time it became known that Stalin had reached Novaya Uda, Stalin himself was already planning his escape. If the biographical chronicle is accurate, it would have been virtually impossible for him to have received the letter in exile. The letter is not mentioned in *Stalin's Early Writings and Activities*, where we would expect to find it prominently displayed.

Nevertheless Lenin was in the habit of sending brief letters of acknowledgement to strangers, especially if he heard some good of them or if they were likely to become Bolsheviks. There was a small community of Georgian Bolsheviks in Geneva, he was following events in the Transcaucasus carefully, and he might very well be induced to write a brief note to Stalin in acknowledgement of a letter of appreciation.

The 'little letter' has some importance in any account of Stalin, because Stalin himself regarded it as the beginning of his acquaintance with Lenin, the first flowering of the affection between them. When he addressed the cadets, he had every reason to magnify his early contacts with Lenin, and the processes of magnification can be observed during the course of his speech. First there is the little *pis'metso*, then it becomes 'comparatively short', then it becomes a long letter containing 'a bold and fearless criticism of the practical work of our party and a remarkably clear and precise account of the *entire* plan of work of the party in the immediate future'. It was Stalin's habit to confuse the grain of dust with the pearl. In the course of his life he told many grandiose lies, but there is often an ascertainable grain of truth in them.*

* There is one possible explanation for the *pis'metso* which, so far as I know, has never been suggested. Stalin may very well have received a brief note from Lenin while in prison, and about the same time or when he was in Siberia he may have read Lenin's 'Letter to a Comrade on Our Organizational Tasks'. This letter, which appeared in the form of a pamphlet, was written in September 1902 before the Bolshevik-Menshevik split, and was reproduced in hundreds of hectographed and printed copies, being easily the most widely read work of Lenin up to this time. Krupskaya reports that the police were continually finding copies all over Russia. A special edition of the pamphlet, printed by the Social Democratic party in Siberia, appeared in June 1903.

Lenin's 'Letter to a Comrade' was far from being a 'little letter'. In the current edition of his *Complete Works* it covers twenty-one closely printed pages.

He may have been telling lies again when some weeks after his escape from Siberia he met Sergo Alliluiev in Tiflis and told a long circumstantial story of his first abortive attempt to escape on Christmas Eve, when his guard was drunk. Armed with a sporting rifle lent by a grocer in Novaya Uda, he made his way on foot through the bitter cold of a Siberian winter, intending to reach the fairly large village of Makarovka twenty miles away. The road ran through a ravine, then climbing on to a plateau it crossed the open taiga before it came to the outskirts of the village. The ravine was safe, but the taiga was known to be infested with wolves hunting in packs. It had been a long and cruel winter, and the wolves were famished.

A few wolves appeared while he was making his way through the ravine, but they fled at the first shot. His ears and nose were suffering from frostbite, but he went on. When at last he came out on the plateau, a whole wolf pack numbering at least ten wolves descended on him. He fought them off and then realized that his feet had grown numb. He was forced to turn back in the direction of Novaya Uda. Ten days later he made another attempt to escape. This time he did not go on foot, but on a sledge. He told Henri Barbusse that he made the journey 'at his own expense' and that he arrived in Batum in the disguise of a soldier.

Of this providential escape, and of many others, there will be more to be said later. Here it is only necessary to observe that all his escapes took place with astonishing ease. He left no trail, had no accomplices, and travelled alone. There was always an air of mystery about him, but he was never more mysterious than when he spirited himself from one end of Russia to the other. He has the air of a conjurer. The rabbits disappear into the hat, the hat disappears, finally the conjurer himself disappears, and the stage is left empty. This time, when he reappears, he is almost unrecognizable. The sullen adolescent has given place to the hardened revolutionary.

THE YEARS OF THE LOCUST

One cannot help laughing when one sees a man making war against his own fantasies.

THE REVOLUTIONARY

IN 1904, WHEN STALIN RETURNED from Siberia, he was still little known. He had preached socialism among small groups of workmen in Tiflis, taken an obscure part in two *mayevkas*, printed his own broadsheets and manifestoes in an obscure village near Batum, and led his own private revolutionary organization in defiance of the Tiflis organization. He had contributed a few remarkable pages to the second issue of *Brdzola* and except for some poems written in his teens and a short inflammatory ode to the martyrs of the Batum massacre, this was the extent of his writings. He had spent nearly a year and a half in prison before being sent into exile in Siberia. There were thousands of young revolutionaries who had done more.

Among those who had done considerably more was the twenty-one-year-old revolutionary called Lev Borisovich Rosenfeld, who went by the name of Kamenev, which means 'a stone'. There was however nothing stonelike about him. He had a quick and cultivated mind, a calm disposition, and a sense of moral purpose. Unlike Trotsky, whose sister he married, he was no fiery orator; he won his arguments by reason and persuasion. He was a handsome man with finely modelled features and an impressively high forehead, and there was about him even when he was young an air of natural distinction. He possessed no vanity at all and seemed unaware of the effect he produced on people. He was born of working-class parents, his father being a Moscow railroadman who went to work on the Transcaucasian railroad when the boy was about thirteen. From the Tiflis gymnasium Kamenev became a law student at Moscow University. Almost immediately he got into trouble and was thrown into the Butyrki prison for making Marxist speeches. In the summer of 1902 he went abroad to be near Lenin, and they remained on intimate terms until Lenin's death.

Stalin and Kamenev had only a few things in common. Each had been to prison, each had led study circles among the shoemakers and railroad workers, each regarded himself as a dedicated Marxist, and held Lenin in great honour. There the resemblance ended. Their manners, their way of thinking, and their approach to problems differed so fundamentally that it was as though they spoke of entirely different Marxisms and entirely different Lenins. What was especially galling to Stalin was that Kamenev was a member of the Bolshevik party and was on intimate terms with Lenin. Stalin himself did not become a registered member of the party until a year later.

Their paths crossed in Tiflis a few days after Stalin's escape from Siberia, when they met for the first time and Kamenev made arrangements for Stalin to hide out in the apartment of a worker called Morochkov. Kamenev was notably reticent about the meeting, and Stalin for his own reasons kept silent about it. On the night of January 18th the police raided Kamenev's apartment, and he fled to Moscow, where he was once more arrested. He was deported again to Tiflis on July 28th, and there he remained except for brief organizational tours until the spring of 1905, when he went to London as a delegate of the Third Congress. As Lenin's personal representative, he was by far the most important member of the party in Georgia, and the most effective. The police, who were hunting for him continually, regarded him as the most dangerous.

When Stalin came to rewrite the history of the Bolshevik party in Georgia, he was to claim that 'the entire revolutionary movement in Transcaucasia from its inception was inseparably associated with the work and name of Stalin'. In fact he was a late-comer, arriving on the scene long after the first seeds were planted by exiles from Tsarist Russia in the early nineties. He claimed that since 1898 he was, if not the sole director, at least the prime mover in the revolutionary struggle in Georgia. The claim was fraudulent. He was merely one of many, and there were at least fifty others who played more outstanding roles. Most of the claims made for Stalin in *Stalin's Early Writings and Activities* could be made more properly of Kamenev.

Stalin's activities in 1904 are shrouded in mystery. Of his writings during that year only two letters and an unsigned article on 'The Social Democratic View of the National Question', which appeared in *Proletariatis Brdzola* have survived. The article is notable because it shows Stalin grappling with the problem of nationalities, on which he was later to be regarded as an authority. Following the accepted Social Democratic programme, he envisages a decentralized state formed of self-governing nationalities free to follow their own customs and to speak their own languages. In this article he attacks the Social Federalists who demanded Georgian autonomy, and tells an ominous story about an amateur anatomist, 'who possessed all the requirements of his profession, a degree, an operating room, the proper instruments and inordinate pretensions, although he was altogether lacking in one minor capacity – he knew nothing about anatomy'. Confronted with the scrambled pieces of a skeleton on his anatomical table, the amateur anatomist simply hurls the pieces against the wall, complaining loudly that too many of them were spurious for him to make a complete skeleton out of them. The story has nothing to do with the argument, but throws some light on Stalin's method of solving problems.

The article is chiefly interesting because it shows Stalin for the first time paying tribute to the proletariat. 'A new class has entered the arena – the *proletariat* – and with it a new "national question" has arisen – *"the national question" of the proletariat.*' For the first time, too, he is heard proclaiming like Lenin that there must be a single, flexible, centralized party, 'whose Central Committee should be able to rouse the workers of the whole of Russia at a moment's notice and lead them in a decisive onslaught against the autocracy and the bourgeoisie'.

Two letters written in September–October 1904, but not published until 1949, have survived. They were written to his friend Davitashvili, who was then living in Germany. They show some evidence of having been carefully edited, for the praises of Lenin are written in a different style from the rest. The first letter begins by asking for copies of *Iskra*, which, as Stalin well knew, was not being edited by Lenin: the Mensheviks had seized control of it. 'What we need here now,' he wrote, 'is *Iskra* (although it is without sparks, nevertheless we have need of it: at all events it has news, the devil take it, and we must thoroughly know the enemy.)' He asks for a copy of Lenin's pamphlet *One Step Forward, Two Steps Back*, but adds that there is no urgent need of it – 'You can put this one aside if you can't send it now'. He asks for all the new publications, and he evidently means both Bolshevik and Menshevik publications – 'We need everything new that is being printed, from simple declarations to large pamphlets, which in any way deals with the struggle now going on in the party'.

This is not the tone of a convinced Bolshevik, who would find little reason to read the works of the Menshevik enemy. He praises Lénin, and then goes on to ask questions which Lenin had answered long ago. He asks: 'Do the masses give their leaders a programme and the principles underlying the programme, or do the leaders give them to the masses?' He is obviously quite seriously concerned with the question, for if the masses spontaneously dictate the programme, why should anyone be concerned with the various divagations of the party line? And if the revolutionary movement arises spontaneously, why should anyone waste his effort in attacking the anarchists and the terrorists, who are both in their various ways expressions of the movement? Finally, following Lenin, he arrives at the conclusion that the theory of socialism is 'completely independent of the growth of the spontaneous movement' and is introduced from the outside, correcting the movement in conformity with the requirements of the proletarian class struggle. The revolutionary elite directs the spontaneous movement. So he writes to Davitashvili:

> The practical deduction to be drawn from this is as follows: we must raise the proletariat to the consciousness of its real class interests, to a consciousness of the socialist ideal, and not dissipate this ideal in trivialities or accommodate it to the spontaneous movement. Lenin has laid down the theoretical basis on which this practical deduction is built. All you need to do is to accept this theoretical premise, and no opportunism will ever come near you. Here lies the significance of the Leninist idea. I call it Leninist, because no one in Russian literature has expressed it so clearly as Lenin. Plekhanov thinks he is still living in the nineties and goes on chewing what has already been chewed eighteen times over – twice two make four.

Stalin writes like an unfledged amateur, impatient for certainties, certain only that a revolutionary uprising must be directed by an elite while arising spontaneously. Plekhanov, who had no sympathy for the self-elected revolutionary elite, is therefore dismissed for his absurd parochialism. But in the second letter Stalin returns to the contemplation of Plekhanov as though he were fascinated by that powerful and compelling figure, whose disciples, Rosa Luxemburg, Vera Zasulich, Karl Kautsky and Paul Axelrod, formed a close-knit clan, 'who cannot betray one another and will always defend one another

without raising the question of their individual guilt or innocence'. He does not explain why they should be asked to
betray another. Once again he finds himself asking those insistent questions concerning the leaders and the led. He was
sorry for Plekhanov, who was so miserably confused that he
had asked all the wrong questions, and he proceeds to ask
the right questions, which, according to Stalin, answer themselves:

> Plekhanov's war on the question of tactics is nothing but
> utter confusion, characteristic of the 'individual' as he passes
> over to the camp of the opportunists. If Plekhanov had
> formulated the question clearly, in this way: 'Who formu-
> lates the programme, the leaders or the led?' Or again:
> 'Who raises whom to an understanding of the programme,
> the leaders or the led?' Or again: 'Is it perhaps undesirable
> that the leaders should raise the masses to an understanding
> of the programme, tactics, and principles of organization?'
> If Plekhanov had put these questions to himself as clearly
> as this, he would have perceived that their simplicity and
> tautology provide their own solution, and perhaps he
> would have been deterred from his intentions and would
> not have come out in such an uproar against Lenin. But
> since Plekhanov did not do this, i.e., since he confused the
> question with phrases about 'the heroes and the mob', he
> erred on the side of *tactical opportunism*. Confusing the
> issue is a characteristic trait of opportunists.

Stalin's attitude towards the leader and the led has considerable importance, because he became an absolute leader who
permitted himself no limits to his autocratic power. It was
precisely on the question of the leaders and the led that the
Russian Democratic party was split to its foundations; and it
is clear that Stalin never seriously permitted himself to believe
that the question was worth raising. By circumstance, by
nature, and by instinct, he regarded himself as a leader. His
hesitations were not those of a man who did not know the
answer, but of a man too young and untrained to know
how to formulate the question.

The two letters to Davitashvili, the second answering the
first, show Stalin for the first time grappling with theory. He
had a minimum of theoretical ability; theory was something
to be avoided. What he was most concerned with in the long
and repetitive series of essays, articles and pronunciamentos

written before his rise to power was the exploration of the tactics necessary for acquiring power. Lenin had led the way with his demand for a revolutionary elite which would achieve power, and Stalin was happy to follow him.

He was not however acquiring very much power in 1904. The biographical chronicle is exceedingly vague about his activities, while granting him in general a position of prominence. In February he is 'directing' the work of an otherwise unknown 'Caucasian Union Committee of the Russian Social Democratic Party'. In June he is in Baku, dissolving a Menshevik committee and installing a Bolshevik committee in its stead. He spends the summer touring through 'the most important districts of Transcaucasia', holding debates with Mensheviks, Federalists and Anarchists, and establishing a Bolshevik Imeretia-Mingrelia Committee. In November he is in Baku 'leading the campaign for the convocation of the Third Congress of the party', and in the following month he 'leads' the general strike of the Baku workers.

These claims are unsubstantiated, and some of them are demonstrably false. He had no large following; it is possible that he had no following at all. He was one of those who lived on the outskirts of the revolutionary movement. When Vladimir Bobrovsky and his wife, Cecilia Bobrovskaya, were sent to the Caucasus by Lenin to take charge of Bolshevik operations in the autumn of 1904 they found no evidence of any remarkable activities by Stalin. Cecilia Bobrovskaya, writing her autobiographical *Twenty Years in Underground Russia* long after Stalin was in power, saw no reason to make generous claims for him. 'I had business,' she wrote, 'mostly with Mikha Tskhakaya, who was known as Gurgen, with Stalin, then still very young, and with the late Alexander Tsulukidze, who was even then very ill.' She had a good deal to say about the activities of the Georgian revolutionaries, but Stalin is never mentioned again.

What then was he doing? Trotsky, rather unfairly, was inclined to believe that he spent a good part of the year celebrating the joys of his marriage with Ekaterina Svanidze, a girl from the village of Didi-Lilo. Two portraits of her have survived, a photograph and a drawing said to have been made by Stalin. They have enough in common to suggest that she was unusually beautiful with her deep-set eyes, straight nose, and strong, well-modelled chin. The marriage is said to have taken place in Gori on June 22nd, 1904.

Iremashvili, who was not always accurate in his dates, says the marriage took place in 1903, while Stalin was in prison. It is not impossible that there were two marriages, the first a brief civil ceremony performed in prison and witnessed by his revolutionary comrades. Such marriages, which were fairly common in Tsarist prisons, were regarded by the revolutionaries as binding. If the girl insisted upon it, there might be a religious marriage when the term of imprisonment was over. It would seem likely that the girl was chosen for him by his mother in the hope that he would settle down and keep out of mischief, and that once he agreed to the marriage he would eventually be forced to accept a religious ceremony.

We know so little about Stalin's private life that even the smallest scraps of information may prove useful. As it happens, Iremashvili has given a reasonably full and convincing portrait of the marriage in his memoirs. I have here combined three separate passages from the memoirs:

He married in 1903. His marriage, according to his lights, was a happy one. True, the equality of the sexes which he himself advocated as the basic principle of marriage in the new state, had no place in his own house. It was not in his character to feel any sense of equality with anyone. His marriage was a happy one because his wife, who could not follow him in intellectual attainments, regarded him as a demigod, and because, being a Georgian woman, she was brought up in the sacrosanct tradition that a woman is born to serve.... This truly Georgian woman watched over the welfare of her husband in fear and trembling. She spent countless nights in ardent prayers waiting for her Soso to return from his secret conferences. She prayed that Koba would turn away from his ideas that were displeasing to God and that he would enjoy a peaceful family life of toil and contentment ... This man, so restless in spirit, feeling that everything he did and every step he took was being closely watched by the Tsarist police, could find love only in his impoverished home. Only his wife, his child, and his mother were exempt from the scorn he poured out on everyone else.

Iremashvili's account of the marriage rings true. It was a marriage that was happy for the husband and miserable for the submissive wife, who could not share his political beliefs and took refuge in her religion. It was therefore not unlike the marriage between the brutal cobbler and the quiet peasant woman who gave birth to Stalin.

A son, Jacob, was born of the marriage, but the date of his birth is unknown. Iremashvili tells us that the boy was one of his students in the Tiflis gymnasium in 1919–1920, but since boys in Russia generally entered the gymnasium at the age of about ten and remained there for the following six years, this information gives no clue to the date of his birth. All we know of him is that he grew up to be a strikingly handsome man, with no taste for politics, quiet and studious, and he seems to have made it a point of honour never to use his father's position for his own advancement. He is said to have studied machine technology at the Baumann Institute in Moscow, but even this is uncertain. Only one date in his life can be considered reasonably accurate, and only one conversation in which he took part has been recorded. The date is July 24th, 1941, when, as a lieutenant in the Red Army, he was captured by the Germans near Lesno. The conversation took place with Hermann Goering, who ordered the prisoner to be brought to his Karinhall estate. Goering vaunted the superiority of German civilization. Jacob expressed contempt for all that was not Russian, and went on to astonish Goering by insisting that Russia would become the mightiest political, scientific and economic power of the world. Asked about his private career, he said he had no personal privileges at all because he was the Premier's son. The report came from sources close to the Vatican.

Of his ultimate fate nothing is known for certain. It is believed that he was removed to a concentration camp reserved for specially important prisoners, and for a while the Germans seem to have played with the idea of offering him in exchange for Field Marshal Paulus. There are also reports that Stalin offered a large sum for news of his whereabouts. An American soldier who conducted a careful inquiry after the war heard that not long before the fall of Berlin, either because he feared what would happen to him when he was recaptured by the Red Army or because he was afraid of becoming a pawn of the Germans during their last desperate efforts to delay surrender, he flung himself on the electrically charged wire fence at Oranienburg concentration camp.

While we know very little about Jacob, we know even less about his mother. To the end she remains a ghostly presence in the background, having no share and no interest in her husband's political activities. She died, according to Iremashvili, in 1907. The cause of her death is unknown; at various times it has been stated to have been pneumonia, tuberculosis, and puerperal fever. She was buried according to the rites of the Orthodox Church.

Stalin accompanied her to the grave, a pale, sullen, shattered man, who had no longer anything to live for except to take vengeance on society and to pursue his ambitions. Iremashvili, who attended the funeral ceremony, was struck by the contrast between the priests in their flowing gold vestments and the shambling and utterly heartbroken revolutionary in their midst. At the cemetery gates Stalin paused, took Iremashvili by the hand, and said as he pointed to the coffin: 'She was the one creature who softened my heart of stone. She is dead, and with her have died my last warm feelings for humanity.' Then he placed his hand on his heart and said: 'It is all so desolate here, so inexpressibly empty!'

There is no reason to doubt that he said exactly these words, which would not appear to be so theatrical to a Georgian as they appear to an American. The words are memorable, because they came from the heart. Never again shall we hear Stalin speaking so humanly.

Iremashvili believed that the death of Ekaterina brought about Stalin's final break with society. Up to this moment there had always been some frail bonds of morality, a sense of the necessity of obeying the conventions which men have invented in order to live peacefully with one another. He would steal, but not murder; he would incite, but he would not come out openly in rebellion. Now the bonds were broken, and there were no instruments of oppression he would not use against the oppressors. 'Beginning from the day he buried his wife,' writes Iremashvili, 'he lost the last vestige of human feelings. His heart was filled with the unutterably evil hatred which his cruel father had already begun to engender in him in his childhood. He became indifferent to his sad and poverty-stricken fate, and crushed with sarcasm his less and less frequently occurring moral impulses. Ruthless with himself, he became ruthless with all people.'

Iremashvili's account is borne out by that of another revolutionary. Razden Arsenidze, whose memoirs appeared in 1963, first met Stalin on his return from exile in 1904. He was struck by Stalin's bitterness and remorseless sarcasm, his lack of restraint. At their first meeting Stalin complained

about the tone of some leaflets printed by the party for distribution among Mingrelian peasants. They were not sharp
enough, not sufficiently high-pitched and warlike. It was carefully explained to him that one does not write leaflets for
peasants in the same combative tones as one writes them for
workmen. Stalin listened to the explanations with a mocking
smile. Arsenidze says he was 'a lean, bony man in those days,
disfigured by smallpox, his skin pale brown, free and forward
in his manner, completely self-sufficient'.

Arsenidze says that sarcasm of a most brutal kind was
Stalin's chief weapon of attack. He was a raging anti-Semite,
and liked to introduce lengthy attacks against Jews into his
speeches. What Stalin seemed to like most about the Bolshevik
party was that it included fewer Jews than the Menshevik
party. 'It exasperates Lenin that God sent him such comrades
as the Mensheviks!' Stalin used to say, according to Arsenidze.
'Martov, Dan, Alexandrov – they are nothing but uncircum-
cised Jews! So is that old *baba* Vera Zasulich! Go and
work with them! You will find that they won't fight and
there is no rejoicing at their banquets! They are cowards
and shopkeepers! The workers of Georgia ought to know that
the Jewish nation produces only cowards and people who are
no use at fighting!'

It is not surprising that Stalin should have been anti-Semitic
in his early years, for he was to show an abundance of anti-
Semitic feeling when he came to power. In 1909 he wrote
that he preferred the Bolsheviks because they were more
Russian than the Mensheviks; his anti-Semitism would seem
to have been accompanied by a growing sense of nationalism.
Yet his bitterness against the Jews is not easily explained, for
traditionally the Georgians were far less anti-Semitic than the
Russians. There were no pales or ghettos in Georgia.

Stalin rejoiced in brutal sarcasm, and sometimes his enjoyment can be detected in his writings. Here, for example, he
attacks his *bête noire*, the Georgian Federalists:

The chameleon's distinguishing feature is that it is forever
changing its colour. It is a well-known fact that every animal has its own particular colouring, but the chameleon's
nature is not satisfied with this. It assumes a lion's colouring when it is with a lion, a wolf's colouring when it is
with a wolf, a frog's when it is with a frog, depending on
which colour is more to its advantage at the time, like a

hypocritical and unprincipled man – he is mine when with me, yours when with you, a reactionary with a reactionary, provided he can somehow creep into a loophole and get what he wants.

He was continually referring to people 'who hide in loopholes', perhaps because it was a subject on which he could speak with some authority. When the liberals came to power following the January 1905 massacre of unarmed workmen in front of the Winter Palace in St Petersburg, he wrote:

> Comrades! Only a few months have passed since 'new breezes' sprang up in Russia. That was the time of 'revelation from on high'. ... The tongues of the liberals loosened at once, and a round of banquets, social evenings, petitions, etc. began. 'We are the salt of the earth; so, for the love of Christ, give us a little freedom,' they implored the Tsar. Socialist Revolutionaries clicked their pistols here and there, and people began to talk about the approach of 'spring'. The Tsar looked at it all and laughed. But all things come to an end. The Tsar got tired of the 'endless pother' of the liberals and sternly cried: 'Now, now, an end to your jokes, enough of your noise!' And they, poor things, piped down and hid in corners.

Although his enemies were continually creeping into corners, they were continually emerging, and so again and again we find him attacking the enemies he had already laughed to scorn.

What role he desired to play in the coming revolution was made clear in an article written for *Proletariatis Brdzola* in January 1905, a week before the massacre which precipitated the revolutionary ferment in Russia. 'The party,' he wrote, 'has now become a centralized *organization*, and has thrown off its patriarchal aspects, becoming in all respects like a *fortress*, whose gates are opened only to those who are worthy.' The party would not be ruled by 'a conglomeration of individuals', but by a small, highly trained elite, with their own programme, tactics and organizational principles. Following Lenin, he saw the coming revolution as an armed uprising of the peasants and the proletariat led by a general staff 'comprising the most experienced among the Bolsheviks', among whom he evidently included himself. To Arsenidze he said

more simply: 'We shall become the policemen of the revolution.'

The revolution however was far in the future. For the
present he had to content himself with the writing of leaflets,
manifestoes and occasional articles in illegal journals, with
conspiratorial work, and with debates with his opponents. He
was not, nor was he ever to become, a gifted orator. Arsenidze, who debated with him, complains that he spoke mechanically, dully, as though reciting the words of Lenin, which he
had learned by rote. But in another passage Arsenidze refers
to his persistence and the hammerlike beat of his sentences,
which made him perhaps a more effective speaker than his
opponent was willing to acknowledge. Arsenidze also reports
that if Stalin was worsted in an argument, he would show no
emotion, but there would be 'a sarcastic smile on the left
side of his face'. In his biographical chronicle Stalin refers
to his debates with Arsenidze, and evidently found them memorable.

In later years Stalin claimed that he presided over a series
of important conferences, assumed direct responsibility for the
work of the party in Georgia, and was instrumental in founding what came to be known as the Avlabar printing shop, a
secret underground press in the Avlabar district of Tiflis.
The press was in a deep cellar fifty feet below the surface
of the earth; there were a number of refinements unusual in
revolutionary printing shops. The changing values which
Stalin attached to the secret printing press form one of the
more bewildering problems in reconstructing the life of Stalin
during this period, for sometimes he seemed to attach extraordinary significance to his singlehanded construction of the
press, at other times he regarded himself as one of many
revolutionaries who operated it, and there were also times
when he would mention it only casually and claim to have
had very little to do with it.

Yaroslavsky, in his official biography of Stalin, provides a
description of the printing press ostensibly taken from the
newspaper *Kavkaz* (The Caucasus) of April 16th, 1908:

Secret Printing Plant

On Saturday, April 15th, in the courtyard of an uninhabi-
ted detached house belonging to D. Rostomashvili in Avlabar, some 150 or 200 paces from the City Hospital for

Contagious Diseases, a well was discovered some seventy feet deep, which could be descended by means of a rope and a pulley. At a depth of about fifty feet there was a gallery leading to another well, in which there was a ladder about thirty-five feet long giving access to a vault situated beneath the cellar of the house. In this vault a fully equipped printing plant has been discovered with twenty cases of Russian, Georgian and Armenian type, a hand press costing between 1,500 and 2,000 rubles, various acids, blasting gelatine and other paraphernalia for the manufacture of bombs, a large quantity of illegal literature, the seals of various regiments and government institutions, as well as an infernal machine containing 15 lb. of dynamite. The establishment was illuminated by acetylene lamps and was fitted up with an electric signalling system. In a shed in the courtyard of the house three live bombs, bomb casings and similar material have been found. Twenty-four persons have been arrested at a meeting in the editorial offices of the newspaper *Elva* and charged with being implicated in the affair. A search of the *Elva* offices revealed a large quantity of illegal literature and leaflets, as well as about twenty blank passport forms. The editorial offices have been sealed up. Since electric wires have been discovered issuing from the secret printing plant in various directions, excavations are being made in the hope of discovering other underground premises. The equipment discovered in this printing plant was removed in five carts. That same evening three other persons were arrested in connection with this affair. All the way to the prison the arrested men kept singing the 'Marseillaise'.

Curiously Yaroslavsky nowhere states that Stalin was among those arrested, and Beria scarcely mentions the printing plant, while the biographical chronicle remains silent about the whole affair. Georgian revolutionaries have stated categorically that he was one of the twenty-seven men arrested. He appears to have been one of the three other persons who were arrested on the evening of April 15th. He was taken to gendarmerie headquarters, and some hours later he was released. In the normal course of events, he would have been interrogated and if found to have had any connection with the illegal printing plant he would have been thrown into the Metekh fortress, where the other prisoners were being held. Arsenidze, who was in the prison fortress at the time, says: 'He was released from gendarmerie headquarters and did not appear in the Metekh prison.'

Arsenidze was surprised. He had been expecting Stalin to join the ranks of the other prisoners, but instead he vanished into thin air.

Everything about Stalin's connection with the Avlabar printing plant and the arrest of the culprits remains mysterious. It has been supposed that he escaped imprisonment because he was able to provide the police with a list of the people connected with the plant, or on the promise that he would become a police informer at the Stockholm conference which he attended later in the month under the name of Ivanovich. But these are suppositions based on no evidence. He was perfectly capable of being an informer, for he was a man totally without scruples. According to Semyon Vereshchak, a Socialist Revolutionary who spent some time in prison with him, Stalin had informed on his fellow students at the theological seminary at Tiflis a few days after he was expelled. He wrote a letter to the Rector giving the names of all the students who had taken part in revolutionary activities, and when the students heard later that Stalin was the informer, he is said to have justified his action by pointing out that once these students lost their claim to the priesthood, they would become good revolutionaries. But this story, too, depends on so little evidence that it cannot be accepted. All we know with reasonable certainty is that Stalin was arrested and a few hours later he was released. He may have been on friendly relations with an officer of the gendarmerie, or he may have convinced the police that he was not the man they were searching for. It is one more of Stalin's puzzling escapes.

When he left for Stockholm he was one of ten delegates representing the Caucasus – the nine others were Mensheviks. It was his first visit abroad. He had no time to observe life in Stockholm. The dreary debates continued day after day as the Bolsheviks and Mensheviks attempted to settle their differences in an atmosphere of acrimony and invective. Lenin urged peasant insurrections and the nationalization of the land under a revolutionary government. Stalin came out in opposition to Lenin and urged that the land should be given to the peasants. His brief speeches, in which he defended the giving of the land to the peasants, are included in his

Collected Works together with an abject apology in which he explains that he had come to this view through lack of insight and understanding. Sixty-two Mensheviks and forty-two Bolsheviks attended the conference, and neither Lenin's nor Stalin's opinion prevailed, for the Mensheviks won a clear majority and were able to insist that the land should be given to the local municipalities. The Stockholm conference had been heralded as a 'unity conference', but no unity came of it. Bolsheviks and Mensheviks were still at loggerheads.

Stalin's speeches were beginning to have the authentic Marxist flavour. He had been reading Lenin's works carefully, and he liked to repeat Lenin's favourite quotations. He especially liked Marx's statement that 'once you have entered upon an insurrectionary career, you must act with the greatest determination and always on the offensive. The defensive is the death of every armed uprising'. The final resolution of the conference denied that the time was ripe for revolution: there must be no armed uprising, only agitation. Stalin, writing his report on the work of the conference, agreed with Lenin that there was no need to delay the armed uprising. The quicker the better and the only problem was where to find the arms and how to train the people. 'Our task today,' he wrote, 'is to achieve the sovereignty of the people. We want the reins of government to be transferred to the hands of the proletariat and the peasantry. Can this be achieved by means of a general strike? No, the only sure path is the armed insurrection of the proletariat and the peasantry.'

It was a theme he was to repeat endlessly during the following years. 'Comrades,' he would say, 'we need only three things. First, arms! Second, arms! Third, arms!'

Stalin's interventions at the Stockholm conference attracted very little attention. Krupskaya in her memoirs written when Stalin was in power seems to have forgotten that he was present at the conference, for she does not mention him, and there is no record that Lenin paid any attention to him. Stalin vividly remembered Lenin, and shortly after Lenin's death he spoke of attending a meeting in Stockholm of dispirited Bolsheviks who kept begging Lenin for advice about how to deal with the Mensheviks. They were outnumbered; they had marshalled their arguments badly; they were sunk in weariness and despair. Through clenched teeth Lenin told them: 'Don't whine, comrades. We shall win because we are right!'

This was not Stalin's first encounter with Lenin, for they had met briefly at the Tammerfors conference held in December 1905 while the uprising in Moscow was at its height. As no records of the conference have survived, there is no way of knowing whether they were in agreement. What Stalin particularly noticed was Lenin's humility, his quietness, and lack of ostentation. He wrote later:

> I met Lenin for the first time in December 1905 at the Bolshevik Conference at Tammerfors in Finland. I was expecting to see the mountain eagle of our party, a great man, not only politically, but if you will, physically, for I had formed for myself an image of Lenin as a giant, stately and imposing. What was my disappointment when I saw the most ordinary-looking man, below middle height, distinguished from ordinary mortals by nothing, literally nothing.
>
> It is the accepted custom for a great man to arrive late at meetings so that the assembly may await his appearance with bated breath, and then just before he appears come the warning whispers: 'Hush – silence – he is coming!' This ceremony seemed to me to have its uses, for it inspires respect. What was my disappointment to learn that Lenin had arrived before the other delegates, had sat down somewhere in a corner, and was unassumingly carrying on a most ordinary conversation with the most ordinary delegates at the conference. I will not conceal from you that I thought his behaviour to be a violation of certain essential rules.

In time Lenin was to come forcibly to the conclusion that Stalin's behaviour was 'a violation of certain essential rules'. But at the Tammerfors conference there was no quarrel between them. Stalin was still a lonely and largely inexperienced member of the party, and scarcely noticed.

THE EXPROPRIATOR

FOR STALIN, AS A dedicated revolutionary, there were four or five principal ways in which he could attract the attention of the revolutionary hierarchy. He could attend party conferences and show himself as a powerful speaker, he could edit an illegal newspaper and in this way put his stamp on the revolutionary movement, he could write books which would be smuggled into all the Bolshevik cells, or he could commit an act of superb revolutionary daring which would make him a memorable figure in revolutionary circles. Finally he could seek out Lenin, the acknowledged leader of the party, and make himself indispensable by showing that he possessed sources of knowledge and influence denied to other revolutionaries. At various times Stalin employed all these methods. He proved to be a mediocre speaker, but he was a skilful editor and he could write passable pamphlets and he possessed a revolutionary flair as an expropriator. Though unconvincing as a public speaker, he had a gift for persuasion in private discussion and Lenin came to regard him as among the few who were knowledgeable about affairs in Georgia.

Towards the end of 1906 Stalin wrote his first full-length pamphlet under the title *Anarchism or Socialism?* He had begun the work during the summer and some six extracts from a preliminary draft appeared in the revolutionary journal *Akhali Tskhovreba* (New Life) under the signature 'Koba' in June and July. This draft appears to have been abandoned, and a completely revised series of articles covering many of the same themes appeared in a variety of revolutionary journals between December 1906 and April 1907. *Anarchism or Socialism?* is particularly notable because we see Stalin strenuously engaged in coming to grips with Marxism and putting forward with extreme seriousness the theory that the dictatorship of the proletariat could under no circumstances degenerate into the dictatorship of one man or a few powerful revolutionary leaders.

Stalin's attempts to come to grips with Marxism are not always informative. He was not an intellectual, had no gift for exposition, and was tempted to give way to bouts of ill temper. The pamphlet is essentially a polemic addressed to a small but powerful group of Georgian anarchists, followers of Prince Kropotkin, who feared the Social Democrats chiefly because of their unconcealed determination to introduce a dictatorship of the proletariat. Kropotkin wrote once that the anarchists had pronounced sentence of death on all dictatorships, whether they came from the right or the left. Stalin, who had been reading Arthur Arnould's *Popular History of the Paris Commune*, answered that under the Paris Commune there had been a dictatorship only in name. What had actually happened was that the people themselves took power, and he quoted approvingly from Arnould that 'the people were the rulers, the only rulers, and they themselves set up their police and magistracy'. No lawyers, deputies, journalists or generals assumed power. Instead there were only the common people, cooks, bookbinders, clerks and workmen, who listened to the voices of the humble and translated what they heard into effective political action. 'If,' wrote Stalin, 'it turns out that the Paris Commune was indeed the dictatorship of a few individuals over the proletariat, then – down with Marxism, down with the dictatorship of the proletariat!' Then he went on to show from Arnould's book that Marxism and the dictatorship were vindicated because Paris had been ruled not by an elite of revolutionaries but by the humble masses acting in unison.

It is possible that he genuinely believed that the masses could take power in Russia, but it is more likely that he held no such belief, for he had spoken long before of the necessity of creating a powerful elite. It was a problem which had troubled him before he wrote *Anarchism or Socialism?* and it was to continue to haunt him until he himself achieved supreme power; then the problem vanished, for he could no longer see any reason why the anonymous masses should rule.

Anarchism or Socialism? begins with a discussion of the nature of anarchism and of Marxist communism. The cornerstone of anarchism is the individual; the masses can only be emancipated when the individual is emancipated. According to Marxist doctrine the individual can only be emancipated when the masses are emancipated. It is a simple confrontation of two opposing theories, and Stalin derives some amusement from the ignorance of the anarchists who did not realize that the Marxist version of historical development rested on scientific foundations while the anarchist version rested on no foundations at all. According to Stalin, man originally lived in a primitive communistic society, which was followed by a matriarchal society where men earned their livelihood by primitive agriculture, and this society in turn was superseded by a patriarchal society where men earned their livelihood by cattle breeding. There followed a slave-owning society; then came feudal society; then came bourgeois society. The dictatorship of the proletariat followed inevitably, and as a result of this dictatorship there would come about a pure communistic society where there were no ministers, gendarmes, police or soldiers, for the state would have withered away. 'The so-called state will retire into the sphere of history.'

Such was the slender basis for Stalin's call for violent revolution. He had interpreted Marxism in such simple terms that it was almost devoid of any meaning, and he seems to have been aware that there were gaps in the argument. 'I am giving you a brief summary,' he says, 'and you will understand it all better if you study Marx and Engels.' Meanwhile doubts would sometimes occur to him, and sometimes he asks himself a pertinent question: 'How do we know that Marx's proletarian socialism is not merely a sentimental dream, a fantasy? Where is the scientific proof that it is not?'

Since there was no proof, Stalin offered his own version of Marxist theory, explaining that capitalism arose when each man began to work for himself, 'stuck in his own corner'. It is an illuminating phrase, one which he had used many times before. In time the individual capitalist began to hire workmen to do his work for him. The processes of production thereupon assumed 'a social, collective character'. But the capitalist expropriated the wealth arising from collective labour, and it is self-evident that the collective of labourers is in a position to destroy the capitalists. 'So it is obvious that the socialist system will follow capitalism as inevitably as day follows night.'

These arguments are more interesting for the light they throw on Stalin than for any effect they might have had on the anarchist Shalva Gogelia, whose articles in the Georgian anarchist newspapers had prompted Stalin's fury. Gogelia had suggested that there was after all nothing new about the *Communist Manifesto*. Had not Marx stolen a good part of it from Victor Considerant's *Democratic Manifesto*? Stalin jumps to the defence of Marx, and pretends to be appalled by the presumption of the anarchists, who have failed to perceive that while Considerant merely proposed: 'All classes, unite!', Marx proposed a far more revolutionary slogan: 'Workers of the world, unite!' Only a criminal fool would think that Marx had borrowed from anyone.

As one reads *Anarchism or Socialism?*, one becomes aware of a vast uncertainty. Stalin seems to be ill at ease among Marxian dialectics. He gives no signs of having read Marx -- his quotations are always those which had appeared in Lenin's articles and pamphlets -- and though he peppers the pages with the familiar nineteenth-century names of Lamarck, Hegel, Cuvier, Herbert Spencer, Proudhon, Helmholtz and many more, employing the names as battering rams in order to reinforce his arguments, he does not give the impression of having read them. He bows to Pascal and salutes Aristotle, but there is no suggestion that he had read either. He turns restlessly and quickly from one problem to another, and he has answers for all of them, but does not seem to know where he is going. Of the arguments of the anarchists he says:

> We can only laugh when we gaze at this spectacle, for one cannot help laughing when one sees a man making war against his own fantasies and destroying his own fictions, while at the same time heatedly asserting that he is vanquishing his opponent.

It is the best paragraph in the pamphlet, and it is possible that Stalin was perfectly aware that he was 'making war against his own fantasies'.

Anarchism or Socialism? was not a book which would commend itself to Lenin, who never read it. Until 1949 it remained in the decent obscurity of the Georgian language, appearing in Russian only in Stalin's *Collected Works*.

In April 1907 the Social Democratic Party held its Fifth Congress in London, and Stalin attended as a representative from Georgia. It was his first and last visit to England. There was some doubt about his qualifications to represent any particular group of Georgian Bolsheviks, and he was therefore given only a consultative voice with no voting privileges. The Congress was stormy, and lasted nearly three weeks. Stalin made no speeches, though he was entitled to speak, and he seems to have made no impression on any of the three hundred delegates, for none of them remembered him in their memoirs. Stalin seems to have attended few of the sessions, for in a lengthy account of the proceedings he wrote on his return to Georgia he mentions only a handful of speakers, paying more attention to Rosa Luxemburg than to anyone else. Lenin is mentioned, but only in passing. Stalin noticed that many of the Mensheviks were Jews and many of the Bolsheviks were Russians, and the only memorable passage in his account of the proceedings reveals his anti-Semitic feeling. After discussing the composition of the delegates according to their professions and territorial origins, he pauses to consider their national distribution.

Of no less interest is the composition of the Congress from the national point of view. The statistics show that the majority of the Menshevik faction consists of Jews – and this of course without counting the Bundists – after which come Georgians and then Russians. On the other hand the overwhelming majority of the Bolshevik faction consists of Russians, after which come Jews – not counting of course the Poles and the Letts, and then Georgians etc. In this connection one of the Bolsheviks (I think it was Comrade Alexinsky) remarked in jest that the Mensheviks formed a Jewish faction, the Bolsheviks a truly Russian faction, and therefore there was something to be said for us Bolsheviks organizing a pogrom within the party.

Stalin went on to describe very briefly the successes and failures of the Congress, coming to the conclusion that the Bolsheviks were on the whole the victors:

Generally speaking the Bolsheviks prevailed, or rather they prevailed to a considerable extent.

Thus, the conference was Bolshevik, though not sharply Bolshevik. Of the Menshevik resolutions the only one to pass was the one dealing with guerrilla uprisings, and that passed only by sheer accident; on this point the Bolsheviks did not give battle, or rather they had no desire to carry it through to the end, purely out of a desire 'to give the comrade Mensheviks something to be happy about'.

In making this statement, Stalin was being exceedingly disingenuous, for the question of guerrilla uprisings was central to the Bolshevik programme. Guerrilla uprisings meant armed insurrection, the seizure of the state machinery by armed force, and from the beginning Lenin had never doubted that this was the way it would have to be. The Mensheviks were continually protesting against the lawless, conspiratorial attitude of the Bolsheviks, and the Bolsheviks in turn derived a sardonic pleasure from contemplating the Menshevik delight in legality. The Bolsheviks had not surrendered to the Mensheviks. Lenin had simply decided not to raise the question publicly because he knew he would be outvoted.

The question of armed insurrection was intimately connected with the question of expropriations, by which was meant armed robbery. From the beginning Lenin recognized the need for large sums of money to bring the Bolsheviks to power. He had no illusions about the financial cost of victory. He wanted a revolution from the top, a sudden devastating blow by a highly skilled revolutionary elite in command of a small but well-armed revolutionary militia. With these weapons he hoped to shatter the whole fabric of existing society. He was in a hurry, and regarded gradualness as treason. With such views he could scarcely be expected to believe that the vast sums needed by the Bolsheviks should be obtained from legitmate enterprises. For his revolutionary purposes he wanted money urgently, now, this very moment, and it was all one to him whether the money came from the contributions of his followers or from armed raids on mail trains or dynamited bank vaults.

Around him there formed a small group of dedicated expropriators. They were men of various skills and various purposes. The most brilliant was Leonid Borisovich Krassin, who had the manners of an aristocrat. He was tall, dark, faintly saturnine. His spade-shaped beard was always neatly groomed, and his clothes were always immaculate, his necktie matching his suit and shirt, the stickpin in exactly the proper place. He earned a high salary as an electrical engineer, and it amused him to place his intelligence and his considerable fortune at the service of the Bolsheviks, to collect money from sympathetic liberal friends, to forge identity papers, and to manufacture bombs.

A completely different kind of person was Semyon Arshakovich Ter-Petrosyan, known as Kamo, who was born in Gori, the son of a well-to-do Armenian contractor. There is a legend that when Ter-Petrosyan was expelled from school for a religious offence, Stalin, three years older, was engaged to tutor him. He always spoke Russian badly, and the story is told that he received the name Kamo from Stalin, who good-naturedly teased him for saying when he was asked to carry some secret documents across the town: '*Kamo otnesti?* (To whom should I take it?)' when he should have said: '*Komu otnesti?*' In rebellion against his wealthy father Kamo became a revolutionary at an early age.

Like Krassin, Kamo was handsome, debonair, and superbly gifted; in every other respect they were different. Kamo combined ferocious daring with an actor's talent for disguise. He was the pure revolutionary adventurer, a throwback to an earlier revolutionary age. To carry illegal literature or printing type from one part of Tiflis to another he would simply disguise himself as a *kinto*, a street peddler, balancing a basket of vegetables on his head, pushing his way through the noisy bazaar crowds and laughing under the eyes of the police, or else he would disguise himself as an elegant young officer, arriving at the railroad station at the last moment, hurling himself with his luggage into a compartment filled with young women and flirting with all of them during the journey; no police inspector seeing him in that compartment would dream of asking him to open his luggage. On the return journey he would be a poor peasant carrying an enormous basket of eggs. Poor and dirty, with a whining voice, he would ask everyone, even a police inspector, to help him protect the eggs from being crushed.

Kamo enjoyed danger; he had the instincts of a matador. He especially liked situations which others preferred not to undertake. At the May Day demonstration in Tiflis in 1903, it was Kamo who unfurled the red flag and kept it flying even when the Cossacks charged down on him. At the end of the year he was arrested in the Batum railroad station while carrying illegal literature. Imprisoned, he vaulted over the prison wall nine months later. Arrested again, he impersonated another student so well that he was allowed to go free. The police put a price on his head, and he wrote an impertinent letter to police headquarters demanding that they increase the price. The police redoubled their efforts, but he slipped through their fingers. For a while he travelled about Georgia hidden under the seat of a third-class compartment. Sometimes he was a merchant, a dancing master, an officer of a Guard's regiment, and he especially liked to disguise himself as a priest. Then for long hours he would sit in an attitude of prayer in the dark corner of some Armenian or Georgian church, and the women who came to whisper to him brought secret messages.

A number of minor expropriations had taken place, including a daring raid at Kutais which brought in fifteen thousand rubles, but the revolutionaries were thinking in terms of hundreds of thousands of rubles. It was decided to hold up the messengers bringing money under armed escort to the State Bank at Tiflis. Lenin, who was hiding in

Finland, had to be consulted. The bombs were to be obtained from Krassin in St Petersburg. Kamo, fresh from some gun-running exploits and a term of imprisonment in Rumania, decided to make the journey. He travelled first-class, wore the uniform of a Cossack officer, and carried a passport bearing the name of Prince Dadiani. In his luggage were watermelons, a present for Lenin; and when he reached Lenin's hiding place in Kuok-kala, he took care to wrap up the melons in a mysterious way, so that they resembled bombs, and he frightened Krupskaya half out of her wits. During the winter of 1906 he spent some weeks at his favourite sport of gun-running between Finland and St Petersburg; by the spring he was back again in Tiflis, carrying a whole armoury of Krassin's bombs. The bombs were not very good ones. The first attempt ended with failure, one of the bombs exploding prematurely and wounding him in the face. His left eye was seriously injured, and it was thought that he might lose the use of the right eye. A sympathetic doctor looked after him in a private hospital. The right eye was saved, but he remained almost completely blind in the left eye to the end of his life.

The exploit for which Kamo was always remembered occurred on June 26th, 1907, at about ten-thirty in the morning. He had learned that a very large sum of money was being transferred from St Petersburg to Tiflis by mail. The greater part of the sum consisted of 500-ruble treasury notes of the series AM 62900 to AM 63650, corresponding altogether to 375,000 rubles, but there were also various bonds and debentures, treasury bonds of the Agricultural Bank, and stocks and railroad shares which could not be negotiated in Russia. Kamo's plan was to capture the money as the carriage of the State Bank, escorted by a detachment of eighteen mounted Cossacks, was leaving Erivan Square and entering Sololakskaya Street. Altogether fourteen men and two women were involved in the plot. Of these only seven or eight were armed, the rest being scouts who would signal the approach of the carriage.

Shortly after ten o'clock Kurdumov, the chief cashier of the State Bank, and Golovia, the chief accountant, accompanied by two armed policemen, entered the post office. They signed for the two heavy mail sacks, and with the help of the two policemen carried them to the carriage. The lieutenant in command of the Cossack guard gave the order, and soon the small procession was making its way rapidly in the direction of Erivan Square. From a café near the post office two young women made a telephone call to another café on Sololakskaya Street. Other telephone calls followed. The conspirators then went to their stations, some to hurl their bombs at the carriage, others to cover the line of retreat of the bomb throwers. Kamo himself, dressed in an elegant uniform, remained in a phaeton drawn up on one side of Erivan Square. A legend, invented shortly after the attack, described how he spent the morning circulating around the square and quietly dropping hints that it would be better for people to go away. The purpose of the legend was to show that Kamo went to some pains to avoid the loss of human life, but he could scarcely have circulated round the square dropping hints without calling attention to himself, and he seems to have remained contentedly in the phaeton while calmly making unobtrusive signals to the conspirators. He had organized and planned the attack. It was not his task to throw the bombs, but to superintend the capture of the money and to give orders if the attempt failed or if an unexpected hitch occurred.

One of the conspirators climbed up on the roof of Prince Shumbatov's palace and from there hurled the first bomb. A moment later six more bombs were hurled. Two Cossacks were killed outright, others were thrown from their horses and still others found themselves being carried off in all directions on the backs of their bolting horses. The force of the explosion hurled the cashier and the accountant from the cab, leaving them badly wounded. Where there had been a small, glittering procession of mounted Cossacks surrounding a carriage emblazoned with the arms of the State Bank, there was now a choking pall of black smoke. Some fifty people were wounded by bomb fragments, many seriously. There was confusion everywhere. Dead and dying horses were lying in the square, children were screaming, police officers were shouting, and the conspirators who had thrown the bombs were in full flight.

In the confusion Kamo was one of the few to observe that the carriage with the mail sacks was still intact. The frightened horses, miraculously unhurt, were bolting in the direction of the Soldatsky market place. Kamo shouted to his driver to pursue the carriage. He had some idea of jumping on to it and in this way taking possession of the mail sacks, but at the corner of Velyaminovskaya Street a conspirator darted off the sidewalk and hurled a bomb which blew off the cab's wheels and wounded the horses, slowing them down. Then he jumped on to the wrecked carriage, seized one of the mail sacks and ran off. Kamo saw what was happening. He recognized the youthful conspirator, a man named Daniko, and went after him, standing up in his seat, firing his revolver and cursing volubly. The bystanders thought he was an army officer who was outraged by the holdup and determined to capture and punish the thief. Kamo caught up with Daniko, took the sack from him, then ordered him into the waiting phaeton, explaining to passers-by that it was only proper that the thief should be taken to the police station and made to answer for his crime. Then he drove off, but not before he had acquired the second mail sack. That night the sacks were hidden in a friend's apartment. A few days later they were taken secretly to the Tiflis Observatory, to find a safe refuge under the sofa in the director's office. Some weeks later they turned up in St Petersburg. Krassin examined them carefully, destroyed the non-negotiable securities, and smuggled the 500-ruble notes out of the country. The Tsarist police broadcast through Europe the serial numbers of the banknotes, with the result that all efforts to change them into foreign currency were unsuccessful.

The Tiflis expropriation, the most famous and most daring of all the expropriations undertaken by the Bolsheviks, brought no money into the party.

Although the expropriation proved to be a disastrous failure, it served to show to what lengths the Bolsheviks were prepared to go in order to raise money. The Mensheviks, who soon learned that Lenin was involved in the affair, bitterly attacked him. Lenin rejoiced in these attacks, for in his view they only demonstrated the insincerity of the Mensheviks, who were perfectly prepared to send their followers into the factories to raise contributions for party funds, while refusing to countenance simpler and more revolutionary tactics. 'We should make the Tsar pay for his revolutionaries,' Lenin said, and he continued to give his blessing to the expropriators.

Stalin was involved in the Tiflis expropriation, but how deeply he was involved and whether he had any decisive voice in the affair remains unknown. According to one account, he was the man who threw the bomb from the roof of Prince Shumbatov's palace. According to another, he arranged the transfer of the mail sacks to the Observatory where, as we know, he had excellent connections. There was a third version which presented him as the sole originator of the plan and its chief executor, but this last version seems unlikely. Stalin himself made no public claim to have taken part in the expropriation. According to the official biographical chronicle printed in his *Collected Works* he would seem to have spent the entire summer and autumn of 1907 in Baku, organizing the oilworkers while campaigning against the Mensheviks and Socialist Revolutionaries. The official biographical chronicle however is notoriously inaccurate, and if it says he was in Baku, there is no reason to suppose that he was not in Tiflis.

In 1930, during the course of a three-hour conversation with Stalin, Emil Ludwig raised the question of the Tiflis expropriation. Stalin had evidently not expected the question to be raised. 'He began to laugh in that heavy way of his, blinked several times, and stood up, for the first and only time in our three-hour interview,' Ludwig reports. 'He walked over, with his somewhat dragging footsteps, to the writing desk, and brought me a pamphlet of about thirty pages, his biography – in Russian; but there was nothing in it, of course, about my question.' It suited Stalin's purpose to evade the issue, but Ludwig naturally found himself wondering which of his many purposes was served by the evasion. Stalin could have denied that he had anything to do with the expropriation, he could have confessed to it, or he could have said it was only a legend. By remaining silent, he gave Ludwig the impression that he had something to do with it, but preferred not to reveal the part he had played.

Without knowing it, Ludwig had touched a wound, for Stalin suffered one of the worst blows of his revolutionary career as a result of the Tiflis expropriation. While Lenin unofficially approved of the 'exes', the local party did not, and Stalin was hauled before a party tribunal and placed on trial, found guilty, and sentenced to expulsion. The revolutionary court was headed by Sylvester Djibladze, who had already tusselled with Stalin in the past. In addition the three or four small revolutionary groups over which Stalin retained control were also expelled from the party. Arsenidze says categorically that from that time 'the Georgian organization was always closed to Koba'.

Arsenidze is not the only authority for the story of Stalin's expulsion from the party. In March 1918 no less a person

than Martov published in his short-lived Moscow newspaper
a brief attack on Stalin which was to have extraordinary
consequences. Martov wrote:

> That the Caucasian Bolsheviks attached themselves to all
> sorts of daring enterprises of an expropriatory nature
> should be well known to the same Citizen Stalin, who was
> expelled in his time from the party organization for hav-
> ing had something to do with expropriation.

By attacking the powerful Commissar for Nationalities
Martov was acting with almost unbelievable daring. He was
the head of the barely tolerated Menshevik party, which was
being permitted to exist for a few more weeks on sufferance.
Though the fact of the expulsion was common knowledge
among Georgian revolutionaries, there were no written
records to substantiate the charges; if there had been any
such records, Stalin was in a position to sequester them.
Realizing that the best defence was attack, Stalin accused
Martov of committing 'a vicious libel'. Lenin, who had remained friendly with Martov in spite of their political differences, took an interest in the matter, and ordered a trial.
Stalin denied the accusation. Where, he asked, were the documents to prove that he had been expelled? Why were they
attacking him on the basis of mere rumours? By what right
could Martov impugn the good name of a high official of
the government? The judge ordered a commission of inquiry to proceed to the Caucasus to gather evidence about
the expulsion and also about an attempt on the life of a
certain Comrade Zharinov, who was said to have exposed
Stalin's part in the expropriations. Boris Nikolayevsky was
placed in charge of the commission, and he was able to gather
affidavits from Sylvester Djibladze, Isidor Ramishvili, and
others who had sat in judgement over Stalin at the court of
honour in Tiflis. When Nikolayevsky returned to Moscow
with the affidavits, the Bolshevik government was no longer
prepared to permit Stalin to stand trial. To his surprise Nikolayevsky discovered that the court had conveniently lost its
records and the trial could not therefore be continued. Martov was dismissed with a reprimand for 'insulting and damaging the reputation of a member of the government'.

The exact terms of the charge brought against Stalin at
the court of honour in 1907 are unknown, but it is clear that
he was not dismissed from the party only for taking part in

an 'ex'. Djibladze, Ramishvili, and the other party members in positions of authority were determined revolutionaries who had no objection to bloodshed. Djibladze had organized the assassination of General Gryaznov, the chief of the Caucasian army's general staff, in January 1906. The first attempt to assassinate the general failed, because the bomb thrower Arsena Djordjiashvili refused to hurl the bomb when he saw that the general was accompanied in his open carriage by his young daughter. The second attempt succeeded – the young daughter had been left at home. Political assassination and terror, expropriations and uprisings by revolutionary militia were the commonplaces of Georgia during those years. The reason for Stalin's expulsion must therefore be found outside the context of the revolutionary situation. It is to be found not in the expropriation itself, but in his character – his brutality, his harshness, his assumption of unauthorized power, his murderous attitude towards other Bolsheviks, and his attempts to use stolen money for his own purposes. To the very end he was to remain an *abrek*, a guerrilla chieftain who refused to acknowledge any power but his own.

An even more sinister accusation against Stalin was being made by Georgian revolutionaries at the time. In 1907 the most venerated person in Georgia was Prince Ilya Chavchavadze, the statesman, novelist and poet, who had founded the periodical *Iveria* in which Stalin's first poems appeared. He was a great and towering figure both in literature and in politics, he was determined to right the wrongs of the oppressed, and he looked forward to a time when there would arise an independent Georgian state. He was seventy years old, and he had spent most of his long life fighting on behalf of Georgia. He was returning to his country house at Saguramo near Mtskheta when he was killed by a band of assassins. The murder took place on August 28th, 1907, two months after Kamo's famous raid on the Tiflis State Bank. Iremashvili, who sometimes found something good to say about Stalin, says outright: 'Koba was the man indirectly responsible for the murder. He was the instigator of all these outrages, the agitator seething with hatred.'

There is no proof that Stalin was responsible directly or indirectly for the murder of Prince Chavchavadze. The motive for the murder was never established. It was commonly believed that it was the work of the Bolsheviks, because the prince had denounced them for their ruthlessness, but there were some who were prepared to lay the blame on the Tsarist secret police, for he had also denounced them; and there were some, too, who thought it was a simple case of murder for robbery. Many years later, in World War II, an old man, a former member of the Tsarist gendarmerie, confessed that he had led the attack on the prince on orders of his superiors, but his confession was not widely believed. It would not be surprising if Stalin had some indirect part in the murder; it would be more surprising if he had a direct part.

Little is known about Stalin's movements during this critical period. Between July 10th and September 22nd no writings appeared from his pen. In his biographical chronicle he claims that he was in Baku, organizing the oilworkers and bringing out a new revolutionary newspaper. Arsenidze says he left Tiflis and only returned for a secret two-day visit in 1909. He had failed to conquer Tiflis and Batum, and he was to have only a little more success in Baku. Beria, the remorseless chronicler of Stalin's victories, ascribes the entire revolutionary ferment in Baku to the guiding hand of Stalin, but in fact he was once again in the position of a minor revolutionary compelled to obey other revolutionaries, men like Prokofy Djaparidze, Avely Yenukidze and Suren Spandaryan, who were to become prominent and powerful members of the party. They gave the orders, and Stalin obeyed them, while all the time attempting to unseat them. His task was to compose editorials for the revolutionary newspaper *Gudok* (The Siren).

During the autumn and winter of 1907 Stalin's activities become increasingly mysterious. He leaves few traces, in Baku or elsewhere. He told Henri Barbusse that about this time he made a secret journey to Berlin to confer with Lenin, whose movements have been documented with extraordinary precision, so that we know where he was on nearly every day of his life; nowhere is there any record of a visit to Berlin in that year. On the contrary the records agree that except for his visit to London to attend the congress, Lenin spent the whole year in Finland.

On many other occasions Stalin talked of this mysterious visit to Germany, and sometimes he spoke of two separate visits. During a discussion about the German character with Churchill and Roosevelt, he went out of his way to say that he well remembered his visit to Leipzig in 1907. He said he accompanied two hundred German communists to attend an international conference, but when the train arrived at the station there was no official to take their tickets and so they waited docilely on the platform for two hours hoping to receive permission to leave the platform. It is a strange story. Stalin did not speak a word of German, and no German communists have spoken of meeting him in 1907. It is also the only anecdote about himself which he related during the Teheran Conference. In some strange way Germany-Lenin-1907 seems to have become firmly fixed in his mind, and he was pleasantly amused by the spectacle of the docile German communists waiting so long on the platform that they missed the conference altogether.

Stalin was always making mysterious journeys, and there is therefore just a possibility that he did go to Germany on some errand connected with the 'exes'.

The Bolsheviks in Baku were among the few revolutionaries who were making their influence felt. For two weeks, during a general strike during the spring of 1908, they were able to impose their authority on the city. Lenin heard of their success and wrote admiringly: 'These are our last Mohicans of the political mass strike.' The Tsarist government, fully aware of the danger of an insurrectionary movement in Baku, struck back. New companies of gendarmes were rushed into the Caucasus, and the strike was broken and the ringleaders were rounded up. On April 7th, 1908, they arrested a certain Gaioz Nizharadze, who proved to be Stalin in disguise.

THE PRISONER

THE BAILOV PRISON in Baku was one of the worst of Tsarist prisons, but this was not the fault of the prison governor or of the guards, who were no more brutal than elsewhere. It was bad because it was hopelessly overcrowded, with fifteen hundred prisoners enclosed in a space intended for four hundred. It was a long, low, ugly building of plastered brick, two storeys high, overlooking a drab industrial district, with a glimpse of the Caspian Sea beyond. If it resembled anything at all, it resembled an abandoned factory filled to bursting point with men in a state of perpetual mutiny. In winter it was bitterly cold, and in summer men crowded near the barred windows, gasping for air.

A strange silence hovers over the circumstances of Stalin's arrest. The usual prison photographs have not survived, and there are no interrogations or reports by police officers. Beria, who quotes police reports made in 1909, 1910 and 1912, all of them reading like genuine documents interspersed with convenient fictions, has nothing to say about the circumstances of Stalin's arrest or of the seven and a half months of imprisonment that followed, except to note that Stalin organized classes and debates, and edited a newspaper *Bakinsky Rabochy* (The Baku Worker) from behind the prison walls. He gives the impression that Stalin in prison behaved exactly like Stalin free, dominating everyone within sight.

A rather different picture is presented by Semyon Vereshchak, a Socialist Revolutionary who met Stalin in prison. Vereshchak is not wholly reliable, but the Soviet authorities never disputed the accuracy of his memoirs and on two separate occasions published extracts from them. Vereshchak was evidently troubled by Stalin's presence in this prison which had become the clearinghouse for all the prisoners in the Caucasus. According to Vereshchak, Stalin was not like other men. He was remote, cunning, treacherous, learned in Marxist doctrine, a friend of bandits, swindlers and thieves. He treated the prison guards with contempt, and he was the hardest man in a hard prison. 'The prison at Baku,' Vereshchak wrote, 'had an extraordinary effect on the inmates, for all became hardened revolutionaries.' But Stalin seemed to possess a hardness denied to ordinary prisoners, a remorseless unpitying quality which took Vereshchak's breath away.

Here is Vereshchak's description of Stalin as he appeared in prison:

One day a new face appeared in the Bolshevik camp. I inquired who the comrade was, and in great secrecy was told: 'It is Koba.' ... Koba stood out among the various factions as a Marxist student. He wore a blue satin smock with a wide open collar, and no belt. His head was bare. A *bashlik* – a sort of detached hood with two tapering scarves – was thrown across his shoulders. He always carried a book. Of more than medium height, he walked with a slow catlike tread. He was slender, with pointed face, pock-marked skin, sharp nose, and small eyes looking out from a narrow forehead, slightly indented. He spoke little and sought no company.

The Stalin of these days was defiant; he submitted to no regulations. The political prisoners at Baku endeavoured to segregate themselves as much as possible from the criminals, and the younger among them were punished if they infringed this unwritten law. Openly flouting the custom, Koba was constantly to be seen in the company of bandits, swindlers and thieves. He chose as his cellmates the Sakvadelidze brothers, one a counterfeiter, the other a well-known Bolshevik. Active people, people who did things, attracted him.

Koba fell into the habit of summoning others to formal discussions. These prearranged debates came to be established institutions, occurring at set hours virtually every day, centring around the agrarian problem, revolutionary tactics and philosophy. The discussions on the agrarian problems were very heated, often climaxed by blows.

All these discussions were made uncomfortable by Koba's appearance and his manners. He lacked wit and conveyed his thoughts rather dryly. Astounding, however, to everyone was the machine-like precision of his memory. He seemed to have memorized the whole of Marx's *Das Kapital*. Marxism was the air he breathed. In this realm he was invincible. No power on earth could move him from a stand once assumed. He was ready to refute every attack levelled against his arguments with an argument from Karl Marx. This readiness in rebuttal made a profound impression on the young party members who were little experienced in politics.

At a time when the whole prison was upset, sleepless, tense, in expectation of a night execution, Koba would calmly compose himself in slumber or else study Esperanto, which he regarded as the future language of the socialist international.

Semyon Vereshchak was a man with considerable psychological insight. Slowly, sentence by sentence, he builds up the portrait of a man who is already wholly corrupt, caring nothing at all for the other people in the prison, whether guards or prisoners, seeking only his own advantage, with an icy calm and a terrifying imperturbability, so that on a night when all the other prisoners are caught up in fear knowing that a man will be hanged in the courtyard outside their windows, he calmly goes to sleep or studies Esperanto.

There were two aspects of Stalin's character which particularly interested Vereshchak: his calm and his treachery. The bored prisoners would sometimes amuse themselves by needling one another. It was vicious needling designed to reduce a man to maniacal fury. A prisoner would be confronted with rumours or entirely imaginary stories about his past life, trapped into shameful admissions, scolded, perjured, and insulted. It was a game which was played especially on long winter evenings, and was called 'chasing into a bubble'. 'We could never drive Koba off his balance,' Vereshchak says. 'We could never get a rise out of him.'

But Stalin, too, had his amusements. He, too, enjoyed spreading rumours. He quietly spread the rumour that a young Georgian, of whom he knew nothing whatsoever, was an *agent provocateur*. The inevitable consequence was that a gang of prisoners waylaid the youth in a corridor and beat him nearly to death. Covered with blood he was removed to the prison hospital on a stretcher. There was an inquiry among the revolutionaries, and it transpired that the Georgian was not an *agent provocateur* and no one knew how the accusation had arisen. 'Many months later,' says Vereshchak, 'it became clear that Koba had started the rumour.'

A similar incident occurred when a Bolshevik stabbed a young workman to death in the belief that he was a spy. The workman was unknown to the Bolshevik. It was an obscure affair, but finally there was the usual revolutionary court of honour to inquire into the guilt or innocence of the Bolshevik. Only then was it learned that Stalin had been the instigator.

Vereshchak says that Stalin instigated protests and demonstrations, but never signed the protests and never took part in the demonstrations. He was always behind the scenes, pulling strings, daring others to commit senseless acts against the authorities. 'He was an astute intriguer with a talent for striking through others,' Vereshchak says; and he tells these stories quietly, never raising his voice to denounce him, never giving the impression of being shocked, and therefore he is all the more credible.

On one occasion – the date, according to Vereshchak was Easter Sunday 1909, but it is more likely to have been Easter Sunday 1908 – there was a riot in the prison and the ringleaders were ordered to suffer the punishment known as 'walking the green street'. In the old days prisoners would be made to walk in single file through two lines of soldiers armed with leafy boughs. The leafy boughs, however, had been exchanged for rifle butts, but the punishment was still called 'walking the green street'. Stalin was suspected of being one of the ringleaders of the riot. Vereshchak says he walked through the line of soldiers with his head lifted proudly, a book under his arm. Yaroslavsky improves on the story by saying that it was a book by Marx. Demyan Bedny improves on it still further by saying that Stalin 'made no effort to protect himself, but walked straight through the ranks with a book in his hand'.

On another occasion, according to Vereshchak, Stalin refused to have anything to do with the rioters. When the riot broke out, he bolted the door and refused to participate even when threatened with a gun.

Vereshchak's description of that overcrowded prison, where it was impossible to sit or lie down without stepping on someone's toes, is one of the masterpieces of prison literature. The sights, the smells, the daily horrors are recorded dispassionately, but it is the portrait of Stalin, in his indifference and cruelty, which compels our admiration. It also compelled the admiration of Stalin, for otherwise he would never have permitted the publication of the two extracts from Vereshchak's book which appeared in *Pravda* on February 7th, 1928, and December 20th, 1929. Both extracts were published under the heading 'Certified Correct'. The dates were significant, for by February 1928 Stalin feared no one on earth and on December 21st, 1929, he celebrated his fitieth anniversary and almost the entire issue of *Pravda* was given over to praises of him.

In prison he continued to write occasional articles for revolutionary newspapers. Six articles written between March and August 1908 have been preserved, many of them dealing with the problems of the oilworkers. He attacked Mensheviks, anarchists, and the owners of the Baku oilfields with equal fury. 'We leave stealthy acts of violence to the notorious terrorist elements,' he wrote. 'As for ourselves, we must come out *openly* against the bourgeoisie, keeping them in a state of terror *all the time until victory is won*.' He had more to say on the subject of terror when on May 28th, 1908, the Russian Exarch of Georgia, Archbishop Nikon, was murdered at the archbishopric in Tiflis by unknown assassins. This murder was as mysterious as that of Prince Ilya Chavchavadze, for Archbishop Nikon was believed to sympathize with the Georgian Church, which the Russian Church had continually oppressed. Robbery was not involved, but the extreme left (the Bolsheviks) and the extreme right (the Black Hundreds) were both suspected. Stalin read a copy of the Menshevik journal *Napertskali* (The Spark) while in prison, and smuggled out his own comments on their report. The Mensheviks had protested against the act of terror, and had suggested that anyone who had any inside information should go to the police. In his article in *Bakinsky Proletary* Stalin objected strenuously to the encouragement of informers. He wrote:

> The story of this murder is well-known. A certain group, having murdered the Exarch, went on to murder a captain of the gendarmerie who was returning from 'the scene of the crime' with his report, and then the group fell on a procession of hooligans accompanying the Exarch's body. Obviously the group that murdered him did not consist of hooligans, nor did it consist of revolutionaries, for no revolutionary group would contemplate such an act at the present time, while we are building up our forces, thus risking the collapse of the solidarity of the proletariat. The position of the Social Democrats in relation to such groups is well-known. Ascertaining the conditions which give rise to such groups and combating these conditions, the Social Democrats at the same time wage an ideological and organizational struggle against these groups, discrediting them in the eyes of the proletariat and dissociating the proletariat from them. But that is not what *Napertskali* says. This newspaper tells the people to betray such groups to the police . . .

Stalin is not completely convincing. He cleverly confuses the hooligans with the police and the mourners, but he is less convincing when he speaks about the well-known hostility of Social Democrats to hooligan groups. The article appeared on July 20th under the signature of 'Ko . . .' He wrote one more article on the oilworkers for *Bakinsky Proletary* on July 28th, and then if we can trust the evidence of the *Collected Works* he remained completely silent for a whole year.

It is a puzzling silence, and we shall have occasion to inquire into the reasons for it. Officially, no articles came from his pen between July 28th, 1908, and August 1st, 1909. More probably he continued to write, but felt that none of these articles deserved to be included in the *Collected Works*. He had provided for such an eventuality in the introduction to the first volume of the works, saying that this was 'the first attempt to collect and publish *nearly* all the works of J. V. Stalin'. In the same introduction he claims that the texts remain unchanged 'except in a few instances where the author has introduced slight changes of a purely stylistic character'. This is a lie. Changes have been made which have nothing to do with their stylistic character.

Beria and the biographical chronicle agree that on November 22nd, 1908, Stalin left the Bailov prison after being sentenced to exile in the town of Solvychegodsk in the *guberniya* of Vologda, and that he remained there until he escaped on July 6th, 1909. The sentence was to be kept in force for two years, during which time he was to remain under police surveillance. It was the mildest punishment possible to any convicted revolutionary.

All the documents connected with the sentence of deportation have vanished, and there is no longer any possibility of discovering why he should have been treated so leniently. Solvychegodsk was a small sixteenth-century town with grassy streets and queer little decorated wooden houses on the banks of the Vychegda river. It was once the fief of the powerful Stroganov family, but they had long ago deserted it to live in St Petersburg. Abandoned and forgotten, it was regarded by the police as an excellent place for sending minor revolutionaries. The biographical chronicle states that on his way he suffered from relapsing fever and was removed to a hospital in Vyatka. The records of the local police show that his behaviour had remained unchanged. 'Coarse and brutal, disrespectful to the authorities. Quarrels with the townfolk. It is suggested that the Governor of Vologda should transfer him to the village of Krioukooka.' Coarse and brutal ... Fifteen years later Lenin reached the same verdict on Stalin, and like the police inspector in Solvychegodsk he suggested that Stalin should be transferred elsewhere.

Six times Stalin was exiled by the Tsarist government. Usually he left some traces of his activities while in exile. He was a memorable figure, and revolutionaries remembered him. Yet no one has written about his months in Solvychegodsk. He vanishes into the northern mists, coarse, brutal, quarrelsome, and disrespectful. The local officials wish he would go away.

He obliged them by escaping in July, staying briefly in St Petersburg, where he may have met Sergo Alliluiev in a chance encounter on a street corner – the meeting is recorded by Alliluiev with the air of a man conferring a favour by filling up a gap in the records. There are gaps everywhere. We hear that he hid for a while in the apartment of a janitor, and then moved on to Moscow where he found shelter in the house of a textile worker. Then he vanishes. Suddenly he reappears in Baku on August 1st, 1909, with an article on the crisis of the party, and the long silence is broken.

The article is written in tones of despair. Again and again he complains that the party is isolated from the masses, the various party organizations have no connection with one another, there is no leadership, and the revolution is farther away than ever. Worse still, the party is losing members, and the great men who rule the party from abroad are smuggling leaflets and pamphlets into the country which show only too clearly that they are in no position to understand what is really happening. In later years it was his pride that he never took refuge abroad. The leaders fled; he remained. So now in this article, written in gall, he bitterly upbraids the party leadership and condemns them for not permitting the advanced workers to control the local organizations. They should be placed in charge immediately, and though they will stumble and make mistakes at first, they will learn in the end to walk independently 'as Christ walked on the waters'.

Again and again in this article, one of the best he ever wrote, he denies his past. He had objected in Tiflis to the workers' taking control. Now he objected because they were not permitted to take control. The intellectuals had failed the revolution; it was time that Social Democracy was returned to the workers. He mentions the places where the workers have set up their own organizations – in the Urals, in the Donets Basin, in Nikolayev, Sermovo, and elsewhere – and hammers out a philosophy of action based on the workers' organizations in a desperate effort to prevent the collapse of Social Democracy in Russia.

This article, called 'The Party Crisis and Our Tasks', is an important document, for it shows him for the first time developing an independent plan of action. Two more short articles followed, and then again there was a long silence. The police were after him. Beria, not too reliably, quotes a report from the archives of the gendarmerie of Tiflis dated October 24th, 1909:

In compliance with the request of the Department of

Police of September 30th ult., No. 136706, the Caucasian District Secret Police Department reports that according to the information of the chief of the Baku Secret Police Department, 'Soso', who escaped from Siberia and is known in the organization as 'Koba', has been identified as Oganess Vartanov Totomyants, a resident of the city of Tiflis in whose name he has a passport, No. 982, issued by the Tiflis superintendent of police on May 12th of this year and valid for one year.

If this report is accurate, it suggests that the police were close on his trail and ready to pounce. Fugitives from Siberian exile could expect to be treated harshly; they could expect long terms of imprisonment followed by even longer sentences of deportation. Once again there is a long silence. Between August 27th, 1909, and February 28th, 1910, no writings appeared under his signature. The biographical chronicle informs us that he spent the autumn and winter busily convening party conferences in Baku and Tiflis, and setting up a secret printing press. We do not know what he was really doing. Georgian revolutionaries believe he was working quietly in the heart of Baku as an accountant in the Mantashev oil refinery, and had almost abandoned revolutionary work.

On March 24th, 1910, the past caught up with him. Informers, or some incautious action of his own, led to his arrest. Beria quotes two police reports made immediately after his arrest:

On March 24th, 1910, Captain Martynov reports that a member of the Baku Committee of the *R.S.D.L.P.* 'known in the party organization as Koba, and a most active party official, occupying a leading position', has been arrested.

The quotation marks are supplied by Beria, and their significance is unknown.

The second report reads:

Djugashvili is a member of the Baku Committee of the Russian Social Democratic Labour Party, known in the organization under the alias of 'Koba' ... In view of his stubborn participation, despite all administrative penalties, in the activity of the revolutionary parties in which *he has always occupied an extremely prominent position*, and in view of his escape on two occasions from the locality of his exile, as a result of which he has not undergone a single one of the administrative penalties imposed upon him, I would suggest recourse to a stricter measure of punishment – exile to the most remote districts of Siberia for *five years*.

The italics are supplied by Beria, and their significance is known. Beria also supplies the dots pointing to an omission in the text, and the information that the report was drawn up by Captain Galimbatovsky. No facsimile of the document has been published, and we are therefore compelled to rely on Beria's good faith in reproducing the document accurately.

Since there is no reason to trust any document submitted by Beria, we are entitled to examine the document closely for evidence of deliberate distortions and falsifications, especially such distortions and falsifications as will serve his purpose. In a footnote Beria claims that both documents were found in the Central Party Archives of the Central Committee of the Communist Party of Azerbaijan, File No. 430. We have every reason to be on our guard when Beria quotes the numbers of a file to give an impression of authenticity; and it is certain that the file had long since left Azerbaijan, for shortly after the October revolution Stalin arranged that all police reports concerning his early life should be transferred to Moscow for safekeeping. This police report and many others therefore reposed in Stalin's private file in the Kremlin.

Now this report, as we shall see, is one of capital importance, and the decision to publish it at all could have come only from Stalin. Taken in its context, it is a damaging document. Stalin must have been perfectly aware that there were dangers in publishing it, but these dangers, in his view, must have been outweighed by the advantages of seeing himself portrayed so early in his career as a man who has always occupied an extremely prominent position in revolutionary circles, and one who in the eyes of the police deserved exemplary punishment. The more severe the punishment, the more dangerous he must be in the eyes of the police, and the more heroic in the eyes of the revolutionaries. Beria's italics point up the advantages: he was a revolutionary who had always occupied an extremely prominent position, and he was about to be given a very heavy punishment.

The facts, as Beria well knew, were otherwise. Stalin was not a prominent revolutionary, nor was he heavily punished.

His punishment was a modest one. He was kept in the Bailov prison for six months and then sent back to Solvychegodsk to complete the term of his exile. Far from receiving exemplary punishment, he received a slap on the wrists.

Beria went to some pains to conceal the modest punishment in the text of his book. The Galimbatovsky report is quoted on page 228. Thirteen pages later, after a rambling account of articles written by Stalin between 1904 and 1912, we come upon the words: 'Comrade Stalin was arrested on March 23rd, 1910 [New Style, April 5th], and exiled to Solvychegodsk, a town in the *guberniya* of Vologda.' He is not sentenced to a long term of exile. He is merely ordered to return to Solvychegodsk to complete his term of exile. The police could not have dealt with him more leniently. He was an exceedingly privileged prisoner.

That he was a privileged prisoner does not necessarily mean that he was in the pay of the police or acted as an informer, for there are other explanations more readily available. We know that there were police officers sympathetic to the Bolsheviks, just as we know that there were members of Stalin's secret police who worked secretly against Stalin. They were few, but they existed. Alternatively, Stalin may have rendered the police some service, for which he would be rewarded. He had already caused men to be murdered in prison by circulating rumours against them, and there was nothing in his character to prevent him from circulating similar rumours to the police. In his own eyes, and in the eyes of Lenin, such actions were far from being reprehensible; Mensheviks especially were expendable.

Georgian revolutionaries in exile have long believed that Stalin was an informer. Arsenidze, for example, has repeatedly declared that to his knowledge Stalin, on being arrested in the spring of 1906, was taken to gendarmerie headquarters by Captain Zasypkin, who proposed that he should become an agent of the Okhrana. Arsenidze does not say that Stalin accepted the offer, but points to his abrupt release from headquarters a few hours later as proof of his guilt. There is in fact no direct evidence that Stalin was an informer; nor, in the nature of things, could there be such evidence. He would commit any crime at all to attain his ends. He may have informed on Bolsheviks sporadically and on Mensheviks continually; he would not have considered that these were crimes.

The history of Stalin's arrests and escapes is a melancholy

one. He is usually arrested when he is at loggerheads with his superiors in the party, he is never given a court trial, his sentence is always imposed by administrative order, and he always escapes from his place of exile with suspicious ease. The dates of his arrests and escapes are recorded in meticulous detail in the biographical chronicle and in *Stalin's Early Writings and Activities*, where six arrests followed by five escapes are carefully noted. But when Beria came to write his tribute on the occasion of Stalin's sixtieth birthday in 1939, he either forgot his former chronology or revised the number of arrests and escapes so completely that doubt is thrown on the entire chronological system. He wrote:

> From the very outset the autocratic regime of the tsar had sensed in Stalin a dangerous and implacable foe. Eight times he was arrested and kept in jail, starting with 1902. Seven times he was banished in some far-away corner of the inclement North and six times he managed to escape from his place of tsarist exile to lead with renewed energy the struggle for the overthrow of the bourgeois and landlord systems.

There would appear to be no possibility of reconciling the two sets of figures. One of the arrests took place under suspicious circumstances shortly before the discovery of the secret Avlabar printing plant, and is not recorded in the official chronologies. If this arrest is added to the official chronology, we have seven arrests, one quick release, and five escapes. By no manner of juggling with the figures can we arrive at eight arrests and six escapes.

These mathematical shifts are not merely of academic interest. Something has gone profoundly wrong in the official chronology. Beria would not have dared to alter the figures without the permission of Stalin. If he altered the figures, it was for a purpose. The most likely purpose would be to record two arrests which had not previously appeared in the official canon, but which had to be included in the canon because they had become known in the Soviet Union or among Russian emigres abroad. They were probably not arrests for political crimes, otherwise Stalin would have claimed full credit for them; they are more likely to have been arrests for murder, robbery or rape. What is certain is that by 1939 it had become necessary to revise the entire system of the chronology of Stalin's arrests and escapes, and the announcement by Beria of the eight arrests served as preliminary notice that the chronology was under revision.

The two otherwise unrecorded arrests may have occurred in 1904, a year in which we have only the most meagre information about Stalin's activities. On January 5th he claims to have escaped from his Siberian exile in the village of Novaya Uda, and thereafter except for an unsigned article which appeared on September 1st and for two letters said to have been written in September and October from Kutais, we have no further trustworthy knowledge of him. As usual he claims that he was forming committees, leading strikes and engaging in debates, but it is just as possible that he was spending some of the time in prison or in exile. From January 5th, 1904, to March 25th, 1908, no arrests are recorded in the official biography. Such freedom from arrest, in a man of Stalin's character, is itself suspicious.

When Stalin arrived at Solvychegodsk in October 1910 to complete his term of exile, he knew that he had only a few more months to serve. Captain Galimbatovsky had proposed that he should be sentenced to exile in some remote districts of Siberia for five years. Instead he spent six months in prison, a month on the journey under guard to Solvychegodsk, which is not in Siberia but in European Russia, and nine months in exile. By June 27th, 1911, he was a free man, restricted only by the order of the Viceroy of the Caucasus that he was not permitted to reside in the Caucasus, and by the order which applied to all political prisoners that he could not live in St Petersburg, Moscow or any of the large industrial cities. He decided to stay in the ancient city of Vologda, halfway between Solvychegodsk and St Petersburg. From there, in God's good time, he hoped to launch his fourth or fifth revolutionary career.

THE BIRTH OF *PRAVDA*

DURING THE LONG WINTER DAYS in Solvychegodsk, when the sun was seen rarely, Stalin was still busy at the work of destroying the world of the Tsars, the capitalists and the landlords. In the darkness, like a mole in the bowels of the earth, he was blindly pursuing his vocation. Here and there he would make some small progress, announce an idea, develop a long-forgotten revolutionary concept, and then retreat into obscurity. He committed small acts of defiance, attended secret meetings of Bolshevik exiles, and once at least his house was searched for incriminating documents. In later years he would remember that this second period in Solvychegodsk was notable for one event above all others: at long last he established contact with Lenin.

He had, of course, met Lenin before in Tammerfors and London, but these were brief meetings which left no residue of affection or trust. Stalin was just one more of the nameless, uneasy revolutionaries who flocked to join the Bolsheviks because there was no other party which seemed ruthless enough to take on the task of destroying the state. He was more anonymous than most. Shiftless and dangerous, he had not yet made any mark on the party. Now, in Solvychegodsk, for the first time, at a moment when the party's fortunes were at a low ebb, we find him writing to Lenin in Paris in a tone of mingled respect, devotion and self-assertiveness, about the problems that beset the party. The letter, addressed ostensibly to Semeon Schwarz, a member of the Central Committee, was clearly intended for Lenin's eyes. He wrote:

Comrade Semeon! I received your letter yesterday, thanks to the comrades. First of all, warmest greetings to Lenin, Kamenev, and the rest.* And now about your letter, and in general about the 'damned questions'.

In my opinion the line of the bloc (Lenin-Plekhanov) is the only correct one: 1) this line, and this alone, answers to the real interests of the work in Russia, which demands that all real party elements should rally together; 2) this

* After the purge of Kamenev, his name was omitted in all official references to this letter. In *The Real Stalin*, by Yves Delbars (London, Allen & Unwin, 1953; p. 60), the letter is quoted with the following addition after 'and the rest'.

I am glad to get their letters, though sometimes I find them too academic. It seems to me that the peaceful atmosphere in which you are living yonder prevents you from realizing the approach of a new tempest which is gathering here. I don't venture to compare my modest personality with the men who have kindled the spark. But I have already had experience of a good few conflagrations here . . . I am practically the only one of our group who is actually concerned with the conflagration. People must listen to what I say.

line, and this alone, will hurry forward the process of emancipating the legal organizations from the yoke of the Liquidators, by digging a chasm between the Menshevik workers and the Liquidators, so scattering them and killing them off. The fight for influence in the legal organizations is the burning question of the day, a necessary stage on the road towards regenerating the party, while a bloc is the only means for cleaning out these organizations from the garbage of Liquidationism.

The plan of the bloc reveals the hand of Lenin – he is a wise peasant and knows where the crayfish hide in winter ...

The most important thing is to organize the work in Russia. The history of our party shows that disagreements are ironed out not in debates, but chiefly in the course of work, in the course of applying principles. Hence the task of the day is to organize work in Russia around a strictly defined principle. The Liquidators at once realized what was happening (they have a keen nose for such things) and have begun to penetrate (have already penetrated) into the legal workers' organizations, and it seems they already have their illegal centre in Russia, which is directing etc. the work. Meanwhile, we are merely 'preparers', still at the stage of rehearsals. In my view our next task, which must not be delayed, is the organization of a central (Russian) group, which would co-ordinate the illegal, semilegal and legal work at first in the main centres (Petersburg, Moscow, the Urals, the South). Call it what you will – the 'Russian section of the Central Committee' – it makes no difference. Such a group is as necessary as air, as bread ...

Now about myself. I have another six months to serve. When the term expires, I shall be entirely at your service. If the need of organizers is really acute, I can fly the coop at once ...

In this letter, written on the last day of 1910, Stalin was writing his passport to power. The need for a powerful auxiliary group representing the Central Committee within Russia was not an original one, but it had proved extraordinarily difficult to bring about; and it was all the more difficult because Lenin, while remaining abroad, insisted on holding all the leading strings in his hands. Yet there had never been the opportunity which existed now, nor had there ever been a time when such an auxiliary group had been so necessary.

Inside Russia the party was weak and disorganized. No natural leaders had yet emerged. There was talk of liquidating the illegal, conspiratorial work of the party altogether and striving for power by parliamentary means; and sometimes Lenin himself would pay lip service to these ideas. The Liquidators, who wanted to liquidate the revolution, were in the ascendant, not because the theory of the violent, conspiratorial overthrow of the government was unsound, but because the workers were opposed to it. 'During the period 1909–1911,' Stalin wrote later, 'the party went through a period of complete disintegration, with wholesale desertions, not only on the part of the intellectuals, but also on the part of the workingmen.' Something new therefore had to be attempted, and Stalin was not averse to attempting it.

In his letter to Comrade Semeon, Stalin presented himself as the heaven-sent regenerator of the party within Russia. He wrote with exactly the right sense of devotion towards Lenin, and exactly the right sense of urgency; and his reward was not long in coming. Lenin began to pay more attention to Stalin than he had ever done in the past.

From Stalin's letter it is clear that he was aiming at something more than being a mere local organizer. What he wanted above all was to become a member of the Central Committee, acting inside Russia with the full authority of the small group of exiles hammering out the party programme from abroad.

Less than a month later, on January 24th, 1911, he wrote a letter to the Moscow Bolsheviks, which was intercepted by the police. It is a strange letter, for Stalin commits the crime, rare among revolutionaries, of mentioning the names of members of the party, with the result that the letter was to prove more useful to the Okhrana than to the Moscow Bolsheviks. This was characteristic of him: he never took much care to safeguard the lives of others. Realizing that he was little known in Moscow, he went to some pains to identify himself. He wrote:

The Caucasian Soso is writing to you. You remember in 1904 in Tiflis and Baku. First of all my ardent greetings to Olga, to you, to Germanov. I. M. Golubev, with whom I am beguiling my days in exile, told me about all of you.

Germanov knows me as K....b....a (he'll understand). I am finishing here in July of this year. Ilyich and Co. are calling me to one of two centres, without waiting for the end of the term. However, I should like to finish my term (a legal person has more possibilities) ... But if the need is great (I am awaiting their answer), then, of course, I'll fly the coop ... We here are stifling without anything to do, I am literally choking.

We have heard, of course, about the 'tempest in the teapot' abroad. Blocs of Lenin-Plekhanov on the one hand, and of Trotsky-Martov-Bogdanov on the other. The attitude of the workers towards the first bloc is, so far as I know, favourable. But in general the workers are beginning to look contemptuously on 'abroad', saying:

'Let them crawl on the wall to their hearts' desire, but the way we feel about it, he who has the interests of the movement at heart should keep busy; as for the rest, it will take care of itself.'

This, I think, is for the best.

Stalin was saying one thing to Comrade Semeon, and something else to the Moscow Bolsheviks. He wanted power, the laying on of hands from Lenin, and at the same time he was prepared to destroy Lenin's authority by deriding it. Lenin, far away, out of touch with the revolutionary developments, had become merely something that crawled on a wall. The letter to Comrade Semeon demonstrated undying devotion to Lenin, while the letter to the Moscow Bolsheviks written three weeks later shows only contempt.

In these two letters the conflict which was later to break out between Stalin and Lenin was already announced.

When Stalin left Solvychegodsk for Vologda he still had no official position within the party. The police were still watching him. He had no money, no group of admiring young workmen who would obey his orders, and no possibility of setting up an illegal printing press. In September he slipped out of Vologda and made his way to St Petersburg, where Sergo Alliluiev let him hide in his apartment. It was a dangerous move, for Alliluiev, as a Bolshevik militant, was being watched by the police and three Okhrana agents were in the neighbourhood of the apartment, keeping it under surveillance. Alliluiev, who genuinely liked Stalin, seems to have been aware of his friend's recklessness and he hinted that

Stalin would be well advised to hide elsewhere. Stalin thought he was suffering from an excess of caution, and obstinately decided to take advantage of Alliluiev's friendship and remain in the apartment. The inevitable happened. On September 9th, after being only two days in St Petersburg, he was arrested. It happened to be the day when Prime Minister Stolypin was shot to death by a lawyer and former *agent provocateur* called Bagrov, and the government, afraid of more assassinations, ordered a roundup of all known revolutionaries. Stalin, who had hoped to become the head of the Bolshevik organization in Russia, was carried off to the House of Preliminary Detention. There he remained for three months. In December he was ordered to return to Vologda and to remain there under police surveillance.

Until February 1912 Stalin was one of those obscure revolutionaries who had accomplished very little and was still little known within the party. Few had read his writings, which had not yet been translated from Georgian. He had written little. In the whole of 1911 not a single article came from his pen. Quite suddenly, at the beginning of 1912, his fortunes changed as the result of a decision made by Lenin at the Prague Conference.

At this conference, which was wholly dominated by Lenin, a new Central Committee was elected. It was composed of seven members: Lenin, Zinoviev, Malinovsky, Schwartzman, Goloshchekin, Ordjonikidze and Spandaryan. These last two came from the Caucasus, which was now for the first time given considerable weight in the Central Committee. In addition there were four alternate members: Bubnov, Smirnov, Kalinin, and Elena Stassova. Unknown to Lenin, Malinovsky was in the pay of the secret police. Lenin reserved the right to coopt anyone he thought fit into the Central Committee, and some time after the conference he decided to add two more members: Stalin, and a certain Belostotsky, a metalworker in the Putilov works who had attended the school at Longjumeau where he impressed Lenin by his ability.

Stalin was not elected to the Central Committee. Lenin simply placed him on the committee as an afterthought. It was an afterthought that was to have an incalculable effect on the history of the party and on the history of the world.

The appointment seems to have been made at the end of February and was officially communicated to Stalin by Ordjonikidze, who passed through Vologda early in March. Stalin was overjoyed by the news. 'I have been to see Ivanovich,' Ordjonikidze reported to Lenin, 'and came to a definite understanding with him. He is very pleased with the way things turned out. The news has made a splendid impression on him.' He had every reason to be pleased. He was no longer to be counted among the anonymous sappers; he had emerged into the daylight of power.

It was at first a very tenuous power, rarely exercised, because there were so few opportunities for exercising it. The first step, of course, was to escape from police supervision in Vologda, and with Ordjonikidze's help he slipped out of the town and immediately made his way to the south, to the Caucasus, where for a while he vanished from sight. As a member of the Central Committee he was expected to send voluminous reports to Lenin, but none of these reports reached their destination. A letter written by Lenin, dated March 28th, 1912, was intercepted by the police. It included a brief reference to Stalin: 'Have heard nothing from Ivanovich. Is he all right? Where is he? How is he?' Nothing is known of Stalin's movements from March 13th, when he left Vologda, to April 23rd, when he appeared in St Petersburg. The biographical chronicle notes that he spent these weeks in Baku and Tiflis 'organizing the work of the Transcaucasian Bolshevik organizations in order to carry out the decisions of the Prague Conference'. Armed with his new authority, he may very well have made a study of revolutionary conditions in Baku and Tiflis, but a visit to St Petersburg was of far greater importance. Here, in the capital, he could exert his authority more effectively. If the Tsarist regime was ever overthrown, it would be as a result of an uprising in St Petersburg, not as a result of an uprising in the Caucasus. St Petersburg was the centre of the revolutionary ferment.

In later years Stalin liked to believe that shortly after his arrival in St Petersburg, he assumed the entire responsibility for organizing and publishing the first Bolshevik daily newspaper, *Pravda*. It was a vast claim, for the establishment of the newspaper was one of the major triumphs of the party. Stalin himself was perfectly aware of the importance to be attached to *Pravda*. He wrote in 1951: '*Pravda* was founded on the instructions of V. I. Lenin on the initiative of J. V. Stalin, who as a member of the Central Committee directed the drafting of the newspaper's platform and took part in making up the first issue.' Two of these statements are true:

Pravda was founded on the instructions of Lenin, and Stalin took part in making up the first issue.

Writing in 1922, on the tenth anniversary of *Pravda*, Stalin made a more modest claim. He wrote:

> It was in the middle of April 1912, one evening at Comrade Poletayev's house, where two members of the Duma (Pokrovsky and Poletayev), two writers (Olminsky and Baturin) and I, a member of the Central Committee (I, being in hiding, had found 'sanctuary' in the house of Poletayev, who enjoyed 'parliamentary immunity') reached agreement concerning *Pravda*'s platform and compiled the first issue of the newspaper.

Now, the beginnings of *Pravda* are known and can be traced very accurately. Unknown to Stalin, the decision to publish a daily newspaper was taken by Lenin during the course of the Prague Conference. As soon as the conference was over, Lenin took the train to Leipzig for a secret meeting with the Bolshevik members of the Third Duma, among whom was included the veteran journalist Poletayev, the editor of the Bolshevik weekly *Zvezda* (The Star), which had been in existence since December 1910. Poletayev was a revolutionary of considerable attainments. Born in 1872, he began his career as a turner in a machine shop in St Petersburg, and at the age of eighteen or nineteen became a convinced revolutionary. He was arrested several times, and each time escaped from prison. A well-read man, and a gifted speaker, he was a member of the Petersburg Soviet in 1905 and later became a member of the Third Duma. Lenin liked and trusted him, and one of the major reasons for calling the secret meeting at Leipzig was to discuss the new newspaper, which would appear under his editorship. By the time Stalin had arrived in the capital, the plans for bringing out the newspaper were already far advanced, a large sum of money had been collected, and stocks of paper had been made available.

Stalin's first task in St Petersburg was to write brief occasional pieces for *Zvezda*, which had recently begun to appear two or three times each week. Eight of his pieces appeared under a variety of pseudonyms – S., K.S., K.S.——n, K. Salin, K. Solin, the last being used three times. The name Stalin had not yet emerged, and he gives the impression of a man groping for his revolutionary identity.

The Bolsheviks chose their pseudonyms with care and

attached considerable importance to them, experimenting continually until they had discovered exactly the right arrangement of syllables. Their pseudonyms were battle flags, disguises, decorations. Sometimes the pseudonyms had the effect of giving the wearer a personality which did not altogether belong to him, but which he strove to acquire. So the young Vyacheslav Scriabin assumed the name of Molotov, from *molot*, meaning 'a hammer', and Lev Rosenfeld assumed the name of Kamenev, from *kamen*, meaning 'a stone', to signify that he was unshakable. The legend that Stalin obtained his name because Lenin recognized his 'steel-like' quality can easily be disproved. Instead, Stalin arrived at his name hesitantly, ambiguously, after many experiments. The name first appeared in January 1913 below a long article in the magazine *Prosveshcheniye* (The Enlightenment) devoted to a study of Marxism and the national question. Previously there had been approximations to this name, curious sallies towards it and away from it. The name, which was to be known all over the world, was strangely elusive.

Before he arrived in St Petersburg he had signed his articles usually with variations on Koba – K., Ko..., Koba Ivanovich. Once for an article written in 1910 he employed the pseudonym K. Stephin. At other times he used the name K. Kato, evidently in emulation of Cato the Elder, whose forthrightness, hatred of luxury and bloodthirstiness had always commended him to revolutionaries. 'Our fathers were sybarites, but we are Catos,' cried Prince Viazemsky, the friend of the poet Pushkin. The name Solin belongs to a different order of things, for it comes from *solniy*, meaning 'salty', perhaps in the sense of 'the salt of the earth'.

The eight articles written in St Petersburg are all in his characteristic heavy-handed style, which was already formed and would not change over the years. A few weeks earlier workmen in the gold mines on the River Lena in the far north of Siberia had come out on strike. The strike committee was arrested, and when the workers marched in procession to protest against their arrest, soldiers opened fire, killing 270 and wounding 250. All over Russia the workers downed tools and demanded an explanation. The revolutionary flame, which had been burning low, flared up again. Stalin's first article was a call to arms against a government which could permit such a massacre. It concluded ominously with the words: 'Greetings to you, the first swallows!' Another article concluded with the single word: 'Fools!' A third article concluded with a translation of a Georgian proverb: 'Life is all-powerful, and it always triumphs.' But it was in the last of the eight articles that Stalin showed himself at his most trenchant, employing the repetitive liturgical style which he always employed at moments of crisis. He wrote:

The nation lay shackled at the feet of oppressors.

The nation needed a popular constitution, and was granted instead a savage tyranny...

The nation needed freedom of speech, press and assembly, and all round we see the smashed workers' organizations, suppressed newspapers, editors arrested, broken-up meetings, and strikers deported.

The nation demanded land for the peasants, and was granted agrarian laws which only increased the land hunger of the peasant masses for the pleasure of a few rural capitalists.

The nation demanded protection of 'person' and 'property' but the prisons and places of exile are overcrowded with 'undesirables', and the chiefs of the criminal investigation departments (remember Kiev and Tiflis) enter into alliance with bandits and thieves to tyrannize over persons and to plunder property.

The nation was promised 'prosperity' and 'abundance', and everywhere peasant farming is on the decline, and tens of millions of peasants are starving, and scurvy and typhus are carrying away thousands of victims.

The nation endured all this, and went on enduring it, and those who could not endure it killed themselves.

But everything must have an end – the patience of the nation has come to an end.

The Lena shooting has broken the ice of silence, and the river of the people's movement has begun to flow.

The ice is broken!...

Stalin never forgot the rhythms of the liturgical chants he heard as a choirboy and seminarian, and at intervals during his life, breaking through the arid monotony of his prose, there would come these curious bursts of song, sometimes printed as free verse, sometimes buried in long paragraphs of prose. Whenever he was confronted with new responsibilities, new powers or new difficulties, his political energy flowed into a liturgical mould. At such moments the poet in him would flash briefly and immediately die out, and years might pass before there was another sudden flare.

For Stalin these were days of violent excitement, for the Bolsheviks were convinced that the massacre in the Lena gold fields would be the signal for revolution. He had reached St Petersburg at exactly the right moment. The article appeared on April 2nd, 1912, at the height of the preparations for publishing *Pravda*. Though Stalin liked to claim that he was the only begetter, he would sometimes make the more modest claim that the fathers of the newspaper were Stalin, Poletayev and Olminsky, the last a veteran journalist and revolutionary who had been a Bolshevik since 1903 and who had worked on *Vperyod* and *Proletary* in the days when the Bolsheviks had only a small following; and in fact they ran the newspaper and Stalin had very little to do with it. In his *Collected Works* he printed an unsigned article, which appeared in the first number, as his own. The article, entitled 'Our Aims', consists of a few modest paragraphs in which the author begs for the sympathy of the workers and urges them to become writers for the newspaper. It is written in the style of Poletayev, who was always encouraging workers to write, and contains none of the characteristic rhythms and vocabulary of Stalin. He did not write it, and claimed to have written it only because it was necessary for him to believe that he presided over the destinies of *Pravda* from the beginning.

Nevertheless he was present at the birth of *Pravda*, took part in the preliminary discussions, and as a member of the Central Committee was able to make his influence felt. A closely printed three-page article on *Pravda*'s origins which appears in Volume XXI of the most recent edition of Lenin's *Complete Works* mentions him only once as one of twenty contributors listed in alphabetical order.

On May 5th, the same day that saw the first issue of *Pravda* on the streets, Stalin was arrested by the police and lodged in the famous house of detention on Shpalernaya Street. Roman Malinovsky, a more important member of the Central Committee, had simply told the police where he could be found. For two weeks he remained in jail. His case was a serious one. The police felt they had dealt leniently with him by permitting him to live in Vologda, and they had expected him to remain there quietly. They now knew through their agent Malinovsky that he was a member of the Central Committee of the Bolshevik party, and they congratulated themselves on

„Правда" родилась в момент революционнаго подъема в знаменитые „ленские дни". Появление на свет массовой рабочей газеты „Правды" в эти именно дни знаменовало собой: 1) ликвидацию периода общей усталости в стране после Столыпинской „тиши да глади", 2) мощное пробуждение русскаго рабочаго класса к новой, второй после 1905 года, революции и 3) начало завоевания широких масс рабочаго класса на сторону большевиков.

„Правда" 1912-го года — это закладка фундамента для победы большевизма в 1917 году.

И. Сталин

Pravda was born during the rising tide of the revolution in the celebrated 'Lena days'. The appearance of *Pravda*, a mass workers' newspaper, precisely at that moment marked: 1) the end of the period of general fatigue prevailing in the country after the Stolypin 'lull and calm'; 2) a powerful awakening of the Russian working class to a new revolution after the Revolution of 1905; 3) the beginning of the winning over by the Bolsheviks of the broad masses of the working people.

Pravda of 1912 was the laying of the cornerstone for the victory of Bolshevism in 1917.

May 5th, 1922 —J. STALIN

having arrested a revolutionary of some importance. The sentence was a comparatively heavy one – three years of exile at Narym on the Ob river in the frozen wastes of north-western Siberia.

Narym was a well-known place of exile, and many hard-bitten revolutionaries were living there. Among them were Sverdlov, Smirnov, Lashevich and Vereshchak, who had been Stalin's cellmate at Baku. In his memoirs Vereshchak recounts a meeting with Stalin in the neighbouring town of Kolpashevo. Stalin was in good humour and talked only of escaping, saying that the best way to escape was by being smuggled on to the river steamer. Escape was virtually impossible in winter when the river was frozen over. During the summer Lashevich succeeded in escaping, and Sverdlov, who had already spent a year in exile, tried to paddle down the river in the hope of boarding a river steamer, but the canoe overturned, he was rescued by local peasants and handed over to the police. According to his own account Stalin succeeded in escaping on September 13th, and reached St Petersburg twelve days later.

The irrepressible fugitive could now take up the work he had left in May, writing articles for *Pravda* and supervising the fortunes of the Bolshevik party in the capital. The election campaign for the Fourth State Duma was in progress, and in October there was a conference of electoral representatives. After Malinovsky, Stalin was the highest-ranking member of the party in St Petersburg and to some extent he could dictate policy. He could, and did, frame the Bolshevik programme, and he was in no mood to take orders from anyone abroad. He wrote the party mandate, which Lenin later approved, and worked tirelessly to bring about the election of Bolshevik deputies. All the time he was living an underground life, avoiding arrest by staying in a different apartment each night. As a result of his efforts only six Bolshevik deputies were elected out of a total of 422. The six were Malinovsky, Petrovsky, Muranov, Badayev, Samoilov, and Shagov. The first four had been metalworkers, the last two had been textile workers.

Lenin, who was then living in Cracow, summoned the six deputies to a conference to discuss the future plans of the party. He was clearly not satisfied with Stalin's activities, and it was decided that he should be relieved of the editorship of *Pravda*, with Badayev replacing him. Stalin spent a few days in Cracow, and then returned to Russia. He had not been dismissed from his position on the Central Committee, but Lenin was in some doubt about how his services could be best used, and insisted that there should be another meeting between them. At the end of December Stalin once again made the journey to Cracow, travelling without papers, and with only a remote idea of how he could cross the frontier safely. Chance favoured him, for at a small frontier town he fell in with a Polish cobbler. Stalin told the cobbler that he was himself the son of a cobbler in Georgia.

'Ah, so you are from Georgia?' the Pole said. 'I have heard of your country. It's wonderful there – mountains, vineyards. I suppose there are Tsarist gendarmes there, just as in Poland?'

'Yes, just as in Poland,' Stalin replied. 'We have no schools in our own tongue, but many gendarmes.'

After a while Stalin said: 'I must cross the frontier today.'

'Then I will take you across,' the Pole replied, and he refused any payment, adding: 'The sons of oppressed nations should help one another.'

Lenin had many purposes in inviting Stalin to this second meeting in Cracow. There were questions about funds to be raised for *Pravda,* and there was also the question of how the funds had been spent – no one seems to have made a detailed accounting. There was also the question of renumeration for Lenin himself; he had little money left, and no means of raising money. There were a hundred questions about future tactics. There was the necessity to find a place for Stalin in the revolutionary organization. For some time Lenin had been devoting considerable attention to the nationalities question, and when they met, he asked Stalin for his views on the subject. As a Caucasian, Stalin was an authority on the oppressed nationalities in Russia, and he spoke at length on the subject. Lenin was all the more impressed when he discovered that they had an identity of views, and he suggested that Stalin should write an exhaustive study on the national question in its relationship to Marxism, adding that he might like to discuss the subject with Bukharin and Trotsky, who were in Vienna. Accordingly, in the second part of January 1913, Stalin took the train for Vienna. Some days later, writing to Maxim Gorky, Lenin said: 'I agree with you it is time to take up seriously the national question. We had with us here a wonderful Georgian who is writing for *Prosveshcheniye* [The Enlightenment] a long article, for which he has collected all the Austrian and other material.'

Stalin knew no German, and therefore had to rely on the good offices of Bukharin for help. Alexander Troyanovsky, another Bolshevik revolutionary living in Vienna, who later became the Soviet ambassador in Washington, also supplied translations from Austrian books on the nationalities question. There was a brief, and unhappy, meeting with Trotsky, who could remember afterwards only 'the glint of animosity in Stalin's yellow eyes'. Trotsky was far from being on good terms with the Bolsheviks. He had denounced the Prague Conference as 'a fraud and a usurpation', which it was, and was in no mood for welcoming one of Lenin's disciples to the secrets of his mind.

Stalin's pamphlet *Marxism and the National Question*, which fills seventy-seven pages of his *Collected Works*, is an impressive document, for it skilfully avoids the chief issues and yet gives an impression of hard, logical thinking. Here and there the style changes abruptly, showing where a phrase, a paragraph, or a page have been added by another hand, but for the most part it is Stalin grappling forcibly with problems which admit of no easy solutions, stifling his rage over their intractability, and compelling them to accept their proper Marxist solutions.

He begins by asserting that a nation is neither racial nor tribal, for, he says, the Italians were formed from Romans, Teutons, Etruscans, Greeks and Arabs, and the French were formed from Gauls, Romans, Britons and Teutons. Clearly, too, Great Britain and the United States are not a common nation, though they speak the same language and share the same traditions. So a nation must have a common territory, and this is its chief characteristic. It must have a common language, a common economy, and national characteristics in common. He has a hard time finding a nation which obeys this formula. Is Georgia a nation? But in Georgia there are Mingrelians, Abkhazians, Adjarians, Svanetians, Lezghians, and Ossets, all speaking different languages, with their own separate cultural traditions. The solution, then, is to deprive them of their language, culture, and traditions by submitting them 'to the common stream of a higher culture'. He is not too happy with this solution, and argues restlessly against Noah Jordania, who was more inclined to permit the cultural minorities to live their own separate lives, and he finds some merit in the right of all nations to secede. At times he wonders whether the national question is really the paramount question, saying that 'the hub of political life in Russia is not the national but the agrarian question', as though the problem could be dismissed out of hand by an appeal to another problem. For a while the problem of national culture absorbs him. Is there a national culture in Russia, where, as he says, the bourgeoisie thirsts for war and the proletariat has declared war on war? He answers that it is impossible to speak of 'the union of all the members of the national-cultural community', for they are divided among themselves. And slowly, patiently, with astonishing adroitness, he begins to destroy the concept of the nation until nothing exists except its right to secede.

Stalin's treatment of the nation bears some relation to Gogol's description of a strange animal called a *nedotichomka*, which had two slits for a nose and a hole for a mouth. Nations exist – he has no doubt about their existence – but where shall you find them? He hammers away at national characteristics. What are they? Where can they be found? He insists that common national characteristics are the mark of a nation, but difficulties are continually arising. It is a national characteristic of Georgians that they like to pursue vendettas, and self-flagellation is a national characteristic of some Transcaucasian Tatars. Who will say what a national characteristic is? If, even in Georgia, there is no common language, no common economy, and no common national characteristics – only some land that is called Georgia – is there such a thing as a Georgian nation? In the last sentence of the last page of *Marxism and the National Question*, Stalin comes to the conclusion that 'the principle of international solidarity of the workers is an essential element in the solution of the national question'. There are no nations; there is only the international community of workers. Marx's slogan 'Workers of the world, unite!' has effectively provided the acid in which the problem is finally dissolved.

Nevertheless, in the course of his study of nations, Stalin shows a shrewd and subtle capacity for argument. He argues plausibly against the German and Austrian socialists who have absorbed nationalism into their socialist beliefs. 'We can always cope with overt nationalism,' he declares, 'but it is much more difficult to combat nationalism when it is masked and unrecognizable beneath its mask, protected by the armour of socialism, and therefore less vulnerable and more tenacious.' In much the same way he argues against secession by the Transcaucasian Tatars, 'who may assemble in their parliament, and succumbing to the influence of their beys and mullahs, decide to restore the old order of things'. In theory, every nation has a right to secede; in practice, nations are merely the provisional fiefs of the old, dying bourgeois system, and the right to secede is scarcely a matter of importance. Let them secede if they like; it will do them no harm. The question of the right to secession was not an academic one. Then as now, Russia was composed of some two hundred nations, all praying for their day of deliverance from the authority of the central power.

Stalin's arguments in *Marxism and the National Question* are often jesuitical. He says, for example, that the minorities have always been oppressed, so that we find Jews being oppressed in Poland, Russians in the Caucasus, Poles in the Ukraine, and all this oppression will end 'when each nation is given complete democracy, for then there will be no room for fear'. Then he pauses and asks himself the destructive question: 'What need is there for a nation when there is complete democracy?' In this way the argument proceeds in circles like the circles on the surface of a pool when a stone is flung in. As so often in Lenin's own writings, the problem vanishes because it has been denied the right of existence.

Stalin's long article appeared in the March-May issue of *Prosveshcheniye*, which was published legally in St Petersburg. Before it appeared in print, Stalin was once more under arrest. He had returned to St Petersburg secretly and was attending a concert given in aid of party funds when the police pounced on him.

This time they were in no mood to show their customary kindness to him. Arrested at the beginning of March 1913, he was kept in prison for three months and then exiled to Turukhansk in the far northern wastes of Siberia for four years. This time they were determined not to let him escape.

SIBERIA

Turukhansk lies at a latitude of 62 degrees North, and is six hundred miles from the nearest railroad station. In those days it was nothing more than a huddle of cottages overlooking the broad reaches of the Yenisei river. Revillon Frères, of Paris, had a trading station there, buying the furs of silver foxes from the neighbouring trappers. Political prisoners were given an allowance of fifteen rubles a month, but there were no shops where they could spend the money. An Arctic silence surrounded them. They vanished into the northern wastes, and sometimes nothing was ever heard of them again.

From being a member of the Central Committee and an editor of *Pravda* Stalin was reduced to being a small speck above the Arctic Circle. Very rarely would he be able to send letters out, and very rarely would he receive magazines and newspapers. He was at the mercy of guards who had orders to kill any escaping prisoners; he had almost no money, and little hope. He had the stamina to survive the long winters, and four years in Turukhansk would do no harm to his body, but it had happened before that prisoners lost their minds in the far north. It was August before he reached Turukhansk; by October the whole province would be under snow. He succeeded in getting a letter to Alliluiev in St Petersburg, begging for money, which might enable him to escape, or to pay for food and kerosene against the coming of the harsh northern winter. He was not alone, for Sverdlov, who was later to become the titular head of the Bolshevik government, had been arrested on the same day and was now his companion in exile. They had little in common, did not particularly like each other, and rarely spoke to one another. Sverdlov spoke three or four languages, read omnivorously, enjoyed argument, and had a passion for ideas; Stalin preferred to brood in silence.

They were taken to the obscure hamlet of Kostino, where there were no more than four or five houses. From the beginning they made plans to escape, and those plans came to the ears of the governor of Yeniseisk, who gave orders that all means were permissible to forestall an escape. In February they learned that they were to be sent some sixty-five miles further north to the hamlet of Kureika. Stalin had received 100 rubles through Alliluiev, and when the authorities learned that he had received the money, they ordered that he should be deprived of his regular allowance for four months. Just before setting out for Kureika, Sverdlov wrote to his sister Sarah Mikhailovna Sverdlova in St Petersburg:

DEAR SARAH,

My next letter will be numbered again. I am writing just a few words now hastily. Joseph Djugashvili and I are being transferred a hundred versts further north – eighty versts north of the Arctic Circle. There will only be the two of us in the village, and two guards with us. The surveillance is being increased, and we are cut off from the mail. The latter comes once a month with a messenger on foot, who is generally late. We will get the post approximately eight or nine times a year. Still, it is better than at Maximkin Yar. Please send everything to my old address: the comrades will forward it all. Djugashvili has been deprived of his subsidy for four months, for having received money. Both he and I need money, but it cannot be addressed to us. By the way I have already written to you that I have a debt and that you can send the money not to me but directly to my creditors. I'll let you know their address. All you have to do is to mark the coupon: 'In payment of Ya. M.'s debt.' I'm waiting for everything I've asked for. I shall write you next from Kureika. I'm not writing to anyone but you in Peter. I'm hoping they'll hear from you.

Much love,

Yours, YAKOV

Write oftener and more. I ask all my friends to do the same. I did write to a few people in Peter after all. My address is the same as usual.

Sverdlov's references to debts, creditors and coupons were hints for money, passports, and addresses, for the purpose of escaping. The letter was written on February 19th, but there was some delay in setting out for Kureika, for they apparently did not reach the hamlet until two weeks later. With the summer came the declaration of war by Germany. On August 12th, 1914, Sverdlov wrote prophetically: 'The horrors of the war and its consequences will exert tremendous revolutionary effect on the backward classes. The reactionaries may commit cruel and repressive acts and excesses, but the victory is not theirs.' He had abandoned nearly all hope of escaping. He followed the war across vast distances of space.

In his first letter from Kureika, Sverdlov described his lodging, a small house crowded with the landlord's children. He complained that people kept dropping in every evening just when he was sitting down to work. There was no privacy, for Stalin shared his room. 'Stalin is a good fellow, but too much of an individualist in everyday life, while I believe in a semblance of order,' he wrote. 'That's why I am nervous at times.' Stalin's disorderly habits could be excruciatingly painful, but Sverdlov suffered them with outward good humour. Stalin did almost no work; Sverdlov was always working, writing articles, giving lessons, making observations for the local meteorological station. He planned the day minutely, and complained that Stalin knew nothing about planning.

Sverdlov was one of the few Bolsheviks with a gift for description. Once he wrote:

> The ice thaw on a great river like the Yenisei is worth seeing. The ice breaks with a cracking noise, splits into enormous blocks. The blocks are driven against each other by the water, they strike against the shore while the water rises higher and higher. One is loath to leave the shore. The north wind rises, the waters of the Yenisei swell, become covered in foam, and they hammer against the high bank where the village stands, washing it away bit by bit, and then the earth falls with a great thud and is carried away by the waves.

In another letter he describes the sun shining through his window late at night:

> Since yesterday the sun has stopped setting. The sun is always on the horizon. It is now eleven o'clock at night, and the sun is straight in front of my window. Only it is blood-red, and hardly gives any warmth. In contrast, there is a lot of snow. It melts and disappears with incredible slowness.

Unlike Sverdlov, Stalin took no joy in the Arctic scenery. He fished, hunted, laid traps for the silver foxes, swam and went skiing. He had a natural talent as a hunter, and the corner of the room which he shared with Sverdlov was filled with traps, nets, and spears which he was continually cleaning or mending. Living in the open air, he became healthier. In summer he hunted geese and ducks. In winter he laid his traps, and dropped nets below the ice to catch the fish. Occasionally he would forget his brooding long enough to flare up in a quarrel with Sverdlov or one of the other political prisoners, then he would become sullen and quiet again. A local woman became his mistress, and in due course she gave him a son.

One by one the revolutionaries who had been sent to Kureika were permitted to settle elsewhere; at last only Stalin remained behind, lonely, aloof, not caring for the company of others, content with his fishing and trapping. Early in 1915 Sverdlov settled in the little hamlet of Monastyrskoye, where there was already a small colony of exiled revolutionaries, which later included five of the Bolshevik deputies to the Duma; they had been rounded up for carrying on revolutionary propaganda against the war. Kamenev, Linde, and Yakovlev lived in the same hamlet.

In the summer of 1915, Stalin visited Monastyrskoye and was photographed with the other Bolsheviks. He stands in the back row, wearing a black felt hat, which gives him something of the appearance of an artist, with Suren Spandaryan on one side of him, and Kamenev, looking already like a high dignitary of state, on the other. Stalin looks calm and rested, a faint smile playing about his lips, the pockmarks clearly visible on his cheeks. When the photograph was reproduced in the Soviet Union, Kamenev was carefully obliterated, vanishing into the leaves of the trees in the background.

The old scratched photograph was revised and edited over the years, and misleading captions were continually being added to it, so that we find Yaroslavsky, for example, describing it as a photograph taken in 1903, and even Deutscher, the careful analyst of Stalin's political fortunes, places under the photograph the words 'Stalin in exile, 1903.' Yet there is no doubt that it was taken in the summer of 1915, not long before the death of Spandaryan and at a time when Kamenev and Stalin were still on fairly good terms. Stalin looks very young on the photograph; we shall find him looking even younger on photographs taken three years later.

He stayed only a few days in Monastyrskoye. Soon he was making the 150-mile journey back to Kureika, to prepare himself for the long winter ahead. Those winters in Siberia taught him many things. Above all, they taught him that the lives of men were of little consequence when weighed against the powers of nature. Twenty years later, at the height of the purges, he told the Red Army cadets that he once saw thirty men struggling against the floods of the river Yenisei. Towards evening the men returned to the village; one was missing. He asked about the missing man, and they shrugged their shoulders, and one of them said: 'He was drowned, and now I have to go and water my mare. We can always make men, but try to make a mare.' 'It seems to me,' Stalin concluded, 'that the indifference of certain of our leaders to people, to cadres, their inability to value people, is a survival of that strange attitude of man to man displayed in this episode in faraway Siberia.'

It was curious that Stalin should have remembered that incident at the height of the purges, but it would have been still more curious if he had forgotten the lessons he learned in Siberia, where indifference to human life and ferocious cruelty to animals were the commonplaces of existence. He was a ruthless hunter, a man with strong nerves, never frightened by the screaming of animals in pain. He spent most of the winter setting traps, moving around Kureika with his dog team. The best foxes were those caught in winter, for they had the softest fur. Once he boasted that he received a hundred gold rubles for his winter catch. His room was filled to the roof with casting nets, seines, blocks, traps, baskets, and guns of all kinds. Somewhere there may have been books and manuscripts, but if so, only one person saw them.

Did Stalin study in exile, and what did he study? Vera Schweitzer, the wife of Suren Spandaryan, who visited him in Kureika, speaks of seeing his table overflowing with books, magazines and newspapers. The works of Karl Marx were prominently displayed, there was a book by Rosa Luxemburg which he was translating into Russian, and at the same time he was revising *Marxism and the National Question*. As she describes him he is the typical revolutionary scholar immersed in his studies, taking advantage of the long quiet days of exile. But no one else observed the great piles of books, and not a single book, tract or article written by Stalin during those years has survived.

The exiles who met him during this period and later wrote their reminiscences are all agreed that he lived in a kind of monastic seclusion, content to be alone, spending most of his time hunting and fishing. Vera Schweitzer was writing twenty years after the event, and there is some evidence that Stalin revised and edited her manuscript before publication. He knew only the smattering of German he picked up during a brief visit to Vienna, and it is difficult to understand how he could have translated Rosa Luxemburg. He may have revised *Marxism and the National Question*, but no trace of the manuscript has survived, although Anna Alliluieva speaks of receiving the manuscript and sending it secretly to Lenin. If Lenin ever received it, he paid no attention to it, for it was never mentioned again.

Writing about this period of Stalin's life, Trotsky poured scorn on the *evasiveness* of the revolutionary who attended only to his nets and fishing tackle when he should have concerned himself with revolutionary theory. Trotsky himself never let a day pass without writing about revolution, even when he must have known that the revolutionary flame was burning low. 'Stalin,' he wrote, 'remained on the sidelines, sullen, alarmed by the flood of nature at springtide and, as always, malevolent.' But this was to mistake the quality of the man. There is no evidence that he was alarmed by the flood of nature at springtide, nor is there any evidence that he was malevolent during the long years of exile. On the contrary his few surviving letters show a pathetic warmth and kindness.

Prophets invariably go to the desert, where they strip themselves of all human associations, alone with the alone. So it was with Stalin. A man can be tempered by fire, but he can also be tempered by ice. In this Siberian wasteland all that was enduring in Stalin's character – his essential nihilism, his utter distrust of human motives, his instinctive cruelty – were being reinforced and strengthened. His native intelligence, his cunning, his coarseness were, as it were, refined by that long imprisonment in the northern snows. He brooded before; now brooding became a part of life, for there was nothing else to do in the intervals of trapping and skinning wild beasts.

He knew danger well. Indeed, he had always known it, but in exile it assumed cosmic proportions. When he returned to Petrograd it amused him to tell stories of that far distant land to the children of Sergo Alliluiev. He told of fishing on the river when a violent storm erupted, and it was pure miracle that he reached the shore alive, for he was within an inch of being drowned. He told them, too, of his triumphs. He was a good fisherman and sometimes the natives would come along and watch him, shaking their heads because whenever he let down his net the fish gathered. 'You know the secret word,' they whispered, and they were in some awe of him, thinking he possessed some mysterious knowledge denied to others.

His years of exile were an advantage to him, for they gave him clarity of purpose, resourcefulness, an instinctive grasp of the realities of power. Living off the land, profoundly self-sufficient, unconcerned with the ceaseless exhausting arguments of his fellow exiles, he could give himself up to the only thing that ultimately mattered to him – the practical means of dominating his environment.

Not all the accounts written by exiles are trustworthy, but all are agreed upon his strange remoteness, his inability to communicate with them. There was something chilling about his dedication to hunting and trapping. Shumatsky described him as living in complete solitude, with almost no need for intercourse with people, visiting Monastyrskoye two or three times a year to spend a few days with Suren Spandaryan and Vera Schweitzer. Karganov, another revolutionary, tells of his visit to the hamlet of Bakhlanika where a criminal known as 'Chayka' (seagull) had been arrested for stealing. The tribesmen asked the political exiles to adjudicate the case. Long speeches were made pointing out the legal aspects of stealing, the defendant made a speech promising restitution, and the jury deliberated at length on the exact punishment to be given to a confessed criminal. Suddenly Stalin sprang to his feet and asked for the floor. 'Chayka,' he said, 'is a professional thief, and he was merely carrying out his professional duties as he saw them. He is waging war against the capitalist order of society, and therefore he should be praised instead of being condemned. He belongs to us!'

Only one authentic letter written by Stalin to Lenin during the war years has survived. It is written awkwardly, with heavy humour and a curiously explosive violence, and for understandable reasons Stalin did not include it in his *Collected Works*. Yaroslavsky says the letter was written jointly by Stalin and Suren Spandaryan, but from internal evidence it would appear to be wholly the work of Stalin. Written from Monastyrskoye on February 27th, 1915, the letter accompanied a collective declaration from the small Bolshevik group. It is quoted here in its entirety because it conveys to a quite extraordinary degree Stalin's preoccupations at the time:

My greetings to you, dear Ilyich, warm, warm greetings. Greetings to Zinoviev, greetings to Nadezhda Konstantinovna. How are you? How is your health? I live as before, chew my bread, completing half of my term. It is rather dull, but can't be helped. How are things with you? It must be much livelier where you are. I recently read Kropotkin's articles – he's an old fool, completely out of his mind. I also read a short article by Plekhanov in *Ryech* – an incorrigible old gossip! *Ekh-mah!* And the Liquidators with their deputies – agents of the Free Economic Society! There's no one to give them a drubbing, devil take me! Are they to be allowed to get off scot-free? Rejoice our hearts by telling us there will soon appear a newspaper which will smite them across the jaw, and lay it on heartily, too, with a vengeance.

In case you should want to write to me, the address is Turukhansk Territory, Yeniseisk Province, Monastyrskoye Village, for Suren Spandaryan.

Yours,
KOBA

PS. Timofey [Spandaryan] asks that his most bitter regards be sent to Guesde, Sembat and Vandervelde in their glorious (ho! ho!) ministerial posts.

The letter is pure Stalin, coarse, impudent, forceful. He could write well enough when he chose, but he was in no mood to display an elegant command of language. His mind was numbed by the long Siberian winter, and he was hopelessly cut off from the world. How remote these exiles were we can judge from the postscript in which Spandaryan ruefully salutes the acceptance of ministerial posts by two French and one Belgian socialist. Vandervelde had in fact entered the Belgian cabinet on August 4th, 1914. Guesde and Sembat became ministers in the French cabinet a few days later. Spandaryan was referring to events which had happened nearly seven months before as though they had happened only a few weeks before.

When Trotsky came to examine this letter in his unfinished life of Stalin, he was appalled by its tone of jaunty bravado. He commented that it bore the characteristic traits of Stalin – slyness, stupidity and vulgarity. 'A man,' Trotsky declared, 'who really values an exchange of theoretical thoughts does not write like this.' The verdict is true, but irrelevant.

What emerges from the letter is the portrait of a man of phenomenal patience, who nevertheless has no patience with people. He confesses to warm feelings for Lenin, Krupskaya and Zinoviev, but treats the rest of the world with cold indifference or grudging contempt. What angers him is that he is in no position to accomplish the downfall of his enemies. 'There's no one to give them a drubbing, devil take me! Are they to be allowed to get off scot-free?' He must have repeated these ominous words many times in the course of his long life.

The biographical chronicle for 1915 consists of only three entries. It mentions the February letter to Lenin and another, never published, dated November 10th. It also records the general meeting of the Bolshevik groups held at Monastyrskoye during the summer. In the winter Lenin wrote to his friend Karpinsky: 'I have a great favour to ask of you. Find out the surname of Koba. Joseph D——? We have forgotten it.'

In fact Stalin was forgotten by nearly everyone. He was a trapper in the far north, who had vanished into the snows. Only one private letter written during this time is known. It was sent to Olga Evgeyevna Alliluieva, his future mother-in-law, and describes a man who has surrendered wholly to his environment and who broods continually without any hope that his brooding will ameliorate a situation which has grown intolerable. Winter was coming down with a vengeance; the village was snowbound; it was deathly cold on a November day when he wrote thanking her for a small parcel.

I am deeply grateful to you, dear Olga Evgeyevna, for your pure and fine feelings towards me. I shall never forget your thoughtful attitude towards me. I am waiting for the time when I shall be freed from prison, and as soon as I am in Petersburg I shall thank you, and also Sergey, for everything you have done. But there are still two years altogether to wait.

I received the parcel. Thank you. I ask only for one. Do not spend anything more on me – you need the money. I shall be content if from time to time you send me a postcard with a view of nature etcetera. In this accursed country nature is reduced to ugliness – in summer the river, in winter the snow, and that's all the nature there is. I am stupidly homesick for the sight of a landscape, even if it is only on paper.

My greetings to the boys and girls. I wish them all good things.

I live as before. I feel well. My health is fine. I am getting accustomed to this place. Nature is severe here – three weeks ago we had 45 degrees of frost.

Until the next letter,
Respectfully yours,
JOSEPH

This letter, dated November 21st, is recognizably by the same hand that wrote the letter to Lenin. There is the same warmth in the greeting, the same awkward repetitions, the same pathetic desire for news of the outside world. It is the letter of a man who has almost, in Dostoyevsky's phrase, 'returned his ticket to God'. All he wants of life is a picture postcard.

The biographical chronicle for 1916 consists of four spare entries. In early February he wrote a letter to the Bolshevik centre abroad, and three weeks later he wrote another to the centre. In March he wrote a letter to a magazine called *Voprosy Strakhovaniya* (Insurance Problems). In December he was sent under escort to Krasnoyarsk to be inducted into the army.

Of the three letters only one has survived – the letter to *Voprosy Strakhovaniya*. This magazine, an offshoot of *Pravda*, was in urgent need of funds, and the small group of exiles collected 6 rubles 85 kopecks as their contribution towards defraying the expenses of publication. Stalin signed the accompanying letter, which was probably written by Kamenev. It read:

DEAR COMRADES,

We, a group of exiles in Turukhansk Territory, gladly welcome the resumption of publication of *Voprosy Strakhovaniya*. At the present time, when the public opinion of the masses of the workers in Russia is so deliberately misrepresented and when genuine workers' representation is thwarted with the active assistance of A. Guchkov and P. Ryabuchinsky, it is a joy to see and to read a real workers' magazine. *Voprosy Strakhovaniya* must exert every effort ideologically to insure the working class of our country against the corrupting antiproletarian preachments of Potresov, Levitsky, Plekhanov and their kind, all fundamentally opposed to the principles of internationalism.

Why Stalin should have claimed to have written this letter is something of a mystery. In later years it became his practice to claim as his own all letters which bore his signature, even if it was one of twenty signatures, and since there was such a paucity of letters connected with his stay in Turukhansk he seems to have accepted responsibility for this letter with good grace. It does not however appear in his *Collected Works*.

Like all Siberian exiles he thirsted for a change of scene, and when he was summoned to present himself for military service at Krasnoyarsk he was in excellent humour. The long journey in the depth of winter merely increased his appetite for change. He was about six weeks on the road, walking part of the way, sometimes riding in a sleigh drawn by reindeer. He reached Krasnoyarsk towards the end of December. There are several accounts of his reception at the army induction centre. Yaroslavsky, the official historian, says he was not accepted because the army knew him to be 'dangerous'. A more credible reason for his rejection was given by Anna Alliluieva, his future sister-in-law, who wrote in her memoirs that when she asked him how he escaped service in the army, he answered with a laugh: 'I was an undesirable element, and so they excused me on account of my arm.' The crooked arm saved him from becoming a Tsarist soldier.

For some reason he was not sent back to Kureika, but permitted to live at Achinsk, a small town on the Trans-Siberian railway 150 miles west of Krasnoyarsk. There were about 6,000 inhabitants in the town, two churches and six or seven mansions belonging to the local merchants; otherwise it was completely indistinguishable from hundreds of other small Siberian towns which consisted of log cabins and streets which were almost impassable in summer because the earth turned to dust and nearly as impassable in the icy winters. But it was strange that he should be sent there, for the government took care that political prisoners should never reside close to the railway. It is possible that he simply slipped out of Krasnoyarsk on the first available train and got off at the next stop. Vera Schweitzer lends some confirmation to this view, for she goes out of her way to say that he went underground as soon as he reached Achinsk. Kamenev was also hiding in Achinsk. Gradually most of the Bolshevik exiles made their way to this obscure town. None of them knew or guessed how close they were to the revolution.

Before the spring came, the February revolution broke out in Petrograd.

ON THE EDGE OF THE ABYSS

Stalin gave the impression of a grey blur which flickered obscurely and left no trace.

– SUKHANOV

THE COMING OF LENIN

IN LATER YEARS Alexander Kerensky, who was raised to power by the February revolution, would sometimes look back on those strange days and say that they reminded him of nothing so much as Russalka, the bewitching goddess of ancient Russian mythology who carried death in her arms. In his New York apartment, old and vigorous, having long outlived his enemies, he would say softly: 'February was Russalka.'

The revolution caught the Russian revolutionaries by surprise. Never was there a revolution which needed the help of revolutionaries so little. In five days the whole feudal structure of Russia collapsed. Quite suddenly the Romanov dynasty, which had ruled Russia for centuries, vanished from the scene. There were short, sharp battles in Petrograd and Moscow; some soldiers shot at their officers, and some policemen were burned alive; yet the total casualties were fewer than 1,500 killed and wounded. Victory came so easily that the people could hardly believe their good fortune. The bewitching goddess smiled on them. For seven months they would enjoy a precarious liberty, then once again autocracy would be imposed upon them.

All over Russia there was that sense of delirious joy, as the floodgates opened. The abdication of the Tsar meant the end of autocracy. In the popular imagination the Tsar was a lonely, remote figure surrounded by scheming adventurers and pro-German advisers. They were 'the dark forces' to whom all defeats could be attributed. With the fall of the monarchy it was believed that 'the dark forces' would automatically be replaced by the shining representatives of justice, mercy and truth.

Everything happened, as the great journalist Sukhanov wrote later, 'with a sort of fabulous ease'. In effect the people had merely shouted and the monarchy was shattered, as a wine glass is sometimes shattered by a note of music. There was a moment – a very brief moment – when the Provisional Government, following the terms of the Tsar's abdication decree, contemplated elevating the Tsar's only brother, the scholarly and liberal Grand Duke Michael Alexandrovich, to the throne. He told the Provisional Government that he would accept the throne only if it were offered to him by a Constituent Assembly, and the restoration of the monarchy was never mentioned again. The news of the February revolution reached the revolutionary exiles in Achinsk, who held a meeting to honour the Grand Duke for having so decisively rejected the crown, and a telegram of congratulations was sent to him. The class war had not yet been instituted; it was still possible for revolutionaries to regard a Grand Duke as a man of sensibility and good will; and among the signers of the telegram was Kamenev. In later years it was held against him that he had somehow contaminated himself by adding his signature in a telegram to a member of the imperial family.

A few days later Kamenev signed another telegram, this time to Lenin. The telegram was sent from Perm, and read: 'Fraternal greetings. Starting today for Petrograd. Kamenev. Muranov. Stalin.' From all over Siberia the exiles were pouring into the capital. Every train was welcomed by representatives of the political parties who eagerly embraced the newcomers from Siberia and made speeches in which the words 'freedom' and 'peace' were constantly recurring, for repetition had not yet dulled the brightness of the words.

From Perm the three exiles, all members of the Central Committee, sent a telegram to the Bolshevik committee in Petrograd. It was a very small committee consisting of two workmen, Alexander Shlyapnikov and Pyotr Zalutsky, both being experienced agitators, and the twenty-seven-year-old Vyacheslav Molotov. In those days Molotov was slight and fragile, with a pale face and wild hair. He had been on the staff of *Pravda* in 1912. He knew Stalin, and for a brief period Stalin had hidden in the apartment of Molotov's aunt, the widow of a civil servant. At that time there were rumours that Molotov and Stalin had formed a solemn alliance to help one another under all circumstances. There was probably some truth in the rumour, for they remained devoted to one another for forty years. Such alliances, amounting to blood brotherhood, were common among the Bolsheviks.

Shlyapnikov's speech of welcome has survived in his voluminous memoirs. He greeted the newcomers in the name of the victory of the working class, and in the course of the speech bitterly assailed the Provisional Government. He was a dyed-in-the-wool Leninist, breathing fire and thunder. With Molotov and Zalutsky he had already resumed the publication of

Pravda, banned during the war, and his editorials were as fiery as his speeches.

The exiles arrived in Petrograd on March 25th. Only ten days had passed since the abdication of the Tsar and the setting up of the Provisional Government. As the days passed, Kamenev was struck with the extraordinary spectacle of a city where the people were drunk with victory, and both the Provisional Government and the Soviet of Workers' and Soldiers' Deputies, which had come to birth at the same time, being the successor of the Soviet of the 1905 revolution, were in command. Shlyapnikov wanted to overturn the Provisional Government. Kamenev, who was a gentle soul with a horror of inflicting pain, wanted a gradual revolution. With no liking for Shlyapnikov's extremist views, he decided to oust him from the control of *Pravda* and to assume the editorship himself. On March 28th *Pravda* announced that the editorial board was composed of Kamenev as editor in chief, with Bulanov and Stalin as editors, all of them being members of the Central Committee.

In this way it happened that the first Bolshevik to assume a position of power and responsibility in Petrograd was a small, retiring, gentle man who had no thirst for bloody revolutions and who wanted to get along amicably with the other political parties.

Kamenev was in fact aghast when he read the violent articles published by Shlyapnikov. Meeting Sukhanov a few days later, he was apologetic. 'Have you been reading *Pravda?*' he asked. 'Of course, it had a completely unseemly and unsuitable tone, and a terrible reputation. When I came here I was in despair. What should be done? I even thought of shutting down this *Pravda* altogether and getting out a new central organ under a different name. But that's impossible. In our party too much is bound up with the name *Pravda*. It must stay. Only we will have to shift to a new course.' In his mind the new course consisted of an alliance of all the revolutionary parties, and Sukhanov, a Menshevik, was accordingly invited to become a contributor.

Shlyapnikov, ousted from his post, was in no mood to take the affront lying down. The new *Pravda* in its first editorial declared that the Bolsheviks would resolutely support the Provisional Government 'in as far as it fights reaction or counter-revolution'. In Shlyapnikov's eyes *Pravda* had gone over to the enemy. 'When the first of the new issues reached the factories,' he wrote, 'it created confusion and indignation among our party members and sympathizers, and spiteful satisfaction among our opponents.' His attack was directed at Stalin as much as at Kamenev, for Stalin's attitude was only a little to the left of Kamenev's. He, too, looked forward to the alliance of the revolutionary parties, and his first article in *Pravda* took the form of a salute to the February revolution and a prayer that 'the dark forces of ancient Russia' should be finally vanquished. He concluded his short article with an appeal that the fundamental demands of the Russian people should be realized: 'Land for the peasants, protection of labour for the workers, and a democratic republic for all the citizens of Russia!'

In this modest way the future dictator spoke two days after he had arrived in revolutionary Petrograd.

A few days later, to signify his adherence to an alliance of revolutionary parties, he became one of the associate members of the Petrograd Soviet of Workers' and Soldiers' Deputies, largely under the control of the Mensheviks. The president of the Soviet was Chkheidze, a Menshevik from Georgia. The two vice-presidents were Skobelev, a Menshevik, and Kerensky, a Trudovnik, a party which derived from the Narodniki of an earlier generation. There was an Executive Committee of seven members, and there were between thirty and forty associate members who possessed rather less power than the full members of the Executive Committee. Among the associate members were the Mensheviks Irakly Tseretelli, Sukhanov and Lieber, and the Bolsheviks Kamenev, Molotov and Stalin.

Stalin's role in the Soviet of Workers' and Soldiers' Deputies appears to have been a modest one. Sukhanov in his *Notes on the Revolution* described him as 'a grey blur which flickered obscurely and left no trace'. Since his description of Stalin's first appearance on the Executive Committee of the Soviet is one of the classic records of the Russian Revolution, it should be given in full:

In those days, beside Kamenev, Stalin also represented the Bolsheviks in the Ex.Com. He was one of the central figures of the Bolshevik Party and perhaps one of the few individuals who held (and hold to this day) the fate of the revolution and of the state in their hands. Why this is so I shall not undertake to say, since 'influence' in these exalted and irresponsible spheres, remote from the people and alien to publicity, is so capricious. In any event it is impossible not to be perplexed by the role of Stalin. The Bolshevik Party, in spite of the low level of its 'officers' corps, the overwhelmingly ignorant and casual rank and file, includes a whole series of great figures and able leaders in its general staff. Stalin, however, during the course of his modest activity in the Ex.Com. gave me the impression – and I was not alone in this view – of a grey blur which flickered obscurely and left no trace. There is really nothing more to be said about him.

Sukhanov compiled his seven-volume history of the Russian Revolution on the basis of careful diary notes made in 1917. Published in 1922 under a casual and misleading title, it remains to this day the most brilliant description of those tortured months when the revolution flung itself headlong into the abyss. In time 'the grey blur' was to become part of the abyss.

Then as later Stalin was working quietly and feverishly behind the scenes. Though he appears to have delivered no speeches in the Tauride Palace where the Soviet met, his influence could be felt in the Bolshevik Party. He was addressing workers' meetings and writing articles for *Pravda*. The Petrograd Soviet had appealed to the people of the world to stop the war, and in his second article for *Pravda* Stalin endorsed the appeal and gave some healthy advice to the Provisional Government 'which must come out openly and publicly in an effort to induce all the belligerent powers to begin peace negotiations immediately on the basis of recognition of the right of nations to self-determination'. He had no animus against the Provisional Government; he wanted it to do exactly what the Mensheviks wanted it to do. Two days later he wrote an article for *Pravda* on 'The Conditions for the Victory of the Russian Revolution'. He announced three conditions: the immediate arming of the workers, the speedy convocation of the Constituent Assembly and the formation of a super-Soviet, 'an all-Russian organ of revolutionary struggle of the entire Russian democracy'. He used the word *rossiisky* rather than *russky*, implying that the super-Soviet would embrace the entire territorial extent of Russia including countries like Finland and Poland which formerly belonged to the Russian empire. This super-Soviet would 'transform itself at the required moment from an organ of revolutionary *struggle* of the people into an organ of revolutionary *power*'.

The reason for bringing about a super-Soviet was clear. Russia was being ruled by the Provisional Government which drew its strength from the provinces. The Soviets in Leningrad, Moscow and other large cities were confronted with the age-old problem of the power of the cities versus the power of the rural districts. What was needed in Stalin's view was an amalgamation of the Soviets to include the peasant Soviets, and the combined Soviets would overthrow the government. Stalin's article which appeared in *Pravda* on March 31st showed that his views were hardening. He did not really know, and could not guess, which way the revolution was turning. 'The inertia of the provinces is receding into the past, and the ground is trembling under the feet of the Provisional Government,' he wrote, but the inertia of the provinces was to plague the revolutionaries for years to come and the Provisional Government was still in the saddle.

'The Conditions for the Victory of the Russian Revolution' is an important document, because it shows Stalin groping with the ultimate concepts of power. He saw, for example, that power would finally fall neither to the Soviets nor to the Provisional Government nor to the army. It would fall into the hands of a revolutionary elite composed of armed workers. On this subject Stalin wrote with quite unusual penetration. He wrote:

> The army is mobile and fluid, and this is especially due to its constant movement from one place to another according to the demands of the war. The army cannot remain permanently in one place, protecting the revolution from counter-revolution. Accordingly another armed force is needed, an army of armed workers naturally connected with the centres of the revolutionary movement. And if it is true that a revolution cannot triumph without an armed force always ready to serve it, then our revolution too cannot succeed without its own workers' guard, vitally bound up with the interests of the revolution.

But when Stalin used the word 'revolution', he was not using it in the same sense as the ordinary people in the streets, who were still celebrating the February revolution, the fall of the Tsar and the establishment of a liberal government.

Already the word 'revolution' was acquiring overtones of terror.

Stalin was still groping, incapable of focusing on any revolutionary principle. He was still obsessed by the vast gulf between the city and the country. 'The tumult and the firing, the barricades, the casualties, the struggle and the victory have all taken place here in Petrograd,' he wrote. 'The provinces have confined themselves to accepting the fruits of victory and expressing confidence in the Provisional Government.' There was the deathly possibility that the revolution envisaged by the Bolsheviks would be stopped dead in its tracks in Petrograd.

But while there was groping in Petrograd, there was none in Geneva, where Lenin was studying the scanty reports on the Russian revolution which appeared in the French, German and Swiss newspapers. He had already come to some unshakable conclusions. Writing the first of his 'Letters from Afar' on March 20th, he announced that the February revolution could have come about only as the result of a happy conjunction of a popular mass movement acting simultaneously with a reactionary conspiracy. Lenin's interpretation of events was wholly mistaken. There was no reactionary conspiracy, and there had been no popular movement outside of Petrograd. From these wrong conclusions Lenin derived a useful revolutionary thesis: it was necessary to destroy the Provisional Government.

Lenin's attitude towards the Provisional Government was one of unalloyed rage. How dared they take power? They would drown Russia in blood, and starve the people, and enslave them. He cursed them like an Old Testament prophet for all the evil they had accomplished and for the evil they would do. He wrote in his first 'Letter from Afar':

The Provisional Government can give the people *neither peace, nor bread, nor freedom*.

Peace – because it is a government for war, a government for the continuation of the imperialist slaughter, a government of *plunderers*, determined to plunder Armenia, Galicia, Turkey, to seize Constantinople and to reconquer Poland, Courland, Lithuania, etc. This government is bound hand and foot by Anglo-French imperialist capital ...

Bread – because it is a government of the bourgeoisie. *At the very best* it may give the people, as the government of Germany has done, 'hunger organized with genius'. But the people have no desire to be hungry. The people will learn – probably they will learn this very soon – that there is bread, and that it can be obtained in no other way than by means *that do not show respect for the sanctity of capital and landownership.*

Freedom – because it is a government of landowners and capitalists, who are *afraid* of the people and already beginning to conclude a bargain with the Romanov dynasty.

It is not only that none of these statements was true, but even with the small scraps of knowledge from which he fed, Lenin must have known they were untrue. The most absurdly untrue statement was the last, for there was never any evidence that the Provisional Government had any desire to conclude a bargain with the Romanov dynasty. Significantly, the official English translation omits these words.

Lenin had already formed his mythology of the revolution: the enemy was the Provisional Government. In time by a process of accretion he would add other enemies, the Mensheviks, the Socialist Revolutionaries, all other parties of the left or right which were in disagreement with him. Already on March 19th he had sent a telegram to the Russian Social Democrats in Sweden who were preparing to return to Russia, denouncing the Provisional Government and especially Kerensky, and calling for an armed uprising, immediate elections for the Petrograd Duma, and complete separation from all other parties. The telegram, which was written in French, read:

> *Notre tactique: méfiance absolue, aucun soutien nouveau gouvernement, Kérensky surtout soupçonnons, prolétariat seule garantie, élection immédiate Douma de Pétrograd, aucun rapprochement autres partis. Télégraphiez cela Pétrograd.**

> ULYANOV

Thereafter *méfiance absolue* was to become the watchword, but the most ominous of the many ominous statements was the claim to complete exclusivity.

* Our tactic: absolute distrust, no support for the new government, above all we are suspicious of Kerensky, the proletariat is the sole guarantee, immediate election of the Petrograd Duma, no reconciliation with other parties. Telegraph this to Petrograd. ULYANOV.

This telegram and the first 'Letter from Afar' – the remaining four letters were not published until after his death, for by the time they reached Petrograd Lenin had caught up with them – caused a sensation among the Bolsheviks in the capital. They comforted the extremist wing of the Bolsheviks, while leaving the more gentle souls like Kamenev and Stalin relatively unaffected, for they could argue that Lenin, writing from another country, was out of touch with the real situation; nor was there any immediate prospect that he would be able to leave Switzerland. Yet there was no doubt that Lenin's pitiless philosophy was disquieting, even profoundly disturbing. Kamenev was still working quietly for an alliance of revolutionary parties. He still talked of a Constituent Assembly in which the Bolsheviks and all the other parties would be represented. To him the Leninist theory of exclusivity was meaningless, and he expected Lenin to change his mind when he reached Russia.

Sukhanov was especially struck by Kamenev's moderate tone, his constant denials that the Bolsheviks were up to mischief. 'His position was ambiguous, and not easy,' Sukhanov wrote. 'He had his own views, and was working on Russian revolutionary soil. But – he was casting a "sideways" look abroad, where they had *their* own views, which were not the same as his.'

Stalin, too, had his own views, and they were not the same as Lenin's. He was not yet ready to follow the hard line, denouncing the Provisional Government and all its works. Writing in *Pravda* on April 6th, he congratulated the Provisional Government for its decree abolishing the restrictions imposed on people of non-Russian nationality and those who did not belong to the Orthodox Church. 'The peoples of Russia who were hitherto under suspicion can now breathe freely and feel they are citizens of Russia,' he wrote. 'This is all to the good.' The decree did not, of course, go far enough. As the Bolshevik expert on the nationalities question, he pointed out that the decree had not faced the problem of the national minorities. Soon Transcaucasia, Turkestan, the Ukraine, Lithuania, and all the minorities in Russia must form federal states each with its own parliament, they must be permitted to conduct their affairs in their national languages, and they must have the right to secede. In an article written four days later for *Pravda*, he claimed that it would be foolish to draw an analogy between the United States in 1776 and the Russia of 1917. The national problem could not be solved by federation, but only by granting the right of secession to all states and by granting political autonomy to regions like Transcaucasia, Siberia, and Turkestan, which possessed a specific national character.

These were not merely theoretical problems. They were being discussed by all the political parties, and it was characteristic of Stalin at this time that he should have chosen the most *liberal* solution, the one which most faithfully reflected the desires of the minorities. For these views he later apologized, giving as his excuse the fact that at the time of the October revolution many states had already seceded and that the Bolsheviks had misjudged 'the power of the national movement'. These articles were written long before the October revolution. The monolithic state was still undreamed of, and the iron-handed rule of the Bolsheviks was a thing of the future. Yet in the last days of his life Lenin was to be haunted with the problem of the right of secession, quarrelling violently with Stalin on the issue of Georgia. For Stalin the matter was a very simple one. As he expressed it in a note written in December 1924, the party simply 'traversed the path from denial of federation to recognition of federation as a transitional form to the complete unity of the working people of the various nations'. In effect he was saying that there could be no right of secession until the formation of the world socialist state had been brought about, when secession would become meaningless.

But in those early days in April before Lenin reached Petrograd, Stalin still affected the liberal position. His approach to political problems showed no trace of intolerance. He was listening, keeping his ear close to the ground, uncertain which direction the revolution would take, and in no position to make his influence widely felt. All the time he was working quietly to bring about a conference of Petrograd Bolsheviks in order to hammer out a programme. On April 11th the conference met in the requisitioned palace of the *prima ballerina assoluta* Kshesinskaya, near the Peter and Paul Fortress. A few days later it moved to the Tauride Palace. There were about eighty delegates. The Central Committee consisted of Stalin, Molotov, Zalutsky, Elena Stassova, and Shlyapnikov, and this order of precedence was not fortuitous – Stalin was the presiding spirit, but he neither dictated to the delegates nor permitted anyone else to dictate to them. He had brought them together, and although he made two lengthy speeches he was chiefly content to listen to their opinions.

In the histories of the Bolshevik party published in the Soviet Union no mention of this conference is made, though it was the first to be held on Russian soil after the revolution, and therefore possessed a quite extraordinary historical significance. It was believed that the minutes were lost until a fairly complete transcript covering seventy pages of printed text was smuggled out of Russia by Trotsky. From internal evidence there is not the least doubt that the transcript is an authentic record of the conference, and it is not difficult to see why it was suppressed. The transcript shows the Bolshevik delegates acting like quivering schoolchildren. There is something curiously tame about their deliberations as they hover among uncertainties, fearfully aware of their vast responsibilities but incapable of coming to any decisions.

Many of the Bolsheviks who attended the conference later acquired high positions in the Soviet government. They included Yenukidze, Smilga, Krestinsky, Olminsky, Drobnis, Serebryakov, Milyutin, Badayev, Goloshchekin, Skrypnik, Madame Kollontay, and Anna Elizarova, Lenin's sister. Neither Lenin nor Trotsky had yet arrived in Petrograd, and the delegates therefore represented a good cross section of those who would later be known as 'second-string Bolsheviks'. They were listed as representatives of their districts – Serebryakov, for example, was the delegate from Kostroma, and Drobnis was the delegate from Poltava. In this way it could be claimed that the conference represented the entire body of Bolsheviks, and it was therefore called the All-Russia Conference of the Bolshevik Party, although the delegates had been hand-picked by Stalin, Molotov, and Shlyapnikov. For some reason Kamenev was not on the presiding committee, but spoke from the floor.

In the disquieting atmosphere of revolutionary Petrograd, where at least ten different parties were loudly proclaiming their interests, it was not to be wondered at that the Bolshevik conference should reflect a multitude of conflicting passions. Between the Bolshevik far left and the Bolshevik far right there could be no alliance. Stalin was somewhere in the middle. He did not adopt this position because he had any particular desire to straddle fences, but because as the chairman of the conference he needed to keep his flock in order He had no message to deliver. It was enough if he proved to be a good chairman. It was, after all, the first party conference he had attended for many years, and never before had he attended a conference as a member of the Central Committee.

Stalin's behaviour throughout the conference was uniformly polite and considerate. He did not speak of the proletariat, but of the people. He gave guarded approval to the acts of the Provisional Government and the Soviet of Workers' and Soldiers' Deputies. He approved, though with reservations, a suggestion that the Bolsheviks should forget their old quarrel with the Mensheviks and form a new union. He saw no reason 'to force events', a Bolshevik phrase meaning 'to come out in armed rebellion'. Everything he said at the conference could be described later as treasonable, for it was aimed at compromise, and so far removed from the hard Leninist line that it was perfectly clear that he had no idea what was going through Lenin's mind and was in no mood to accept Lenin's analysis of political conditions in the first 'Letter from Afar'.

Speaking of the two governments in Petrograd, Stalin described them as being both useful and commendable, for each had a part to play. The Provisional Government was commended for being the 'consolidator of the victory of the people', which had come about under the leadership of the Soviet of Workers' and Soldiers' Deputies. He elaborated at some length on this dual power, saying:

Power has been divided between two organs, of which neither possesses full authority. There is, and there must be, friction between them. They share the power jointly. The Soviet of Workers' and Soldiers' Deputies is in reality the leader of the insurrectionary people, an organ of control over the Provisional Government. And the Provisional Government on the other hand has assumed the role of consolidator of the victory of the people. The Soviet of Workers' and Soldiers' Deputies has mobilized the forces and exercises control. But the Provisional Government in its obstinate and confused way has consolidated the victory already won by the people. Such a situation has disadvantages, but it has advantages also. It is not to our advantage at present to force events, thus antagonizing the bourgeois layers, which will in future inevitably withdraw from us. It is necessary for us to gain time by putting a brake on

the splitting away of the middle bourgeois layers so that
we may prepare ourselves for the struggle against the Provisional Government. But such a situation will not endure
endlessly. The revolution is deepening.

These were the words of a man respectful of the power of
the Provisional Government, and determined not to provoke a
premature revolt. He did not discount the possibility of an insurrection at some time in the future, for he added ominously:
'We must hide our aims until the Provisional Government exhausts itself.' But like the veteran Bolshevik Krestinsky, Stalin was in no hurry. Krestinsky imagined the time
might come when the Provisional Government might actually
perform the role of servant to the Bolsheviks. 'The Soviets
are only embryos of power,' he declared, using a phrase which
had already been employed by Lenin, but from this premise
he derived a totally un-Leninist conclusion, for he added:
'So long as the Soviet power remains unorganized, we will
tolerate the Provisional Government even if it parts company
with us. What will happen then? It is schematically possible
that the Provisional Government after a shake-up in its personnel will faithfully serve us. Then we will not have to replace it.'

It was a strange conference, the child of compromise and
mediation, with occasional prophecies of doom and sudden
flares of self-righteousness. Mensheviks, members of the Soviet
of Workers' and Soldiers' Deputies, attended by invitation,
and Lieber, a fiery and tormented man, seems to have been
the first to accuse the Bolsheviks of deliberately seeking the
kind of revolution demanded by the nihilists of the nineteenth century. 'We are facing an abyss, not a party!' he
shouted. 'No – an abyss into which we are plunging the
proletariat!'

But such interruptions were rare, and the general tone of the
delegates was solemn, quiet, uneasy. When Molotov demanded a hard line, an abandonment of all the efforts to compromise, Stalin gently rebuked him: 'There is no use running
ahead and anticipating disagreements. There is no party life
without disagreements. We will live down trivial disagreements within the party.' Stalin was the gentle pacifier, the
sensible one, the man rooted in realities. He was no trum-
peter. He was a man doing his job.

The days passed. One day Kamenev rose and reported on

his negotiations with the Mensheviks and the Socialist Revolutionaries. The negotiations were progressing favourably. Stalin approved. There might be some minor disagreements, and probably the negotiations would be protracted, but he could see no reason why the three parties could not hammer out a common programme. Krassikov, an Old Bolshevik who had withdrawn from the party and who had only recently emerged from seclusion, might ask bitterly: 'What has happened to the dictatorship of the proletariat?' and Shlyapnikov would remember Lenin's constant objection to compromise, but there was scarcely anything in the speeches which would have brought a blush to the cheeks of the Mensheviks. The Bolsheviks under Stalin were children whimpering in the wilderness.

The conference began on a Wednesday, continued for four days and then went into recess. The Saturday was Easter Eve, and some lingering respect for the Christian holiday suggested that there were advantages in putting political quarrels aside. The church bells pealed, while the Russians celebrated Easter Sunday with *kulich* and *pascha* and paraded in the streets in their best finery. Monday, too, was a holiday, with the factories closed and little traffic in the streets. Telegrams on such a day were apt to be delayed, and so it happened that Maria Ilyinichna Ulyanova received late in the morning a telegram which had been sent the previous day from Torneo on the Swedish-Finnish frontier. The telegram read:

ARRIVING MONDAY EVENING ELEVEN O'CLOCK TELL PRAVDA
—ULYANOV

Lenin was on his way to Petrograd. Soon – much too soon for anyone's comfort – the halting chorus of the Bolshevik conference would give way to Lenin's shrill trumpet note. No longer would Stalin direct the course of the conference. His place would be taken by a small, red-bearded man with a rasping voice and a strange capacity to dominate any assembly in which he was present.

With the coming of Lenin to the Finland Station on that Easter Monday the second revolution began.

WHEN STALIN WAS busily creating his own legend, it pleased him to imagine that he was John the Baptist to Lenin's Christ. He came to believe that in Lenin's absence he was the acknowledged leader of the Petrograd Bolsheviks, the possessor of the secret doctrine, and when it was known that Lenin was arriving in Petrograd, he imagined he gave orders for the massive reception at the Finland Station and then sped to Belo-Ostrov to be the first to welcome him on Russian soil. He saw himself with Lenin on the train and at the Finland Station, and he was standing beside the armoured car when Lenin mounted the turret and proclaimed the world-wide socialist revolution while the searchlights played on him. In those April days and all through the summer and again in November Lenin and Stalin were inseparable.

These satisfying dreams were incorporated in the legend, and related in the official biographies, but they were not true. He had not been the acknowledged leader of the Petrograd Bolsheviks, but merely one of many leaders. His claim that he was the first to welcome Lenin at Belo-Ostrov acquired the sanction of hundreds of commissioned drawings and paintings which showed him welcoming Lenin with open arms or standing beside him at the train window, but they rested on his unsupported testimony. He claimed that he accompanied Maria Ulyanova, Lenin's unmarried sister, and a delegation of Petrograd and Sestroretsk workers and working women to Belo-Ostrov, but none of the workers who later wrote their reminiscences remembered seeing him there. Sergo Alliluiev said he saw Stalin leaving the Finland Station after Lenin's arrival, but he was the only eyewitness. If he was present, as he stated so categorically in his biographical chronicle, he wore his anonymity well.

A few Bolsheviks did make the journey to Belo-Ostrov. Raskolnikov, the young ensign who later commanded the Baltic Fleet and was one of those chiefly responsible for winning the October revolution, heard the news of Lenin's coming from his friend Leonid Stark, a Bolshevik sailor, later to become one of the commissars of the Military Revolutionary Council. Raskolnikov at once telephoned to Kamenev and they arranged to take the next train to Belo-Ostrov. With them went Teodorovich, an Old Bolshevik who was given the thankless job of Commissar of Supplies in the first Soviet government, and Kamenev's wife, Olga Davidovna, who was the sister of Trotsky. At Belo-Ostrov they found that a small delegation of Bolsheviks had already arrived. Shlyapnikov, Maria Ulyanova, and Madame Kollontay were drinking tea in the station buffet. Raskolnikov remembered there was no vast delegation of workmen and working women; he counted about twenty. They were all surprised by the news. They had not expected Lenin to come so soon. It was already known that he had come through Germany on a sealed train, but they were afraid he might be arrested during the journey through Finland. Military police were walking up and down the platform, and as soon as Lenin stepped out of the train it was likely that they would carry him off to prison. The same thought was passing through Lenin's mind as the train approached Belo-Ostrov.

But in fact no one made the slightest move to arrest him, and after the passport formalities were completed, the Bolsheviks went up to him and paid their respects to him. He was all smiles. Kamenev had hardly settled down beside Lenin for the short journey to Petrograd when Lenin suddenly burst out: 'What have you been writing in *Pravda*? We read a few numbers and gave you a thorough cursing!' In this way Lenin announced his dissatisfaction with the Bolsheviks in Petrograd, but the words were spoken good-humouredly. It was not a tongue-lashing. He was calm and cheerful, playing with Zinoviev's son, and sometimes, as though he was speaking about someone else altogether, he would say: 'Won't they hang me when we reach Petrograd?' Then Shlyapnikov or Raskolnikov would explain that nothing of the kind would happen. The Finland Station was decorated with red-and-gold flags in his honour, sailors from the Baltic Fleet were even then standing on the platform to form a guard of honour, and high officers of the Soviet of Workers' and Soldiers' Deputies would be there to welcome him. Lenin scarcely believed it. When he stepped off the train in Petrograd, carrying a bouquet of roses given to him by Madame Kollontay, he looked dazed and faintly annoyed. The square outside the station was crowded with workers bearing banners which glittered in the light of searchlights. No revolutionary had ever had such a homecoming.

That same night in the Kshesinskaya Palace Lenin announced briefly a programme which was later to become known as the April Theses. With unparalleled audacity he described a new kind of state in which there would be no army, no police, and no bureaucracy, and the government would derive its power from the workers' militia. He envisaged outright war against the Provisional Government and he hinted that every political party which did not assent to his programme should be proscribed. He spoke of the state vanishing in the far greater world union of the Socialist International. He demanded an end to the war and a social revolution which would give power not to the Soviet of Workers' and Soldiers' Deputies but to the dictatorship of the proletariat.

An article embodying the April Theses was published in *Pravda* on April 20th, and on the following day Kamenev wrote a vigorous rebuttal, saying that Lenin's ideas were categorically at variance with those expressed during the All-Russian Congress by the representatives of *Pravda*, among whom Stalin was clearly included. He wrote:

> With regard to Comrade Lenin's general line, it appears to be unacceptable inasmuch as it proceeds from the assumption that the bourgeois-democratic revolution *has been completed,* and it builds on the immediate transformation of the revolution into a socialist revolution. The tactics that follow from an analysis of this kind are greatly at variance with the tactics defended by the representatives of *Pravda* at the All-Russian Congress both against the official leaders of the Soviet and against the Mensheviks who dragged the Soviet to the Right.

Kamenev's verdict was shared by most of the Bolsheviks in Leningrad. It was generally believed that in his haste to see the communist revolution Lenin had lost the sense of the practical. He demanded that the April Theses be put into operation immediately, and the Bolsheviks were as yet in no mood to obey his dictatorship.

Stalin remained aloof from the discussion. His articles at this time reflect no revolutionary passion; they are the kind of articles that can be written automatically. He no longer possessed a dominant position on *Pravda*. On the masthead he was merely listed as one of some forty contributors.

Meanwhile by the sheer power of his dominating personality Lenin was gradually winning the Bolsheviks to his views.

All those who had ever spoken in favour of the Provisional Government were damned; all those who could not see that the entire world was tottering on the edge of revolution were simpletons, or worse. He demanded an end to the war, and if the governments refused, then he promised that 'we shall ourselves unleash a revolutionary war and summon the workers of the world to join us'. He spoke as though he was already in command of Russia.

For two weeks Stalin remained on the sidelines, examining at a distance this strange apparition which was breathing fire and thunder. It was his practice to watch carefully and weigh his opinions laboriously. As he said in a preface to a collection of speeches published seven years later: 'I held a mistaken position, which I shared with the majority of the party. I left them at the end of April and adopted the theses of Lenin.'

Stalin was often inaccurate about dates, but this date was completely accurate, for on April 30th he wrote an article in celebration of May Day which showed that he had burned his bridges and had come over to the side of Lenin. He wrote:

Amid the thunder of the Russian revolution, the workers of the West too are rising from their slumber. The strikes and demonstrations in Germany, the manifestations in Austria and Bulgaria, the strikes and meetings in the neutral countries, the growing unrest in England and France, the mass fraternization at the fronts – these are the first swallows of the socialist revolution that is brewing.

The ground is burning underneath the feet of the capitalist robbers, for the red flag of the International is again waving over Europe.

Not one of these statements was even remotely true. The strikes and demonstrations in Europe were either the figment of Lenin's imagination, or they were such small affairs that they were easily put down. There was no mass fraternization at the fronts, though Lenin was always dreaming about it. The red flag was not waving over Europe, and the Russian revolution was proceeding with surprising calm. If there was thunder it was in the voice of Lenin as he jeered and cajoled and spun his vast theories about a state in which there were no soldiers, no policemen and no bureaucrats.

In the history of the Russian Revolution this article by

Stalin deserves a special place. For the first time he spoke with the authentic accents of his master.

Various explanations have been given for the sudden *volte-face* by which Stalin, from being a moderate, became an extremist. According to Angarsky, the decision came about when Lenin approached Stalin in the *Pravda* office and praised him for being a man of action, while all the rest of the Bolshevik leaders were no more than 'intellectual nincompoops'. 'Come,' Lenin is reported to have said, 'we two shall form an alliance. The Provisional Government must be overthrown, and we shall overthrow it when the masses are with us! I guarantee they will be with us very soon, because we shall promise them everything they can demand from a victorious revolution. Will you join me?'

Saying this, Lenin pushed his grey cap over his ears, went straight up to Stalin and clapped him over the shoulder. The compact was sealed.

We may believe the story or not, as we please; but there is little doubt that something very similar occurred. Stalin respected strength, and Lenin in those days was a man of formidable strength, and in addition he was one of the very few in Russia who knew where he was going. At the end of April Stalin became Lenin's man.

Now when he made speeches he spoke with greater authority, for he had Lenin behind him. In the middle of May, when a new Central Committee of nine members was formed, Stalin was elected by a large vote. The Central Committee members were Lenin, Zinoviev, Kamenev, Milyutin, Nogin, Sverdlov, Smilga, Fyodorov, and Stalin. As usual the Central Committee had been hand-picked by Lenin, and the voting was a mere formality.

Now, as never before, Stalin belonged to the revolutionary elite. By the will of Lenin he was concerned with great decisions, where previously he had stood aloof from the battle. In later years he would point to Kamenev as one of those who had failed their revolutionary duty during the weeks before Lenin arrived in Petrograd, forgetting that he had been himself as much a compromiser as Kamenev, giving praise to the Provisional Government and the Soviet of Workers' and Soldiers' Deputies where it was due. Henceforth he was to be dedicated to the violent overthrow of both the Soviet and the Provisional Government.

Now nine years later, in an autobiographical letter written in

reply to greetings from the railroadmen of Tiflis, Stalin recalled vividly the impression made upon him when for the
first time he became 'one of the leaders of the great party of
the working class'. He wrote:

> I recall the year 1917 when by the will of the Party, after
> many wanderings through prisons and places of exile, I
> was entrusted by the Party with certain work in Leningrad.
> There, among Russian workers and in direct contact with
> the great teacher of proletarians in all countries, Comrade
> Lenin, in the storm of mighty clashes between the prole-
> tariat and the *bourgeoisie*, while the imperialist war was
> running its course, I first learned what it meant to be one
> of the leaders of the great Party of the working class. There
> among Russian workers – the liberators of oppressed
> peoples and the pioneers of the proletarian struggle of all
> countries and all peoples – I received my third baptism in
> the revolutionary fire. There, in Russia, under Lenin's guid-
> ance, I became a master worker of revolution.

If Stalin was a master worker, Lenin was the dynamo. He
was a whole party in himself, writing so many articles and
making so many speeches that he seemed to be in perpetual
motion. Against the Provisional Government, which was in a
state of perpetual crisis, he waged implacable war – threats,
abuse, sudden attacks, sporadic retreats were his weapons. The
Provisional Government was confronted by enemies on all
sides. It lived from day to day. It was attempting to restore
public order and, in Stalin's phrase, to 'consolidate the social
revolution', and at the same time it was attempting to fight a
war with Germany. If it passed good laws, the Bolsheviks
would leap up and cry that they were not good enough. If it
spoke of continuing to fight against Germany, the Bolsheviks
would cry that it was simply the Tsarist government under a
new name. Whatever it did, whether good or bad, Lenin
would attack it mercilessly.

The advantages were on the side of Lenin, for the Provisional Government was dealing with a situation which had
become anarchic. Factories were closing down for lack of
supplies, the soldiers were deserting from the front, the peasants were pillaging the estates of the landlords, transport was
paralysed, and the scarcity of products was bringing about a
disastrous inflation. Only the armament factories, which had
been developed during the first years of the war, were run-

ning successfully, with the result that the Bolsheviks were to become the inheritors of vast supplies of ammunition and weapons.

By May a third of the proletariat of Petrograd had come over to the Bolsheviks and to the group of Mensheviks which had reluctantly joined forces with them. The cry 'All power to the Soviets' meant 'No power to the Provisional Government'. But from the beginning it was clear that Lenin had little sympathy for the Soviets. When the Revolution was won, he announced that the power had passed, not into the hands of the Soviets, but into the hands of a small Military Revolutionary Committee.

Meanwhile, like all the other Bolsheviks, Stalin lived in Lenin's shadow. He performed such administrative duties as were assigned to him, wrote occasional articles for *Pravda,* made speeches, and attended the interminable conferences brought about to discuss tactics. At the April conference he was the *rapporteur* on the national question. His speech, which echoed the opinions Lenin expressed in a letter to Shaumyan in 1913, attacked the problem of the national minorities in a manner calculated to make the minorities tremble. Certainly they would be permitted to secede; certainly they would be permitted to employ their own languages and retain their own culture. 'But while the people have the right to secede, we also possess the right to agitate for or against secession in accordance with the interests of the proletarian revolution,' he said, adding that he personally would be opposed to the secession of Transcaucasia, 'bearing in mind the common development of Transcaucasia and Russia.' 'Of course,' he went on, 'if Transcaucasia were to demand secession, it would encounter no opposition from us.'

A month earlier he had spoken about the sacred right of secession, and how any government which opposed this right was doomed to failure. Now the tables were turned, and he would permit secession only 'in accordance with the interests of the proletarian revolution'.

Yet the proletarian revolution was still far from being accomplished, and the Bolsheviks were still a minority in Petrograd. They were in no position to bring about the revolt. On May 17th Stalin wrote in *Pravda* that 'the revolution is growing in breadth and depth', and now at last the provinces were taking the lead, as Petrograd had taken the lead in the February revolution. If the provinces were indeed clamouring to join the Bolsheviks, then the battle was already won, but in fact the Mensheviks and the Socialist Revolutionaries were still vastly more powerful in the provinces than the Bolsheviks. Lenin himself seemed to be losing his nerve. In his speeches and conversations he continually urged the Bolsheviks to attack the government and seize power, but there was neither any machinery for making war against the government nor in those spring days were the Bolsheviks in control of the large sums of money that were later to fall into their hands. The memory of the great processional triumph on Easter Monday was fading. The Bolsheviks were still only a small party living on the edge of legality. They were divided among themselves, curiously ineffective, without roots in the countryside, and without purpose or direction. As the summer came on, even Lenin seemed to have lost his charismatic power.

On May 17th there occurred an event which was to have a decisive effect on the revolutionary struggle. Trotsky, after a brief period of imprisonment in a Canadian concentration camp, arrived in Petrograd. As chairman of the St Petersburg Soviet in 1905, he was one of the very few Russian revolutionaries who had exercised effective revolutionary power in the past. He was not hag-ridden by doctrine, but possessed a free intelligence, a gift for clear exposition, and a deep sense of the drama of revolution. When he spoke, his eyes seemed to glow with a revolutionary flame; he had a voice like thunder. When he arrived at the Finland Station there were brief speeches of welcome, and then he marched straight to the Petrograd Soviet, where it was decided to grant him the role of adviser, a purely honorary position with no voting rights. The Executive Committee of the Soviet was overwhelmingly composed of Mensheviks and Socialist Revolutionaries. They knew his power over the masses, and they were under no illusions about the danger of an alliance between Lenin and Trotsky. In those days it was generally believed that Trotsky was too independent, too self-seeking, and altogether too conscious of his revolutionary fame to ally himself with anybody.

In fact Lenin and Trotsky complemented one another to an extraordinary degree. They were like two sides of the same coin. Where Lenin was dogmatic, diffuse, and intolerant, Trotsky, with his clearer brain and vaster appetite for experience, showed himself to be tolerant and capable of tossing dogma to the winds. He was the apostle of adventurous expediency, with a flair for romantic action and a taste for the murderous improvisations of revolution. Once Lenin had written: 'Trotsky – strictly conspiratorial comprehension of the party.' The statement was true, but it was not the whole truth. Trotsky was a master conspirator, one of those who had raised conspiracy to a pitch of genius. While Lenin held himself aloof, Trotsky went down among the masses to proclaim the necessity of a second and more violent revolution. His speeches delivered at the Modern Circus to audiences composed of workers, soldiers, and their women were violently inflammatory; and these speeches, which were nearly always delivered late at night, were continued early the next morning in the factories and shipyards and to audiences of Baltic sailors. He spoke endlessly, always with passionate fervour. He was setting the faggots alight.

By the beginning of June Lenin and Trotsky had concluded a firm alliance. With that alliance the revolution was already half won. They were the superb technicians of revolt, and neither in the Soviets nor in the government was there any group of men capable of unseating them. The moment the alliance was formed, each man became immeasurably more powerful.

Meanwhile Stalin still worked in the shadows. He attended the long three-week Congress of Soviets of Workers' and Soldiers' Deputies which opened at the beginning of June, where he delivered an address, now lost, on 'The National Movement and National Regiments'. The army, in the process of disintegrating, was reverting to a regional character. Ukrainians, Tatars, Bashkirs, Letts and Caucasians were drawing together and forming new regiments, refusing to obey the orders of anyone who did not belong to their nationality. Stalin was particularly concerned with the growth of the Caucasian regiments, and did everything in his power to promote their formation. From time to time he wrote editorials in *Pravda* notable for their inflated rhetoric. 'The dead have now laid hold of the living,' he wrote in one editorial, and in another: 'We are confronted with the sinister phantoms of hunger and ruin.' And sometimes he would point to the revolutionary fervour in England, France and Germany as cause for celebration. 'Over there in the West, in the belligerent countries, the dawn of a new life, the dawn of the great workers' revolution is breaking,' he wrote, calling upon the proletariat of Petrograd to imitate their brothers in London, Paris or Berlin, although there was not the slightest evidence in the summer of 1917 that England, France or Germany were any closer to revolution than they had been in 1914.

In the Congress of Soviets the Mensheviks were in the ascendant. On June 18th the Menshevik leaders called for mass demonstrations in the streets, and some 400,000 workers paraded through Petrograd with banners inscribed with the words: 'All Power to the Soviets.' It was a slogan which the Bolsheviks regarded with incurable distrust, while aware that it could be made to serve their own purposes. A wildly enthusiastic Stalin watched the marchers and described the demonstrations in *Pravda*:

> A bright, sunny day. Endless column of demonstrators. From morning to evening the processions make their way to the Mars Field. Endless forest of banners. All factories and workshops are closed. Traffic is at a standstill. The demonstrators march past the graves with banners lowered. The 'Marseillaise' and the 'Internationale' give place to 'You were the victims'. The air resounds with an uproar of voices. From time to time there is heard 'Down with the ten capitalist ministers!' and 'All power to the Soviet of Workers' and Soldiers' Deputies!' And from all sides there comes the thundering approving chorus: 'Hurrah!'

The demonstration was ordered by the Mensheviks, but the Bolsheviks watched it closely, took part in it, and arranged that their own slogans should appear prominently. The demonstration had been called to show confidence in the Soviets and in the Provisional Government, and the Bolsheviks noted approvingly that few of the demonstrators showed any confidence in the Provisional Government. The workers who came out *en masse* were hoping that the Soviets would take power, but the Soviets were irresolute.

Lenin was not irresolute. A few days before, at the Congress, when the Menshevik Tseretelli said: 'At this moment there is no political party in Russia which would say, "Hand over the power to us, quit, we will take your place",' Lenin gave the ringing answer: 'There is such a party! My party is prepared at any moment to take over the entire power!'

Now, watching nearly half a million workmen surging through the streets of Petrograd in obedience to the Mensheviks, Lenin pondered the vast possibilities of mass demonstrations. What if the Bolsheviks ordered a demonstration, armed the workers, placed detachments of soldiers and sailors among them, and simply took over the power? The idea appealed to him, and there were times when he would discuss it convincingly, and at other times he would wonder whether even a *levée en masse* would prove successful. During the June days he, too, suffered from the irresolution which alternates in revolutionaries with a fearful recklessness.

THE JULY DAYS

A REVOLUTION RARELY MOVES in a straight line. It goes by fits and starts, according to the impulses, the hesitancies, the changing moods of the adversaries. Since revolutions imply concentrations of force on many levels, by many men with many different ideas, there is rarely any steady emerging pattern. Revolutions constantly change direction in midpassage; sometimes they even go back on themselves, and repeat themselves, and find themselves confronted with the same insoluble problems. In spite of the Marxist contention that revolutions obey well-known historical laws, no one has ever been able to state the laws comprehensively. By the very nature of things there are too many ambiguities in a revolution to permit us to believe that its course is predictable.

In July 1917 the course of the Bolshevik revolution was going from bad to worse. Lenin and his colleagues were prepared to take desperate measures, but found themselves in a position where even the most desperate measure of all was likely to be more destructive to the Bolsheviks than to the Provisional Government. Power was in their grasp; they could seize the government and proclaim the new Soviet state and set about destroying all their enemies; and they knew that within a week the Provisional Government would be in power again, and they would be proscribed. They were strong in Petrograd; they were not strong anywhere else. If they seized power, there would be civil war at once, and they were not yet in a position to fight a civil war. There were waverings in the Bolshevik high command. Some wanted to seize power, others were content with a violent demonstration, and there were still others who thought of husbanding their forces. Lenin had slipped away to Finland to recover from a heavy cold, and though he preached and never ceased preaching the immediate seizure of power, he seems to have known that little would be gained by it.

In the absence of Lenin the Bolshevik high command determined upon a show of force. There would be no insurrection, no seizure of public buildings, no attempt to arrest the government. Instead there would be a massive display of armed demonstrators which would have the effect of testing the strength of the Provisional Government. Lenin, still suffering from his cold, was hastily summoned from Finland.

This strange half-insurrection broke out on the evening of July 16th, when the First Machine Gun Regiment marched on the Tauride Palace accompanied by most of the workers from the Putilov factory. They chanted slogans: 'Down with the Provisional Government! All power to the Soviets!' They tied up traffic, and truckloads of soldiers and factory workers raced through the streets firing at random, causing small riots, and getting completely out of hand. It was in the middle of summer, the days very bright and the sunset interminable. The Petrograd Soviet was in session. By ten o'clock in the evening they decided that something had to be done to curb the mounting excitement; and the members of the Soviet went out in the streets and addressed the rioters to discover why they were rioting and how they could be brought to order. Among them were the Bolsheviks who had ordered the demonstration. The rioters were told to disperse; they refused, and promised to come out in greater force the following day. To their surprise and horror the Bolsheviks discovered that they could no longer control the mob.

On the following day some twenty thousand sailors from Kronstadt sailed up the Neva, landed on the north bank, and marched to the Kshesinskaya Palace, where Lenin greeted them from the balcony with a perfunctory speech in which he spoke of the inevitable victory of the Soviets and appealed for 'firmness, steadfastness and vigilance'. They were not the words one addresses to revolutionary troops on the eve of battle, or even of a skirmish. As Sukhanov observed, there was nothing to prevent Lenin from seizing power – 'Any small group of ten or twelve men could have arrested the government', which was then sitting in the unprotected apartment of Prince George Lvov, the premier. But at this moment there were no advantages in arresting the government, and there was nothing to be gained by continuing the riots, which continued through the day, becoming increasingly dangerous as the morning wore on. At two o'clock in the afternoon a small battle took place at the corner of the Sadovaya and the Nevsky Prospect. The demonstrators were fired on, or they fired into the crowd; no one seemed to know what happened. Afterwards there was volley on volley of gunfire. In a memorable photograph taken immediately after the first shots were fired, the people of Petrograd can be seen hurtling away from the point of danger like so many shapeless pieces of shrapnel.

For the rest of the day there were sporadic outbursts of gunfire. Shots were fired from roof tops and bell towers, from speeding trucks and the windows of government offices. According to the Bolsheviks the casualties amounted to four hundred dead and wounded. The official commission of inquiry which was set up immediately after the two-day riot gave 114 people wounded and 20 dead. It added that most, or perhaps all, of the dead were killed by shots fired from trucks careering at great speed.

Stalin's role during the July half-insurrection was a marginal one. As a member of the Soviet and also of the Central Committee of the Bolshevik party, he was one of those assigned to act as liaison officers. His task was to stress the peaceful and democratic intentions of the Bolsheviks, and to encourage the Petrograd Soviet to believe that the Bolsheviks would not demonstrate, had no intention of demonstrating, and would do their utmost to prevent the demonstration. It was a role which he played with considerable finesse. At the Sixth Congress of the Bolshevik party held a few days later, he described his role at some length, referring again and again to the peaceful intentions of the Bolshevik party and explaining how they eventually took charge of the demonstration only when it was forced on them. He said:

At four o'clock a meeting of the Central Committee was called at the Tauride Palace. The Central Committee decided to abstain from action. At a meeting of the Bureau of the Central Executive Committee of the Soviets, I announced in the name of the Central Committee of our party that we had determined not to demonstrate. I reported all the facts to them, informing them that the machine-gun regiment had sent their delegates to the factories and workshops. I proposed that the Bureau take all necessary measures to prevent the demonstration. That was entered into the minutes at our request. The Socialist Revolutionaries and Mensheviks, who are now accusing us of preparing the demonstration, forget this.

At five o'clock the City Conference voted not to demonstrate. All the members of the Conference dispersed throughout the districts and factories in order to restrain the masses from action.

At seven o'clock in the evening the Kshesinskaya Palace was approached by two regiments bearing banners with the slogan 'All power to the Soviets'. Two comrades made speeches, Lashevich and Kurayev. Both of them tried to persuade the soldiers not to demonstrate, but to return to their barracks. They were met with wild shouts of 'Down with them!' – a thing which had never happened before. At the same moment a demonstration of workers appeared under the slogan 'All power to the Soviets'. For all of us it became clear that a demonstration could not be prevented. Then a private conference of the members of the Central Committee decided in favour of intervening in the demonstration, of directing the soldiers and workers to act in an organized way, to go peacefully to the Tauride Palace, elect delegates and through them declare their demands. This decision was greeted by the soldiers with a roar of applause and the singing of the 'Marseillaise'.

At about ten o'clock the members of the Central Committee and of the City Conference, together with the representatives of the regiments and the factories, assembled in the Kshesinskaya Palace. It was thought necessary to decide the question all over again, to intervene and take control of the movement already under way. It would have been nothing short of criminal for the party to have washed its hands of the movement at that moment.

In claiming that the Bolsheviks took charge of the demonstration by default, Stalin was writing a lawyer's brief on behalf of gentle persuasiveness. The argument was dubious, and in publishing his speech in his *Collected Works*, Stalin severely edited it, omitting all references to his own part in the affair, saying nothing at all about his announcement to the Central Executive Committee of the Soviets that the Bolsheviks would take no part in the demonstration and his request that these words should be entered into the minutes.

The impression he wanted to convey at the time he delivered this speech was of a man who simply carried out the instructions of the Bolshevik party. When he published his *Collected Works* he wanted to convey the quite different idea that he was among the leaders of the activist movement within the party; he was not one of those who held back or sat on the sidelines.

In fact he sat on the sidelines throughout the July days, refusing to take any initiative, at the mercy of his fears. He had many things to be afraid of. The Provisional Government was biding its time. The bridges were up, and the demonstrators from the factories were therefore isolated from their bases. Only the First Machine Gun Regiment, heavily infiltrated with Bolsheviks, had come out on the side of the demonstrators; the other regiments declared their neutrality. There were also more pressing fears. The Provisional Government had ordered a massive advance on the German lines, and the July demonstration coincided with this advance. The Provisional Government could therefore appeal to the people, reminding them that the demonstrations led by the Bolshevik party were deliberately designed to give aid and comfort to the enemy. Worse still, the government was known to be in possession of documents showing that Lenin had received funds from the Germans and was acting as a German spy.

These documents had been compiled and edited by Grigory Alexinsky and Vasily Pankratov, the first a former member of the Bolshevik party, leader of the party's faction in the Second Duma, and at one time a close friend of Lenin, while Pankratov was one of the more vocal and experienced members of the Socialist Revolutionary party, who had spent fourteen years in prison for his political activities. They were not straw men, and their words carried weight, though the evidence amounted to little more than the uncorroborated statement by a captured Russian ensign called Ermolenko who had been given a safe-conduct by the Germans through Russian lines in order to agitate for a separate peace, and who reported that Lenin had been sent across Germany in a sealed train for the same purpose.

Today, when we know a good deal more about the large sums of money sent to the Bolshevik party from Germany through the agency of Yakov Ganetsky, the question of whether or not Lenin was a German agent seems merely a matter of semantics. With or without the money Lenin would have continued to foment revolution, and he would do this not to help the German General Staff, but in order to further his dreams of a communist revolution which would one day embrace the whole world. No evidence has been brought forward to show that he acted consciously as a German agent. His interests and the interests of the Germans coincided to a remarkable degree. He seems not to have known or to have been completely indifferent to the source of the money that permitted him to hire printing presses, buy stocks of paper, and pay agitators.

In the summer of 1917 the charge that Lenin was a German agent was a formidable one. Alexinsky and Pankratov published their allegations in the newspaper *Zhivoe Slovo* (The Living Word) at the height of the demonstrations. Stalin was well aware of the danger to the Bolshevik party, and in his speech at the Sixth Congress he said:

> The turning point was the publication of the documents about 'Lenin's treason'. It became clear that the material had been ready at the military headquarters for a long time. After that it became clear that by publishing these documents they intended to provoke the anger of the soldiers against the Bolsheviks. Obviously they calculated upon playing on the mentality of the soldiers who were expected to be influenced more than anything else by the news that Lenin was a German spy.
>
> Although Minister Tseretelli called the newspapers by telephone and asked them not to print unsubstantiated reports, nevertheless the 'documents' were published by *Zhivoe Slovo*.

Stalin spoke in tones of regret, as though some unforeseen catastrophe had occurred, which even Tseretelli's intervention had been unable to prevent. He would say later that Tseretelli wanted to proclaim a dictatorship and to disarm the workers and soldiers, that he was the worst of all the enemies of the Bolshevik party, but these accusations derived perhaps from a sense of indebtedness. Tseretelli had done everything possible to prevent the circulation of the allegations against Lenin. He had helped to save the honour of the Bolsheviks, and scarcely expected to receive their gratitude.

Throughout the July days Stalin kept a diary in which he or one of his secretaries – for the style has little in common with his other writings – recorded events as they happened day by day and sometimes hour by hour. This diary formed the basis of his speech at the Sixth Congress. Here he is describing some of the events on the day following the collapse of the demonstrations, including his own abortive attempt to save the Kshesinskaya Palace from being commandeered by the forces of the Provisional Government:

July 19th. No demonstrations. Fresh troops have been brought up from the front and are marching in the streets. The Cadets have been brought in from the suburbs of Petrograd. The agents of the Military Intelligence Service are swarming on the streets, examining passports and arresting people at random ... Our comrades Zinoviev and Kamenev have been negotiating with Lieber about protecting the members of our party and party organizations from the attacks of hooligans and about restoring the editorial offices of *Pravda*, etc. The negotiations ended in an agreement by which the armoured cars were to be removed from the Kshesinskaya Palace, the bridges were to be opened for traffic, the sailors who had remained in Petrograd were to return to Kronstadt, the troops left in the Peter and Paul Fortress were to be allowed to depart unhindered, and a guard was to be set at the Kshesinskaya Palace. But this agreement was not carried out ... The order to clear the Kshesinskaya Palace was received by Kuzmin, the commander of the Petrograd district. At once I set off for the Central Executive Committee of the Soviet with the proposal to settle the affair without bloodshed. 'What do you want? To shoot at us?' I asked. 'We are not rising against the Soviet.' Bogdanov told me he wanted to avoid bloodshed. We set out for headquarters. The military met us in none too friendly a manner, and told us the order had already been given. I got the impression that these gentlemen would like a bloodbath at all costs.

In a report made to the Petrograd Conference of the Bolshevik party, in which he covered much of the same ground, Stalin described the meeting with Kuzmin at greater length. Kuzmin was clearly nettled by the appearance of the Menshevik Bogdanov and the Bolshevik Stalin. He had everything ready for the attack on the Kshesinskaya Palace and the Peter and Paul Fortress nearby. Artillery, cavalry and infantry were at their battle stations. An ultimatum ordering the Bolsheviks to leave the palace and the fortress within three quarters of an hour had already been issued. Stalin's task was to prevent bloodshed, and to see whether the ultimatum could be rescinded or extended. 'We argued with him not to resort to armed force,' Stalin related, 'but he resented the fact that the civilians were hampering him with their constant interference, and it was only reluctantly that he agreed to comply with the insistent demand of the Central Executive Committee of the Soviet.' The order of the Central Executive Committee was that the buildings should be evacuated peacefully, and this was done, but only under the threat that force would be used against the Bolsheviks if they resisted. Stalin's role in the affair was therefore that of a temporizer who attempts to prevent a display of force. He went to the sailors who had occupied the fortress and appealed to them to leave quietly, and he seems to have sent a message to the same effect to the Bolsheviks in the palace. His efforts of mediation were not particularly successful. The ultimatum was extended by a few minutes, but the terms remained exactly what they were before. The Bolshevik revolutionary Ilyin-Genevsky, one of the many who attempted to parley with Captain Kuzmin, wrote in his memoirs how he learned what the terms were. 'Lieutenant Mazurenko stood there with his hand on his black belt, his face stern and inexorable. When we asked him what he desired of us, he answered curtly, "Disarm and surrender".'

The Bolsheviks disarmed and surrendered; they had no alternative, for the Kronstadt sailors guarding the Peter and Paul Fortress and the Kshesinskaya Palace were no match for the troops of the Provisional Government who surrounded them. The Bolsheviks had now lost the only two strongholds which had fallen into their hands. The fortress and the palace were not the only losses. During the early morning of July 18th the offices of *Pravda* were completely wrecked, the printing press put out of order and the typewriters smashed. As Stalin explained at the Sixth Congress, this was as damaging a blow as the others: without a printing press they were unable to explain their position to their followers. 'Why didn't you flood Petrograd with leaflets?' he was asked, and he explained sadly that the Bolshevik printing press had been wrecked and no other printing house dared to accept orders from the Bolsheviks.

The July demonstration intended to test the power of the Provisional Government had only shown the weakness of the Bolsheviks. Once, when describing the Pugachev rebellion

which ravaged Russia in the eighteenth century, the poet
Pushkin described it as 'a real Russian revolt, wild and senseless'. Lenin said of the July demonstration that it was 'something less than a revolution'. In fact it was a wild and senseless revolt, which petered out.

On the same day that the Peter and Paul Fortress and the
Kshesinskaya Palace fell, the Provisional Government issued
an order for the arrest of Lenin. He had been working in
the *Pravda* office only half an hour before it was raided; he
continued to have a miraculous series of lucky escapes. At
first it was decided to hide him in the workers' district of
Vyborg, but it was soon realized that this was too dangerous.
He decided to hide in the house of Sergo Alliluiev, who lived
in a fifth-floor apartment at 17a Tenth Rozhdestvenskaya
Street, not far from the heart of Petrograd. Stalin, as we have
seen, was a close friend of the family, and he seems to have
had some part in arranging the hiding place. Lenin was in
the mood of a man baffled by defeat, and when Krupskaya
and Maria Ilyinichna came to visit him he was debating
whether to surrender to the Petrograd Soviet, which had also
ordered his arrest as a dangerous and irresponsible agitator.
Zinoviev was in the same hiding place. Together they discussed
the advantages of facing their accusers at a public trial. Finally
they agreed that this was the better course. When Krupskaya
came to see him, Lenin announced: 'Grigory and I have
decided to appear in court.'

Lenin was not behaving stupidly. The logic of events demanded that he should wipe out the defeat of the July demonstration by an act of superb daring. Speaking from the dock
in a public trial, he would be able to incite the populace to
further acts of rebellion. Many Bolsheviks in Petrograd believed this was the proper course to take. Lenin had almost
made up his mind to surrender unconditionally to the Soviet
when wiser counsels prevailed. Stalin, Nogin and Ordjonikidze came to visit the hiding place. There was a long debate,
and finally it was decided that Nogin and Ordjonikidze should
meet with representatives of the Soviet to demand absolute
guarantees for the safety of Lenin while in prison. They returned empty-handed. No absolute guarantees could be given.
Stalin had disliked the idea from the beginning, saying that
nothing was more likely than that Lenin would be murdered.
There was no more thought of surrendering.

During the following days it was decided that Lenin and

Zinoviev must leave the capital, and the task of hiding them was given to Nikolay Emelianov, a factory worker at Sestroretsk, a small town on the northern coast of the Gulf of Finland. Emelianov owned a house in the nearby village of Razliv. Lenin was to stay there until a better hiding place could be discovered.

While they were waiting for the final arrangements to be made, Stalin suggested that Lenin should shave off his beard and moustache. When Lenin agreed, Stalin offered to act as the barber. His offer was accepted, and so it happened that alone among the members of the Central Committee of the Bolshevik party Stalin could claim to have put a razor to Lenin's face. According to the Alliluievs Lenin without his beard and moustache looked like a Finnish peasant.

On the night of July 24th Lenin and Zinoviev, accompanied by Stalin and Sergo Alliluiev, slipped out of the house and made their way to the Primorsky station in the north of the city. It was a long and dangerous journey. Lenin was wearing Alliluiev's overcoat and cap, drawn low over his eyes. Emelianov was waiting for them close to the station. He had already bought three tickets. He had devised a plan by which the three of them – Lenin, Zinoviev and Emelianov – would jump on a freight train at the last moment before it left the station, and everything worked out according to the plan. At Razliv Lenin and Zinoviev were safe. A few visitors came: Shotman, Dzerzhinsky, Sverdlov, Ordjonikidze. In later years it pleased Stalin to think that he too had made the journey to Razliv.

A few days after Lenin and Zinoviev left the apartment, Stalin came to live with the Alliluievs. When the suggestion was made by Alliluiev's wife, Stalin replied that he would be putting them in danger. Police spies were everywhere; he was a marked man; if he was found, everyone in the apartment would be arrested. Olga Alliluieva, who was genuinely fond of him, said she was not frightened by police spies and knew how to deal with them. She told later how she brought him new clothes and heard him pacing endlessly in his small room 'with leisurely strides'. So the days passed, while he paced like a caged animal, determined upon revolution, but irresolute about the means with which revolution can be brought about, and sometimes there would come a message from Lenin, and occasionally he would bestir himself sufficiently to write an article for *Pravda*, and then again there was only the sound of a man pacing with leisurely strides in a small room.

ON THE EVE

'NOVEMBER 7TH–8TH. V. I. LENIN and J. V. Stalin direct the armed uprising.'

In this way Stalin described in his biographical chronicle how he conducted himself during the Revolution. In later years he explained how he gave orders and directives, announced the aims of the revolutionary movement, secured with great difficulty the necessary agreements with other parties, and decided upon the exact time when the armed uprising should take place. He liked to imply that he had already organized the Revolution and set it in motion before Lenin was summoned from his hiding place.

The amplitude of Stalin's claim is all the more surprising because there is no evidence that he played any effective role in the uprising. He remained in the shadows, neither for the revolution nor against it, waiting for others to make decisions. No orders signed by him have survived; no speeches are recorded. He wrote a few articles of paralysing dullness, and he may have written an unsigned article which appeared in *Rabochy Put* five days before the revolution broke out – an article which possesses a kind of fierce and malevolent splendour, written in the style of Trotsky and concluding with the words: 'The revolution is not disposed either to pity or to bury its dead.' The article is a polemic against Gorky, and was exactly the kind of article that Trotsky enjoyed writing. There are at least four other articles in Stalin's *Collected Works* which bear indisputable signs of being written by another hand.

Stalin claimed to be the dominating member of a five-man 'Party Centre' which assumed command of the revolutionary forces. Although he often repeated the claim, he never offered any evidence to sustain it. It was a fact of history, which everyone was expected to know and therefore it was not incumbent upon Stalin to provide his credentials. The minutes and orders of the mysterious centre were never published, and the very existence of the centre remained unsuspected until shortly after the death of Lenin when Emelian Yaroslavsky, Stalin's favourite historian, discovered a statement in the minutes of one of the October conferences saying that the centre had been constituted, its members being Sverdlov, Stalin, Bubnov, Uritsky and Dzerzhinsky. This single sentence, with Stalin placed second, provided the sole justification for the existence of the centre. It did not prove that Stalin was the dominating member of anything.

If he was not directing the revolutionary forces, what was Stalin doing?

There is only the scantiest information about his activities during those months when the revolution was coming to a climax. Few people saw him. In the voluminous records of the October revolution and in the equally voluminous memoirs of those who took part, he is rarely mentioned. We know that from August onwards he lived in Sergo Alliluiev's apartment at Tenth Rozhdestvenskaya Street near the Smolny, and that he continued working in some editorial capacity on *Rabochy Put*. We know that he attended two important conferences at which Lenin, having returned secretly from Finland, insisted upon an immediate uprising, against the advice of Kamenev and Zinoviev, who proclaimed that an uprising at this time was premature and dangerous. Being convinced that Lenin was about to precipitate a premature revolution Kamenev and Zinoviev wrote an article for Gorky's paper *Novaya Zhizn* attacking the members of their own party for being so determined to break the public peace. When Lenin urged that the two culprits should be expelled from the party, Stalin replied: 'Expulsion from the party is not a cure – we must preserve unity.' It was the voice of moderation. Four days before the uprising he threatened to resign as one of the editors of *Rabochy Put*, unless the expulsion of Kamenev and Zinoviev was called off. As Lenin paid no attention to his threat, it can be assumed that Stalin was still a member of the party in good standing when the revolution broke out.

All through these days Stalin walks in a cloud. It is not only that we rarely have a glimpse of him, but it is astonishingly difficult to discover whether he was doing anything at all. Most of the time he seems to have been in the fourth-storey apartment at Tenth Rozhdestvenskaya Street, or in the *Pravda* office in Basseinaya Street, or in the ground floor room in the Smolny Convent reserved for Bolshevik leaders after the Smolny was commandeered by the Petrograd Soviet.

We never see Stalin in action. He is a dim, brooding presence, who sometimes takes messages or offers a curt reply to an inquiry, and then he vanishes into a strange limbo. Invisible, mischievous, strangely irresolute and inarticulate, he remains 'a grey blur'.

One of the few who recorded their meetings with him in those days was an old factory worker, Nikolay Sveshnikov, a member of the party since 1911, who assumed the thankless task of treasurer of the Vyborg branch of the party. The local party office was at 62 Bolshoy Sampsonievsky. This was a command post of some considerable importance because the Vyborg workers excelled all others in Petrograd in their revolutionary fervour. The Vyborg party secretary was a woman, Evgenia Yegorova, who went by the party name of 'Zhenya'. Krupskaya worked in her office, and Lenin would arrange to send his messages from his nearby hiding place to her. They would be copied and then sent to the other Bolshevik leaders who were also in hiding. Nikolay Sveshnikov became one of the messengers who from time to time brought Lenin's letters to Stalin. In his reminiscences he wrote:

One day 'Zhenya' said: 'Nikolay, you will have to take notes to Comrade Stalin from time to time.'

She gave me the address of a place in Peski. Although Stalin was a legally elected member of the Bolshevik faction of the Petrograd Soviet, he found it more convenient that the authorities should not know his exact address. I remember, as though it happened yesterday, how I received Lenin's message – I guessed it must come from Lenin – from 'Zhenya', and then I made my way by streetcar and on foot to one of the Rozhdestvenskaya streets where Stalin was staying in the home of Sergo Alliluiev.

Once Stalin asked me whether I knew whom the messages came from. I answered that no one had told me, but I guessed they were from Ilyich. Stalin smiled. As usual he asked me to wait for a little while. Some twenty or thirty minutes later I returned to the Vyborg District Committee and gave everything to 'Zhenya'. The message was taken to Lenin by the woman in whose home he was hiding.

These messages were presumably instructions to members of the Bolshevik Central Committee, for at this time very few of Lenin's articles were being published in *Rabochy Put*.

Lenin arrived in Petrograd from Finland on October 20th, and Sveshnikov could therefore have been employed as a messenger for only a few days.

On October 23rd there took place in an apartment belonging to Sukhanov the meeting which, according to Bolshevik historians, decisively affected the course of the Revolution, for it was at this meeting that Lenin called for the insurrection.

Of the twenty-one members of the Central Committee eleven were present – Lenin, Zinoviev, Kamenev, Trotsky, Stalin, Sverdlov, Uritsky, Dzerzhinsky, Madame Kollontay, Bubnov, Sokolnikov. Also present were the candidate members Lomov and Varvara Yakovleva, who acted as secretary. Galina Flaxerman, the wife of Sukhanov, was the only other person present, and her role was limited to serving tea and cakes. Sverdlov was chairman, and he began by delivering three reports on Bolshevik operations at the front. Lenin was the main speaker, and he urged that there should be no more delay in bringing about the revolt. It was a curious speech, for as Yakovleva recorded it, he would speak in one breath of the urgency of ordering the revolt immediately and in the next breath he would point out that the workers of Petrograd had only 40,000 rifles. 'This will not decide the issue, this is nothing,' he said. He reminded them that the garrison troops after their behaviour during the July days could no longer be relied upon. Nevertheless he had convinced himself that the moment had come for the transfer of power. Later in the evening he drew up an extraordinary document proclaiming that the German naval mutiny, and the possibility that Germany and the Allies would make peace in order to crush the Russian Revolution made it inevitable that an armed uprising should take place. Kamenev and Zinoviev argued against the resolution, and their arguments continued through the night until the early morning. When the vote was taken, ten had accepted the necessity for an immediate uprising, two were against. It is reasonably certain that if the full committee which included Rykov, Nogin and Milyutin had been present, there would have been stronger opposition to the insurrection. Lenin sketched out the draft of the resolution with a stubby pencil in a child's notebook. He wrote that the time for the insurrection was 'fully ripe'.

It is known that at the meeting Lenin, Zinoviev, Kamenev, Sverdlov, Uritsky, Dzerzhinsky, Lomov and Trotsky all spoke.

Apparently Stalin had nothing to say, for the minutes contain no record of any speech made by him.

Towards the end of the meeting, it was decided on Dzerzhinsky's proposal to create a political bureau of seven members. The first reference in the minutes is curiously worded. It says: 'After an exchange of opinion, the proposal is carried. A political bureau of 7 is created (the editors + two + Bubnov).' It is not clear what is meant by 'the editors', but it is possible that Yakovleva simply used this phrase to describe Stalin, who was the editor of *Rabochy Put*, Sokolnikov, who was his assistant, Kamenev, who had edited *Pravda*, and Zinoviev, who had been one of the editors of *Proletary* and was now editing *Prosveshcheniye*, the monthly theoretical journal which had ceased publication in 1913 and was now being revived. 'Two' probably indicates Lenin and Trotsky. This would agree with the statement which appears at the end of the minutes where the decision about the political bureau is repeated: 'It is decided to form a bureau of 7: Lenin, Zinoviev, Kamenev, Trotsky, Stalin, Sokolnikov, Bubnov.'

The meeting in the apartment of Sukhanov, who was spending the night in the editorial office of *Novaya Zhizn*, lasted from about half past three in the afternoon to three or four o'clock in the morning. Some of the Central Committee members stayed on, and slept on the sofas. Others made their way through the misty dawn to their hiding places. Among these was Lenin. In the early hours of the morning, clean-shaven, wearing a grey wig and heavy spectacles which gave him, according to Yakovleva, the appearance of a Lutheran priest, he slipped out of the apartment and made his way to the ugly workers' dwelling on the Bolshoy Sampsonievsky where he was hiding.

Although a momentous decision had been reached by the Central Committee, there were still no outward signs that the uprising would take place. Petrograd slept its long sleep, while the rain fell, and a chilling wind blew in from the Baltic. Men huddled around braziers in the damp, cold streets. Winter was coming down.

For Lenin, as for the other members of the Central Committee, the decision made on the twenty-third was not absolutely binding. The machinery for bringing about an uprising had not been carefully worked out, and no date had been set, although it was generally agreed that if there was an uprising at all, it should be on November 2nd, the day before the opening of the Congress of Soviets. The date of the Congress of Soviets had been chosen by the Socialist Revolutionaries and the Mensheviks in the Petrograd Soviet.

With the revolution scarcely a week away, the revolutionaries were behaving with an air of casual improvisation. There were no hard outlines, no battle plans, no carefully thought-out programme. Decisions which were to affect the fate of Russia and the world for generations to come were made by small groups of men who met secretly and then returned to their hiding places.

To put an end to this crushing weight of indecision Lenin decided to call a conference of the Central Committee, the Petrograd party committee, the factory committees, the railwaymen and the Petrograd Council of Trade Unions. Kalinin, then mayor of the Lesnoy subdistrict of Vyborg, solved the problem of providing a suitable meeting place by offering his official residence, a large two-storey wooden building with gingerbread architecture set back from the street in a large garden. The meeting began at seven o'clock in the evening of October 29th.

Although this was intended to be the ultimate, determining conference which would launch the revolution, the meeting was ill-attended.* Only twenty-five people attended, among them nine members of the Central Committee. Trotsky was not present. Sverdlov acted as chairman, his deep raucous voice dominating the assembly. Lenin presented his case for an immediate uprising in a speech lasting nearly two hours. He was in good humour, and he kept pacing backwards and forwards across the room with his thumbs caught under the armholes of his vest in the familiar posture which somehow gave him a professorial air. He had to shout because the rain was pouring down in torrents. He was all for immediate action, without any further examination of the problem. 'The masses have expressed their confidence in the Bolsheviks,' he declared, 'and they demand of us not words but deeds, a decisive policy in the struggle against war and against eco-

---

* Of the twenty-five who attended twenty-three can be identified. They were Boky, Dzerzhinsky, Fenigstein, Joffe, Kamenev, Krylenko, Latsis, Lenin, Milyutin, Rahja, Ravich, Schmidt, Shlyapnikov, Shotman, Skalov, Skrypnik, Sokolnikov, Stalin, Sverdlov, Uritsky, Volodarsky, and Zinoviev. There was an anonymous 'comrade from the railroad workers', and a certain T., otherwise unidentified. T. was not Trotsky.

nomic ruin.' In his reminiscences Shotman says the audience listened 'in rapt silence, holding their breaths'.

But not all the audience was prepared to accept Lenin's domination. Krylenko shouted: 'The pot has boiled enough!' and Rahja said: 'The masses will pour out on the streets, for they are facing starvation!' but there were older and more responsible leaders who still objected strongly to Lenin's authoritarian urgency. 'It worked to our advantage that there was no July uprising,' Milyutin declared, 'and if there is no uprising now, we shall not perish.' Joffe, his intricate brain moving among insistent dialectics, pointed out that the resolution was not to be regarded as an order to act, but 'as a rejection of the tactic of refraining from action'. Kamenev was equally intricate. 'We are not strong enough to enter into an uprising with an assurance of victory,' he said, 'but we are strong enough not to permit extreme expressions of reaction.' And he added more convincingly: 'Two tactics are fighting here: the tactic of conspiracy, and the tactic of faith in the moving forces of the Russian revolution.' He was still hoping that the Bolsheviks would abandon the course of insurrection and exert their power through the Constituent Assembly by winning the greater number of votes in a parliamentary democracy.

Lenin laughed when it was suggested that he was engaged upon a conspiracy. How could it be a conspiracy when everyone knew what they were doing? As Sokolnikov said, 'Our greatest security and our strength lies in the fact that we are openly preparing for an uprising.' He knew that negotiations with the garrison troops were being pursued, and said categorically: 'It is not a question of fighting against the troops, but of one part of the troops fighting against another.' In the end this is what happened. The October revolution was largely a battle fought between the troops, with the armed workers taking a very small part.

Many of the twenty-five hand-picked delegates seemed to be moving towards revolution like sleepwalkers. 'We are marching on, half-consciously, to defeat,' said Fenigstein. Dzerzhinsky also seemed to be advancing blindly towards the revolution. 'When the uprising comes,' he said, 'the technical forces will also appear.' It was one of the more fatalistic statements made at the conference, for when at last the uprising occurred, everyone was woefully unprepared.

Fenigstein was followed by Stalin, who rarely took part in

debate and who showed, if we can trust the accuracy of the minutes of the meeting, a sensible detached attitude to the revolution. The key words in his speech were 'with expediency'. According to the minutes, he said:

> The date of the insurrection must be chosen with expediency. It is only in this sense that the resolution should be understood.
>
> They say it is necessary to wait for the government to attack, but we must be clear what attack means. The raising of the price of bread, the sending of Cossacks to the Donets Basin, etc. – this is already an attack. How long are we to wait if there is not going to be an armed attack? Objectively, what Kamenev and Zinoviev propose would enable the counter-revolution to prepare and organize its forces. We would be retreating endlessly and we would lose the revolution. Why should we not ensure for ourselves the possibility of choosing the date of the uprising and the conditions, so as to deprive the counter-revolution of the possibility of organizing.
>
> Comrade Stalin then proceeded to analyse international relations, suggesting that there should now be greater confidence. There are two policies: one policy points towards the victory of the revolution and looks to Europe, as for the other – it has no faith in the revolution and expects to be merely in opposition.*

This was the only speech known to have been made by Stalin in October, and therefore deserves close study. It shows him to be concerned with a subject which was to weigh heavily in his thoughts to the end of his life – the nature of provocation. A military attack on the revolution was, in his view, only one of the forms of provocation. The rising cost of bread, the dispatch of Cossacks to put down an agrarian revolt could also be regarded as provocation. Almost any action by the government could be regarded as provocation. This was not Lenin's way of looking at the revolution. For him the revolution was necessary, inevitable, and it existed in its own right.

'We must be clear what attack means,' says Stalin, and we

---

* When Stalin incorporated these minutes in his *Collected Works*, he gave them the title 'Speech at a Meeting of the Central Committee.' It was in fact a speech delivered before a more or less representative body of Bolsheviks.

are given no assurance that he is himself clear what it means.

Alone of the speakers he spoke of choosing a time and place. Volodarsky and Ravich spoke of slogans, Sokolnikov of the lessons of the February revolution, Latsis of the sentiments of the masses. Milyutin, Kamenev and Zinoviev agreed that it would be impossible to overthrow the Provisional Government in the next few days. Only Stalin said that a date for the insurrection must be chosen 'with expediency'. He could claim later that he was among the very few at the Lesnoy conference who were absolutely determined on revolution.

Nothing is known about the analysis of international relations mentioned in his speech. Probably it followed closely on Lenin's earlier discussion, which relied heavily on the German naval mutiny and the extraordinary belief that unless the revolutionaries acted at once, the Germans and the Allies would combine to crush the revolution. When Stalin said there were two policies, one pointing to Europe and the other to stagnation, he was consciously or unconsciously amending the doctrine he had announced at the Sixth Congress in July where Preobrazhensky had outlined a similar programme only to be outvoted. In later years Stalin would explain how at the Sixth Congress he had spoken of 'socialism in one country' and never wavered from that faith, but in fact he wavered often. Yet in demanding that a date should be chosen for the uprising, he spoke with even greater assurance than Lenin. When Kamenev said at the Lesnoy conference that an uprising was simply impossible, because nothing had been done by the Central Committee to bring it about, Lenin had been shocked into the recognition that he was absolutely ignorant about what measures had been taken. 'I could not refute this argument,' he wrote two days later, 'because I did not know what was being done.' It is a curious and revealing statement, and it could only mean that on October 29th, 1917, Lenin did not know and could not guess what effective measures were being taken to bring the revolution about.

The minutes of the Lesnoy conference conclude with the statement:

> Central Committee continues in session alone and adopts the following resolution: the Central Committee to organize a military revolutionary centre composed of the following: Sverdlov, Stalin, Bubnov, Uritsky, and Dzerzhinsky. This

centre to become a part of the Revolutionary Committee of the Soviet.

On this baffling statement Stalin was to rest his claim that he was one of the prime movers of the revolution. No other evidence of a military revolutionary centre under Bolshevik auspices exists, and in fact such a centre existed only on paper.

In this way, very tentatively, in grave ignorance, the Bolsheviks embarked on the revolution which was to have such vast consequences. The revolution was only a week away. At this time Lenin did not know what was happening or where the revolution was going. The real decisions were being made by Trotsky as chairman of the Soviet of Workers' and Soldiers' Deputies and by the talented band of amateur strategists who worked with him.

At the Lesnoy conference Lenin won a majority of votes. Of the twenty-five who were present twenty voted for his resolution, two voted against, and three abstained. A week before, he had convinced eight people that the time for revolution had come; at the Lesnoy conference he convinced nineteen. But these pathetically small numbers were no measure of the revolutionary power that was being exerted by the workers and soldiers of Petrograd. In the Smolny Trotsky was busily engaged in preparing for battle.

At last, just before dawn, the Lesnoy conference came to an end. The rain had ceased, and in the misty morning the delegates dispersed as they had come, one at a time. Lenin was the last to leave, wearing his thick spectacles and the familiar grey wig. It was remembered that shortly after leaving the house a gust of wind blew off the wig, which fell in the mud. Unconcerned, Lenin picked up the muddy wig, set it on his head, thrust his hands deep in the pockets of his overcoat, and made his way to his hiding place.

THE ARTS OF POWER

*The entire Party and the Soviet work is being recon-
structed along new lines. The military control has been
cleaned up and reorganized. The provincial Cheka
has been purged and staffed with new workers.*

COMMISSAR

THE REVOLUTION WHICH BROKE OUT in Petrograd in November 1917 was the work of many dedicated revolutionaries, and of these there were perhaps three hundred who played a more effective role than Stalin.

One of those who played an essential role was the now-forgotten Pavel Evgenievich Lazimir, the President of the Military Revolutionary Committee, who died when he was scarcely twenty. We have brief glimpses of him, a few documents signed by him, and then he vanishes in the typhus-ridden battlefields of the Ukraine, leaving others to reap the fruits of his revolutionary talents. History, in Trotsky's phrase, 'threw him into the rubbish heap'. Yet there is a sense in which it was he, as much as anyone else, who was responsible for the success of the revolution.

Until the middle of October the revolutionary wing of the Petrograd Soviet envisaged the overthrow of the Provisional Government by means of an uprising of armed workmen. It was Lazimir, a Left Socialist Revolutionary delegate to the Soviet, who proposed instead to give the leading place to the disaffected garrison troops. On October 24th he drew up a plan of operations and a set of rules for a military *coup d'état*. On the following day the plan was discussed at length in a closed session of the Executive Committee of the Soviet and adopted, and the Military Revolutionary Committee formally came into existence.

Sukhanov, who was present at the closed session, had no illusions about its intentions. 'The Military Revolutionary Committee,' he wrote, 'intended to concentrate in its own hands *all military power* in the capital and the provinces, and in this way arrogate to itself all power whatsoever.' Since Trotsky was a Bolshevik, and the Military Revolutionary Committee would be under his supervision as chairman of the Petrograd Soviet, Sukhanov feared that the new committee would sooner or later become the military arm of the Bolshevik party.

At various times Trotsky wrote two different accounts of how Lazimir became President of the Military Revolutionary Committee. Writing in *Proletarskaya Revolutsiya* in 1922 he described how the idea of such a committee had been forced on him by events, and he had merely permitted Lazimir to advance it because as a Left Socialist Revolutionary it would come from him with better grace than from a Bolshevik. He had therefore deliberately plotted to involve Lazimir in the conspiracy. Writing his *History of the Russian Revolution* he repeats that there was a plot to involve Lazimir, but speaks with some reverence of Lazimir's original plan and explains how he improved upon it. 'Lazimir's preliminary rough draft,' he wrote, 'was edited by Trotsky in two directions: the practical plans relating to the conquest of the garrison were more sharply defined, the general revolutionary goal was still more glazed over.' There is about that bleak account of how the committee was formed more than a hint that he was deliberately tampering with the evidence. The majority of the soldiers in the Petrograd Soviet were Mensheviks or Socialist Revolutionaries, and they were perfectly capable of drawing up plans for a revolution which would deprive the Provisional Government of its power by a massive infiltration of garrison troops. Mekhonoshin, a Bolshevik who became one of the most important leaders of the committee, gave Lazimir full credit for bringing it about.

For two weeks Lazimir signed the committee's orders in his rich and flowing calligraphy. Sometimes the orders were countersigned by Nikolay Podvoisky and Vladimir Antonov-Ovseyenko, both dedicated Bolsheviks. The rough, good-humoured Podvoisky and the poetic-looking Antonov-Ovseyenko were perfect foils for one another. Together these three revolutionaries gathered around them an impressive collection of amateur soldiers, few of them with any practical experience of battle. Antonov-Ovseyenko had been a captain in the Tsarist army, but neither Trotsky nor Podvoisky who together assumed command of operations had any military training.

On November 5th, late in the evening, the Military Revolutionary Committee took its first decisive step by sending Lazimir, Mekhonoshin and Sadovsky to Colonel Polkovnikov, the commander of the Petrograd military area, with orders to inform the colonel that he was to submit to the orders of the Military Revolutionary Committee. He was told that his commands would be invalid unless they were countersigned by one or other of the three commissars. Firmly, and without bravado, the colonel refused, and the three commissars returned to the Smolny to set in motion the last stages of the conspiracy. The garrisons were honeycombed with their agents. They were in telephone contact with the garrison troops, who were ordered to disobey their officers and to obey only the orders of the Military Revolutionary Committee. Lazimir's dream of a bloodless revolution in which a small, closely-knit revolutionary group would assume command of the troops was now closer to fulfilment.

On that same evening John Reed, the American journalist, visited the Smolny and talked briefly with Lazimir.

> In room 10 on the top floor, the Military Revolutionary Committee sat in continuous session, under the chairmanship of a tow-headed, eighteen-year-old boy named Lazimir. He stopped, as he passed, to shake hands rather bashfully.
>
> 'Peter-Paul Fortress has just come over to us,' said he, with a pleased grin. 'A minute ago we got word from a regiment that was ordered by the Government to come over to Petrograd. The men were suspicious, so they stopped the train at Gatchina and sent a delegation to us. "What's the matter?" they asked. "What have you got to say? We have just passed a resolution, 'All Power to the Soviets'." The Military Revolutionary Committee sent word back, "Brothers! We greet you in the name of the revolution. Stay where you are until further instructions!"'
>
> All telephones, he said, were cut off: but communication with the factories and the barracks was established by means of military telephonograph apparatus.

At this moment the revolution was only twenty-four hours away.

Throughout those two weeks while the Military Revolutionary Committee gathered its forces and captured one by one all the military installations in the city without firing a shot, Stalin remains invisible. Trotsky, Lazimir, Antonov-Ovseyenko, Podvoisky, Chudnovsky and a hundred others have left traces of themselves. We know what they were doing, and we can weigh the consequences of their actions. They speed through the streets of Petrograd, address meetings of soldiers, give orders on the telephonograph, and receive deputations in the Smolny, which was humming like a gigantic hive. If Stalin was there, he was one of the lesser bees in the hive.

When at last Stalin emerges into public record, it is on the

evening of November 6th. Lenin had slipped out of his hiding
place, making his way by streetcar and on foot to the Smolny.
He had left a brief note: 'I am going where you did not
want me to go. *Au revoir*, ILYICH.' The note had been found
and brought to Evgenia Yegorova, the capable woman in
charge of party affairs in Vyborg. Krupskaya also saw the
note. Both were disturbed, and since it was obvious that Lenin
intended to reach the Smolny, it was decided to send Nikolay
Sveshnikov to find out what had happened to him. Sveshnikov
tells of his brief and curiously ambiguous meeting with
Stalin that night:

> Late at night on November 6th 'Zhenya' sent me to the
> Military Revolutionary Committee to see Stalin and find out
> where Lenin was. In the evening he had left the house where
> he was staying, leaving a note saying that he had gone at
> such and such an hour. We were worried that something
> might have happened to him, but at the same time were
> glad that he himself had decided to intervene and to put
> an end to the waverings of the Central Committee. I remem-
> ber how I ran to Stalin, had a hard time getting him to
> come out from the meeting of the Military Revolutionary
> Committee and asked about Ilyich, saying that Nadezhda
> Konstantinovna had asked me to make inquiries. Stalin
> told me that Nadezhda Konstantinovna had been informed
> about everything. Back in the district I learned that Ilyich
> himself had been at the Military Revolutionary Committee.

This is the only glimpse we have of Stalin, and it is oddly
unsatisfying. Krupskaya relates in her memoirs that as soon
as she heard that Lenin had left his hiding place, she and
Yegorova found a truck leaving Vyborg for the Smolny,
climbed into the back, and without any difficulty reached the
headquarters of the revolution on the famous night when the
Military Revolutionary Committee sprang into action. Krupskaya could not remember whether she saw her husband, and
she says nothing at all about seeing Stalin.

On the following day, which was the day of the insurrection, Stalin vanishes completely. He becomes a ghost again,
lurking invisibly in the background. *The History of the Civil
War in the USSR*, that extraordinary thousand-page compilation describing the Bolshevik rise to power, scrupulously
edited by Gorky, Molotov, Voroshilov, Kirov, Zhdanov and
Stalin himself, and written by an eight-man committee which

included one of Stalin's secretaries, mentions him only once in the seven chapters devoted to the events of that day. It says:

> Stalin, Sverdlov and Dzerzhinsky, the members of the Party centre, were constantly in attendance at the Military Revolutionary Committee. It is they who planned the details of the insurrection. They selected the units that were to occupy the Telephone Exchange and Telegraph Office. The Military Revolutionary Committee detailed units to protect the Neva bridges so as to maintain contact with all the districts and with the centre.

Everything about Stalin's participation in the uprising has the appearance of being in some curious way *contrived*. His movements are uncertain, but their very uncertainty seems to be deliberate. When at last he is permitted to appear in a monumental work of dubious historical scholarship, he is merely one of three people, of whom the only concrete thing that can be said is that 'they selected the units that were to occupy the Telephone Exchange and Telegraph Office'. There is very little doubt that Stalin, Sverdlov and Dzerzhinsky were working in the Smolny that day, and it may be that one of their endeavours was the selection of the units to occupy the Telephone Exchange and Telegraph Office.

After half a day of sporadic fighting around the Winter Palace, the uprising came to an end in the early hours of the following morning. A telephonogram was received at the Smolny: '2:04 am. Winter Palace taken. Six men killed (Pavlovtsy regiment). CHUDNOVSKY.' Lenin was so certain that the Winter Palace would fall that he had proclaimed the overthrow of the Provisional Government four hours earlier. By the terms of the proclamation written hurriedly on a half sheet of paper, state power now rested securely in the hands of the Military Revolutionary Committee of the Petrograd Soviet, but this was a convenient revolutionary fiction. The real power lay in the hands of Lenin and Trotsky, who proceeded to form a government, which was duly announced by Kamenev early in the morning of November 9th. The fifteenth and last member of the government to be announced was Stalin, who was given the post of Commissar for Nationalities. He was not the least important member of the government. It was simply that the question of nationalities did not, at this particular moment, have very much bearing on the revolutionary situation. The Bolsheviks had captured Petrograd: they had not yet captured Russia.

The traces of Stalin's activities become increasingly visible after the uprising. For the moment he had little work to do, and he could therefore employ his talents as he pleased. He particularly enjoyed drawing up decrees, and a considerable number of the early decrees published by the Bolsheviks were drawn up by a small committee consisting of Kamenev, Stalin, and Larin, the chief of the legislative branch of the new government. These were for the most part enabling decrees, giving the local organizations authority to requisition warehouses, stores and restaurants, but they also included occasional decrees of vast and unprecedented scope, and these too, as Larin recalled in his memoirs, were sent off to be printed, bearing the signature of Lenin written in Stalin's handwriting. Decree No. 12, for example, conferred legislative powers on the fifteen-man government, although the Congress of Soviets had not granted these powers and had no intention of granting them. 'Until the convocation of the Constituent Assembly,' declared this extraordinary decree, 'the preparation and drafting of the laws shall be carried out by the Provisional Government of Workers and Peasants elected by the All-Russian Congress of Soviets of Workers', Soldiers' and Peasants' Deputies.' Lenin was shocked when this decree was shown to him. He knew nothing about it, although it bore his signature. Finally he accepted it with good grace, for it confirmed him in his desire to impose a personal dictatorship over Russia. It is unlikely that Kamenev or Larin would have dared to write it, and it must be assumed that this sweeping decree by which power was to remain wholly beyond the reach of the people was the work of Stalin. Since the Bolsheviks never had any intention of granting legislative functions to the Constituent Assembly, the decree merely outlined the formula for a permanent dictatorship.

The decree appeared on November 12th, four days after the seizure of power. Three days later there appeared another decree signed by Stalin and Lenin in that order. Stalin, as Commissar for Nationalities, was solving once and for all the problem of the nationalities:

RIGHTS OF THE PEOPLES OF RUSSIA TO SELF-DETERMINATION

The November revolution of the workers and peasants began under the common banner of emancipation.

The peasants are being emancipated from the power of the landlords, for the landlord no longer has any property rights in the land – that right has been abolished. The soldiers and sailors are being emancipated from the power of autocratic generals, for henceforth generals will be elective and subject to recall. The workers are being emancipated from the whims and arbitrary will of the capitalists, for henceforth workers' control will be established over mills and factories. Everything living and viable is being emancipated from hateful shackles.

There remain now only the people of Russia who have suffered and are suffering under an arbitrary yoke. Their emancipation must be considered at once and their liberation effected with resoluteness and finality.

During Tsarist times the peoples of Russia were systematically incited against one another. The results of this policy are well-known: massacres and pogroms on the one hand, slavery and bondage on the other.

There can be and there must be no return to this shameful policy of provocation. Henceforth it must be replaced by a policy of voluntary and honest co-operation of the peoples of Russia.

During the period of imperialism after the March revolution, when the government passed into the hands of Cadet bourgeoisie, the unconcealed policy of instigation gave way to one of cowardly distrust of the peoples of Russia, of cavilling and provocation camouflaged by verbal declarations about the 'freedom' and 'equality' of peoples. The results of this policy, too, are well-known – the growth of national enmity, the impairment of mutual trust.

An end must be made to this unworthy policy of falsehood and distrust, of cavil and provocation. Henceforth it must be replaced by an open and honest policy leading to complete mutual confidence among the peoples of Russia.

Only as a result of such a confidence can an honest and lasting union of the peoples of Russia be formed.

Only as a result of such a union can the workers and peasants of the peoples of Russia be welded into a revolutionary force capable of resisting all attempts on the part of the imperialist-annexationist bourgeoisie.

The Congress of Soviets, in June of this year, proclaimed the right of the peoples of Russia to free self-determination.

The Second Congress of Soviets, in November of this year, reaffirmed this inalienable right of the peoples of Russia more decisively and definitely.

In compliance with the will of these Congresses, the Soviet of People's Commissars has resolved to adopt as the basis of its activity on the problem of nationalities in Russia the following principles:

1. Equality and sovereignty of the peoples of Russia.

2. The right of free self-determination of the peoples of Russia, including the right to secede and to form independent states.

3. Abolition of all privileges and disabilities based on nationality or religion.

4. Free development of national minorities and ethnographic groups inhabiting Russian territory.

All concrete measures appertaining to the above declaration are to be decreed immediately upon the formation of a special commission for nationalities.

JOSEPH DZHUGASHVILI (STALIN)
Commissar for Nationalities
V. ULYANOV (LENIN)
President of Soviet of People's Commissars

Stalin was inordinately proud of this decree, the only one in which his name stands above that of Lenin. He claimed to be the sole author of the decree, and this claim, unlike so many others that he made, is completely credible, for most of it is recognizably in his style and the balanced liturgical passages in the long second paragraph could have been written by no one else.

Like many of the decrees issued in the early days of the Soviet power, it was largely an exercise in propaganda designed to give an air of authority to a government which was still tentative and uncertain of itself. As Trotsky observed, these decrees were almost acts of desperation, for Lenin was singularly aware that his government might fall and every member of it might be hanged; nevertheless the decrees would remind people in future ages of what they had attempted to do. Many motives were combined in these decrees, which mingled promises and threats, savage denunciations, lyrical evocations of the new freedom, sudden insights, and astonishing vagueness about the means with which the decrees would be carried out. Only a week had passed since the revolution;

already the Bolshevik leaders were rewriting history. It was
not true, for example, that during Tsarist times the people of
Russia were systematically incited against one another. Only
the most blinkered mind could claim that the government
after the February revolution passed into the hands of the
Cadet bourgeoisie and showed a cowardly distrust of the
peoples of Russia. All this was deliberate propaganda. Stalin
was painting the enemy as black as possible, while reserving
the brightest colours for the new regime. Inevitably the decree
tries to do too much, and just as inevitably Stalin overplays
his hand. The new government promises 'honest co-operation',
'an honest policy', 'an honest and lasting union'. Finally the
government offers such vast freedoms that the minorities themselves might reasonably wonder what price would have to be
paid. Sometimes these decrees have the appearance of protestations of innocence. Sometimes, too, they reflect the excitement of those times when there was no clear demarcation
between reality and dreams, and everything seemed possible.

The test for the decree on the nationalities came on November 27th when Stalin addressed a Congress of the Finnish
Social Democratic Labour Party at Helsinki. It was an unusual and memorable occasion, for he came as a messenger
of the Council of People's Commissars to right the historic
wrongs which had poisoned the relations between the two
countries since the time of Alexander III. He promised freedom – absolute freedom. No more would Finland suffer under the tutelage of the Russians. He declared that the Soviet
government would do everything in its power to restore fraternal confidence between the workers of Finland and Russia.
'Everyone knows,' he said, 'that the restoration of confidence
would be inconceivable unless the right of the Finnish people
to free self-determination was firmly recognized.' Speaking
gravely, the heavy Georgian accent demonstrating that he was
himself a member of a once oppressed minority, Stalin affirmed that the time for words had passed, and that a concrete act was needed. The Council of People's Commissars
would grant freedom to Finland and an honest alliance with
Russia, and in this way the gains of the October revolution
would be consolidated.

Here and there he was able to suggest that imperishable
freedom would be granted only under conditions. There must,
of course, be a Social Democratic party in power and the
lessons of the October revolution must be taken to heart by

the Finns. The peroration to his speech provided a warning that the lessons would be enforced. He said:

> Comrades! Information has come to us that your country is living through roughly the same crisis of power that Russia lived through on the eve of the October revolution. Information has come to us that they will intimidate you with threats of hunger, sabotage, and so on. Permit me to inform you on the basis of experience derived from the actual practice of the Russian revolutionary movement that these dangers, even if real, are by no means insuperable. These dangers can be overcome if you act resolutely and without faltering. In an atmosphere of war and economic disruption, and in the atmosphere of a revolutionary movement which is flaring up in the West and of the growing victories of the workers' revolution in Russia – there are no dangers or difficulties which can withstand your attacks. In such an atmosphere there is only one power, socialist power, which can maintain itself and conquer. In such an atmosphere there can be only one kind of tactic, the tactic of Danton: Audacity, audacity, and again audacity!
>
> And if you should have need of our help, we shall give it to you, extending to you a fraternal hand.
>
> You may be assured of this.

For the first time Stalin was speaking as a conqueror, and inevitably he used those liturgical, balanced phrases which marked his speeches whenever he was excited or deeply moved. The help he promised was soon forthcoming. Experienced revolutionaries were sent in increasing numbers from Petrograd to Finland, large sums of money were placed at the service of the Finnish Social Democratic Party, and a regime favourable to the Bolsheviks came into power. Independence however was not granted 'without hesitation'. On January 4th Stalin was able to announce before the Central Executive Committee that the Council of People's Commissars had decided to recommend independence in principle. The final treaty was not signed until March 1st, 1918.

Meanwhile the Commissars in the Smolny, threatened with civil war and the almost insuperable problems of attempting to govern a country on the verge of anarchy, were brutally aware that even the simplest problems were not solved easily. How, for example, does one form a commissariat? Stanislav

Pestkovsky, a Pole who had been a member of the British Labour Party while studying at the London School of Economics – his knowledge of economics was to serve him in good stead, for Lenin appointed him director of the State Bank – met Stalin in one of the corridors of the Smolny and asked him whether he had already formed a commissariat. Stalin confessed he had not yet formed it, and did not know how to go about it.

'The important thing,' said Pestkovsky, 'is to obtain a mandate.'

Stalin obtained the mandate by the simple process of entering the office of the Council of People's Commissars and getting it typed by a secretary. Then a vacant space was found in one of the crowded offices and Pestkovsky wrote on a sheet of paper: 'People's Commissariat for the Affairs of the Nationalities' and tacked it on the wall. Everything was now attended to except the money to run the Commissariat. This problem was solved by borrowing 3,000 rubles from Trotsky's Commissariat of Foreign Affairs.

Improvisation was the order of the day, and Lenin proved to be the master improviser. He held to the axiom that there was nothing simpler than ruling a country. 'Anyone can do it,' he said, and when people complained of their own inadequacies as potential rulers on the grounds of their inexperience, he would say: 'None of us has any experience. It is not experience that matters. The important thing is to do it.' Sometimes he would provide breathtaking neat solutions for almost insoluble problems.

Stalin was present when Lenin accomplished one of his neatest solutions. Lenin was determined to make peace with Germany and accordingly he telegraphed General Nikolay Dukhonin, the acting commander in chief of the Russian army, commanding him to end hostilities. The order was telegraphed on November 21st at about three o'clock in the afternoon. Lenin expected an immediate reply, but none was received. Thirteen hours later, in the middle of the night, Lenin in a rage arrived at the Petrograd army headquarters and announced that he wanted a direct line to General Dukhonin at Moghilev, the command post on the western front. With Lenin went Stalin and Krylenko, one of the three Commissars for War, a former ensign.

After interminable delays General Dukhonin was brought to the telephone. Lenin demanded an immediate reply to the telegram. The general explained cautiously that he had indeed received a telegram signed by Lenin, Trotsky and Krylenko, ordering a cessation of hostilities with Germany, but nothing was said about whether Turkey and Rumania were included in the terms of reference, how the negotiations should be conducted, or in whose name he should conduct them.

'The text of the telegram is perfectly clear and precise,' Lenin replied sharply. 'It is simply a question of opening immediate negotiations with all the belligerent powers. It is a matter of extreme urgency, and I demand that reports be sent to me from hour to hour with details on how the negotiations are being carried on.'

When General Dukhonin pointed out that such negotiations could be carried on only by the central government, Lenin flew into a rage, deprived him of his command, and appointed Ensign Krylenko to be commander in chief of the Russian army. Six years later in a speech he delivered shortly after Lenin's death Stalin remembered that early morning confrontation. He spoke of it as 'a terrifying minute – *zhutkaya minuta*'. During that minute Lenin found an astonishingly simple method to put his own orders into effect.

I recall [said Stalin] how Lenin, Krylenko and I went to Staff Headquarters in Petersburg for those negotiations on the telephone. It was a terrifying minute. Dukhonin and General Headquarters categorically refused to obey the order of the Council of People's Commissars. The commanding officers were completely under the sway of headquarters. As for the soldiers it was impossible to know what this army of 14 million men would say, since they were subordinated to the so-called army organizations, which were hostile to the Soviet power. In Petersburg itself we knew that a mutiny of military cadets was brewing. Moreover Kerensky was marching on the city. I recall how after a short pause on the line the face of Lenin shone with an extraordinary light. Clearly he had arrived at a decision. 'Let us go to the radio station,' Lenin said. 'It will render us a service. We will issue a special decree removing General Dukhonin and appointing in his place Comrade Krylenko as commander in chief, and we will appeal to the soldiers over the heads of their officers, calling on them to arrest the generals, suspend military operations, establish contact with the

Austro-German soldiers and take the cause of peace into their own hands.'

What Stalin found so intoxicating in Lenin's decision was its vast audacity. It was 'a leap into the unknown', one of those acts of daring which took the breath away. That Lenin's act was essentially reckless and derived from a misplaced and almost mystical belief in *brataniye*, the brotherhood which would automatically emerge from the trenches once the hated officers were removed, did not occur to him; or if it did, he did not care. Lenin had found the key. His broadcast, delivered a few hours later, was the signal for the disintegration of the army.

Krylenko held the post of commander in chief of the disintegrating army for only a few weeks. One of his first acts was to give orders to the soldiers, or permit them, to beat Dukhonin to death.

Lenin's 'leap into the unknown' came to nothing. The problem of liquidating the war was to prove astonishingly difficult, and there ensued over a period of four months the long-drawn tragicomedy in which the Bolsheviks attempted to make peace on their own terms by using psychological weapons to neutralize the overwhelming power of the German army in the field. These psychological weapons were sometimes successful, for Lenin possessed an instinctive knowledge of the German mind, but they were rarely successful for long; and so it would happen that the Germans would periodically awaken from the stupor caused by the totally unexpected behaviour of the Bolsheviks and they would order a further advance, a further strenuous turn of the screw. An air of unreality enfolds the protracted negotiations which took place at Brest Litovsk. These shadowy negotiations were conducted with little help from Stalin, who automatically opposed any suggestion made by Trotsky and therefore often found himself in opposition to Lenin. Both Trotsky and Lenin sometimes gave way to the belief that if the Germans advanced deep into Russia, their advance would set off a shock wave of revolutionary assistance from the West. Stalin, with his usual disdain for foreigners, believed it would have exactly the reverse effect. 'There is no revolutionary movement in the West,' Stalin said. 'There is only a potential, and we cannot rely on a mere potential. If the Germans take the offensive, this will have the effect of giving more power to the counter-revolution.' But Stalin lacked the imagination of Trotsky, who devised the formula 'no peace and no war', thus giving the Soviet delegates an excuse for not signing. Stalin objected to the formula, only to be scolded by Lenin who said: 'Stalin is not right when he says we cannot not sign.' The flurry of negatives reduced Stalin to silence. In those days only Zinoviev seemed to understand that the question of whether the Soviet government should sign an agreement with the Germans was purely academic, for the Germans had the overpowering superiority in arms, and eventually they would be forced to sign. On March 3rd, 1918, the Brest Litovsk treaty was signed, and the war with Germany at long last came to an end.

The war against Germany had no sooner ended than the Civil War began.

TSARITSYN

AS COMMISSAR FOR NATIONALITIES, Stalin was rarely in a position where he could have a decisive influence on events. He had a small staff, a small budget, a weekly newspaper called *The Life of the Nationalities,* and a devouring passion for exerting power. He had followed the government from Petrograd to Moscow, and as soon as there arose the question of obtaining a building to house his commissariat, he characteristically took possession of a building already assigned to the Supreme Council of National Economy. His method of acquiring property was a simple one. He invaded the building late at night armed with thumb tacks and sheets of paper on which he had written: 'This building has been taken over by the People's Commissariat of Nationalities.' Then it belonged to him.

His chief task was to organize the national minorities, and since there were over two hundred minorities in Russia, each with its own specific and nearly insoluble problems, he might have been content to work with the minorities to the exclusion of everything else. The Second Congress of Soviets in November had proclaimed the inalienable right of the peoples to self-determination, and Stalin's task, in theory, was to see that Ukrainians, Kirghiz, Armenians, Georgians, Latvians and Tatars, and all other minorities, were enabled to exercise the rights granted to them by the Decree on Nationalities which he had signed jointly with Lenin. The Decree on Nationalities was addressed to nearly half the population of Russia, for some 65,000,000 out of 140,000,000 belonged to national minorities. It promised the nationalities everything they wanted. Stalin had not the least intention of acting upon it.

In *Marxism and the National Question* he had already outlined the proper course to be pursued by the Bolsheviks towards the national minorities. Minorities would have the right to full independence; they would have equal rights with Russia and with one another; they would have their own schools, their own languages, their own churches; under certain conditions they would have the right to secede. These rights would be granted only when 'full democracy' had been established, and on conditions which served the purpose of the dictatorship. National independence movements would be suppressed.

Stalin's task was to install pro-Communist leaders in all the national minorities, and to execute or otherwise rid the country of potential minority leaders with a thirst for independence. To select and train pro-Communist leaders, to advance them to positions of power, to install them at the head of obedient governments, and to see that they were well supplied with weapons were tasks that demanded an absolutely ruthless determination, an iron nerve and exquisite cynicism. His aim was to ensure that none of the promised rights would be granted. The right of self-determination would be granted only to 'the toiling masses' when they accepted the Bolshevik dictatorship; it would then be too late for self-determination.

It was a time of incredible confusion, with new armies, and new governments, arising in the provinces every day. Here and there the Bolsheviks had their outposts, but the territory ruled by the Central Executive Committee was shrinking daily. Stepan Shaumyan seized Baku for the Bolsheviks, Budu Mdivani seized Kutais and was promptly arrested, Tiflis remained under the control of the Mensheviks and an obliging German army of occupation. The Ukraine was being ruled by its Rada, a provisional government which had no intention of submitting to the Bolsheviks and refused to allow the passage of Red Army troops through its territory. Small nationalist groups, intensely hostile to the Bolsheviks, were springing up. The time for carrying out a programme of self-determination for 'the toiling masses' had obviously not yet come, and Stalin, while continuing to hold the leading strings over the national minorities which were already in Bolshevik power, had time to fish in other waters.

He was particularly interested in military affairs, discussed them with Lenin, and showed a surprising command of detail. Lenin sometimes relied upon him to give detailed instructions to the Commissariat of War. A decree issued by the Sovnarkom at eleven o'clock at night on April 22nd, 1918, commanding that urgent measures be taken to defend Kharkov, is signed by Lenin with a postscript: 'For details have a talk with Stalin.' Since he had more time to spare than the other Commissars, Stalin became a Jack-of-all-trades, interfering wherever he pleased and doing very much as he chose. When it became apparent that Moscow, ringed with enemies, would starve unless food supplies were brought in, it was decided to send him to the south with extraordinary powers. He was given the title of Director General of Food Supplies for the South of Russia, and the decree confirming his appointment was signed by Lenin, Bonch-Bruyevich, and the secretary of the Sovnarkom, Nikolay Gorbunov. In the photographs of the decree published after Stalin's rise to power, the signature of Gorbunov was usually erased. Gorbunov was executed by Stalin in 1938, and was posthumously rehabilitated many years later.

The decree is an interesting document because it appears to have been written by Stalin himself. The extraordinary powers are spelled out in considerable detail, but the precise nature of his duties is never stated. Everyone is ordered to obey him under all circumstances. The decree is almost an invitation to licence, but it conveys not the least suggestion that he was being invited to take up a military command.

On June 4th, 1918, Stalin left Moscow for the south with two armoured trains and a detachment of Red Guards, ostensibly on a tour of inspection which would take him to the North Caucasus, the only extensive granary still left in Bolshevik hands. Two days later he arrived at Tsaritsyn, and on the next day he sent off his first telegram to Lenin. It is possible that this telegram has been severely edited, for it was not published until 1936, at a time when Stalin was seeking to identify himself as a close comrade-in-arms of Lenin. In Tsaritsyn he found railroad transport completely disorganized, and there was chaos and profiteering in the

Council
of People's Commissars
May 31st, 1918

APPOINTMENT

People's Commissar Joseph Vissarionovich STALIN, member of the Council of People's Commissars, is hereby appointed by the Council of People's Commissars Director General of Food Supplies for the south of Russia invested with extraordinary powers. Local and provincial Sovnarkoms, Sovdeps, Revcoms, staffs and commanders of detachments, railroad organizations and stationmasters, organizations involved in commercial shipping by sea and by river, post-telegraphs, provisioning organizations, all commissars and emissaries are obliged to obey the orders of Comrade Stalin.

grain markets. River transport was being held up, apparently because Czechoslovak troops were in command of points along the river between Nizhni Novgorod and Tsaritsyn. Stalin telegraphed: 'Within a week we shall proclaim a "Grain Week", and promptly dispatch to Moscow about one million poods with a special escort of railwaymen.' He added that he would be leaving in a day or two for the south.

He did not go to the south, for in his view there were more urgent matters to attend to than sending grain to Moscow. The military situation in Tsaritsyn was deteriorating, and he decided to assume effective command of the city, clearing it of all doubtful elements and giving the weight of his support to the local Cheka. A black barge was moored in midstream, and there, almost nightly, the prisoners he had sentenced to death were shot and their bodies flung overboard. He was given extraordinary powers to deal with the grain situation, and he was now exerting these powers to deal with the military situation. By July 7th the Cossacks of General Krasnov were threatening the city. On that day Stalin wrote to Lenin:

COMRADE LENIN!

I am hurrying to the front. I am writing only on business.

The line south of Tsaritsyn has not yet been restored. I am driving and scolding everyone who deserves it, and I hope it will soon be restored. You may rest assured we shall spare no one, neither ourselves nor others, and we shall get you the grain in spite of everything. If our military 'specialists' (the shoemakers!) had not been sleeping and wasting time, the line would not have been broken, and if the line is restored it will not be thanks to the military, but in spite of them.

South of Tsaritsyn large quantities of grain have accumulated on the rails. As soon as the line is cleared we shall send you grain on the through trains.

Have received your communication. Everything will be done to forestall possible surprises. You may rest assured that our hand will not flinch . . .

The hand did not flinch. By this time he was the virtual dictator of the city, spending very little time on provisions for Moscow – three barges of grain were sent north in June – and exerting all his energy in ferreting out real or imaginary conspiracies, ordering executions, appointing and removing officials. In his letter to Lenin he wrote: 'Give somebody (or

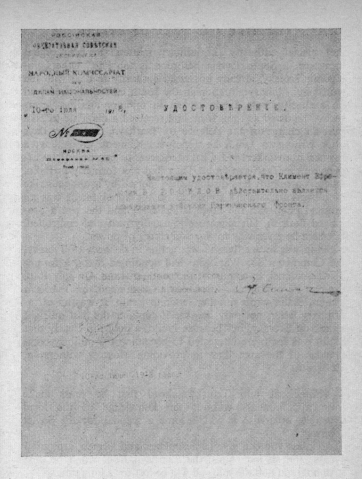

CERTIFICATION

It is hereby certified that Kliment Yefremovich VORO-SHILOV is in active command of the armies on the Tsaritsyn front.

Member of the Council of People's Commissars
Commissar for Nationalities

STALIN

Tsaritsyn, 10th July, 1918

me) special authority (in military matters) to take urgent measures in South Russia before it is too late.' Others, including Trotsky, already possessed authority to deal with the worsening military situation in the south, and Stalin received no authority from Lenin to act in military affairs. Nevertheless he acted as though he had received a mandate to take over-all charge of the defence of Tsaritsyn, and three days after writing to Lenin he appointed Kliment Voroshilov, a former ironworker and Chekist officer, to command the armies on the Tsaritsyn front. They had met formerly in Baku, where Voroshilov had distinguished himself by leading a strike of oilworkers. Stalin's signature on the appointment was an unusual one, with the large letters STA and the rest a prolonged flourish. His signature is usually neat and controlled, but here he gives way to the excitement of power.

Stalin was aware that he was acting in defiance of Trotsky, the Commissar for War, who had appointed Sytin, a former Tsarist colonel, to command the southern front. On July 10th, the day he appointed Voroshilov to command the Tsaritsyn armies, Stalin wrote another letter to Lenin. It was an extraordinary letter, not only because it contains the first outright attack on Trotsky, but because it shows only too clearly that Stalin was far more interested in becoming the military commander of the area than in providing Moscow with grain. He wrote:

Knock it into Trotsky's head that he must make no appointments without the knowledge of the local people, otherwise it will become a scandal for the Soviet power.

Unless you can give us aeroplanes and airmen, armoured cars, and six-inch guns, the Tsaritsyn front won't be able to hold out and the railroad will be lost for a long time.

There is a great deal of grain in the south, but to get it there we need a well-organized apparatus, which does not have to face obstacles from troop trains, army commanders, etc. Further, the military must assist the provisioning agents. The food question is definitely connected with the military question. For use in my work I need military powers. I have already written about this, but there has been no reply. Very well. In that case I shall myself, without any formalities, throw out the army commanders and commissars who are ruining the work. The interests of the

Царицынъ. Сталину

Говоритъ Ленинъ.

Не можете ли передать в Баку токо
что полученную телеграмму по radio
из Ташкента:

X ##

Затем о продовольствiи долженъ сказать,
что сегодня вовсе не выдали ни в Питеръ
ни в Москвѣ. Положенiе совсѣмъ плохъ.
Сообщите, можете ли принять экстренныя
мѣры, ибо кромѣ какъ у васъ достать неот-
куда. И Ярославлъ возстанiе бѣлыхъ пода-
влено. Симбирскъ вчера обошли или чехами.
Жду отвѣта!

TO STALIN AT TSARITSYN

Lenin speaking.

Could you transmit to Baku the telegram I have just received by radio from Tashkent?

With regard to provisions I must tell you that nothing was
delivered today either in Petrograd or in Moscow. The situation is as bad as it can be. Let me know whether you can
take urgent measures, for it is only from you that anything
can be obtained. The uprising of White Guards at Yaroslavl
has been smashed. Simbirsk has been taken by the White
Guards or by the Czechs. I am awaiting your reply.

REPLY OF STALIN

Everything we could send off to Turkestan was sent yesterday during the night. We have retransmitted your radio appeal to Baku. There are large reserves of grain in the North Caucasus, but it is impossible to direct them to the north. The rails are cut.

Absolutely impossible to provide grain until the rails are joined up. An expedition has been sent into the provinces of Samara and Saratov, but we cannot now come to your help by sending grain. We hope to have the trains running in ten days or so. Find ways to hold out, distribute meat and fish, which we will be able to send you in large quantities. Things will be better in a week.

TO STALIN AT TSARITSYN

Send fish, meat, vegetables, every kind of provision, and in as large quantities as possible.

---

work dictate this, and of course not having a bit of paper from Trotsky is not going to stand in my way.

This letter to Lenin is clearly a justification of a *fait accompli*. He takes care not to mention that he has already made military appointments on his own initiative, and he is evidently angered by Lenin's silence. He had asked for full military powers, and he had not received them.

In the last words of the letter Stalin proclaims his right to 'throw out' army commanders and commissars at will, without reference to any authority but his own. He is not fighting Trotsky only; he is fighting Lenin as well. What he wants from Lenin, what he is determined to get, is power.

Lenin, however, was in no hurry to give him power. Lenin desperately wanted the grain, and by July 24th, grown weary of the long delays and by Stalin's habits of procrastination, he telegraphed to Stalin complaining that no grain had arrived and that the food situation was chaotic, although the news from the fighting fronts was excellent. The telegram was sent on a Hughes telegraph machine, the forerunner of the modern teletype machine, and Lenin's original manuscript, written in an unusually sharp and angry handwriting, has been preserved, while Stalin's reply was recorded by the same machine.

Stalin answered with vague promises of help. The railroad has been cut, but large quantities of meat and fish will be sent in some unspecified manner. 'Find ways to hold out,' he says. Eleven days later, in answer to Lenin's further appeals, he explains that seven hundred wagon loads containing over a million and a half poods of grain are waiting in sidings in the North Caucasus, but unfortunately there is no way of sending them to Moscow. As for the cattle – 'We have more cattle here than we need' – it is impossible to send them to Moscow, because there is not enough hay to keep them alive during the journey. He suggests that against the time when the cattle arrive in Moscow, Lenin should busy himself by establishing a slaughterhouse.

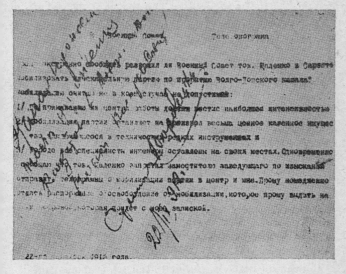

In that strange exchange of correspondence nothing is so bewildering as Lenin's patience. He was not by nature a patient man, but he seems to have measured Stalin by a yard-stick inapplicable to other men. He permitted Stalin a latitude which he permitted to no one else. Stalin coolly counter-manded the orders of Trotsky. Across such an order he, or Voroshilov, would write: 'To be ignored.' Similarly when a telephonogram arrived urging the call-up of surveyors for the projected Volga-Don Canal, Stalin and Voroshilov amused themselves by scrawling across it: 'We'll build the canal after we have drowned the Cadets in the Volga and the Don. Members of the Military Soviet – Stalin/Voroshilov.' Stalin seems to have been particularly proud of this message. When he came to power, he gave it a special place of honour in the Museum of the Revolution in Moscow.

The scrawl across the telephonogram was a foretaste of things to come. Here, brutality and coarseness were mingled with contempt, but also with a sense of inferiority. It was not necessary for them to insist that they were members of the Military Soviet, the highest power in Tsaritsyn, nor was it necessary for them to show such deliberate defiance of orders. Stalin claimed that the battle for Tsaritsyn was the most formidable, the most decisive, and the most difficult of all the battles that were being fought in the south. Then, as later, he was completely unable to see beyond the range of his own special interests.

Stalin saw himself as commander in chief of all the forces in the south, an intrepid and merciless figure, prevented only by Trotsky and Sytin from exercising his command. He was not content to be merely a member of the Military Soviet on the Tsaritsyn front; he must assume vast and nebulous powers over the entire region from Nizhni Novgorod in the north to Tiflis in the south. He saw himself as, above all, a military commander, and as the weeks went by, his letters to Lenin spoke more and more about military matters and less and less about grain. He wrote on August 31st, 1918:

DEAR COMRADE LENIN!

The fight is on for the South and the Caspian. In order to keep all this area in our hands (and we *can* keep it!), we must have several light destroyers and a couple of submarines (ask Artem for the details). I beg you to break through all obstacles, facilitate and set in motion the immediate delivery of our requirements. Baku, Turkestan, the North Caucasus will be ours (unquestionably!) if our demands are immediately met.

Our affairs at the front are doing well. I have no doubt they will do still better (the Cossacks are becoming completely demoralized).

I press your hand, my dear and beloved Ilyich.

Your
STALIN

When this letter was first published in the magazine *Bolshevik* in 1938, the claim was made that Lenin drew lines through Stalin's signature and through the words 'Ask Artem for details', then gave the letter to his secretary. It was claimed that the letter was then sent out as a directive under Lenin's name.

This claim originated with Stalin, and is suspect for many reasons, not the least of them being that the letter, even with the omissions, does not assume the form of a directive. Lenin is urged 'to break through all obstacles, facilitate and set in motion the immediate delivery of our requirements'. It is unlikely that Lenin would be influenced by so categorical a demand. No destroyers and submarines were available, and none were sent. Stalin, who had failed miserably to supply grain, was in no position to make categorical demands.

The date of the letter is puzzling: it was the day after the attempted assassination of Lenin by Dora Kaplan. Towards eleven o'clock in the evening of August 30th Sverdlov had broadcast the news of the attempted assassination, urging the workers to institute a mass terror against the enemies of the regime. It is almost inconceivable that Stalin on August 31st could have remained in ignorance of that broadcast. The news was sent by radio and telegraph to all the Soviet armies, and was repeated many times. There was scarcely anyone in Russia who did not hear the news. Stalin and Voroshilov heard it, and replied at once by telegraph to Sverdlov:

> The Military Soviet of the North Caucasian Military Area, having learned of the villainous attempt of the hirelings of the bourgeoisie upon the life of the greatest revolutionary of the world, the tested leader and teacher of the proletariat, Comrade Lenin, answers this vile attempt by organizing open and systematic mass terror against the bourgeoisie and its agents.

What is puzzling is that Stalin should have sent off his letter demanding the destroyers and the submarines on the same day that he answered Sverdlov's appeal for mass terror, and that he should later have claimed that the letter became a directive with all the authority of Lenin behind it. Lenin himself could not have seen the letter for many days, and by that time the situation had changed drastically.

Stalin's campaign against Trotsky was being waged relentlessly. Trotsky said later that he was under the impression that Voroshilov was responsible for the continual acts of insubordination on the Tsaritsyn front, and it was only much later that he realized the full extent of Stalin's responsibility. By the beginning of October his patience was wearing out. He gave orders that any commander who refused to obey the commands of the Military Revolutionary Soviet of the southern front would be executed; and in order to exact obedience Trotsky was prepared, if necessary, to hurl his own Red Armies against Tsaritsyn. He thought he would have little difficulty in destroying Stalin's Tenth Army – it could be done, he said, in twenty-four hours. On October 5th he issued an ultimatum to Stalin in the form of a telegram to Lenin. He wrote:

> I insist categorically on Stalin's recall. Things are going badly on the Tsaritsyn front in spite of superabundant forces. Voroshilov is capable of commanding a regiment, not an army of 50,000. However I shall leave him in command of the Tenth Army at Tsaritsyn, provided he reports to the Commander of the Army of the South, Sytin. Thus far Tsaritsyn has not even sent reports of operations to Kozlov. I have required reports of reconnaissances and operations sent twice daily. If that is not done by tomorrow, I shall remand Voroshilov and Minin to court martial, and shall publish the fact in an Army Order. According to the statutes of the Revolutionary Council of War of the Republic, Stalin and Minin, as long as they remain in Tsaritsyn, are nothing more than members of the Revolutionary Council of War of the Tenth Army. We have only a short time left for taking the offensive before the autumn mud sets in, when the local roads will be impassable for either infantry or mounted troops. No serious action will be possible without co-ordination with Tsaritsyn. There is no time to lose on diplomatic negotiations. Tsaritsyn must either submit or take the consequences. We have a colossal superiority of forces, but there is utter anarchy at the top. I can put a stop to it in twenty-four hours, provided I have your firm and clear-cut support. At all events this is the only course I can see.

Stalin seems to have known about the ultimatum, for on the following day he left abruptly for Moscow in the hope of dissuading Lenin from retaining Trotsky as Commissar for War. According to the biographical chronicle he was able to convince Lenin that he should be appointed a member of the Military Revolutionary Council of the Republic, which would give him a higher military rank than before. Armed with these new powers, he returned to Tsaritsyn, only to discover that Trotsky was more adamant than ever. For weeks Trotsky had been insisting that Stalin must go. Now at last, on the eve of an offensive against General Krasnov, Trotsky decided that nothing was to be gained by any further diplomatic negotiations. Lenin dispatched Sverdlov to Tsaritsyn by special train in the hope that Sverdlov would be able to force Trotsky and Stalin to hammer out their differences. He failed.

Once again Trotsky said that Stalin and his military assistants must go, and that a new commander must take over the Tsaritsyn front. Here is how Trotsky described the meeting:

> 'Do you really want me to dismiss them all?' Stalin asked me in a tone of exaggerated subservience. 'They're fine boys!'
> 'These fine boys will ruin the Revolution, which can't wait for them to grow up,' I answered him. 'All I want is to draw Tsaritsyn back into Soviet Russia.'

The angry thrust proved to be effective; and Sverdlov, who had no very great liking for Stalin, ordered Stalin removed from command of the army of Tsaritsyn. Swearing vengeance, Stalin was forced to accompany the president of the republic back to Moscow to take up whatever duties were suitable to his talents.

To the end of his life Stalin regarded his work at Tsaritsyn as the cornerstone of his revolutionary career. He came to believe that his defence of the city had saved the revolution. In an interview with a correspondent from *Pravda* at the end of the month, he explained that the capture of Tsaritsyn would have resulted in the rout of the entire Red Army on the southern front, and it was for this reason that the enemy concentrated his heaviest fire on Tsaritsyn. As usual, Stalin regarded his own acts as supremely important and vital to the Revolution. In fact, Tsaritsyn was lost in June 1919, and its loss did not seriously affect the strategical position of the Red Army. Not until January 1920 did Tsaritsyn fall again into Communist hands.

When Lenin was dead, Stalin decided to change the name of the city which had seen so many agonizing defeats and so few triumphs; and he called it Stalingrad.

TROUBLE SHOOTER

IN THE EYES OF LENIN there was no more capable trouble shooter in the Soviet Union than Stalin. He admired Stalin's forcefulness, his brutality, his devotion to the Soviet cause. That Stalin had proved to be a failure as a provisioning officer and as a military commander was perhaps to be expected; he had little knowledge of food provisioning and no military training. He belonged to the ranks of the second-rate revolutionaries like Radek, who could never be entrusted with power but who could nevertheless be entrusted with watchdog positions of great importance. Stalin's name – that name which had been reached after so many hesitations – gave the impression of a man who was firm, ruthless, unhesitating. Lenin seems to have been perfectly prepared to regard Stalin as 'a man of steel'.

Though Stalin had failed at Tsaritsyn, there were formidable opportunities still open to him. There were, for example, ceremonial functions: the name of Stalin looked well on official telegrams. When Karl Liebknecht, the German Communist leader, was released from prison in October, Lenin invited Sverdlov and Stalin to sign the official telegram of congratulations. The original document has been preserved, and it is evident that Stalin was invited to sign the telegram as an afterthought. He was the last to sign, and his cramped signature can be seen on the right of the document.

By telephone
October 23rd, 1918

> To the Russian Ambassador
> in Berlin.

Immediately convey to Karl Liebknecht our very warm greetings. The release from prison of the representative of the revolutionary workers of Germany is a visible sign of the new epoch of triumphant socialism, now being revealed for Germany and for the whole world. On behalf of the Central Committee of the Russian Communist Party (Bolsheviks).

LENIN   SVERDLOV   STALIN

Meanwhile in Moscow Stalin attended meetings of the Council of People's Commissars, made speeches on the national question, wrote articles, and attempted to make himself indispensable. When the Third Army surrendered Perm to Admiral Kolchak and thus opened the way for the conquest of the Urals by the Whites, Lenin immediately thought of sending Trotsky to take command, and then it occurred to him to send Stalin or Smilga on a mission of inquiry. He wrote to Trotsky:

> To Trotsky at Kozlov, or wherever the Chairman of the Revolutionary Council of War of the Republic may be:
> Moscow, December 31st, 1918

> There are several party reports from around Perm about the catastrophic condition of the Army and about drunkenness. I am forwarding them to you. They ask that you go there. I thought of sending Stalin. I am afraid Smilga will be too soft with Lashevich, who is said to drink and is unable to restore order. Telegraph your opinion.

LENIN

Trotsky telegraphed his opinion immediately; he favoured sending Stalin with full powers to restore order, purge the officers and punish the guilty. There was no question of Stalin taking up a military command. The Central Committee decided that he should not go alone, and Dzerzhinsky was ordered to accompany him. With that formidable combination of two men adept in all the arts of terror, it was thought that the line could be stabilized. On January 5th, 1919, Stalin and Dzerzhinsky reached Vyatka. On the same day they wrote

their first report to Lenin. The report includes a bitter indirect attack on Trotsky:

To the Chairman of the Council of Defence,
    Comrade Lenin.

    The investigation has begun. We shall inform you how
the investigation goes on from time to time. For the time
being we consider it necessary to inform you about one
requirement for the Third Army, which cannot be delayed
any longer. The fact is that the Third Army (which had
more than 30,000 men) has now only a complement of
about 11,000 weary, exhausted soldiers, who can hardly
withstand the pressure of the enemy. The units sent by the
commander in chief are unreliable, some are even hostile,
and they need to be seriously filtered. To save the remnants
of the Third Army and avert the rapid advance of the
enemy towards Vyatka (according to information received
from the commanders at the front and the Third Army,
this is a very real danger), it is *absolutely* necessary *urgently* to transfer from Russia at least three *thoroughly* reliable regiments and to place them at the disposal of the
army commander. We earnestly request you to bring pressure to bear on the appropriate military authorities for
this purpose. We repeat: unless this is done, Vyatka will
meet the same fate as Perm. This is the general opinion
of the comrades on the spot, and all the facts at our disposal lead us to endorse it.

                              STALIN
                    F. DZERZHINSKY
5/I. 1919. *Vyatka*
8 o'clock in the evening

Stalin evidently attached quite extraordinary importance to
this letter, which was first published in *Pravda* in December
1929, nearly eleven years after it was written. Twenty years
later, in 1949, a facsimile reproduction of the original letter
appeared in the fourth volume of Stalin's *Collected Works*,
and there would be nothing in the least surprising in the
inclusion of the facsimile if it were not for one disturbing
and highly intriguing fact – throughout the entire thirteen
volumes of the *Collected Works* no other facsimile appears.
Stalin and Dzerzhinsky followed this letter with a stream of
dispatches all implying bitter criticism of Trotsky without

Разслѣдованіе начато. О ходѣ разслѣдованія будемъ сообщать покуда. Пока считаемъ нужнымъ заявить Вамъ объ одной, не терпящей отлагательства, нуждѣ III-ей арміи. Дѣло въ томъ, что отъ III-ей арміи (болѣе 30 тысяч) остались лишь около 11 тысячъ усталыхъ, издерганныхъ солдатъ, еле сдерживающихъ напоръ противника. Присланныя главкомомъ части ненадежны, частью даже враждебны къ намъ и нуждаются въ серьезной фильтровкѣ. Для спасенія остатковъ III-ей арміи и предотвращенія быстраго продвиженія противника до Вятки (по всѣмъ даннымъ, полученнымъ отъ команднаго состава фронта и III-ей арміи, эта опасность совершенно реальна) абсолютно необходимо срочно перекинуть изъ Россіи въ распоряженіе командарма по крайней мѣрѣ 3 совершенно надежныхъ полка. Настоятельно просимъ сдѣлать въ этомъ направленіи нажимъ на соотвѣтствующія военучрежденія. Повторяемъ: безъ такой мѣры Вяткѣ угрожаетъ участь Перми, таково общее мнѣніе причастныхъ къ дѣлу товарищей, къ которому мы присоединяемся на основаніи всѣхъ имѣющихся у насъ данныхъ.

Сталинъ

Ф. Дзержинскій

5/I 1919. Вятка
8 часовъ вечера.

once mentioning his name. In a letter to Lenin which for some reason was not included in Stalin's *Collected Works*, they wrote:

> 1200 reliable bayonets and swords were sent to the front; the next day two squadrons of cavalry. On the 10th the 62nd Regiment of the 3rd Brigade (previously thoroughly filtered) was sent. These units made it possible for us to check the advance of the enemy, to raise the morale of the Third Army and to begin our advance upon Perm, so far successful. A thorough purge of Soviet and Party institutions is going on in the rear of the Army. Revolutionary committees have been organized in Vyatka and at country seats. Strong revolutionary organizations have begun to be set up in the villages. The entire Party and the Soviet work is being reconstructed along new lines. The military control has been cleaned up and reorganized. The provincial Cheka has been purged and staffed with new workers.

About the time this dispatch was being written, Lenin, annoyed by the delay in the investigation over the loss of Perm and perhaps hoping to put an end to the police work in which Stalin and Dzerzhinsky were showing a continuing interest, fired off an angry telegram demanding explicit answers to explicit questions. He had sent them to report on the surrender of Perm; instead they were busily engaged in a private war with Trotsky and disrupting the army and the Cheka by shooting everyone they suspected to be a counter-revolutionary and putting their own appointees in command. He wanted to know how many soldiers had gone over to Kolchak, and why they had surrendered, and what machinery had been dismantled and saved, and why the bridge had not been blown up, and what was the present fighting strength of the army, and whether political control was being maintained, and whether adequate measures were being taken to halt the retreat.

The characteristic Stalin-Dzerzhinsky tone changed abruptly. There were no more sentences like: 'The entire Party and the Soviet work is being reconstructed along new lines.' They explained that the collapse was due to the employment of unreliable front-line units led by 'callow youths, not commissars', and to the incompetence of the Military Revolutionary Council, 'whose so-called directives and decrees disorganized the administration of the front and the armies'. But when it came to answering Lenin's explicit questions, they were in difficulties. It soon became clear that the fall of Perm was due less to the incompetence of the Military Revolutionary Council than to the suddenness of Kolchak's attack. The industrial plant of Motovilikha – familiar to readers of Pasternak's brilliant story 'The Childhood of Luvers' – had already been dismantled and the machines had already been loaded on to railroad cars when the enemy swooped down and captured them. Five-sixths of the workers, together with the entire technical staff, had been trapped in Perm. Stalin-Dzerzhinsky blamed the Military Revolutionary Council for not blowing up the bridge, but had to admit that the comrade deputized to blow up the bridge was killed by White Guards a few minutes before the charge was about to be fired. Lenin had asked for a complete report on the losses, but received only a sketchy list based 'on the scanty data available'. These staggering losses included 297 locomotive engines, five million rubles' worth of medical supplies, 150 trainloads of food, 29 guns, 10,000 shells, 2,000 rifles, 8 million cartridges. Lenin asked about political control of the Third Army, and they answered: 'Outwardly the system of control seems the usual one and "according to the manual". Actually there is no system at all – the administration is utterly incompetent, has no liaison with the combat area, and the divisions are virtually autonomous.' Nevertheless 'thanks to Stalin and Dzerzhinsky', 900 fresh and completely reliable soldiers were being dispatched to the front to bolster the morale of the Third Army. Lenin, who always weighed one part of a document against another, could have taken small comfort in weighing 900 soldiers against the catastrophic losses.

The Stalin-Dzerzhinsky dispatches were merely preliminary reports. At the end of the month they were back in Moscow with a detailed report covering thirty pages, which analysed the reasons for the fall of Perm and blamed the 'inexcusable blunders' of the Military Revolutionary Council. They drew a picture of 'the general disruption and disorganization of the army and the rear, and the mismanagement and irresponsibility on the part of the army, party and Soviet institutions', and they admitted that the people of Perm had no particular desire to serve their Soviet masters. They added a sombre list of important military officials who had gone over to the enemy and described the panic which set in during the last days:

Banin, the engineer in charge of the defence works, and all his staff, railway engineer Adrianovsky and all the experts of the local railroad administration, Sukhorsky, chief of army transport and all his staff, Bukin, chief of mobilization of the Area Military Commissariat and all his staff, Ufimtsev, commander of the guard battalion, Valyuzhenich, commander of the artillery brigade, Ekin, chief of special formations, the commander of the engineer battalion and his second in command, the commandants of Perm I and Perm II stations, the entire accountants' division of the army supply department, half the members of the Central Collegium – all these and many others remained in Perm and went over to the enemy.

All this could only increase the general panic which seized not only the retreating units but even the revolutionary committee which had been set up on the eve of the fall of Perm and which had failed to maintain revolutionary order in the city, and the District Military Commissariat which lost contact with the various sectors of the city, resulting in the fact that two companies of the guard battalion who were afterwards massacred by White Guards failed to withdraw from Perm in time, and the ski battalion, also massacred by the White Guards, was also lost. The provocative firing (on December 23rd and 24th), skilfully organized by White agents in various localities of the city, also aided and enhanced the general panic.

This was not, of course, the full story. The Third Army was in a pitiable plight, drawn out in a thin line along a 300-mile perimeter, having fought continuously without relief for six months. Stalin-Dzerzhinsky reported that whole battalions of Red Army soldiers had thrown themselves down in the snow, begging their commissars to shoot them. 'We haven't the strength to stand, let alone march,' they declared. 'We're finished. Shoot us, comrades!' The real enemies were not treachery and incompetence, but weariness, hunger, cold, lack of faith in the revolution. The commissioners noted that the word 'commissar' had become a term of opprobrium. Mass desertions were commonplace; there were never enough reserves. Finally the losses in men and equipment had been even greater than at first surmised. The long report attacking the Military Revolutionary Committee concluded with a plea for a special Control and Inspection Commission under the

Council of Defence. To the end of his days Stalin was to rejoice in the invention of control commissions. Here he outlines the first of many such commissions:

Shortcomings in work arise not only from the laxity, negligence and irresponsibility of some of the workers, but also from the inexperience of other workers. In several places the Commission was able to find absolutely honest, tireless and devoted workers, who nevertheless committed a whole series of blunders as a result of inexperience. If the Soviet power had a special apparatus to accumulate the experience gained in the work of building the socialist state and to pass on this experience to the young workers who are ardently desirous of helping the proletariat, then the building of socialist Russia would proceed much faster and less painfully. This apparatus should be the already mentioned Control and Inspection Commission under the Council of Defence. This Commission in its operations could well supplement the work of the centre in tightening discipline among the workers.

Lenin read the report. He was not overly impressed with the attacks on the Military Revolutionary Committee – he had known that Stalin was waging a private war against Trotsky for some time, and in military affairs his impulse was to trust Trotsky, the practised warrior, rather than Stalin, who had shown no particular talent for military affairs. But the Soviet government was in desperate straits, every available talent was needed, and Stalin, too, must have his place in the scheme of things. Lenin may have read the last paragraph of the report more carefully than the rest, for he immediately appointed Stalin to head the proposed Control and Inspection Commission under the Council of Defence. In this way Stalin would be removed from his dangerous interference in military affairs, becoming in effect nothing more than an inspector general with wide-ranging powers behind the lines but with no active duties at the front. With commendable modesty Stalin had hinted that the function of his Commission would be largely advisory; it was merely a question of putting the accumulated experience of the past into the hands of young party workers. But in fact Stalin was playing for higher stakes. As the months passed the Commission became increasingly powerful and voluble; its inspectors and investigators were everywhere; they owed their formidable positions and their loyalty to Stalin alone; and they influenced military policy by the simple expedient of writing favourable reports on persons who favoured Stalin's purposes and unfavourable reports on persons who challenged Stalin's authority. The Commissar for Nationalities had never possessed any real power until this moment. Now at last he was in a position where his influence was decisive.

Just as Stalin attached quite extraordinary importance to the letter from Vyatka, giving it unusual prominence in his *Collected Works*, so too did he attach quite extraordinary importance to the long report on the fall of Perm written in collaboration with Dzerzhinsky. This document lay in the secret files of the Council of Defence for sixteen years. Suddenly, on January 16th, 1935, the complete text was published in *Pravda*. At the time no explanation could be given for the sudden emergence of a report describing a battle fought and lost long ago, with the harrowing details of vast losses sustained, of treachery in the ranks, of Red Army men lying down in the snow and asking to be shot. Gradually the reasons for the publication of the report became clear. On December 1st, 1934, Sergey Kirov, the secretary of the Leningrad Committee, was shot dead either at the orders of Stalin or with his connivance. A new wave of terror began. Zinoviev and Kamenev were placed under arrest, and there began the long, arduous, and always dangerous series of trials of important Bolsheviks, which came to be known as the Great Purge. When he published the report on the fall of Perm, Stalin knew exactly what he was doing. He was saying: 'Look what happened in Perm. There was unbelievable chaos, unbelievable treachery, unbelievable misery. But I stepped in. I became the head of the Control Commission, and established revolutionary order where none existed before. This is what I did in the past, and this is what I shall do again.'

In January 1935 all Russia was trembling, wondering what was portended by the strange murder of Kirov. In those anxious weeks there were few clues to what was passing through Stalin's mind, as he plotted against the people he felt called upon to rule. But an attentive reader of 'A Report to Comrade Lenin by the Commission of the Party Central Committee and the Council of Defence on the Reasons for the Fall of Perm in December 1918' might have paused when he came upon two revealing sentences buried in the final chapter of the report. They read: 'All Party and Soviet work is being reorganized on new lines. The military control has been cleaned up and reorganized.' What Stalin had done in Vyatka when his powers were limited, he now intended to do with full power over the length and breadth of Russia.

But all this belonged to the future, and Stalin was still in Moscow, debating with himself whether to work out a coherent scheme of inspection, or whether to content himself with work in the Council of People's Commissars, which was still the fountainhead of power. For some reason Lenin was no longer showing any enthusiasm for the Inspectorate: there was not enough available manpower, and the lessons of the fall of Perm were of no particular importance at a time when the battle fronts were changing rapidly. Offered a post on the south-western front early in February, Stalin rejected it out of hand. For the moment he was more concerned to make his presence felt in the Kremlin.

Between writing articles in *Izvestiya* and *Zhizn Natsionalnostei* (The Life of the Nationalities), Stalin busied himself with an intensive study of the problems which would be raised at the forthcoming Eighth Congress of the party, to be held in March. The republic was still in mortal danger, and Lenin had called for a brief congress to hammer out some necessary principles of action. Among other things, he wanted to advance the thesis that the party needed to conciliate the middle peasants and there should be an end to forced collections of grain. There were important questions to be settled about the nature of the world-wide revolution which Lenin confidently expected, and about the place of the nationalities in a multinational state. But the most important matter to be discussed related to the conduct of the war, and on this subject Stalin had some fixed opinions and some troubling reservations. The discussion on military affairs was never published in full, but Stalin permitted brief extracts from his own speech at the Congress to appear in a pamphlet called *On the Opposition: Articles and Speeches*, which appeared in 1928, and later in his *Collected Works*. In his report on the fall of Perm he had pointed to treason and inefficiency as the two main causes of the Soviet defeat, but at the Eighth Congress he admitted that there was a far more important cause – the peasants simply did not want to fight for the dictatorship of the proletariat. It had been necessary to use machine guns to force them into battle, and on some occasions, when it was feared that they would desert *en masse*, machine-gunners were ordered to mow them down in cold blood. As Stalin saw it, the peasants could be made into an effective fighting force only by rigorous training. He said:

There has been a series of mutinies at the rear and at the front, and excesses have been committed at the front, and these show that the non-proletarian elements comprising the greater part of our army have no desire to fight voluntarily for communism. Our task therefore is to re-educate these elements with a spirit of iron discipline, to make them follow the proletariat not only in the rear but also at the front, to compel them to fight for our common socialist cause, and in the course of the war to complete the building of a true regular army, which alone is capable of defending the country.

So the question stands:

Either we create a true workers-peasants army, a strictly disciplined regular army, and defend the republic, or we do not, and in that case our cause is ruined.

Stalin's admission that the peasants were in rebellion against the Red Army was an important one, for it showed that he was no longer playing the game of politics; he saw things as they were, and for the moment he was in no mood to seek his private advantage. At the Congress Lenin came out strongly on the side of Trotsky, and there was therefore nothing to be gained by overt attacks on Trotsky. Even Vladimir Smirnov, who at this time led the opposition to Trotsky, conceded that the employment of Tsarist officers served a useful purpose; and while he protested against the introduction of military ranks and salutes and special forms of address and special billeting for the officers, he took care not to press the idea that the defence of the Republic could be entrusted solely to guerrilla forces or a *levée en masse*. When the vote was taken 95 were against Trotsky, while 174 supported his policies. Stalin's vote was in support of Trotsky, whose behaviour at the Congress was not calculated to impress his listeners with his humility. After a short speech, in which he treated the audience to a brilliant survey of the civil war, Trotsky announced that Ufa was being threatened by the Whites and it was his duty to see at once to the defence of the city. He left immediately for the front. Some days later he received a message from Zinoviev saying that while the Congress approved of his policies, it had come to the conclusion that he should pay more attention to the political commissars. It was a very gentle slap on the wrists.

On March 24th, the day after the Congress ended, Stalin married Nadezhda Alliluieva, the sixteen-year-old daughter of Sergo Alliluiev, the old locksmith in whose apartments in the Caucasus and Petrograd he had taken refuge when he was being hounded by the police. Nadezhda had worked in Lenin's secretariat, and was already a revolutionary in her own right. Small, well-formed, with a white skin and the dark eyes of her Georgian mother, she was one of those young women who combine a natural gaiety with a calm intelligence. She had been Stalin's mistress and was already pregnant.

The marriage created very little stir, and there was nothing in the least unusual about it. Georgian women customarily marry when they are very young, between the ages of thirteen and sixteen, and Nadezhda was physically and spiritually more Georgian than Russian. No high officials attended the wedding, which took place in a registry office. The witnesses were Nadezhda's brother-in-law, Stanislav Redenss, a Latvian Communist working in the Cheka, and Avely Yenukidze, Stalin's closest friend, then secretary of the Central Executive Committee. There was no honeymoon. A small house inside the Kremlin near the Spassky Gate was found for them, and there they remained for the thirteen years of their marriage.

At thirty-nine, Stalin was considerably more than twice the age of his bride. He was set in his ways, methodical, ponderous, curiously reserved and unreachable. In those years he could still sometimes affect an almost youthful appearance, twirling his thick moustaches to a point, the dark curls escaping from under his military cap. But the overwhelming impression was of a man with a rather heavy, slow-moving intelligence, incapable of sentiment, speaking rarely and only after he had carefully rehearsed his thoughts, in love with power. He was not the kind of man to settle down to domesticity.

THE CONQUEROR OF KRASNAYA GORKA

THE CIVIL WAR MOVED like a series of spasms across the broken face of Russia. There was no focus, no concerted plan. Battles would erupt inexplicably, and just as inexplicably they would die down again. The Red Army was the product of elaborate improvisation, while the White armies still fought according to the military manuals of another century. The White generals never succeeded in producing a social programme which would encourage the peasants to fight for them. Hidebound, quarrelsome, fighting with a kind of desperate halfheartedness, they succeeded only in making the Communist dictatorship inevitable.

In May General Yudenich led an army from Estonia against Petrograd. His aim was to encircle the city and provoke anti-Soviet uprisings. It was a dark hour for the Communists. Zinoviev, in charge of Petrograd, lost his nerve, the commander of the Soviet Seventh Army was in secret correspondence with the enemy, and the foreign embassies in Petrograd were largely sympathetic to Yudenich and in control of vast sums of money which could be used to encourage the uprising. On May 14th General Rodzyanko captured Pskov. The garrisons defending the outskirts of Petrograd had already gone over to him. It seemed that Soviet Petrograd had only a few more hours to live.

In this extremity Stalin asked for and received extraordinary powers. He was to go to Petrograd as a plenipotentiary of the Council of Defence with orders 'to adopt all measures necessitated by the situation on the Western Front'. He was sent to Petrograd as a trouble shooter, a one-man court martial and executioner. He arrived on May 19th in an armoured train to discover that Rodzyanko's advance had come to a halt, and that the threatened reinforcements from Finland were nowhere in sight. 'The Finns,' he told Lenin by direct wire six days later, 'are maintaining a stubborn silence, and strangely enough they are not taking advantage of the opportunity.' He asked that troops be rushed up to Petrograd, and complained when only six hundred arrived. He urged that two trainloads of reinforcements be sent up daily for a period of three or four weeks. Meanwhile he continued to make tours of inspection and to hold drumhead courts martial. The front was relatively quiet, and there was not the least sign of the promised uprising. The ruthless plenipotentiary had very little to be ruthless about.

The silence on the western front was broken on June 13th when two forts guarding the approaches to Petrograd went over to the enemy. These forts were Krasnaya Gorka (Red Hill) and Seraya Loshad (Grey Horse), and their loss was a serious matter. The naval base of Krondstadt remained in Bolshevik hands. The guns of Krasnaya Gorka opened fire on the base, and the two battleships *Petropavlovsk* and *Andrey Pervozvanniy* were damaged, but not seriously. With Kronstadt holding out for the Soviets, it was a comparatively simple matter to reduce the two forts.

For a long while Stalin had been determined to cover himself with military glory and now the opportunity presented itself. From headquarters in Oranienbaum he ordered a massive attack on Krasnaya Gorka by land, sea and air. The attacking force consisted of units of the Baltic Fleet, eight hundred troops summoned from Petrograd, and a few aeroplanes. Though having no military command, Stalin as a plenipotentiary of the Council of Defence was in a position to over-ride the decisions of officers on the spot. He was told that it was impossible to send a landing party to the fort by sea, and that the only practical way to reduce it was by a strong attack in the rear. He sent ships with landing parties against the fort, and ordered the guns of the two battleships to cover the attack. Krasnaya Gorka fell at midnight on June 15th, followed a few hours later by Seraya Loshad. As soon as the news reached Oranienbaum, Stalin sent off a jubilant telegram to Lenin:

Confidential.

Immediately after the liquidation of Krasnaya Gorka came that of Seraya Loshad. Their guns are in full working order. A quick check of all forts and strongholds is being carried out.

The naval specialists assert that the capture of Krasnaya Gorka from the sea runs counter to naval science. I only deplore this so-called science. The swift capture of Gorka came about as a result of the rudest intervention by me and by other civilians in operational matters, even to the point of countermanding orders on land and sea and imposing our own.

I consider it my duty to announce that I shall continue to act in this way in future in spite of all my reverence for science.

July 16th, 1919.   STALIN

Stalin attached considerable importance to this telegram, permitting a facsimile to appear in the luxurious memorial volume published in celebration of his sixtieth year. The facsimile telegram agrees with the version published in Stalin's *Collected Works* except for the word 'check' (*proverka*) in the third line, which was garbled in transmission. Nevertheless there are some reasons for believing that Stalin has doctored the original text. There is not the slightest doubt that Stalin took charge of the attack on the forts and was elated by his success and sent a telegram to Lenin. But the use of the phrase 'rudest intervention' (*samoe gruboe vmeshatelstvo*) is oddly disturbing, for when Lenin was writing his last testament he singled out as a grave defect in Stalin's character precisely this quality of rudeness which Stalin celebrates in the telegram. He described Stalin as *grub*, meaning rude, coarse, vulgar, and went on to declare that this defect in his character was a sufficient reason for removing him from office. Stalin doctored a good many of his historical records, and it is just possible that he inserted an entire sentence to demonstrate that he accepted Lenin's verdict of his character, rejoiced in it, and was perfectly aware of it long before Lenin brought it into prominence in his testament. The telegram was first published in *Pravda* in December 1929, when Stalin was busily re-creating and recasting his activities during the civil war.

According to Trotsky, Lenin was annoyed by the telegram with its tone of 'provocative braggadocio', and by Stalin's indifference to the elementary rules of good taste and good manners. But in fact Stalin had never displayed any particular ability to display good manners, and the telegram was perfectly characteristic of him. So, too, was a long note sent to Lenin by direct wire two days later in which he drew attention to the arrest and execution of 67 officers at Kronstadt, who were implicated in a vast conspiracy. He wrote:

We have unearthed a vast conspiracy in the Kronstadt area. The battery commanders of all the forts in the entire fortified area of Kronstadt are involved. The aim of the conspiracy – to take possession of the fortress, to compel the surrender of the fleet, to open fire on the rear of our troops, and to clear the road to Petrograd for Rodzyanko. The relevant documents have fallen into our hands.

The impudence with which Rodzyanko and his small force advanced on Petrograd has now become clear to me. The insolence of the Finns is also understandable. Understandable too are the wholesale desertions of our combat officers. So is the strange fact that at the moment of the betrayal of Krasnaya Gorka the British [warships] vanished from the scene. The British clearly considered that direct interference on their part (intervention!) would not be 'convenient', preferring to turn up after the fortress and the fleet had fallen into the hands of the Whites, with the object of 'helping the Russian people' to establish a new 'democratic regime'.

Clearly Rodzyanko and Yudenich (to whom can be traced all the threads of the conspiracy, financed by England through the Italian, Swiss and Danish embassies) based their scheme on the successful issue of the conspiracy which, I hope, we have nipped in the bud (all persons implicated have been arrested, the investigation is continuing).

My request: let there be no relaxation with regard to the arrested embassy officials, keep them in strict confinement until the completion of the investigation, which is revealing a wealth of new threads.

I shall give you a more detailed account in three or four days, by which time I hope to come to Moscow for a day, if you have no objections.

I am sending the map. Until this moment it was quite impossible because I was away all the time on front-line business, mostly at the front.

STALIN

18th June 1919,
3 o'clock in the morning.

For some reason this document, too, remained for many years in the secret archives of the party. It was not published until February 1941. There was nothing particularly secret about the contents of the report, for on July 8th, 1919, Stalin on his return to Moscow delivered a very similar report to a *Pravda* correspondent. The document is chiefly interesting because it describes Stalin's involvement in the arrest, summary trial and execution of the Kronstadt officers implicated in 'a vast conspiracy', which appears not to have been a conspiracy at all. It was simply that the officers disagreed with Stalin's tactics for reducing the forts, and they paid for their disagreement with their lives.

Stalin was now riding high. He had shown that he possessed military ability, and the time had now come for a concerted attack against Yudenich. He took charge, or at least permitted himself to believe that he was in charge. Four days later another telegram was dispatched to Lenin. It read:

> The turning point for our troops has come. For an entire week there has not been a single case of individual or group desertions to the enemy. Deserters are returning in thousands. Desertions from the enemy to our camp have grown more frequent. In one week 400 men have come over to us, nearly all of them with their arms. Our offensive began yesterday afternoon. Although the promised reinforcements have not yet arrived, it was impossible for us to remain on the line we occupied – it was too close to Petrograd. So far the offensive has developed successfully. The Whites are on the run. Today we took the line Kernovo-Voronino-Slepino-Kaskovo. We have taken prisoners and captured two or more field pieces, automatic rifles, cartridges. The enemy vessels have not shown up; they are evidently afraid of Krasnaya Gorka, which is now in our hands. Urgently send two million rounds of ammunition at my disposal for the Sixth Division.

Voroshilov, who published this telegram in a symposium in honour of Stalin's fiftieth birthday in 1939, says it offers 'a full picture of the tremendous creative work performed by Comrade Stalin in liquidating the perilous situation which had arisen around Red Petrograd'. The telegram does not quite achieve this purpose. Petrograd was not in danger; the capture of the forts was no more than a very small incident in a long-drawn campaign; and the offensive, described with a curious lack of detail by Stalin, was little more than a casual sortie by Red Guards. Trotsky showed some annoyance over Stalin's postscript: 'Urgently send two million rounds of ammunition at my disposal for the Sixth Division.' In his usual correct fashion, Trotsky was alarmed at the thought that Stalin had appealed directly to Lenin for ammunition instead of approaching the Director of Supplies, who co-ordinated the issue of ammunition to the various fronts; still more infuriating was Stalin's request that the ammunition should be placed 'at my disposal', thus providing him with the opportunity of offering a personal gift to the division commander of his choice. In Trotsky's view Stalin was 'violating every semblance of order'. So he was, and he was perfectly aware of it. At all costs he wanted military renown, and he was prepared to go to any lengths to achieve it. Unhappily the situation at Petrograd gave him no opportunity to demonstrate the full extent of his military genius – there were many skirmishes, but no battles – and after a few days spent in organizing small units of the Baltic Fleet, Stalin returned to Moscow. He had not covered himself with glory, but he had once again shown himself to be a capable trouble shooter.

Stalin arrived in Moscow on July 3rd, in time to take part in a momentous full-scale debate on the conduct of the civil war. For many weeks he had been calling for the resignation of Trotsky and of Joachim Vatzetis, the former colonel of a Latvian rifle brigade, who was titular commander in chief of the Red Army. He wanted a position of importance in the Council of Defence, a clean sweep of the high command, and the downfall of Trotsky. Trotsky, who was Commissar for War, Chairman of the Revolutionary War Committee, and a member of the Central Committee, replied to the accusations against him by offering to resign from all his posts. He offered to retire completely from the government and devote himself to writing. No one had expected such an unqualified resignation of power, but no one doubted the sincerity of the offer. Lenin was disturbed. He knew Trotsky well enough to know that he meant what he said, and he called for a unanimous motion to retain Trotsky in all his positions. His resignation was declared 'absolutely impossible' and 'of the greatest detriment to the Republic'. So it happened that on July 5th Stalin affixed his signature to the document begging Trotsky to stay.

If we can believe the biographical chronicle, Stalin spent the following months organizing the resistance of the Red Army from headquarters in Smolensk, Serpukhov, and Sergeyevsk. According to a pleasant interpretation first put forward by Voroshilov in 1929, Stalin assumed this new appointment only after the Central Committee had agreed unconditionally:

1. That Trotsky must not interfere in the affairs of the southern front or cross its lines of demarcation.
2. That a number of people whom Comrade Stalin regarded as incapable of restoring the situation among the troops must be immediately recalled.
3. That new people selected by Comrade Stalin, capable of coping with these tasks, should be immediately dispatched to the southern front.

In reality no such conditions were agreed upon, for they would have been immediately vetoed by Trotsky who, as Commissar for War, was ultimately responsible for all appointments in the battle areas. The three conditions were a convenient fiction invented to suggest that Stalin was in a position of military authority, when in fact he remained a roving trouble shooter with no clearly defined powers except the power to hold drumhead courts martial and to report at intervals to Lenin. He seems to have made very few reports, and only two are included in his *Collected Works*.

The first, written from Smolensk in August, is notable for its tone of unrelieved pessimism. He wrote:

TO COMRADE LENIN.

The situation on the Western Front is becoming more and more menacing.

The old, threadbare and weary units of the XVI Army, which is being hard pressed by the Poles who comprise the most active enemy on the Western Front, are not only unable to withstand their onslaughts or to defend themselves, but they are incapable of covering the retreat of their batteries, which are naturally falling into the hands of the enemy. I am afraid that, with the units in such a state, the XVI Army in its retreat to the Berezina will find itself without guns or baggage trains. There is also the danger that the battered and absolutely demoralized cadres of the majority of the regiments will quickly find themselves incapable of assimilating reinforcements, and it must be said that these reinforcements are arriving after monstrous delays....

There is nothing in the letter to suggest that Stalin exercised any form of military command. He writes as an observer baffled by continual defeats. Disaster is everywhere. He appeals for reinforcements of trained and seasoned troops, and he must have known that none are available. The mood of the Vyatka and Tsaritsyn letters is notably absent. Not once does Stalin say that he has taken matters in his own hands.

The second letter, written from Serpukhov in October, is of considerably more importance, for it shows Stalin in the unaccustomed light of a strategist. The letter, suitably edited, was used to demonstrate Stalin's superiority over Trotsky as a strategist. Voroshilov, after observing that all comment on the letter was superfluous, proceeded to discuss it at length, warmly commending Stalin for his decisive role, his clear and characteristically farsighted interpretation of strategic problems, and his understanding that the shortest geographical route is not necessarily the most desirable. Voroshilov says the letter demonstrates Stalin's claim to be 'a proletarian revolutionary and the real strategist of the civil war'.

Stalin, too, regarded the letter with high favour, and ordered it to be printed in bold letters and in red ink in the memorial volume *Pervaya Konnaya*, which celebrated his feats during the civil war.

This letter, so often quoted and misquoted, refers to the calamitous period during the autumn of 1919 when the southern front had broken and Denikin was driving north against Moscow. Kursk fell on September 21st, Orel followed three weeks later, opening the road to Tula, where the chief munition factories were concentrated, and beyond Tula there was Moscow, undefended except for the Red Guards. The situation was made more desperate because the Don Cossacks were in open revolt. The original plan of the Soviet high command was for an offensive across the regions of Kharkov and the Donets Basin, but this plan was abandoned. Instead it was decided to stage a diversionary attack across the Don steppe between Tsaritsyn and Novorossisk. On September 14th, a week before the fall of Kursk, the government changed its mind and decided to march on Kharkov and the Donets Basin. Stalin, writing a month later, seemed to be completely unaware that these new dispositions had been made. He clamoured for the original plan and poured scorn on all the arguments in favour of a campaign in the Don steppe. The letter should be quoted in full because it provides our only extensive glimpse into the mind of Stalin as strategist.

COMRADE LENIN!

Some two months ago the commander in chief did not object in principle to launching an attack from west to east through the Don Basin. And if he rejected it nevertheless, it was on the plea of the 'heritage' left by the retreat of the southern troops during the summer, that is to say because of the haphazard redistribution of troops in the area of the present south-eastern front, the reforming of which (the grouping) entailing considerable loss of time to the advantage of Denikin. It was *only* for this reason that I raised no objection to the officially adopted direction for the offensive. But now the situation and the distribution of forces has radically changed: the VIII Army (the major one on the former southern front) has advanced into the area of the southern front and directly faces the Donets Basin; Budyenny's Cavalry Corps (another major force) has also moved into the southern front area; a new force has been added – the Latvian division which within a month after it has been reorganized will again represent a formidable force to Denikin.

You see that the old grouping (the 'heritage') no longer exists. What then is there to compel the commander in chief to keep to the old plan? Obviously, only his obstinacy, or if you like, his factionalism, that short-sighted and dangerous factionalism, destructive of the Republic, cultivated at headquarters by the 'strategic' bantam cock Gusev.* The other day the commander in chief gave Shorin the directive to advance from the Tsaritsyn area on Novorossisk through the Don steppe along a line which our aviators might find it convenient to fly, though our infantry and artillery would find it quite impossible to wander over. There is no need to prove that this harebrained (proposed) advance into the middle of a population *hostile* to us, where there are absolutely *no roads*, threatens us with utter defeat. It should not be difficult to understand that this advance on the Cossack villages, as recent experience has shown, can only rally the Cossacks in defence of their villages around Denikin, so enabling Denikin to pose as the saviour of the Don and so creating a Cossack army for Denikin; in other words it can only strengthen Denikin's hand.

Precisely for this reason it is essential now, without delay, to change the old plan which has already been changed in practice, and to replace it with a plan by which the main blow will be directed from the Voronezh area through Kharkov and the Donets Basin against Rostov. Here in the first place we shall find ourselves in a sympathetic and not hostile environment, a circumstance which will facilitate our advance. In the second place we shall gain a most important railroad system (Donets) and the main artery feeding Denikin's army, the Voronezh–Rostov line (the loss of this line

* In his authorized biography, Henri Barbusse omitted Gusev's name when quoting from the letter and added a note: 'An allusion to Trotsky.'

will have the effect of leaving the Cossack army without supplies in winter, because the Don River which supplies the Army of the Don will have been frozen over, while the East Donets railroad, Likhaya–Tsaritsyn, will be cut). In the third place by this advance we cut Denikin's army in two. One part, the Volunteer Army, we shall leave for Makhno to devour, while the other, the Cossack army, we shall threaten with an attack from the rear. Fourthly, we shall be in a position to set the Cossacks quarrelling with Denikin who, if our advance is successful, will endeavour to move the Cossack units to the west, which the majority of the Cossacks will refuse to do if by that time we have put before them the issue of peace, of negotiations for peace, and so on. Fifthly, we shall secure coal, and Denikin will not be able to get any.

This plan must be adopted without delay, since the headquarters' plan of transferring and regrouping of regiments threatens to nullify our recent successes on the southern front. I say nothing of the fact that headquarters has ignored and virtually rescinded the recent decision of the Central Committee and of the government: 'Everything for the southern front.'

In short: the old plan which has already been abolished in reality must under no circumstances be galvanized into life – that would be dangerous for the Republic, and it would certainly improve Denikin's position. It must be replaced by another plan. Not only are conditions and circumstances ripe for this, but they urgently call for such a change. In this case the grouping of regiments will also proceed on different lines.

Without this my work on the southern front will be meaningless, criminal and futile; and this will give me the right, or rather compel me, to go anywhere, even to the devil himself, rather than to remain on the southern front.

> Yours,
> STALIN

Serpukhov,
October 15th, 1919

On the basis of this letter Stalin was to claim in his *History of the Communist Party of the Soviet Union: Short Course* that 'the Central Committee of the Party accepted Comrade Stalin's plan, and in the second half of October 1919, after fierce resistance, Denikin was defeated by the Red Army in the decisive battles of Orel and Voronezh'. He wishes to imply that on receiving his letter the Central Committee abruptly saw the light of reason, changed course, ordered Stalin's plan to be put into operation, and thereby saved the South for the Soviets.

Although Stalin published the letter in *Pravda* in December 1929, during that famous year when his exploits during the civil war were being widely reassessed, there is no reason to believe that it is a forgery. Only Stalin could have written it. The hesitancies, repetitions and obfuscations are so characteristic of his style that it is inconceivable that anyone could have imitated them. The slow, ponderous and deliberate argument circles around a single point – the army of Denikin. The name 'Denikin', mentioned twelve times, acquires an accumulative force. Stalin sees the campaign in terms of vast anonymous forces moving over a map towards a point marked 'Denikin', and this point will be obliterated from the map only if Stalin's advice is acted upon. There is no carefully reasoned argument proceeding from inevitable cause to inevitable effect. There is no attempt at pinpointing dates and times. 'Some two months ago ... The other day ...' When? Where? He evidently has not inquired, and in any case he is not really concerned with the orders of the commander in chief. In his painstaking way he succeeds in drowning his ideas in verbiage. He describes a line of attack which could be pleasantly accomplished by aviators, but would prove difficult for artillery and infantry. The heavy sarcasm grows heavier as he recounts the advantages to be gained by Denikin as the Red Army forces the Don Cossacks to fight for him, so offering hostages to the enemy.

When Lenin outlined a plan to be followed, he was accustomed to number his arguments 1, 2, 3. He had an orderly mind, and possessed a keen appreciation of the drama of order. Stalin's mind was disorderly. He gropes around the problem, hurls himself at it from all sides, and therefore continually repeats himself. He does not solve a problem so much as wear it down. He is the master of that form of argument which consists in introducing entirely extraneous ideas to mislead and obfuscate. What he feared above all was to be deprived of an active role in affairs. He cries out that unless his plan is adopted without delay, his work will become 'meaningless, criminal and futile', and he might as well go to the devil.

There is no evidence that his plan was adopted. Orel fell to the Red Army on October 20th, Voronezh five days later. A letter written on October 15th could not have led to a complete change of plan by the high command. Why then did Stalin write the letter? The only possible interpretation would seem to be that he was out of touch with affairs, did not know what dispositions had been made, and was perhaps deliberately misinformed. The letter told Lenin nothing he did not know, but it was particularly illuminating for the insights it offered into Stalin's character. Lenin's reply to the letter has never been published.

When Stalin wrote this letter, he was still suffering from a stinging rebuke he had received from the Politburo. Among the decisions reached at the September 14th meeting was one 'to inform Comrade Stalin that the Politburo considers absolutely inadmissible the reinforcement of one's practical suggestions with ultimatums about resignation'. Now Stalin was not a man to suffer reprimands lightly, and this particular reprimand must have been all the more galling since he could vividly remember that when Trotsky offered to resign all his posts in July, Stalin himself was one of the signatories of the testimonial begging him to remain in office. Stalin had always despised Trotsky, and he was aware that the feeling was mutual. But from despising a man to hating him with unalloyed hatred there is more than one step. Stalin made all these steps in the autumn of 1919.

The letter which Voroshilov proclaimed to be Stalin's civil war testament is now seen under another light. Far from demonstrating Stalin's genius as a military strategist, it shows him to have been an incompetent adviser on military affairs, easily frightened, giving way to compulsive despairs, incapable of logical argument or of any *human* evaluation of the forces at work. He relies heavily on maps, railroad lines, undigested statements about the grouping of armies intended to suggest a profound knowledge of military affairs, but to the very end he remains the amateur uncomfortably attempting to reproduce the language of professionals. Lenin, if he ever saw the letter, must have regarded it with annoyance. He rarely tolerated rudeness from his subordinates; still less did he tolerate defiance; and the final paragraph was both rude and defiant. 'My work ... meaningless, criminal and futile ... compel me to go ... to the devil ...'

Very little is known about Stalin's actions in the remaining months of 1919. We hear of three directives issued to troops under his command. These were first published by Voroshilov in an essay entitled *Stalin, Builder of the Red Army*, which appeared in 1939. The first directive, which purports to be addressed to all army commanders in the Orel and Voronezh areas, reads:

> ... In working towards the objectives army commanders must avoid advancing in line formation, but should concentrate their forces for flank attacks upon the main forces of the enemy operating in the major direction, bearing in mind that success can be achieved only by manoeuvre. I draw special attention to the expediency of using cavalry for attacks upon the flanks and rear of the enemy, concentrating it in large formations on the flanks, thereby ensuring the proper meeting of forces.

This directive, according to Voroshilov, was numbered 10726, and dated October 9th, 1919. The second directive, numbered 11144/op., was dated October 20th, 1919, and reads:

> I confirm for the information of all army commanders: Remembering the conditions which enabled us to achieve success at Orel and Voronezh, do not scatter your forces, but instead strike a concentrated, smashing blow in the chosen direction, with speed and determination, and on a narrow front. Maintain at all times firm contact with your detachments and with your neighbours.

The third directive, dated November 24th, 1919, came in the form of a telegram addressed to all army commanders:

> I fully agree that the troops must be broken of the pernicious habit of 'elbow liaison' and taught to secure their flanks by their own resources. It is my opinion that this should be instilled in the troops by instruction and training, and more especially the higher officers, and not by completely repudiating the need of demarcation lines ... Above all the troops must be taught to rid themselves of the fear of open spaces on their flanks. While maintaining close contact with the adjacent detachments, it is not necessary to seek 'elbow liaison', but they should operate through the utmost possible concentration of striking power on the most important operative directions. Demarcation lines,

however, are necessary in order to indicate to the detachments their main, basic direction, as well as to regulate the disposition and movements of the rear.

These three directives are quoted by Voroshilov to demonstrate Stalin's profound genius in military strategy and perhaps also to demonstrate his connection with the battles of Orel and Voronezh. The directives, however, are not written in Stalin's customary style, and would seem to have been written by a field officer attached to headquarters.

What was Stalin really doing between July and December 1919? According to the biographical chronicle he was constantly travelling from one front to another, giving orders and directives, organizing shock brigades, sending a stream of reports to Moscow, and occasionally attending a meeting of the Central Committee at the Kremlin. From July 9th to December 18th there are altogether sixty-five entries in the biographical chronicle. We read, for example:

October 30th	J. V. Stalin leaves Serpukhov for the battle area of the southern front.
November 3rd	J. V. Stalin returns to Serpukhov after his visit to the front.
November 4th	J. V. Stalin leaves for Moscow.
November 6th	J. V. Stalin attends a meeting of the Politburo of the CC, RCP. (b). On the proposal of J. V. Stalin the resolution to send reinforcements to the southern front is adopted.
November 9th	J. V. Stalin returns to Serpukhov, headquarters of the southern front. J. V. Stalin signs a directive of the Military Revolutionary Council of the southern front for developing the offensive along the whole front and for the complete destruction of the Kursk group of Denikin's army.
November 11th	On the proposal of J. V. Stalin the Military Revolutionary Council of the southern front resolved to form a Cavalry Army.

For page after page these precise undocumented statements follow one another, but there is more than a suggestion that they have been carefully fabricated. The entry for November 11th gives Stalin full responsibility for forming the Cavalry Army, but there is no documentary evidence that he had anything to do with it. The actual document sent to the Military Revolutionary Council in Moscow makes no mention of Stalin. It reads:

To the Military Revolutionary Council of the Republic.

The Military Revolutionary Council of the southern front at its meeting of November 11th inst has resolved, in view of conditions prevailing at the present time, to form a Cavalry Army of the 1st and 2nd Cavalry Corps and one Rifle Brigade (a second brigade to be added subsequently).

The composition of the Military Revolutionary Council of the Cavalry Army to be: Commander – Comrade Budyenny; members – Comrades Voroshilov and Shchadenko.

Authority: Decision of the Military Revolutionary Council of the Southern Front, November 11th, 1919. No. 505/a.

Confirmation of the above is requested.

Voroshilov, writing in 1929, says that Stalin took the initiative in forming the Cavalry Army in the face of opposition from the Central Committee. Revising his essay ten years later, he exonerates the Central Committee and says outright that the Army was formed 'in spite of Trotsky's active resistance'.

From the fragmentary evidence provided by Stalin there are grounds for believing that during the second half of 1919 he exercised no military command, issued no directives to the armed forces, took no part in the formation of the Cavalry Army, and acted merely as a roving commissar whose reports had no effect whatsoever on the course of the fighting.

Stalin was a man who thirsted for military glory, and he was prepared to go to any lengths to achieve the outward forms of honour. At Trotsky's suggestion it had been decided to revive the giving of medals and decorations for extraordinary acts of valour. At a meeting of the Central Committee Kamenev put forward the suggestion that the Order of the Red Banner should be offered to Stalin. Trotsky, who was present, says that Kalinin protested indignantly, for everyone knew that Stalin had played only a minor role in the civil war. Bukharin commented: 'Stalin can't live unless he has what someone else has.'

Accordingly Stalin was awarded the Order of the Red

Banner in a decree dated November 20th. At a gala meeting at the Bolshoy Theatre a week later, the citation was solemnly read aloud. It was a carefully worded citation, paying tribute to Stalin's work in reducing the fort at Krasnaya Gorka, while referring only briefly and in the most general terms to his work on the southern front. The citation read:

> At a time of mortal danger, when the Soviet power was surrounded on all sides by a tight ring of enemies, and when in July 1919 the enemies of the Workers-Peasants Revolution advanced on Krasnaya Gorka – in this difficult hour for Soviet Russia, the Praesidium of the All-Russia Central Executive Committee of Soviets summoned Joseph Vissarionovich Stalin to assume a battle post, and by his energy and tireless labour he succeeded in rallying the wavering ranks of the Red Army. Thereafter, while in the battle lines and under fire, he inspired the ranks of the fighters for the cause of the Soviet Republic by his personal example. For his outstanding services in the defence of Petrograd, and also for his selfless labours on the southern front, the All-Russia Central Executive Committee of Soviets resolves to award J. V. Stalin with the Order of the Red Banner.

In later years Stalin would speak of himself as the victor of Orel and Voronezh, the untiring organizer of the Red Army, the strategist who caused the defeat of Denikin's army. But these triumphs passed unobserved in the citation, where he was credited only with 'selfless labours on the southern front', and with 'rallying the wavering ranks of the Red Army' before Krasnaya Gorka, that obscure fort on the Gulf of Finland.

When the citation was read, there was only polite hand-clapping.

GENERAL SECRETARY

THE CONQUEROR OF KRASNAYA GORKA was now forty years old, a veteran of nearly a quarter of a century of intrigues and adventures. No doubt the photograph taken on the southern front has been adroitly touched up – the photograph reveals a skin of alabaster purity, whereas we know it to have been thickly pockmarked – but there is no denying the youthful look, the eagerness in the eyes, the expression of calm and conscious superiority. The thick dark curls escape from under the leather cap over an unclouded forehead, the moustaches are twirled into points, and there is something dapper about him. He holds a pipe, and a cigarette still burns in the ashtray. He smiles faintly, and we are aware that he is one of those who are never plagued with problems; he knows the answers before he has heard the questions. No one looking at him would guess that he had already instituted at least three separate reigns of terror.

Stalin was not alone in his appearance of youthfulness. Radek, too, looked absurdly young for a revolutionary, and it was said of Bukharin that when he smiled he looked like a child. Dzerzhinsky, too, although he had taken to wearing a saturnine beard, had a smooth-featured boyish face. Many of the revolutionaries were spiritual adolescents, solving all problems by shooting their way out of them. Only Lenin, who looked middle-aged when he was twenty, gave an impression of complete maturity, but it was an erroneous impression. More than any of the others he was a man of youthful and dangerous daring.

Lenin's relations with Stalin remained friendly. He continued to find virtues in Stalin which scarcely existed, and he took comfort in Stalin's vices, his self-assurance, his ruthlessness, his criminality. Stalin never seemed to accomplish the great missions with which he was entrusted, but he succeeded in giving the impression that, even though he failed in the mission, he had accomplished great things. He was creating his legend. He was a conqueror, for had he not captured Krasnaya Gorka and Seraya Loshad? Tsaritsyn, Perm, Vyatka were cities associated with his memory. He had become the organizer of victory, the champion of the oppressed nationalities, the man who took Lenin's orders and saw that they were carried out. Of this period Stalin was to write later an admiring tribute to himself. It appears in *Joseph Stalin: A Political Biography* edited by the Marx-Engels-Lenin Institute, but largely written by Stalin himself. He wrote:

It was Stalin who directly inspired and organized the major victories of the Red Army. Wherever the destinies of the revolution were being decided in battle, there the party sent Stalin. It was he who drew up the chief strategic plans and who directed the decisive military operations. At Tsaritsyn and Perm, at Petrograd and in the operations against Denikin, in the west against the Polish gentry and in the south against Wrangel, everywhere Stalin's iron will and strategic genius caused victory for the revolution. It was he who trained and directed the military commissars, without whom, as Lenin said, there would have been no Red Army. With Stalin's name are linked the most glorious victories of the Red Army.

Voroshilov, Stalin's colourless drinking companion, made the same claim for Stalin in more general terms. 'Wherever alarm and panic might at any moment develop into helplessness and catastrophe,' he wrote, 'there Comrade Stalin was always sure to be found.'

Most of Stalin's claimed victories were defeats. In at least two of them they were such disastrous defeats that he was threatened with courts martial, and escaped punishment only because he was under Lenin's protection.

In April 1920 Poland attacked Russia, and soon the Polish armies were penetrating deep into the Ukraine. Kiev fell early in May, to the consternation of the Bolshevik high command, which was under the delusion that all the countries bordering on Russia were merely waiting for the opportunity to become satellites of the Soviet Union. The Ukrainians fought back, the Poles were compelled to withdraw after occupying Kiev for little more than a month, and the question arose whether the Red Army should pursue the retreating Poles to the gates of Warsaw. Lenin was inclined, as he said, 'to test Europe with the bayonets of the Red Army', and against the advice of Trotsky, Radek, and Dzerzhinsky he ordered the advance. Stalin wavered, but later joined the army of invasion as a political commissar. On June 17th he wrote to the Military Revolutionary Council of the Red Cavalry:

DEAR FRIENDS,

Keep in mind the following circumstances:

As a rule there are *military missions* ... of foreign European states attached to the Polish units. The members of the missions actually direct the Polish troops. Therefore it is absolutely essential (whenever possible) to arrest them and send them under reliable escort to the Military Revolutionary Council at the Front.

There are usually various Red Cross establishments in the towns occupied by the Poles. These institutions are hotbeds of Polish espionage. Their personnel must also be detained and conveyed to the Military Revolutionary Council.

When they retreat, the Poles leave arms with the kulaks for the purpose of subsequently unleashing banditry in the rear of our troops. It is therefore imperative that our advancing forces confiscate all arms from the population, that they do not fail to disarm the population.

Impress upon the commanders, commissars, as well as upon all the men without exception that we are marching ahead to liberate the toiling peasants from the *Polish* gentry, that ours is a war of liberation ...

Show consideration for the Galician Ukrainians (Ruthenians) taken prisoner – not only peasants, but also intellectuals. Impress upon them that if the Galician Ukrainians who are oppressed by Poland support us, we shall march on Lvov with the aim of liberating the city, turning it over to the Galician Ukrainians to form their own independent state, even if it is not a Soviet state but one that maintains a favourable (sympathetic, friendly) attitude to the RSFSR. ...

For some reason Stalin did not include this letter in his *Collected Works*. It was an oddly mild letter, for while the Red Cross is a hotbed of espionage and the kulaks are to be regarded as bandits, the peasants and intellectuals are to be treated with commendable gentleness. The last lines are perhaps the most significant, and they go some way to explaining Stalin's extraordinary behaviour during the campaign.

The main force under Tukhachevsky was directed against Warsaw, while a smaller force under Yegorov was directed against Lvov. There seems to have been no concerted plan, and the two armies acted separately. As the political commissar attached to Yegorov's headquarters, Stalin had a deciding voice. The French General Maxime Weygand was acting as military adviser to the Poles, and the dispositions of the Polish armies had been carefully worked out. Tukhachevsky advanced up to the gates of Warsaw, and was hurled back. A few days before, when it became evident that Tukhachevsky's army was in danger of being trapped, orders went out to Yegorov to abandon the march on Lvov and to strike at the flanks of the Polish·troops near Warsaw. Stalin, following a custom he had practised with some success at Tsaritsyn, countermanded the order. His vanity demanded that he should enter Lvov in triumph at the same time that Tukhachevsky entered Warsaw. He had prepared everything to the last detail. Galician Ukraine would become an independent state. He had no authority for forming an independent state, but he was not accustomed to asking for authority; he would act first and the authority would come later. The orders of the commander in chief were explicit; if he defied them, he knew he would have to bear the consequences. Yegorov could only obey the orders of the political commissar. He therefore ordered the army to take Lvov. Soon the Poles attacked, and the army of Yegorov was in full retreat. Lenin, who had hoped to build a bridge across Poland into Germany, was understandably mortified. So was Stalin, who took his long-delayed revenge a quarter of a century later. After the Second World War, Lvov, for centuries a Polish city, was incorporated into the Soviet Union.

The Polish campaign was a disaster, and Lenin, who had ordered the campaign and built so many hopes on it, now sought for scapegoats. Yegorov and Stalin were threatened with courts martial: a fate they richly deserved for refusing to obey orders. As Trotsky observed, Stalin had been fighting his own private war, but there was a sense in which Lenin had also been fighting a private war unrelated to political realities. Since he knew that he was himself responsible for the debacle, he called off the courts martial.

For Stalin the war in Poland was not a defeat; it was merely a disturbing incident in his quest for political power. He had so many offices and so many powers that a failure in one direction could always be balanced by victories in another. He was Commissar for Nationalities, but this was almost the least of his titles. He was a member of the Politburo, a member of the Military Revolutionary Council, acting Inspector General of the Red Army, and roving political commissar. In the previous year, on the suggestion of Zinoviev, he had been appointed to the newly created Commissariat of Workers' and Peasants' Inspectorate, which had been set up to control every branch of the administration 'with a view to eliminating the many faults of inefficiency and corruption'. The Commissariat, known as Rabkrin, had sweeping powers to investigate every official in the country. It policed the administration, exposed abuses, cut through red tape, watched over finances, and saw to it that the major administrative posts were in the hands of men who would obey Stalin's orders instantly. Lenin believed that government was largely a task for accountants. Stalin, as head of Rabkrin, set his accountants to watch the accountants, until the bureaucracy became so intricate and involved that it was in danger of perishing under its own weight.

That Stalin should have been given such sweeping powers testifies to Lenin's confidence in him. In the history of his quest for power, the appointment to Rabkrin occupies a seminal place, for it involved him in the day-by-day operations of the government and gave him unprecedented powers over the entire army of bureaucrats. The other members of the Politburo lived on a loftier plane altogether. Trotsky commanded the army by the sheer power of his intelligence and his formidable rhetoric. He was temperamentally unfitted for the detailed work of managing the army in its day-by day operations. He saw the army in its vast outlines, as fields of force. Stalin saw the army and the bureaucracy as a machine politician might see them: he would place his own men in the critical positions. He was not concerned with high policy. His chief concern was to capture the bureaucratic machine, and he succeeded abundantly, beyond all expectation. The Rabkrin was his own invention. He had told Zinoviev what to say, and Zinoviev had fallen into the trap.

Of the five members of the Politburo – Lenin, Trotsky, Kamenev, Bukharin and Stalin – only Stalin concerned himself with power on local levels. Kamenev acted as adviser and helpmate of Lenin, Bukharin concerned himself with propaganda and theoretical affairs, living in the cloudy regions where Marxian dialectics could be applied to the problems arising out of the civil war. Long before Zinoviev and Tomsky were elected to the Politburo, Stalin was already in a position to control the machinery of government. He had appointed his own men to key administrative posts, set his spies to watch over them, collected voluminous data on all of them, and ensured their loyalty. Lenin's orders affecting the bureaucracy passed through his hands. He could distort them as he pleased. Already he had a stranglehold on the machinery of government.

Stalin was also head of the Orgburo, or Organization Bureau, which effectively controlled party members, appointing and dismissing party members as he pleased. Like Rabkrin, the Orgburo claimed to be merely a supervisory device to see that men worked efficiently and honestly in obedience to the dictates of the Politburo. Stalin made it the servant of his will. His powers were already formidable. Though he worked behind the scenes, was rarely seen in public, and made no great impression on the people, he had quietly accumulated so much power that he was almost as powerful as Lenin. In a speech made in October 1920 he said:

> Comrades, a country is not governed by those who elect delegates to parliament according to the bourgeois system, or to the Congress of Soviets according to the Soviet system. No, a country is in fact governed by those who have really mastered the executive apparatus of the state, by those who direct this apparatus.

He was the master of the apparatus, and while in Moscow, and to some extent while he was travelling on his interminable inspection trips, he directed it.

A few days after delivering this speech Stalin set out on an inspection tour of the south. Georgia had proclaimed its independence in May 1918 and a Menshevik government was firmly in the saddle. Baku was in Soviet hands, while Batum, which had been occupied by British forces until July 1920, now belonged to Georgia. Lenin dreaded the possibility of losing Baku with its vast oil deposits, and always kept a watchful eye on its defence. When it occurred to him that the government of Georgia might surrender Batum to the British or the French, who would then march on Baku, he sent a hurried note to Stalin to inquire into the situation. Lenin's note, which was later tapped out on a telegraph machine, has survived:

> To Baku, to be forwarded
> To the member of the M(ilitary) R(evolutionary)
>   C(ouncil) of the Rep(ublic)   STALIN
> 29th October.

> I regard it as an established fact that Georgia will surrender Batum to the Entente, probably secretly, and that the Entente will then march on Baku. Examine the question and attach great urgency to measures for strengthening the approaches to Baku by land and sea, and measures for bringing up heavy artillery etc. Communicate your decisions.
>   LENIN

Баку и по месту
нахождения
Члену РВСРесп Сталину
29/X
Считаю несомненным что Грузия
отдает Батум Антанте вероятно тайно
и что Антанта пойдет на Баку обдумайте
и приготовьте спешно меры укрепления
подступов к Баку с суши и с моря подвоз
боевой армии и прочее сообщите ваше
решение
Ленин

Certainties, probabilities and ambiguities were always
crowding on Lenin. There had come to him the fleeting idea
that Baku was once more in danger, and that Stalin, who was
travelling in the south, would be its protector. Stalin was in
Vladikavkaz, and immediately left for Baku, where he learned
that there was no immediate danger. Georgia had no intention of surrendering Batum to the Entente and so risk her
independence by calling down the wrath of the Soviet Union.
A treaty of peace and friendship had been concluded between the two countries. Noah Jordania and Isidor Ramishvili had known Lenin well, and believed that he could be
trusted to leave Menshevik Georgia in peace. For a few more
months the independent republic of Georgia was permitted
to survive.

Before leaving Baku, Stalin addressed the Baku Soviet and
recited the achievements of Soviet power. The civil war was
coming to an end, and the Communist Party, which had
numbered scarcely a quarter of a million men at the time of
the revolution now numbered some 700,000 men, all of them
veterans of the storm through which Soviet Russia had
passed, all of them 'forged out of steel'. His figures were
not very accurate, and when he spoke of them being 'forged

out of 'steel', he was paying tribute to his own name. He spoke ominously about the Social Democrats of Georgia, calling them 'social innkeepers'. In his peroration he summoned up the figure of Martin Luther, saying:

Our way will not be easy, but undoubtedly we are not the sort of men to be frightened by difficulties. Paraphrasing the well-known words of Luther, Russia could say:
'Here I stand on the borderline between the old capitalist world and the new socialist world. Here on this borderline I unite the efforts of the proletarians of the West and of the peasants in the East in order to shatter the old world! May the god of history come to my aid!'

The god of history was coming to his aid much faster than anyone could have expected.

Outwardly there were no signs that he had been especially marked by providence. He had accomplished little during his journey to the south. He had proclaimed the independence of Daghestan and the Terek region. He continued to make speeches, but they were without any particular force. The energy seemed to be draining out of him. When he returned to Moscow at the end of November, he was a sick man, nervous, excitable, and in pain. The doctors diagnosed appendicitis, and rushed him to hospital.

For three or four days his life hung in the balance. Dr Rozanov, who performed the operation at the Soldatensky Hospital, said later that a deep incision had to be made around the appendix and the patient's condition was such that there could be no guarantee that the operation would be successful. Lenin, always solicitous for the health of his commissars, sent a stream of messages inquiring about his health. There was some talk of sending him to a sanatorium for his convalescence, but Lenin had no high opinion of the sanatoriums then available, and when Dr Rozanov suggested he should go back to Georgia to recuperate, Lenin said: 'You're right! There he'll be further away from everything and no one will bother him.'

Stalin however was in no mood to be sent away, and he remained in Moscow all through the winter and spring, occasionally attending meetings of the Politburo, receiving delegations, and, very rarely, writing articles. At the Tenth Congress of the Communist Party held in March, he spoke in

favour of a federal republic, belaboured Great Russian chauvinism, and spoke with sympathy of the Kirghiz, Chechens
and Ossets, 'nations which are doomed to incredible suffering
and extinction'. One of these nations, the Chechens, he was
himself to destroy many years later. The tone of the speech
was gentle, giving the impression of a man who genuinely
believed in the need for giving autonomy to the oppressed
nations of Russia.

In his speech he said nothing about independent Georgia,
which lay in ruins. From his sickbed in February he had
planned the destruction of Menshevik Georgia with an unre-
lenting use of the weapons of terror. He sent his agents into
the country to stir up disorders and to bring about mutinies
and desertions in the pathetically small Georgian army. A
detachment of the Red Army was sent to the Armenian-
Georgian border with orders to cross over at a signal from
Stalin. More and more troops streamed south. Sheinman, the
Soviet envoy to Georgia, professed to the Georgian government the most peaceful intentions, while actively engaged in
subversion. Riots broke out in the Lori district south of Tiflis.
Stalin reported to Lenin that a Bolshevik uprising was taking
place in Tiflis; the Red Army was near; surely they should
be permitted to give comfort and aid to the revolutionaries?
Lenin agreed, and on the same day, February 16th, 1921,
Stalin gave the signal for invasion. Stalin's friend Sergo Ordjonikidze was the commander. Nine days later the Red Army
entered Tiflis, looting, raping and murdering on a scale which
was unheard of since the time of Tamerlane. It was Stalin's
revenge against the city where he had spent his youth.

The destruction of the independent state of Georgia was
brought about with cold-blooded cynicism, at a time when
the Bolsheviks were calling loudly for the sovereign independence of all nations. The Georgians had offered no provocations, and there had been no disorders except for some
street riots deliberately provoked by the Bolsheviks. A pact
of friendship had been signed by the two countries. In
Stalin's eyes the crime of Georgia was that it was being ruled
by moderate socialists.

Three months before, Stalin had hinted at the fate awaiting Georgia. In an interview with *Pravda* he said: 'Georgia,
which has been transformed into the principal base of the
imperialist operations of England and France, and which therefore has entered into hostile relations with Soviet Russia, that

Georgia is now living out the last days of her life.' It was not true that Georgia had become the principal base of the imperialist operations of England and France. It was true that Georgia was the principal target of Stalin's imperialist ambitions.

About the time the Red Army was sacking Tiflis, Stalin found himself studying the voluminous report of the State Commission for the Electrification of Russia, known as Goelro. The electrification of Russia was a subject very close to Lenin's heart, and since Lenin had already commended the report, Stalin added his commendation:

COMRADE LENIN,

During the last three days I have had the opportunity of reading the collection of articles, *A Plan for the Electrification of Russia*. My illness made this possible (nothing bad but some good comes out of it!). An excellent book, well put together. A masterly draft of a truly *single* and truly *state* economic plan, *not in quotation marks*. The only Marxist attempt in our time to place the Soviet's superstructure of economically backward Russia on a really practical technical and production basis, the only possible one under present conditions. Remember Trotsky's 'plan' of last year (his theses) for the 'economic revival' of Russia on the basis of the mass application of the unskilled *peasant* and worker masses (the labour army) to the remnants of pre-war industry. How pathetic, how backward when compared with the Goelro plan! A medieval craftsman, imagining himself to be a hero out of Ibsen, called to 'save' Russia through an ancient myth ... And what value are the dozens of 'single plans' which to our shame appear from time to time in our press – the childish prattling of preparatory school pupils? ... Or again, the philistine 'realism' (more properly *Manilovism*) of Rykov, who continues to 'criticize' the Goelro and is immersed up to the ears in routine ...

In my opinion:

1. Not one more minute must be wasted on idle talk about a plan.

2. *A practical beginning* on the work must be *put in hand* immediately.

3. To this *beginning* must be devoted at least one third of the work (two thirds will be required for 'current' neces-

sities) in transporting materials and men, restoring enterprises, distributing labour forces, delivering foodstuffs,
organizing supply bases and supplies, and so on.

4. Since the workers of Goelro, for all their excellent
qualities, lack a sound practical outlook (one feels a professorial impotence in the articles), we must without fail
include in the planning commission men who are alive and
practical and who act on the principles – 'Report fulfilment', 'Complete on time', and so on.

5. *Pravda, Izvestiya* and especially *Ekonomicheskaya
Zhizn* (Economic Life) must be enjoined to popularize 'the
plan of electrification' both as a whole and as regards its
concrete points dealing with individual schemes, bearing in
mind that there is *only one* 'single economic plan' – the
plan for electrification – and that all other plans are idle
chattering, empty and harmful.

Your
STALIN

So he wrote, praising Lenin's master plan for the electrification of Russia in an oddly unconvincing way, saying in one
breath that the report drawn up by the Scientific and Technical Council is 'a masterly draft of a truly *single* and truly
state economic plan, *not in quotation marks*', these last words
intending to convey that he was not speaking ironically but
with the utmost seriousness, and with another breath declaring that he senses 'a professorial impotence' in that symposium drawn up at Lenin's orders. He is continually
repeating that the plan must be implemented, but he has not
the least idea how it should be done. He says that 'a
practical beginning on the work must be *put in hand* immediately', but his only practical contribution consists of a
strange formula by which a third of the available labour
force should be set to work on it, while two thirds are retained for current necessities. Lenin, too, liked to make these
numerical assessments on a grandiose scale, and there is more
than a suspicion that Stalin is imitating the master.

The attack on Trotsky as 'a medieval craftsman, imagining
himself to be a hero out of Ibsen', clearly refers to Ibsen's
The Master Builder. Solness dreams of building castles in the
sky and falls to his death by over-reaching himself, a fate
which Stalin had long since hopefully reserved for Trotsky.
Stalin uses another literary image when he turns his attention

to Rykov, accusing him of Manilovism. Manilov is a colourless, faintly ingratiating pipe-smoking character in Gogol's *Dead Souls*, of whom it is related that 'while everyone else has some peculiarities, Manilov has nothing'. Stalin had a habit of calling anyone he disliked 'a Manilov'. In fact, there was a good deal of the colourless Manilov in Stalin himself.

As the summer came on, Stalin fell ill again, apparently with tuberculosis, though no medical report was ever published. Lenin forgot his previous antipathy to sanatoriums and permitted him to stay in the sanatorium at Nalchik, south of Piatigorsk, halfway between the Black Sea and the Caspian. From time to time messages would be sent by Lenin to Ordjonikidze to inquire about the health of Stalin. 'Please let me know the state of Stalin's health and the opinion of the doctors,' Lenin wrote. 'Communicate name and address of doctor treating Stalin. How many days has he spent working during his vacation?' The dates these telegrams were received by Ordjonikidze are solemnly recorded in Stalin's biographical chronicle.

Though he was still not fully recovered, Stalin decided in July to visit Tiflis, the city he had conquered from his sickbed. Surrounded by Chekist guards he appeared on the platform at a mass meeting held in the working-class district of

Tiflis. The theatre was crowded with workers, who shouted:
'Murderer! Traitor! Renegade! Curses on you!' Old
women, who had sheltered him when he was hiding from the
secret police, hissed at him. The veteran revolutionary Isidor
Ramishvili arrived in the theatre and received an ovation.
Eager workmen carried him to the platform and set him
down before the astonished Stalin, who had conquered Tiflis
only to discover the ingratitude of the conquered. Bravely –
for the Chekist guards in their leather uniforms were very
much in evidence – Ramishvili delivered a speech in which
he castigated Stalin for the rape of Georgia and the imposition
of a bloody dictatorship of the proletariat, which was merely
his own personal dictatorship exercised from the Kremlin.
Stalin stood behind the speaker, quietly biding his time. Ramishvili was followed by Alexander Dgebuadze, who made an
even more personal attack on Stalin, saying: 'Why have you
destroyed Georgia? What have you to offer by way of atonement?' Stalin turned pale. He had nothing to offer by way of
atonement. He managed to say a few words about the glorious
opportunities now opened to the workers by the onward
march of communism, and then, his voice drowned by the
screaming and shouting audience, he fled behind his guards,
while the workmen sang the 'Internationale' and the Georgian
hymn of freedom. Afterwards they laughed and congratulated
themselves for having frightened the bogeyman off the stage;
in the following days they had reason to regret their laughter.

Stalin sought for scapegoats and found one in Philipp Makharadze, the Bolshevik commissar of Georgia. Makharadze
received a tongue-lashing at party headquarters the next day.
Stalin held him personally responsible for the humiliation
poured upon him in the theatre.

On July 6th he addressed the Tiflis Communists on the
immediate tasks confronting them. The immediate task
proved to be an unpalatable one, for he inveighed against the
spirit of nationalism and gave them as their first and most
urgent task 'to cauterize all nationalist survivals with red-hot
irons'. He spoke of the happy days in the past when the
spirit of nationalism had been commendably absent:

I remember the years 1905–1917, when among the workers and labouring people of the Transcaucasian nationalities there could be observed only complete brotherly
solidarity, when the bonds of brotherhood bound Armeni-

ans, Georgians, Azerbaijans and Russian workers into a single socialist family. Now, on my arrival in Tiflis, I am astounded by the absence of the former solidarity among the workers of the nationalities of Transcaucasia. A spirit of nationalism has arisen among the workers and peasants, and there is a strong feeling of distrust ...

This distrust, however, was very largely of his own making, and his memories of the workers of Transcaucasia between the years 1905 and 1917 cannot have been as substantial as those of the men who listened to him, since he was no longer living in Transcaucasia during the greater part of this period. He must have had some feeling of guilt, for he went on to offer a loan of several million gold rubles and unlimited free oil from Baku, provided that the Georgian Communists agreed to merge with Armenia and Azerbaijan in a single Transcaucasian Federation, a more unpalatable prospect than any other he had offered. Nothing came of the idea. He left for Moscow, leaving instructions for a full-scale purge of nationalists, and the Georgian Communists were glad to see him go.

For the Georgians, Stalin was no longer one of them. He was Moscow, armed with terrible powers, impervious to pity, sombre and menacing. He could not be argued with. The workers of Tiflis had laughed at him and cheered his enemies; they had drowned his words in catcalls; and they knew that in his own way and in his own time he would exact a fearful punishment.

On his return to Moscow Stalin still bathed in the affections of Lenin. He could do nothing wrong. Even Rabkrin, that monumental accounting machine designed to watch over all the other accounting machines, proved to be unassailable. On September 27th Lenin wrote a long letter to Stalin pointing out its inadequacies. He had been reading a report on the affairs of Rabkrin, and it was obvious that nothing was working well. It did not seem to know what it was doing, followed no basic principles, and merely complicated an already complicated situation. 'It is more concerned,' Lenin wrote, 'with catching men out and proving their guilt.'

It was a scathing letter, written during a period when Lenin was beginning to be oppressed by the monstrous bureaucracy he had himself created. Everywhere he looked he saw the machinery of government grinding to a halt in a morass of red tape. The fault, according to Lenin, lay with the bureau-crats, and it never seems to have occurred to him that there were any faults in bureaucracy. The letter demanded an im-mediate answer, and Stalin, who answered it the same day, may have known that his political life was in danger unless he provided a satisfactory alibi. He established two alibis. First, the report on the affairs of Rabkrin was merely a preliminary draft, and therefore should not be taken seriously. Second, the author of the report, a certain Loninov, had failed to include any statement of the concrete steps which were being undertaken to remedy an admittedly unsatisfactory situation. The new statement would be submitted to Lenin in a day or two. In this way Stalin placed the blame squarely on Loninov. Shielded by his two alibis, he continued in Lenin's good graces.

Because Stalin was the man who got things done, or ap-peared to get things done, Lenin was prepared to go to any lengths to defend him. At the Tenth Congress of the Party held during the following March, opposition to Stalin was gaining ground. His high-handedness and brutality could scarcely be attacked, for these were qualities which Lenin demanded of a good revolutionary. It was decided to attack him where he was most vulnerable. He had acquired too much power, and too many portfolios. It was inconceivable, said the old Bolshevik Evgeny Preobrazhensky, that any man could hold down two such important posts as head of Rab-krin and Commissar for Nationalities. Lenin answered by saying that it was not only perfectly conceivable, but essential, that Stalin should hold these posts. He was 'a man of author-ity', Lenin explained, and he hinted that there were very few such men in the world. He said:

Preobrazhensky has frivolously complained that Stalin is in charge of two commissariats ... But what can we do to maintain the existing situation in the People's Commissariat for Nationalities and to get to the bottom of all these Turkestan, Caucasian and other questions? After all, they are political problems! And they are problems that must be solved; they are problems that have been occupying European states for hundreds of years and which have been solved in the democratic republics to only the smallest ex-tent. We are solving these problems, and we must have a man to whom any representative of the nationalities may come and discuss matters at length. Where are we to find such a man? I think that even Preobrazhensky could not name anybody else but Comrade Stalin.

The same is true of the Workers' and Peasants' Directorate. The work is gigantic. But to handle the work of investigation properly, we must have a man of authority in charge, otherwise we shall be submerged in petty intrigues.

Such was Lenin's testimonial to Stalin in a speech delivered on March 28th, 1922. Never in his life had he ever praised anyone in this way. When he said 'The work is gigantic', he conveyed clearly that he regarded Stalin as a giant, one who solved all problems by main strength and by employing the full weight of his authority. At this moment he had the utmost confidence in Stalin, and could not have guessed how soon he would find this confidence misplaced.

Five days later, still under the spell of Stalin, he proposed that Molotov should be removed from his position as General Secretary of the Central Committee and replaced by Stalin. In theory, this was not too great a burden; in the past the General Secretary was little more than the chief filing clerk attached to the Central Committee, whose task was to see that the resolutions of the committee members were properly tabled and that their decrees and directives were sent to the proper commissariats. The General Secretary had no influence on policy, or only such influence as secretaries generally possess by being in a position to withhold documents, by manoeuvring favourite documents on the agenda, and by taking charge of the order of business. It was not in itself an important post, and no one paid any particular attention to the new appointment when it was announced in *Pravda*. Molotov and Kuibyshev were appointed assistants to the new General Secretary, and it was assumed that they would do most of the work.

Stalin retained the post for thirty years, relinquishing it only in October 1952. It was the greatest of all the gifts he received from Lenin, for it enabled him to capture the Central Committee.

Nine days later, on April 11th, Lenin offered an even greater gift to Trotsky by proposing that he be appointed deputy chairman of the Council of People's Commissars. Rykov and Tsyurupa had already been appointed deputy chairmen, and Trotsky seems to have felt that the appointment was beneath his dignity. He was not a man to share honours with others. He knew his own value. Was he not the man who had built up the Red Army and held the whole world at bay? It never seems to have occurred to him that Lenin had proposed the honour in order to ensure the succession. Trotsky haughtily declined to fill the office, and at that moment he signed his own death warrant. If he had accepted the honour, he might have been able to claim the succession. Without it, he was weaponless.

Marxists believe as an article of faith that the actions of individual men are of no consequence compared with the iron laws of history. These inexorable laws dictate the coming of revolutions, the rise and fall of classes and civilizations, the birth of wars; and those who know the laws of history can foretell the future. But no one, that April, could have foretold the consequences of an imperceptible event which took place in the following month.

Just before ten o'clock in the morning of May 26th, 1922, a small blood vessel burst in Lenin's brain.

It was the beginning of the end. He was to live for nearly two more years, but never again would he have firm control over Russia's destiny. On that May morning the god of history stood beside Stalin, beckoning him to take power.

THE BATTLE WITH LENIN

I propose to the comrades to find some way of removing Stalin . . .

LENIN, January 1923

ONLY VERY RARELY do dictators live long lives. Their occupation is a hazardous one, and they often burn themselves out by middle age. When Lenin suffered his first stroke, he was fifty-two, and he had ruled over Russia for little more than four years and six months.

Though ill, he was still a force to be reckoned with. His right arm and leg were partly paralysed, there was some impairment of his speech, but otherwise he looked nearly as well as before the stroke. Soon he was receiving visitors, reading the newspapers, calling the Kremlin on the telephone, and loudly protesting the orders of the doctors, who insisted that he should take a long rest and reduce his work to a minimum. Inactivity terrified him. Worse than inactivity was the thought that he might become a useless encumbrance to those around him. When Dr Auerbach came to call on him, he said: 'Tell me the truth. If it is paralysis, what use would I be, and who would have need of me?' It was the only time in his life he ever begged for mercy.

Occasionally visitors were permitted to meet him in his country house at Gorki, not far from Moscow. Stalin, as might be expected, was the first visitor, arriving two weeks after the stroke. Lenin was in good humour, and already on the road to recovery. He asked questions continually, like a man who has been famished of news. 'I am not allowed to read newspapers,' Lenin complained, 'and I must not talk politics. So I avoid every scrap of paper on the table in case it should turn out to be a newspaper and lead to a breach of discipline.' Stalin, who recorded his conversations with Lenin in *Pravda*, remembered that they joked together about the doctors with their absurd idea that men of politics could be prevented from talking about politics. What especially pleased Lenin, according to Stalin, was that there were prospects of a good harvest.

On July 28th Lenin felt much better, and accordingly there was an extraordinary meeting at Gorki, attended by Trotsky, Zinoviev, Kamenev, and Stalin, to discuss the preparations for the forthcoming Twelfth Congress of the party. The meeting appears to have lasted six days. No doubt they met for a few hours each day and then broke up, to afford Lenin the time to rest. During the previous week Kamenev and Bukharin had paid brief visits to Gorki. Throughout August and September visitors came more frequently. Krassin came twice, to discuss the subject of the concessions which might, or might not, be offered to the British industrialist Leslie Urquhart. Zinoviev, Kamenev, Dzerzhinsky, Rykov, Rakovsky, Tomsky, Kinchuk, Kalinin, Pyatakov, Sokolnikov, Manuilsky, Preobrazhensky, Vladimirov, Skvortsov, Svidersky and Meshcheryakov, who was the chief of the government printing office, came once. Only one man came frequently. This was Stalin.

Until recently little was known about Lenin's visitors during this critical period while he was in temporary retirement, though he still held the leading strings of government. It is a matter of some concern to know who visited him during those days, when decisions of critical importance were being made. In 1964, for the first time, a more or less complete accounting of his visitors appeared in the biographical chronicle given in an appendix to Volume XLV of Lenin's *Collected Works*. According to this list Stalin visited Lenin seven times; in his own biographical chronicle he records only three visits during the same period. It is possible that Stalin had good reason to conceal the number of his visits. He did not come to Gorki only to discuss grave and urgent matters of state; he came to spy out the land, to see that his own trusted agents surrounded Lenin, and to ensure himself of the accuracy of the doctors' reports. He came regularly as clockwork, once every two weeks. He was watching Lenin closely.

By the middle of August Lenin no longer suffered from the blinding headaches and insomnia which were the aftermath of the stroke. Though he moved his right arm and leg with some difficulty, the paralysis was receding, and he spoke clearly, though more slowly. Stalin, who saw him for the fourth time on August 19th, said he showed no trace of overwork or fatigue. 'He was our old Lenin,' Stalin observed, 'screwing up his eyes and gazing shrewdly at his visitor.'

He was the old Lenin, threatening fire and brimstone upon his enemies. He shared with Stalin a hatred of the Socialist Revolutionaries and the Mensheviks, and Stalin records Lenin's curse on them:

'Well, they have made it their aim to defame Soviet Russia.

They are helping the imperialists to wage war against Soviet Russia. They have fallen into the slime of capitalism, and are sliding into an abyss. Let them wallow. They have long since died as far as the working class is concerned!'

When Stalin reminded him that the emigré press had reported his death, Lenin answered: 'Let them lie and console themselves. One should not take from the dying their last consolation.'

Stalin goes to some lengths to suggest that Lenin was quite exceptionally cordial to him. Towards the end of September there was a change in their relationship. The ostensible cause of the strained relationship was an argument on the nationalities question, but there may have been other disagreements. It is also reasonable to suppose that while Lenin was absent from the Kremlin, Stalin was shouldering many of the burdens of government, and it was unlikely that he would view Lenin's recovery with pleasure. He was a man who enjoyed the burdens of power.

They were still on good terms in August. A famous photograph taken during that month shows them sitting pleasantly together. Lenin leans back, his hands folded on his lap, while Stalin leans forward, as always when he was being photographed. He wears knee boots, dark trousers, and a white summer tunic. Power has made him put on weight, he has a bulging waistline and his cheeks are fleshy. He looks like an eminently successful businessman.

The rift, when it came, developed over a matter of principle. Exactly what powers should be entrusted to the states forming the federal republic? Should all power radiate from the capital, or should the states themselves be in a position to exercise power? On what terms should the states be permitted to secede? These were matters which Stalin had discussed at considerable length in his pamphlet on *Marxism and the National Question*, but they were still far from solution.

Lenin wanted a comparatively loose federation of states with two Central Executive Committees, one representing the republic as a whole, the other representing the individual states. As Stalin realized, such a system involved the creation of an upper and lower house roughly comparable to the Senate and House of Representatives in the United States. He wanted all power concentrated in Moscow, with only the local administration of police, education and public health in the hands of the states. With considerable skill he was devising a formula by which the states would enjoy vast *apparent* powers, while in fact all real power was retained by the government. Lenin saw through the formula, and on the eve of his return to Moscow he wrote to Kamenev emphasizing the need for a careful revision of Stalin's 'Resolution on the Admission of the Independent Republics into the Soviet Union'. Among other things Lenin insisted that the new republic should bear the name of 'Union of Soviet Republics of Europe and Asia'. The grandiose name deliberately avoided the word 'socialist', so demonstrating that the union represented many states at different levels of social development.

Lenin saw that he would have difficulty in converting Stalin, the expert on nationalities, to his new beliefs; and after some unsatisfactory telephone calls with Sokolnikov and Stalin, he decided to write an urgent appeal to Kamenev and all members of the Politburo. He wrote on September 26th :

COMRADE KAMENEV! You probably have received already from Stalin the resolution of his commission on the admission of the independent republic into the RSFSR.

If you have not received it, get it from the secretary and please read it immediately. I spoke about it yesterday with Sokolnikov, today with Stalin, tomorrow I will see Mdivani [a Georgian Communist, suspected of separatism].

In my opinion the question is supremely important. Stalin has a slight aspiration towards hurry. You must think it over well. Zinoviev, too. (You once had the intention of taking the matter up and did so to some extent.) Stalin has already agreed to one concession, in Section I, instead of saying 'entry' into the RSFSR to say 'formal unification with the RSFSR in a union of Soviet Republics of Europe and Asia. I trust the spirit of this concession is obvious. We acknowledge ourselves on an equal basis with the Ukrainian Republic and the other Republics, and together with them on the basis of equality we enter into a new union, a new federation, 'the union of Soviet Republics of Europe and Asia' . . .

Stalin has agreed to postpone introducing the resolution in the Politburo until my arrival. I arrive Monday, October 2nd. I should like to have an interview with you and Rykov for a couple of hours – in the morning, say, from one to two, and, if necessary in the evening, say five to seven, or six to eight.

Here is my preliminary project. On the basis of a conversation with Mdivani and other comrades, I will fight for it and change it. I urge you to do the same and answer me.

What is clear from the letter is that Lenin foresaw a long-drawn struggle with Stalin and that he would have to exert every ounce of political expertise. He was not dealing with a subordinate, but with a man who had accumulated such vast powers that he could speak as an equal.

Stalin, who received a copy of the letter, replied the same day. The complete letter has never been published, but two extracts of it are known, and in both Stalin goes to quite extraordinary lengths in attacking Lenin's idea. The idea of the two Executive Committees is summarily dismissed, Lenin is accused of 'national liberalism', and for having suggested that Stalin has 'a slight aspiration towards hurry'. Lenin is repaid in the same coin. Here are the two extracts from Stalin's reply:

Lenin's correction to paragraph 2, proposing to create along with the Central Executive Committee of the Russian Republic, a Central Executive Committee of the Federation, should not, in my opinion, be adopted. The existence of two Central Executive Committees in Moscow, one of which will obviously represent a 'lower house' and the other an 'upper house', will give us nothing but conflict and debate....

On the subject of paragraph 4, in my opinion, Comrade Lenin himself 'hurried' a little, demanding a fusion of the Commissariats of Finance, Food Supply, Labour and National Economy with the Commissariats of the Federation. There is hardly a doubt that this 'hurriedness' will supply fuel to the advocates of 'independence', to the detriment of the national liberalism of Lenin. Lenin's correction to paragraph 5 is, in my opinion, superfluous.

Stalin's letter was an astonishing and illuminating document, for it showed him for the first time capable of insulting Lenin. He was saying in effect: 'How dare Lenin interfere? What does he know about the matter?' Stalin considered himself to be an expert on the nationalities question. He had spent many years studying the question, on which he had changed his opinions many times. He was now engaged in a trial of strength with Lenin, which was to have terrible consequences.

Outwardly the two men were pursuing a purely theoretical discussion on the nature of the Soviet state and the precise form it would acquire. In fact they were engaged in a deadly struggle for power.

On October 2nd, still under doctors' orders to limit the amount of his work, Lenin returned to the Kremlin. There were even more pressing matters than the nationalities question to attend to, and apart from a few conferences with Kamenev, Sokolnikov and Mdivani, and his decision to send three men to Georgia to examine the problems of the entry of Georgia into the Soviet Union, he seems to have spent very little time thinking about the question. The three men to be sent to Georgia were Felix Dzerzhinsky, Vikenty Mits-kevich-Kapsukas and Dmitry Manuilsky, and Stalin had very little difficulty convincing them that Georgia wanted to be incorporated in the Soviet Union even though the entire body of the Central Committee of the Georgian Communist Party had resigned in protest against Stalin's heavy-handed tactics. For the moment Lenin permitted himself the fatal luxury of postponing a head-on collision with Stalin.

He was very ill, still suffered from incapacitating headaches and insomnia, and worked much more slowly than usual. Rykov and Tsyurupa, on whom he often relied for advice, could no longer bear any of his burdens, for they were ill and unreachable: they were in sanatoriums in Germany. He saw about ten people a day; the interviews were limited by the doctors to fifteen minutes each, but Lenin was rarely in a mood to listen to his doctors. He still conducted his affairs methodically, and in the early evenings he attended the Council of People's Commissars.

On October 6th a plenary session of the Central Committee adopted Stalin's resolutions on the admission of the independent republics into the Soviet Union. There were some slight textual modifications to placate Lenin, but Stalin's original plan prevailed. Lenin was too ill to attend the meeting. He read the documents, and was appalled by them. A visit from Dzerzhinsky who was about to leave for Georgia gave him no comfort, and a further talk with Zinoviev, to whom he expressed his fears, was equally disturbing. He may have guessed that Zinoviev was already in alliance with Stalin. In the letter of September 27th he had demanded a basis of equality between the republics, and it was precisely this basis of equality which Stalin was destroying. In the text Stalin permitted the republics 'complete freedom to leave the union', but this complete freedom was negated by Stalin's insistence on 'the absolute need for unification'. On this rock Lenin was to break his heart.

But for the moment, in the intervals of headaches and bouts of insomnia, he was more concerned with the emergence of a vast destructive bureaucracy which threatened to transform the Communist Party into a morass of bureaucrats. There must be – it was intolerable that there should not be – some way to reduce the power of the bureaucrats, and he drew up a memorandum on the subject of the bureaucracy which was strangling the Soviet Union when it was scarcely five years old.

In Lenin's absence the plenary session had adopted a proposal put forward by Stalin, Bukharin and Pyatakov to permit the private import and export of a very restricted number of goods. A week later Lenin wrote a long, excited letter to Stalin complaining once again of his 'undue haste'. The letter which covered five and a half closely written pages and two postscripts took the form of a blast at Stalin for his incomprehension of the nature of the socialist state, which could not under any conditions permit private trading with foreign countries. The state monopoly must be maintained. Had not the Twelfth Party Congress confirmed the inviolability of the state monopoly of foreign trade? Lenin implied that there had been a deliberate plot to pass the measure in his absence.

'I am extremely sorry,' he wrote to Stalin, 'that illness prevented me from attending the meeting that day and that I am now compelled to solicit for a certain exception to the rules. But I think the question needs to be weighed and studied, and it is dangerous to be so hasty.'

Stalin did nothing. He simply tabled the proposal, which was not discussed again until two months later. By that time Lenin's condition had changed abruptly for the worse.

All through October and November Lenin was aware of the growing power of Stalin. Wherever he turned, Stalin was watching him. Stalin's will pervaded all affairs of state, and ultimate decisions were continually being made by him. He seemed to know, and did know, far more about Lenin's activities than Lenin knew about Stalin's.

Until recently it was generally assumed that Stalin must have had a spy in Lenin's secretariat, and from time to time suspicion would fall on one or other of those members of the secretariat whose names have been recorded. It seemed inconceivable that Stalin should have been in a position to thwart Lenin's moves so successfully unless there was a spy who had access to his papers and overheard his telephone conversations. In 1964, with the publication of Lenin's daybook, comprising entries from November 21st, 1922, to March 6th, 1923, the name of the spy became known for the first time. *Nadezhda Alliluieva, Stalin's wife, was the spy.*

In Stalin's rise to power Nadezhda Alliluieva played an important role, but she was never so important as when she worked in Lenin's office as a secretary during the weeks prior to his second stroke. Lenin liked her. She was a good secretary, capable, efficient, and pretty. She had been one of Lenin's secretaries as early as 1917, when she was scarcely out of school, and Lenin trusted her implicitly, regarding her as one of the family. She had accompanied Stalin to Tsaritsyn and typed out his chilling death sentences. She was her husband's creature, without any will of her own. She was the perfect secret agent.

At this period Lenin was already engaged in a bitter feud with Stalin. Everything depended on being able to maintain secrecy in his own organization. For six days a week Alliluieva worked every morning in Lenin's office. She took dictation, and wrote up the daybook with its brief account of meetings and telephone calls and whatever else might be of interest. Because Lenin worked only a few hours each morning, she had a good deal of time on her hands. She was in a position to remove copies of letters and show them to Stalin. Another secretary took over in the evenings, and on Sundays she was free to spend the whole day with her husband.

The entries she wrote in the daybook do not seem to have the stuff of tragedy in them; they are quiet and colourless. The drama however lies close to the surface, for all this information and much more inevitably found its way to Stalin. Here are some of the entries written by Alliluieva:

23rd November. At 11 this morning Vladimir Ilyich attended a meeting of the Politburo. He left no instructions.

If Vladimir Ilyich asks about the letter of Hoover, he must be told that everything is in Chicherin's hands. Haskell leaves today at 7:20.* The letter will be given through Landers (this is what Vladimir Ilyich ordered). No appointments for the evening.

27th November. About 12 o'clock Vladimir Ilyich came to his study, said nothing, and soon left. Through Nadezhda Konstantinovna he asked for all the material on foreign trade. This was sent to the apartment. No instructions, no visitors, and no letters.

30th November. Vladimir Ilyich came to the study at 1:10, rang and asked for *Posledniye Novosti*, No. 763, of October 13th. He was interested in an article by Peshekhonov. I found it and took it to his apartment. Vladimir Ilyich was exactly five minutes in his study, and immediately went home. No instructions, no letters. Lydia Alexandrovna [Fotieva] asked me to note, simply for my information, that the letters for Haskell and Chicherin in the name of Lenin should be given to Kamenev.

1st December. Vladimir Ilyich rang for Lydia Alexandrovna at 11:30 and asked her to set up an appointment for Molotov at 12.

4th December. Vladimir Ilyich came to the study at 11:5.†
At 10:40 he rang, and asked that Avanesov should be summoned at 11. Avanesov arrived at 11:15 and left at 12:10. They discussed foreign trade. At 12:30 Vladimir Ilyich went to Gorbunov's room, then returned and dictated to Volodicheva over the telephone. At 2 he went home.

These diary entries are not particularly exciting in themselves, yet they reveal that she had an observant eye, knew exactly what was happening, and had access to Lenin's private files. She knew what Lenin talked about, and what rooms he entered.

* Colonel William N. Haskell was Herbert Hoover's representative in Russia for the American Relief Administration.

† Presumably a mistake for 10:5.

Lenin's sickness was growing worse, and the doctors prevailed on him to take a rest. On the evening of December 7th he left for Gorky, where he remained for five days. Alliluieva still went to his office every morning, and she still wrote up the daybook. If someone called, or if Lenin telephoned in from the country to ask one of the secretaries to take dictation, she was there to record the fact. When he returned on the morning of December 12th, she was still there, patiently recording the time of his arrival and departure. She could look through all the documents lying on his desk. She had time on her hands. The entry she wrote in the daybook for December 18th reads:

> 18th December, morning. The plenum of the Central Committee is meeting. Vladimir Ilyich is not present. He is ill. No orders or instructions.
> 18th December, evening. The plenum is meeting. Vladimir Ilyich is not present. The evening meeting of the plenum has ended.

Two days before, Lenin had suffered his second stroke. Power, which he had wielded so brilliantly and so devastatingly, had already fallen from his hands.

For a few more months he was able to think and dream, to compose letters and articles, to draw on his immense reserves of strength in order to hammer out the shape of the socialist state. Stalin was the enemy, and from his sickbed Lenin prepared a series of documents, which he called 'bombshells', intended to remove Stalin from his position of eminence. It was almost too late, but there was still hope that he could act in time. There were days when he fought with wild courage, and other days when he was sunk in lethargy; then his spirits would revive, and the battle would go on. It was a battle of naked wills, fought secretly within the Kremlin wall, with accusations and indictments and articles taking the place of swords. It was nothing less than a battle for the soul of Russia, and on the outcome of this battle the fate of Communism would depend for generations to come.

It was an unequal battle, for Stalin commanded vast resources. Lenin commanded only the services of his wife, his sister and his secretaries, and perhaps one or two other people whose names are unrecorded in history. For Lenin it was a lonely battle, and the most desperate he ever fought.

THE BOMBSHELLS

IN LENIN'S SECRETARIAT Lydia Alexandrovna Fotieva held a special place. She was a quiet, retiring, sensible woman, a spinster, forty-three years old, who had spent more than half her life as a revolutionary. She had a broad forehead, a snub nose, a long upper lip, and she wore her hair drawn back over her forehead. In a crowd, with a shopping bag over her arm, she would have been taken for a housewife or a schoolmistress. There was nothing in the least to distinguish her from hundreds of thousands of other women, and no one, seeing her, would have guessed that she was a dedicated conspirator, who fought against Stalin with all her strength. In those difficult months she was Lenin's ally. She knew all his secrets, carried on the fight for him when he was completely incapacitated, and fought bravely, stubbornly, with a complete disregard for her own safety. In the end she made serious errors of strategy, and these turned to Stalin's advantage. The story of the struggle between Lenin and Stalin should be told at some length, because it shows how cold-bloodedly Stalin wrested power from his adversary.

Lydia Fotieva met Lenin first in Geneva when she was twenty-three, and immediately fell under his spell. After being arrested and imprisoned by the Tsarist secret police, she made her way to Switzerland. Here she met Lenin's sister, Maria Ilyinichna, who introduced her to Lenin. She helped Krupskaya to code and decode the messages which were being smuggled in and out of Russia. When Lenin transferred the government from Petrograd to Moscow, she became his chief secretary. She was an intimate friend of the family, and was especially close to Krupskaya.

The secretariat continued to function after Lenin's second stroke, for he was still able to dictate and to make his desires known. All except one of the former members of the secretariat continued to work for him. The exception was Alliluieva, who never worked for him after December 18th. She resigned, or she was dismissed. She had done her work well. Stalin could congratulate himself that he knew all the secrets of the secretariat. These advantages however were to be denied to him during the following months. He tapped telephones and had people followed, but he no longer knew what Lenin was dictating to his secretaries.

While Lenin lay in bed in his Kremlin apartment, he would sometimes remember that just before he fell ill, he had had an unfortunate meeting with Dzerzhinsky. 'On the eve of my sickness,' he told Fotieva in January, 'Dzerzhinsky spoke to me about the work of the commission and about "the incident", and this made a very painful impression on me.' It was so painful an impression that it may have brought about the second stroke, for the meeting with Dzerzhinsky, which took place on December 12th, was immediately followed by a series of minor attacks which culminated in the stroke on the morning of December 16th. What particularly disturbed him during this meeting was the discovery that Dzerzhinsky was in total agreement with Stalin on the Georgian question and that they were deliberately plotting against him. On the next day he summoned Stalin to his office. Fotieva notes in the daybook that Stalin arrived at 12:30 and remained until 2:35. No details of this long meeting have been published, but Stalin may have been conciliatory, for Lenin was in a good humour for the rest of the day. He knew he was seriously ill, and would have to wait many weeks before he would be strong enough to make an open attack on Stalin. For the moment he was husbanding his resources.

On the following evening he dictated a letter to Fotieva in which he mentioned his intention to speak at the next Congress if it was humanly possible. He spoke of winding up his affairs and leaving with a quiet mind, and in the same breath he spoke of his uneasiness and his determination to continue working. The letter was addressed to Stalin, but intended for all the members of the Central Committee. He wrote:

I have now wound up my affairs and can leave with a quiet mind. There is only one thing that disturbs me very much, and that is that I shall not be able to speak at the Congress. The doctors are coming to see me on Tuesday and we shall then consider whether there is the slightest chance of my being able to speak. I think it would be very awkward, to say the least, for me not to speak. The outline of my speech was prepared during the last few days. I therefore suggest that while continuing to make arrangements for someone else to speak in my place, the question should be left open until Wednesday when I shall know whether I may perhaps be able to appear myself with a speech much shorter than usual, say of about three quarters of an hour. A speech like that will in no way interfere with the one made by my substitute (whoever you may choose for the purpose), but I think it will be useful, both politically and for me personally, as it will remove the cause of a great uneasiness. Please bear this in mind, and if the opening of the Congress is to be put off any longer, inform me in good time through my secretary.

The crippling attack came the next day, and for a week, as he lay paralysed, he saw only the doctors, Maria Ilyinichna, and Krupskaya. Nevertheless he was strong enough on December 21st to whisper to Krupskaya a message which he wanted delivered by hand to Trotsky. The message read:

Comrade Trotsky, it seems we succeeded in taking the position without a single shot by a mere manoeuvre. I suggest we do not stop but press the attack.

There was a postscript suggesting that Trotsky should reply by telephone. The postscript was fatal. Stalin had long ago arranged to tap the telephone wires, and when Trotsky called Krupskaya, Stalin learned, as he had perhaps suspected long before, that Lenin and Trotsky together were forming a powerful alliance against him.

On the following day Stalin went into action. He knew that Lenin had suffered a second stroke, and he also knew that Krupskaya suffered from a variety of diseases and was on the verge of a nervous breakdown. He decided on shock tactics. Over the telephone he screamed abuse at her, using the foulest gutter language. He ordered her not to meddle in political matters, commanded her never to discuss politics with her husband, and threatened to have her brought to trial before the Control Commission. He dared not attack Lenin directly, but he could attack Lenin's wife, knowing that she was vulnerable. He had chosen the moment well. By a series of shattering psychological blows, he hoped to do her irremediable harm.

The most charitable explanation of Stalin's outburst is that he was drunk, but it is not an explanation which found favour among those who knew him. He knew the value of psychological hammer blows, and he usually knew what he was doing. He was murderously determined to silence her, and if possible to silence Lenin, who by his mere existence stood between him and the attainment of supreme power. He called her a whore, and referred to her barren womb. He threatened, cajoled, screamed. Not one but many frustrations lay concealed in that outburst of terrible rage.

Though Krupskaya was an experienced revolutionary, she was firmly addicted to all the bourgeois virtues. She was well-meaning, kindly, prim, and hated to inflict suffering. She belonged by instinct and inheritance to the minor aristocracy, and she was particularly sensitive to the tones of the human voice. Outraged by Stalin's abuse she immediately wrote to Kamenev and Zinoviev demanding their protection. The letter to Zinoviev has not been published, but the letter to Kamenev was the first document quoted by Nikita Khrushchev in his secret report in 1956. She wrote:

LEV BORISOVICH!
Because of a short letter which I had written in words dictated to me by Vladimir Ilyich by permission of the doctors, Stalin allowed himself yesterday an unusually crude outburst directed at me. This is not my first day in the Party. During all these 30 years I have never heard from any comrade a word of rudeness. The business of the Party and of Ilyich are not less dear to me than to Stalin. I need at present the maximum of self-control. What one can and what one cannot discuss with Ilyich I know better than any doctor, because I know what makes him nervous and what does not, in any case I know better than Stalin. I am turning to you and to Grigory [Zinoviev], as much closer comrades of V.I., and I beg you to protect me from crude interference with my private life and from vile invectives and threats. I have no doubt as to what will be the unanimous decision of the Control Commission, with which Stalin sees fit to threaten me. However I have neither the strength nor the time to waste on this stupid quarrel. I am a human being, and my nerves are stretched to the utmost.

N. KRUPSKAYA

Krupskaya was a woman who knew how to keep her own counsel, and it was some weeks before Lenin was informed about the full details of the 'stupid quarrel', which was, as she knew, far more than a quarrel. It is possible, however, that she hinted to Lenin about the telephone conversation, not telling him anything that would be too painful, while at the same time conveying a sense of acute displeasure over Stalin's 'crude interference' (*gruboe vmeshatelstvo*). A few days later, when Lenin was writing the documents which came to be known as his Testament, he significantly employed the same adjective which Krupskaya had used. In describing Stalin's character he said simply that he was 'too crude'.

Stalin's cold-blooded attempt to silence Krupskaya and through her to destroy Lenin was characteristic of the man, who was already determined to achieve supreme power. But the fault lay not only with Stalin. The Communist system, as proclaimed by Lenin, involved the negation of the most elementary laws of human morality. Lawful was whatever served the interests of the revolution or the passing impulses of the revolutionary dictator. In the name of the revolutionary law hundreds of thousands of completely innocent people had been killed. In the name of the same revolutionary law the revolutionary leaders were to fight among themselves until only the most ruthless survived.

Nevertheless there is something strangely perplexing in Stalin's behaviour at this time. As Boris Nikolayevsky has pointed out, Stalin possessed extraordinary self-restraint, knew how to conceal his true feelings when necessary, and he could skilfully play whatever role he pleased. When he screamed in rage against Krupskaya, it was calculated rage. He knew what he was doing, and he was prepared to take the risk, for he was playing for high stakes. If Lenin recovered, Stalin knew he would have to pay a heavy penalty.

Meanwhile Lenin was showing extraordinary resilience. He was in no mood to give up the battle, and he insisted on working, even though the doctors permitted him to work for only a few minutes each day.

On the day following Krupskaya's letter to Kamenev, the doctors held a conference with the Politburo. Stalin attended the conference. The doctors said they wanted Lenin to divorce himself completely from political affairs. He must not read newspapers or think about politics. But they knew that this was a counsel of perfection. There was no chance that Lenin would obey them. Even if his wife, his sister and his secretaries were taken from him, he would still compose political articles in his head and find someone to take down dictation. So they agreed to permit him to dictate for a few minutes a day, but he was forbidden to receive visitors or to expect any replies to his letters. No political news was to be brought to him either by friends or by his family. He was to be kept in a complete vacuum, and the doctors were ordered to report periodically to Stalin on how well their orders were obeyed. In fact, Lenin refused to obey the orders, fought against them strenuously, and with the help of Krupskaya, Maria Ilyinichna, and his secretaries he was able for a period of ten weeks to dictate a long series of political analyses and articles deliberately intended to influence the development of the Communist state and to remove Stalin from power.

Lenin's method was a simple one. He announced that unless he was allowed to dictate to a stenographer every day, he would simply refuse all medical treatment. Though bedridden, suffering excruciating headaches and exhausted by long bouts of insomnia, he categorically refused to live in a vacuum. Already on December 23rd he told his doctor that he intended to dictate for five minutes that evening. The doctor gave his reluctant permission, and that same evening, shortly after eight o'clock, Maria Volodicheva took down the opening paragraphs of a long letter addressed to the Congress, in which he suggested that the time had come for a vast expansion of the Central Committee.

On the following evening he dictated to Volodicheva a continuation of his argument, but where previously he had spoken in generalities he now came down to particulars. He saw very clearly that without his restraining influence the party was in danger of being split wide open by Stalin and Trotsky, who had emerged as the two most powerful contenders for the throne. He said:

I propose to examine a number of considerations of a purely personal character.

It is my view that an essential factor in the problem of stability is the existence within the Central Committee of such members as Stalin and Trotsky. The relationship between them constitutes in my view the chief danger of the split which could have been avoided and the avoidance of which, in my opinion, would be served, incidentally, by increasing the number of members of the Central Committee to fifty or a hundred persons.

Comrade Stalin, having become General Secretary, has concentrated immeasurable power in his hands, and I am not sure that he always knows how to use that power with sufficient caution. On the other hand Comrade Trotsky, as was proved by his struggle against the Central Committee in connection with the question of the People's Commissariat of Railroads, is distinguished not only by his exceptional abilities – personally, to be sure, he is perhaps the most able man in the present Central Committee – but also by his exceptional self-assurance and exceptional enthusiasm for the purely administrative aspect of affairs.

These two qualities of the two most eminent leaders of the present Central Committee might, quite innocently, lead to a split, and if our party does not take measures to prevent it, a split might arise unexpectedly.

He went on to discuss the personal characteristics of Zinoviev, Kamenev, Pyatakov, and Bukharin, whom he described as 'one who may be considered legitimately as the favourite of the entire party'. Already the letter to the Congress was assuming a testamentary form. He was passing in review all those who might be expected to become the leaders of the Soviet state, analysing them and giving his considered opinion on their merits. He was aware that these statements would powerfully affect public opinion if produced at exactly the right time, and he took care that they should be kept secret. Several times Volodicheva was warned that they must be kept in a safe place.

Day after day he dictated to his secretaries, and those last urgent messages are among the most concentrated of his writings. He detested dictation. He liked to see the words in front of him, to follow the emerging shapes of his sentences as they appeared on paper, but he reconciled himself to dictation. By January 4th he had come to the conclusion which was forced on him by events – some way must be found to rid the party of Stalin. He dictated to Fotieva that evening the sharpest attack he had ever delivered on any of his fellow revolutionaries. It was an accurate and pitiless denunciation of a man whom Lenin himself had raised to a position of eminence and power. He said:

Stalin is too crude, and this fault, though tolerable in dealings among us Communists, becomes unbearable in a General Secretary. Therefore I propose to the comrades to find some way of removing Stalin from his position and appointing somebody else who differs in all respects from

Comrade Stalin in one characteristic – namely, someone more tolerant, more loyal, more polite and considerate to his comrades, less capricious, etc. The circumstance may seem to be a mere trifle, but I think that from the point of view of preventing a split and from the point of view of what I wrote about the relations between Stalin and Trotsky, it is not a trifle, or else it is a trifle which may acquire a decisive importance.

Such was the extraordinary document which stands at the heart of Lenin's testamentary writings. It is worth examining closely, for it implies at least as much as it says. It implies, for example, that Lenin had already received from Krupskaya a guarded version of the famous telephone conversation. It implies that in Lenin's view Stalin was not only 'crude' – the word *grub* suggests buffoonery at one end of its spectrum of meanings and the working of intolerable hardship on people at the other end – but it also conveys Lenin's realization that Stalin was intolerant and capricious to a degree which threatened the safety of the state.

Now, in the vocabulary of the Russian Communists 'to remove' could only have one meaning. It could mean only 'to liquidate'. When Lenin said: 'I propose to the comrades to find some way of removing Stalin from his position', he meant that Stalin must be destroyed. Three weeks before, he could have issued an order for the arrest and summary trial and execution of Stalin, but he was no longer in a position to issue such an order. Yet Stalin had not yet achieved an impregnable position. If this letter was read at the Congress it would come like a bolt from the blue, with all the authority of the half-legendary father of the Revolution behind it. Above all, it was necessary that the letter should be read before Stalin had acquired a preponderance of power. It was necessary to act quickly. For some reason Lenin could not bring himself to act quickly. The 'Letter to the Congress' was placed in an envelope in the secret archive, to be held in reserve like a bomb with a delayed fuse.

There was one other implication in the letter which is usually passed over in silence. When Lenin proposed to the comrades to appoint 'somebody else who differs in all respects from Comrade Stalin in one characteristic – namely, someone more tolerant, more loyal, more polite and considerate to his comrades, less capricious, etc.', he was delibera-

tely pointing a finger at Trotsky. In his mind the battle between Trotsky and Stalin could be simply resolved by the
elimination of Stalin. The question whether Trotsky would
have made a suitable head of a Communist state is irrelevant.
In Lenin's eyes there was no alternative. There must be an
end to Stalin, once and for all, and Trotsky must become his
inevitable successor.

In the silence of the Kremlin a deadly combat was being
waged. In their different ways Lenin and Stalin were seeking
to encompass each other's deaths. They were like two scor-
pions in a bottle, both poised to inflict the fatal wound.

But as the days passed, the sense of urgency gradually
vanished. Other problems insistently demanded solution, and
Lenin set to work to compose a series of essays dealing with
the fundamental problems of the revolution. Dictating in short
bursts nearly every evening, he discussed the appalling backwardness of proletarian culture, the need to organize the village schoolteachers, the relationship between the villages and
the towns, and the urgent task of trading 'in the European
manner'. He wrote a long essay on co-operatives, and a
series of notes on Sukhanov's brilliant diary describing the
1917 revolution. He did not like Sukhanov's interpretation of
the revolution, which seemed to him commonplace and vulgar. In these articles and essays he would sometimes proclaim
that state power was now firmly in the hands of the proletariat, forgetting that it was increasingly falling into the
hands of Stalin. It was as though Stalin no longer possessed
any existence for him. For nearly three weeks, from January
4th to January 24th, he seems to have put Stalin out of his
mind. Then, abruptly, after finishing an article called 'How
We Should Reorganize the Workers' and Peasants' Inspection', Lenin called for the documents on the Georgian question which were in the possession of Dzerzhinsky, and asked
Lydia Fotieva, Maria Gliasser and Nikolay Gorbunov to
study them thoroughly and submit a report on them.

He was now back at work, infringing the rules laid down
by the doctors. He had, in fact, been infringing them from
the beginning. Feeling stronger, he expanded the time allowed
for dictation to a full half hour every evening. Once, on January 17th, he dictated for nearly three quarters of an hour.
He was beginning to feel strong enough to mount the frontal
attack which would lead, he hoped, to the downfall of
Stalin.

There were many grounds for attacking Stalin, and it now occurred to him that the simplest and most obvious was on the grounds of his high-handed method of silencing all opposition in Georgia. There had been many murders. There had also been a brutal physical attack on Budu Mdivani, the president of the Georgian Council of Ministers. In Lenin's eyes an attack of this kind revealed a corrupt and chauvinistic temper, and Dzerzhinsky's long report on this and other incidents had left a painful impression on him. Summoning his three secretaries, Lenin told them he was moved by the need 'to complete the examination and to re-examine all the data of Dzerzhinsky's commission in order to correct the huge mass of injustices and biased opinions which are certainly to be found there'. He wanted to know exactly what had happened, and where the responsibility lay. On the basis of their report he would himself draw up the indictment against Stalin.

As Fotieva discovered, it was no easy matter to acquire the report. Since Lenin had last seen him, Dzerzhinsky had returned to Tiflis under Stalin's orders; his task was to liquidate the opposition in Georgia. Nor could Stalin be reached on the telephone. Finally, on January 27th, Dzerzhinsky returned to Moscow, and Fotieva learned, without too much surprise, that he had given the entire dossier to Stalin. In her entries in the daybook she describes the difficulties that confronted her as she sought on Lenin's behalf to obtain possession of the documents:

January 27th. I asked Dzerzhinsky for the documents of the Commission on 'the Georgian question', but he said they were in Stalin's possession.

January 29th. J. V. Stalin informed me on the telephone that he could not give out the documents without the permission of the Politburo. He asked me whether I was not telling Vladimir Ilyich more than I should about current affairs. For example the article about Rabkrin shows that he was in possession of information about current problems. I replied that I had not spoken about them and had no reason to believe that he was fully informed on current affairs.

January 30th. Vladimir Ilyich called and asked me about Stalin's reply, and then said he would fight until they gave him the data. [Here follows a brief discussion on the article about Rabkrin.] Then Vladimir Ilyich said that yesterday in answer to the question whether he would be able to address the Congress on March 30th, the doctor said no, adding that by that time he would be able to get out of bed, and a month later he would be allowed to read the newspapers. Turning to the question of the Georgian Commission, Vladimir Ilyich said with a smile: 'But it's not a newspaper, so I can read it now.' His mood was evidently not so bad. There were no compresses on his head.

February 1st. Vladimir Ilyich summoned me (6 pm). I told him the Politburo had agreed to give him the documents. He explained what should be particularly noted when they were being examined, and in general how we should approach the work. Vladimir Ilyich said: 'If only I were free...' And after this beginning, he began again and said smiling: 'If only I were free, I would be able to do it all so easily.'

It is assumed that the study of the documents will take four weeks.

Although there are some omissions in the published version of the daybook – there is, for example, no diary entry for January 28th – Fotieva's entries have an authentic ring. What is clear is that Lenin was absolutely determined to obtain the documents, and Fotieva, Volodicheva, Gliasser and Gorbunov became his willing accomplices.

In her account of these last days Fotieva mentions Gorbunov only once, but it is probable that he played a leading part in obtaining the documents. He was a resourceful and quick-witted man, who was often called upon to carry out confidential assignments. On one occasion Lenin entrusted him with extraordinary powers. Not long after the revolution, when the Soviet government was transferred to Moscow, Lenin ordered Gorbunov to remain in Petrograd. It was a particularly dangerous time. The transfer of the government to Moscow was undertaken in the greatest secrecy; the White armies were approaching the city; no one knew what attitude the people of Petrograd would assume when they learned they were being abandoned by the government. So that Gorbunov could act with authority, he was given a number of blank order forms signed by Lenin. He had merely to write any order he pleased, and it would automatically receive the sanction of Lenin's signature. Only one other man, Trotsky, received these blank order forms.

Exactly how Stalin was induced to surrender the documents is unknown. Gorbunov, who was shot by Stalin in 1938, throws no light on the subject in his fragmentary memoirs. Fotieva, who carefully studied the documents, hints that some of the papers had been removed before they came into her possession. 'The file,' she says, 'proved to be much thinner than we expected.' Lenin, however, was overjoyed. His health markedly improved. 'He was in good spirits, dictated well without pausing and rarely searched for a word. He speaks quite normally, does not give the impression of someone dictating, and stresses his points with energetic gestures.' So Volodicheva wrote shortly after the receipt of the documents, and Fotieva reports that he went into great detail about how they should be studied and how long it would be before the completed report reached his hands. It was generally agreed that the final report would be ready by March 1st.

All through the remaining days of January and February Lenin looked forward to the report. His health fluctuated. One day his mind would be active, and he would dictate with astonishing energy and clarity; the next day he would be in a fever, suffering from headaches, loss of memory and insomnia, incapable of pronouncing more than a few words to his secretaries, a prey to dark thoughts. He was engaged in a highly secret operation, and it disturbed him that even his doctors seemed to know a good deal more about what he was dictating than they might be expected to know. On February 12th he shared these suspicions with Fotieva. On February 14th he told her that it was necessary for her to hurry 'because this is something I want to present to the Congress, and I still hope it can be done'.

There is considerable mystery about the report produced by Lenin's secretaries on the Georgian question. It was never published. As we know, the dossier was in the hands of the secretaries on February 1st, and they were instructed to complete the report in three weeks. On or about February 5th, when the secretaries were beginning to become familiar with the dossier, Maria Gliasser called on Lenin and announced that the secretaries had reached the unanimous conclusion that all of them should read through the entire dossier. They had decided to abandon the original plan of distributing the material among them in three roughly equal parts. Lenin asked how much longer it would be before the complete report was in his hands, bearing in mind that he intended to present it before the party congress which opened on March 30th. Maria Gliasser answered that it would be ready before the opening of the Congress.

Lenin was perplexed by these delays, and he proceeded to cross-examine Maria Gliasser at some length. He wanted to know exactly what was happening. How many hours a day were they working on the documents? How were the documents being kept? He explained once more that he wanted a general review of all the data outlined by the commission, and he also wanted answers to questions he would later put before them. His mind was working clearly, he was in no pain, and he knew exactly what they must do. He showed his customary solicitude, saying he was sorry he had imposed this burden on them and bewailing the fact that it might be necessary to impose even greater burdens, because so much additional information would probably have to be unearthed; it might even be necessary to obtain information from the Caucasus. Then he said that within a week he would decide how much time he could afford to give them and exactly how they were to draw up the final report. He was racing against time. Finally, he ordered that the report must be completed by March 3rd.

The question of the report by the secretaries may not seem to be a matter of very great importance, but it should be remembered that Lenin was engaged in a desperate struggle with Stalin, a struggle which occupied his waking thoughts almost to the exclusion of everything else. He was fighting with the only weapons remaining to him – his thoughts, which others wrote down for him. As the days passed, he seems to have become increasingly aware of the hopelessness of the cause he had undertaken, but until the very end he was still drawing up his grand strategy for the final confrontation with Stalin.

The last entries in the daybook have a sombre colouring. They describe the last days of a fallen titan:

February 12th. [*Written by Fotieva*] Vladimir Ilyich is worse. He has a very bad headache. He called me for a few minutes. According to Maria Ilyinichna, the doctors disturbed him so much that his lips trembled. The day before Dr Foerster said that all newspapers, visitors and political information were categorically forbidden to him. When asked what was meant by political information, Dr Foerster answered: 'Well, there is your interest in the census of employees.' Apparently it was the knowledge that the doctors knew so much about him that disturbed Vladimir Ilyich. Apparently, too, Vladimir Ilyich was under the impression that the doctors did not give information to the Central Committee, but the Central Committee gave its instructions to the doctors.

He talked to me about the same three themes, and complained of his headache. I laughed and said I would hypnotize him and in two days the headaches would go.

February 14th. [*Written by Fotieva*] Vladimir Ilyich called me at one o'clock. He had no headache. He said he was quite well. He said it was a nervous disease, and so at times he was perfectly well, that is, his head was absolutely clear, and at other times he grew worse. That was why we had to make haste in carrying out his orders, because there was something he was bent on putting through the Congress, and was hoping to manage it. If we procrastinated and thereby ruined the plan, he would be very unhappy. The doctors came and our conversation was interrupted.

He called again in the evening. He spoke with difficulty and was evidently tired. He again talked of the three themes. More especially, and at some length, on the one which was most disturbing to him, that is, the Georgian question. He asked us to hurry. He gave a few instructions.

March 5th. [*Written by Volodicheva*] Vladimir Ilyich called about 12. Dictated two letters: one to Trotsky, the other to Stalin, saying that I should personally send the first to Trotsky by telephone, demanding an answer as soon as possible. He asked that the second be put aside for a while, saying that things were going badly today. He felt unwell.

March 6th. [*Written by Volodicheva*] He asked for the reply to the first letter (the reply had been dictated over the telephone). He read over the second (to Stalin), and asked me to hand it personally to Stalin and bring back the answer. He dictated a letter to the Mdivani group. He felt unwell. Krupskaya begged him not to send the letter to Stalin, but it was done in the course of March 6th.* But on March 7th I asked whether I should fulfil the instructions of Vladimir Ilyich. Krupskaya had a conversation with Kamenev, and the letter was sent to Stalin and Kamenev, and later to Zinoviev, when he returned from Petrograd. Stalin's reply came immediately after he had received the letter of Vladimir Ilyich (the letter was handed by me personally to Stalin, and he dictated to me his answer to Vladimir Ilyich). The letter to Vladimir Ilyich has still not been read to him, because he is ill.

There ends the daybook; no more was written. The last entry, from the words 'Krupskaya begged him not to send the letter' to the end, was written in shorthand, and remained undeciphered until 1956 when Volodicheva was called in to transcribe it. Then it became known for the first time that Volodicheva was entrusted with the last official act in Lenin's career.

The letters to Stalin and Trotsky have survived. The first letter was a blast at Stalin for his obscene telephone conversation with Krupskaya, the second was an urgent appeal to Trotsky for help.

To Comrade Stalin:
Copies for Kamenev and Zinoviev
DEAR COMRADE STALIN!

You permitted yourself a rude summons of my wife to the telephone and you went on to reprimand her rudely. Despite the fact that she told you she agreed to forget what was said, nevertheless Zinoviev and Kamenev heard about it from her. I have no intention of forgetting so easily something that has been done against me, and I do not have to stress that I consider anything done against my wife as done against me. I am therefore asking you to weigh carefully whether you agree to retract your words and apologize, or whether you prefer the severance of relations between us.

Sincerely:
LENIN

* Clearly the letter was not sent on March 6th, but on the following day.

To Comrade Trotsky:
DEAR COMRADE TROTSKY!

I earnestly ask you to undertake the defence of the Georgian case in the CC of the party. At present the case is under the 'advisement' of Stalin and Dzerzhinsky, so that I cannot rely on their impartiality. Quite the contrary. If you would agree to undertake its defence, my mind would be at rest. If for some reason you cannot agree, return the entire dossier to me. I shall consider that a sign of your disagreement.

With the very best comradely greetings:
LENIN

Such were the letters which Lenin dictated about noon on March 5th, composing them in agony and despair, and what appears to have been a curious sense of inadequacy. It was not his custom to write letters with escape clauses. Both Trotsky and Stalin were offered alternatives: they could, if they wished, wriggle out of the duties he had imposed upon them. He asked Trotsky to undertake the 'defence'. If he had been well, he would have said the 'attack'.

On March 7th Fotieva and Gliasser called on Trotsky, who was living in the Kavalersky Building nearby. The entire file on the Georgian question was placed in his hands, together with all the relevant notes and correspondence. Lenin was staking everything on Trotsky's help. There appears to have been considerable preliminary correspondence between Trotsky and the secretaries, and from time to time this had been read to Lenin, for Gliasser told Trotsky: 'He was more cheerful when he heard the letters we exchanged.' The two secretaries also brought a note from Volodicheva, which had been dictated by Lenin, saying that Kamenev was leaving shortly for Georgia and suggesting that Trotsky might have some message for him. When Trotsky asked whether he had permission to show the documents on the Georgian question to Kamenev, Fotieva said she would first have to consult Lenin, so she went back to Lenin's apartment. It would have been simpler to have telephoned, but by this time everyone seemed to be aware of the danger of wiretapping.

Fotieva returned with the message: 'Absolutely no. Vladimir Ilyich says Kamenev would show the letter to Stalin, who would make a rotten compromise in order later to double-cross us.'

Trotsky was a sick man suffering from lumbago and a variety of disorders brought on by the exhaustions of the civil war, and Lenin was very ill indeed. The two men were plotting from their sickbeds. They were in desperate need of allies, but Kamenev was now dismissed as a potential ally. Trotsky wanted to know more about the implications of the quarrel between Lenin and Stalin, for he apparently knew nothing at that time about Lenin's threat to break off comradely relations with Stalin.

'Does it mean,' Trotsky asked Fotieva, 'that Ilyich does not believe it possible to conclude a compromise with Stalin even along correct lines?'

'Yes,' Fotieva answered. 'Ilyich does not trust Stalin. He wants to come out openly against him before the whole party. He is preparing a bombshell.'

At this point Trotsky seems to have asked for further elucidation, for he records that Fotieva returned to Lenin's apartment and half an hour later brought back a copy of a short letter, dictated to Volodicheva on the previous day. It was addressed to Budu Mdivani and Philipp Makharadze, the two Georgian revolutionaries who had protested against Stalin's high-handed incursions on Georgian politics. It read:

To Comrades Mdivani and Makharadze
Copies for Trotsky and Kamenev
DEAR COMRADES!

I am with you in this matter with all my heart. I am outraged by the arrogance of Ordjonikidze and by the connivance of Stalin and Dzerzhinsky. On your behalf I am now preparing notes and a speech.

With esteem:
LENIN

Trotsky was puzzled to discover that a copy of the letter was being sent to Kamenev. Did this mean that Lenin had altered his opinion of Kamenev? Fotieva explained the changed attitude by Lenin's worsening health.

'His condition is getting worse every hour,' she said. 'You must not believe the reassuring statements of the doctors. He can speak now only with difficulty. The Georgian question worries him terribly. He is afraid he will collapse before he can undertake anything. When he handed this note to me, he said: "Before it is too late ... I am obliged now to come out openly before the proper time!"'

'This means I can talk to Kamenev?' Trotsky interrupted.
'Obviously.'
'Then ask him to come and see me.'

Kamenev arrived at Trotsky's apartment an hour later. He
had been visiting Lenin and talking to Krupskaya about the
letter of apology which they hoped Stalin would write. Volodicheva had been sent with Lenin's letter to Stalin, and they
were waiting anxiously for the reply. About two hours passed.
Lenin was gradually gathering the threads of his conspiracy
against Stalin together. It was beginning to look as though
he was back in harness, and with Trotsky's help he would be
able to overthrow Stalin. But it was not to be. By the time
Volodicheva returned with the letter of apology which Stalin
dictated to her, Lenin had suffered his third stroke. That
afternoon Lenin played his strongest cards, and lost.

The third stroke deprived Lenin of his greatest gift – his
resourcefulness. He could no longer play the role of conspirator extraordinary. Speechless, completely paralysed on his
right side and partially paralysed on his left, he was at the
mercy of his doctors. Yet he seemed indestructible, and he
gradually regained the use of his legs and even learned to
speak a little. In time he understood what was read to him,
and learned to write. But the brain was injured beyond recovery, and during the remaining months of his life he wandered like a ghost through the gardens of Gorki.

Had Lenin's stroke been delayed for a few weeks or a
few days, the history of Russia would have been different.
His last words and last letters spoke of his anguished determination to crush Stalin for the evil he had done, the evil
he would continue to do. He had found his enemy; it was not
the bourgeoisie or the capitalists, but the coarseness and brutality which lay at the heart of the Bolshevik system.

On many occasions during those last troubled weeks Lenin
could have brought his quarrel with Stalin to a crisis. His
mind was not on the present, but on the Congress, which he
continued to believe he would be able to attend. At the
Congress, if he had been well, it would have been a simple
matter to destroy Stalin: he had merely to read the indictment,
and he would have all the members of the Congress agreeing
with him and voting Stalin out of office, or putting him on
trial.

By delaying the attack against Stalin Lenin committed a
fatal error, but the error was compounded by the secretaries,

who were so frightened by the responsibility he had entrusted to them that they decided to work slowly through a voluminous pile of documents, all three of them reading the entire dossier. They hesitated, brooded, and endlessly discussed the steps they should take, while Russia trembled in their hands.

Lenin was fighting Stalin with words, not with actions. At the time of his third stroke he was preparing a comprehensive indictment based on the mountains of evidence which had been sifted by his secretaries. With this indictment he hoped to overthrow Stalin. It was all wasted effort. A simple sharp letter addressed to all the members of the Central Committee might conceivably have brought about Stalin's downfall. In the past Lenin had relied upon such simple solutions, realizing their devastating force. Instead he supervised a report on a report and dictated a series of memoranda directed against Stalin, which rested harmlessly in his secret archive. When the time for action came, it was too late.

THE FIGHT FOR POWER

ON MAY 12TH, 1923, Lenin was carried out of his apartment on a stretcher and driven in an ambulance to Gorki. Except for one brief visit later in the year, he never saw Moscow again.

Although Lenin suffered three strokes in the space of a single year, he proved to be a singularly resilient patient. The indomitable will survived; he refused to break. Each time he was struck down, he rose again. Even after his third stroke, many believed he would resume his place in the government. Years before, speaking with Lunacharsky in Paris, Romain Rolland had said: 'Lenin cannot be broken, he can only be killed . . .'

At first the doctors despaired of his recovery, and the bulletins issued from the Kremlin described a man who had almost exhausted his chances of remaining alive for more than a few days. Yet within a week he was rallying, and on March 22nd the doctors pronounced that he might well recover both his speech and the use of his limbs. They spoke guardedly of a four- or five-month rest in the country, and they added that by the late summer he might be back in harness again.

This tempered optimism was not brought about by political pressure, for the doctors who signed the bulletins included famous specialists imported from Germany and Sweden who had nothing to gain and much to lose by submitting to pressure. They had studied the history of the case, and they were aware that he possessed remarkable reserves of strength.

By the end of July he was hobbling around his bedroom with the help of a cane. He could not talk, but he was giving orders with gestures. He could understand Krupskaya when she read to him, and with her assistance he was already beginning the long and arduous course of instruction which would lead him eventually to write and speak again, though he was never to write more than a few words or to speak more than a few sentences. His favourite word, which he learned very early and used continually, was 'Vot!' It means 'here', but he gave it a wide spectrum of meanings. Later in the year he used the word repeatedly during a lengthy interview with a prominent Communist, who was astonished by the way Lenin was able to convey a wealth of ideas with a single word.

In September Lenin surprised his guards by making his way downstairs by clinging to the banisters. Soon he was walking in the gardens. He refused to be held a prisoner in the palatial house, and made it clear that he was determined to exercise his freedom. He wanted to see no guards around him, and he refused the attentions of some doctors, while approving the attentions of others. When he was walking in the gardens, the officers of the secret police, disguised as woodcutters or gardeners, made themselves scarce, for he had long ago penetrated their disguise. It was the same in the house. He would see only Krupskaya, Maria Ilyinichna, the maidservant Evdokia Smirnova, and a few close intimates. Once while walking in the garden, he caught sight of a doctor, who was observing him. He expressed his anger, and the doctor took care never again to give the impression of spying on him.

All through the autumn Lenin gave the impression of a man actively engaged in the pursuit of health. He put on weight. He spent more and more time in the open air. Sometimes he would invite Dr Rozanov to pick mushrooms with him, and the doctor observed that he had not lost his gift for seeing them ten yards away, when they were invisible to anyone else. He wore spectacles, but his sight was good, thanks largely to Dr Auerbach, the eye specialist, for whom Lenin had a very special regard. On October 9th Molotov announced that the doctors, who had been hesitant to pronounce a verdict, were now unanimously of the opinion that he was well on the road to recovery and only some unforeseen accident would prevent him from returning to work. Molotov also said that the doctors were agreed that he should spend the rest of the year in Gorki. There were no advantages to be gained by sending him to a warmer climate.

While Lenin was recuperating at Gorki, the battle for the succession was being fought halfheartedly. As long as he remained alive, the question of his successor remained largely academic, for his mere existence posed a threat to whoever chose to proclaim himself the inheritor of the crown; and the threat became all the greater as the year advanced and Lenin's rapid recovery became known.

Those who regarded themselves as the successors formed alliances, assumed postures, and made the gestures which they thought were demanded of them. Power was divided among four men: Stalin, Zinoviev, Kamenev, and Trotsky, who as Commissar for War retained his vast influence over the affairs of the nation. It was an unholy alliance, for each member of the quadrumvirate despised or hated the other members. Each had an independent view of the nature of the Communist state and his own role within it. Stalin, Zinoviev and Trotsky were men of overwhelming ambition, who would stop at nothing to occupy the position formerly occupied by Lenin and now in theory occupied by Kamenev, who presided over the Council of Commissars while possessing only a tithe of Lenin's forthrightness, energy and authority.

During the spring and summer of 1923 the battle lines were not yet drawn. The quarrel between Stalin and Trotsky had not yet emerged into the open. There could be heard the rumblings of the coming storm, but there was little to indicate what direction it would take.

Lenin had hoped to destroy Stalin by indicting him for ruthlessly crushing the independence of Soviet Georgia, and in the following months it might have been expected that there would be a stormy confrontation between Stalin and Trotsky acting as the mouthpiece of Lenin. Lenin was outraged by the behaviour of Stalin, Ordjonikidze and Dzerzhinsky, and was prepared to make war against them. Even though ill, he was still a power to be reckoned with. He had never lost a battle, and it was scarcely to be expected he would lose this one.

In fact there was no battle. Trotsky and Kamenev made halfhearted attempts to bring Lenin's views on the 'Georgian question' to the attention of the public, and then permitted themselves to be over-ridden by Stalin. Trotsky's role in the affair was curiously ambiguous, for after he had washed his hands of it, he demanded from Stalin a written declaration that he had acted properly. Not surprisingly Stalin conveniently forgot to provide the certificate of good health.

For more than a month after Lenin's third stroke Trotsky made no effort to open the attack. Kamenev was in the Caucasus, Fotieva was ill, Krupskaya and Maria Ilyinichna were keeping their vigil around Lenin, and Trotsky may have felt a strange uneasiness at the thought of being almost the sole survivor of what was in effect a conspiracy to destroy Stalin. He had the documents in his possession. He could have used them with devastating effect. Instead he quietly sent them back to Lenin's secretariat, presumably hoping that they would be lost without a trace among the documents in Lenin's extensive secret archive.

In all probability nothing at all would have become known about Lenin's implacable war against Stalin if Fotieva, returning to work after a long bout of illness, had not decided to take matters in her own hands. After Krupskaya she was Lenin's closest confidante; she knew his intentions; and she seems to have been outraged that nothing had been done. The documented report on the 'Georgian question', written by the three secretaries, did not have Lenin's authority behind it, even though it was produced under his supervision. Still, there was a weapon closer at hand. This was an article dictated by Lenin during the last days of 1922. The article was entitled 'Concerning the National Question of "Autonomization",' and it contained a blistering attack on Stalin, Ordjonikidze and Dzerzhinsky. Intolerance, brutality, Great Russian chauvinism, and a complete incapacity to understand the needs of the proletariat are listed among their crimes. Stalin, in particular, is singled out as a brutal and arrogant police inspector who is infatuated with his power. Lenin compares him bluntly with Derzhimorda, the coarse policeman in Gogol's *The Inspector General*, and speaks of 'the fatal role played by the haste and administrative impetuousness of Stalin', and of how 'responsibility for this whole truly Great Russian campaign should be placed squarely on the backs of Stalin and Dzerzhinsky'. Ordjonikidze had set himself up as the head of the Georgian government, and for this he, too, must be punished. But the most withering attack on Stalin came in a passage where he is not mentioned by name, but only as 'a Georgian':

A Georgian who treats this side of the matter with frivolity, who frivolously chatters about the charges of 'social nationalism' (while he himself is not only a real and authentic 'social nationalist' but also a brutal Great Russian Derzhimorda), that Georgian actually harms the interests of proletarian class solidarity, because nothing so much impedes the development and strengthening of proletarian class solidarity as national injustice.

Significantly Lenin had detected in Stalin that quality which had been concealed from everyone else – his appalling frivolity.

This was the article which Fotieva with single-minded devotion to Lenin decided to use in the battle against Stalin. On April 16th she telephoned to Kamenev, who had returned from the Caucasus, and described the contents of the article, reminding him that he had known about the existence of the article for some time since, presumably under Lenin's instructions, she had spoken to him about it on December 31st, 1922, the day it was completed. She emphasized that Lenin attached the utmost importance to it. Would he care to read it? She offered to send him the copy preserved in Lenin's secret archive. Kamenev received the article and a covering letter from Fotieva late in the afternoon, and realizing its seriousness immediately wrote a note to the Central Committee urging its publication. He wrote:

Only a moment ago, at 5:35 pm I received the enclosed note from Comrade Fotieva. I am sending this note to the Central Committee because it contains nothing that pertains to me personally. In my opinion the Central Committee should immediately decide affirmatively the question of publishing the article by Vladimir Ilyich.

L. KAMENEV

Kamenev did not enclose the article with his note to the Central Committee. He seems to have thought that the prestige of Lenin's name was sufficient, and the Central Committee would immediately authorize the publication of the article sight unseen. It was a clever manoeuvre, but it did not work. Trotsky had seen a copy of Fotieva's letter to Kamenev, and immediately wrote to Stalin and the Central Committee, enclosing a copy of Lenin's article from his own files. He wrote:

To Comrade Stalin
To all members of the Central Committee

I have today received the enclosed copy of a letter from the personal secretary of Comrade Lenin, Comrade Fotieva, to Comrade Kamenev, concerning an article by Comrade Lenin on the national question.

I had received Comrade Lenin's article of March 5th together with three notes by Comrade Lenin, copies of which are enclosed...

The article is of fundamental importance. It also contains a sharp condemnation of three members of the Central Committee. As long as even a shadow of hope existed that Vladimir Ilyich had left some instructions concerning this article for the Party Congress, for which it was obviously meant, judging by all signs and especially by Comrade Fotieva's note – so long have I avoided mentioning this article.

In the situation which has now arisen – as is also evident from Comrade Fotieva's letter – I have no alternative but to make this article known to the Central Committee members because in my opinion this article has no lesser significance from the viewpoint of party policy on the national question than the former article on the question of the relationship between the proletariat and the peasantry.

If on the basis of motives of an inner party nature, whose significance is self-evident, no Central Committee member will make this article in one form or another known to the Party or to the Party Congress, I, for my part, will consider this as a decision of silence, a decision which – in connection with the Party Congress – removes from me personal responsibility for this article.

L. TROTSKY

The letter was received in Stalin's office at 8:10 pm on April 16th, and for the first time, thanks to Trotsky, Stalin was in a position to read Lenin's article. He knew he must act quickly and decisively to prevent the article from being published. Trotsky himself had indicated the method to be followed by raising the question whether Lenin had left any formal instructions concerning it. Stalin immediately got on the telephone to Fotieva, and in his most threatening and browbeating manner demanded why she was meddling in affairs which did not concern her. He had threatened to put Krupskaya on trial, and now he threatened Fotieva. Her courage, which had been great during the afternoon, now failed her. She could not deny that Lenin had intended to publish the article in connection with the speech he intended to make at the Congress, but she was prepared to admit under Stalin's promptings that it was not in its final form and ready for the printer. She offered to consult Maria Ilyinichna; the offer was accepted. The statement which she drew up after consulting Maria Ilyinichna read:

COMRADE STALIN:

I have today sought the advice of Maria Ilyinichna on the question whether Vladimir Ilyich's article, which was sent to you, should be published because of the fact that Vladimir Ilyich had expressed the intention to publish it in connection with a speech he intended to make at the Congress.

Maria Ilyinichna has expressed the opinion that the article should not be published because Vladimir Ilyich had not issued a clear order concerning its publication; she only grants the possibility of making this article known to delegates at the Congress.

From my own point of view I need add only that Vladimir Ilyich did not consider this article to be in its final form and ready for the printer.

L. FOTIEVA

16 IV 1923
9 o'clock in the evening

With this statement from Fotieva Stalin was able to lay the ghost at least until such time as Lenin recovered. The importance and relevance of Lenin's article, the fact that he had intended to publish it, all these were of no importance. The important thing was that the article was 'not in its final form'. Therefore he refused to permit it to be printed. Within a few minutes of receiving Fotieva's letter, he drew up a statement of his own in which he attacked Trotsky for keeping the article secret for over a month, and pronounced his own verdict on whether it should be published. The statement, which went to all members of the Central Committee, was especially notable for a curious twisting of the knife in the final paragraph:

> The articles of Comrade Lenin are without a doubt of distinct and fundamental significance, but I am greatly surprised that Comrade Trotsky, who had already received them on March 5th of this year, considered it admissible to keep them secret for over a month without making their contents known to the Politburo or the Central Committee plenum until one day before the opening of the Twelfth Congress of the Party. The theme of these articles – as I was informed today by the Congress delegates – is subject to discussion and rumours and stories among the delegates. These articles, as I have learned today, are known to people who have nothing in common with the Central Committee. The Central Committee members themselves must seek information from rumours and gossip, while it is self-evident that the content of these articles should have been reported first of all to the Central Committee.
>
> I think that Comrade Lenin's articles should be published in the press. It is only regrettable that – as is clearly evident from Comrade Fotieva's letter – these articles apparently cannot be published because they have not been reviewed by Comrade Lenin.
>
> J. STALIN
>
> 10 o'clock in the evening

The final paragraph shows the hand of a master. There is something breathtaking in Stalin's neat solution of the problem.

By order of Stalin this statement was sent to all members of the Central Committee, together with the relevant documents. The letter in which Trotsky refused to accept responsibility in the matter so long as members of the Central Committee remained silent was placed first. Then came Lenin's article; then came the two letters of Fotieva to Kamenev and Stalin;

then came Stalin's statement. The arrangement was deliberate. The emphasis now was on Trotsky, not on Lenin. Trotsky had received an important document from Lenin and failed to communicate its contents to the Central Committee. Why? What secret purpose lay behind his refusal to divulge its contents for so long? Trotsky's own explanations were tortuous and unconvincing. The reader coming freshly upon his letter, knowing nothing of what lay behind it, might be excused for believing that Trotsky possessed a guilty secret. If the reader, intrigued, went on to read Lenin's article, he would have noted the virulent attacks on Stalin, Ordjonikidze and Dzerzhinsky, and wondered all the more why Trotsky failed to use the weapon which had been handed to him. Was he afraid of Stalin? Was he preparing a coup? Why the secrecy? When he reached the last document the reader would discover that Stalin had found a formula which effectively disposed of the whole issue.

Trotsky realized he was under attack. The next day he wrote to the members of the Central Committee a reply to Stalin's statement. 'Comrade Lenin's article,' he wrote, 'was sent to me secretly and personally by Comrade Lenin through Comrade Fotieva, and notwithstanding my expressed intention to acquaint the members of the Politburo with the article, Comrade Lenin categorically expressed himself against this through Comrade Fotieva.' So he began, painting himself as the innocent victim of an unhappy conspiracy and hiding behind Fotieva's skirts. He claimed that he knew nothing about the instructions Lenin gave with regard to the article; no doubt there were some instructions, and perhaps Krupskaya, Maria Ilyinichna or the secretaries knew about them. 'I did not deem it proper,' he wrote, 'to question anyone about it for reasons that do not require clarification.' But in fact the reasons did require clarification, and Trotsky knew this better than anyone.

Trotsky went on to claim that when he received the copy of the letter to Kamenev, he immediately telephoned Fotieva and asked her whether Lenin had made any arrangements about the publication of the article. Fotieva, according to Trotsky, said that Lenin had never formally expressed his wishes on the matter. This was the loophole through which Trotsky hoped to escape from his responsibility. As we have seen, Stalin employed the same loophole to prevent the article from being published. Lenin was not in the custom of giving instructions about his articles, because they were published automatically.

'Since Comrade Lenin had not formally expressed his wishes on the matter, it had to be decided on the principle of political feasibility,' Trotsky continued. 'It stands to reason that I could not personally assume responsibility for such a decision and therefore I referred the matter to the Central Committee. I did it without wasting a minute after I learned that Comrade Lenin had not given any direct and formal instructions as to the future fate of the article, the original of which is kept by his secretaries.' He concluded his letter with an acknowledgement that there would inevitably be some who would question his reasoning. 'If anyone thinks I have acted improperly in this affair, I for my part propose that the matter be investigated either by the conflicts commission of the Central Committee or by some special commission. I see no other way.'

There can scarcely have been a more pitiful letter written by a revolutionary leader. His defence was no defence; with every succeeding paragraph he showed himself in a worse light. The task which Lenin had imposed upon him had proved to be beyond his strength, and he was now desperately seeking for a compromise. Speaking about Kamenev, Lenin had said there was a danger that he would make 'a rotten compromise' with Stalin. Trotsky, not Kamenev, made 'a rotten compromise'.

Stalin, however, was not yet in a mood to accept Trotsky's interpretation of the affair. On the same day that Trotsky wrote his letter to the Central Committee, he went to see Stalin. Trotsky asked for a formal declaration substantiating his claim that he had acted in the best interests of the party. For Stalin it was a moment of exquisite triumph. He had cunningly prepared the pit, and Trotsky was falling headlong into it. He spoke approvingly of Trotsky's actions, and promised to draw up a declaration to the effect that Trotsky was not compromised in any way. The declaration would be drawn up immediately and circulated among members of the Central Committee. Trotsky left Stalin with the feeling that he had won a powerful ally, and the whole unhappy incident could now be forgotten. He was asking for a formal acknowledgement of his obliging innocence. Revolutionary ardour had been exchanged for polite formalities.

That interview, which took place on April 17th, 1923, was

to have incalculable consequences. The stage was now set for
the coming battle between Stalin and Trotsky. Within forty
days of Lenin's third stroke Stalin was sowing the dragons'
teeth and Trotsky was running for cover.

In his struggle for power Stalin showed that he would
employ any weapon, even the most unscrupulous, in order to
achieve his aims. Ironically, he was able to use the weapon
intended to destroy him and to turn it against Trotsky.

When by eleven o'clock the next morning Trotsky learned
that the promised bill of health had failed to arrive, he seems
to have realized that he had overplayed his hand. In a desperate effort to mend matters, he wrote off an extraordinary
letter to Stalin, imploring him to write the formal declaration
and threatening to appeal to the conflicts commission of the
Central Committee if it was not received by the end of the
day. It is a timid, crude, and vacillating letter, and it should
be quoted at length because it reveals Trotsky at the beginning of his long struggle with Stalin as a suppliant:

COMRADE STALIN:

Yesterday in personal conversation with me you said it
was perfectly clear to you that in the matter of Comrade
Lenin's article I did not act improperly and that you will
formulate a written declaration to that effect.

Until this morning (11 o'clock) I have not received such
a declaration. It is possible that you were delayed by your
report of yesterday.

In any event your first declaration remains until the
present moment unrepudiated by you and gives certain comrades a justification for spreading a corresponding version
among certain of the delegates.

Since I cannot permit even the shadow of vagueness in
this matter – for reasons which, of course, you have no
difficulty in understanding – I deem it necessary to expedite
its termination. If in reply to this note I do not receive
from you a communication to the effect that in the course
of today you will send to all members of the Central Committee a declaration that would exclude the possibility of
any sort of equivocalness in this matter, then I shall conclude that you have changed your intention of yesterday
and I will appeal to the conflicts commission, requesting an
investigation from beginning to end.

You can understand and appreciate better than anyone

else that if I have not done this so far, it was not because it could have hurt my interests in any way.

April 18th, 1923

In writing this letter Trotsky was well aware that his interests had been hurt. He was known to have been in possession of a compromising document, and as soon as possible he had thrust the document away from him. Stalin had nothing to gain by granting Trotsky a clean bill of health; he had much to gain by silence. It may have amused him that the great Commissar for War, who had brought the Soviet armies to victory, was begging for a scrap of paper with his signature, but if so, it was a wry amusement. He had won the first round in the battle for the succession.

Meanwhile he had more important things to do than listen to Trotsky's whining. The Twelfth Congress of the Russian Communist Party was in session, and on the day following the receipt of Trotsky's letter he addressed himself to the 'Georgian question', secure in the knowledge that none of the delegates except Trotsky, Mdivani and Makharadze knew that Lenin had intended to address the Congress from a very different point of view. Stalin laughed the 'Georgian question' out of existence. There was really no 'Georgian question' at all, for everything had happened in accordance with decisions properly arrived at in the Central Committee, which had in all matters followed the instructions of Lenin. Why was Mdivani continuing to oppose federation? Such untoward behaviour could only mean that he was contemptuous of the Central Committee's decisions. The Central Committee had quite properly recalled him, and now in defeat he was claiming to be the victor. With heavy scorn Stalin asked what kind of victory it was which ended in defeat? He said:

Mdivani will have us believe that in spite of being recalled, he has won a victory. In that case I do not know what defeat is. I suppose you know that Don Quixote of blessed memory also regarded himself as a victor when he was tossed head over heels by the sails of a windmill. I think that there are certain comrades working in a certain corner of Soviet territory known as Georgia who have bats in their belfries.

I pass on to Comrade Makharadze. He declared here that he is an Old Bolshevik in the national question, of the school of Lenin. That is not true, comrades. In April 1917

I and Comrade Lenin made war against Comrade Makharadze at a conference. At that time he was against the
self-determination of nations, against our fundamental programme, against the right of nations to exist as independent
states. From this point of view he fought against the party.
Later he changed his opinion (that is certainly to his credit),
but all the same he should not have forgotten it! He is
really not an Old Bolshevik on the national question, but
only a more or less young one.

In this way, with innuendoes, counter-accusations, and vitu-
peration, Stalin attacked Mdivani and Makharadze as
though they were a couple of clowns who had presented themselves at the Congress when they would be better occupied at
the circus. Whom did they represent? No one except themselves. Who gave them the right to speak for Georgia? No
one. When they proclaimed that the regime in Georgia lacked
any kind of freedom and was intolerable to live under, he
asked them to produce documents which would prove that
anyone had in any way limited the freedom of the Georgians,
and he went on to demand that they should be more explicit
about the word 'regime'. What regime were they talking about
– the ancient regime of the corrupt aristocracy, or the new
regime instituted by the Soviets? Two commissions had been
sent down to investigate, the first headed by Dzerzhinsky, the
second by Kamenev. 'Of course,' Stalin commented, 'there is
nothing to prevent us from sending down a third commission,'
and with that he concluded his examination of the 'Georgian
question'. He had won the first round against Trotsky, and he
had won the first round against Mdivani and Makharadze.
Only a month and a few days had passed since Lenin had
had his third stroke.
Stalin dominated the Twelfth Congress by the sheer weight
of his invective. He had the backing of Dzerzhinsky and the
Cheka. He quoted Lenin constantly, and in the process of
quotation he was usually able to traduce Lenin's meaning.
Lenin had spoken of a crash which was bound to occur because the state was floundering in a morass of bureaucracy.
Lenin had been speaking of the bureaucracy on the highest
levels, but Stalin significantly chose to believe that he was
speaking about minor officials who were feathering their nests
while the rest of the country starved. There was nothing
wrong, according to Stalin, in the state apparatus; the policy

was correct, the leader – presumably he meant himself – was behaving according to all the proper principles, but somewhere down the line there were hesitations, distortions, disobedience. 'The state apparatus is of the right kind, but its component parts are still alien to us, bureaucratic, half Tsarist-bourgeois.' So perhaps they were, but a vast and increasing number of the component parts were his own appointees. That invincible belief in the implicit rightness of the state apparatus and the intolerable obtuseness of its component parts was to accompany him throughout his life, and it never seems to have occurred to him that the state apparatus and its component parts were one and the same.

When one of the delegates rose to demand free speech, a democratic regime and freedom from arbitrary arrest, Stalin had a field day. He said it was absurd and beyond belief that anyone should be so ignorant, or so innocent, as to believe that a revolutionary party should subject itself to all the hazards of free speech. What was there to speak about? Did the delegate seriously believe that important matters should be discussed and debated by every one of the 400,000 members of the party? 'The party would be transformed into a debating society with everyone eternally talking and deciding nothing,' he declared. 'Above all, the party must be a party of action, for we are in power.' He left it to be understood that action and debate necessarily negated one another, and that 'we' meant Stalin.

A few weeks later Stalin ordered the arrest of the Tatar Communist Mirza Sultan Galiyev, chairman of the Tatar Council of People's Commissars, on the grounds that he was aiming to build up a separate Tatar state and had been in secret correspondence with Kemal Ataturk. Kamenev and Zinoviev gave their assent to the arrest when evidence from his intercepted mail was shown to them. Stalin wanted to have Sultan Galiyev shot, but the question of his execution was deferred, and he was not shot until 1929. Kamenev and Zinoviev were perfectly aware of the significance of the arrest. For the first time a high Communist official was being thrown into the Lubyanka. In time it was to become the general fate of high Communist officials to vanish in this way, but in those early days it was a matter of sufficient rarity to cause comment. 'With the arrest of Sultan Galiyev,' Kamenev said later, 'Stalin for the first time tasted blood.' But Kamenev did not speak as an innocent man; he spoke as one who had himself signed the order of arrest and was therefore compromised.

It was a pattern to be repeated endlessly in the following years, as Stalin sharpened his weapons. The Politburo was obedient to him, because it was compromised by him. Guilt was spread so wide that all shared it; and when at last Stalin turned on the Politburo, he could rid himself more easily of them because he had corrupted them.

Already, long before Lenin's death, Stalin was climbing towards a position of supreme power. Zinoviev, Kamenev, Bukharin and many others realized that they were threatened. In September, when Zinoviev and Bukharin were taking their holiday in the watering place of Kislovodsk, they discussed what could be done. Voroshilov and Ordjonikidze were taking their holiday at Rostov, and were invited to join the open conspiracy. Kamenev, Rudzutak, Lashevich and Evdokimov were also invited. For safety's sake it was decided to hold the conference in one of the famous caves near Kislovodsk called 'the Cave of the Dead Mule'.

There, sitting on the damp rock, in the half-darkness, they debated what Zinoviev called 'the balance of power'. They saw power slipping from their hands and they hoped in some mysterious way to restore it. Power now rested in the Secretariat of the Central Committee, and most especially in the General Secretary. To broaden the basis of power, they suggested that a new political organization should be introduced with Zinoviev, Trotsky and Stalin possessing more or less equal powers, and there was some talk of asking Stalin to resign. Voroshilov, who was taking careful notes, said later that he viewed the meeting in the cave as a conference of conspirators which could only lead 'to harm and fiasco'. But the problems were urgent, and it was decided to invite Stalin to the conference. Ordjonikidze was deputed to send off an explanatory telegram. Stalin replied: 'I have other things to do beside chattering with a bunch of nincompoops.' This reply was not final, for some days later Stalin arrived at Kislovodsk, determined to rout the cave dwellers and to show who was master of the situation. What he objected to, as he explained two years later at the Fourteenth Congress, was the extraordinary effrontery of the cave dwellers. He said:

They wanted to abolish the Politburo and to transform

the Secretariat into a political and organizational body consisting of Zinoviev, Trotsky and Stalin. What was the meaning of this platform? It meant that the party was to be led without Rykov, without Kalinin, without Tomsky, without Molotov, without Bukharin. The platform came to nothing, not only because it did not represent any principles, but also because the party cannot be led at the present time without the comrades I have mentioned. To a question sent to me in writing from the depths of Kislovodsk, I refused to have anything to do with the scheme, and said that, if the comrades desired, I was ready to retire from the scene, quite quietly, without open or hidden discussion, and without making any demands for the protection of 'the rights of minorities'.

But that was Stalin speaking long after the event, when his memory of 'the meeting of the troglodytes' was clouded by the knowledge that he had already successfully outmanoeuvred them. When he offered to resign, he was in fact taunting them; and when he suggested that the party could not be led by Zinoviev, Trotsky and Stalin alone, because that would mean depriving it of the best brains available, he was taunting them even more derisively. Nothing came of the conference at Kislovodsk. The powers of the General Secretary remained unchanged, and the conspirators returned to Moscow, baffled and empty-handed.

Stalin stood alone, above all the tribes of commissars, content to wield power as he saw fit. No one dared to oppose him, though many made ineffectual gestures of opposition. Already he had acquired the authority formerly possessed by Lenin. He had taken possession of the machinery of state; he had his own men in all the administrative posts; he was chief of state, and his word was law. Sometimes he would turn anxious eyes in the direction of Gorki, for Lenin, recovering from his third stroke, was the only man who had the authority to remove him.

'I was ready to retire from the scene, quite quietly, without open or hidden discussion,' Stalin said, and these words, in that strange language he had invented, meant: 'I will destroy anyone who gets in my way.'

THE DEATH OF LENIN

DURING THE AUTUMN of 1923 Lenin's health began to show a marked improvement. He spent more and more time in the open air, studied speech and writing more diligently, and showed an astonishing capacity to make his wishes understood. His cheeks filled out, the colour came back to his face, the haggard look was gone. The doctors were saying he would recover; in six months he might be back in the Kremlin.

In August Dr Rozanov, noting Lenin's improvement, decided to take a month's holiday. On his return at the beginning of September he found that his patient had improved beyond all expectation. He was livelier, happier, more tolerant. The weak leg had grown stronger and he was able to walk more easily with the aid of orthopaedic boots. He did not look like an invalid; he was always breaking out into laughter. Of one of his visits Dr Rozanov wrote: 'He invited us to stay for dinner, and while at table he continued to take part in the conversation, employing, it is true, a vocabulary which was still limited, but one which we had nevertheless learned to understand. When I visited him, he was always gay.'

Dr Rozanov observed one cloud on the horizon: Lenin was troubled by the presence of the male nurses. Since the nurses were members of the secret police, it was not unreasonable that Lenin should dislike to have them hovering around him. Slightly more perplexing was his sudden antipathy to the German neurologist, Dr Otfried Foerster, with whom he had hitherto been on very cordial terms. They usually joked when they met. Now, whenever he caught sight of the doctor, Lenin would suffer almost a nervous crisis. 'When autumn came,' says Dr Rozanov, 'Lenin refused to have anything to do with Dr Foerster, and if by chance he caught sight of the doctor he would become wildly irritable. In the end there was nothing for the doctor to do but to prescribe treatment based on the observations of those who were around the patient.'

Yet there was perhaps nothing remarkable for the sudden dislike of the German doctor, and the explanation was clearly stated in a letter written by Maria Ilyinichna to Dr Rozanov in mid-August. She wrote that Lenin was improving day by day, he was learning to speak and was so impatient with his speech lessons that he had to be held back, and in her view there was no longer any necessity for continual surveillance. In September the nurses were ordered to keep out of sight.

An extraordinary event occurred in October. Quite suddenly Lenin decided to return to Moscow. He had sometimes spoken of going to Moscow before, saying he was lonely when Krupskaya and Maria Ilyinichna made their weekly visits to the city, but he was always prevailed upon to remain behind.

On that day in mid-October* Lenin had obviously made up his mind to accompany his wife and sister to Moscow. He ate his lunch quickly, put on his fur cap, and explained that he was not going to be left behind. Because he was so agitated, Dr Osipov was called in, but the moment the doctor appeared Lenin became so infuriated by his presence that it was thought best to leave him alone. The moment the doctor left the room, Lenin made his way to the garage and climbed into the Rolls-Royce. The chauffeur was already in the car. Lenin made it clear that he was going to Moscow, and when Krupskaya and Maria Ilyinichna reached the garage his mood was inflexible. There was a brief discussion, and finally it was agreed that there was no harm in permitting him to make the journey. In the Rolls-Royce were Lenin, Krupskaya, Maria Ilyinichna, and the chauffeur. Pyotr Pakaln, the chief of the GPU guards at Gorki, also went with them. In the following car came a number of guards, Dr Osipov, and the doctor's

* There is some mystery about the exact date of the journey. Alexander Belmas, the GPU guard, says it took place 'one day in October'. The authoritative *Lenin v Kremle* gives the eighteenth. The official chronology in the early editions of the *Sochineniya* gives the tenth, but the latest edition of the *Sochineniya* says that he left on the eighteenth and returned the next day. Fotieva, who is usually accurate about dates, had already said he spent the night at the flat and drove back on the nineteenth, and the current official version would seem to rely on Fotieva's statement. The story about Lenin's discovery that the drawer was rifled is given by Valentinov in his unpublished memoirs, now in the Russian Archives, Columbia University. In discussing the journey I have followed the account given by Dr V. N. Osipov in a speech entitled 'On Some Character Traits of V. I. Lenin at the Time of His Illness', delivered in Leningrad on the third anniversary of Lenin's death. The speech was subsequently printed in *Krasnaya Letopis*, No. 2 (23), 1927, pp. 237–246. Dr Osipov gives the date of the journey to Moscow as the twenty-first.

brother. On the way they met Dr Rozanov, and Lenin ordered the car to be stopped to pick him up.

It was past three o'clock when they left Gorki, and it was already growing dark when they reached Moscow. He spent the night in his own apartment, and the next morning he decided to drive through the streets of Moscow and visit the agricultural exhibition, where he was recognized and saluted passers-by by doffing his cap. He spent some time in his study, choosing books from the shelves, and sitting at his desk. There is a story, told by Valentinov, that when he opened a secret drawer in his desk, he discovered that it had been rifled, and was so appalled that he broke down in tears. Later in the day the two cars returned to Gorki. According to Dr Osipov he never showed the least desire to go to Moscow again.

A few days later, towards the end of October, an old friend Ossip Piatnitsky, veteran of many early struggles, came to visit him, with a small group which included the Old Bolshevik Dr Boris Weissbrod and Ivan Skvortsov, the theoretician. Krupskaya was present, and so were both of Lenin's sisters. Lenin was in a good mood. 'I saw the same face, the same wonderfully intelligent eyes, the same smile which I had seen hundreds of times before,' Piatnitsky reported later. He noted that Lenin had some difficulty in speaking, and when Skvortsov spoke about the recent Moscow elections, he seemed listless, but he listened intently to a discussion of the new street lighting in the poorer sections of Moscow and the extension of the streetcar system. When Piatnitsky, who was a member of the executive committee of the Communist International, spoke about disagreements in the Italian and British Communist parties, then again Lenin was listless, but when they spoke about the revolutionary situation in Germany Lenin was suddenly wide awake. 'It seemed to me,' Piatnitsky wrote, 'that I was in his office and he was listening to a report on the situation of the German working class, and from the expression of his face, his remarks and his total absorption in the subject, it was clear that he was showing a lively interest.'

A few days later, on November 2nd, he met for the last time with a delegation of workers. They came from Glukhovo, a small town near Arzamas, and they had brought with them a gift of eighteen cherry trees to be planted in the conservatory at Gorki. According to Pelageya Kholodova, one of the women workers, Lenin greeted them with the words: 'How glad I am that you have come,' but it is possible that he merely sketched out the sentence, filling out the gaps with gestures. It was an emotional meeting. They all kissed him, and the last to leave, a sixty-year-old worker, threw his arms around him and said through his tears: 'Yes, Vladimir Il-yich, I'm a toiling blacksmith. I'll forge all you want! ...' For two minutes they clung to one another, and then the small delegation watched him leave the room. Invited to stay over-night they learned the next morning from Maria Ilyinichna that Lenin was particularly pleased with the illuminated scroll they had given him and read it over and over again.

January 7th, 1924, was Christmas Day according to the calendar of the Greek Orthodox Church. All the neighbour-ing children were invited to a Christmas party, which was held in the palatial living-room. The Christmas tree was loa-ded with presents. When Lenin came in, the children were running about merrily; he looked pleased and happy, per-mitted some of them to sit on his knee and helped to give out the Christmas presents.

About a week later Zinoviev, Kamenev and Bukharin paid a short visit to Gorki. They saw him walking in the park. He was in good humour, and they were especially struck by the sweetness of his smile. 'Everything is going well with us,' Krupskaya said. 'He went out hunting, but wouldn't take me with him – he said he didn't want a nurse. His studies and his reading go on well. He is in good heart, cracks jokes, and laughs uproariously.'

While Lenin gave the impression of a man quickly recover-ing his health, Trotsky's repeated illnesses had become a mat-ter of concern to his physicians. He was suffering from what he called 'a dogged, mysterious infection' which he was un-able to shake off. The infection followed a cold he had caught after slipping into some icy water in October. He was examined by the Kremlin doctors on December 21st. Their report mentions influenza, catarrh in the upper respiratory organs, enlargement of the bronchial glands, persistent fever, loss of weight and appetite. For some reason the report was not published in *Pravda* until January 8th. By that time all arrangements had been made for him to take a prolonged vacation in the Caucasus. Ten days later he set off on the slow journey to the south.

On the previous day, at the Thirteenth Party Conference

called to prepare the groundwork for the Congress which would be held in the spring, Stalin delivered a vitriolic attack on Trotsky, listing his 'errors', the gravest of them being his resolute determination to ignore the will of the party. There were six 'errors'; one would have been enough to hang him. Trotsky was presumptuous, he was continually demanding that the voices of the students should be heard, he was attempting to split the party from the apparatus, and he was proclaiming the freedom of groups within the party. Having described Trotsky as a traitor to the cause, Stalin thereupon read a secret clause, which had been adopted on Lenin's proposal, at the Tenth Party Congress. This secret clause threatened expulsion to members of the Central Committee who violate party discipline or indulge in factionalism. Stalin had many weapons with which to destroy his enemies, but this was one of the few which had been prepared for him by Lenin. For the moment he held the weapon in reserve. The resolution of the conference affirmed that the party was more closely united than ever before, and threatened political destruction on 'anyone who makes an attempt upon the unity of the party ranks'.

A full account of the conference was published in *Pravda*. Krupskaya, following her custom, read it to Lenin. 'When I read it to him on January 19th,' she wrote later, 'he was very disturbed. I told him that the resolution had been reached unanimously. I read the resolution to him again the next day, and Vladimir Ilyich listened attentively, and sometimes asked questions.'

Lenin had every reason to be disturbed by the resolution, for it was directed as much against himself as against Trotsky. Lenin could have derived no comfort from the resolution, which had been passed unanimously, for with that resolution Stalin proclaimed that anyone who opposed him would be destroyed.

For days a storm had been hovering over Gorki, but on that January 19th the weather turned clear. Muffled up against the cold, Lenin went for a drive in a sleigh, propped up with pillows. Bukharin was with him, and when a young retriever brought back a bird and laid it at Bukharin's feet, Lenin said: '*Vot sobaka*' – meaning 'Look at the dog', or 'What a good dog it is!' When he returned for lunch, he is said to have spoken a good deal about a young hound which was nervous and untrained but showed remarkable aptitude. 'She is all right,' he is supposed to have said, 'if you give her time and do not hustle her too much. She is young and stupid still and over-eager, but she will learn if you give her time.' Such, at any rate, was the semi-official report given out by the Soviet Foreign Office and reported by Walter Duranty. With a mixture of words and gestures, he could say quite complicated things, and he may very well have said something like this.

In the evening Krupskaya read to him. From the well-stocked library at Gorki, which amounted to three thousand volumes, she chose one of his favourite authors, Jack London. She read from the paperback German Tauchnitz edition. The story she chose to read was a surprising one, a tale of harsh and unrelieved suffering. It is not the kind of story one reads to a man who is ill. Three years later she wrote:

> Two days before his death I read to him in the evening Jack London's *Love of Life* – the book is still lying on the table in his room. It is a very strong story. Across a wilderness of ice, where no human being has set foot, a sick man, dying of hunger, is making for the harbour of a big river. His strength is giving out, he cannot walk but keeps slipping, and beside him there glides a wolf, also dying of hunger, and they fight together, and the man wins – half dead, half demented, he reaches his goal. Ilyich was extraordinarily pleased with the story.
>
> The following day he asked me to read him more Jack London stories. His strong stories, though, are mingled in a quite extraordinary manner with feeble ones. The next story happened to have quite a different character – saturated with bourgeois morality. A ship's captain promises the owner he will sell his cargo of grain at a good price, and sacrifices his life in order to keep his word. Ilyich laughed and dismissed it with a wave of his hand.
>
> That was the last time I read to him.

Jack London's *Love of Life* is a terrifying story, the climax coming when the dying man hurls himself on the famished wolf, kills it, and drinks its blood. Then, with renewed energy, he makes his way blindly over the ice, and at last is seen by the crew of a whaleboat. 'They saw something which was alive but which could hardly be called a man. It was blind, unconscious. It squirmed across the ground like some monstrous worm. Most of its efforts were ineffectual, but it was persistent, and it writhed and twisted and went ahead perhaps a score of feet an hour.'

Presumably Krupskaya chose this story in order to instill courage in him after the misery of reading the resolution at the Thirteenth Conference. Krupskaya and Lenin, the two old revolutionaries, were not in a happy mood that evening, for too many ominous shadows were present in the room.

Some time after supper, at about eight o'clock in the evening, Lenin complained of a sharp pain in the eyes. Alarmed, Maria Ilyinichna telephoned the famous eye specialist, Dr Michael Auerbach, in Moscow. He reached Gorki by ten o'clock, and was a little surprised to discover five doctors, Foerster, Guetier, Rozanov, Kramer and Osipov keeping vigil outside Lenin's rooms. 'Lenin led me into his study with extraordinary good humour,' Dr Auerbach reported a few days later, 'and showed great solicitude for me.' His eyes still hurt him, and the doctor examined them, but found nothing wrong. He came to the conclusion that Lenin must have accidentally touched his eyeballs with his hands while making gestures, and that the pain would soon pass away.

According to Dr Auerbach, Lenin was in high spirits, and talked a good deal. Lenin was especially anxious that the doctor should stay the night, because a storm might spring up and it was bitterly cold; and when the doctor said he would have to see patients early the next morning and must return to Moscow immediately, Lenin begged him to wrap himself up well. They shook hands, and the doctor took his leave. He could not have guessed that Lenin had only a few more hours to live.

The next morning Lenin rose late. He was listless, and slept much of the day, but there was nothing particularly strange in this. When a friend asked about Lenin's health during the morning, Maria Ilyinichna said: 'He's sleeping now. There's one thing quite certain – he's going to be completely cured by the summer.' He drank some tea during the morning, took a little lunch, and returned to bed. At six o'clock in the evening some servants listening outside the door heard him breathing with difficulty. Dr Foerster, who was on duty, was immediately summoned. Because Lenin was still conscious and because he could not bear the sight of the doctors in his room, Dr Foerster hid behind a screen, ready to give whispered advice, but soon the breathing became more regular and he left the room, only to be summoned back a few minutes later. Lenin was breathing with difficulty again. Two other doctors – Elistratov and Osipov – were summoned. Convulsions set in. By half past six it became evident that only a miracle could save him. He died at 6:50 pm, having been violently ill for less than an hour.

At eleven o'clock the next morning an autopsy was conducted on the body. Nine doctors attended the autopsy, which was not completed until nearly four o'clock in the afternoon. They produced a voluminous report arriving at the simple conclusion that he died of 'disseminated vascular arteriosclerosis'. A week later Dr Weissbrod, who had attended the autopsy, wrote in *Pravda*: 'We are not yet in a position to collect all details now and to integrate all information about Lenin's disease.' He seemed to be hinting broadly that he was not satisfied with the autopsy report. Many others were dissatisfied with the report. Over the years Communists who had known Lenin would come together and discuss in whispers the strange rumour that he had been poisoned by Stalin.

There are many mysteries about Lenin's death, and one of the most mysterious is the autopsy report, with its curious omissions and inadequacies. The brain is described at considerable length, and is shown to have been in a state of complete sclerotic decay. Semashko, the Commissar of Public Health, who was present at the autopsy, reported that the doctors were thunderstruck to discover that the blood vessels of the brain were calcified and metal instruments touching the brain gave off a ringing sound. It is inconceivable that Lenin should have shown a continuing improvement of health during many months, and walked and talked the day before his death, if his brain was so calcified. Throughout the autopsy report the emphasis is on sclerosis. Dr Rozanov in his memoirs says that the autopsy revealed 'sclerosis of the vessels of the brain, *only sclerosis*', and for some reason the words are italicized. Dr Weissbrod wrote later that sclerosis had reached into the abdomen, a detail not mentioned in the autopsy report. There is no explanation why the autopsy was begun so late. More than sixteen hours passed between the time of Lenin's death and the beginning of the autopsy.

There was no toxicological examination, no description of the contents of the stomach. 'The stomach is empty. Its walls are collapsed,' reads the report, although completely empty stomachs are rarely found in autopsies, and it is known that

Lenin took two small meals during the day. The report mentions irregularities in the spleen and liver, without going into detail. In general the doctors avoided a discussion of all the organs where traces of poison might be found. They made no examination of the blood.

Throughout, the autopsy report gives the impression of being a contrived document, deliberately intended to show that the main cause of death was sclerosis, 'only sclerosis'. It was not a difficult verdict to reach on the basis of Lenin's medical history, but whether he actually died of 'disseminated vascular arteriosclerosis' is another matter. A man may have cancer and die by falling off a roof. If the doctors reported that he died of cancer, it could only mean that they had failed to observe the cracked skull.

Until the publication of the memoirs of Alexander Belmas, the GPU guard attached to the security forces at Gorki, it was almost impossible to come to any conclusions about Lenin's death. It was widely rumoured that he was poisoned, but rumours are not evidence. Belmas provided the evidence that something went hopelessly wrong at Gorki by describing the last three days of Lenin's life in a manner at variance with the reports of all the others who saw Lenin at that time. He says that Lenin was desperately ill during those three days, that they kept a constant vigil, and that telephones were continually ringing as people called to ask about Lenin's health. Belmas wrote in his diary:

19th January. Nadezhda Konstantinovna and Maria Ilyinichna took up an uninterrupted vigil by the bedside of Ilyich. The telephone kept ringing. Calls were coming in from the Central Committee, the Sovnarkom and GPU, all asking about the health of Lenin. We were all anxious and silent. Only Maria Ilyinichna went about reproving anyone who made a noise; she complained about the telephone and the noise we made with our feet. I took off my felt boots, so that they would make no noise.

20th January. About one o'clock at night Lenin became unconscious. Everyone was stricken with grief. People came from the Central Committee, and with them came all Lenin's doctors. Kramer, Foerster, Rozanov, Obukh, Guetier, Semashko were all there. While they were discussing what to do, the attack came to an end, but Lenin remained weak. He had eaten nothing since the previous day.

21st January. Telephone ringing, everyone fearfully calling up about Lenin's health. The doctors have not left him, and there are two others, his wife and his sister, who have maintained the vigil for the third day.

The memoirs of Belmas were first published in the *Istorichesky Arkhiv* (Historical Archive) in 1958, and caused little comment. It was just one more of the many accounts of Lenin's last days. At the time no one realized that this account differs from all the others in many remarkable respects, and most of all in describing the atmosphere of doom in the house as Lenin fights for his life over a period of three days. All other observers found Lenin remarkably tranquil and healthy during two of these days. If Belmas is telling the truth, the others are lying.

Now, there exists a considerable body of detailed evidence about Lenin's last days. Semashko, Rozanov, Weissbrod, and Auerbach have all left records; they were skilled professional men, and their accounts fit into a discernible pattern. Vladimir Sorin, a high party official from Moscow, who was staying in a nearby cottage, relates the events of these days at considerable length, and his testimony fits into the same pattern. Krupskaya, too, tells a completely credible story about a man who is rapidly regaining his health, who understands everything that is said to him, and whose speech shows remarkable progress. She reads him the stories of Jack London, he goes out on a sleigh, and is distressed by the news from the Thirteenth Congress, but is otherwise cheerful and in good spirits, at a time when, according to Belmas, he is hovering between life and death.

All we know of Alexander Belmas is that he was a Latvian, twenty-five years old, who had joined the party in 1920 and fought in the civil war. In the autumn of 1922 he was attached to Lenin's personal guard, and he remained a member of the guard until Lenin's death.

Although Belmas was a member of the security forces at Gorki, it does not follow that he knew what was happening. There were between thirty and forty guards on the establishment, some disguised as gardeners and carpenters, others as medical orderlies. Lenin would have nothing to do with them, and they took care not to be seen by him. They were not allowed upstairs, and were never permitted to enter Lenin's private apartments. What scraps of information they possessed must have come from the doctors or from Maria Ilyinichna and Krupskaya. For most of the time Lenin lived quietly in his bedroom or his study. He lived with his family in an enclosed world, in one of the wings of the house, as far from the guards as possible. Belmas therefore was one of those who watched from a distance, and he could very easily have been wrong. He thought Lenin was ill and dying, when those who were closer to Lenin thought he was well on the road to recovery.

If we imagine that Stalin gave orders to poison Lenin, then we would expect him to consult with Pakaln, the head of the security forces at Gorki, and with Yagoda, the chief of the toxicological laboratory attached to the Kremlin. He would consult, too, with the doctors – not all of them, but those he regarded as most useful and sympathetic to him. The most useful, if he could be suborned, was the sixty-one-year-old Fyodor Alexandrovich Guetier, Lenin's family physician. Guetier was also the family physician of Trotsky. He was a mild-mannered man of great charm and considerable talent, the founder and senior physician of the Botkinsky Hospital. When the Soviet government was first installed in Moscow, he was placed in charge of the medical and sanitary facilities of the Kremlin. Lenin trusted him implicitly. Guetier was the last person anyone would suspect to be implicated in the murder of Lenin. Nevertheless it is possible that he had something to do with Lenin's death.

The name of Fyodor Alexandrovich Guetier appears briefly in an account of Lenin's last hours published by Yves Delbars under the title *Le Vrai Staline* in 1951. Delbars was in close contact with emigrés from the Soviet Union, including an un-named member of Stalin's secretariat, who was probably Bazhanov. Grigory Kanner was also a member of the secretariat. This is the story told by Delbars:

On January 20th, 1924 Kanner saw Yagoda enter Stalin's office, accompanied by two of the physicians who were attending Lenin. 'Fyodor Alexandrovich,' said Stalin to one of these physicians, 'you must go at once to Gorki, for an urgent consultation in respect of Vladimir Ilyich. Genrick Grigorievich [Yagoda] will accompany you.'

That same evening Kanner, who was in and out of the

room, overheard a few snatches of conversation between Stalin and Yagoda. 'There will soon be another attack. The symptoms are there. He has written a few lines (Kanner saw a few lines in Lenin's distorted handwriting) to thank you for sending him a means of deliverance. He is terribly distressed by the thought of a fresh attack...'

On January 21st, 1924 the fatal attack developed. It was terrible, but it did not last long. Krupskaya left the room for a moment in order to telephone. When she returned Lenin was dead. On his bed-table were several small bottles – empty. At a quarter past seven the telephone rang in Stalin's office. Yagoda announced that Lenin was dead.

It is not necessary to believe the entire story, as related by Delbars. It reads like a story told at second or third hand, where the salient facts may be correct while some of the details have the air of improvisation. Kanner cannot be asked to confirm the story, for he was executed in the purges.

In 1955, more than thirty years after Lenin's death, there appeared for the first time a circumstantial account of Lenin's death by poison in Elizabeth Lermolo's book, *Face of a Victim*. A state prisoner, she was kept in solitary confinement, but occasionally she found means of talking with other state prisoners, and these conversations as reported in her book are exceptionally convincing. In one of her prisons she met an Old Bolshevik, Gavril Volkov, who claimed that he had been in charge of the kitchens at Gorki and had taken Lenin his second breakfast on the morning of his death. Here she tells his story:

And then on January 21st, 1924 ... At eleven in the morning, as usual, Volkov took Lenin his second breakfast. There was no one in his room. As soon as Volkov appeared, Lenin made an effort to rise and extended both his hands, uttering unintelligible sounds. Volkov rushed over to him and Lenin slipped a note into his hands.

As Volkov turned, having hidden the note, Dr Elistratov, Lenin's personal physician, ran into the room, apparently having been attracted by the commotion. The two of them got Lenin back to bed and gave him an injection to calm him. Lenin quieted down, his eyes half closed. He never opened them again.

The note scratched in a nervous scrawl, read : 'Gavrilushka, I've been poisoned ... go fetch Nadya at once ... tell Trotsky ... tell everyone you can.'

Elizabeth Lermolo describes her life in the 'isolators' without embroidery and without straining for effect. Much that she has to relate was confirmed by Khrushchev in his speech at the Twentieth Congress three years after the publication of her book. We can trust her to report accurately what she heard.

It would seem to be beyond dispute that the different clues we have been following all lead to the same conclusion. Stalin had good reason to rid himself of Lenin, who was rapidly recovering his health. He therefore decided to strike before he was himself struck down. The official government announcement published in *Izvestiya* reads: 'Nothing indicated that death was so near. Lately the health of Vladimir Ilyich has been showing significant improvement. Everything indicated that his health would be restored in future. Entirely unexpected, yesterday evening...' Precisely because Lenin was recovering, he was dangerous.

Stalin would have felt no compunction in murdering Lenin. He possessed abundant means for bringing the murder about, and in addition he possessed an alibi known to all the members of the Politburo. He had already manoeuvred Trotsky from the scene; between himself and supreme power there remained only Lenin. He was not a man to let such an opportunity slip. Only Lenin and Trotsky were capable of threatening his power, and he therefore decided to strike at them simultaneously. Towards his enemies, whoever they were, he was always pitiless.

That Lenin despised and feared Stalin, and that Stalin in turn despised and feared Lenin are matters of historical fact. They were both cruel and vindictive, capable of any ruses in order to achieve their ends, and it was perhaps inevitable that they should find themselves in mortal conflict. In January 1923 Lenin wrote: 'I propose to the comrades to find some way of removing Stalin.' Exactly a year later Stalin, without appealing to the comrades, seems to have found some way of removing Lenin.

THE TRIUMPH OF POWER

Successes have their dark side, especially when they come about with comparative ease. People not infrequently become drunk with such successes.

THE NEWS OF LENIN'S DEATH reached the Kremlin within a few seconds. The Central Committee was informed, and it was decided to leave for Gorki within the hour. Rykov was ill, but Stalin, Zinoviev, Kamenev, Bukharin, Kalinin and Tomsky formed themselves into a delegation to pay tribute to the dead leader who had raised them to their high positions. Zinoviev, one of the first to be informed, reached out for a sheet of paper to record his first melancholy impressions. 'We are going by auto-sleigh to Gorki,' he wrote. 'Just as in the past we always hurried at his summons, so now we shall fly to him on wings....'

They did not fly to him on wings, for instead of leaving in an hour they left in two hours and a half, and it was nearly midnight when they arrived at Gorki. The delay was probably caused by the difficulty of collecting cameramen and photographers, journalists and others who would record the scene. Merkhulov, the sculptor, accompanied them; later that night he would make the death mask of Lenin. Plans had to be made for the funeral; a thousand decisions had to be reached; orders of precedence had to be exactly calculated. The ceremonies would be as formal and complex as those for a dead emperor.

That night the sky was still clear, but the snow lay heavy on the ground. The new leaders of Russia made their way to the room in the north wing where Lenin lay on a table, his beard and moustaches neatly trimmed, his body clothed in a new double-breasted suit, a plump pillow supporting the head. According to Zinoviev, he looked calm and healthy, and others, seeing his fists still clenched, wondered whether he might not rise from the table. They kissed his forehead, spoke in whispers with Krupskaya, discussed the funeral, and returned by train to Moscow. They had intended to hold a meeting of the plenum of the Central Committee at two o'clock in the morning, but did not reach the Kremlin until three o'clock. Then they talked about Lenin until the dawn came. All through the night until well into the next morning the death of Lenin was kept secret.

Stalin appointed himself master of ceremonies, chief

mourner, officiating priest, and principal legatee. Originally he planned to hold the funeral on the twenty-fifth in the Red Square, and it is possible that he spoke in good faith when he told Trotsky, then in Tiflis, that he should continue his vacation because he would not be able to return in time. The date of the funeral was postponed for many reasons, and perhaps the most compelling was the need to use the funeral for purposes of propaganda. Mass demonstrations were arranged, and special trains were run from faraway places to enable the workers and peasants to come to Moscow.

Early in the morning of January 23rd Stalin and the Politburo made their second journey to Gorki. Among those who accompanied the delegation was Mikoyan, the enduring spectator of so many Russian tragedies. With the delegation came the scarlet coffin with the glass lid in which Lenin would be brought back in triumph to Moscow. Now Lenin no longer wore the dark double-breasted suit in which he had been dressed shortly after his death. Instead he wore a semi-military khaki jacket which for some reason was felt to be more in keeping with his role as a revolutionary. Then, very slowly and in silence, they carried the open coffin downstairs. Once outside they laid the coffin on the ground. There was a light snowfall, and some drops of snow fell on Lenin's uncovered face.

There occurred at this moment perhaps the strangest of many strange events which accompanied the long-drawn-out funeral of Lenin. It was an event at once so ordinary and so filled with appalling grandeur that few people observed it, and only one person, Mikhail Koltzov, chose to record it. While the coffin lay on the ground, and the snow fell, Stalin, chalk-white, went up to it and bent over it, gazing down at the body lying at his feet. He was still gazing steadily at Lenin when the glass lid was placed over the coffin.

Under leaden skies the coffin was carried through the streets of Moscow to the Hall of Trade Unions, where it was to lie in state for four days. The new masters of Russia took turns to stand in the honour guard at the bier. With exemplary caution Stalin arranged that cinematograph cameras should be present, to record for posterity the tense expression on his face as he stood on guard, and as he mopped his brow against the heat of the arc lamps set up by the cameramen.

Stalin dominated the funeral by his prevailing presence. During those days he signed a stream of telegrams, gave orders, stage-managed the commemoration meetings and the processions, and took care that he should be seen. Stalin's biographical chronicle is not wholly inaccurate in claiming that he was the prime mover in all the events of those days. Here, for example, are the entries for the day of the entombment:

January 27th

8 am	Stalin stands in the honour guard at the bier.
8:30 am	Stalin stands at the head of the bier.
9 am	Stalin and workers' representatives carry out the coffin.
4 pm	Stalin, Molotov and others carry the coffin into the crypt.

The words 'and others' conceal a multitude of crimes. The others were Kamenev, Zinoviev, Bukharin, Tomsky, Dzerzhinsky, and Rudzutak. Of these Dzerzhinsky was the only one who may have died a natural death.

On the evening before the entombment Stalin delivered his funeral oration, which included his vow to follow in the footsteps of Lenin. He attached some importance to the oration, and carefully noted that it was delivered between 8:24 and 8:40 pm. He said:

In departing from us, Comrade Lenin enjoined on us to hold high and keep pure the great calling of member of the Party.

We vow to thee, Comrade Lenin, that we will with honour fulfil this thy commandment.

In departing from us, Comrade Lenin enjoined on us to guard the unity of our Party as the apple of our eye.

We vow to thee, Comrade Lenin, that we will with honour fulfil this thy commandment.

In departing from us, Comrade Lenin enjoined on us to guard and to strengthen the dictatorship of the proletariat.

We vow to thee, Comrade Lenin, that we will not spare our strength to fulfil with honour this thy commandment.

In departing from us, Comrade Lenin enjoined on us to strengthen with all our might the union of workers and peasants.

We vow to thee, Comrade Lenin, that we will with honour fulfil this thy commandment.

In departing from us, Comrade Lenin enjoined on us to strengthen and extend the union of republics.

We vow to thee, Comrade Lenin, that we will with honour fulfil this thy commandment.

In departing from us, Comrade Lenin enjoined on us to remain faithful to the principles of the Communist International.

We vow to thee, Comrade Lenin, that we will not spare our lives to strengthen and extend the union of the working people of the whole world – the Communist International.

With these words Stalin announced himself as the high priest of the cult of Lenin, and the commander of the faithful. The speech was composed with great care and deliberation. He used the sacerdotal 'thee' and 'thy', previously reserved for the deity or the saints, with deliberate effect. Arrogance, duplicity and cynicism were implicit in this strange liturgical chant which combined an astonishing audacity with a hardheaded determination to inaugurate a permanent cult of Lenin. But it is important to observe that the cult and the attendant mythology had very little relation to the real Lenin; it was concerned only with those particular aspects of Lenin which were useful to Stalin.

Once he had decided to inaugurate the cult of Lenin, Stalin was not slow to comprehend the consequences. Shortly after Lenin's death Krupskaya wrote a brief and poignant paragraph, printed in *Pravda*, urging that there should be 'no external reverence for his person'. She begged that there should be no memorials raised to him, no palaces named after him, no vast celebrations held in his honour. 'To all these things,' she wrote, 'he attached so little importance during his life: they were so burdensome to him.' Instead, she suggested that those who honoured his name should build crèches, schools, libraries and hospitals, and above all that they should follow his principles. Stalin, who had little sympathy for Krupskaya, decided to pay no attention to her advice. The Second All-Union Congress of Soviets, meeting on January 26th, five days after Lenin's death, voted 'unanimously' that Petrograd, which only nine years before had borne the name St Petersburg, should bear forever the name of 'Vladimir Ilyich Ulyanov-Lenin, the greatest of all leaders of the proletariat'. One after another there came decrees designed to perpetuate Lenin's image and his name. The anniversary of his death was to become a day of national mourning. In all the chief cities of the Soviet Union his statue was to be erected, and all the words he ever wrote were to be solemnly collected and edited in a complete edition of his writings. This task, however, was never seriously undertaken. Every five or six years a new 'complete edition' of his works appeared, and although each successive edition was larger than the one before, each suffered from the fatal flaw of being so carefully edited, with all dangerous material scrupulously omitted, that the real Lenin could be seen only dimly. No comprehensive edition of his letters was ever published, with good reason. The letters would have shown him *en pantoufles*, warmly human and coldly ironic by turns. Overnight he had become a god, and no human traits must be permitted to betray his divinity.

Stalin, by introducing the cult of the dead Lenin, was reinforcing his own role as the deified successor. He was 'the faithful comrade-in-arms', the man who always stood reverently beside Lenin at moments of danger or at moments of great decision. There began to appear, at first slowly and then in increasing numbers, drawings and paintings which showed them in silent discussion, with Lenin usually sitting at a table while Stalin, waving his pipe, hovered over him. They had rarely been photographed together. Soon the existing photographs would be doctored to show them sitting very close to one another. But in those early days the processes of falsification were still cautious and tentative. In the newspapers praise of Stalin was generally accompanied by praise of Zinoviev and Kamenev, but already Stalin's name was appearing in the more prominent positions, and within the enclosed circle of the Politburo he was already the dominant personality.

He was not, however, well-known outside the Politburo and the Central Committee, and the task of acquiring a dominant public image was a difficult one. To be effective, he must put himself forward as the modest and retiring comrade on whom Lenin had bequeathed the leadership of the party. He was neither modest nor retiring, and the leadership had not been bequeathed to him. On the contrary Lenin had exerted every effort during the last hours of his active life to destroy him politically.

Lenin had left altogether three bombshells directed against Stalin. The first was the article called 'Concerning the National Question of "Autonomization",' and the second, to which he attached an even greater importance, was the critical analysis of the 'Georgian question' prepared by his secretaries. Both of these bombshells failed to explode, and no longer threatened him. There remained the document known as Lenin's Testament, in which Stalin was excoriated as a man too crude to be permitted to retain any position of authority. It was in this document that comrades were urged to 'remove' Stalin. That single sentence represented the gravest threat to Stalin's assumption of a personal dictatorship.

Although the Testament had been kept secret, rumour and gossip had been at work, and there was a general belief that Lenin, though dead, still had some unpleasant surprises in store for Stalin. Both Kamenev and Trotsky seem to have had a general idea of the contents of the Testament, and it is possible that Fotieva had given them copies to read. The Testament was being held in reserve: it was a bombshell with a long-delayed fuse, for when Lenin died, more than a year had passed since it was written.

Three months after Lenin's death and on the eve of the Thirteenth Congress Krupskaya decided to act. She had no part in the Fotieva-Trotsky conspiracies, which had failed largely because they lacked the authority of her name and influence. This time she held nothing back. She could do no less, because Lenin had instructed her to see that this document and the others he had written during his illness should be submitted to the next party conference after his death. The authority behind the documents was no longer Fotieva-Trotsky; it was Lenin-Krupskaya.

On May 18th, a few days before the Congress opened, she sent the documents to Kamenev with a covering note:

I am transmitting the notes which Vladimir Ilyich dictated during his illness from December 23rd to January 23rd – 13 separate notes. This total does not include the article on the national question (Maria Ilyinichna has it). Some of these notes have already been published, for example the article on the Workers-Peasants Inspectorate and on Sukhanov's book. Among the unpublished notes are those of December 24th–25th, 1922, and those of January 4th, 1923, which contain personal appraisals of some Central Committee members. Vladimir Ilyich expressed the definite wish that this note of his be submitted after his death to the next Party Congress for its information.

Vladimir Ilyich's notes mentioned above and transmitted to Comrade Kamenev are all known to me and were earmarked by Vladimir Ilyich for transmittal to the Party.

N. KRUPSKAYA

Krupskaya was leaving nothing to chance. Twice she emphasized that the documents had received the final *imprimatur* from Lenin. Her determination that they should be read at the Congress could not be lightly denied, and on the following day the Plenum Commission of the Central Committee, composed of Zinoviev, Smirnov, Kalinin, Bukharin, Stalin, and Kamenev, voted to submit the documents to the Congress for its information.

Although a vote had been taken, this was not the end of the matter, for it was soon realized that the Testament might split the Central Committee wide open. Stalin's allies went to work. It was decided to hold a meeting of the Central Committee to discuss the Testament at greater length. Careful preliminary alliances were formed. It was certain that the bombshell would have an explosive effect, but it was believed that the worst effects could be mitigated. Trotsky and Radek were present. So, too, was Boris Bazhanov, one of Stalin's secretaries, who has described the consternation following the reading of the Testament. 'A painful embarrassment paralysed all who were present,' he wrote. 'Stalin, sitting on the steps of the rostrum, felt small and miserable. Although he was controlling himself, you could see plainly from his face that his fate was at stake.'

The situation was saved by Zinoviev, who had now entered into a close alliance with Stalin. Never before and never again was he to show quite such skill in treachery as he displayed on this occasion. 'Comrades, no one can doubt that every word of Ilyich is sacred to us,' he declared solemnly. 'More than once we have sworn to fulfil what the dying Ilyich commanded of us. All of us know that we shall keep that vow. But there is one point where, we are happy to say, Lenin's fears have proved groundless. I am speaking on the question of our General Secretary. All of you have witnessed our harmonious co-operation during these last months, and all of you, like me, have had the satisfaction of seeing that what Lenin feared has not taken place.' Kamenev made a less tendentious appeal in Stalin's favour. Trotsky remained silent, pride and contempt stamping his features as he surveyed the enormity of the crime which was being enacted before his eyes. Once, during the reading of the Testament, Radek leaned over and said: 'Now they won't dare to go against you,' and Trotsky answered prophetically: 'On the contrary, now they will have to see it through to the bitter end.' It was decided that the Testament should be read only to specially selected delegates, and never to publish it. Three years later when the question of the Testament was raised again before the Central Committee, with Zinoviev and Kamenev demanding the publication of the document, Stalin retorted that the matter had already been debated, and there was no purpose in reviving an ancient quarrel; and when he was pressed to reconsider, he answered that the delegates of the Congress had all heard it, and had he not admitted Lenin's charge against him, and offered to resign from his post, and no one, not even Trotsky, had chosen to accept his resignation. At this meeting he even quoted Lenin's most powerful attack on him. In 1927 he could afford to quote these damaging statements, for by this time he had almost consolidated his personal dictatorship and no longer needed Zinoviev and Kamenev as allies.

Only Krupskaya fought against the verdict of the Central Committee. About this time she sought an audience with Stalin and bitterly upbraided him for suppressing the Testament. The incident was reported by Christian Rakovsky, who says it took place in the presence of Lev Mekhlis, then Stalin's secretary and later the political chief of the Red Army, and of Sergey Syrtsov, head of the Orgburo and a prominent Soviet politician. Rakovsky quoted Mekhlis as saying that Krupskaya was hysterical with despair and kept shouting at the top of her voice. 'I warn you,' she shouted, 'that if you don't read the Testament during a session of the Central Committee, I shall publish it myself – I am the testamentary legatee. I have to fulfil a mission which he entrusted to me on the day of his death.'

Stalin permitted her to shout, but refused to change the policy he had decided upon. When she left his office, he burst into a rage and cursed her, as he had cursed her once before on the telephone, screaming abuse at a woman who had already fled from his presence.

Krupskaya never dared to carry out her threat. She did not publish the Testament, though she may have been responsible for the occasional mimeographed copies which circulated in

Moscow. From one of these mimeographed texts the Menshevik journal *Sotsialistichesky Vestnik*, then published in Berlin, printed a more or less accurate version of the Testament in July 1924, and two years later, Max Eastman published the complete text in *The New York Times*. Trotsky went to some pains to deny that Max Eastman had obtained the text from him, but he could scarcely do otherwise. As so often when Trotsky found himself in danger, he compounded his errors, denied the existence of the Testament and, a priori, any conspiracy to conceal it. 'All talk about concealing or violating a Testament is a malicious invention and is entirely directed against Vladimir Ilyich's real Testament.' These words pleased Stalin so much that he quoted them in a speech printed in his *Collected Works*, which appeared after World War II, many years after Trotsky's death. Stalin seems to have long savoured the exquisite moment of triumph when he made Trotsky deny the existence of the Testament.

But the Testament existed, and even Stalin must have been aware that it could not be suppressed forever. So raw, so urgent a document could never entirely perish. It was one of those writings which seemed to have an independent life of their own, clamouring to be heard. Three years after Stalin's death it was finally released with the full authority of the Soviet government.

It was released in slow stages, tentatively, experimentally. In February 1956 it was circulated privately to leading members of the party as one of the supporting documents to Khrushchev's secret speech at the Twentieth Congress. On June 30th, 1956, it appeared in the theoretical journal *Kommunist*. A few days later it appeared in pamphlet form in an edition of a million copies, and this edition was followed by others in German, French, English, Swedish, Polish, Czech and Chinese. But even when it was broadcast to the world in massive editions, the Communist Party viewed it with alarm. Lenin's purpose when he wrote the Testament was to correct abuses of power; he wrote in molten anger because power had already been abused. There was no hiding Lenin's bitterness and horror, but there was also no hiding the special praises he heaped on the heads of Trotsky, Bukharin, Kamenev, Zinoviev and Pyatakov, all of whom were later murdered by Stalin. None of these former members of the Soviet government had been rehabilitated in 1956, and the mythology of Communism demanded that they should remain forgotten.

The Testament was therefore a two-edged weapon, for while striking at Stalin the document struck with equal persuasiveness at abuses of Soviet power wherever they occurred.

When the Testament was finally published in 1956, it was decided to blunt its impact with an introductory survey in which Lenin was rapped lightly over the knuckles for his inexplicable lapses in judgement; it was explained that he was ill when he wrote the Testament and not perhaps in full command of his faculties. Communist cells were encouraged to set up study circles to examine the Testament in the light of current Communist doctrine, and students were warned to attach no weight to Lenin's appraisals of the five men he particularly admired. In exactly the same way Stalin explained away the significance of the Testament thirty-two years earlier when he permitted it to be seen only by specially selected delegates to the Congress.

What the contemporary Communists failed to observe was that the Testament was a human document which could not be divided into passages of greater or lesser authenticity. If Lenin was justified in attacking Stalin, he was also justified in praising Trotsky, Bukharin, Kamenev, Zinoviev and Pyatakov. If he warned, as he did, against the coarsening of the fibre of Communist society, it was not because he was inept in his judgement, but because the coarsening had already taken place, and he was himself largely responsible for it. The Testament was therefore a supreme act of confession and a grim warning, which has never been heeded.

With the Testament successfully disposed of, Stalin could now go about the task of securing undivided control of the government. He still hoped that the revolution in Russia would be buttressed by revolution abroad, but more and more he was beginning to see that 'socialism in one country' was a useful slogan which could be implemented by a rigorous programme of industrialization; and sometimes his eyes would turn with a kind of yearning towards America. In April 1924 he delivered a series of lectures, later published under the general title *Problems of Leninism,* in which he concluded that 'the combination of Russian revolutionary *élan* with American efficiency is the essence of Leninism in party and national work'. But both revolutionary *élan* and American efficiency were oddly lacking in those days when there was no Lenin to guide the revolution and his successor had not yet stamped his imprint on the party.

There comes a time in all revolutions when they become irresolute and hesitant, becalmed in their Sargasso Seas. They wait idly for visitations – a chance breath of wind, squalls, tempests, the emergence of the inevitable dictator. In the summer and autumn of 1924 the rulers of Russia were looking hungrily for conquests, but there were no conquests in sight. The bureaucratic machine seemed to have ground to a standstill, while the leaders deliberated, quarrelled, froze into attitudes, or looked for scapegoats; and there were some who realized that the revolution came to an end with the death of Lenin. What followed could only be the working out of an ancient despair.

Zinoviev might declare: 'It has become a thousand times more necessary than ever that the party should become monolithic,' and Stalin might speak repeatedly of the need to purge the party until only its fine essence remained, but the unanswered questions still haunted the party members. Monolithic for what? What is the party for, and where is it going?

While Lenin was alive, the party possessed a programme, which was logical and coherent because it reflected the orderly processes of Lenin's mind. In the summer and autumn following Lenin's death logic and coherence seemed to have vanished. The revolution was marking time, its titular leader being the colourless Alexey Rykov, who was chairman of the Council of People's Commissars, a man who looked old and withered at the age of forty-three. Kamenev, who wielded far greater power, served as Rykov's deputy. The triumvirate Stalin, Kamenev, and Zinoviev had no basis in revolutionary law, and was merely an accommodation between three rivals for power. Trotsky, though Commissar for War, with the Red Army still loyal to him, held himself aloof from the struggle. Where Lenin had been, there was only a vacuum.

Though Trotsky held himself aloof, he was not above taking part in sniping raids against Zinoviev and Kamenev. In October Trotsky published his pamphlet *The Lessons of October*, in which he reminded his readers that when Lenin said: 'We must strike now – to delay is criminal,' Zinoviev and Kamenev had answered: 'An armed uprising now will bring total defeat to the proletariat and the revolution.' In the tones of a dry schoolmaster Trotsky pointed out that neither Zinoviev nor Kamenev was infallible. He had too much scorn for them to come out openly against them, and he carefully omitted the name of Stalin, as though it were beneath his dignity to consider the minor role played by Stalin during the revolution.

The Lessons of October is not one of Trotsky's major works; there is no fire in it, no drama, no sense of mastery. Here and there a sentence or a half paragraph stands out among the dreary wastes, as when he describes the Hungarian revolution under Bela Kun : 'This revolution, triumphant without a battle and without a victory, was left from the beginning without a leadership.' But there are not many such sentences. He writes like an exhausted man, torn between his duty to seek the causes of the October revolution and his desire to snipe at those who disagreed with him, who did not share his precise and complicated notion of what the revolution was about.

Stalin, on the contrary, never showed any awareness of the complexities of revolution. What he especially enjoyed were those dramatic moments when the enemy was baited and trapped, as when Lenin simply telephoned from military staff headquarters in Petrograd, got the commanding general of the Russian army on the line, and dismissed him. For Stalin a revolution was essentially simple, and he liked to quote the saying, once fairly common among Bolsheviks, that 'Lenin swims in revolution like a fish in water'.

When Stalin speaks of Lenin, he is always illuminating. He did not see Lenin as an adroit and superbly gifted strategist; instead, he saw Lenin as a magician or a prophet. Shortly after Lenin's death, Stalin described him as 'a clairvoyant, who divines the movement of classes and the probable zigzag paths of the revolution, seeing them as though in the palm of his hand'. But it was not by clairvoyance or divination or palmistry that Lenin acquired power. He acquired it by the severe and merciless study of revolutionary logic, and by his knowledge of the strengths and weaknesses of the enemy. Stalin lacked the sense of revolutionary logic, and he had little understanding of the strengths and weaknesses of the enemy. When Zinoviev and Kamenev attacked Lenin on the eve of the uprising, Stalin remained silent, waiting to see what would happen. With Lenin dead, he was still waiting to see what would happen.

The revolution, if it was to survive, needed a watchword and a sign, but none of the triumvirs was capable of inventing one. In his *Problems of Leninism* Stalin grappled with Marxist theory, only to show, as Riazanov once observed to his face, that it would have been better if he had left theory alone. He misinterpreted, simplified, and painfully elaborated the obvious. His method was that of the eighteenth- and nineteenth-century schoolmaster, who offers a series of quotations and inquires into the meaning of a few words which seem to have importance, then goes on to the next quotation without explaining the meaning of the last. Here and there he repeats a few favourite themes. American efficiency is continually celebrated. It is that 'indomitable force which neither knows nor recognizes obstacles, which blasts its way with real perseverance through all barriers, and once it has embarked on a task carries it through to the end'. Again and again he compares practical revolutionary work with the fantasies and dreams of the theoreticians, the Bukharins and the Trotskys. The romantic posturing Bolsheviks, the handsome strong-jawed men in leather jackets, every muscle rigid with determination – so Boris Pilnyak described them in his novel *The Naked Year*, written with troubled and affectionate irony – these, too, Stalin dismissed because they possessed no vision and did not know what the revolution was about. Visiting a factory in November, he wrote out his dreams for the future.

Such dreams, however, were small comfort to the people of Russia. They were the dreams of a bureaucrat. *Forge ahead, future increase, high level, firmly weld together* were the words used *ad nauseam* by political agitators; there was no passion in them. Stalin was a leader in search of a cause, and there was still no cause in sight.

In his search for a cause Trotsky had discovered 'the permanent revolution'. Trotsky believed that if the revolution was contained within the borders of one country, it would perish, for a communist revolution was by its nature international. Lenin, too, had believed this, and prayed and hoped that the conflagration begun in Russia would blaze even more brightly in Germany; then Russia and Germany together would carry it to the ends of the world. Stalin had repeated the formula in *Problems of Leninism*. By the end of the year the formula was revised. The permanent, ever-widening revolution was no doubt desirable, but socialism in one country was also desirable 'for the development, support and awakening of the revolution in all countries'. 'Socialism in one country' could be used as a stick to belabour 'the permanent revolution'.

These doctrinal differences represented profound differences of attitude almost as old as Russian history. While Trotsky dreamed incessantly of the world revolution, Stalin entered upon the path of national communism, realizing only too well

My desire for the workers

of Dynamo, as for the workers of all Russia, is that industry should forge ahead, that the number of proletarians in Russia should in the near future increase to 20 or 30 millions, that collective farming should thrive and bring private farming under its influence, and that a high level of industry and collective farming should firmly weld together the proletarians of the factories and the tillers of the soil into one single Socialist army ...

November 7th, 1924   J. STALIN

that communism had not yet been established in Russia. He was not against the world revolution; it was simply that he knew it was not coming about at any speed measurable by the Kremlin experts who watched over the birth of revolutions.

So, very patiently, slowly and hesitantly, he began to put his own house in order, and to those who followed Trotsky, he said ominously: 'We are ready for you, comrades.'

THE MAN WHO NEVER STOOPS

AS THE YEARS PASSED, Stalin continually found reasons for reviewing the October revolution. Time after time he would begin a speech on some theme connected with the present, but inevitatbly his mind would revert to the past and he would say: 'Comrades, what happened during the October revolution?' His answers were rarely the same. Sometimes he would flounder in rhetoric, drowning the revolution in quotations from Marx; sometimes he would give the impression of a man earnestly seeking for answers; sometimes he would speak of himself as the man who had single-handedly brought the revolution about; at other times he scarcely mentioned the role he had played. The revolution puzzled, disturbed and annoyed him. A vast outpouring of energy had occurred, and he seems never to have been quite sure what brought it about.

He saw himself as one of those – perhaps the principal one – who had pulled the strings and summoned Lenin out of hiding and taken command of the revolutionary army, and it pleased him to believe the myth that Trotsky had almost nothing to do with the revolution. Already in November 1924 he was saying: 'Neither in the party, nor in the October uprising, did Trotsky play any *special* role, nor could he do so, for he was relatively new in our party during the October days.' But if Trotsky did not lead the revolution, and if Lenin remained in hiding, then by a process of elimination there remained only one man who was capable of leading the revolution to victory. As for Trotsky, he was merely one of those who contributed to the victory by appearing at the last moment when the revolution was on the march and the enemy was already in flight.

These convenient fictions were frequently repeated, and in time they became articles of faith; it is possible that Stalin even came to believe them. Only a few months after Lenin's death he was interpreting history as he pleased; even very recent history was altered to justify the myth that Lenin and Stalin together had brought about the revolution. There were occasions when Stalin was kind to Lenin. 'You must not believe the ridiculous gossip you hear about Lenin being in hiding,' he said. 'As for Trotsky he was a coward during the time of the Brest Litovsk negotiations, and the greatest victories during the civil war were won *in spite of him*.'

Already Lenin was gradually fading into the mists of history, his embalmed body grimly pointing to an ancient past, the Red Square becoming a nesting place of relics. The prophet, the clairvoyant, the genius who manipulated whole classes and who had only to whisper to make the whole world tremble became at last the author of copybook maxims. So Stalin wrote on the first anniversary of Lenin's death:

Помните, любите, изучайте Ильича, нашего учителя, нашего вождя.

Боритесь и побеждайте врагов, внутренних и внешних, — по Ильичу.

Стройте новую жизнь, новый быт, новую культуру — по Ильичу.

Никогда не отказывайтесь от малого в работе, ибо из малого строится великое, — в этом один из важных заветов Ильича.

И. Сталин

Remember, love, study Ilyich, our teacher and leader.

Fight and vanquish the enemies, internal and foreign – according to the way of Ilyich.

Build the new life, the new existence, the new culture – according to the way of Ilyich.

Never refuse to do little things, for from little things are built the big things – this is one of Ilyich's important behests.

J. STALIN

Significantly, Stalin mentioned the internal enemies first, giving them their proper pride of place. For the rest of his long life he was to grant them his close attention. Some of the enemies were real, most were imaginary, and the imaginary enemies were by far the most dangerous.

Long before he came to wield undivided power, Stalin was corrupted by it. The signs of corruption could be seen in the increasing brutality of his speech, his ferocious rages, the fear he instilled in the Politburo, and the oriental magnificence of his gestures. Petrograd had become Leningrad. Why should not Tsaritsyn become Stalingrad? On April 10th, 1925, he issued a decree ordering that Tsaritsyn should be renamed Stalingrad in perpetuity. One after another the ancient names went down like skittles. Perm became Molotov, Tver became Kalinin, and Ekaterinburg, where the Tsar and the entire imperial family were murdered, became Sverdlovsk. Elizavetgrad, where Zinoviev was born, became Zinovievsk, Samara became Kuibyshev, and an obscure village on the Volga, formerly known as 'The Fleas', was named after the obscure Rudzutak. Even Kamenev had a small town named after him. Gatchina, where Trotsky won a famous victory, became Trotsky. Tomsky appears to have been the only member of the Politburo who refused to have a town named after him. Not all these gifts were bestowed at once, for the names of cities kept changing through the thirties. Vladikavkaz, for example, did not become Ordjonikidze until 1932.*

---

* The actual dates of the first changes of city names are illuminating. The first to be changed was Petrograd in January 1924. The second was Uzovka, the steel town in the Ukraine with the largest and deepest mine in the Soviet Union, which became Stalin in June 1924. Elizavetgrad became Zinovievsk and Ekaterinburg became Sverdlovsk in September 1924. Tsaritsyn became Stalingrad seven months later.

As he changed the names of cities in accordance with his whims, Stalin sometimes showed a nice sense of historical perspective. Sverdlov had ordered the execution of the Tsar, and it was appropriate that his name should perpetuate the crime. Simbirsk, where Lenin was born, became Ulyanovsk. Nizhni Novgorod, because it was associated with Gorky's novels and stories, became Gorky. Gatchina did not bear the name of Trotsky for long. When Trotsky fell from favour, it became Krasnoarmeisk in honour of the Red Army, but this name, too, was later abandoned. The small town of Pishpek, the capital of Kirghizia, lying at the end of the long railway line from Moscow, acquired a more enduring name. It was called Frunze after Mikhail Frunze, one of the generals of the civil war, who became Commissar for War early in 1925. Seven months later, fearing his rising power and suspecting that he was friendly with Trotsky, Stalin ordered him to submit to an operation in the Kremlin clinic. He died under the knife.

During the following year Boris Pilnyak wrote an extraordinary story called 'The Tale of the Unextinguished Moon', in which he describes how an army commander called Gavrilov, who had distinguished himself in the civil war and organized a revolution in China, was summoned to Moscow. He has no idea why he has been summoned. On a grey autumn morning his private train rolls into a deserted siding, where the newspapers are brought to him. He opens a newspaper and reads a brief announcement that 'Comrade Gavrilov has arrived in Moscow in order to submit to an operation for stomach ulcer'. It is an ominous beginning, but the story grows far more ominous when Gavrilov presents himself to 'Number One, the man who never stoops', who sits behind a large desk and talks of the days when they were both fighting in the civil war.

'Do you remember when you and I led the ragged troops against Ekaterinoslav,' Number One says. 'You had a rifle, and I had a rifle, and then a shell killed your horse, and you went ahead on foot. The Red Army men began to turn tail and flee, and you shot one of them with your revolver to stop the rout. Commander, you would have shot me, if I had shown fear.'

Gavrilov asks Number One to come to the point. Surely it was not for an exchange of reminiscences about the civil war that he has been summoned to Moscow.

'I called you because you must undergo an operation,' Number One replies. 'The revolution needs you. I have called in the specialists, and they say you will be on your feet in a few months. The revolution demands this of you.'

Gavrilov protests. His own doctors have told him there is no need for an operation; he feels perfectly well, and though there is an ulcer, it will heal.

Number One says: 'Do you remember the time when we discussed whether four thousand men were to be sent to certain death? You ordered them sent, and you did the right thing ... Excuse me, there is nothing more to be said.'

Gavrilov has no alternative. He must submit to the operation because Number One has decided he must die.

'The Tale of the Unextinguished Moon' was so patently about Stalin and Frunze that it caused a furore. Published in *Novy Mir*, it was immediately censored. It was dedicated to Alexander Voronsky, the editor of *Krasnaya Nov*, an Old Bolshevik and a formidable figure in the publishing world, and in the following issue of *Novy Mir* Voronsky rejected the dedication as an insult to him as a member of the Communist Party. He described the story as a cruel distortion of history. Surprisingly Pilnyak survived until the great purges of the thirties.

In the story 'the man who never stoops' is a figure of menacing power. His purposes are obscure. From time to time the nightmares of the civil war rise to torment him, but his voice is steady and he knows where he is going even if he cannot discern how he will reach his goal. At the funeral of Frunze Stalin spoke of his boundless grief over the death of 'the purest, most honest and most fearless revolutionary of our time'. 'Perhaps,' he said, 'it is indeed necessary that old comrades should go down to their graves easily and simply, but young comrades do not rise to take their place as easily or as simply.'

Though Stalin already wore an aspect of brooding menace, and was determined to achieve power for his own purposes rather than for the purposes of the revolution, he liked to present himself as a man who always avoided violence. He wrote to a comrade early in 1925:

I am determinedly opposed to the policy of throwing out all comrades who disagree with us. I am opposed to such a policy not because I am sorry for them, but because such a policy gives rise within the party of a regime of intimidation, a regime of bullying, a regime which kills the spirit of self-criticism and initiative. It is not good when the leaders of the party are feared but not respected.

In the same spirit Stalin spoke to students at Sverdlov University during the summer, emphasizing that everything must be done to moderate the struggle with the peasants 'by means of agreements and mutual concessions, never permitting the struggle to assume an acute form'. He repeated the warning in the autumn. 'We must employ the method of persuasion,' he declared. He spoke often of the necessity of avoiding clashes, but he was continually manufacturing clashes. The opportunity for a clash with Zinoviev and Kamenev came with the Fourteenth Party Congress in December 1925. The struggle for power was fought brazenly. Trotsky held himself aloof, apparently indifferent to the fate of all congresses. Stalin waged a determined battle against Zinoviev and Kamenev, whose powers, once formidable, because they controlled the organizations in Leningrad and Moscow, seemed to wilt before the fury of his attacks. 'Those,' said Stalin, 'who think it it possible to build socialism with white gloves are grievously mistaken.' He had long ago abandoned the methods of peaceful persuasion.

Kamenev, who knew Stalin better than most men, attacked him at the Congress with extraordinary force and energy. He declared:

We are against creating the theory of a leader; we are against making a leader. We are against having the secretariat combine in practice both politics and organization and place itself above the political organ ... We cannot regard it as normal, and we think it harmful to the party, to prolong a situation in which the secretariat combines politics and organization, and in fact decides policy in advance. I must say what I have to say to the end. Because I have more than once said it to Comrade Stalin personally, because I have more than once said it to a group of party delegates, I repeat it to the congress: *I have reached the conviction that Comrade Stalin cannot perform the function of uniting the Bolshevik general staff.*

Kamenev was not alone in this view, but no one else had dared to express it so effectively. Unhappily, he was only too vulnerable, for Stalin could always point out that he had

Stalin at fourteen

Stalin's mother in 1933

Stalin, Kamenev and others, 1915

Lenin and Stalin at Gorki, August 1922

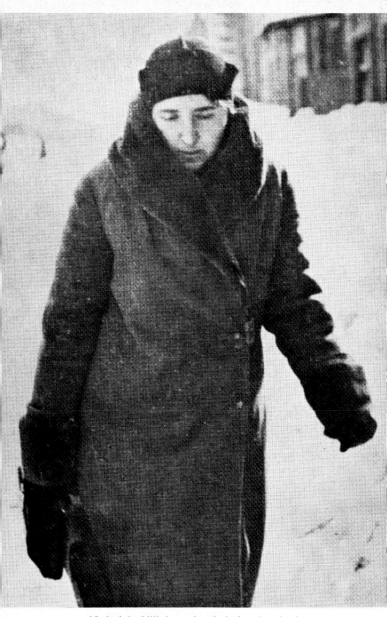

Nadezhda Alliluieva, shortly before her death

betrayed the revolution once before, and could be expected to betray it again. Zinoviev and Kamenev were 'the strike-breakers of the October revolution'. They were therefore not competent to understand the revolutionary process. They attacked 'socialism in one country' and 'the transformation of the Soviet Union from an agricultural into an industrial country', but they had no simple and effective slogans to put in their place. Zinoviev was defended by the Leningrad party members, Kamenev by some of his Moscow supporters, but their combined force was hopelessly outnumbered by Stalin's appointees. The voting was 459 to 65. Stalin could now congratulate himself that he no longer needed to fear any effective opposition to his dictatorship. The triumvirate was dissolved. Supreme power lay in his hands, while Zinoviev, Kamenev and Trotsky went down to defeat.

Up to the time of the Fourteenth Congress Stalin had been a comparatively little-known figure. 'What kind of man is he?' Trotsky had been asked earlier in the year, and he replied with bewildering inaccuracy: 'The most eminent mediocrity in the party.' Stalin was not a mediocrity, but a machine politician of extraordinary talents, able to manipulate the Congress until it became the obedient servant of his will. A certain Katalynov was saying at the end of the Congress that only one thing mattered: whether a man was a Stalinist or not. 'If the man is not a Stalinist, crush him, throttle him, throw him out, do everything short of kicking him.' Previously the name of Stalin was rarely mentioned; now it was on everyone's lips.

After his victory at the Fourteenth Congress, Stalin went about the task of crushing his enemies with quiet efficiency. Zinoviev was the first to feel Stalin's wrath, perhaps because he had been closer to Stalin than anyone else and had helped him on the road to power. Zinoviev was removed from the leadership of the party organization in Leningrad, and was replaced by Kirov. In the summer Zinoviev was expelled from the Politburo. In the autumn he was removed from the chairmanship of the Third International, and at the same time Trotsky and Kamenev were removed from the Politburo. It was not enough to remove them from their high positions. Their friends and accomplices, all those who were loyal to them, were removed from positions of power. The party machine worked silently to produce a monolithic unity; all were to be made obedient to the sovereign will of the leader.

The slow processes of liquidation continued. Zinoviev, Kamenev and Trotsky were deprived of their posts, their secretarial staffs, their chauffeurs and their automobiles; they were prevented from writing in newspapers and magazines; they were threatened and intimidated; but they were still members of the Central Committee, and they still had power to sway men's minds. There were many ways in which they could be destroyed. Stalin could laugh them to scorn; he could attack their ideas head on and pulverize them; he could reduce them to insignificance by the sheer weight of his propaganda; he could have them watched and followed so strenuously that they would scarcely dare to open their mouths; he could infiltrate their ranks with so many spies that they would wonder whether there was anyone they could trust; and he could set one against the other. He could plant documents on them, and arrest them on trumped-up charges. He could destroy their private lives. All these methods were employed. The question whether to destroy them physically or whether to let them destroy themselves was largely an academic one.

Long before Zinoviev, Kamenev and Trotsky were removed from the Central Committee in the autumn of 1927, they were politically destroyed. They possessed no offices; they had become private citizens; their influence extended no further than the length of a room; they had descended into that limbo from which there is rarely any return. Though they were living, they were already dead.

Though they presented no effective danger to his regime, their continual presence was a reminder of many unsolved problems. In their different ways Zinoviev, Kamenev and Trotsky represented three aspects of the revolution which were, quite simply, indestructible. While Zinoviev represented the exhausted romanticism of the revolution, Kamenev represented the cool revolutionary intelligence, and Trotsky represented the brilliant manipulation of revolutionary ideas. What they represented was enduring; and others would arise to speak in their authentic voices. For Stalin it was a nightmare. Although he was in control of the machinery of state, and had the will and the power to destroy opposition, the opposition remained. It remained, because at the moment when he became dictator, he brought it into being.

Although there was no way to unseat the dictator except by force, the opposition contented itself by making ineffective gestures. On November 7th, 1927, the tenth anniversary of the revolution, there were parades in the streets in Moscow and Leningrad, with opposition groups carrying banners and red flags, placards and strips of paper with scrawled slogans: 'Let us carry out Lenin's Testament'; 'Against opportunism, against a split, and for the unity of Lenin's party'. The organizers of the procession hoped the people of Moscow would be electrified into action by the appearance of a handful of placards. Nothing happened. The parades were dispersed by the police. A more solemn protest was demanded, and this was provided by Adolf Joffe, the veteran Soviet diplomat, who thought that by killing himself he would in some mysterious way dramatize the plight of the opposition. Just before killing himself on the evening of November 17th, he wrote to Trotsky:

DEAR LEV DAVIDOVICH,

All my life I have thought that a man of politics ought to know how to leave the scene at the right time, as an actor leaves the stage, and it is better to go too soon than too late.

More than thirty years ago I embraced the philosophy that human life has meaning only to the degree that, and so long as, it is lived in the service of something infinite. For us humanity is infinite. The rest is finite, and to work for the rest is therefore meaningless. Even if humanity too must have a purpose beyond itself, that purpose will appear in so remote a future that for us humanity may be considered as an absolute infinite. It is in this and this only that I have always seen the meaning of life. And now, taking a glance backwards over my past, of which twenty-seven years were spent in the ranks of our party, it seems to me that I have the right to say that during *all* my conscious life I have been faithful to this philosophy. I have lived according to this meaning of life: work and struggle for the good of humanity. I think I have the right to say that not a day of my life has been meaningless.

But now it seems, comes the time when my life loses its meaning, and in consequence I feel obliged to abandon it, to bring it to an end ...

I know that the general opinion of the party is opposed to suicide, but I believe that none of those who understand my situation will condemn me for it. If I were in good health I would have found strength and energy to struggle against the situation created by the party. But in my present state I cannot endure a situation in which the party silently tolerates *your exclusion from its ranks*, even though I am absolutely certain that sooner or later a crisis will come which will oblige the party to cast off those who have led it to such disgrace. In this sense my death is a *protest* against those who have led the party to a situation such that it cannot react in any way to this opprobrium.

If I may be permitted to compare something big with something little, I will say that the immensely important historical event, your exclusion and that of Zinoviev, an exclusion which must inevitably open a period of Thermidor in our revolution, and the fact that I am reduced, after twenty-seven years of revolutionary work at responsible posts in the party to a situation where I have nothing left but to put a bullet through my head – these two facts illustrate one and the same thing – the present regime in our party. And perhaps the two events, the little and the big one together, will jar the party awake and halt it on the road leading to Thermidor ...

Do not be afraid today if certain ones desert you, and especially if the many do not come to you as quickly as we all wish. You are in the right, but the certainty of the victory of your truth lies precisely in a strict intransigency, in the most severe rigidity, in the repudiation of every compromise, exactly as that was always the secret of the victories of Ilyich.

I have often wanted to tell you this, and have only brought myself to it now, at the moment of saying goodbye.

I wish you energy and courage equal to those you have always shown, and a swift victory. I embrace you. Goodbye.

Your,

A. JOFFE

Joffe's testament, for it was nothing less, deserves to be quoted at length not only because it is a poignant human document, but because it throws a sharp light on the intolerable situation in which so many of the Old Bolsheviks found themselves. He wrote with a mind made luminous by despair. What he saw only too clearly was that the exclusion of Trotsky meant the liquidation of the revolution; not that Trotsky's presence necessarily gave purpose to the revolution, but that his *absence* was like a wound that could never be healed, for no one else would be able to stand up against the arbitrary dictatorship of Stalin, nor was there anyone in sight with

Trotsky's gifts of intelligence and leadership. In writing this letter half an hour before shooting himself, Joffe was hoping that in some mysterious way his sacrifice would give strength to Trotsky, but he must have known that it was already too late, and that Trotsky himself lacked precisely those qualities which were needed to destroy Stalin. 'The certainty of the victory of your truth,' wrote Joffe, 'lies precisely in a strict intransigency, in the most severe rigidity, in the repudiation of every compromise, exactly as that was always the secret of the victories of Ilyich.' But it was not Lenin so much as Stalin who showed strict intransigency, severe rigidity, and a horror of compromise.

There is a sense in which Joffe's letter is a salute to the victor. Joffe had evidently hoped that Stalin would never see it. Before shooting himself he placed the letter in an envelope on the bedside table, and gave instructions that Trotsky should be informed of his death and of the existence of the letter. Not long afterwards Trotsky heard an unfamiliar voice over the telephone: 'Adolf Abramovich has shot himself. There is an envelope for you beside his bed.' By the time Trotsky reached the deathbed,* the letter had vanished, and there was already a GPU officer in the house, rifling through Joffe's papers. Trotsky asked for the letter and was told there was no letter. The GPU officer was obviously lying. The letter had already been removed to GPU headquarters. For a little while longer Trotsky stayed at Joffe's apartment, gazing down at the head on the bloodstained pillow, 'the calm and infinitely tender face' of his friend. Then he slipped away.

The suicide of Joffe created a sensation. He was the first high Bolshevik official to commit suicide. He had led the Bolshevik delegation at Brest Litovsk in December 1917, he signed the Brest Litovsk treaty in March 1918, he was ambassador to Germany in the stormy days of 1919, he signed the peace treaty with Poland after the disastrous war of 1920, and he was the delegate to the Genoa Conference in 1923. Later he was sent on a special mission to convert Dr Sun

---

* The GPU officer must have acted with extraordinary speed. Joffe committed suicide in his apartment on Leontievsky Street, and Trotsky was living in an apartment in the House of the Soviets on Cheremetievsky (later Granovsky) Street, near the University. The two streets were connected by the Bolshaya Nikitskaya, one of the main thoroughfares radiating from the Kremlin. Trotsky could have made the journey in ten minutes.

Yat-sen, the Chinese leader, to communism and was afterwards appointed ambassador to Japan. He had been high in Lenin's confidence, and he had a firm place in Soviet history. His death, coming so soon after Stalin's rise to power during the October meeting of the Central Committee, when Zinoviev and Trotsky were expelled, raised many awkward questions among foreign journalists.

Trotsky was a man without power, but not powerless. He still had a following – how large it was, and how many members of the armed forces were included in it, Stalin could only guess. Trotsky demanded that the letter be handed over to him. There was no reply. He informed the foreign press that the letter had been purloined by the secret police. Finally Stalin relented, and a copy of the letter was given to Christian Rakovsky to give to Trotsky.

Joffe's testament ranks with Lenin's testament as one of the great human documents of the revolution. It was not only that he had seen with fearful clarity the coming of Thermidor, the end of the revolution, but he was also deeply responsible for bringing it about. The revolution, which had started with such high hopes, suffered from a fatal flaw: it could not survive except as the personal dictatorship of one man. Joffe seems to have thought that the dictatorship of Trotsky would have been more tolerable than the dictatorship of Stalin, but this was merely to clutch at straws.

On November 19th Joffe's coffin was borne through the streets of Moscow to the cemetery of the Novodevichy Monastery. Trotsky, Rakovsky and Smirnov led the procession through the whirling snow gusts. When they reached the cemetery gate, they discovered that orders had been issued by the Central Committee that only twenty people would be allowed to accompany the coffin to the grave. The crowd forced its way in, defying the police. At the graveside Rakovsky seized the red flag which covered the coffin, and said: 'Like you we shall follow the flag to the very end, and we make this oath to you now on your tomb.' Trotsky said: 'The life of Joffe, not his suicide, should be the model for those he has left behind. The struggle goes on. Everyone must remain at his post!' But these were empty gestures. There could be no struggle, for Stalin had seen to it that the opposition was deprived of weapons. The opposition could not even guarantee the life of Trotsky, who hid in a brick shed on the cemetery grounds when the funeral was over, until a safe passage could be made for him. There Louis Fischer, the American journalist, saw him briefly as he paced up and down like a caged tiger. He was almost demented with grief, and he may have known that this was his last appearance at a political rally in Russia. Two months later he was exiled to Alma-Ata in Kazakhstan, where among apple orchards and flowers, in a reed-thatched farmhouse, he sat down to translate a vitriolic pamphlet by Karl Marx, and the works of Thomas Hodgkin, an obscure English utopian socialist.

When he spoke about the opposition, Stalin liked to tell one of Krylov's fables about a hermit and a bear who grew very fond of one another. One day, when the hermit was sleeping, a fly settled on his nose. The bear, full of solicitude, waved the fly away, but it obstinately returned. Out of love for the hermit the bear decided to put an end to the fly once and for all, so that the hermit could sleep peacefully. So the bear picked up an enormous stone, and just at the moment when the fly settled again on the hermit's forehead, he brought the stone down on the fly, and cracked open the hermit's skull.

'You see,' Stalin would explain with savage irony, 'the opposition is just like that bear.'

DIZZY WITH SUCCESS

As STALIN GREW increasingly powerful, hovering like a vast shadow over a country where there was no organized opposition and where every manifestation of opposition was mercilessly uprooted, there arose inevitably among those who feared the total domination of Stalin small splinter groups of men who hoped that in some mysterious way the total dictatorship of one man could be avoided. Communist historians, and Stalin himself, speak of the Right Opposition and the Left Opposition, as though these were actual political parties with fixed programmes and clearly defined aims. But there were no political parties: only baffled men searching desperately for a solution. There was a ground swell of opposition, ill-organized, with continually shifting allegiances, uncertain in its aims, seeking for leadership and finding none.

The men who fought against Stalin had no weapons, no programmes, and no hope of winning any victories. They were terrified, lost and confused. They behaved as people behave when they are caught in the beams of powerful searchlights; blinded, they turned this way and that way, stretched out their arms, and made ineffective gestures. There was no need for the searchlights to be turned on continually. At intervals the lights would be turned off, and in the darkness the dim shapes of the conspirators could be seen moving like ghosts through the familiar countryside. When the lights were turned on again, they assumed the same postures as before.

The handful of leaders who formed the opposition were men who had already outlived their time. All of them had betrayed the revolution, all were compromised. Even Bukharin, the only one of them who possessed a keen intelligence and the capacity to lead the revolution into new and safer channels, was so deeply compromised that he could no longer take independent action. His powers had been stripped from him. Already he resembled a victim offering himself up for the sacrifice.

The final break between Bukharin and Stalin occurred early in July 1928. The exact date was probably July 10th, for on the following day Bukharin, accompanied by Sokolnikov, called on Kamenev in a state of abject terror. Their meeting was attended by the usual mystifications pleasing to the conspiratorial nature of the Russian mind. No telephone calls were made, no bells were rung, the door of Kamenev's apartment in Moscow opened silently to receive the two visitors. Kamenev was calm and spoke guardedly; Bukharin was in a state bordering on collapse; Sokolnikov seems to have said nothing at all, regarding himself merely as the intermediary between these political figures who were formerly so powerful.

What Bukharin had to say probably came as no surprise to Kamenev. He spoke like a man who had reached the end of the road, still shuddering from his last interview with Stalin. At this interview he learned that the prospects for the revolution were more terrible than any he had imagined. He urged Kamenev not to take any notes. No one must know about this meeting, and it must never be discussed on the telephone. He spoke in feverish, disconnected sentences, jumping from one subject to another as the mood came to him.

'Stalin's line will be the ruin of the revolution,' he said. 'It will bring us all to the abyss. For several weeks I refused to speak with Stalin. He is nothing more than an unprincipled intriguer who subordinates everything to his appetite for power. At any given moment he will change his theories in order to get rid of someone. Our relations have reached the point when all we can say is, "You are lying!" If he pretends to make concessions, it is only to have a better grip on our throats!'

He pointed out that Stalin's line was one of almost unbelievable crudity and simplicity. Hating the peasants because they had never fully accepted the revolution, he was determined to sacrifice them. Just as capitalism had developed through loans and through the exploitation of the colonies and of the workers, so the Russian Communists, having no colonies and no means of acquiring large-scale loans, were exploiting the one remaining class which lent itself to exploitation – the peasantry. Stalin believed as an axiom that the more socialism grew, the more resistance there would be, and he was determined to break this resistance. The inevitable result of 'this idiotic and illiterate theory' was that the leader of the country would have to use unexampled force. 'In this way,' said Bukharin, 'we are left with nothing but a police state.'

In foreign affairs, according to Bukharin, the prospects were no better. Stalin had succeeded in expelling the Comintern from the Kremlin. He was showing extraordinary weakness in his relations to foreign powers, and did not understand how to deal with foreigners. All the time, in dealing with the Comintern, Stalin wanted to demonstrate his brilliant theoretical powers, and he had even threatened to read a paper at the forthcoming Congress. Bukharin did not stop to ask himself why he was so mortally afraid of Stalin reading a paper to the assembled representatives of the Communist parties abroad. It was perhaps only one more sign that Stalin was attempting to take power, all power, into his own hands.

Again and again during that strange monologue Bukharin kept asking: 'What is going to happen?' and answering the question in much the same way. 'The party is doomed,' he said. 'The state and the party have become one.' Stalin was simply leading the country to 'famine and ruin'. His policy could only lead to civil war, and he would be forced to drown the rebellions in blood. 'Stalin will strangle us all. He knows only vengeance – the dagger in the back. We must remember his theory of sweet revenge.' The theory of sweet revenge was five years old. One summer night in 1923 Stalin had opened his heart to Dzerzhinsky and Kamenev, and said: 'To choose one's victim, to prepare one's plans minutely, to slake an implacable vengeance, and then to go to bed – there is nothing sweeter in the world.' Bukharin now realized that he was to become one of the sacrificial offerings.

As he talked, it seemed to him that there was only one force which could stop Stalin in his tracks: the concerted action of all the remaining Old Bolsheviks who were not hopelessly entangled in Stalin's net. He must have known that concerted action was now impossible. Panic-stricken, he did not know where to turn. He spoke about secrecy – everything must be done with the utmost secrecy – and yet at the end of the meeting he agreed that a full report of their discussion should be sent to Zinoviev, who was in exile in Voronezh. Kamenev accordingly wrote out an account of the discussion in the form of a series of statements, dialogues and later observations, and sent it by special messenger to Zinoviev. A few hours or days later the notes were in the hands of Stalin, who is reported to have said: 'Now they are in their coffin, and all we need is to dig the grave.'

The incompetence and stupidity of the conspirators played into the hands of Stalin. The original revolutionary flame had withered until it was no more than a quivering breath of smoke among the ashes. They had lost contact with reality, with the result that one blunder led to another and they perished like men devoted to death.

Stalin seems to have been pleasantly surprised by the ease with which he had destroyed the opposition, and from time to time in his speeches he would point to it with some pride, while warning the comrades 'not to become the prey of self-satisfaction and self-admiration'. He called for more and more self-criticism, for it was only by self-criticism that men could eliminate their shortcomings. The leaders, too, must submit to self-criticism, for they had risen immeasurably high and were in danger of losing contact with the masses. 'If the leaders at the top find themselves looking down at the masses,' he said, 'then nothing but ruin came come to the party.'

As the years passed, he was becoming more and more remote from the people. He had come to depend on others, especially the members of his huge secretariat, to inform him about the needs of the country. He saw the world through the windows of the Kremlin, and rarely left Moscow.

In January 1928, accompanied by Malenkov, he made his first and last inspection tour of Siberia, ostensibly in order to discuss grain deliveries with the local farmers. The real reason was a more intimidating one. The farmers had been speculating in grain prices, and he was determined to put an end to it. They were not delivering the grain the government demanded at the prices the government wanted to pay. They had formed powerful combinations, and were sufficiently far from Moscow to feel independent.

At first there was little to suggest that this was anything more than a perfectly normal inspection tour. He paid special attention to the areas where the grain delivery had been poor, visited the villages, looked at barns, stables and threshing floors, asked whether the farmers had complaints and whether they were being well-treated by local officials, and showed himself to be affable and courteous. In a little notebook he entered the punishments to be meted out. He was apparently good-humoured even when the farmers were insolent. He tells the story of how he spent two hours arguing with grain owners in an attempt to persuade them to deliver the grain, and how a kulak came up to him with a pipe in his mouth and said: 'Let me see you dance, young fellow, and then I will give you a bushel or two.' The story was told at a plenary session of the Central Committee a year later, and Stalin described the incident as taking place between a Bolshevik agitator and a kulak in Kazakhstan, but none of his listeners doubted that Stalin was the 'young fellow' who had been ordered to dance for a bushel of grain.

Stalin spent three weeks on the tour. He was continually on the move, addressing meetings, travelling by day and staying in obscure villages by night, filling out the notebook with notations about the hoards of grain which were being concealed from the government authorities. In one of the speeches he made during the tour, he said:

I have been sent to you in Siberia for a short visit. My mission is to help you fulfil your grain delivery quota. I have also been ordered to discuss with you the possibilities for agricultural development and the plans for developing collective farms and state farms in your area ... You know, of course, what the effect of the shortages will be if they are not made good. What will happen will be that our towns and industrial centres and the Red Army will be in difficulties, they will be poorly supplied, and they will be threatened with hunger. Clearly we cannot allow that ... You tell me the grain delivery quotas are too high and cannot be fulfilled. Why cannot they be fulfilled? Where does this idea come from? Isn't it true that your harvest this year is a record one? And isn't it true that the Siberian grain delivery quotas are almost the same as last year? Then why do you say the plan cannot be fulfilled? Look at the farms of the kulaks! Their barns and granaries are brimming with grain, and grain is lying in the open for lack of storage space . . . I have seen dozens of your prosecuting and judicial officials. Nearly all of them are living in the homes of kulaks, they board and lodge with them, and of course they are only too anxious to live in peace with them. Clearly, nothing effective or useful to the Soviet state can be expected from these prosecuting and judicial officials. It it not at all clear why these gentry have not been cleared out and replaced by more honest officials.

I propose (1) the immediate delivery of all grain surpluses from the kulaks at government prices, (2) kulaks refusing to obey the law be prosecuted under Article 107 of the Criminal Code of the RSFSR, and their grain surpluses confiscated by the state, with the proviso that 25 per cent of the confiscated grain be distributed among the poor and less well-to-do peasants at low government prices or in the form of long-term loans.

You will soon see these measures producing splendid results.

Among the other measures introduced was the abrupt dismissal of all Communists who had any contact with kulaks, whatever their former revolutionary services. Kulaks were officially described as 'alien elements'; their grain was taken from them, and if they resisted or protested, they were placed on trial and received exemplary punishment. The iron broom was being swept across Siberia. The kulaks had only a few more months to live.

On Stalin's return to Moscow the campaign against the kulaks began. Kulak farms were raided, the grain was expropriated, and the farmers were arrested. There was as yet no general programme of expropriation; during the spring and the summer the raids and requisitions were haphazard and tentative. Some very rich farmers were murdered, while others nearly as rich were left in peace. In July 1928 Stalin was saying that the question of expropriating the peasants had never arisen. In December 1929 he was saying it was no longer sufficient to expropriate the kulaks: a merciless war must be waged against them. For the farmers, whether rich or poor, there was now no law, no court of appeal, no means of escape. The secret police were encouraged to deal with the recalcitrant peasantry as they saw fit. The kulaks and the 'middle peasants' took to arms. They hid their grain, burned their crops, destroyed their farm implements and slaughtered their cattle. Not only the kulaks and the 'middle peasants' perished; the poor peasants, too, were caught up in the senseless programme to carve up the whole of agricultural Russia into collective and state farms overnight.

The law of the land became whatever the secret police desired. The captured farmers became the prisoners of the secret police, which thus acquired a vast labour force which could be made to work on starvation rations and sent wherever some bureaucrat in Moscow thought work was desirable. The GPU employed millions of slaves, who built railroads, dug canals, and cut down forests. Into the coffers of the secret police immense wealth poured, as the slaves were sent down into the mines or made to harvest the natural wealth of Russia. Hundreds of thousands of slaves perished in the arctic winters; they were soon replaced.* The power of the secret police had never been greater, for it dominated the entire economic life of the country. Stalin had described the GPU as 'the terror of the bourgeoisie, the vigilant guardian of the revolution, the naked sword of the proletariat'. But now the GPU terrorized the proletariat and the peasantry alike, and no one was safe from it.

Stalin murdered and exiled the peasants because their murder and exile only increased his personal power. He was not concerned with the fate of millions of men; he was concerned only with his power, his ability to control every aspect of the economic life of the country. By collectivizing the farms and nationalizing peasant labour, he made the peasantry completely dependent upon the state: they would sow what he ordered them to sow and reap what he ordered them to reap. The result was that ten million peasants perished. Not even Hitler with his mechanical gas chambers showed so much talent for mass murder.

Thirteen years later Winston Churchill asked Stalin point-blank whether the cares of fighting a war were greater than

* The first slave labour camps were established by Lenin on Solovetsky Island in the Arctic in 1922.

those he had known when he was forcing collectivization upon a rebellious peasantry. It was late at night, and Stalin was in a relaxed mood.

'Yes,' Stalin said, 'the collective farm policy was a terrible struggle.'

'I thought you would have found it bad,' Churchill answered, 'because you were not dealing with a few score thousand of aristocrats or big landowners, but with millions of small men.'

'Ten million,' Stalin said, holding up his hands.

He held up his hands so that Churchill could count the fingers, but even so it was beyond belief. Equally beyond belief was the explanation which Stalin advanced, speaking in the tones of a man who had watched helplessly while a natural disaster, earthquake or volcanic eruption, occurred. He said:

'It was fearful. Four years it lasted. It was absolutely necessary for Russia, if we were to avoid periodic famines, to plough the land with tractors. We must mechanize our agriculture. When we gave tractors to the peasants, they were all spoiled in a few months. Only collective farms with workshops could handle tractors. We took the greatest trouble to explain it to the peasants. It was no use arguing with them. After you have said all you can to a peasant, he says he must go home and consult his wife, and he must consult his herder. After he has talked it over with them he always answers that he does not want the collective farm, and he would rather do without the tractors.'

'These were what you call kulaks?'

'Yes,' he said, but he did not repeat the word. After a pause, 'It was all very bad and difficult – but necessary.'

'What happened?' I asked.

'Oh, well,' he said, 'many of them agreed to come in with us. Some of them were given land of their own to cultivate in the province of Tomsk or the province of Irkutsk or farther north, but the great bulk were very unpopular and were wiped out by their labourers.'

There was a considerable pause. Then, 'Not only have we vastly increased the food supply, but we have improved the quality of the grain beyond measure. All kinds of grain used to be grown. Now no one is allowed to sow any but the standard Soviet grain from one end of our country to the other.'

In this way, during a time of disasters, Stalin defended an earlier disaster which he had inflicted upon his country. Most of his statements were calculated untruths. He had not vastly increased the food supply by introducing the standard Soviet grain from one end of the country to another, and when he spoke of giving lands to the farmers in Siberia and the far north, he may have enjoyed the irony, but he was not committing himself to the truth. The only truthful statement he made to Churchill was: 'It was all very bad and difficult.'

How bad and how difficult appears from the losses in livestock which were a direct result of the collectivization programme. They were not such losses as plague or drought or famine could bring about. The figures in the official handbook of agricultural statistics have a bloodless look about them, but they register the calamities of those years with a terrifying monumentality:

LIVESTOCK POPULATION (MILLIONS OF HEAD)

	1928	1934
Horses	32·1	15·4
Cattle	60·1	33·5
Pigs	22·0	11·5
Sheep	97·3	32·9

Such violent and comprehensive disasters are rarely visited upon a country not in a state of war. Nothing quite like this had ever happened to Russia before, and not until Hitler attacked the Soviet Union was disaster to become so commonplace again. Soviet rural economy had still not caught up with these staggering losses in 1947.

Stalin did not regard these losses with any great seriousness. Marxist theory, liberally supported by quotations from Lenin, endorsed the destruction of the kulaks as a class. If Bukharin and others were against 'dekulakization' and showed by quotations from Marx and Lenin that it was unnecessary and dangerous, so much the worse for them – they had failed to understand the spirit of Marxism and were traitors to the revolution.

Stalin professed to be delighted with the reports that streamed into his Kremlin office. Everything was going well. In the space of four months 50 per cent of all the peasants in the entire country, and even higher proportions in the areas of south-eastern European Russia which normally produced a grain surplus, had been collectivized. The only danger was that the comrades might become 'dizzy with success'. He warned the comrades that successes have 'their dark side'. He said:

> Successes have their dark side, especially when they come about with comparative ease, or, as they say unexpectedly. Such successes sometimes induce a spirit of vanity and conceit: 'We can do everything!' 'There is nothing we cannot do!' People not infrequently become drunk with such successes, their heads go round and round as they contemplate their success, they lose their sense of proportion, they lose the capacity to come to grips with reality, they show a tendency to overrate their own strength and to underestimate the strength of the enemy.

These observations appeared in an article in *Pravda* on March 2nd, 1930, when the harm had already been done. In the same article he hinted that there might be some slight need to curb the excesses of those who were bringing about the collectivization of the peasantry. The peasants must be shown the advantages of collectivization; it must be demonstrated to them quietly and gently that they will be happier under the new dispensation. Lenin had said there must not be the slightest compulsion, and of course there had not been any compulsion at all, except on the part of a few comrades who were 'dizzy with success'. On them fell the blame and the ignominy for punishing some of the 'middle peasants'. As for the kulaks, those bloodsuckers, spiders and vampires, they deserved all they got.

In this spirit, encouraging the gentle and striking out at the strong, Stalin showed himself to be the partisan of gentle persuasion. It was a role he played without conviction. He knew exactly what he was doing. The loss of ten million peasants and some 120 million horses, cattle, pigs and sheep was a small price to pay for the victory of an idea which in its simplest terms was merely: 'Collectivize everything, and see what happens.' He said in 1933: 'From the standpoint of Leninism, the collective economies, and the Soviets as well, are, taken as a form of organization, a weapon and nothing but a weapon.' As Martin Buber observed, one cannot in the nature of things expect a little tree that has been turned into a club to put forth leaves.

In December 1929, at the height of the collectivization campaign, Stalin celebrated his fiftieth birthday. The celebrations were designed to put to shame the puny honours paid to the Tsars. All over Russia there were parades and processions, speeches and gala performances to honour the birthday of a man who was so far above other men that he could only be addressed in hyperbole. He was no longer Stalin, but Great Stalin, the Leader, the unparalleled Builder of Communism, the Father of Peoples. The pages of *Pravda* were filled with adulation of the great genius who had providentially descended to earth to show by example and precept how men should live; and though the name of Lenin was occasionally mentioned, as of someone who had lived in a remote age and set the wheel of doctrine in motion, Stalin now appeared as a massive figure in his own right, who derived his authority from his own effortless power. He was the predetermined saviour. 'The role of Stalin,' wrote Kaganovich, 'was already predetermined in the dawn of development of our party, when the foundation stones were being laid, when the first party circles were being organized.'

Peasants in the frozen prison camps in the north signed testimonials to the kindness of Stalin in permitting them to live in socialist prisons. *Pravda* announced that Communist prisoners in the capitalist jails of Poland, Hungary and Italy had succeeded in their thousands in smuggling messages of congratulation out of their prisons. To celebrate his birthday the Communist Party of Germany called for a Stalin levy. Everywhere there were posters describing Stalin as 'the best of the best of those forming the iron battalion of the Bolshevik guard'.

The Bolshevik rulers vied with one another in describing his virtues. Ordjonikidze, soon to die at Stalin's orders, declared that there had never been an occasion when Stalin had disagreed with Lenin, who had esteemed him above all other comrades. What distinguished Stalin from all other comrades was his boundless faith, his infinite loyalty to Lenin, and his sense of the inherent justice of Communism. Voroshilov described the great military strategist who had forced the gates of Krasnaya Gorka and stiffened the resistance of the defenders of Tsaritsyn. Of all the articles in praise of Stalin, Voroshilov's 'Stalin and the Red Army' was perhaps the most interesting, for it included unpublished documents on Stalin's military career, showing that 'he always correctly determined the chief directions to be taken for the main blow at the enemy'. Many passages of Voroshilov's article were written by Stalin himself.

Although the exaltation of Stalin reached new and hitherto unsuspected heights on Stalin's fiftieth birthday, Stalin himself maintained a proper humility. In answer to the hundreds of thousands of messages of congratulation, he published a reply which appeared on the front page of *Pravda* the day after his birthday:

> Your congratulations and greetings I place to the credit of the great party of the working class which bore me and reared me in its own image and likeness. And just because I place them to the credit of our glorious Leninist party, I make bold to tender you my Bolshevik gratitude.
>
> Comrades, you need have no doubt that I am prepared in the future, too, to devote to the cause of the working class, to the cause of the proletarian revolution and world communism, all my strength, all my ability, and, if need be, all my blood, drop by drop.
>
> *With deep respect,*
> J. STALIN.

Although the birthday celebrations were stage-managed and choreographed to an unprecedented degree, and the praise heaped upon him was so fulsome that it would have been indigestible to anyone with a weaker stomach, nevertheless the occasion deserved celebration. Stalin had emerged at last as the undisputed victor. Those who had formerly laid claim to the throne were in full retreat, despairing even of the honour of being permitted to hide in the throne's shadow. Trotsky was safely in exile, expelled from Russia ostensibly under Article 58/10 of the Criminal Code for 'preparing an armed struggle against the Soviet power'. His only remaining weapon was his vitriolic pen, for during the months of his exile in Alma-Ata he had lost whatever support he had once possessed among the intelligentsia and in the Red Army. When the charge was originally presented to him he wrote that it was 'criminal in substance and illegal in form'. So perhaps it was, but he had committed so many illegal acts in his life and had so little taste for legality that he may have been aware of the irony of his last official statement in the Soviet Union. Irony attended him throughout his long exile. When he was sent to Turkey under armed guard, the London *Times* commented on his arrival in Constantinople that he had probably been sent by Stalin to foment revolution in the Near East.

By ridding himself of Trotsky, Stalin prepared the way for a quarter of a century of absolute rule. He liked to describe this period as 'the great change'; and so it was. His power was secure, unalterable and final; it would end only with his death. He would permit others to live, but only on his own terms.

To those who visited him, Stalin presented a modest and retiring appearance. American Communists who visited him in May 1929, shortly after the expulsion of Trotsky, heard with surprise that among their major sins was their declaration that they were Stalinites. 'My dear comrades, that is disgraceful,' Stalin said. 'Do you not know that there are no Stalinites, that there must be no Stalinites?' Between May 6th and May 14th he delivered three lectures on the factions which had broken out in the American Communist Party. These lectures, which are not included in his *Collected Works*, perhaps because he felt that the American Communist Party had little relevance to the history of world Communism, are remarkable for their underlying bitterness. He disliked the American Communists, and warned them: 'Comrades, the Comintern is not a stock market. The Comintern is the holy of holies of the working class. The Comintern, therefore, must not be confused with the stock market.' One of his graver charges against the American Communists was that they had underestimated the power of the Communist movement in America. He, Stalin, knew better. The Communist movement in America was exceptionally powerful, even if its leaders were not aware of it. It was magnificently equipped to deal with the heightening crisis in capitalism. Unfortunately the leaders were fools, factionalists and deviationists, who refused to obey the orders of the Kremlin and showed signs of being immune to the revolutionary bacillus. They were tricksters, manipulators, intriguers and backstage wirepullers – no words were too harsh to describe them.

Stalin knew very little about the political situation in America. 'I think the moment is not far off when a revolutionary crisis will develop in America,' he declared. 'And when a revolutionary crisis develops in America, that will be the beginning of the end of world capitalism as a whole.' The wish was father to the thought. Many wishes were father to many thoughts. He had reached that peculiar stage, common among dictators, when the line between desire and reality breaks down.

Meanwhile the glorification of Stalin continued with unabated vigour. In February 1930, when Russia was in the grip of starvation, it occurred to him that the time had come when he should receive some signal honour for his revolutionary efforts, and accordingly he awarded himself with his second Order of the Red Banner, the first having been received for his victory at Krasnaya Gorka. He always took pains to record the exact dates of the honours he received, and so the biographical chronicle records under the date February 23rd that 'in response to the request of numerous organizations and general meetings of workers, peasants and Red Army men, J. V. Stalin was awarded a second Order of the Red Banner for his outstanding services on the front of socialist construction'.

Now more than ever he regarded himself as the constructor of a new civilization, the architect of a nation. He would give shape and form to the nation until it bore his own image and likeness. He would draw lines across the map, and there would be canals dug by his millions of slaves. Where there were deserts and empty spaces, he would order the building of towns. Because he was a man of steel, he would transform Russia into a country of metal. A few days before his fiftieth birthday, on the twelfth anniversary of the October revolution, he declared that Russian backwardness would come to an end and a new metallic Russia would surge forward until it had outstripped the capitalist countries. He said:

We are advancing at full steam along the path of industrialization towards socialism, leaving behind the age-old 'Russian' backwardness. We are becoming a country of metal, a country of automobiles, a country of tractors. And when we have set the USSR on an automobile, and the muzhik on a tractor, let the capitalist gentlemen, who boast so loudly of their 'civilization', try to overtake us! We shall then see which countries are to be classified as backward and which as advanced.

He never realized his dream. During the quarter of a century that remained to him, the Soviet Union never advanced at full steam along the path of industrialization. It lurched along, pausing at intervals to catch its breath, the whole country at the mercy of the all-powerful secret police.

He ruled by terror, which is always inefficient and wasteful, with the result that his plans of industrialization were continually breaking down. To the end of his life he would repeat the same cry: 'Let the capitalist gentlemen try to overtake us!' It was a strange cry, for the Soviet Union continually lagged behind.

A ROOM IN THE KREMLIN

By 1930 THE IMAGE which Stalin chose to present to the world was fully formed. Until his death he would continue to rule over Russia, imposing his erratic will on a people who came to regard him as a force of nature and therefore beyond all normal human laws. He grew older, but the face, the appearance, the gestures were always the same. He was to grant himself such titles as even the Roman Emperors never dreamed of, but there was nothing in the least imperial in that solid, heavy, moustached face which peered down from a million posters. In the year of his death, when he was over seventy, grey and flabby, with watery eyes and swollen ankles, he was still being represented in portraits as a man of early middle age.

The image which Stalin chose to present to the world was deliberately contrived and painstakingly adapted to circumstances. There was art in it, and not a little cunning. At times he would imitate Napoleon, thrusting two fingers between the buttons of his greatcoat, standing with set jaw and feet apart in the attitude of a conqueror, but this was a pose which he adopted chiefly when reviewing troops in the Red Square from the top of Lenin's tomb; it was not natural for him, nor was it very characteristic of him. The public pose which he maintained through the greater part of his life after achieving supreme power was a more modest one. He liked to say he was a quite ordinary revolutionary, whose only merit was that he had followed faithfully and humbly in the footsteps of Lenin, and he deliberately cultivated an air of ordinariness and humility. He would remind listeners that he was not a great theoretician like Lenin: his greatest merit was that he was a practical man who was able to put the theories into practice. In fact he was a bold theoretician with no particular gift for putting theories into practice except by destroying all the evidence that proved the theories wrong, and he was very far from being a humble follower of Lenin.

The mask concealed the man. The humble air, the grave, slow speech, the ever-present pipe, the elaborately simple uniform consisting of a plain brown military coat and dark trousers thrust into leather boots, all these were the props with which he played out his actor's role. The mask was placid, unemotional, stoic in the face of adversity, calm in danger, with no gift for dissembling, efficient and fatherly. The real man was something else. He was vain, hysterical, wildly emotional, quick to take offence, cynical and ruthless. Men were statistics, to be moulded at his pleasure: a few million more or a few million less made no difference to him. 'I have grown up on battlefields,' Napoleon told Metternich at a famous interview in Dresden, 'and a man like me cares little about the lives of a million men.' So it was with Stalin, whose fatherly affection for the people took the form of mass executions on a scale which has had no equal in history. His calm was illusory. Storms were continually blowing through him, and there were long periods in his life when he was in danger of being torn apart by powerful and conflicting forces over which he had no control. His rages were phenomenal. He knew the uses of sudden explosions of anger, and it amused him to keep his staff in a state of hysterical suspense, not knowing where the next blow would fall. He had little physical courage and panicked in times of danger.

The public mask however prevailed, and since he controlled all available resources of propaganda he was able to ensure that the image of the calm and fatherly Stalin should be the only one, for he permitted no other. He disliked being photographed, and the countless posters showing his benign features were usually drawings which were oddly unlike him, for they gave him a higher forehead, a bushier moustache, and thicker hair than he possessed. These drawings were usually in three-quarter face, a pose which showed him to advantage, and they attested more to the obedience of the artists than to their skill in portraiture.

This was the image that Stalin presented to the masses. Visitors to the Kremlin, seeing him at arm's length, were sometimes shocked to observe how little the public image resembled the man himself. They saw a short man, about five feet four inches tall, with a coarse pock-marked skin, a stiff brush of hair springing from a surprisingly low forehead, brown eyes shot with hazel, thick lips which sometimes parted to show ugly, short, gold and black teeth. It was a face in which the several parts seemed not to fit together. There was a curious heaviness and sullenness about him. He moved slowly and deliberately, and it seemed that every motion was calculated and pondered in advance. His eyes were watchful, rather crafty, and sometimes they appeared to flash yellow. He rarely spoke, preferring to listen or half-listen while he doodled endlessly with a blue or red crayon. There was nothing imposing about his physical presence, no grace of manner, no magnetism, no sense that he was one of the world's chosen ones. His voice was heavy, and he spoke with a pronounced Georgian accent. His speech did not fall into the natural rhythms of Russian, but into a strange, rather halting rhythm which was wholly his own.

Such was his outward appearance, and it was as misleading as the public image. The inner man was alert, intelligent, sensitive to the smallest nuances of a conversation, weighing everything he heard and evaluating every statement with uncommon precision. When he seemed to be absorbed in doodling, his senses were wide awake. He rarely looked men in the eyes and he could therefore learn little from the fleeting changes in the appearance of the eyes, which often show what men are really thinking. He relied on his ears, which were abnormally sensitive to alterations of rhythm, the slurring or quickening of the voice which announces that something is being concealed or said falsely. He had trained himself like a good police inspector to detect whether men told the truth or whether they were lying or whether they were mixing truth with falsity. Men, for Stalin, were largely disembodied voices.

The inner man was remote from the world as in a grave, curiously inert, so alien from the ordinary world of men that he was never able to form intimate friendships. Men were statistics, voices, echoes, and they seemed to come from a long way away. Their existence troubled him, and he preferred to be alone with his own thoughts, brooding on men's insufficiencies and never for a moment forgetting that every man was a potential source of danger. Even when he was in a position of unchallengeable authority, under heavy protective guard, never appearing in public except when he was standing on Lenin's tomb, he was continually devising new and more complicated methods of self-protection. He was a desperately lonely and desperately frightened man.

In the war he waged with himself he gave no quarter. At all times he was watching himself, mercilessly criticizing himself. He was one of those who, in Paul Valéry's words, had 'killed the marionette'. He was utterly uninterested in the ordinary conventions of life or in its social aspects. He had stripped himself bare of the ornaments with which men normally surround their lives. His temper was authoritarian, ascetic, quietly deliberate; it was as though he spent his days in going from one monk's cell to another, walking with a measured tread. Everything that was superfluous was omitted, torn out, exhausted. He read Gogol attentively, and he was amused by some of the more mordant passages in *Dead Souls*, but he showed a greater interest in Balzac, whose *La Comédie Humaine*, with its penetrating portraits of a decaying bourgeoisie, remained a constant study. Painting and sculpture meant nothing to him, though he enjoyed seeing larger-than-life-size sculptures of himself and he could sketch well enough to show an artist how he wanted himself depicted. He preferred drawings to paintings. He enjoyed music, particularly the operas of Verdi, and in later years he developed a considerable interest in the cinema, but his taste both in music and the cinema was confused, and he was likely to agree with the last authority he spoke to and change his opinion when the next authority came on the scene. His mind, like the rooms he inhabited, was bleak, cheerless, clinical.

His office in the Kremlin was fifty feet long and twenty feet wide. Two large photographs of Lenin and Karl Marx hung on the wall, high up, out of reach, in plain wooden frames. On his desk there was another, much smaller photograph of Lenin, a battery of five telephones, and a holder for his red and blue crayons. Unlike Lenin, whose desk was in a continual state of disorder, with scissors, mucilage, blotters and sealing wax lying among conglomerations of books, letters, documents and newspapers, Stalin kept his desk clean. Lenin had a working library within reach, maps hung on the wall, and there were piles of newspapers on the floor. In Stalin's office there were no books, no newspapers, no maps in sight: if he wanted them, he would simply call in a secretary and order them to be produced.

Lenin's small and untidy office opened on a conference room where the meetings of the Central Committee were usually held. Stalin's office was also his conference room, and meetings were held at a long table set against the wall immediately below the portraits of Lenin and Karl Marx. Ten people could sit comfortably at the table, which was furnished with water carafes, plain glasses and ashtrays. The walls were dark green, the carpet of the same colour. There were no flowers, no plants, nothing to distract the attention. Visitors came through a door at the far end of the room, and he would usually wave them into a chair beside the long table. He rarely met them at his desk.

His secretariat worked in an adjoining room; only in the direst emergencies were they permitted to enter his office without being summoned. After 1928, when he visited Siberia, he rarely left his office except during his annual holidays in the south. In that bare and austere office he worked day after day, year in, year out, like a monk in his cell.

His private quarters in the Kremlin were similarly barren of ornament. He lived in a small three-storey house, once inhabited by the Tsar's servants. The lower floor was occupied by guards; on the remaining floors there were three small bedrooms and a dining-room, reached through a narrow hallway. There was no kitchen, for meals were sent in. White linen curtains hung over the windows. The bedrooms were furnished as simply as those of a respectable second-class hotel, spotlessly clean, without ornament. The dining-room was oval-shaped, with the table occupying most of the space. One bedroom was used by a servant, another by his daughter Svetlana. His sons Jacob and Vasily, if they were staying in the Kremlin, slept on the dining-room divan or in a small alcove leading out of the dining-room. It was such a house as might have been occupied by a factory foreman with unusually severe tastes. The only comfortable object was a well-stuffed armchair in which Stalin liked to smoke his pipe or a cigarette after his meals. He smoked cigarettes frequently, but took care that he always had a pipe within reach.

The small house was merely a machine for living in; he had no affection for it. He had no sense of possession, no bank account, no income. He needed no income, for everything he wanted would be brought to him instantly after he had given an order on the telephone. He possessed all of Russia. Ships, railroad trains, fleets of automobiles, country estates, everything he could conceivably desire was given to him almost before he asked for it. He indulged himself in country houses. At various times he owned nearly a score of them, but except for the fortress-palace at Sochi and the Nadezhda estate on the Caucasian coast of the Black Sea, where he usually spent the summer, there was no sense of permanent possession. He would leave the Kremlin in August, when the dust and heat of Moscow became intolerable, and take the train for the south; and these journeys were always executed with military precision, with decoy trains sent on ahead, and with security guards patrolling every inch of the track. He had a fear of heights, and only once in his life travelled by aeroplane.

He was guarded as no one else has ever been guarded. Thousands upon thousands of men were employed to protect him. When he left the Kremlin for one or other of his country estates, he would be driven in a black Packard by way of the Mozhaisk Chaussee through streets where trusted security guards stood at every twenty yards. Usually decoy automobiles would be sent on ahead. The country estates were ringed by guards, and every known electronic device was used to prevent unauthorized persons from entering the magic circle in which he lived. At his feet in the automobile there was always a machine gun.

Just as Lenin would always draw up the ground plan of every house at which he stayed, and carefully work out all possible escape routes, so Stalin, with even more thoroughness, supervised his own protection, pored over maps and tracings, and invented more and more complicated ways of evading an assassin's bullet. Once he was in power, he never walked through the streets of Moscow, for he had a morbid fear of assassination. The inevitable result was that he became the prisoner of his private guard.

His revolver, like his pipe, was always within reach, but he permitted no one to come into his presence armed. Even very high officials were thoroughly searched before they were allowed to see him. Once Molotov, returning from a hurried mission to London, was thrown bodily to the ground when it was discovered that he was still carrying a revolver when walking up to Stalin's office in the Kremlin. Molotov complained about the treatment he had received, and Stalin merely reminded him that he was lucky to have gotten away with his life.

By 1930 Stalin was already withdrawing from the world. The ordinary preoccupations of people no longer had any meaning for him. He delivered speeches, welcomed ambassadors, attended state functions, and paid a periodical tribute to the Russian ballet, occupying the box previously reserved for the Tsar, but more and more he was a monk in a cell ringed round by armed men, remote from the world and lost in his meditations. He suffered from the vice which the medieval monks accounted as among the deadliest of the seven deadly sins—*accidia,* the noonday madness of illimitable boredom. Pride, too, assailed him, and this was even more dangerous. From this period there begins to be heard the mechanically reiterated cry: '*Slava velikomu Stalinu!* Glory to great Stalin!'

Pride tormented him and boredom plagued him; there was no escaping them. The cry would grow louder until it became the deafening accompaniment of all his actions, his imperial progress. No other Russian in history, not even Lenin, received such flattery. When the poets compared him with the sun, when his statue was placed on the highest peak of the Caucasus, when cities were named after him, he accepted these gifts as his due, and it never seems to have occurred to him that there was poison in them. He drank eagerly from the cup, which was constantly replenished. He dreamed of world rule and his own deification, accepted or invented the title of 'Father of the Peoples', and saw himself as the destined Moses who would lead the world's children to the promised land.

The small pock-marked man in the Kremlin rarely spoke about his true beliefs. No secretaries reported his intimate conversations for posterity. The rare foreigners who were permitted to enter the Kremlin went away baffled by the thickness of his protective armour. Those who wondered how a man could hold such vast power and still remain sane were puzzled to find him wearing the robes of humility.

One of the few who succeeded in penetrating a little way through the disguise was the German author Emil Ludwig who had a three-hour interview with him on December 31st, 1931. In the following spring the Russian transcript of the interview was published in the magazine *Bolshevik*. Ludwig had considerable experience of interviewing historic personages and had written extensively about leading figures of the past. He had some preconceived opinions about Stalin, and many of these remained with him after he left Russia. Writing in 1942, he described Stalin as 'a healthy, moderate man who in fifteen years of rule has never manifested a single symptom of delusions of grandeur'. He believed that Stalin had faithfully kept the oath he swore at Lenin's tomb, and was impressed by the dictator's good nature and affability. Sometimes he asked hard questions, and the replies are illuminating.

It occurred to Ludwig that Peter the Great had forced the transformation of Russia and that in some way Stalin could be regarded as his successor. Stalin denied the charge peremptorily. 'These historical parallels are always dangerous,' he replied, 'but if you insist upon it, I can only say the following: Peter brought only one stone to the temple. Lenin built it. As for myself, I am only a pupil of Lenin, and my only desire is to be worthy of him.'

Ludwig noted silently that Stalin had deliberately omitted 'the Great', and that something was wrong in this disingenuous pose of humility. He said he had always understood that Marxism denies the role of heroes in history: it is not the heroes but the masses who changed the course of historical events.

'No,' replied Stalin, 'Marxism does not in the least deny the role played by outstanding individuals or that history is made by the masses. Of course in *The Poverty of Philosophy* and in other works by Marx you will find the statement that history is made by the masses. But people do not make history according to the promptings of their imagination or according to their fancy. Every new generation encounters definite conditions already in existence, and its greatness is measured by the way it brings a correct understanding to these conditions and changes them. If they fail to understand these conditions and decide to alter them according to the promptings of their imagination, then they will find themselves in the same situation as Don Quixote. That, at least, is how we Russian Bolsheviks understand Marx, and we have been studying Marx for a good many years now.'

Ludwig said he understood from his German professors that the materialistic conception of history denied the role of heroic personalities in history.

'The German professors are wrong,' said Stalin. 'They are vulgarizers of Marxism. Marxism has never denied the role of heroes. On the contrary Marxism recognizes the considerable role they play, but with the reservations I have just stated.'

According to Stalin, history was made by the masses, but it was also made by the heroes. Peter the Great was a hero of feudalism, and Lenin of communism; Peter the Great was a drop in the sea, Lenin the whole ocean. And having announced this conclusion, Stalin was confronted with one of those sharp and tiresome questions which Ludwig was able to ask only because Stalin had liked and read his books and was prepared to be affable. The question was: 'Who decides?'

To this question there could be only three answers: (a) the heroes, (b) the masses, or (c) both together. Stalin, confronted with the three alternatives, suddenly reversed his former argument in defence of heroes and announced: 'No, individual people cannot decide,' and went into an elaborate argument on the need for collective authority. Individuals are always making mistakes, the country would never tolerate power in the hands of one person, and it is only by open discussion among the best available minds that proper solutions can be arrived at. 'There are about seventy members of the Central Committee,' he said, 'and among them you will find our best industrial leaders, our best co-operative leaders, our best supply managers, our best soldiers, our best propagandists and agitators, our best experts on the nations constituting the Soviet Union and on national policy.' These seventy members form an 'Areopagus' where the collective wisdom of the party is expressed. It is odd that Stalin chose the word 'Areopagus', for this was the hill of the war god, lying close to the Acropolis in Athens, where the Athenians held their highest court dealing especially with capital crimes. The Athenians were not governed from the Areopagus, but from another hill altogether.

'Who decides?' Ludwig had asked, and Stalin was saying, 'The seventy decide.'*

Then Ludwig asked why the government was so severe and ruthless against its enemies, and Stalin answered by recalling

---

* At another time Stalin said the decisions were made by the three or four thousand front-rank leaders of the party. In a speech to the plenum of the Central Committee in 1937 he said: 'In our party, if we have in mind its leading strata, there are three to four thousand leaders whom we call the party's general staff. Then there are 30-40,000 middle rank leaders, who are our party's corps of officers. Then there are about 100-150,000 of the lower-rank party command staff, who are so to speak our party's non-commissioned officers.'

the early years of the Revolution when the Bolsheviks showed at first a conciliatory attitude towards their enemies, only to discover that they were surrounded by traitors. He gave the example of General Krasnov who organized a counter-revolutionary campaign against Petrograd, was captured and released 'on his word of honour as a soldier', and went on to organize the Cossacks against the Soviets. 'We learned by experience,' said Stalin, 'that the only way to deal with these enemies was to inflict upon them the most merciless policy of suppression.'

'This policy of cruelty,' Ludwig replied, 'seems to have aroused a very widespread fear. I have the impression that a large part of the population is afraid of the Soviet power, and that the stability of the regime reposes on a basis of fear. What I would like to know is your own state of mind when you are confronted with the knowledge that in order to strengthen your power you must inspire terror. You do not use these methods when you are with your comrades, your friends – you do not make them afraid. But the people are terrified.'

Ludwig had spoken with extraordinary boldness. It was a hard question, perhaps the hardest of all, but Stalin made light of it. It was simply not true that the Soviet power rested on a basis of terror. Was it possible that a government could retain power for fourteen years by intimidation and terror? Terror was the instrument used by the Tsars; it had proved a useless weapon, for the Tsars had been overthrown. When Ludwig reminded Stalin that the Romanovs had ruled for three hundred years, Stalin pointed to the uprisings of Stenka Razin and Emelyan Pugachev, the attempted *coup d'état* by the Decembrists in 1825, the revolutions of 1905, February 1917 and October 1917. The people had never been submissive under the Tsars. There was a pause while Stalin laughed quietly, and then he took up the thread of his argument on terror. He said:

Of course, there remains a certain small section of the population that really fears the Soviet power and fights against it. I am thinking of the remnants of those dying classes now in process of liquidation – I am thinking of a small fraction of the peasantry – the kulaks. We are not concerned with the question of instituting a reign of terror among these groups, for such a policy really doesn't exist.

Everyone knows that we Bolsheviks do not confine ourselves to using weapons of terror, but go further – our aim
is to liquidate completely the whole class of the bourgeoisie.
*The kulaks also fear the other section of the peasant popu-
lation. This is a hang-over from the earlier class system.
Among the middle classes, for example, and especially the
professional classes, there is something of the same kind of
fear, because these latter had special privileges under the
old regime. Moreover, there are traders and a certain section of the peasants still maintain the old liking for the
gentry.*

But if you take the working population of the USSR,
the workers and the labouring peasants, you will find that
not more than ten per cent† are against the regime, *or are
silent from fear or are waiting for the moment when they
can undermine the Bolshevik state.* The vast majority sup-
ports the Soviet system because this system serves the fundamental interests of the workers and peasants. *We often have
to put on the brakes. They would like to stamp out the last
remnants of the intelligentsia. But we would not permit
that. In the whole history of the world there never was a
power that was supported by nine tenths of the population
as the Soviet power is supported.*

*That is the reason for our success in putting our ideas
into practice. If we ruled only by fear, not a man would
have stood by us. The working classes would have destroyed
any power that attempted to continue to rule by fear.
Workers who have made three revolutions have had some
practice in overthrowing governments. They would not
endure such a mockery of government as one merely based
on fear.*

In his conversation with Ludwig, Stalin gives the appearance of being on the defensive. He turns the question aside,
admits little, laughs scornfully at those who would think
Russia could be ruled by terror. Far from being a man who
inspired terror, he claims he is one of those who prevented
acts of terror. The workers would like to have killed off the
entire intelligentsia, but he, Stalin, had prevented them. 'Every-

---

* The words in italics are omitted in the transcript given in
Stalin's *Collected Works.*

† According to Ludwig, Stalin said that fifteen per cent, not
ten per cent, were against the regime.

one knows that we Bolsheviks do not confine ourselves to using weapons of terror,' Stalin said, thereby admitting that weapons of terror were used abundantly, although other weapons are also used. He makes light of terror; yet it is the thread on which the conversation hangs.

In this way throughout the conversation we are made aware of a cautious ambivalence. It was the same when they came to discuss America. Ludwig remarked that he had observed in Russia an intense respect, amounting to worship, of everything American. Stalin answered that on the contrary the Russians had no especially high regard for everything American, but then he went on to modify the statement adroitly, saying that the Russians admired the vigour and health of Americans, their whole approach to work, their habits of democracy and 'the efficiency the Americans display in everything – in industry, technology, literature and life'. He said no, and then yes. He was always saying no, and when he said yes it was usually too late.

Of his own survival he spoke dispassionately, as though he was merely the product of forces; and when Ludwig asked him whether he believed in fate, he said: 'Fate is contrary to law. It is something mystic, and I do not believe in it. Of course there were reasons why I came through all these dangers. It could not have happened merely by accident.' A few moments later Ludwig left the Kremlin, remembering how Stalin had 'laughed in his dark muffled way' when he spoke of fate.

Ludwig had spoken to Stalin in his bare Kremlin office, where the only decorations were the photographs of Marx and Lenin, and the carafes and ashtrays set at orderly intervals on the conference table. Everything was barren, orderly, painfully neat. The office reminded him of nothing so much as a doctor's consulting-room. Continually doodling with a red pencil, rarely looking up, Stalin answered all the questions addressed to him, though rarely convincingly. His mind worked unhurriedly, unemotionally. Once, when Trotsky's name was mentioned, he shot a dour look at Ludwig, but otherwise showed no emotion. 'He is the most silent man I ever saw, silent until he suddenly attacks you,' Ludwig observed.

In that silent room with the dark-green walls Stalin spent nearly thirty years of his working life. If the room resembled a doctor's consulting-room, it also resembled those faded and austere rooms which are favoured by high ecclesiastical figures: rooms where silence accumulates, where clocks chime, and from time to time a penitent enters to receive absolution. Here all human emotion came to a stop. Law, punishment, guilt, penitence, these were the abstractions which haunted the lonely room where the dictator worked through the night. At regular intervals the chimes from the Spassky tower disturbed the silence. They were the only sounds to break the austere tranquillity of his nights.

So he worked, in silence and without joy, codifying the laws, doodling, inspecting with a connoisseur's eye long lists of persons condemned to death, restlessly experimenting with whole classes, whole provinces, devoted to the working-out of some mythological plan of salvation which he alone could bring to the world. Sometimes he seemed uncomfortable and out of place, like a stranger in his own home.

DEATH AND THE MAIDEN

IN HIS ATTITUTE TOWARDS the arts Stalin followed the classic path of the modern dictator. No art was valid unless it served his superior purpose. In the ideal world of his imagination no idea was permitted to enter a man's head unless it had received the stamp of his approval.

From time to time authors would send their books to Stalin, and wait in fear and trembling for a word of encouragement or denunciation. He read voluminously, kept up with the latest books, and amused himself by playing the role of literary arbiter. His favourite poet was Demyan Bedny, the author of literary jingles, but he enjoyed the work of Mayakovsky, who had written in one of his more famous poems:

> *Together with reports on pig iron and steel*
> *I want a report on verse production on behalf of*
> *the Politburo from Stalin.*

Stalin appears to have permitted Mayakovsky more than a customary licence, and he was able to produce a play, *The Bedbug*, a devastating satire on Communist life, without being arrested. After Mayakovsky committed suicide in 1930, having become increasingly disenchanted with Communism; Stalin exercised his authority to canonize the dead poet by proclaiming him 'the greatest poet of our socialist epoch'. He detested sentimental poetry of any kind, and he said of the love poems of Anna Akhmatova that it would be sufficient if only two copies were printed – one for him, and one for her. Towards Pasternak he was forbearing and sometimes kind, and there was a short period when they were on fairly intimate terms. Stalin had himself written poetry which was not without merit, and he seems to have recognized in Pasternak a depth of genius lacking in the other poets of the time.

Even Pasternak was compelled to obey the dictates of Stalin. Only one man was immune to Stalin's authority. This was the veteran novelist Maxim Gorky, who occupied an unassailable place in Russian letters and was a law to himself. When the Bolsheviks came to power, he attacked them fearlessly in the pages of his journal *Novaya Zhizn,* and though he made his peace with Lenin in the summer of 1918 he never publicly withdrew his early denunciations in which he described Lenin as a remorseless experimental scientist working upon the living flesh of the Russian people. In August 1921 he went into exile, staying at Sorrento in Italy.

Gorky abroad was still a power to be reckoned with. He represented sanity and generosity in a world given over to frustrations and ferocious hate. He was not loved by the Soviet government, but he was respected. He commanded no organized following and possessed no gift for politics. He had no fondness for Mussolini's Italy, and like all Russians living abroad he suffered from bouts of nostalgia which were like an illness. He was aging rapidly. When Soviet officials wrote to him, reminding him that he would celebrate his sixtieth birthday on March 14th, 1928, and where better could he celebrate it than in Russia among his own people and in the new and vigorous society created by Communism, he raised few objections. He was mortally weary of exile, and for many months he had been dreaming of an excuse for returning home.

Stalin took charge of the negotiations for the return of the prodigal. He, too, had attacked Gorky in the past, denouncing him in the early days of the revolution as one more of the incompetent *petit bourgeois* who remained silent when the Tsar drove the peasants to despair, but protested vigorously when the Bolsheviks stood up to defend the cheated peasants and workers. But these attacks belonged to the remote past, to the period when tempers were exasperated by the violence of revolution. Now he wrote to Gorky with the utmost cordiality, offering him every conceivable honour and position including a seat on the Central Executive Committee, the ruling power of the Soviet Union. Nizhni Novgorod would be renamed Gorky in his honour. A literary institute would be set up in order to propagate his works, a publishing house would be placed at his disposal, unlimited funds would be given to him for travelling expenses and for starting new magazines. He would become the acknowledged legislator of Russian literature, the mentor of all Russian writers, the sole court of appeal. Even a strong man would have been tempted by these blandishments, and Gorky was no longer the strong man he had been in the past. In the spring he returned to Russia and received a hero's welcome.

Everywhere he went he was suffocated with veneration. People pointed him out in the streets, young writers sent him manuscripts, his house became a place of pilgrimage. He visited factories, and spoke of the vast improvements in factory life since the days of his youth. In Nizhni Novgorod he was once an assistant in an underground bakery, unforgettably described in his short story 'Twenty-six Men and a Girl'. Now he was taken to the mechanized bakery in Leningrad, a vast palace-like building gleaming with chrome and white paint, where it was explained to him that the bakers worked only seven hours a day to produce all the bread needed by Leningrad, and he remembered that in his youth he had worked twenty hours a day in the sweatshop. He wrote in the visitors' book: 'This factory is the most wonderful thing I have seen in Leningrad. There is nothing which bears more eloquent testimony to the revolution accomplished in everyday living.' He became the fervent apostle of the industrial revolution sweeping over Russia.

So vast were the changes overtaking the country that he sometimes spoke of himself as an old man wandering into a new world, carrying his box of 'sacred relics', his memories of an ancient feudal past. He had been a man of a hundred trades, errand boy, ragpicker, baker, bricklayer, watchman, icon painter, lawyer's clerk, stevedore, railroad worker. In all these trades he had worked long hours for a pittance. Now the machines were taking over the work of men, and he was grateful. He was not blind to the conditions of the industrial workers. They still worked long hours and were miserably paid, but at least the millennium was in sight. Throughout those early months, as he travelled across the length and breadth of Russia, he seemed to be in a state of euphoria.

Wherever he went the local soviets would meet in plenary session to pay tribute to him, to heap more and more honours on his head. He would make droll speeches, reminding them that he was like a child in their midst, unworthy of all the attention paid to him; he had returned to Russia to learn about the phenomenal achievements of Communism. Occasionally there would appear a note of warning. At the plenary session of the Moscow Soviet held in May 1928 he said: 'Comrades, you must bring more kindness into your relationships. You must be less harsh among yourselves. You have found it possible to be kind to me, then why should you be less so among yourselves?' The plea for kindness was deadly serious, but it was greeted with laughter. For the rest of his life he would plead for kindness and hear the laughter.

Stalin had taken his measure. He knew Gorky's weaknesses, as he knew those of most men, and played upon them. More and more honours were heaped on Gorky. He received the Order of Lenin, the highest decoration in the Soviet Union. Countless factories, clubs, schools and theatres were named after him. The Tverskaya, the main thoroughfare in Moscow, became Gorky Street overnight, and even the Moscow Art Theatre became the Gorky Theatre. But there was a purpose behind all these honours, and a price to be paid. Gorky gradually lost his independence. He became the willing tool of Stalin, the apologist for all Stalin's arbitrary decisions. Saying that he was lost in admiration before the genius of Stalin, he would tell stories emphasizing Stalin's humanity, his kindness, his respect for the opinions of others. The newspapers and magazines of the time were filled with photographs of Stalin and Gorky walking arm in arm or pausing to enjoy a joke. They seemed to be inseparable.

The honeymoon lasted for little more than a year. Gradually, as the euphoria wore away, Gorky came to realize the harsh realities behind the shining façade. Stalin's ruthlessness and cruelty appalled him, though he would sometimes attempt to rationalize them. Once again, as in the time of Lenin, he saw that he would have to play the role of mediator, though he was no longer young enough to play it effectively. He counselled moderation and generosity, and spoke of a time when the dictatorship would be less burdensome to the people, more humane and more flexible. Stalin countered with arguments for the need of an iron dictatorship during 'a transition period', which threatened to be endless.

In the winter of 1929 Gorky returned to Italy, not as an exile but as an old man in failing health who needed the sunshine. From Sorrento he wrote a long letter to Stalin in which he proposed a number of literary ventures and went on to suggest some long-overdue changes in the Soviet scene. He particularly objected to the crudities of the anti-religious campaign, and said so. He objected to the practice of self-criticism amounting to self-incrimination, which was officially encouraged by the government. All over the country innocent people were being forced to confess to sins they had never committed because the government inspectors needed a substantial quota of guilt; if the sins were small enough, the guilty ones were sometimes reinstated in the party. In Gorky's view these witch-hunts weakened rather than strengthened the party, and it was time they were abolished. But the most important passages of Gorky's letter were devoted to the Soviet youth, burdened by the oppressions of the regime. They were not machines to be hammered into shape, but infinitely creative and resourceful elements in society, to be protected and encouraged; they would become more resourceful and creative if they were permitted to express themselves more freely.

In Stalin's view such opinions amounted to heresy; they were all the more unpalatable because they came from Gorky. He delayed replying for some weeks. Finally, in a long letter written in January 1930 – he attached some importance to the letter and included it in his *Collected Works* – he denied all the underlying assumptions of Gorky's letter and insisted that there could be no changes and everything must go on as before. He wrote:

DEAR ALEXEY MAXIMOVICH!

Loads of apologies, and please do not be angry with me for my late (so very late!) reply. I am dreadfully overworked. And then, too, I have been rather ill. This is certainly no excuse, but it may serve as some kind of explanation.

1) We cannot do without self-criticism. We simply cannot, Alexey Maximovich. Without it, inevitable stagnation, corruption of the apparatus, growth of bureaucracy, undermining of the creative initiative of the working class. Of course self-criticism offers material for our enemies. In this

you are absolutely right. But it also offers material (and a stimulus) for our forward progress, for releasing the constructive energy of the workers, for the growth of competition, for shock brigades, etc. The negative aspect is counterbalanced and outweighed by the positive.

It may be that our press gives too much prominence to our shortcomings, and sometimes even (involuntarily) advertises them. That is possible and even probable. You demand therefore that our shortcomings should be counterbalanced (I would prefer to say 'outweighed') by our achievements. You are of course right about that too. We shall most certainly repair this defect, and without delay. You need have no doubt on this score.

2) Our youth is of various kinds. We have the whiners, the weary, the despairing (like Zenin). Then there are those who are bold, full of joy in life, strong-willed, and indomitably determined to achieve victory. Now, at a time when we are breaking our old bonds with life and forging new ones, when the familiar roads and pathways are being torn up and the new, unfamiliar ones are being laid down, when whole sections of the population who used to live in plenty are being thrown off the rails and are falling out of the ranks, making way for millions of people who were formerly oppressed – it cannot be that these youths should represent a homogeneous mass of people sympathizing with us, with no differences and divisions among them. Firstly, among the youths there are the sons of wealthy parents. Secondly, if we take the youths who belong to us (in social status), not all of them have the daring, the strength, the character, the understanding to picture the tremendous destruction of the old and the feverish building of the new as something that *has to be* and is therefore *desirable*, something that has little resemblance to the heavenly idyll of 'universal bliss' that will afford everyone the opportunity to 'take his ease' or 'bask in joy' . . .

So Stalin answered Gorky's cry for more freedom with the statement that there could be no freedom whatsoever for the enemies of the regime and very little for its supporters. For the rest, he contents himself with generalizations, fragments from half-forgotten speeches, and deliberate evasions which, by their very frequency, have the effect of rebukes. We do not know what Gorky made of that long letter, but we can guess that he was not wholly satisfied. He was learning slowly that he was completely powerless to change Stalin's mind.

He spent his winters in Italy, but every spring he returned to Russia like a homing pigeon. If he could do little to change Stalin's mind, he could sometimes do much to alleviate the lot of writers who found themselves in disfavour; and once more as in the early years of the revolution he became the mediator between the unarmed intelligence and the armed tyranny. He found jobs for writers who were starving, protected those who had incurred the displeasure of the authorities, and sometimes he was able to obtain passports for those who were in danger of arrest. At intervals he worked without very much enthusiasm on an extraordinary compilation called *The History of the Civil War in the USSR*, which celebrated Lenin and Stalin as the sole begetters of the revolution and mentioned Trotsky only in passing. It was a work of a thousand closely printed pages, and had very little relation to history as it actually occurred.

Among those whose lives were saved by Gorky was a great novelist and short story writer, Evgeny Zamyatin, a former engineer and naval architect, whose novel *We*, precursor of Huxley's *Brave New World* and Orwell's *1984*, had been published in America and Czechoslovakia to the consternation and alarm of the Soviet authorities. *We* described a future Communist society given over to a completely soulless and mechanical regimen. The narrative is in the form of a diary written by the designer of an interplanetary rocket intended to rescue the inhabitants of undiscovered worlds from 'the savage state of freedom'. There comes a time when the engineer rebels in the belief that reason will ultimately conquer over the stupidities of the mechanical state. He reads in the official newspaper: 'The enemies of happiness are not asleep. Hold on to happiness with both hands! Tomorrow all work will be suspended – all numbers will report for the Operation. Those who fail to appear will be submitted to the Machine of the Benefactor.' At this point he revolts, only to discover that time has run out and there is only a faint hope that the Machine can be destroyed.

We challenged the entire Soviet system, and though it was never published in Russia manuscript copies appeared and it was widely discussed. Zamyatin's name was known to be on the list of writers whose existence served no useful purpose. In June 1931 he wrote to Stalin requesting permission to leave the country since he was no longer free to pursue his writing and such a life was tantamount to a death sentence. Gorky placed the letter in Stalin's hands and urged that very careful consideration should be given to Zamyatin's request. Stalin was startled. He had expected an abject plea; instead he found a dignified and reasoned argument with ironical overtones. The request was refused, and Zamyatin was in more danger than ever. Gorky interceded for a second and third time until finally Stalin allowed Zamyatin to go free. Once more Gorky had saved a writer from torture, imprisonment, or death.

To the end Gorky's relations with Stalin remained ambiguous. Very early after his return from exile he seems to have realized that the powers which were promised him were scarcely more than nominal and decorative. He was a sick man, and his literary talents were failing. Yet in spite of the sense of failure which continually overwhelmed him, he worked on doggedly. 'The future belongs to the young,' he kept saying, and he was never happier than when he was among young students and workers. He gave them courage at a time when courage was desperately needed: it was his greatest service to the Soviet Union.

On October 11th, 1931, an incident occurred which later came to assume the dimensions of a legend. It was a very simple incident: the chief of state paid a call on an aging novelist. In any other country such a visit would not have been accounted remarkable, but Stalin's visit to Gorky's apartment came to be regarded as a major event. The dictator, who rarely left the Kremlin, showed himself to be a humble admirer of the novelist, and Gorky was shown to be on terms of easy familiarity with the dictator. Countless paintings and drawings of the scene were commissioned. Articles were written on the deep and abiding friendship between the two men, and these articles would be illustrated by photographs of Stalin and Gorky smiling pleasantly at one another around a table. In Stalin's biographical chronicle there appeared the entry: 'J. V. Stalin, V. M. Molotov and K. Y. Voroshilov visited A. M. Gorky, who read to them one of his works, the fairy tale "Death and the Maiden".'

The official biographical chronicle is often inaccurate, and in fact Molotov was not present at the meeting. Voroshilov, Commissar of Defence, was present in full military uniform, and in one of the photographs taken during the visit he can be seen smiling pleasantly and a little maliciously at Gorky,

while Stalin broods ruminatively over his pipe. As usual Gorky
was tieless, and he wore his familiar skullcap.

'Death and the Maiden' was a fairy tale in verse written
in 1892, when Gorky was at the beginning of his literary
career. It is contemporary with his first stories, and may have
been the earliest of his writings. Since it included among other
things an undisguised attack on Tsarist tyranny, it appeared
originally in a heavily expurgated form, and the full text was
not published until 1917. The first verse describes the Tsar
returning from a lost battle and coming upon a maiden hidden
among bushes. The maiden bursts out laughing at the Tsar,
and he orders her to be strangled.

> *The Tsar was riding away from the war, the dark fury*
> *Rising within him, gnawing at his heart,*
> *When he heard a voice among the elder bushes –*
> *A maiden was laughing, laughing.*
> *The Tsar's red brows knit terribly together,*
> *He struck his horse with his spurs*
> *And flew after the girl like an advancing storm.*
> *And his voice set his armour ringing.*
> *'You there!' he cried from the evil depths of his throat.*
> *'Tell me, young maiden, why are you laughing?*
> *The enemy has stolen the victory from me,*
> *All my troops have been slaughtered like cattle,*
> *Half my retinue has been made captive.*
> *I am returning to build a new army,*
> *I am your Tsar, sorrowing and despairing.*
> *How dare you laugh at me so stupidly?'*
> *The maiden rearranged her blouse,*
> *And made answer to the Tsar:*
> *'Go away! I am speaking with my beloved!*
> *Little father, it is best if you go away!'*
> *The Tsar shuddered, shaking with rage,*
> *And he addressed his loyal retinue:*
> *'Seize her! Throw her in prison,*
> *Or better still – strangle her!'*
> *With hideous distorted mouths like demons*
> *The obsequious grooms and vassals of the Tsar*
> *Hurled themselves upon the maiden*
> *And gave her into the hands of Death.*

It was a strange poem to read to a dictator, but there were
stranger things to come, for Death and the Tsar are seen to

be the same, and both are groping for some meaning in their lives. Death complains that he is utterly weary of his incessant traffic in decaying flesh, in burials and sepulchres, and the terror he inspires has long since become burdensome to him. He wonders what to do with the maiden. Shall he strangle her at once, or permit her to spend her last night with her lover? Death remembers that if there were no lovers, there would be no birth and therefore no death, and so he permits the maiden to sleep with her lover, and Death too goes to sleep, but it is not a peaceful sleep. Death has nightmares. He sees Cain and Judas, the murderer and the traitor, appealing feverishly for salvation from the archangels, only to be cast down into the evil-smelling marshes lit by ghostly blue flames, while Christ stands above, reading from a book where every page is as vast as the Milky Way. Then Death awakes and sings sadly of the fate that overtakes all men, even the tyrants 'who hunt down the people and are themselves hunted'. Far away, naked in the morning dew, her lover beside her, lies the maiden, and Death, appalled by her beauty, swoops down upon her to claim her for his kingdom, while the maiden sings:

> There is no god in heaven
> More beautiful than the sun,
> And there are no fires
> More marvellous than the fires of love.

Hearing those words, Death is silent. He recognizes at last that love is stronger than death.

The poem is raw and passionate, and only a young poet could have written it. In its total effect 'Death and the Maiden' is entirely convincing. Gorky meant every word of it when he wrote it, and it is unlikely that he had changed his opinion forty years later when he read it aloud to Stalin.

We do not know what Stalin thought of it. He seems to have been amused by it; for on the last page of the poem he scrawled a curious testimonial. He wrote:

> These verses are more powerful
>   than Goethe's 'Faust'
>   (*love conquers
>   death*)
>   J. STALIN 11/X-31

Stalin may have written these words facetiously, with a lazy, good-humoured desire to please, not caring very much what he wrote. The handwriting is hurried and flamboyant, and suggests that he had drunk four or five glasses of vodka. We know that he had read *Faust*, and it is possible that some of the songs sung by the maiden or by Death may have reminded him of Marguerite's songs. He felt the need to celebrate the occasion, and wrote the first thing that entered his head; and what is remarkable is that these words, sprawling diagonally across the page, give an overwhelming impression of banality. They are the product of an unpleasantly commonplace mind, incapable of any generous impulse or any real feeling for poetry.

Many years before, when Gorky was leading the life of a vagabond under the Tsar, he was arrested and thrown into the prison at Nizhni Novgorod. Some verses were found on him, and when he was brought into the office of General Poznansky for interrogation, he found the general sitting at ease and reading the verses.

'There's some good verse of yours here,' the general said. 'Yes, indeed ... you should go on writing! Good verse ... a pleasure to read ...'

In his patronizing way Stalin was only saying what General Poznansky had said many years before.

Why did Gorky read 'Death and the Maiden' to his two powerful visitors?

Like many writers who are more famous for their prose, Gorky attached a disproportionate significance to his verses, took pleasure in reading them aloud, and eagerly awaited criticism or blame. He read his fairy tale in verse 'The Fisherman and the Fairy' to the story writer Vladmir Korolenko, and many years later he could remember every detail of the long conversation that followed. He read his verses to Anton Chekhov, who on one famous occasion honoured him by asking him to read them all over again, and then commented mildly that it would be better if two lines were omitted. Gorky believed that his verses were at least as important as his prose, and he was in the habit of choosing very carefully among his poems for the ones most appropriate to his audience. So we may imagine that 'Death and the Maiden' was chosen quite deliberately as a proper entertainment for a dictator. The poem celebrated life against all the forces of tyranny and death. Ever since the October revolution Gorky's aim had been to make the dictatorship more humane and less rigid. When Stalin and Voroshilov entered his apartment he saw

Смерть молчит, а девушкины речи
Зависти огнем ей кости плавят,
В жар и холод властно ее мечут,
Что же сердце Смерти миру явит?

Смерть — не мать, но — женщина, и в ней
Сердце тоже разума сильней;
В темном сердце Смерти есть росинки
Жалости и гнева и тоски.

Тем, кого она полюбит крепче,
Кто ужален в душу злой тоскою,
Как она любовно ночью шепчет
О великой радости покоя!

— «Что ж, — сказала Смерть, — пусть будет чудо!
Разрешаю и тебе — живи!
Только я с тобою рядом буду,
Вечно буду около Любви!»

С той поры Любовь и Смерть, как сестры,
Ходят неразлучно до сего дня,
За Любовью Смерть с косою острой
Тащится повсюду, точно сводня.
Ходит, околдована сестрою,
И везде — на свадьбе и на тризне
Неустанно, неуклонно строят
Радости Любви и счастье Жизни.

56

no reason to break off the dialogue he had maintained for so long with the Bolsheviks. In his gentle way he was proclaiming that love and gentleness prevail.

All through the following year the relations between Gorky and Stalin remained amicable. They were frequently photographed together; once or twice Stalin attended a literary meeting where he was introduced to young novelists and poets. He helped to organize the festivities arranged to honour the fortieth anniversary of Gorky's literary and revolutionary activity. In September 1932 there were public exhibitions of Gorky's books and manuscripts, his plays were performed everywhere, and Stalin attended a meeting at the Bolshoy Theatre where Gorky was proclaimed the laureate of the Soviet Union. The ceremonial meeting took place in the evening of September 25th. That morning on the front page of *Pravda* there had appeared Stalin's brief protestation of undying friendship. He wrote:

> DEAR ALEXEY MAXIMOVICH,
>   From my soul I greet you and firmly grasp your hand. I wish you long years of life and labour to the joy of all working people and the terror of the enemies of the working class.
>
>   J. STALIN

Two weeks later, on October 7th, there was another meeting at Gorky's apartment. Some doctors had approached him with the idea of establishing an Institute of Experimental Medicine, and he had simply telephoned the Kremlin and suggested a meeting between the doctors and leading government officials. Stalin, Voroshilov and Molotov all attended the meeting, and after a brief discussion Stalin promised that funds would be set aside for the institute. A few days later Gorky invited Stalin to meet some poets, and it was remembered afterwards that Stalin behaved towards them with unusual deference and remarked that writers were 'engineers of human souls'. Stalin's wife was especially close to Gorky, and when she died mysteriously early in November, Gorky may have remembered that it was almost exactly a year since he had read 'Death and the Maiden' to the dictator.

For a little while longer Gorky remained in Stalin's good graces. His immense following among the workers, the youths and the intellectuals gave him a moral influence possessed by no one else in the Soviet Union. When he appeared in the factories, workers wept. When he cried out in his hoarse, tubercular voice that it was good to be alive in the age of Stalin, 'the man of steel, the greatest leader of our time', they cheered him, and because Gorky described Stalin as a man of simple virtues, they believed him. It was the time when the Baltic-White Sea Canal was being built by hundreds of thousands of slave labourers recruited by the GPU. Gorky visited the camps and settlements of the canal builders, and praised the GPU officers for gently coaxing these former enemies of the people into useful and productive life. 'The creators of the canal have brought honour and glory, valour and heroism to our country,' he wrote. 'They have shown the way out of the anarchy to which these poor men were reduced by the barbarities of capitalism, and they have taught them the truths of socialism by means of socially useful labour.' By 'the creators of the canal', Gorky meant the GPU officers headed by Genrikh Yagoda, with whom he was on terms of friendship. It seems never to have occurred to him that Yagoda was a man of bestial cruelty.

Though Gorky was blind to the terror of the secret police, he was perfectly aware that Stalin was engaged in a ferocious battle with the Old Bolsheviks, and he used his influence to moderate Stalin's bottomless mania for vengeance. He was especially close to Kamenev. When Kamenev's life seemed to be in danger, Gorky arranged a confrontation between them in the Kremlin.

Inevitably Stalin became irritated by Gorky's humanity. From being an ally Gorky had become a source of danger. He moulded public opinion, he corresponded with writers all over the world, and he was the first to whom the injured complained. He was continually pleading for the poor, the disinherited, the imprisoned. Stalin wanted him to write a book celebrating Stalin. Gorky did not openly refuse, but procrastinated. Stalin suggested that he should write an article on 'Lenin and Stalin', and again Gorky procrastinated. It was his way of protesting against the growing persecution of the Old Bolsheviks. Gradually their friendly meetings came to an end, and few of the calls which Gorky put through to the Kremlin were answered. In despair he asked for permission to go abroad. Stalin replied that his health would be improved by a journey to the Crimea. An article against Gorky appeared in *Pravda*. Then at last Gorky realized that there was nothing to be done except to live out the terror.

What Gorky asked or demanded no longer had any consequence. Stalin could do as he pleased with his prisoner. More police guards watched outside Gorky's house. A ring of silence closed round him.

Long ago Chekhov had said: 'There will come a time when Gorky's work will be forgotten, but Gorky, the man, will never be forgotten.' The giant with the pale-blue eyes and the walrus moustache was among the immortals, even though none of his writings after his return to Russia added to his fame. In theory he was beyond the reach of governments. He belonged to the country, not to Stalin. He could not be exiled or shot, and it was beyond belief that he could be imprisoned. He could, however, be permitted to die.

Alexander Poskrebyshev, who was Stalin's confidential secretary, later wrote an affecting account of Gorky's last days. 'Whenever Gorky felt very ill,' he wrote, 'Comrade Stalin always came to visit him, cheering him up and serving as a great moral support. Comrade Stalin visited him just before he died, and Gorky's friends relate how cheered he was by this visit and how he talked about it until he lost consciousness.'

Poskrebyshev's account remains uncorroborated; nor is there anything in the character of Poskrebyshev to suggest that he ever told the truth. Gorky died on June 18th, 1936, at the height of the purges. Two years later Yagoda confessed to having murdered him. In June 1936 Yagoda was head of the secret police, taking his orders from Stalin.

THE DEATH OF NADEZHDA ALLILUIEVA

WHEREVER STALIN MOVED, death followed him. It was the companion of his daylight hours and of his nights. His closest friends died at his orders, and he had almost no enemies, for he killed all those he could reach. His wife died when she was still young. It is just possible that she committed suicide, but it is more likely that he killed her.

Nadezhda Sergeyevna Alliluieva-Stalina, to give her full

name, might have settled down to a life of uneventful domesticity. She had been a beautiful young woman with enormous dark eyes and full lips, but by the age of thirty she was worn out. She had served her husband well at Tsaritsyn, and again when she was a member of Lenin's secretariat. She was a good mother to her two children, Svetlana and Vasily, and she possessed all the domestic virtues. No breath of scandal ever touched her. She liked to efface herself, and she took care never to take advantage of her high position.

Though she was gentle, there was iron in her. As the daughter of the veteran Bolshevik Sergo Alliluiev, she had been a revolutionary in her teens. She had known Lenin, Zinoviev and Stalin when they hid in her father's apartment. As a child she ran errands for the revolutionaries; she knew all there was to know about secret stores of guns and about illegal newspapers, and she was fifteen, scarcely more than a child, when she worked as a secretary at the Smolny and saw the revolution coming to birth. At sixteen she was already an experienced revolutionary. At this age she became Stalin's mistress, and was made pregnant by him, and she was still only sixteen when they were officially married on March 24th, 1919. The gentle, calm woman who superintended Stalin's household in the Kremlin had a turbulent childhood and a turbulent adolescence.

Half Georgian, half Russian, her father descending from priests who at some time in the early nineteenth century gave themselves the name of Alliluiev, meaning 'hallelujah', she was born in September 1902. She spent her childhood in the Caucasus, had little formal schooling, and was brought to St Petersburg when she was about twelve to live in the poverty-stricken Vyborg quarter. By this time her father had become a full-time revolutionary. In time all of his children were to become revolutionaries.

Of the three children Anna, the oldest, was the most intelligent, the most loquacious and the most uninhibited. She had Nadezhda's good looks, but was far more high-spirited. She married a Pole, Stanislav Redenss, who eventually worked himself up to be chief of the Moscow Administration of the secret police. He vanished in the purges, and Anna herself spent six years in a concentration camp. She wrote well, and her brief memoirs include a well-rounded account of Stalin in the days when he was still little known. At Stalin's orders the memoirs were withdrawn shortly after publication.

Paul, the second child, had the fine Alliluiev features, the enormous eyes and the firm chin. He resembled Nadezhda, and was very close to her. When Nadezhda married Stalin, Paul came to live with them. There was nothing unusual in this arrangement, for Stalin was continually travelling and Nadezhda, alone in her small apartment in the Kremlin, needed someone close to her. Paul was a man without any guile, almost feminine in his gentleness. He followed a family tradition by marrying a daughter of a priest, and having little interest in military affairs and no interest in police work, he chose to become an expert in foreign trade, accompanying official trade delegations abroad. Since much of the trade was concerned with buying military equipment, he gradually found himself deeply involved in tanks. By 1936, almost against his will, he became chief of the Political Department of the tank corps and shortly afterwards Commissar of the Tank Forces of the Soviet Union. He died in 1939, and the obituary, signed by Voroshilov, announced with deep sorrow that his death had occurred 'while carrying out his official duties'. It is more likely that he was one more victim of the purges. There had been a time when he knew Stalin well, and such knowledge was dangerous.

When Paul stayed in the Kremlin apartment, he had ample opportunity to observe the relationship between Nadezhda and Stalin. On the whole they were such as one might expect in a marriage between a sixteen-year-old girl and a man more than twice her age. She busied herself about the apartment, went marketing, looked after her babies, and attended to her husband's comforts. Her son Vasily was born in 1919; there followed a long rest from childbearing, for her daughter Svetlana was not born until six years later. Vasily comes from the Greek *basileus*, meaning 'king', but among Russians the name has a deeply religious connotation and derives from St Basil the Great, the Cappadocian theologian who was among the first to inaugurate rules for the Christian monks. All over Russia there were churches dedicated to St Basil, and the most beautiful of them all stood on the Red Square. Svetlana comes from *svet*, meaning 'daylight' or 'radiance'. It is a name with pagan origins. Both Vasily and Svetlana were common names, which they shared with hundreds of thousands of Russian children.

Nadezhda was gentle, but she was not meek. Stalin's drinking bouts and sudden explosions of temper usually took place at weekends when he gathered some cronies around him in a country house just outside Moscow. There were occasional quarrels, but they were apparently not very serious. He could be very tender to her when he wanted to be. He could be foulmouthed when he was drunk, but he held his liquor well and was rarely so drunk that he did not know what he was saying. In 1926, after a scene in which he raged at her drunkenly, she simply slipped out of the apartment with her two children and the servant Alexandra, and fled to Leningrad. Stalin appealed to her to return, but did not follow her. She gave him two weeks to cool his heels and then returned quietly. They resumed their lives together as though nothing had happened.

It was not a happy marriage, but it was not unhappy. She had a quiet, relentless will of her own, represented by a firm pointed chin, and she usually got what she wanted.

By 1929 her children were growing up and she was becoming bored and impatient with household affairs. Stalin was calling for a rapid speed-up in industrialization, and as a result thousands of Moscow students were clamouring to enter industrial and technical colleges, to learn engineering and the applied sciences. Nadezhda was determined to serve her country. Stalin had emerged as the supreme dictator of Russia, spent more and more of his time in his Kremlin office and in his country houses, and had less need of her. She discussed her plans with Paul and finally decided to enter the Industrial Academy on the Novaya Basmannaya under an assumed name. Stalin stormed when he heard about her plans, but later he accepted her decision with good grace. There was no publicity, and the government never made capital of the fact that the twenty-seven-year-old wife of the dictator was going to college. During the first months no one recognized her. She was a good student, reserved, a little shy, arriving just before classes began and leaving immediately after they were over. She usually drove her own car. Sometimes a police guard was detailed to follow her. She had a horror of attracting attention, and since few students could afford or were in any position to own cars, she always parked the car in a side street. The Novaya Basmannaya is in the north-east of Moscow near the suburbs, and it was obviously impractical for her to walk or to take the tram.

The Industrial Academy gave a streamlined three-year course in chemistry, physics, mathematics, machine-drawing and engineering. Students were expected to work hard and to spend long hours over their homework. She enrolled in the winter of 1929 and she remained a student until her death.

Inevitably Stalin sent spies to watch over her behaviour. Her conversations were reported to him; a voluminous file on her activities at the Academy was prepared; and since during the first year she expressed few opinions and was careful not to ask many questions of the other students, she was in no danger. Gradually she took more and more part in extracurricular activities. Her presence was becoming known, and sometimes students would turn to her for advice. It was the time of the forced collectivization of the farms, there were peasant revolts all over the south, and many of the students coming from the villages were horrified and appalled by what was happening. Nadezhda was the daughter of an old locksmith who had defied the Tsarist government, and her roots on her mother's side were among the peasantry: she could not always hold her tongue. She attended debates held by the Komsomols at which opinions against collectivization were sometimes expressed too freely. The police spies would report her attendance, and there were unhappy arguments when she returned to the Kremlin.

She was aging rapidly. One of the few photographs taken of her shows her walking through the snow, muffled in a heavy winter coat, and wearing a fur cap. She carries a small dark portfolio, and it is possible that the photograph was taken when she was on her way to her lessons. She looks forty, although at the time she could not have been more than twenty-eight or -nine. There are traces of her former beauty, but her expression is one of settled melancholy, as of someone attending a funeral or withdrawing from the world.

This haunting photograph is very nearly all that remains of Nadezhda Alliluieva, whose names were so singularly inappropriate, for she had little to hope for and rarely rejoiced. We see her walking in a terrifying loneliness down the snowbound street, lost in her dreams, and then she vanishes forever.

On November 7th, 1932, the fifteenth anniversary of the Revolution was celebrated with a military parade on the Red Square. This was followed by processions of workmen and athletes. As usual Stalin took the salute from Lenin's mausoleum. Nadezhda was seen among the crowds watching the display of military power. She looked pale and worn, took little interest in what was happening around her, and hung on her brother's arm. In three weeks she would receive her diploma as a chemical engineer, and her nervousness was perhaps no more than the inevitable nervousness of a woman who will soon leave the familiar surroundings of a college. She did not yet know what she would do with the knowledge she had acquired, but there were innumerable factories and laboratories in the Moscow region where her services would be welcomed. She could become an engineer working for the Soviet Union without leaving her family in the Kremlin.

Among the Soviet hierarchy the anniversaries of the Revolution were celebrated like Christmas. All-night parties continued sometimes through the day and the following night; innumerable toasts were drunk; presents were exchanged; there was a constant round of visits. On the night of November 8th Stalin attended a party given at the country house of Voroshilov. He was accompanied by Nadezhda, and a small circle of intimate friends now reduced by the butcheries of the previous twelve months. At such parties he was always inclined to drink dangerously. Something said by Nadezhda – it may have been about another woman, Rosa Kaganovich, who was also present, or about the expropriations in the villages which were dooming the peasants to famine – reduced Stalin to a state of imbecile rage. In front of her friends he poured out a torrent of abuse and obscenity. He was a master of the art of cursing, with an astonishing range of vile phrases and that peculiarly obscene form of speaking which the Russians call *matershchina*. Nadezhda could stand it no more, rushed out of the room, drove to the Kremlin and went straight to the small house where she had spent most of her married life. She died about four o'clock in the morning.

The official communiqué announced only that her death was 'sudden and premature'. No further official announcement was made, although a semi-official report that she had died of acute appendicitis was circulated. Since she was not in good health and had looked wan and exhausted during the last months, it was generally accepted that the official report was true or alternatively that she had taken an overdose of sleeping pills. There were also rumours that she had shot herself through the head.

In that year millions of people had died in the famine-stricken regions of Russia, and the death of a young woman was not a matter which caused a great deal of speculation, even if that woman was the wife of the dictator. She was thirty years old. In her short life she had had little impact on the Russian scene. Under the Soviets, the private lives of high officials were rarely discussed, and little or nothing was published about them in the newspapers.

Nadezhda's death however was not forgotten. It was as though in her quiet way she became more alive after her death than she had ever been when she was among the living. People remembered that she had attended the party at Voroshilov's house and had fled in disgust, and sometimes they asked themselves how her 'sudden and premature' death came about. She became a minor legend.

In 1955 Elizabeth Lermolo published her extraordinary account of her life in various isolators in Russia. Among the prisoners she met was Natalia Trushina, a young woman who had formerly worked in Lenin's secretariat. At the time of Nadezhda's death she was employed as a housekeeper in Stalin's household, looking after the children when Nadezhda was at her studies. On the night of November 8th she was wide-awake. Here is her account as reported by Elizabeth Lermolo:

About one o'clock at night, the doorbell rang at the Stalin apartment. Natalia ran to open it, thinking that it was early for the Stalins to be back. To her surprise it was Nadya escorted by Voroshilov. In the vestibule, Nadya hastily thanked Voroshilov, bade him goodnight and rushed to her room. Voroshilov, looking rather nonplussed, left after a moment, and Natalia hurried to Nadya who was sitting on the bed, staring blankly into space.

'It's the end,' Nadya said. 'I've reached the limit. Until now I've been a sort of wife to him, but not any more. I'm nothing. The only prospect is death. I shall be poisoned or killed in some prearranged "accident". Where can I go? What can I do?'

Nadya became hysterical. Natalia tried to calm her, saying that Stalin's flirtations were well-known to her, that he would tire of the present attraction as he had of others, and that she, Nadya, would soon be an engineer and free to go away and do as she liked.

When Nadya had quieted a bit, Natalia took her into the bathroom and she started to undress. Then, for no apparent reason, she fainted.

Natalia, alarmed, did the first thing she thought of. She grabbed the telephone and called the Voroshilov apartment and asked that Stalin return home at once. When he arrived a few minutes later, flustered and impatient, Natalia directed him to the bathroom. Nadya had regained consciousness by now but would not come out.

Through the partially opened door, Natalia heard the quarrel that followed. Nadya accused Stalin of carrying on shamelessly with 'that woman' in the presence of a large company, of hurting her and humiliating her. Stalin, after listening in silence for a long while, answered her with a tirade. He told her that she had retained none of her old revolutionary ardour, that she had become transformed into a conventional housewife, that as far as the revolution was concerned she was just so much excess baggage. 'You are no longer the companion needed by a leader of the world revolution!' he said.

The quarrel went on and on. Nadya out of her hurt pride argued like any woman who as wife and mother is conscious of certain rights. Stalin kept protesting that his position put him above bourgeois concepts of morality, that he needed someone to rekindle his spirit, revive his will to leadership.

At this, Nadya was infuriated. 'Rosa, I suppose, revives you! ... I know the kind of leader you are. More than anyone else, I know the kind of revolutionist you are!' And she went on to accuse him of usurping the leadership of the party dishonestly, of involving her in his shady schemes. She was, she said, ashamed to look her comrades in the eye because of his blood purges and liquidations. Her voice rose hysterically.

'Shut up, damn you!' Stalin roared at last.

Then Natalia heard a blow, a fall, someone gasping. Filled with foreboding, not quite knowing what she was up to, Natalia pushed open the door of the bathroom. There on the floor was Stalin savagely choking Nadya with both his hands and saying, 'You would, would you?'

Natalia screamed, whereupon Stalin broke away from Nadya and with his face turned tore out of the bathroom.

Nadya lay on the floor, not breathing. At her temple was a large wound that could have been the blow from an instrument. There was blood, and near her on the floor was a bloodstained revolver.

Natalia Trushina went on to describe how Poskrebyshev, Stalin's secretary, suddenly appeared, forbade her to call a doctor, removed the revolver, ordered the blood mopped up, and saw to it that the unfortunate incident was smoothed over. From time to time during the night Soviet dignitaries came to the house to console Stalin. Long before morning Nadezhda's disfigured face had been restored with the help of scissors, cold cream and face powder, and the hair had been rearranged to conceal the wound.

Natalia Trushina's account of Nadezhda's death may not be completely convincing in all its details, but it has the ring of truth. Events follow one another in a haphazard order, as they do in life; a novelist could scarcely have invented the scene in the bathroom. Her account is partly confirmed by a report published in the *Novoye Russkoye Slovo* on December 21st, 1949, which relates how a woman doctor, who was the acting head of the Kremlin hospital, was awakened in the early hours of the morning and asked to come immediately to Stalin's apartment. 'On her arrival she saw the lifeless body of Alliluieva on the floor. Nearby, leaning against the writing desk, stood Stalin, pale and stunned and almost insensible. On the desk lay the revolver. Alliluieva never had a revolver.' Alexander Orlov reports that an officer of Stalin's bodyguard told him how they had heard a shot coming from the bedroom. 'When we rushed in,' he said, 'she was lying on the floor, in a black silk evening dress, her hair done in curls. The pistol was on the floor.' The officer decided it was safer not to pursue the subject further and made no attempt to discover whether Nadezhda shot herself or was shot by Stalin.

For two days the body lay in state and mourners were invited to pay tribute to the dead wife of the dictator. Usually, when a body lies in state in Russia, it lies on a kind of platform at eye level, the head reposing on a pillow. Instead Nadezhda lay in her coffin, her body entirely concealed, her face shadowed by flowers; death had refined her features; she looked young again.

In the normal course of events her body would have been cremated and her ashes placed in the Kremlin wall. For some reason Stalin ordered that she should be buried in the ancient aristocratic cemetery of Novodevichy, where the first wife of Peter the Great and his three sisters were buried. Novodevichy means 'the new maidens', and there is a tradition, perhaps apocryphal, that from the nearby convent there set out the tribute offerings of new maidens once demanded by the Tatars of the Golden Horde.

The funeral took place on November 11th. To the surprise of Yagoda, who as head of the secret police was in charge of the funeral arrangements, Stalin insisted on following the coffin to the grave. The distance from the Kremlin to the cemetery was about four miles. Stalin emphasized that he intended to make the journey on foot, not in an automobile with bulletproof windows, and Yagoda was therefore compelled to see that every window overlooking the funeral procession was closed and guarded by the secret police. Extraordinary precautions were taken. Police cars were stationed at every crossing. Squadrons of mounted police and security guards accompanied the procession when it set out from the Red Square in the afternoon. Among the small group walking with Stalin were Nadezhda's sister Anna and her husband Stanislav Redenss, her brother Paul, and Avely Yenukidze, who had been especially close to Nadezhda, performing the duties of a family friend, and sometimes acting as a mediator between Stalin and his wife. The ornate black-and-silver funeral coach was like a relic from the time of the Tsars. The snow whirled, and the wind whistled through the deserted streets.

In his heavy greatcoat Stalin looked gaunt and sombre, his face deeply lined. Those who saw him at the time were certain his grief was unfeigned; he was like a man who has been poleaxed by grief, no longer knowing where he was or what he was doing. So it had been after the death of his first wife Ekaterina Svanidze twenty-five years before. At that time he had placed his hand on his heart and said: 'She was the only person who could soften my hard heart. Now she is dead, and with her have died any feelings I had for humanity.'

When Ekaterina Svanidze died, there was a funeral service according to the rites of the Orthodox Church, and she was buried on consecrated ground. There was no funeral service for Nadezhda; nor perhaps, as a revolutionary, would she have desired one. But for six or seven hundred years the cemetery had been consecrated ground.

Stalin did not walk beside the bier for long. After a few minutes he slipped quietly into a waiting car, while the others continued to shuffle through the snow. He had spoken so determinedly of following his wife to the grave on foot that in some quarters it was accounted as cowardice that he should have driven off in a heavily armoured official automobile, but there are more charitable explanations. He was waiting for the cortege when it arrived at the Novodevichy cemetery. He said a few words over the grave and then left for the Kremlin.

The rumours that Nadezhda had committed suicide revived when it was learned that she had been buried in a corner of the cemetery where many suicides found their resting place. It was pointed out as especially significant that she lay close to Adolf Joffe, who had killed himself rather than face the wrath of Stalin on another November day five years before, but in fact there was no part of the cemetery specifically reserved for suicides. The great anarchist, Prince Peter Kropotkin, who had died of starvation, lay nearby.

In his grief Stalin did something so astonishingly out of character that it can be explained only by the depths of his feeling for Nadezhda. He ordered a white marble stele of classic simplicity to be erected over the grave. The head of the stele flowered into a portrait of Nadezhda as she had been in her youth, her hair drawn severely back, her chin resting pensively on her hand. Out of the white marble came a face and a hand, nothing more. The white stele, on one side streaked with blue veins, was a work of exquisite refinement and taste.

Inevitably the messages of condolence poured into the Kremlin. They came from all over Russia and for the most part they were written in that strangely empty manner with which men attempt to come to grips with their grief. Thirty-three Soviet authors, among them Boris Pilnyak and Mikhail Koltzov, decided to send a collective letter of condolence. Collective letters were in fashion in the Soviet Union, and it was thought that the general sorrow of authors could best be expressed in this way. The poet Boris Pasternak was invited to sign the letter, but he refused. Instead he wrote a strange codicil:

> I share the feelings of my comrades. On the evening before, I found myself thinking profoundly about Stalin for the first time from the point of view of an artist. In the morning I read the news. I was shaken exactly as though I had been present, as though I had lived through it and seen everything.
>
> BORIS PASTERNAK

With this terrifying and enigmatical statement, suggesting unsuspected powers of clairvoyance, clearly written under the pressure of great emotion, Pasternak was apparently emphasizing his isolation from other writers and at the same time indicating a close affinity with Alliluieva, in whose death he had mysteriously shared. It is certain that Stalin read the letter, and it is possible that he was deeply moved and troubled by Pasternak's implied claim that he had been *poetically* present at her death and knew how she died. Some, who wondered how Pasternak survived the purges which broke over Russia during the next eight years, came to regard this statement as his passport to safety. In his enigmatical fashion the poet had challenged the dictator on his own ground.

To the messages of condolence Stalin replied with a brief acknowledgement which appeared on the front page of *Pravda* on November 18th. It read:

> I convey my heartfelt thanks to the organizations, institutions, comrades and others who have expressed their condolences on the occasion of the passing of my close friend and comrade Nadezhda Sergeyevna Alliluieva-Stalina.
>
> J. STALIN

It was a singularly bleak and official acknowledgement, but he was not a man with any gift for parading his emotions in public. Whether he murdered her, or whether she committed suicide, he was responsible for her death, and knew it. This knowledge weighed heavily on him and remained with him to the end of his life.

In the spring he paid many visits to the grave. On these occasions the guardians of the cemetery would order everyone out, and after a long interval, during which security guards would search until they were certain that no one was hiding among the tombs, a long black high-powered automobile would make its way slowly along the lanes between the gravestones. Then, surrounded by armed guards, he would stand for a while and gaze at the marble head until someone brought him a chair and then he would sit down. He seemed to derive strength from contemplating her. Sometimes he came at night. Beside the grave an intricate floodlighting system was installed, and these midnight visits continued to the end of his life.

It was, and is, an ugly overgrown cemetery, with its broken marble crosses, crumbling vaults, and rusting iron chains. Yet she was in good company, for some of the greatest Russians lay close to her. Chekhov was there, and so were Scriabin, Rimsky-Korsakov, Soloviev and Pisemsky. The beautiful Smolensk Cathedral, built by the Tsar Vasily III, the father of Ivan the Terrible, looked down on those disorderly graves.

In the whole cemetery the most beautiful monument was the slender marble shaft which bore the words:

Nadezhda Sergeyevna
ALLILUIEVA-
STALINA
1902–1932
Member of Bolshevik Party
from
J. V. Stalin

THE MASSACRES

The time has come to realize that of all the valuable capital the world possesses, the most valuable and the most decisive is people.

THE MASSACRES

ONCE HE ACQUIRED supreme power in the winter of 1928, Stalin set about massacring the Russian people with a cold-blooded ruthlessness which had no equal in history up to this time. For the sake of the collectivization campaign whole provinces were decimated. The secret police had orders to shoot not only those who actively opposed Stalin's policies, but also all those who failed to show sufficient enthusiasm for them. To wait patiently, to stand on the sideline, became a crime against the state. To show the least sign of human feeling for the dispossessed was to invite disaster. The effective power in the state no longer rested in the Politburo. It rested in the secret police, who executed Stalin's will no matter what senseless orders he gave to them. Throughout the thirties Russia became a vast prison camp supplied with abundant shooting galleries.

There was however method in Stalin's madness. In *Hadji-Murad* Tolstoy tells the story of Shamil, the Caucasian chieftain who defied one after another the armies sent against him by the Tsar. One day Hadji-Murad, who had surrendered to the Russians, told how Shamil had lured a neighbouring prince to his camp, murdered him and then ordered the murder of the prince's mother and children. The Russians were appalled, and asked why Shamil committed such atrocities. 'Don't you understand?' Hadji-Murad said. 'Once you have jumped over with your forelegs, jump over with your hindlegs as well. Once you begin killing a clan, kill them all. Leave no future avengers.'

Stalin was determined to leave no future avengers. If he killed a man, he would see that the man's wife was rendered harmless and the children were removed to a state institution. Then there were the man's relatives to contend with, and they too were often removed. And so, in widening circles, he would find himself compelled to kill as far as the range of the man's influence extended. There is no end to this process. Carried to its logical conclusion, he would have to kill everybody.

Very early in his life he had embarked on a career of murder, and there was no end in sight. Human lives were of no concern to him, for had he not inaugurated a vast system of social welfare? So there came about the peculiarly Russian expedient known as the *chistka*, derived from the common adjective *chistiy*, meaning 'clean'. A *chistka* is a cleansing or purification. It is usually translated by 'purge', but this is to give it a largely innocuous interpretation. There is no exact English equivalent, and it seems better to use the word 'massacre'.

These massacres were devised for one purpose, and one purpose only: to maintain Stalin and a small group of dedicated Communists in power. Their form and nature changed according to the changing nature of the Communist state. Since they appeared to be effective – the dead give all the appearance of being powerless – the massacres were manipulated and elaborated according to precise and carefully worked out instructions. There was, in most cases, no trial and no court of appeal. The selection of victims was often arbitrary, the method of killing was entirely at the discretion of the police officers, the task being carried out with more or less bureaucratic efficiency. In *State and Revolution* Lenin declared that 'in order to abolish the state it is necessary to convert the functions of the public service into the simple operations of control and accounting'. Under Stalin bureaucratic inefficiency in government service reached its peak, but the simple operations of control and accounting were employed with phenomenal success by the secret police. Instead of abolishing the state, Stalin set about abolishing the people.

This perverse judgement on mankind arose from the very nature of communism. As Engels, and later Kautsky had foreseen, the communist state involved the surrender of popular liberties, restrictions on the movement of workers, the elimination of any kind of opposition to the dictatorship of the proletariat. Surrender, restrictions, elimination were nineteenth-century words, which found sterner Russian equivalents in the twentieth century. The fashionable Communist word was 'liquidation', a word used so often that it almost lost its original meaning. The bureaucracy was forced to invent a technological language for massacre: there were subtle differences in meaning between 'exterminate' and 'liquidate'. For some reason the words 'death penalty' were never employed, and the Communist leaders contented themselves with a deliberate circumlocution. So there would appear on the long

Kirov

Beria

Zinoviev

Bukharin

Yalta, February 1945

Potsdam, August 1945

Front row: Molotov, Kaganovich, Bulganin, Voroshilov, Beria, Malenkov
Second row: Khrushchev, Mikoyan, Zhukov, Sokolovsky, Koniev,
Vasilievsky almost completely hidden by Beria

The Lenin Mausoleum when Stalin was buried there

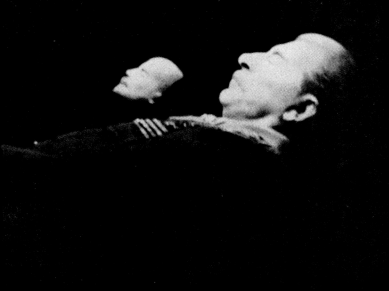

lists of people compiled by the NKVD* the dread letters
VMN, for *vysshnaya mera nakazaniya,* meaning 'supreme
measure of punishment'. Stalin, Molotov, Beria and many
others amused themselves in their rare moments of leisure by
perusing these lists and pencilling these letters in front of the
names of their victims or scrawling the letters across a whole
page.

The massacre system was not invented by Stalin. He inherited it from Lenin, merely insisting on certain characteristic
refinements. Lenin himself showed only a perfunctory interest
in the massacre system, which he inaugurated, regarding it
merely as an inevitable and on the whole tiresome instrument
of revolutionary power. Having complete trust in Uritsky and
Dzerzhinsky, the appointed chiefs of the secret police, he was
content to leave them in charge. His temper was scholarly,
not vindictive. He was sorry when people were killed, but his
sorrow was abstract. A vast social movement had come into
existence, and inevitably people would be killed, just as it was
inevitable that people would be killed if they found themselves in the path of an avalanche. Marx and Engels rejoiced
in the thought of the punishment they hoped to inflict on the
capitalist and bourgeois classes, and liked to repeat: 'The
executioner is at hand.' Such an attitude of mind was entirely
foreign to Lenin's nature.

The classical document in the history of the Communist
massacre system was written, not by Lenin, but by the little-
known Yakov Sverdlov, on the night of August 30th, 1918, a
few hours after the attempted assassination of Lenin by Dora
Kaplan. Sverdlov wrote the document when it was still unknown whether Lenin would recover. He apparently wrote it
in the blood-spattered apartment to which Lenin had been
taken, for it is known that he spent a good part of the evening
in this room crowded with doctors who were busily attempting
to stanch Lenin's wounds. It was written hurriedly, in a mood
of mounting hysteria. Most of the few facts contained in the
document were wrong. He spoke of two people involved in
the attempt on Lenin's life; there was only one. He said that

* The NKVD (People's Commissariat for Internal Affairs) came
into existence in 1934 as the successor to the GPU (State Political
Board). The Cheka (Extraordinary Commission) was founded by
Lenin in December 1917 and was renamed GPU in February
1922. The names changed, but their functions remained the same.
Cheka, GPU, and NKVD, all meant the secret police.

the attempt would undoubtedly be traced to the Right Socialist Revolutionary Party and to hirelings of the English and French governments, and in fact Dora Kaplan was not a hireling of any government and she did not belong to the Right Socialist Revolutionary Party.

ALL SOVIETS
OF WORKERS', PEASANTS', RED ARMYMEN'S DEPUTIES, ALL ARMIES, ALL, ALL, ALL

A few hours ago a villainous attempt was made on the life of Comrade LENIN. The role of Comrade Lenin, his significance for the workers' movement in Russia and the workers' movement of the entire world are well-known to a very wide circle of workers in all countries.

The true leader* of the working class has not lost his close contact with the interests and needs of the class which he has defended for many decades.

Comrade LENIN, who has been appearing all the time at workers' meetings, appeared on Friday at the MICHEL-SON factory in the Zamoskvoretsky district in the city of Moscow. As he left the meeting, Comrade LENIN was wounded. The two people who shot at him have been arrested. Their identities have been revealed. We do not doubt that we shall come upon the tracks of Right Socialist Revolutionaries and of hirelings of England and France.

We call upon all comrades to maintain the most complete calm and to strengthen their work in the fight against counter-revolutionary elements.

The working class will respond to attempts on the lives of its leaders by still further consolidating its forces and by a merciless mass terror against all the enemies of the revolution.

Comrades! Know that the security of your leaders is in your own hands. Close ranks still more firmly, and deliver a decisive and mortal blow to the domination of the bourgeoisie. Victory over the bourgeoisie – the best guarantee, the best consolidation of the gains of the October Revolution, the best guarantee for the safety of the leaders of the working class.

---

* Sverdlov uses the word *vozhd*, the exact equivalent of *Führer* and *Duce*. It was a title which Lenin never accepted for himself.

ВСѢМ СОВѢТАМ

РАБОЧИХ, КРЕСТ., КРАСНОАРМ. ДЕПУТ.

всѣм арміям, всѣм, всѣм, всѣм

Нѣсколько часов тому назад совершено злодѣйское покушеніе на тов. ЛЕНИНА. Роль тов. Ленина, его значеніе для рабочаго движенія Россіи, рабочаго движенія всего міра извѣстны самым широким кругам рабочих всѣх стран.

Истинный вождь рабочаго класса не терял тѣснаго общенія с классом, интересы, нужды котораго он отстаивал десятки лѣт. Тов. ЛЕНИН, выступавшій все время из рабочих митингах, в пятницу выступал перед рабочими завода МИХЕЛЬСОН в Замоскворѣцком районѣ гор. Москвы. По выходѣ с митинга тов. ЛЕНИН был ранен. Двое стрѣлявших задержаны. Их личность выясняется. Мы не сомнѣваемся в том, что и здѣсь будут найдены слѣды правых ж-эров, слѣды наймитов англичан и французов.

ПРИЗЫВАЕМ ВСѢХ ТОВАРИЩЕЙ К ПОЛНѢЙШЕМУ СПОКОЙ СТВІЮ, К УСИЛЕНІЮ СВОЕЙ РАБОТЫ ПО БОРЬБѢ С КОНТР-РЕВОЛЮЦІОННЫМИ ЭЛЕМЕНТАМИ

НА ПОКУШЕНІЯ, НАПРАВЛЕННЫЯ ПРОТИВ ЕГО ВОЖДЕЙ, РАБОЧІЙ КЛАСС ОТВѢТИТ ЕЩЕ БОЛЬШИМ СПЛОЧЕНІЕМ СВОИХ СИЛ, ОТВѢТИТ БЕЗПОЩАДНЫМ МАССОВЫМ ТЕРРОРОМ ПРОТИВ ВСѢХ ВРАГОВ РЕВОЛЮЦІИ.

Товарищи! Помните, что охрана ваших вождей в ваших собственных руках. Тѣснѣе смыкайте свои ряды, и господству буржуазіи вы нанесете рѣшительный, смертельный удар. Побѣда над буржуазіей—лучшая гарантія, лучшее укрѣпленіе всѣх завоеваній октябрьской революціи, лучшая гарантія безопасности вождей рабочаго класса.

Спокойствіе и организація! Всѣ должны стойко оставаться на своих постах! Тѣснѣе ряды!

Предсѣдатель В. Ц. И. К. Я. Свердлов.

30 Августа 1918 года. 10 час. 40 мин. вечера.

Calm and organization! All must remain steadfast at their posts! Close ranks!

President V. Ts. I. K.* Ya. Sverdlov
30th August, 1918, 10:40 pm.

What was most remarkable about that terrifying document was the hysterical mingling of appeals to calm and invitations to murderous licence. Everyone must remain at his post, and at the same time everyone must embark on mass terror. The word 'all' is continually repeated, and Sverdlov can even write that Lenin was appearing *all the time* at workers' meetings when in fact he attended them no more than once a week. When he speaks of 'the security' of the leaders, he uses the word *okhrana*, the name of the dreaded Tsarist secret police who were the security forces of the Tsar. At times Sverdlov is oddly defensive, as when he insists on the role played by Lenin in the workers' movement and claims that Lenin never lost contact with the workers. Yet the most revealing passage in the document comes at the end, when he speaks of victory over the bourgeoisie as the best guarantee for the safety of the Communist leaders. Was it to guarantee the safety of the leaders that the Revolution had been fought?

As he wrote, Sverdlov seems to have been trembling for his own life, thinking more of the remaining Communist leaders than of the man who seemed to be dying before his eyes. Only a frightened man could have written these words. Panic – a murderous panic – had taken hold of him. As a result of this appeal to mass terror the jails were emptied, for the prisoners were shot. In Petrograd alone five hundred were shot the next day.

Sverdlov's statement that two people shot at Lenin can easily be explained. Uritsky, the leader of the Cheka in Petrograd, had been assassinated that same day. In his confused mind the two incidents appear to have become one incident. It is possible that he was so exhausted, so horrified, that he scarcely knew what he was writing.

With this document the floodgates were opened. The words 'mass terror', rarely used before, became commonplace. There had been sporadic murders before. The Tsar, the Tsarina, and

* 'V. Ts. I. K.' stands for *Vserossiiskoe tsentralnyi ispolnitalnyi komitet,* or All-Russian Central Executive Committee. Sverdlov was president of the committee from 1918 to his death in March 1919.

their children were executed; hundreds of members of the aristocracy had perished; Mensheviks and Right Socialist Revolutionaries had been shot for no better reason than that they were powerless in the face of Lenin's dictatorship. The terror was unorganized, slipshod, sporadic, visited impartially on all professions and all classes. It had not yet been used to terrify a whole nation into obedience.

After Sverdlov's order of the day the pace quickened. The youthful Saint Just, who had supplied Robespierre with an intellectual justification for terror and who died at the age of twenty-seven on the guillotine, had announced that 'a Republic is established by the destruction of whatever is opposed to it', and it was in this spirit that the Bolshevik terror was extended throughout the length and breadth of the land ruled by Bolsheviks. Mass terror means total terror. It terrorized the terrorists almost as much as it terrorized the victims; and it left the whole country in the grip of fear. As Lenin lay on his sickbed, the most frightened man in Russia was probably Sverdlov, the inheritor of Lenin's power.

When the civil war came to an end, the terror resumed its sporadic course, no longer total. It became an instrument of intimidation rather than a murder machine. Lenin and the triumvirate who succeeded him were more interested in consolidating their victories than in demanding perpetual sacrifices, and they were particularly concerned to prevent the terror from spreading into the party, although it is in the nature of terror to destroy the terrorists. Stalin was perfectly aware of the danger. At the Fourteenth Congress in December 1925, when the revolutionary leaders were already at each other's throats, he declared: 'The method of chopping off heads and bloodletting is dangerous and infectious. Today you chop off one head, another tomorrow, and a third the day after – what in the end will be left of the party?' His own head was still in danger, and he was inclined towards caution. Four years later, when he was firmly in the saddle, the need for caution was no longer one of his main preoccupations, and he began slowly at first and then with increasing momentum to employ the weapon of terror against all those who had helped him to power.

Stalin's massacre system was launched in 1928 and was employed uninterruptedly for a quarter of a century, coming to an end only with his death in 1953. It was the product of experiment and improvisation, of desperate stratagems and

strange alterations. Inevitably it was coloured by the personalities placed in operational command of the system, of whom
the two most notorious were Genrikh Yagoda and Nikolay
Yezhov. Yagoda and Yezhov were both men of quite extraordinary criminal talents, small, unprepossessing, and vicious.
They were chosen for their ruthlessness and inordinate
capacity for obeying the whims of their master. Yezhov was
finally dismissed in November 1938, and Stalin may have
exercised a deliberate irony when he appointed 'the great
liquidator' to the post of People's Commissar for Water Trans-
portation. The appointment was a brief one, and he soon
disappeared without a trace.

Although Yagoda and Yezhov gave a particular colour to
the terror, they were not its authors. Stalin retained absolute
command, reserving for himself the right to liquidate the
liquidators. The murderous telegrams bore the signature of
the heads of the secret police, but these signatures bore the
authority of Stalin, who approved and encouraged their
actions. Yagoda and Yezhov were merely puppets. By 1937
the massacre machine had become so hungry for victims that
it no longer needed to be fed with names; it was fed with
numbers.

To NKVD, Frunze. You are charged with exterminating
10,000 enemies of the people. Report results by signal.
YEZHOV.

Such telegrams were dispatched at intervals to all points
of the compass. By a conservative estimate seven to eight
million people – according to others, twenty-three million
– perished in the great *chistka* of 1937-1938. Never before had
so much punishment been inflicted upon a people.

This *chistka* was merely the culmination of a system which
had been steadily perfected until it achieved maximum efficiency. During the time of Yezhov everyone in Russia lived
in mortal fear, for the terror had reached down into the
remotest village, into the farthest reaches of the Communist
empire. It was not enough that people must be deprived of
their liberty; they must be deprived also of their reason for
living. Totalitarian terror had achieved its most terrible
triumph when it reduced a once-proud nation to a state of
despair.

When Yezhov sent telegrams ordering the extermination of
thousands of people who were identified only as enemies of

the people, he had very nearly reached the ultimate stage in tyranny. In theory there is nothing to prevent the massacre machine from devouring everybody and then turning on its own operational commanders. In practice the machine was corrupted by the simple fact that its operational commanders had wives, children, and relations, and were rarely enthusiastic about committing them to the machine. In a hundred different ways the effectiveness of the machine was blunted. But of its effectiveness in instilling terror there was never any doubt.

The failures of the machine arose from the nature of its pursuits. Since it was dedicated to a meaningless terror, it necessarily employed meaningless methods and spoke in a meaningless language. The demand for the execution of ten thousand enemies of the people could be instantly transformed into a demand for the execution of a hundred thousand people or a million people. There was no theoretical reason why the process should not be continued indefinitely. The meaningless numbers in the telegrams indicated that the massacre machine was not directed against any class; it was directed at everyone.

The terror was absurd, but it was not self-defeating. It would endure as long as there were people alive capable of submitting to it.

Sverdlov had indicated the real reason behind the terror: it was to guarantee the lives of the leaders, but how many leaders were there? Stalin might dispute that there was only one, for the lives of the members of the Politburo were as expendable as all the rest. By the end of 1938, of the members of the Bolshevik government which was installed in Moscow twenty years earlier only three remained alive: Stalin, Trotsky, and Madame Alexandra Kollontay. Trotsky was in exile, and Madame Kollontay was the Soviet ambassador in Stockholm. The great majority had been killed by Stalin. Madame Kollontay was perhaps permitted to live because she was an invalid, but no such permission had been granted to Trotsky, who was to die two years later at the hands of one of Stalin's agents.

To accomplish the deaths of Soviet leaders Stalin introduced novel techniques. It was not enough that they should be led quietly to an underground cellar and then shot in the back of the head. What was demanded of them was a supreme act of contrition, a superb renunciation. They must die singing his praises. They must beg to be killed. The punishment must be deliberately prolonged, and every last ounce of guilt must be extracted from them; the fact that they were guiltless was regarded as irrelevant. A complicated ritual must be performed. Stalin did not ask that the prisoners should bend their knees to him; they must bend their whole bodies, their whole spirits, their entire lives in celebration of his glory.

The absurdities of terror were orchestrated with remarkable art. Men who had long been distinguished in the Communist movement were to prove from their own lips that they were craven fools, traitors, counter-revolutionaries, hirelings of foreign governments. In set speeches they affirmed that there were no crimes they were incapable of committing, and one after another they testified that they had committed crimes even worse than those for which they were accused. Their confessions were read out in open court, and the defendants went to some pains to explain that they had written these confessions not under duress, but out of deep emotion and gratitude towards the leader who had spared their lives so that they could abase themselves before him. One by one Radek, Kamenev, Zinoviev, Bukharin, Krestinsky, and a hundred others – men who had known Lenin and worked by his side when it was dangerous to be with him – accused themselves publicly of treachery. The world debated why they should behave in this way, but the reason, in so far as there was a reason, had been clearly given by Sverdlov when he called for a mass terror to guarantee the safety of the leaders. Once they themselves had been leaders; now there was only one leader; and their sacrifice was therefore demanded to ensure his safety.

The great trials of the thirties followed inevitably from the nature of totalitarian Communism. The unnumbered and anonymous masses who were killed were not asked to abase themselves, for their self-abasement would have served no purpose. The leaders had to abase themselves because their self-abasement served to augment the safety of Stalin. Minor figures, too, had to abase themselves, to suffer interminable interrogations which were recorded in countless blue folders in the files of the NKVD, and this was done in order to give dignity to the work of the NKVD, by permitting the officers to believe that they were performing a useful function. But in fact the chief purpose of the NKVD was to terrorize everyone, not merely the unfortunate ones who were arrested. It scarcely mattered to them whom they arrested; the names were interchangeable. Their purpose was mass terror: to terrorize the masses. In this they succeeded. Through the operations of the NKVD the entire machinery of state served to exalt and safeguard one individual.

It was not for this that Marx and Engels had worked, though they had dimly foreseen the consequences of their erratic philosophies. They had called for the dictatorship of the proletarian masses. Under Lenin and Stalin the dictatorship of the masses degenerated into the dictatorship of one man, whose life was so infinitely valuable that he had to be preserved at all costs, even at the cost of total terror.

Sverdlov's document throws light on events that happened ten years later, for Sverdlov on that evening of August 1918 was in the same position as Stalin in the winter of 1928. Quite suddenly Sverdlov was in a position of total power. Because Lenin was wounded, he was the head of the state, with power to exert his will in any manner he desired. He did not know the political opinions of Dora Kaplan, and did not care, for he had already made up his mind that the enemies were the bourgeoisie, foreign hirelings, and the Right Socialist Revolutionaries; and if he had been told that she was a poor milliner with a long revolutionary background, who had served a lengthy term of imprisonment for attempting to shoot a Tsarist official, this knowledge would have seemed to him of no importance and entirely irrelevant to his main purpose: the consolidation of the dictatorship. In the same way Stalin did not know who his enemies were, though he knew they were all around him. Sometimes he invented names for them, and he seems to have invented the term 'Trotskyist', and may even have believed that there was a world-wide Trotskyist conspiracy devoted to his downfall. If there had been no Trotsky, he would have sent Zinoviev abroad for the same purpose. He devised plots against himself, and he was careful to keep close watch on these plots in case they miscarried with fatal results to himself. By 1934 he had reached the stage when he could trust no one, not even his closest associates, and he devised one plot after another to rid himself of them.

The closest of his associates, the man he had groomed for the succession, was Sergey Kirov. The plot to murder Kirov was one of the most intricate he ever devised, so that to this day we do not know exactly how the plot was worked out to the last detail, though we can trace its progress with fair accuracy. The bullet that killed Kirov was not fired by Stalin, but we know who gave the bullet to the half-demented murderer, and on what authority. Kirov died, as so many others died, in order to guarantee the safety of the leader.

The murders went on, because they could not be stopped. Sometimes the insatiable massacre system seemed to pause in order to contemplate its own audacity, and then it would resume its operations with even greater speed and efficiency than before. Only one thing could stop it – another and even more terrible massacre system. This was provided by the Germans in due course.

THE MURDER OF KIROV

At four-thirty in the afternoon of December 1st, 1934, an obscure young Communist, Leonid Viktorovich Nikolayev, was prowling along the corridors of the Smolny in Leningrad in search of mischief.

Though he wore the regulation leather jacket, carried a party card, and had served the party on the battlefield and as one of the supervisors of a prison camp in the far north, there were many things to distinguish him from the other Communists who were gathering in the Smolny to attend a party meeting. In the first place he was singularly unpleasant in appearance. He was short, club-footed, with an enormous head, protruding ears, and a wide mouth. His arms were far too long for his body. His only redeeming feature was a pair of soft blue eyes, which seemed to have been borrowed from his mild and trusting mother, while the rest of his body derived from his hard-drinking father. He was a sickly child, disliked by his father, who constantly beat him. Once he was struck so hard that he lost consciousness, and it was thought that his epileptic fits resulted from this beating. He was vindictive, crafty, and given to long periods of brooding. Those who knew him well remarked his phenomenal eagerness to leave his mark upon the world: in this he succeeded beyond all expectation.

The strange sickly Nikolayev, so unlike the conventional picture of the dedicated Communist, seemed to have stepped straight out of the pages of Dostoyevsky. He thirsted for glory, lived in apocalyptic dreams, and saw himself as one of the chosen ones who were destined to usher in a new age. Yet he had no talent for exerting his will on the masses. He was a bad speaker and an indifferent writer. The Party leaders distrusted him when they did not despise him; and they could find no use for him. Gradually he came to inhabit a no man's land where dreams and reality shade into one another. While he was prowling through the corridors of the Smolny he was already close to madness, and perhaps he was already insane.

Born in 1905, the year of the abortive revolution, he grew up in unremitting poverty. His father died when he was very young, leaving the family destitute. The father, Viktor Nikolayev, was a Bulgarian, an unbeliever, a man given to sudden explosions of temper and fitful rages, who beat his wife as unmercifully as he beat his children. His wife belonged to the sect of the Old Believers, and she had her children baptized secretly. At the time of her husband's death in 1908 she had three children by him: Ekaterina, who was ten; Leonid, who was three; and Pyotr, who was still nursing. She made her living as a cleaning woman in a streetcar depot, but her earnings were pathetically meagre. In the evenings, to make ends meet, she worked as a housekeeper for a Finnish baron. Two years after her husband's death she gave birth to the baron's illegitimate daughter, who was given the name of Anna.

With the baron's help the Nikolayevs were able to live in decent poverty. They had a small apartment in Vyborg Side, the industrial section of St Petersburg, and since the mother was often away, the children were left to their own resources. Leonid was a lonely, embittered child, bad at his lessons, with few playmates. He saw little of his older sister, who soon became a milliner's apprentice. He was twelve years of age when the October revolution broke out. The armed workers of Vyborg paraded through the streets, shouted themselves hoarse, and scattered revolutionary handbills, but took little part in the fighting. They were stirring times, and young Leonid, with his proletarian background, became a member of the Young Communist League, and like all the other Vyborg schoolboys he joined parades and ran errands for the new masters of the city. St Petersburg, now Petrograd, had become the capital of a small and shrinking Communist empire, a dangerous and exciting place to live in. But their fortunes were worse than before, for the baron had fled to Finland and the whole family depended on the mother's earnings as a streetcar cleaner. She had been cleaning streetcars since 1903, and she went on cleaning them until 1934, when she was arrested and thrown into prison.

In October 1919 General Yudenich attacked Petrograd in force. He occupied Tsarskoye Selo and Gatchina and would have gone on to capture the city if Trotsky had not hurled against the invaders every available man, woman, and boy. Leonid fought as a soldier in the Red Army during the hard campaigns of that winter. When the civil war was over, he occupied an obscure position in the Cheka. He became a member of the party in 1920. In 1923 he went to live in the nearby city of Pskov, where he worked in the local party committee, and here he met and married an Esthonian woman, Milda Drauleh, some years older than himself. Though she was a homely and rather ugly woman, he was intensely jealous, accused her of going out with other men, and occasionally beat her. She was a Christian, and he was an atheist. She wanted a gay time, and he wanted to dedicate himself to the service of the party. He was always searching for ways to improve himself and to incur favour in the eyes of the party leaders, and when in 1929 the post of supervisor to a forced-labour battalion in Murmansk was offered to him, he accepted it eagerly. It is possible that his superiors in Pskov simply wanted to get rid of him.

In Murmansk he had power of life or death over about a thousand prisoners. He enjoyed his position of authority, but hated the weather and the interminable bureaucratic wrangling with high officials of the Cheka, who sent him streams of orders which it was impossible for him to fulfil. The prisoners died like flies. The labour norms always remained unfulfilled. He would explain at great length why the work could not be done, but there was always an order saying it *must* be done. At last, early in 1934, broken in health, his nerve shattered, he was relieved of his post and sent to Leningrad. The only job that could be found for him was that of guard at the Smolny. From a position of power and responsibility, he had fallen to a position where there was no power and almost no responsibility. Previously he had enjoyed the rank and wages of an officer of the Cheka; now he was no more than a policeman whose sole duty was to check the passes of party members.

Into his diary Nikolayev poured the accumulated rage of his soul. He described in great and intricate detail all his meetings with party officials, and he showed how each one of them had betrayed him. He alone, the proletarian from Vyborg, had demonstrated the true faith; he alone had carried the banner of the Revolution purposefully and honestly. He painted a picture of the state as it should have been, and then he described it as it was, plague-ridden with bureaucrats. He began to read the biographies of the revolutionaries of the nineteenth century, those small and scattered groups which were nevertheless capable of inspiring the Tsar with terror. But though he read these books, he made no mention of them in his interminable diary which he filled with portraits of self-seeking officials and visionary descriptions of a world in which true revolutionaries would have their proper place in the sun. More and more he found himself looking back to the early days of the Revolution, when, as he expressed it, 'there was a comradeship of blood'. But there was no longer any comradeship: only betrayal, and a rage in his soul.

He might have weathered the storm if he had not been dismissed from his post and from the party sometime in the late spring of 1934. The ostensible reason for the dismissal was that he was continually complaining to high officials. He was an inveterate letter writer, and he had written denunciatory letters to every official who had ever made him miserable, and if he received no satisfaction he would write to their superiors. Following his abrupt dismissal, there were more letters, more denunciations. The party had pity on him. His unsatisfactory behaviour was ascribed to nervous exhaustion following his experiences in Murmansk. He received back his party card, but not his job as a guard at the Smolny. He had a wife, a mother and two children to support. Once more there was a deluge of letters and more barbed entries in the diary. Desperate before, he was now more desperate than ever.

He wrote to Stalin, to Kirov, to the chairman of the Control Commission who had been responsible for his dismissal from the party and for his later reinstatement. He had become 'a case history' in bureaucratic circles in Leningrad, where his strident letters were sometimes discussed with amused tolerance by overworked officials. The NKVD showed interest in him. Ivan Zaporozhets, the deputy director of the NKVD in Leningrad, was sufficiently interested to arrange a meeting. Nikolayev was glad to have a listener. He spoke mysteriously of a book he was writing, which he called *A Letter to My Children*. This was the diary in which he recorded all the sufferings he had endured. He explained that this book was the true history of the Revolution, and showed the bureaucrats in their true light. He would not, however, show the book to anyone. It was secret, to be published only after his death. And as Nikolayev rambled on about the vast injustices he had suffered and about the labour norms in Murmansk and about his desire to topple the bureaucrats from their places of authority, it became clear that his mind was already unhinged and that he was an easy prey to suggestion.

A report on Nikolayev was sent to Stalin. The secret book, hidden inside a piano, was easily discovered by an agent of the NKVD, who had the pages photographed. The book was then quietly replaced. There was now not the least doubt that Nikolayev was on the verge of a nervous breakdown. Frustrated, poverty-stricken, confronted by the entire bureaucracy of the Soviet Union whom he regarded as traitors to the Revolution, he was perfectly capable of killing any high official who stepped in his path. If he had been armed and if Stalin had appeared in front of him, he would have shot him dead. He would have shot Kirov or Philip Medved, the head of the Leningrad NKVD, or any one of a hundred other officials. But he was not armed – his revolver had been taken from him when he was dismissed from the Smolny. What would happen if a gun were given to him?

Zaporozhets must have debated for a long time on the consequences of putting a gun in his hands. He was playing a deadly game with a potential assassin, and any mistake might prove fatal to his plans. During the course of the late summer and autumn Nikolayev was under the constant vigilance of NKVD agents. Zaporozhets had to work cautiously, for Philip Medved, his superior, was a close friend of Kirov. His instructions came from the Kremlin. Perusing the photographed sheets of the diary, he derived some satisfaction from the knowledge that he had successfully channelled Nikolayev's thinking towards a single objective – the killing of Kirov. It remained only to give him a revolver, to stand back, and then to telegraph the news to the Kremlin.

One day in November Nikolayev found himself in possession of a Nagan revolver. With his precious diary and the revolver in a briefcase, he went to the Smolny, where he was a familiar figure. He received a pass and went through the first doors leading to the stairway. He was hurrying along when a guard summoned him and ordered him to open the briefcase. He did so, and when the guard saw the revolver, he was immediately placed under arrest. The least punishment for carrying a gun into the party headquarters was three years' imprisonment, but this was imposed only under exceptionally extenuating circumstances. If he had been brought to trial, a much heavier sentence awaited him. He was not brought to trial, for later in the day Zaporozhets ordered his release. The briefcase with the revolver and the diary was returned to him.

Zaporozhets had not given up hope of bringing about the murder of Kirov at the hands of a demented party member. This first attempt was to be regarded as a trial run. For the next and final attempt he made sure that any guards stationed in the corridors of the Smolny would look the other way when Nikolayev appeared. He also arranged that Kirov should be called out of his office while Nikolayev was prowling in the corridor. Kirov would receive a message that he was wanted on the direct Kremlin line and would immediately run down the corridor to the special telephone installed for this purpose. The timing had been worked out to the last second.

Kirov was in his office, putting the last touches to a speech he intended to deliver in a few minutes to party officials. He was alone except for a secretary and a bodyguard, a middle-aged man named Borisov. Kirov was forty-eight; he had spent more than thirty years of his life as an active member of the party, always in positions of danger, and unlike Stalin, who was constantly surrounded by an impenetrable wall of guards, he had never felt any need to be guarded. Borisov was more a friend than a guard, a quiet and cheerful man who adored Kirov and was always in his company.

A few moments after 4:30 pm on that cold Wednesday afternoon Zaporozhets called Kirov's secretary and said the Kremlin was on the line. At that moment Borisov was preparing tea and cakes on a tray. There was nothing unusual in receiving a call from the Kremlin. The tea and cakes could wait until Kirov returned.

Nikolayev was standing close to the door, which opened out on the corridor. He had already removed the Nagan revolver from the briefcase and was no more than four or five feet away when Kirov came out. The moment Kirov appeared, Nikolayev fired at the back of Kirov's head, and then he did something which was not included in the plans so carefully contrived with the help of Zaporozhets. He fainted, and the revolver, with which he had intended to kill himself after killing Kirov, fell from his hands and slithered across the floor.

The sound of the shot echoed through the Smolny. Soon there were twenty people running along the corridor. They saw Kirov lying beside a man in a leather coat, and assumed that both had been assassinated. Kirov had fallen with his feet wedged against the door, and some moments passed before Borisov was able to open it. In those moments Nikolayev awoke from his fainting spell, realized what he had done, and decided to carry out the second part of the compact he had made with himself. Because the revolver was out of reach, he drew a razor from his pocket and cut his own throat. Now there were two pools of blood in the corridor. Kirov was carried into his office where he died a few minutes later without regaining consciousness. Nikolayev, less fortunate, was to survive for nearly a month.

The hunt for the assassin continued. The entrance to the Smolny was closed off by armed guards, and by order of Zaporozhets everyone in the building was searched. He was evidently hoping to gain time. At first no one except Zaporozhets knew that Nikolayev was the murderer. Then someone remembered that while people were streaming past the two bodies and making the circuit of the corridors in search of the assassin, the appearance of one of them had changed. Nikolayev, who had been lying very still, with no blood on him, was observed a few minutes later to be in another position altogether and to be bleeding from the neck. Borisov was among those who noticed the change, and he seems to have guessed that there was some connection between the call from the Kremlin and the murder of his friend. He may have confided his fears to Zaporozhets, for a few hours later he disappeared. On the evening of the following day he was killed. The method of killing him was a curious one. He was being taken in an NKVD truck to an interrogation, when the truck swerved into a wall. The driver and the NKVD guards were unharmed, but Borisov was dead.

When the news of Kirov's murder reached Stalin, he ordered a special train to take him to Leningrad. Genrikh Yagoda, the recently appointed chief of the secret police – he was the successor of Vyacheslav Menzhinsky, who had died from 'paralysis of the heart' the previous May – flew to Leningrad early the next morning. Stalin arrived in the late afternoon to find that Yagoda had already taken charge of the investigation. This was unfortunate, for Yagoda apparently knew very little about the plot, and Stalin announced that he would himself conduct the investigations, making his headquarters at the Smolny.

Stalin took complete command, and himself cross-examined everyone connected with the case from the head of the local NKVD to the last wretched prisoner roped in because his name appeared in the diary or because at some time in his life he had been associated in some remote capacity with Nikolayev. Hundreds were rounded up. Even completely unimportant people, who had met Nikolayev only once or twice, were thrown into prison and solemnly escorted into the presence of Stalin, who took a strange pleasure in accusing them of a crime he had himself planned. His purpose in coming to Leningrad was to ensure that he held all the threads of the plot in his own hands. It was apparent that Zaporozhets had bungled the job.

Meanwhile Stalin wore his mourning robes gracefully. He delivered a brief oration beside Kirov's coffin. He bent down and kissed Kirov on the forehead, and tears streamed down his cheeks. In much the same way he had kissed the dead Lenin, and wiped away the tears. He decreed that Kirov's body should be taken to Moscow for a public funeral, and that his ashes should be interred near Lenin's tomb in the place reserved for the martyred heroes of the Revolution.

As though Kirov had gone on a long journey, farewell letters were written to him and printed prominently in the newspapers. One letter, signed by Stalin and eighteen Communist leaders including Ordjonikidze, Molotov, Kalinin, Mikoyan, Voroshilov, Kaganovich, Zhdanov, Kuibyshev, Rudzutak, Chubar, Kossier, and Yezhov, concluded with the words:

You were dear to all of us, Comrade Kirov, as loyal friend, beloved comrade, dependable companion-in-arms. To the last of our days and our struggle we shall remember you, dear friend, and will feel the weight of our loss. You were ever with us in the days of the hard-fought battles for the triumph of socialism in our country, you were ever with us in the years of vacillation and difficulties within our party. With us you went through all the hardships of recent years, and we have lost you at the moment when our country has scored great victories. In all this struggle, in all our achievements, much was due to you, to your energy, your strength and fervent love for the cause of Communism.

Farewell, our dear friend and comrade, Sergey!

Because Kirov had held high rank as commander of the Eleventh Army during the civil war, another letter signed by the leading generals including Tukhachevsky, Yakir, Kork, Yegorov, Smirnov, Budyenny, Gamarnik and Viktorov was also published. The dead man's victories were proclaimed, his loving care for the Red Army was celebrated, and it was not forgotten that he had received the highest decoration for military leadership, the Order of the Red Banner. 'To the treacherous shot of the enemy which has snatched you from our ranks,' the letter concluded, 'the Red Army will reply by further consolidating its fighting power and rallying still closer around our party and its leader Comrade Stalin.' It was a useful formula, to be repeated many times during the following years. More than half the signatories were later murdered by Stalin.

These orations, letters and decrees were only a small part of Stalin's work during his visit to Leningrad. For most of the time he preferred to act as the patient investigator, the superintendent of police, earnestly inquiring into the causes of the crime, examining the evidence and interviewing witnesses. Nikolayev was the most important witness, but an unsatisfactory one. The wound in the throat was not serious, though he had lost a lot of blood. Thrown into a prison cell, he attempted to kill himself by smashing his head against the wall, but these attempts at suicide were as unsuccessful as the first. With head and throat bandaged, he was brought into Stalin's presence. Asked why he had killed Kirov, he shrugged his shoulders. Had he any animosity against Kirov? He answered that he had none. He was unrepentant, glorying in his terrorist act, saying that he had committed no crime, but had followed in the path of the terrorists of the Narodnaya Volya, men like Zhelyabov and Nechayev, who were prepared to sacrifice their lives to put an end to tyranny. Asked for the names of his accomplices, he answered that there were none, and that it was unthinkable that there could be any. He knew he was doomed and there was nothing to be gained by dissimulation, and therefore he took care to implicate Zaporozhets. He seems to have been perfectly aware that he was being used by the secret police, and it may have amused him to know that, far from being their willing victim, he had employed them from the beginning to accomplish his own ends. He was tortured, but no further information could be got from him. In disgust Stalin abandoned the interrogation of Nikolayev. From time to time prisoners, rounded up by Yagoda, would be taken into a small room and shown a small, heavily bandaged and barely conscious figure lying under a white blanket. They were told: 'There's your friend Nikolayev. Look what you have done to him!'

Stalin's task was made more difficult by Nikolayev's silence. No confession implicating any opposition groups was ever extracted from him. Though admitting the providential aid of Zaporozhets, he insisted that he alone was responsible for committing the murder. For Stalin's purposes such easy explanations offered hostages to fortune, and he may have realized too late that consequences of a murder are sometimes unpredictable.

The first government communiqué referred to an anonymous assassin sent by 'the enemies of the working class'. The communiqué resembled the Sverdlov document in that it pointed to a mysterious un-named assassin, when the identity of the assassin was known, and in the fact that it marked the beginning of a new upsurge in the activities of the massacre machine. It read:

> On December 1st at 4.30 pm in the city of Leningrad, in the building of the Leningrad Soviet (formerly the Smolny), Comrade Sergey Mironovich Kirov, Secretary of the Central and Leningrad Committees of the CPSU (Bolsheviks) and member of the Presidium of the Central Executive Committee of the USSR, fell by the hand of an assassin sent by the enemies of the working class. The assassin has been arrested. His identity is being ascertained.

On that same day Stalin and eighteen prominent Bolsheviks signed a letter in which Kirov is described as 'the inspired tribune of the revolution, a man who combined sincerity and gentleness towards friends and comrades with the radiant warmth and modesty of a true follower of Lenin'. It was perhaps the only time that a Bolshevik leader was officially praised for gentleness. By implication the letter contrasted the anonymous assassin, representing mysterious forces acting against the working class, with the friendly Kirov, who personified the virtues of the working class. And in fact there was some truth in this simple contrast, for Nikolayev was essentially anonymous, colourless and diffuse, living on the fringes of existence, and Kirov was the descendant of a long line of proletarians. Nikolayev scarcely knew what he was doing, and there was never a moment in his life when Kirov did not know exactly what he was doing.

Stalin's purpose in coming to Leningrad was therefore to bring conscious order into a situation which threatened to become chaotic. Yet in those early days he was still feeling his way, still unsure of himself. That he should himself take part in the cross-examination of Nikolayev and the people whose names were found in Nikolayev's diary suggests that he had little faith in Yagoda's capacity to report accurately on the crime. Altogether he cross-examined some twenty or thirty people, including some who were only remotely connected with Nikolayev.

Among those who were arrested after the murder of Kirov was the young and beautiful Elizabeth Lermolo, who had married a White Guard officer and been forced to divorce him. As the former wife of a convicted counter-revolutionary she had been sentenced to a five-year term of exile in Pudozh in northern Russia. Nikolayev had spent a few days in Pudozh during the summer, visiting an aunt. One day in the communal kitchen he suffered an epileptic fit, and Elizabeth Lermolo had helped him to a chair. The young Communist was grateful for her help, and there were occasional brief conversations, which often developed into monologues, with Nikolayev elaborating on the theme that the revolution had fallen into the hands of bureaucrats who no longer valued the services of true Bolsheviks. She listened politely, puzzled that anyone carrying a party card should speak so openly and so bitterly about the affairs of the party, and she remembered later that he carried with him a book about Zhelyabov and Sophie Perovskaya and the other heroes of the Narodnaya Volya. Then he vanished, and she thought no more of him until she was arrested by the NKVD as a material witness in the murder of Kirov. From Pudozh she was flown to Leningrad and almost immediately taken to a large room where Stalin sat at a conference table covered with a green baize cloth, while his secretary, Alexander Poskrebyshev, elderly, bald-headed and pock-marked, wearing a military tunic without insignia, sat behind a desk. Poskrebyshev was not only the head of Stalin's personal secretariat, but he was also the chief of the Central Committee's Secret Division, and therefore he was in a position to wield power second only to Stalin. He succeeded Tovstyukha, who died of tuberculosis in 1927, and thereafter for more than a quarter of a century he remained Stalin's *alter ego*.

Elizabeth Lermolo was one of the few who survived arrest for complicity in Kirov's murder, and her memoirs are therefore all the more valuable. She writes about her arrest and long imprisonment with detachment and grace. At first she was puzzled by Stalin's appearance, for he scarcely resembled his official portraits:

> This was Stalin himself before me – Stalin whose presence filled all of Russia but who kept himself secret except to a few. I sat down and stared fixedly at him. He looked neither as well preserved nor as imposing as he did in his official portraits. I tried to detect in his face some semblance of greatness, an indication of heroic will – but I was aware only of the large, flabby features, the sallow, pock-marked skin, the watery eyes.

For about an hour Stalin cross-examined her relentlessly, apparently in the hope of trapping her into an admission that she was a member of a conspiratorial group. She was asked how and where she had met Nikolayev, what he had said, and why he had entered her name in his diary. Trembling, she explained how she had helped to lift him in a chair when he was in convulsions, and she reported Nikolayev's conversations at length. At intervals Agranov, a deputy minister, who was also in the room, would come running forward with a lighted match for Stalin's pipe, which was always going out, and sometimes Stalin would interrupt a discourse to bark an order to Poskrebyshev, who would immediately take the order down in longhand. At one point Stalin was able to extract from her the admission that she had lent Nikolayev's aunt two rubles to help pay for his railroad passage back to Leningrad.

> 'You lent her the two rubles?' Stalin asked me.
> 'Yes, I did.'
> 'And how long did it take Nikolayev to repay the debt?'
> 'I never did remind the old woman about it.'
> 'What about Nikolayev?'

'Nor did I remind Nikolayev. As a matter of fact I did not know his address.'

Stalin protested that this was impossible. 'How is it he knew your address? He had it written out very clearly in his notebook.' The illogic of this seemed to escape him. Obviously Nikolayev's aunt and I had the same address. 'And besides you should have reminded Nikolayev,' Stalin scolded me. 'Debts should be honoured. Didn't you need the money? Everyone needs money.'

Soon Stalin realized that no advantage was to be gained by pursuing the two rubles further, for no one enters a conspiratorial organization for two rubles, and accordingly he changed his tactics. He asked for the names of all the people Nikolayev had met in Pudozh, and he wanted to discover from her what groups or organizations could have dared to kill Kirov. As Elizabeth Lermolo recounts her interrogation, we see Stalin groping towards three or four alternative solutions to the mystery which he had himself created. He was like a detective running casually through a list of all the possible murderers. Suddenly he asked her whether she knew who Kirov was.

I said that I did.

'And you know that he is no longer alive?'

Yes, I knew that. It was broadcast over the radio.

'How did he die?' Stalin then wanted to know.

Sensing a trap, I said hesitantly, 'He was killed by Nikolayev, wasn't he?'

'Yes. Kirov was slain by Nikolayev at the instigation of the enemies of the working class. Did you anticipate that the friend you made in Pudozh would turn out to be such a scoundrel? Where did he get the revolver? Do you know?'

'How should I?' I answered.

Turning to the deputy minister, Stalin asked him for a report on the weapon found on Nikolayev and was told that when Nikolayev was reinstated in the party no revolver was issued to him because he had no assignment which required one.

'In other words, Agranov,' Stalin interrupted him, 'to commit the murder Nikolayev obtained the revolver either from some Communist, or from the counter-revolutionaries. Right?'

'Quite right, Joseph Vissarionovich,' replied Agranov.

'Is that clear to you, too?' Stalin turned to me.

I shrugged my shoulders, having no reason to confirm or deny what he conceived to be an obvious fact.

Again he questioned me about the weapon – had Nikolayev procured it from the Social Revolutionaries or the Zinovievites? When I again disclaimed knowledge of the matter he addressed himself to the man at the desk.

'Poskrebyshev, be sure to remind me to issue an order to disarm all civilian Communists.'

Stalin now regarded me closely. 'You say you heard nothing about the revolver. Maybe so. But you certainly must have heard how the exiles felt about our late comrade Kirov?'

In reply I told him of the talk I had heard about Kirov and his plans for reform.

'So-so? ... If the exiles pictured Kirov as such a great benefactor, why did they conspire to assassinate him? Why did they incite Nikolayev to kill Kirov?'

'Did the exiles incite Nikolayev? I didn't know that.'

'Who else?' said Stalin. 'Of course everyone now is trying to pin the blame on the Zinovievites. But perhaps the Zinovievites had nothing to do with it ... Tell me, do you think it would be a good idea to abolish the NKVD, to liquidate the concentration camps, to enrich the peasants?'

I suggested that the entire population would benefit, and possibly the government.

'That's what you think? Good enough.' Then after a pause he said, 'When was it that the Zinovievites and the White Guardists decided jointly to eliminate Kirov?'

Keeping impatience from my voice, I explained that the White Guardists whom I knew in Pudozh had never in my hearing expressed any desire to assassinate Kirov. As for the Zinovievites and their type of Communists, I had no contact with them.

Stalin was disbelieving. 'Possibly you do not realize that some of the Communists you knew there belong to the Zinoviev faction. I'll name some of them: Katalynov, Levin, Mandelshtam, Shatsky, Myasnikov.'

I knew none of these people, and said so.

'Strange,' Stalin commented. 'They seem to know you, and know you well ... Now let's approach the problem from another angle. As you know, Kirov has lately been getting rid of all loyal Communists in his party apparatus – men like Nikolayev – and replacing them with Zinovievites. How do you explain this odd behaviour on Kirov's part?'

Elizabeth Lermolo's testimony has been quoted at some length because it is important in itself in explaining the attitude of a prisoner confronted by Stalin, and also because it goes far to explain Stalin's mood in the days immediately following the murder of Kirov. We see him turning restlessly around the central problem: *On whom can we put the blame for the crime?* One by one he examines the possibilities. The exiles in Pudozh, the White Guards, the Socialist Revolutionaries, the Zinovievites – all are examined in turn, weighed, and found wanting. He knows the answer to the problem, but has not yet decided on the official, public answer which will ultimately be incorporated in the textbooks. For the moment he was content to announce that Kirov had been killed by an enemy of the working class. He could afford to wait. He asked Elizabeth Lermolo a few more questions, and then abruptly dismissed her. As a material witness to the crime, she was given an indefinite sentence of imprisonment in the isolators reserved for state criminals, where she remained for ten years, escaping only when the isolator she happened to be in was abandoned in the face of advancing German troops.

Elizabeth Lermolo was luckier than many of the other prisoners. On December 27th Nikolayev was placed on trial, together with thirteen other prisoners. Nikolayev, as was to be expected, pleaded guilty. So, too, did Antonov and Zvyezdov, who apparently had been instrumental in giving him the Nagan revolver. The remaining prisoners, including Katalynov, Levin, Mandelshtam, Shatsky and Myasnikov, all of whom had some slight acquaintance with Nikolayev in Pudozh, vehemently protested their innocence. The trial lasted two days, and all fourteen were sentenced to death. They were shot the next day.

Though Nikolayev was safely dead, no one had any illusions that the *affaire* Nikolayev had come to an end. It was only just beginning.

THE RITUALS OF TERROR

THE OFFICIAL FUNERAL of Kirov was held in Moscow, with Stalin, Voroshilov, Kaganovich and Kalinin carrying the urn with the ashes across the Red Square, for the death of so famous a man demanded its own special ritual. They walked in silence, surrounded by NKVD guards, on a raw, blustery day with the snow on the ground and the clouds racing low across the sky. Half of Moscow had turned out to watch the slow procession and to see the urn placed in the wall behind Lenin's mausoleum.

Every religion demands its own ritual, its vestments and holy vessels, but the religion of Communism under Stalin was still in the experimental stage, and no one, not even Stalin, had troubled to work out a convincing ceremony. The ritual involved a slow march, the vestments were the usual drab fur-lined greatcoats worn by high officials in winter, but it was observed that the Red Army guards called in to supplement the NKVD guards had been issued new uniforms without insignia. The holy vessel consisted of a long wooden tray provided with handles and shaped like one of those great platters in which butchers carry carcasses of beef. In the centre of this platter there rose a miniature wooden temple with four Doric columns; the urn in a wooden box reposed within the temple, which was roofed with garlands. On this tray there were also a few small sprays of flowers, presumably placed there by the four men who carried it on their shoulders.

There were, of course, advantages in employing a ceremonial tray, with its distant resemblance to a coffin. The burden could be shared equally, and the gradations of power were clearly indicated by the positions of the four men. Stalin and Voroshilov walked in front, Kaganovich and Kalinin took up the rear. Nor were the proportions of the miniature wooden temple quite so arbitrary as they at first appeared: these squat columns were intended to resemble the columns that decorated Lenin's mausoleum.

Among those who observed the ceremonies in the Red Square was the American journalist Louis Fischer, who had a profound knowledge of the inner workings of the Soviet state. He was very close to the small procession, and he had a good view of Yagoda, who was marching close to the urn, looking now at Stalin and now at the guards. 'He looked,' said Fischer, 'like a hunted animal. Stalin must have given him a good drubbing.' But it is more probable that Yagoda was simply scared out of his wits that someone might throw a bomb. Fischer noted that 'Stalin was really sad, for Kirov was his bosom friend', and he went on to observe that when the time came for Stalin to mount the steps of Lenin's mausoleum, he did not follow the established custom of arriving a little late, so permitting the lesser officials to be the first on the reviewing stand, but instead, on this day, as on no other day, he 'walked up the steps first, and alone, and stood alone on the stand for a minute, turning his head slowly from one side to the other as if to say, "Here I am. I am not afraid."'

In this way, in silence, savouring his triumph and with the full knowledge that the murder of Kirov could only serve his own purposes, Stalin looked down on the crowds in the Red Square, whom he held in the hollow of his hand.

The consequences of the murder of Kirov were felt all over the Soviet Union, but nowhere were they felt more keenly than in the Kremlin itself.

Security measures within the Kremlin had always been rigorously enforced. In the past visitors to Stalin's office would first have to show a special pass, and they were usually searched and interrogated twice by security officers stationed in the corridors leading to the office. Now they were searched and interrogated *four times*, and orders went out that the entire Kremlin area was to be regarded as a special military area where even the most innocent visitors who had come to see the medieval churches were to be carefully watched. The NKVD established an office in the Museum of History on the Red Square, and anyone who stopped to admire the Kremlin towers or the Lenin mausoleum might find himself accosted by an NKVD officer and led off for investigation. New and increasingly stringent regulations were issued for supervising processions and demonstrations in the Red Square. None of the soldiers marching in parade was permitted to be armed with live ammunition. The distance between Stalin as he stood on the reviewing stand and the first columns of marchers was increased. When he attended the theatre, he no longer showed himself in the royal box, but hid behind curtains. Suddenly the protective wall around

Stalin had become so high that he could no longer see the world he ruled over. He had become another Ivan the Terrible.

Alone, behind his wall, Stalin presided over the destiny of Russia with no real knowledge about the situation in the country, but with an absolute determination to enforce his will. Only two rivals had emerged to threaten his power – Trotsky and Kirov – and one was in exile, the other dead. After the murder of Kirov the entire country became his private concentration camp, where the inmates were expected to behave with submissive and cheerful infantilism, to deny and even to forget that they had ever possessed another master, and to celebrate him continually in their hymns. At intervals sacrifices had to be offered to him.

The murder of Kirov had not changed Stalin's attitude to the world. What had changed was the intensity of his hatred and his fear, and of his awareness that he was in mortal danger. His temper, always authoritarian, guilt-ridden and inclined to acts of sudden violence, was now exasperated by the knowledge that he must now rule by terror, or not at all. The murder of Kirov was the signal for the massive employment of terror *on all fronts*. He was no longer waging war against the *kulaks* or small groups which opposed this or that measure; he was waging war against the Russians in general, against an entire people. For this purpose he possessed an admirable assortment of weapons: murderous audacity, laws which he could promulgate or repeal at leisure, a secret police trained since the days of Lenin to be immune from pity and capable of carrying out any massacre without a qualm.

Among the laws promulgated to give a legal basis to the terror was one dated the same day as the murder of Kirov, although it had been prepared in advance for just such an eventuality. 'The law of December 1st, 1934', was officially promulgated that same evening, presumably after the news of the murder had reached the Kremlin, and some two days later it was approved by the Politburo, and in the form of a decree was signed into law by Yenukidze. Since the signature of Kalinin, the chairman of the Central Executive Committee of the USSR, appears to have been absent, there is some doubt whether the decree had any real basis in Soviet law; but there was no doubt about its effectiveness. It was a law comparable with Robespierre's *loi du 22 prairial* which permitted trial of the accused in his absence without any proper defence or without any judgement except the summary judgement of the court composed of appointees of the dictator. The law of December 1st, 1934, read:

1. The investigating agencies are directed to speed up the cases of persons accused of the preparation or carrying out of acts of terrorism.
2. Judicial organs are directed not to delay the execution of death sentences pertaining to crimes of this category in order to consider the possibility of pardon, because the Presidium of the Central Executive Committee does not consider possible the receiving of petitions of this kind.
3. The organs of the Commissariat of Internal Affairs are directed to execute the death sentences against criminals of the above-mentioned category immediately after the passing of sentences.

This law put an end to legality; the anarchic will of the Commissar of Internal Affairs, dominated by Stalin, now ruled. The first paragraph ordered trials on a conveyor-belt system, the second paragraph ruled against mercy, the third paragraph commanded instant death. Since anyone at all could be accused of 'the preparation of acts of terrorism', the law was evidently designed not so much to punish terrorists as to provide an instrument for political domination by terror. As Khrushchev pointed out in his secret speech of 1956, where the law is quoted in full, it inevitably became the basis for acts of abuse against socialist legality *on a mass scale*. Prisoners who confessed under torture could not hope that their cases would ever be reviewed. Anyone who fell into the hands of the NKVD could now regard himself as doomed, for he had no recourse. Innocent and guilty were alike caught in that intolerable doom, which was senseless because it served neither the purposes of the state nor those of the people.

The law of December 1st, 1934, was merely the codification of lawlessness. For a long time, indeed from the very beginning of the Revolution, the dictator had ruled according to his passing moods, his prejudices, and his sense of the judgement he thought necessary to visit on the people. Murder was his weapon, and the rituals of murder were carefully elaborated in a series of public pronouncements and secret instructions. From time to time it would be necessary to place a curb on murder. The reins were slackened, the people were given a temporary breathing space, and then after a proper interval the reign of terror would be resumed. It was a strange way to govern, and it was effective only because the people had grown accustomed to being ruled by a government which had elevated *senseless murder* to a fine art.

Among the documents known as 'the Smolensk archives', which were captured by the Germans and later fell into American hands, there can be found the secret instructions signed by Molotov as premier and Stalin as party secretary ordering a halt to senseless arrests. The secret instructions were addressed to all party and government officials, to the secret police, and all courts and procuracies. They read:

> The Central Committee and the Sovnarkom are informed that disorderly mass arrests in the countryside are still a part of the practice of our officials. Such arrests are made by the chairmen of village soviets and secretaries of party cells, by *raion* and *krai* officials; arrests are made by all who desire it, and who, strictly speaking, have no right to make arrests. It is not surprising that in such a saturnalia of arrests, organs which have the right to arrest, including the OGPU and especially the militia, lose all sense of moderation and often perpetrate arrests without any basis, acting according to the rule: 'Arrest first, and then investigate.'

Accordingly it was ordered that the arrests should cease, and only the duly appointed secret police and militia should be empowered to make arrests under due process of law. The secret instructions were dated May 8th, 1933, seven months before the murder of Kirov. There is no evidence that they had any effect. The reign of terror which followed Kirov's murder was merely an extension of a reign of terror that already existed. In the past terror had been dissipated; now it was held a little more firmly in the hands of the government.

The theory behind the terror was a simple one, and was stated most clearly by Stalin in a speech he delivered in January 1933. In this speech, by one of those strange ambiguities which were among the commonplaces of Stalin's mind, he insisted that the longed-for 'withering away of the state' could only come about when 'the remnants of the dying classes' were finally crushed. The terror was needed to bring about 'the withering away of the state'. It was also needed in order to transform the Soviet Union into a monolithic state powerful enough to survive and eventually break through 'capitalist encirclement'. He said:

> The state will die out, not as the result of relaxation of state power, but as a result of its maximum consolidation, which is necessary for the purpose of crushing the remnants of the dying classes and for organizing the defence against capitalist encirclement, which is far from being annihilated and will not soon be annihilated.

The theory that the state could only wither away by being made stronger was an eminently satisfactory one, for it permitted Stalin to extend the uses of terror beyond any limits previously known to mankind. By 'maximum consolidation' he meant 'maximum terror'. There was no escape from the logic of his conclusions, and like Shigalov in Dostoyevsky's *The Possessed* he could say: 'My conclusion is in direct contradiction of the original idea with which I started. Starting from unlimited freedom, I end with unlimited despotism.'

Possessing these beliefs, and the instruments to enforce them, he set about destroying one by one all the friends of Lenin who had brought the Bolshevik revolution into existence. It was not that he hated or feared them. It was simply that they had no place in the state as he envisaged it.

THE TRIAL OF ZINOVIEV AND KAMENEV

OF ALL THE MEN who had been intimate with Lenin in the long years of exile, Zinoviev was the one of whom it could be prophesied that he was least likely to become a successful revolutionary. Such talents as he possessed were those of a romantic orator. He was not a gifted writer; he made no contributions to revolutionary theory; he had very little talent for conspiracy. His one redeeming feature in the eyes of the Bolsheviks was his steadfast loyalty to Lenin, whom he had known since 1905 and whom he had followed blindly through all the various crises of the party until at a famous meeting in Petrograd on October 23rd, 1917, he voted with Kamenev against the seizure of power and was accused of cowardice. He was not a coward. He was a man who carefully weighed the consequences of his actions, and he knew exactly what he was doing when he protested against a premature revolt. He had an acute sense of the possible. Trotsky was to point out later that the revolution succeeded as the result of an extraordinary chain of circumstances, which was unlikely to be repeated. Its success could not have been foreseen.

Grigory Evseyevich Apfelbaum, who assumed the name of Zinoviev, was born in Elizavetgrad in 1882. He was short and dark-skinned, with heavy jowls, grey-blue eyes, a strong nose, a heavy jaw. He was proud of his thick mop of dark curly hair, as luxuriant as a woman's. In conversation he had a low caressing voice, which became strident when he was delivering speeches, and he was the master of expansive gestures. In public, haranguing a mob, he gave an impression of power; in private he seemed oddly feminine. He had a viperish tongue, and was an inveterate and dangerous gossip. He dressed shabbily, and took no care of his appearance. Only three men could claim to have been Lenin's intimates: they were Zinoviev, Kamenev, and Bukharin. Closest of all to Lenin was Zinoviev.

It was not strange that they should be so close to one another: they were a study in contrasts. Lenin had a mind like whipcord, harsh, unyielding and logical, and a small, tough, resilient body. Zinoviev was flabby, physically and intellectually, but he was also a man of quite extraordinary charm and willingness to please. He worshipped Lenin, ran errands for him, cheered him when he was downcast, and acted as the perfect foil, since there was nothing in him of the dedicated scholar and there was an earthiness in him which prevented him from losing touch with reality. Lenin could spin theories until his mind almost broke under the strain, while Zinoviev would applaud and try to reduce them to human terms. When he spoke in public, they called him 'the water pourer'.

Lev Borisovich Rosenfeld, who assumed the name of Kamenev, was exactly the same age as Zinoviev, but no two men could have been more different. Zinoviev was all on the surface, Kamenev was an introvert who thought deeply and carefully before he spoke. His father was Jewish, his mother Russian. He might have become a contemplative scholar if he had not been arrested while a law student at Moscow University. He had been a Marxist when he attended the gymnasium at Tiflis; prison made him a dedicated revolutionary. Deported to Tiflis, he instituted Marxist cells among the shoemakers and the railroad workers until the autumn of 1902 when he went to Paris, joined the *Iskra* group, and came under the spell of Lenin. From Paris he returned to Georgia to organize the Bolshevik faction, but had to flee again after the abortive 1905 revolution. Lenin sent him back to Russia to work on *Pravda* in 1913, and he spent most of the war years in exile in Siberia.

What Lenin chiefly admired in Kamenev was his calm intelligence and resourcefulness. He was an intellectual who spoke the language of the workers from long acquaintance with them. He was gentle and unassuming and at the same time exceedingly forceful when the occasion arose. 'Kamen' means stone, and there was a hard core to him. In the early photographs, with his dark, neatly trimmed beard, his pince-nez, and high collar, he resembled the familiar portrait of Chekhov. 'His attitude to his enemies was gentle,' Stakevich said of him, 'and it was as though he were ashamed of the irreconcilability of his position.' Sukhanov, the great journalist who recorded the early months of the revolution with extraordinary accuracy and penetration, described him as 'a man who may resist a little but never strongly'. For once Sukhanov was wrong. Kamenev was an unyielding Marxist, and if he seemed more gentle than the majority of Bolsheviks it was because he was genuinely fond of people. He had been a member of the Duma, he read widely in four or five languages, and he was devoted to his wife Olga, the sister of Trotsky. Like Zinoviev he had followed Lenin blindly except for the occasion when he spoke out against a premature seizure of power.

When Lenin came to power, Zinoviev became chairman of the Petrograd Soviet and Kamenev became chairman of the Moscow Soviet. In effect they became the governors of the two most important Soviet provinces. They were both members of the Central Committee. Zinoviev became the first chairman of the Communist International. When Lenin fell ill, it was Kamenev who acted as his deputy and signed the decrees which affected the lives of everyone in Russia.

Stalin's hatred of Zinoviev and Kamenev was of long standing. Given Stalin's temperament, it could hardly be otherwise, since Zinoviev and Kamenev were the logical heirs, the men who in the normal course of events would inherit the Soviet empire. To defeat them was to assure his own victory, for in Lenin's circle they had been the most prominent and the most skilled in the exercise of power. To crush them, to annihilate them completely, so that nothing would be left of them, to destroy utterly all the legends which had grown around their names and to rewrite the history books so that their contributions to revolutionary history should pass into oblivion – this was only part of the aim. The more crucial aim was to destroy them spiritually, to reduce them to meaninglessness.

What he wanted from them was that they should deny themselves. Their accomplishments, their contributions to the Bolshevik cause, the books they had written, their friendship and affection for Lenin – all these were to be wiped away as though they had never been. They were to be shown to the world and to history not as men, but as caricatures of men, incompetent, treacherous, incapable of honest emotion. They were to prove from their own mouths that their lives had consisted of ludicrous improvisations. They were not real revolutionaries, but shadows posturing as revolutionaries, and therefore they must grovel at his feet, demand pardon, and ask to be shot.

It must always be a strange and baffling task to accomplish the spiritual death of another man, and though it is now clear that this was Stalin's intention from the beginning, it is also clear that Stalin gave profound thought to accomplishing his purpose. There were pitfalls everywhere. Both Zinoviev and Kamenev were public figures, their ways of thought and smallest idiosyncracies being well known to the public. They were not men who could be changed overnight into public enemies of the government, for until recently they had been the government. To destroy them spiritually he needed patience – almost more patience than he possessed.

There exist, of course, ready-made machines for accomplishing the spiritual death of a man. The medieval torture chambers were devised to extract confessions, but they had other purposes as well. They could instil so much fear in a man that he would deny everything, even his most sacred beliefs. They could render his life so meaningless that he would prefer to be dead. When Aimery de Villiers-le-Duc, a Knight Templar, was brought to trial in Paris in AD 1310, he confessed that after seeing fifty-four of his fellow knights driven away in a cart to be burned at the stake, he was filled with such fear that he found himself perfectly capable of confessing any crime to avoid the same fate. 'I feel I would confess anything at all,' he told his inquisitors, 'and if they asked me whether I had killed Christ Himself, I would cheerfully admit it from fear of the fire.' Under torture he had confessed whatever he was ordered to confess. 'But you must not tell the guards what I am saying,' he added, 'because they will send me to the stake.'

Aimery de Villiers-le-Duc was fulfilling the classic role of the man doomed to be reduced to meaninglessness. He was so broken and confused that he was asking the inquisitors to protect him from the guards who tortured him, forgetting that it was the inquisitors who ordered him to be put to the torture.

Under torture a man will convict himself of any crime, implicate those who are nearest and dearest to him, surrender his will completely to the will of the adversary, and he will regard it as an act of mercy if he is put to death. Only a very few men have been able to withstand the extremes of torture. But torture is an unsatisfactory weapon, for once it is removed, the body fights back to sanity and health, and the prisoner has the opportunity to deny his confessions. Torture is temporary.

There are more effective ways than torture to accomplish a man's death. Simply by promises and threats he can be reduced to meaninglessness.

Although Zinoviev and Kamenev were both tortured, it was not necessary to torture them. All that was necessary was for the dictator to say: 'Unless you confess I shall destroy your family. Your confessions will prove that you have no place in history, but have always behaved like vermin. You will abase yourself before me and proclaim to the world that I am the destined saviour of the proletarian revolution. If you do this, I promise to save your life.' Even though the prisoner knows that the promise will almost certainly not be kept, he has no alternative but to cling to this faint hope. Like Aimery de Villiers-le-Duc he must seek for protection from the one source which is determined to destroy him.

For the dictator to obtain the fullest satisfaction, the confessions of the prisoner must be made publicly in the light of day, and there must be no suggestion that the confessions have been forced out of the prisoner. Above all he must appear to have confessed of his own free will, as one who is overwhelmed by his own guilt. But by the very nature of a public trial, confessions are suspect. Only if the prisoners rehearse their confessions in great detail, only if they speak the words like actors simulating a passion they have never felt, can these trials be given the illusion of verisimilitude. Both Zinoviev and Kamenev were brilliantly miscast. They were atrocious actors, and the script, largely written by Stalin, was bungled. There were prolonged rehearsals, every actor knew the exact role he was expected to play, the prosecutor was word perfect, and the audience was carefully chosen. In spite of all this the trial was a miserable failure.

The trial, which opened on August 19th, 1936, and closed five days later, came to be known as 'the trial of the sixteen', for although Zinoviev and Kamenev played the roles of the principal defendants, it was obvious that they could not have entered upon a conspiracy alone. The fourteen other defendants seem to have been chosen at random. They played the roles of counter-revolutionary agents, gunrunners and wreckers. Among them were former high officials and some obscure secret agents, whose roles were largely decorative. They were the spear carriers who could sometimes be heard shouting: 'Down with Trotsky! Down with Kamenev! Down with Zinoviev!' Sometimes they would step forward on the stage and confirm what someone else had said.

The cast could therefore be divided into three separate parts: the principals, the supporting actors, and the spear carriers.

PRINCIPALS

Grigory Evseyevich ZINOVIEV.
Lev Borisovich KAMENEV.

SUPPORTING ACTORS

Grigory Eremeyevich EVDOKIMOV. Former sailor, agitator, and deputy chairman of the Petrograd Soviet. He was among the official speakers at Lenin's funeral.

Ivan Petrovich BAKAYEV. Member of the Bolshevik party since 1906, agitator during the October revolution in Petrograd, former chief of the Petrograd Cheka.

Sergey Vitalevich MRACHKOVSKY. Member of the Bolshevik party since 1905, organizer of the Bolshevik uprising in the Urals in 1917, and subsequently commander of the Urals military district.

Vagarshak Arutyunoch TER-VAGANYAN. Leader of the Armenian Bolsheviks and of the Soviet Revolution in

Armenia. Editor, under Lenin, of the party magazine *Under the Banner of Marxism*:

Ivan Nikitich SMIRNOV. Member of the Bolshevik Party since 1903, five times arrested, each time making his escape. Became leader of Soviet forces in Siberia, and was largely responsible for the victory of the Fifth Army over Kolchak.

Efim Alexandrovich DREITZER. Member of Trotsky's bodyguard, twice decorated with Order of the Red Banner during the civil war. Fought against Kolchak and in the Polish campaign.

Isak Isayevich REINGOLD. Former Assistant People's Commissar for Finance. Close friend of Kamenev.

Richard Vitoldovich PICKEL. Formerly in charge of Zinoviev's secretariat, and former member of the Leningrad Cheka.

Eduard Solomonovich HOLTZMAN. An old Bolshevik, former member of the Leningrad Cheka.

MINOR ROLES

Fritz DAVID (Ilya-David Israilovich Kruglyansky). Former trade union editor of *Rote Fahne*, and former secretary of Wilhelm Pieck, the German Communist leader.

Valentin Pavlovich OLBERG. Former *Impreccor* correspondent and teacher of history at Stalinabad. In 1933 he acquired Honduran citizenship while living in Czechoslovakia.

Conon Borisovich BERMAN-YURIN. (Hans Stauer). Left Russia in 1923 as correspondent of Soviet Youth League papers, subsequently a freelance journalist.

Moissei Ilyich LURYE (Alexander Emel). Contributor to *Impreccor* and member of the German Communist Party.

Nathan Lazarovich LURYE. Of Polish-Russian descent, became a member of the German Communist Party. Fled Germany in 1932.

Such were the men who confessed to being traitors, murderers, and subverters of the Communist state. When the charge was read out, all except one pleaded guilty. The exception was Ivan Smirnov, who confessed that he had been in correspondence with Trotsky, but denied any personal participation in terrorist acts. Throughout the trial, to the visible annoyance of the prosecutor, he wavered from abject confession to defiant proclamations of innocence. He alone seemed to be fighting for his life, tossing his mane of white hair. At intervals Kamenev would seem to rise out of his stupor and hint at a defiance he was never able to express fully. The remaining prisoners seemed desperately anxious to tighten the noose round their necks.

The prisoners who stood in the dock, guarded by blue-capped Red Army soldiers, looked like ghosts of themselves. They suffered from prison pallor, for most of them had been in prison for a long period. Smirnov had been in prison for two years. Zinoviev, Kamenev, Evdokimov and Bakayev had all been arrested after the murder of Kirov. On January 16th, 1935, they were sentenced to varying terms of imprisonment and exile – Zinoviev to ten years, Kamenev to five, Evdokimov and Bakayev to eight. In the summer it was decided to place them on trial again, and on July 27th, 1935, these sentences were revised upward, Kamenev being sentenced to ten years' imprisonment. At first Zinoviev had been deported to Kurultay in Kazakhstan, and Kamenev to Minusinsk, but for more than six months they had been cooped up in prisons in Moscow, facing daily interrogations, threats and tortures.

The NKVD had done its work well: it had reduced most of the prisoners to a state bordering on catatonic lunacy. For month after month they had been compelled to make their depositions, to implicate one another, to invent scenes and incidents which could not have taken place. The story line was constantly being changed at Stalin's orders with the result that the final trial represents an unhappy combination of many stories, all equally improbable. During the interrogations the NKVD officers were constantly having to consult their notes to see whether they were following the current story line, and the prisoners knew this. They were baffled by it, and at the same time they drew what courage they could from the uncertainties in Stalin's mind.

Of all the prisoners Stalin detested Zinoviev most. Vain, mercurial, incompetent as a leader of men, he gave an impression of weakness – a lamb in a lion's skin. Stalin imagined he would have no great difficulty in breaking him down. But in fact Zinoviev proved to be singularly obdurate, and when confronted by other prisoners who had testified to his criminal activities he would sometimes reduce them to silence with a withering look or an appeal to their conscience. For a man who suffered from asthma he withstood torture surprisingly well. Kamenev, who suffered from heart trouble, was more pliant. Yezhov, ordered by Stalin to extract a full confession from him, had only to remind him that the lives of his wife and children were at stake to reduce him to a state of nervous prostration, from which he would rally and go over to the offensive. He despised his torturers all the more because he was by nature gentle and generous. What troubled him more than anything else was his knowledge that the revolution, to which he had devoted his life, had failed in exactly the same way as the French Revolution. Sometimes he would lecture Yezhov on the dangerous course the revolution was taking. 'The French Revolution taught us many lessons,' he said, 'but we did not profit from them. We did not know how to save our revolution from Thermidor. Therein lies our real fault, and for that history will condemn us.'

Yezhov however was not a man who could appreciate the finer points of revolutionary theory; nor was Stalin in any mood to argue with Kamenev. There had been a brief period in 1933 when through the intervention of Gorky an uneasy truce had been arranged between them. But now Stalin was implacable. Told that Kamenev had resisted all persuasion by the NKVD officers, Stalin flew into a temper. 'Do you know how much the state weighs, with all its factories and machines, the army and all its armaments, and the navy? Well, no one can withstand that astronomical weight. Do not tell me that Kamenev can withstand all that pressure!' He was saying that no one could resist him because the sheer physical weight of the Soviet power was behind him, and it was no more than the truth.

The machinery for extracting confessions was cumbrous and inefficient. In the past there had been innumerable trials and the NKVD had successfully extracted whatever confessions it needed, but never before had revolutionaries of the eminence and calibre of Zinoviev and Kamenev been placed on public trial. Stalin acted cautiously. He sometimes permitted the machine to grind to a stop. There were endless conferences, endless revisions of the script. No one knew from day to day exactly what turn the confessions would take. At first it was intended to implicate them in a plot to assassinate Stalin and seize power and then surrender large areas of Russia to Germany and Japan. Intercepted documents of the German General Staff, providentially discovered by Soviet Intelligence agents, were to be introduced as evidence. This idea was abandoned when it became clear to Stalin that it would be dangerous to provoke Hitler, and when the trial took place witnesses were warned against mentioning their contacts with Germany and especially with members of the German government. Yet from time to time the name of Rudolf Hess would be mentioned, only to be struck off the record by Ulrich, the president of the court.

The scenario, as it finally emerged, was so intricate and tortured that even Stalin must have been hard put to enjoy his handiwork. There was no clearly developed line. There were conspiracies within conspiracies, secret meetings within secret meetings, strange journeys by night in aeroplanes, a German cinema magazine with writing in invisible ink, a Honduran passport, a visit to a hotel which had never existed. To explain Trotsky's connection with the plot, all that was necessary was to introduce a 'united Trotskyite-Zinovievite centre' which planned a long series of assassinations. It was responsible for the assassination of Kirov, and attempted to assassinate Stalin, Kaganovich, Voroshilov, and other leading members of the government. Strangely, no attempt was ever made on Molotov. The omission was perhaps deliberate – Stalin would hold it against Molotov that he had been spared by the conspirators. The 'united Trotskyite-Zinovievite centre' consisted of Zinoviev, Kamenev, Evdokimov, Bakayev, Smirnov, Ter-Vaganyan and Mrachkovsky, and these seven men were assisted by a number of shadowy agents mostly recruited from the German Communist Party. The leaders left the killing to their agents, who showed an astonishing incapacity to shoot straight or even to come close to the person they were attempting to assassinate. Berman-Yurin, who was supposed to shoot Stalin during a meeting of the Communist International, failed to arm himself with an admission card. Reingold revealed that Bogdan, Zinoviev's secretary, had been ordered to shoot Stalin in his office, but he had lost his nerve and shot himself instead. Nathan Lurye, ordered to shoot at Voroshilov when he was riding in his automobile, judged that the automobile was moving too fast. Once in Chelyabinsk he had *thought* of going to a factory where Kaganovich and Ordjonikidze were speaking in order to shoot them, but he had thought better of it. Olberg claimed that he had *intended* to throw a bomb at Stalin during a May Day celebration, but he too had thought better of it. There was something oddly frivolous about these attempted assassinations, and there is more than a suggestion that Stalin, intensely disliking the thought of his own assassination, was not prepared to entertain the idea seriously. Frivolous, too, were the chemical inks, the host of unsubstantiated messages from Trotsky written on the margins of books and magazines which had long since vanished. The conspirators used a code word from *The Arabian Nights*. There would be nothing remarkable in this except that Vyshinsky, the chief prosecutor, remembered that during the pre-trial examination Zinoviev had said: 'It is all fantastic, like tales from *The Arabian Nights*.' Fantasies – the stark and disorganized fantasies of Stalin – seemed sometimes to assume physical shape and hover in the courtroom.

Even the existence of the 'united Trotskyite-Zinovievite centre' was never proved. It was simply stated as a fact, to be glossed over whenever difficulties arose. When Vyshinsky put Smirnov on the stand on the evening of August 20th, there came a moment when the 'united centre' seemed about to burst like a soap bubble, and the prosecutor was forced to appeal for confirmation from Mrachkovsky, Zinoviev, Evdokimov and Bakayev, who hurried to his rescue. According to the official transcript the following dialogue took place:

VYSHINSKY: So when did you leave the centre?

SMIRNOV: I never thought of leaving the centre because there was nothing to leave.

VYSHINSKY: Didn't the centre exist?

SMIRNOV: What are you talking about?

VYSHINSKY: Mrachkovsky, did the centre exist?

MRACHKOVSKY: Yes.

VYSHINSKY: Zinoviev, did the centre exist?

ZINOVIEV: Yes.

VYSHINSKY: Evdokimov, did the centre exist?

EVDOKIMOV: Yes.

VYSHINSKY: Bakayev, did the centre exist?

BAKAYEV: Yes.

VYSHINSKY: Smirnov, now tell us how you can take the liberty to maintain that no centre existed?

If we can trust the official transcript, Smirnov made no reply, nor was there any need for him to say anything more about the centre, for he had said enough. The official transcript is an unreliable document, printing the prosecutor's charges and his fifty-page summing-up, while giving only comparatively brief passages from the cross-examinations. The London *Times* correspondent says that for three hours Smir-

nov deliberately misinterpreted questions or did not reply:
these three hours are represented by only nine pages of the
transcript. Vyshinsky in his summing-up admitted that Smirnov had been an unsatisfactory witness, continually denying
the charges. 'He denied everything,' said Vyshinsky. 'The
whole of his examination on August 20th consisted solely of
of the words: "I deny that, again I deny, I deny."' But in
fact Smirnov did not only deny; he would sometimes leave
curious clues about the methods by which the confessions had
been extracted, and sometimes – and these were perhaps the
most terrible moments of all – he would repeat the same
phrase over and over again like a cracked gramophone record,
giving to the words a formidable weight. After the trial it
was related that while the prisoners were in a state of exhaustion, an officer of the NKVD would enter their cells and with
a megaphone recite interminably the stories they were ordered
to tell in court. Here in a hallucinatory way Smirnov seems
to be repeating words that he has heard many times before:

VYSHINSKY: Did you have direct communication with
  Trotsky?
SMIRNOV: I had two addresses.
VYSHINSKY: I am asking you, was there any communication?
SMIRNOV: I had two addresses.
VYSHINSKY: Answer me, was there any communication?
SMIRNOV: If having addresses can be called communica-
  tion ...
VYSHINSKY: What would you call it?
SMIRNOV: I said I received two addresses.
VYSHINSKY: Did you maintain communication with Trotsky?
SMIRNOV: I had two addresses.
VYSHINSKY: Did you have personal communication?
SMIRNOV: There was no personal communication.
VYSHINSKY: Was there any communication by mail with
  Trotsky?
SMIRNOV: There was communication by mail with Trotsky's
  son.

All through the trial there is the sense of an intricate dance
on the edge of madness. The lines so carefully written out and
memorized are spoken by the wrong person at the wrong
time, logic is abandoned, and the prosecutor himself becomes
touched with the prevailing frivolity. Only one piece of solid
evidence was brought forward at the trial: the Honduran

passport belonging to Olberg. Not a single document in the handwriting of Zinoviev or Kamenev or any of the other defendants was produced, but Vyshinsky was not in the least put out by the absence of supporting evidence. For some reason extraordinary importance was attached to the passport:

VYSHINSKY: Permit me to show you this. Is this your passport?

(*The commandant of the court presents the passport.*)

OLBERG: Yes, that's the one. It really was issued by a real consul in the name of the Republic of Honduras. There is such a republic in South America.

VYSHINSKY: Perhaps your parents had some relation with the republic?

OLBERG: No.

VYSHINSKY: Then your forefathers ... ?

OLBERG: No.

VYSHINSKY: Then you yourself – where are you from?

OLBERG: I am from Riga.

It transpired that Olberg had bought the passport in Prague through the medium of a Gestapo agent, paying 13,000 Czech kronen supposed to have been received through Trotskyist agents in Prague. Soon the passport was forgotten. No one ever discovered the role it was intended to play in the scenario. At intervals during the trial other stage properties were introduced, but they tended to disintegrate the moment they were touched, and it was only rarely that their significance was made clear. One of these stage properties was a thesis for a diploma:

OLBERG: I received a letter from her stating that our old friend insisted that the thesis for the diploma be submitted on May 1st.

VYSHINSKY: Thesis for the diploma – what is that?

OLBERG: The assassination of Stalin.

VYSHINSKY: And the old friend – who is that?

OLBERG: The old friend – that is Trotsky.

But these were puerile lines, and like the Honduran passport the thesis for the diploma soon vanished into the limbo of forgotten things. These stage properties were never seriously put forward as evidence: their function was simply to give an air of verisimilitude to the incredible.

Like the other spear carriers, Olberg seemed to be miscast.

Others played their roles a little more convincingly. Fritz David was a Stalinist official for many years, working in Russia and Germany. He had excellent contacts, and worked at a number of good jobs; there seemed to be no reason for him to engage in conspiratorial activities. He said he met Trotsky in November 1932, and there was a general discussion about the need to embark on terroristic activities. Trotsky proposed that he undertake 'the historic mission of killing Stalin'. It was decided that Stalin should be killed at the Seventh Congress of the Comintern, which took place in 1935, three years after the meeting between Fritz David and Trotsky. Berman-Yurin told the sequel at the trial. 'A few days later I met Fritz David,' he said, 'and he declared that he had been unable to shoot. He, Fritz David, sat in a loge, there were a lot of people in the loge, and there was no possibility to shoot. Thus, this plan of ours also failed.'

The recital of plans that failed occupied a good deal of the court's attention, and indeed the whole trial was a study in simple mechanical failures. Everything went wrong. There were gaps in the scenario, which no one troubled to fill. The wrong actors played the wrong parts. The play never moved forward, but seemed to revolve around a single point. It was not only that there was no sense of progression, but it was never made clear what exactly was demanded of the actors. From time to time the defendants would cast appealing gestures to Vyshinsky or to the judges. At such times the judges would call a recess to discuss the matter with Stalin, who appears to have become increasingly irritated and impatient as the trial continued without discovering a focus, without ever achieving an authentic dramatic progression.

Yet there were moments, rare moments, when the play escaped completely from the script-writers and became another play altogether where, very dimly, there could be observed the working out of some strange destiny which had nothing to do with the destiny Stalin had reserved for his prisoners. When Kamenev said: 'I became blind – I lived to the age of fifty and did not see this centre in which, it turns out, I myself was active, in which I participated by action and by inaction, by speech and by silence,' he was hinting at the real nature of the drama in which he was compelled to perform. It was a drama of guilt, and in such a drama silence helped the theme forward and words only hindered its silent development. It was a drama in which all the antagonists were guilty in different proportions. Stalin was absolutely guilty, Kamenev and Zinoviev were relatively guilty. Between the absolute and the relative war had been declared.

According to the programme notes, the end of the drama had long ago been foreseen. The accused would acknowledge their guilt and go down to their deaths proclaiming the innocence of Stalin. They would not beg for mercy, but would ask to be shot, for they were unworthy to live in the same land as Stalin and breathe the same air. Vyshinsky delivered a four-hour speech in which he recited the crimes of the defendants and added a few more for good measure. In the final peroration he demanded that they should be shot like mad dogs. The defendants were then permitted to make their final appeals. Only one, Moissei Lurye, asked for mercy. The rest accepted their guilt with relief, proclaiming that they merited no indulgence and deserved to die.

EVDOKIMOV: We were bandits, assassins, fascists, agents of the Gestapo. I thank the prosecutor for having demanded for us the only penalty we deserve.

MRACHKOVSKY: I depart as a traitor to my party, as a traitor who should be shot.

REINGOLD: We have already been shot politically. It is not for me to plead for mercy.

BAKAYEV: I am guilty of the assassination of Kirov.

OLBERG: I ask for the opportunity to atone for my monstrous crimes.

BERMAN-YURIN: It is too late for contrition.

FRITZ DAVID: I curse Trotsky.

NATHAN LURYE: My regret comes too late.

TER-VAGANYAN: May I somehow fill the abyss!

So they spoke, very quietly and laboriously, for these were difficult sentences to frame even though they had been well schooled. Zinoviev, too, admitted his crimes, though less eagerly. Kamenev said he preferred death to imprisonment, for it would be too great a punishment to watch the giant progress of the socialist state from behind bars. Then, lowering his voice, he spoke of his sons, one of whom was an aviator in the Red Air Force. 'I have stained my sons' names,' he said. 'I want them to know my last wish, which is that they should work, fight, and if need be die only under the banner of Stalin. If I have failed to serve my socialist fatherland in life, then let this service be rendered by my death.'

When the prisoners had given their last pleas, the judges retired to deliberate on the proper verdict. At 2:30 am on August 24th, the president of the court, Ulrich, read the verdict condemning all the prisoners to be shot. He spoke in a dry voice, in short pithy sentences. Zinoviev stood with his head bowed and his hands joined as though in prayer, but most of the prisoners seemed unmoved. They had been told that the death sentences were merely a formality, and that lesser sentences would be granted when they made their last appeal for clemency. They were told that final decisions would be reached within the next seventy-two hours.

On August 25th the front page of *Pravda* printed the smiling portraits of Stalin and Voroshilov at the Tushino airfield, where an air regatta was being held. In small type, in the bottom corner of the fourth page, there was the brief announcement that the President of the Central Executive Committee had rejected the appeals for clemency and all the prisoners had been shot.

Very little is known about the mechanics of execution in the Soviet Union, although there is evidence of automatic self-executions in the late thirties. In such executions the condemned man is ordered to walk down a narrow corridor made of white tiles, and when he steps on a certain tile, an electrically controlled gun fires into his head. A moment later the body falls into a chute and water-spouts are automatically opened. The tiles are washed clean, and the narrow corridor is then ready for its next victim.

When Zinoviev, Kamenev and the other defendants were executed, self-execution had not yet come into existence, and prisoners were shot according to the whims of the executioners. Some days later circumstantial reports of the executions appeared in the foreign press. Victor Serge, a Communist who knew the Lubyanka prison well and wrote with remarkable honesty about the Soviet system, believed that these reports were based on information from NKVD officers who attended the executions. 'In all likelihood,' wrote Victor Serge, 'these reports are true.' Here are the reports:

Kamenev was shot first. He did not resist, offered no complaint. He left his cell in silence, and as if in a dream descended into the execution cellar. After the first revolver shot, fired apparently from behind, he let out an 'ah!' of stupefaction and fell down. He was still alive. Lieutenant

Vasiukov, who was present, cried out in a hysterical voice: 'Finish him,' and gave the dying man a kick with his boot. A second bullet in the head finished Kamenev.

Zinoviev was in solitary confinement on the first floor of the GPU prison. After having been first to sign the petition for pardon, he went to sleep. Though it was warm, he was shivering. He had on flannel drawers and woollen socks. They awakened him at one in the morning. He sat up in a daze, his whole frame trembling.

'Zinoviev, get up. We have orders to transfer you to another place.'

Pale as death, he remained seated, saying nothing.

'Dress yourself.'

He lay down. One of the jailers began to pull on his boots. Zinoviev did not move, but the sweat poured from his face. Another jailer passed his arm under his back and raised him. Zinoviev groaned and tore the hair from his temples. He seemed to have gone mad.

'Let's go!'

Zinoviev continued to groan, dangling his head. One of the jailers threw water on his face. Then he came out of his stupor and stood up.

'Take your things.'

He began stupidly to collect his things. Half a minute later he was led out of the cell. A group of eight guards was waiting at the door. At this moment, Zinoviev understood everything, his legs trembled, he almost fell. They held him up, he resisted a little, with sobs and cries. At the end of the corridor he had a real attack of hysteria. Hanging on the arms of the guards, he cried like a woman. Lieutenant Evangulov ordered the guards to open a cell, which was instantly done. Zinoviev was pushed in.

The lieutenant took him by the hair with his left hand, made him bow his head and, with his right hand, fired a bullet into his brain.

THE GREAT STALIN CONSTITUTION

'LIFE IS BETTER, COMRADES, life is gayer,' Stalin was continually saying, beaming with pleasure because he had brought so many benefits to his country. As he spoke, he would conjure up the vision of a new age of freedom, in which everyone laughed and sang at his work, and there was no poverty anywhere in Russia. The tide had turned; the revolution had succeeded beyond all expectation; and the millennium was approaching.

In those days he was continually speaking of the triumph of socialism, which had been brought about because the workers no longer enriched the capitalists, but worked for themselves, for their own class, for the Soviet society, where power was always wielded 'by the best members of the working class'. Now at last freedom had come about, because the Soviet society had created the material conditions for a prosperous life for the people. He would point to the newly created dams and hydro-electric works, the factory smokestacks, the tractors, the smoothly running collective farms, and say that nowhere in the world was there such a contented people living under such a benevolent government.

Not only was life better and gayer, but everything was moving faster. The trains were moving faster. The People's Commissariat of Railways, which had assured everyone that a commercial speed of 13 or 14 kilometres an hour was the limit which could not be exceeded without contradicting 'the science of railway operations', had received, in Stalin's words, 'a slight tap on the jaw'. The new Commissariat of Railways guaranteed a commercial speed of 18 or 19 kilometres an hour. Work, too, as a result of the energetic contributions of the Stakhanovites, had also become faster; higher norms could now be demanded of all industries. As Stalin contemplated the industrial progress of the Soviet Union, he found the statistics shooting upward, outstripping the dreams of the State Economic Commission.

The phenomenon of 'Stakhanovite labour' exactly suited the needs of the government. In August 1935 a worker named Alexey Stakhanov cut 102 tons of coal during a single shift at the Donets Basin. This was roughly fourteen times the established quota. This extraordinary feat was accomplished with the help of two prop men in 5 hours and 45 minutes. As a result, all over Russia, socialist competition was encouraged, and special bonuses were given for heroic feats of labour. A certain Maria Demchenko achieved a harvest of over 500 centners of sugar beet per hectare in the Ukraine, where the normal harvest of sugar beet was 130 centners per hectare. Some of these feats were fraudulent, and most of the workers feared them, for it gave the State Planning Board the opportunity to demand such high norms that, if they had been carried out, the workers would have died of exhaustion. Nevertheless the spirit of competition was successfully cultivated by the government. It was not free competition, but compulsory competition forced upon the workers by government decree, demanding the expenditure of more and more energy for less and less profit. Stakhanov, a genial and kindly miner, became at last a symbol of forced labour.

Once, in 1924, Dzerzhinsky had told Stalin that he had a precise vision of what Russia must become. 'Our country must become metallic,' he said. It was a vision which pleased Stalin, who never forgot those simple and terrible words. In January 1933, when the balance sheet of the first Five Year Plan was being reckoned up, he celebrated the triumph of metallic Russia in one of those liturgical chants with which he always celebrated his victories. He said:

> We did not have an iron and steel industry, the basis for the industrialization of the country.
> Now we have one.
> We did not have a tractor industry.
> Now we have one.
> We did not have an automobile industry.
> Now we have one.
> We did not have a machine-tool industry.
> Now we have one.
> We did not have an important and modern chemical industry.
> Now we have one.
> We did not have a real and important industry for the production of modern agricultural machinery.
> Now we have one.
> We did not have an aircraft industry.
> Now we have one.

It was a very long hymn, covering nearly two pages of his *Collected Works*, and there was never any mention that the industrial output in 1914 under the Tsar was very nearly as great as the industrial output in 1933 under a Communist dictator. He spoke as though there were no factories in pre-revolutionary Russia, and as though there had been no help from American engineers, and engineers from all over Europe, to bring the industrial miracle about. He said nothing about the organization of forced labour under the secret police. He boasted of the cyclopean works accomplished, but never referred to the price paid in misery and suffering.

There still remained in the Politburo men who were appalled by the terrible demands made on the people. The pace was too fast, the pressure too sharp, the weight of the dictatorship too onerous. Those who complained were quickly eased out of their positions. Only in the Central Committee were there a few voices brave enough to proclaim the need for a change. When Bukharin and Rykov protested, Yezhov denounced them as conspirators. In a speech delivered in the autumn of 1936 he attacked them for organizing a monstrous conspiracy directed against the party and the state. Without advancing any evidence, he pointed to Bukharin's long record of criminal conspiracy, dating back to 1918 when 'Bukharin and his fellow conspirators planned to assassinate Lenin, Stalin and Sverdlov'. 'It is now established,' said Yezhov, 'that Bukharin and Rykov, like Trotsky, Zinoviev and Kamenev, are agents of the Gestapo.'

With incredible courage Bukharin replied to the attack in a three-hour speech in which he excoriated the dictatorship. 'Yes,' he said, 'it is true that there is a monstrous conspiracy directed against the party and the state. The conspirators are Stalin and Yezhov.' He went on:

> Stalin wants to establish his absolute power over the party and the state, and to reach this position it is necessary for him to ride roughshod over all obstacles. That is why we are to be eliminated. But in order to eliminate us, you must use the weapons of fraud, lies, and provocation. By means of political terror and unheard-of methods of torture, old party members make dispositions which even you do not believe. A crowd of paid informers ranging from Radek to common criminals is at your disposal. You need the blood of Bukharin and Rykov to bring about the *coup d'état*, which you have been planning for so long and which your police apparatus is preparing ... I say the party and the Central Committee must return to the traditions which existed at the time of Lenin. The police conspirators must be brought to order. The NKVD, not the party, governs the country today, and it is the NKVD, not the Bukharinites who are preparing a *coup d'état*.

Stalin answered that it was above everything ridiculous to

accuse him of wanting the blood of Bukharin, but he warned Bukharin that to pour abuse on the NKVD was to play the enemy's game. Yezhov's motion to place Bukharin on trial as an agent of the Gestapo was defeated, but Bukharin must have known that his days were numbered.

Stalin rode the storm in a mood of tranquil expectation. Although overwhelmingly defeated in the Central Committee – only one third voted for him, and two thirds were solidly behind Bukharin – Stalin had no intention of accepting defeat. The prospect of having to arrest or kill off most of the Central Committee in order to assert his dictatorship seems to have presented him with few problems. The techniques for liquidation had long ago been worked out.

For the moment, however, he decided to play a waiting game. For a few weeks he lulled the opposition into a sense of security. He had promised that he would carefully study the directives of the Central Committee, and it was assumed that he had suffered a change of heart. The meeting of the Central Committee seems to have ended on September 9th, for on the following day *Pravda* announced that 'the investigation of the charges against Comrades Bukharin and Rykov has been dropped'. Stalin was going for his annual holiday by the Black Sea. As Stalin travelled south in his special train, accompanied by Zhdanov, Kirov's successor as governor of the Leningrad area, the intolerable strain seemed to have lifted. Perhaps, after all, the terror would die a natural death and the Central Committee, the supreme legislative body in the Soviet Union, would be permitted to rule.

By this time Stalin had already worked out his strategy. He was far from having the intention of liquidating the terror; what he needed was someone even more merciless than Yagoda. His choice fell upon the sinister Yezhov who had delivered the ranting speech at the meeting of the Central Committee. From Sochi on September 25th he sent an extraordinary telegram to Kaganovich, Molotov and other members of the Politburo friendly to him announcing a new and even more terrible era of liquidations.

The telegram read:

We consider it absolutely necessary and urgent that Comrade Yezhov be named to the post of People's Commissar of Internal Affairs. Yagoda has definitely shown himself to be incapable of unmasking the Trotskyite-Zinovievite bloc.

The GPU is four years behind in this matter. This is noted by all party workers and the majority of the representatives of the NKVD.

STALIN, ZHDANOV

The existence of this telegram was unknown until it was revealed by Khrushchev in his secret speech in 1956. Like the law of December 1st, 1934, it ranks among those rare documents which are designed for the purpose of destroying civilization at its roots. Those colourless sentences were written in the chill, bureaucratic style customary to Stalin, and like so many of his writings they contained palpable untruths. It was simply not true that Yagoda had failed to unmask the Trotskyite-Zinovievite bloc. He had done as much as any man could do to invent that non-existent conspiracy, and then to search out and punish those who had taken no part in it, because it was impossible to take part in something which had no existence. Nor was it true that 'all party workers' – in the dialect of Stalin the word 'workers' meant 'officials' – believed that the GPU was four years behind in the matter. No doubt the majority of the NKVD desired a more extensive terror, an even greater share in the rule of the country, but it was precisely this desire which the Central Committee had hoped to modify. The last sentence in the telegram simply reversed the decision of the Central Committee.

The historian Boris Nikolayevsky was the first to note the sinister significance of the words: 'The GPU is four years behind in this matter.' What Stalin was saying was that mass repressions in the party should have begun in September 1932 when he first demanded the execution of Ryutin and other party members who found fault in his dictatorship. He had raised the question of their execution in the Politburo and at the plenum of the Central Committee which met from September 28th to October 2nd, 1932. At both meetings he had failed to carry the other members with him. Stalin was not one to forget anniversaries. The date of the telegram was four years to the day since he first raised the question of mass death sentences in the Politburo.

This formidable telegram was immediately transformed into a decree. On September 26th, a few hours after it was received in the Kremlin, the decree was promulgated under the signature of Kaganovich, the Second Secretary of the Central

Committee, and of Molotov, the Chairman of the Council of Ministers. For excellent reasons Stalin did not want his name to be attached to it. The new law resembled the law of December 1st, 1934, which was signed by Yenukidze. With the instinct of a criminal, Stalin made certain that he had an alibi.

By the terms of the decree Yagoda was removed from office, and his place was taken by Yezhov. *Yagoda* means 'berry', *yezhov* comes from *yezh*, meaning 'hedgehog'; but there was small comfort to be derived from the fact that the hedgehog had eaten the berry.

In the eyes of the Russians Nikolay Ivanovich Yezhov had one slight claim to distinction – he was the first Russian since Tsarist times to be in charge of the secret police. His predecessors had been Uritsky, who was a Jew, Dzerzhinsky and Menzhinsky, who were both Poles, and Yagoda, who was a Jew. Yezhov was a small, thin, unprepossessing man, oddly like Yagoda in appearance. From being a factory worker at Rostov he had worked his way up through a number of minor posts in Stalin's secretariat until in the spring of 1935 he became chairman of the Party Control Commission and secretary of the Central Committee, and in quick succession he rose to be a member of the Politburo and a member of the Organization Bureau of the Central Committee. He had Stalin's confidence. Dazzling prospects were held out to him. Though still young, he was given positions previously occupied by veteran members of the party. When he became chairman of the Party Control Commission he replaced Kaganovich. Twelve months before he became head of the NKVD he was completely unknown in the country at large, and even within the party. From being a shadow he became a power. The two years of his reign of terror were given the name of *Yezhovshchina*.

Yezhov's task was to unmask the Trotskyite-Zinovievite bloc, and since the bloc had no existence, his powers were circumscribed by the fact that he had to deal with imaginary conspiracies. This was not a matter of great difficulty, because imaginary conspiracies can take place anywhere, at any time, and for any purpose. 'The liquidation of the remnants of the enemy classes' could proceed at a rhythm dictated only by Yezhov's murderous impulses. Like Yagoda he spent most of his time superintending the torture of innocent people, forcing them to confess to crimes they had never committed, and then executing them on the basis of their false confessions. This was simple, and presented few problems. Nor was there any particular difficulty in drawing up vast death lists: a child could do it. More troublesome was Stalin's compulsive desire to stage public trials at which the defendants would confess their sins to the world and produce a plausible and well-documented account of their conspiracies. A considerable portion of Yezhov's time was therefore devoted to the preparation and staging of the trials; and it was hoped that he would prove more satisfactory than Yagoda. Stalin was anxious to stage a trial at which Bukharin and Rykov would receive their just punishment, and accordingly a 'parallel Bukharinite centre' was invented to explain Bukharin's tenuous connection with Trotsky. On October 16th, 1936, before Stalin had returned from his vacation, Bukharin was arrested while at work in the office of *Izvestiya*, of which he was editor in chief, and driven to the Lubyanka. Then he vanished from sight for fifteen months.

Yezhov's first task was to draw up the scenario of the 'parallel Bukharinite centre'. It was not an easy task, for in spite of his frail health, Bukharin was a match for his inquisitors. Against Yezhov, who used a sledge hammer, he fought with a rapier. He employed all the formidable resources of his penetrating mind to parry and thrust at the adversary.

The surprising thing is that Stalin did not simply liquidate Bukharin. There was very little to be gained by putting him on trial. He was tortured and nearly blinded by being made to stand in front of a battery of bright lights; he was left alone in a small cell for days and weeks on end; he was made to stand for hours without moving until his legs became swollen; he was told that if he did not confess his wife and young child would be slowly strangled; nevertheless for more than a year he refused to confess, and even at the trial which took place in March 1938 he conducted himself with astonishing dignity, sometimes going through the motions of confession, but always in such a way that it was clear that he regarded the trial as a fraud and his partial confessions as a miserable tribute exacted by an implacable dictator; and having confessed, he would deny his confessions. Yezhov's reports on Bukharin's behaviour in prison must have been unsatisfactory, for his trial was continually being postponed.

Meanwhile, with supreme cynicism, Stalin set about refurbishing his public image. The most lawless of men, he represented himself as a man forever mindful of the laws, another Justinian or Napoleon drawing up careful legal codes which would permit everyone to live in harmony and peace. The document known as 'the Stalin Constitution' has a chilling perfection; and had no more to do with the government of the country than lists of names in a telephone book.

'The Stalin Constitution', which passed into law in December 1936, at a time when the *Yezhovshchina* was at its height, must be considered among Stalin's more playful inventions. At a time when mass executions were taking place daily and some seven million people were reduced to slave-workers in labour camps, Stalin solemnly declared that the government accepted fullheartedly the provisions of the Constitution which declared:

> *Article 125.* In conformity with the interests of the working people, and in order to strengthen the socialist system, the citizens of the USSR are guaranteed by law:
>> (a) Freedom of speech,
>> (b) Freedom of the press,
>> (c) Freedom of assembly, including the holding of mass meetings.
>> (d) Freedom of street processions and demonstrations.
>
> These civil rights are ensured by placing at the disposal of the working people and their organizations printing presses, stocks of paper, public buildings, the streets, communications facilities and other material requisites for the exercise of these rights.
>
> *Article 127.* Citizens of the USSR are guaranteed inviolability of the person. No person may be placed under arrest except by decision of a court or with the sanction of a procurator.
>
> *Article 128.* The inviolability of the homes of citizens and privacy of correspondence are protected by law.

This constitution, 'the most democratic in the world', was the work of many students of foreign constitutions and many strange compromises. At various times Zinoviev, Radek, Bukharin and Vyshinsky worked on it, and while it shows some signs of Vyshinsky's characteristic delight in giving with one hand while taking with the other – the freedoms in Article 125, for example, are rendered harmless by the apparently innocuous words: 'In conformity with the interests of the working people' which must be translated: 'In conformity with the decisions of Stalin who in his acts and person represents the working people' – it also shows signs of Bukharin's characteristic breadth of spirit and desire for a more absolute freedom than any government can afford to grant. Some of those who worked on the constitution meant what they said; and in its finished form it represents a curious mingling of idealism and tyranny. Like Lenin's *The State and Revolution*, 'the Stalin Constitution' offers a picture of paradise under the guise of a police state.

In March 1936, when the authors of the constitution had been at work for many months, Stalin granted an interview to Roy Howard, the president of the Scripps-Howard newspapers, in which he ranged over a wide number of subjects. During the course of the interview Stalin discussed the purpose of the constitution. To Roy Howard's surprise the chief purpose of the constitution was to provide the utmost safeguards for human liberty. 'We have not constructed our society in order to shackle individual liberty, but in order that the human personality may feel itself really free,' Stalin declared. 'We have constructed our society for the sake of real personal liberty – liberty without quotation marks.'

'Liberty without quotation marks', as defined by Stalin, had very little relation to liberty as it was understood elsewhere, and he went on to explain that he understood by liberty only that form of it which existed within the Soviet Union. 'Real liberty,' he continued, 'can exist only when exploitation has been abolished, where there is no oppression of some by others, where there is no unemployment or poverty, where a man is not haunted by the fear of being deprived tomorrow of work, home, and bread. Only in such a society is real, personal, and every other liberty possible.'

Perhaps he derived some comfort from these admirable statements, but it is more likely that they were uttered with exquisite cynicism. There were clauses in the constitution which guaranteed the inviolability of private property, the independence of the judiciary, universal suffrage by secret ballot, the right to work, old-age pensions, free schooling and the eight-hour day, but there were no clauses which stated clearly and unequivocally that the NKVD had no right to make arbitrary arrests, put prisoners to torture, and shoot them in the back of the neck. The law of December 1st, 1934, was still on the statute book, and it made a mockery of the constitution, for it effectively disposed of all constitutional rights.

When Stalin spoke to Roy Howard, he had already decided that the new constitution should be passed into law towards the end of the year. Why he should delay for so long is something of a mystery; it is just possible that in March he contemplated a relaxation of the terror and intended to present the constitution as the capstone for a new era of tranquillity between the government and the people. He attached extraordinary importance to the constitution, saying over and over again that it signified a new phase of development and that it was both 'a summary and a seal' of an epoch which had passed away. It was as though a part of him believed that the age of terror had passed, and a new age of peace and tranquillity would be ushered in. In June the draft constitution was thrown open for nationwide discussion; and for five months the people of the Soviet Union were invited to discuss their rights and liberties. The public debate on the constitution could do no harm, and was in fact officially encouraged. Meanwhile the terror became increasingly more savage and arbitrary.

Stalin's formal speech on the new constitution was delivered on November 25th, 1936. The first half of the speech was devoted to the new liberties which had emerged as a result of 'the undoubted victory of Leninist national policy'. Peace had descended on earth, there was no more exploitation of man by man, in all spheres of economic and social life there was a sense of solidarity and mutual aid, mutual distrust had vanished, and for the first time in history fraternal co-operation had been established within the framework of the state. There were no longer any antagonistic classes in society. An entirely new working class had emerged. Indeed, everything was new. In the new state there was no unemployment, no poverty, no luxury: everyone worked for the common good. All the citizens possessed equal rights, and no distinction was made between men and women, the propertied and the propertyless, the educated and the uneducated. 'It is not property status, nor national origin, nor sex, nor office, but personal ability and personal labour that determines the position of every citizen in society.'

So he goes on, drawing up his blueprint for a paradise on earth, sometimes overreaching himself in the desire to exalt this new and beautiful creation which has suddenly, as though by a miracle, appeared on the earth; and in the peroration we hear once again the liturgical music which Stalin always employed when he was in a state of excitement:

> The Constitution does not confine itself to stating the formal rights of citizens;
> It stresses the guarantees of these rights, the means by which they can be exercised.
> The Constitution does not merely proclaim equality of rights for citizens;
> It ensures this equality, granting legislative embodiment to the fact that the reign of exploitation has come to an end and the citizens have been emancipated from exploitation.
> The Constitution does not merely proclaim the right to work;
> It ensures this right, granting legislative embodiment to the fact that there are no crises in Soviet society, and there is no more unemployment.
> The Constitution does not merely proclaim democratic liberties;
> It ensures them legislatively by providing definite material resources.

Such was the hymn which Stalin wrote in honour of the new age, and like the hymn to Lenin which he recited in 1924 it moves awkwardly among ideas which are essentially religious, and even pietistic, with the constitution assuming the place of the God from whom all favours flow. In this new age the liberties of men are not merely stated but guaranteed; equality is assured, and the right to work arises from the abundance of employment. The religious fervour of the hymn is nowhere more appropriately expressed than in the phrase in which Stalin proclaims that 'there are no crises in Soviet society'. When the speech was delivered, there were more crises than any man could cope with.

If often happened that Stalin would write a speech and deliver it many months later. He would, as it were, hold the speech in reserve, as he held his thoughts in reserve, waiting for the moment when they could be used with the greatest effect. The temper of the speech is calm, sentimental, assured;

there is no jerkiness in the style; it moves complacently towards the peroration with its vision of a society at peace with itself. There is some reason to believe that the first part of the speech was written in June. The second part of the speech, written in November, is of sterner stuff.

In the second half of his speech Stalin raged bitterly against those who opposed the constitution, especially the foreigners who regarded it as 'a scrap of paper and a manoeuvre to deceive the Soviet people'. He raged too against those who remained silent, for, as he observed, 'silence is also a form of criticism'. He added that it was a stupid and ridiculous form, but nevertheless it must be taken into account. The semi-official *Deutsche Diplomatische-Politische Korrespondenz* had come out bluntly with the statement that the constitution was nothing more than a Potemkin village, a façade erected to deceive the people. This was a serious charge, but he made no effort to answer it except by repeating that the Soviet government had introduced the eight-hour day, universal suffrage, and cultural facilities unheard-of before the war. 'The Soviet government,' he declared, 'has abolished unemployment, has introduced the right to work, the right to rest and leisure. These are facts, not promises.' But a right does not become a fact until it is enforced, and there was nothing in the constitution to suggest that the Soviet government possessed any machinery for enforcing its admirable constitution.

The *Deutsche Diplomatische-Politische Korrespondenz* went on to argue that the Soviet Union was not a state, but merely 'a more or less strictly defined geographical concept', whence it followed that the constitution could not be regarded as a real constitution. It was not a particularly good argument, and came with ill grace from Germany, which was also 'a more or less strictly defined geographical concept', formed out of many states with widely different traditions. Angrily Stalin retorted by telling one of the satirical stories of the nineteenth-century aristocrat Mikhail Saltykov-Shchedrin:

What can one say about such critics, that is, if we can call them critics?

They remind me of the story of the great Russian writer Shchedrin, who portrays a stupid, pigheaded and narrow-minded official, self-confident and zealous in the extreme. This bureaucrat succeeded in establishing 'law and order' in the region 'under his charge', and he did this by exterminating thousands of its inhabitants and burning down scores of towns, and then he looked around him and somewhere on the horizon he espied America – a country which was little known and where it appeared that there were liberties of some sort which served to agitate the people, and where the state was administered in a different way. The bureaucrat espied America and waxed indignant: 'What country is that? How did it get there? By what right does it exist? I understand the country was discovered accidentally several centuries ago, but that is no excuse – it must be shut up again so that not a vestige of it remains.' Thereupon he wrote the order: 'America is to be shut up again!'

It seems to me that the gentlemen of the *Deutsche Diplomatische-politische Korrespondenz* and Shchedrin's bureaucrat are as like as two peas.

By appealing to Shchedrin's story Stalin was merely avoiding the issue. He never answered the attacks on the constitution; he sidestepped them, laughed at them, and presented himself as the apostle of mildness. It was odd that he chose Shchedrin's story about the discovery of America. It was not America, but Russia, which was 'to be shut up again'.

According to the new constitution Stalin was prepared to grant freedom and equality to all his former enemies. Article 135 offered universal suffrage to everyone above the age of twenty-three 'irrespective of race or nationality, sex, religion, education, domicile, social origin, property status or past activities'. Such sweeping changes in conventional Soviet policy demanded discussion. It was pointed out to Stalin that he was admitting former aristocrats and landowners, priests, White Guards, and people who had been formally disenfranchised into the fold. Stalin made light of these objections. 'It was never the purpose of the Soviet government to punish these people indefinitely, but only temporarily, up to a certain period.' He made it clear that the time had come for 'universal suffrage without restrictions'. To those who insisted on raising trivial objections he declared: 'What is there to be afraid of? If you fear wolves, keep out of the woods!'

Someone suggested that the wolves might be dangerous if they succeeded in infiltrating into the government. Stalin made light of this argument, too. 'It would only show that our propaganda is badly organized,' he said, 'and we should fully deserve such a disgrace.' He reminded his audience that as far back as 1919 Lenin had declared himself in favour of universal suffrage without restrictions. 'Comrades,' he said solemnly, 'seventeen years have passed since that day, and is it not time we carried out Lenin's behests?'

On December 5th the Stalin constitution was formally voted into law, but another year had to pass before the elections to the Supreme Soviet were held, when 91 million votes were cast, and of the 1,143 seats in the Supreme Soviet 855 went to Communist party candidates. At that time the Communist party numbered 3 per cent of the population.

A month later, as a present to himself for having successfully coped with the problem of inaugurating a new constitution, Stalin put Radek, Sokolnikov and fourteen others on trial for treason. The second of the great Moscow trials had begun.

THE TRIAL OF RADEK

RADEK WAS A SMALL, malicious, voluble, monkey-like man, with a vast talent for revolutionary propaganda. Revolution was the sea he swam in, and it is inconceivable that he could swim in any other. In 1902, when he was seventeen, he was already a revolutionary in his native Poland, and he went on to become one of those Central European revolutionaries who were only too happy to join any revolutionary movement, whatever its origin. He had no principles, and very few ideas. He had charm, cunning, and vast energy. Lenin once spoke of his 'misplaced political zeal', but he was a zealous disciple of Lenin, who admired and despised him in equal proportions.

His real name is unknown. He would say that he was born Karl Berngardovich Sobelsohn, but the given name and the patronymic are suspect. Radek was a brilliant pseudonym, for it immediately marked him as a radical. He had other pseudonyms, among them 'Parabellum', and under this name he wrote regularly in revolutionary journals in prewar years. At the Zimmerwald Conference in 1915 he joined forces with Lenin and Zinoviev, and he accompanied them in the famous sealed train across Germany in 1917. He hoped to enter

Russia with them, but the Provisional Government refused to admit him on the grounds that he was an Austrian citizen, and he seems to have been acutely aware of a sense of foreignness among the Russian Bolsheviks. Born a Galician Jew, he spoke four or five languages with varying degrees of accuracy, but mastered only Polish. When he made speeches in Russian, his audience was usually awed by the vehemence of his gestures, but few understood what he was saying.

There was nothing commonplace or predictable about Radek. With his thick mane of curly hair, his heavy red side-whiskers, his dead-white skin, and small bright eyes magnified by black-rimmed spectacles, he did not look like a revolutionary. Russians sometimes said he resembled a nineteenth-century court assessor. Trotsky said: 'He looks like a monkey, and like nothing else.' One of his greater griefs was that Lenin never appointed him to a high executive position, apparently because he could never be trusted to keep a secret.

Under Stalin his fortunes were continually changing. One year he was in exile, the next he was a court favourite. In 1933, during one of his periods of exile, he wrote an astonishing pamphlet designed to permit him to bask once more in Stalin's favour. The pamphlet was called *The Architect of Socialist Society*, and purported to be a lecture delivered in 1967, the fiftieth anniversary of the October revolution, before the College of Interplanetary Communications. In 1967 Stalin is still alive, and the world revolution has still to be brought about, although there are signs that it cannot be long delayed. Stalin stands alone, a figure of fabulous authority, commanding the destiny of the planet. On him Lenin has laid the mantle of leadership, and he has followed the path ordained for him without ever making a misstep, with single-mindedness of purpose and grave humility. He had attacked all the errors of his enemies, among them Trotsky and Radek who had once mistakenly thought that 'the building of socialism in a single country was quite as ridiculous as the idea of some benevolent provincial governor under the Tsars introducing liberalism into a single country'. But those days were over; the former enemies had long ago submitted to his superior knowledge, his gifts of prophecy, his indisputable genius. The pamphlet ends with the vision of Stalin, surrounded by his lieutenants, on the eve of world conquest:

Stalin stood in his grey military greatcoat on Lenin's

mausoleum, surrounded by his immediate comrades in arms
– Molotov, Kaganovich, Voroshilov, Kalinin, and Ordjonikidze. Thoughtfully and calmly he gazed at the hundreds of
thousands of proletarians marching past the mausoleum
with the firm tread of shock troops, the future conquerors
of the capitalist world. Towards this calm and compact
figure of the leader there rolled a wave of love and confidence from those masses who marched with the firm conviction that there, on Lenin's mausoleum, stood the general
staff of the future victorious world revolution.

Stalin was understandably touched by the visionary portrait
of himself on the eve of his greatest conquests, and accordingly instructions were given that the pamphlet be published
in hundreds of thousands of copies and all party cells were
ordered to make a special study of it. Radek was recalled
from exile and made editor in chief of *Izvestiya* and adviser
on foreign policy. Later he became one of the chief artificers
of the Stalin constitution. In October 1936 he was arrested.
His trial, which opened in January 1937, followed the form
already established at the trial of Zinoviev and Kamenev. He
was not alone. There was a supporting cast consisting of seven
distinguished Old Bolsheviks, and there were the usual spear
carriers, all of them being former NKVD agents. The scenario
was written by Stalin and Yezhov, and was no more credible
than the scenario written for the trial of Zinoviev and Kamenev. Stalin appeared to have exhausted his talent for falsification, and the trial therefore resembled a pale imitation of
the first, with one major difference. Radek, usually compliant,
sometimes roused himself and attacked the scenario with a
display of biting sarcasm and brutal wit.
The supporting cast included Grigory Pyatakov, one of the
two men Lenin had recommended to the party in his Testament – the only man he recommended unreservedly – and
Nikolay Muralov, a former military governor of Moscow, who
had fought in the revolution of 1905 and the two revolutions
of 1917. The veteran Bolshevik Grigory Sokolnikov had been
one of the chosen few to accompany Lenin from Switzerland
in the sealed train. A member of the party since 1905, he was
a former Commissar of Finance and a former ambassador to
London. Leonid Serebryakov, Yakov Drobnis, Yakov Livshits,
and Mikhail Boguslavsky were all men who had devoted many
decades of their lives to the party and had reached high posi-

tions. Livshitz, for example, had been Assistant Commissar for Railways and at the time of his arrest he was chief of the Southern Railway.

There were nine spear carriers: Knyazev, Rataichak, Norkin, Shestov, Stroilov, Turok, Hrasche, Pushin, and Arnold *alias* Vasilyev. They played an obscure role at the trial, always supporting the prosecution but sometimes telling stories so improbable that even Vyshinsky seemed troubled by them. Early in the trial, during the examination of Pyatakov, Shestov was introduced for the purpose of providing corroborative evidence about a meeting with Sedov, Trotsky's son, in Berlin. The following exchange took place:

VYSHINSKY: What did Sedov tell you?

SHESTOV: He simply handed over to me a pair of shoes.

VYSHINSKY: So you did not receive letters but shoes?

SHESTOV: Yes. But I knew that they contained letters.

VYSHINSKY: So you were given letters contained in shoes?

SHESTOV: Yes.

VYSHINSKY: In which shoe were the letters – in the right or the left?

SHESTOV: A letter was secreted in each shoe. He said that there were marks on the envelopes of the letters. On one there was the letter 'P' – that meant that it was for Pyatakov, and on the other was the letter 'M' – that meant that it was for Muralov.

VYSHINSKY: You gave a letter to Pyatakov?

SHESTOV: I gave him the letter marked 'P'.

VYSHINSKY: From which shoe, from the right or the left?

SHESTOV: I cannot say exactly.

VYSHINSKY: And the other letter?

SHESTOV: The other letter marked 'M' I gave to Muralov.

VYSHINSKY: May I question Muralov? Accused Muralov, did you receive the letter?

MURALOV: I did.

VYSHINSKY: With a shoe or without a shoe?

MURALOV: No, he brought me only a letter.

VYSHINSKY: Did he bring you the letter sealed or unsealed?

MURALOV: Sealed.

VYSHINSKY: What was on the envelope?

MURALOV: The letter 'M'.

In this tortuous way the evidence of the conspiracy was unfolded. Secret meetings, assassination attempts, wrecking activities were described at great length, but without conviction, by men who seemed to have forgotten their lines and were continually having to be reminded by Vyshinsky about what they had said in the pre-trial examinations and what they were supposed to say at the trial. According to many observers the atmosphere of the trial was curiously muted. The novelist Lion Feuchtwanger, who was sympathetic to the regime, said it 'was less like a criminal trial than a debate carried on in a conversational tone by educated men who were trying to get at the truth'. Pyatakov especially gave the impression of an earnest pedagogue, for he expounded, pointed his finger, and gave the impression of an elderly historian 'delivering a lecture on the life and deeds of a man who had been dead for many years'. Feuchtwanger had no sympathy for Radek. There was something sinister about this man in a brown, ill-fitting suit, whose 'ugly fleshless face was framed by a chestnut-coloured old-fashioned beard'.

Though Feuchtwanger was prepared to give the regime the benefit of every doubt, he was not a fool. He was impressed by the fairness and good temper of the judges and the prosecutor and by the self-evident guilt of the accused. He admired the industrial progress of the Soviet Union, and when his Intourist guides spoke of 'our factories', 'our agriculture', 'our theatres', and 'our army', he was inclined to believe that the Soviet system fostered a naïve pride in its citizens. But sometimes doubts assailed him.

While the trial was still going on, Feuchtwanger was given an audience by Stalin. The novelist was struck by the dictator's vanity. Everywhere he went in Moscow, he saw hundreds of posters showing Stalin in his glory. There was an exhibition of Rembrandt's paintings, but even this exhibition had to be dominated by a larger-than-life-size bust of Stalin. Sitting with Stalin in his Kremlin office, Feuchtwanger asked why there was this vulgar and excessive cult of a single person. Stalin explained that it was not his fault, he had never been consulted, it was what the people wanted, and he shrugged his shoulders at the vulgarity of the immoderate worship of his person. Feuchtwanger returned to the attack. He asked why there had to be a bust of Stalin at the Rembrandt exhibition. Taken aback, and looking for an easy answer, Stalin suggested that it might be an attempt by 'wreckers' to discredit him. As for the cheering crowds he could only excuse their 'naïve joy', since they were not cheering him personally, but as the representative of the socialist system.

At one point Stalin said: 'There is one eternally true legend – that of Judas.'

Feuchtwanger left Stalin's office with mixed feelings. He had not the least doubt of Stalin's genius – 'he is the type of the Russian peasant and worker who has risen to genius and is predestined to victory,' he wrote later – but he had some doubts about the strength of Stalin's character. There was no nobility in him, and he was consumed with vanity. Long after Feuchtwanger left the Kremlin office, he was haunted by the dictator's 'soft, dull, sly, laugh'.

Meanwhile the trial of the many Judases continued in the small courtroom, where Ulrich half dozed and Vyshinsky trembled with excitement. Radek admitted to having been in treasonable correspondence with Trotsky, and mentioned three letters he had received, one in April 1934, a second in December 1935, and a third in January 1936. The case against Radek rested on these letters, which had long ago vanished. 'Where are the documents in the case?' Vyshinsky thundered, and answered by saying that it was not important that they were no longer available: the case against Radek did not depend on evidence. It depended, in fact, on his obvious guilt. Sometimes, like the defendants, Vyshinsky gave the impression of a man who was already weary of the charade.

At the evening session of the third day of the trial, the charade came to an end as the defendant Valentin Arnold took the stand. A breath of life entered the courtroom with the appearance of Valentin Arnold, *alias* Valentin Vasilyev, *alias* Karl Rask, *alias* Aimo Kulpenen. For some reason Vyshinsky was concerned to draw from the defendant a full account of his early life. Arnold told it well. He had deserted twice from the Russian army, wandered all over Russia and Finland, sailed off to New York, joined the American army, sailed off again to Buenos Aires and Scotland and California, and at last returned to the Soviet Union. While employed as a chauffeur, he made halfhearted attempts to kill Ordjonikidze and Molotov, and seems to have been genuinely sorry that he failed. 'A man like me,' he said proudly, 'has had an awful lot of adventures.' He enjoyed telling his adventures, but they had nothing to do with the trial.

In his concluding speech Radek made all the gestures demanded of him as a confessed traitor. He assumed the role of the penitent sinner, recited his infamous dealings with Trotsky, and announced the enormity of his crime. But he was a man who had spent a lifetime as a polemical journalist with a mischievous skill in debate and a fabulous capacity for extricating himself from dangerous situations; and now, fighting for his life, he was still capable of mischief.

Speaking slowly, wearing the loose brown suit he had worn throughout the trial, his monkey-like face fringed with the chestnut-coloured beard, his eyes looking enormous as they peered through the thick lenses of his spectacles, he announced that he had entered into the conspiracy with a full knowledge of what he was doing.

'There are no arguments,' he declared, 'by which a grown man in full possession of his senses could defend treason to his country. Neither can I plead extenuating circumstances. A man who has spent thirty-five years in the labour movement cannot extenuate his crime by any circumstances when he confesses to a crime of treason to the country. I was already a grown man with fully formed views when I met Trotsky.'

Having stated the case for the prosecution, he embarked on a tactical manoeuvre to introduce the case for the defence, his own defence, which was not included in Vyshinsky's plan to destroy him. He merely pointed to the evidence, or rather the entire lack of evidence.

'When I hear that the people in the dock are mere bandits and spies, I object to it!' he declared. 'There is the evidence of two people – the testimony of myself who received the directives and the letters from Trotsky (which, unfortunately, I burned), and the testimony of Pyatakov, who spoke to Trotsky. All the evidence of the other accused rests on this testimony. If you are dealing with mere criminals and spies, on what can you base your conviction that what we have said is the truth, the firm truth?'

It was a breathtaking moment, for quite suddenly and without raising his voice Radek had destroyed the entire case against him. With this deft blow he reduced the evidence to a few pieces of charred paper. The entire case rested on his own admissions and those of Pyatakov, all the subsidiary evidence being derived from their self-accusations. For the moment he was telling the truth. Yet 'the truth, the firm truth' escaped him, as it escaped his prosecutors. There was not one truth, but many truths, and he went on to elaborate on the many kinds of truths, all hidden in their separate cocoons, which constantly assail the practised revolutionary. The passage, which has been little noticed, should be quoted at length because it demonstrates the extraordinary intricate quality of Radek's mind. The passage hints at intrigues within intrigues, of whole schools of immorality clashing against one another. There is a mysterious reference to Gavrilo Princip, the Serbian nationalist who assassinated Archduke Francis Ferdinand and precipitated the First World War. According to Radek, Princip took to the grave 'a fragment of a secret'. It was a secret about war, and it was known to Lenin. Radek did not say what the secret was, or if he did, it was not published in the official transcript of the trial, but he offered at least one clue. He said:

Naturally, the State Prosecutor and the Court, who know the whole history of Trotskyism and who know us, have no reason to suspect that we, bearing the burden of terrorism, added high treason just for our own pleasure. There is no necessity to convince you of that. We must convince, firstly, the diffused wandering Trotskyite elements in the country, who have not yet laid down their arms, who are dangerous and who must realize that we speak here shaken to the depths of our souls, and that we are speaking the truth, and only the truth. And we must also tell the world that what Lenin – I tremble to mention his name from this dock – said in a letter, in the directions he gave to the delegation that was about to leave for The Hague, about the secret of war. A fragment of this secret was in the possession of the young Serbian nationalist Gavrilo Princip, who would die in a fortress without revealing it. He was a Serbian nationalist and felt the justice of his cause when fighting for the secret which was kept by the Serbian nationalist government. I cannot conceal this secret and carry it with me to the grave, because while in view of what I have confessed here, I have not the right to speak as a repentant Communist, nevertheless the thirty-five years I worked in the labour movement, despite all the errors and crimes with which they ended, entitle me to ask you to believe one thing – that, after all, the masses of the people with whom I marched do mean something to me. And if I concealed this truth and departed this life with it, as Kamenev did, as Zinoviev did and as Mrachkovsky did, then when I thought over these things, I would have heard in my hour of death the execrations of those people who will be slaughtered in the future war, and whom, by my testimony, I could have furnished with a weapon against the war that is being fomented.

What was the strange secret to which Radek referred – the secret possessed by Lenin and the Serbian government, of which a fragment was in the possession of Gavrilo Princip?

As it happens, Lenin's instructions to the delegation leaving for The Hague have survived. The delegation was not to the Hague Conference of July 1922, but to the International Congress of Co-operators and Trade Unionists which took place six months later. Lenin's *Notes on the Question of the Tasks of Our Delegation at the Hague* were written on December 4th, 1922, in a mood of towering cynicism, a few days before he suffered the heart attack which removed him from power. Here are some passages from his instructions to the delegates:

> The people must be told about the great secrecy with which war arises, and how helpless the ordinary workers' organizations are in the face of war that is really impending, even if these organizations call themselves revolutionary.
>
> Again and again it must be explained to the people in the most concrete manner how matters stood in the last war, and why they could not be different.
>
> Boycott war – is a stupid phrase. Communists must take part even in the most reactionary war.
>
> We must relate and analyse what happened during the last war, declaring to all present that they do not know this or that they pretend that they know it, whereas, in fact, they shut their eyes to the very crux of the question which, if not understood, puts all effort to combat war utterly out of the question.

These were the instructions which Lenin gave to the small group of Bolsheviks who attended the conference at The Hague between December 10th and 15th, 1922. The delegation was led by Radek and Madame Kollontay. Very little of importance resulted from the conference, but in Radek's eyes this last confrontation with Lenin possessed a supreme importance. When he left Moscow, Lenin was still in command of the government. When he returned from the Hague, Lenin was a sick man fighting for his life.

To Radek these last instructions therefore had something of the effect of a testament or the words of a dying man spoken from a deathbed. When Lenin spoke of 'the great secrecy with which war arises' (*velika taina v kotoroi voina rozhdaetsya*), he was hinting at mysteries, but he was also expressing himself about something which he and Radek understood extremely well – the vast power possessed by conspiratorial societies. Wars begin obscurely as a result of dubious conspiracies and secret stratagems. 'The secret of war', which Radek mentioned in his concluding speech, was the very simple and terrible truth that wars are the result not of great historical forces, but of mysterious and little-known conspiratorial acts. The people are helpless in the face of these acts, for they know nothing about them.

So now, making his last tortured speech, which was his last testament, Radek was saying as clearly as a man could that there were secrets which could not be divulged about this trial, and that there were conspiracies taking place in the Soviet Union which would never enter the history books. He was himself a part of this conspiracy, and he would have to die without ever revealing what he knew.

As though to reinforce this argument Radek introduced the figure of Gavrilo Princip, the idealistic nineteen-year-old assassin of the Archduke, who possessed a fragment of the secret and 'would die in a fortress without revealing it'. Radek knew that the assassination at Sarajevo was not the simple act of a profoundly nationalistic boy, but the result of a complicated intrigue in which Princip was merely the tool of shadowy conspirators like Artamanov, the Russian imperial military attaché at Belgrade, and the redoubtable Colonel Dimitrjević, known as Apis, the chief of the Serbian intelligence service and the leading figure in the secret society 'Union or Death'. This secret society had vowed to bring about the union of Serbia with the Slavic lands in the Balkans, an aim which could scarcely be achieved without a major war. At his trial Princip declared that he shot the Archduke as a protest against the poverty the Austrians had brought to Serbia, and this was in fact the reason why he steeled himself to kill the Archduke, but it was not the reason why Dimitrjević put the revolver in his hands and gave him a capsule of prussic acid so that he could kill himself afterwards. Dimitrjević was executed in February 1915. Princip, too young to be sentenced to the death penalty, was kept in an underground cell in the fortress of Theresienstadt, where he died in 1918. He had entered the conspiracy blindly, knowing little if anything about the motives of the archconspirators. His share of the secret was very small.

By identifying himself with Princip, Radek was insisting on his own innocence while hinting at the existence of a vast conspiratorial underworld in which he had become an unwilling tool. It was not true. He knew the conspirators well, he had been compromised by them, and he was well aware of the fate reserved for those who compromise with Stalin. But that last speech was not unworthy of a man who had devoted his life to conspiracy, and there was a lingering nobility in that strange paragraph in which Princip, the memory of Lenin, and 'the great secrecy with which war arises' are all brought together to form an abstruse plea of innocence.

Most of the other prisoners combined abject confessions of guilt with fragmentary protestations of innocence. Sokolnikov confessed everything, but took care to point out that although he was at the very heart of the conspiracy, he did not know what was going on. 'Even the members of the centre could not know everything,' he said. Muralov, the heavy-set leader of the Moscow uprising in 1917, was even more scornful, and in his last speech he declared that it was in man's nature to make mistakes and only a fool could lay claim to infallibility; and after this parting shot at Stalin he must have known he could expect no mercy.

Surprisingly many of the prisoners spoke with vigour and trenchancy, while a few, like Radek, gave the impression of enjoying the role they had been called upon to play, perhaps because they had been assured of leniency and believed the assurance. Pyatakov was the most abject. 'In a few hours you will pass your sentence,' he said, 'and here I stand before you in filth, crushed by my own crimes, a man who has lost his party, who has no friends, who has lost his family, who has lost his very self.'

The trial came to an end shortly after seven o'clock in the evening of January 29th. Eight hours later, at three o'clock in the morning, the court convened to announce the verdict of death for all the accused except Radek, Sokolnikov, Arnold and Stroilov, who were sentenced to long terms of imprisonment 'with deprivation of political rights for a period of five years'. Pyatakov and Serebryakov were condemned to be shot as the ringleaders, eleven others were condemned to be shot because they had directly carried out the ringleaders' orders, while Radek and Sokolnikov were described as conspirators who had not directly participated in 'acts of a diversive, wrecking, espionage and terrorist nature', and were therefore given lighter sentences.

Feuchtwanger, who was present in the courtroom, reported that Radek's face lit up with joy and relief when he heard the verdict, but others thought he gave a mocking smile and shrugged his shoulders in disbelief.

Before morning Pyatakov, Serebryakov and eleven others lay dead in the cellars of the Lubyanka. Later in the day Nikita Krushchev, a loyal party member and close friend of Stalin, delivered before an audience of two hundred thousand party members gathered in Moscow a long speech to celebrate the killing of the prisoners. At the conclusion of the speech he read out words which could only have been written by Stalin himself, so closely do they follow the liturgical pattern of Stalin's thought:

These men lifted their villainous hands against Comrade Stalin.

By lifting their hands against Comrade Stalin, they lifted them against all of us, against the working class, against the working people.

By lifting their hands against Comrade Stalin, they lifted them against the teaching of Marx, Engels, and Lenin.

By lifting their hands against Comrade Stalin, they lifted them against all the best that humanity possesses.

Stalin is our hope.

Stalin is our expectation.

Stalin is the beacon which guides all progressive mankind.

Stalin is our banner.

Stalin is our will.

Stalin is our victory.

THE MURDER OF THE GENERAL STAFF

THERE ARE MURDERERS who are perfectly content to commit a single murder, and if they survive the inevitable inquiries by the police they spend the rest of their lives relishing the memory of the crime and the agony of the victim. There are other murderers whose whole lives are dedicated to murder, and who cannot stop murdering because it has never occurred to them to find any reason for stopping. They murder habitually, hopelessly, finding no pleasure in it. They know they are damned and it is all one whether they are damned for a thousand murders or a million. In the mathematics of murder, $1,000 = 1,000,000$.

By 1937 Stalin had reached the stage when murder had become as habitual as shaving or eating. Three or four times a week the death lists compiled by Yezhov at his orders would be presented to him, he would read through the lists casually, add his initials, and then forget about them. These lists did not comprise the names of a small number of high officials, but included hundreds and sometimes thousands of obscure people working inside and outside the government. In many cases the lists were mere formalities: the people had already been shot. These drab pages filled with names represented the only currency he recognized: they were his bills of trading in the endless terror he was visiting upon Russia.

There is not the least doubt that these death lists existed. In his speech at the Twentieth Congress of the Party in 1956, Khrushchev mentioned that 383 death lists were sent to Stalin during the years 1937 and 1938. Evidently Khrushchev had ordered a search for these lists and they had been brought for his inspection. There is no reason to believe that 383 was in any sense a final figure. According to Khrushchev the names on the death lists comprised 'thousands of Party, Soviet, Comsomol, army and economic workers', but for some reason he did not feel obliged to say how many thousands, or to explain why the lists were limited to five kinds of workers. In fact there were far more than 383 lists, and in addition there were the famous telegrams to the local NKVD headquarters which took the form of vast, anonymous death sentences: 'Execute at once a thousand men in your city.'

In his *Notes from the Underground* Dostoyevsky describes the classic nihilist exercising his spite upon the world. 'Let everyone perish,' he declares, 'so long as I have my cup of tea.' Stalin was 'the man from the underground', bored and fretful, permitting everyone to perish so long as he had his cup of tea. His victims did not die because Stalin felt that they endangered his dictatorship, nor because there was some peculiar need for sacrificial offerings, nor because he felt any particular hatred of them. They died quite simply because he was bored by human existence.

To the end of his life Stalin continued to initial three or four death lists weekly. He felt neither pleasure nor pain; only a profound indifference. His soul was burdened with so many crimes that he had long ago forgotten that it was possible to live without committing them. Murder was the air he breathed, his sole justification, the key that turned all the locks. Though most of his murders were the casual acts of a bored man, a few arose out of pure hatred.

The trial of Radek and the execution of thirteen of the defendants in January 1937 was followed almost immediately by the execution of Sergo Ordjonikidze, the heavy-set and affable Georgian, who had been in prison with Stalin in 1902. Ten years later he had been Stalin's sponsor when he applied to become a member of the Central Committee. Ten years later still he was responsible with Stalin for the bloody overthrow of the Menshevik regime in Georgia. In 1929 he was one of the four men – Kaganovich, Voroshilov and Yenukidze were the others – who were selected to write the laudatory tributes on Stalin's fiftieth birthday, which were translated into fifty languages and distributed all over the world. In his tribute Ordjonikidze celebrated Stalin as the companion-in-arms of Lenin, and the man who had singlehandedly led the revolutionaries in Georgia since 1905. Neither statement was true, and the tribute as Ordjonikidze wrote it shows signs of having been carefully edited and revised to satisfy the vanity of the dictator. For his services to Stalin Ordjonikidze was appointed Commissar of Industry. He possessed very little scientific bent, and it was generally believed that the real work was done by the Vice-Commissar, Georgy Pyatakov. When Pyatakov was arrested, Ordjonikidze had protested vehemently; and he continued to protest so vehemently that Stalin in spite of their long friendship ordered his execution. The newspapers announced that he died of a heart attack on February 18th, 1937.

The funeral took place three days later in the Red Square. Stalin, Kaganovich, Voroshilov, Khrushchev, Mikoyan and Yezhov accompanied the ashes to the small grave in the Kremlin wall. Speeches were made in honour of the dead leader, 'the faithful follower of Lenin and Stalin'. Many years later, when Khrushchev investigated the death of Ordjonikidze and learned for the first time that the story of the 'heart attack' was a pure invention to conceal a crime, he put the blame squarely on Beria. In his speech at the Twentieth Congress he said that Ordjonikidze 'always opposed Beria and complained against him to Stalin, but instead of examining the affair and taking the appropriate steps, Stalin permitted the liquidation of Ordjonikidze's brother and brought Ordjonikidze to such a pass that he was compelled to kill himself.' In fact Ordjonikidze's brother was killed later, and Beria had little or nothing to do with the crime. It was simply one more of Stalin's millions of murders, remarkable only because Ordjonikidze was his close friend.

Even at the time the story of the 'heart attack' was widely disbelieved. Ordjonikidze was known to have been in excellent health; it was also known that he had fought dangerously for the life of Pyatakov and had told intimate friends that he feared for his life as a result. One account of his death related how officers from the secret police came to his apartment in the middle of the night and offered him the alternative of shooting himself or accompanying them to the cellars of the Lubyanka. According to this account, he said farewell to his wife and shot himself. A few moments later a police doctor, waiting in an anteroom, certified that Ordjonikidze died from heart failure. But this story is not entirely credible – Stalin rarely gave his victims a choice in their manner of dying. It is more likely that he was simply shot to death with no questions asked, without trial, without formality.

Stalin's passion for vengeance knew no limits. It was not enough to kill Ordjonikidze. In the following weeks he went on to kill his wife, his mother, and his daughter. He would have killed Ordjonikidze's father as well, if it were not that the father had died long before. In his speech at the Twentieth Congress Khrushchev made a brief reference to the mass slaughter of an entire family, saying: 'Beria also handled cruelly the family of Comrade Ordjonikidze.' Khrushchev was inaccurate when he introduced Beria as the murderer, but there was no doubt of his accuracy when he used the word 'cruelly'.

Two weeks after the murder of Ordjonikidze Stalin delivered a long rambling speech to the plenum of the Central Committee on the need for more exacting punishments on 'the wreckers in our midst'. This is not one of the speeches written by his secretaries: the passion is too raw, the hate too violent, the familiar incantatory and liturgical style too personal to be successfully imitated. The speech, which was delivered on March 3rd, was not published in *Pravda* until March

29th. There it appeared under the ominous heading: 'On the Inadequacies of Party Work and Measures for Liquidating Trotskyist and other Double-Dealers.' In this speech Ordjonikidze was not mentioned, but there were occasional references to Pyatakov, Radek and Sokolnikov as a dangerous trio who had worked treacherously towards the dismemberment of the Soviet Union and the restoration of capitalism. Pyatakov had been sentenced to death, Radek and Sokolnikov to long-term imprisonment. There was something very odd in the linking of these three figures, as though they were the most dangerous of all the traitors who confronted him, the supreme wreckers of their time. But there was something still odder in the litany of hate which formed the concluding portion of the speech:

We must smash and overthrow the filthy theory that with every forward movement we make the class struggle will die away, that in proportion to our successes the class enemy will become tamed. This is not only a filthy theory but a dangerous theory, for it lulls our people to sleep, leads them into a trap, and makes it possible for the class enemy to rally for the struggle against the Soviet power.

On the contrary, the more we move forward, the more successes we enjoy, then the more hateful become the remnants of the vanquished exploiter classes, the more quickly they turn to sharper forms of struggle, the more mischief they commit upon the Soviet state, the more they grasp at the most desperate resources, as the last resort of the doomed.

We must smash and overthrow a second filthy theory which says that those who are not always wrecking things and are occasionally successful in their work cannot be wreckers. This strange theory reveals the naïveté of its authors. Quite clearly wreckers are not always wrecking, for in that case they would soon be found out.

On the contrary, the real wreckers must from time to time be successful in their work in order to gain the people's confidence and in order to continue at their wrecking games.

We must smash and overthrow a third filthy theory which proclaims that the systematic fulfilment of economic plans reduces wrecking and the results of wrecking to zero. Such a theory can only serve one aim – to arouse the bureaucratic conceit of our administrators, soothe them, and weaken their struggle against wrecking.

We must smash and overthrow the filthy theory that proclaims that the Trotskyist wreckers do not have the use of large reserves, that they are, as it were, 'scraping the bottom of the barrel'. This is untrue, comrades. Only naïve people could think in this way. The Trotskyist wreckers do have reserves, and these consist above all of the remnants of the vanquished exploiter classes in the Soviet Union. They consist also of a whole series of groups and organizations outside the borders of the Soviet Union hostile to us.

Stalin's theory that as the Soviet state grew stronger so did its adversaries had no logical foundation. It was demonstrably untrue, but he was not interested in truths. He was in a fugue state of maniacal vindictiveness, not knowing where to turn, no longer capable of distinguishing between friends and enemies. Those who read the speech must have been acutely aware that another and even more terrible blood bath was about to take place. They were not mistaken. Six days later Yagoda and his chief lieutenants, numbering about two thousand, were arrested. Yagoda himself was kept in the Lubyanka for interrogation and eventually a public trial, while most of his lieutenants were shot out of hand.

There are few occasions in history when blood baths can be termed 'ironical' and 'desirable'. This was one of them. Yagoda may have known he was doomed from the moment when he was demoted to Commissar for Communications the previous September. For a little more than six months he was permitted to wonder when the axe would fall. Arrested on April 4th, 1937, for 'crimes in office', which included embezzlement of state funds and riotous living, he was soon in a state of collapse, begging piteously for freedom or at least for a chance to be brought into the presence of Stalin.

Yagoda's real crime was not treachery. On the contrary, no one had ever shown such profound and reverent obedience to Stalin. He had been Stalin's man almost from the day in 1920 when he became a member of the presidium of the Cheka at the age of twenty-nine. As Vyshinsky said later at his trial: 'Yagoda was not an ordinary murderer; he was a murderer with a guarantee that he would not be found out.' This pharmacist with a genuine talent for administering poison was a genius in the art of torture and mass murder. For sixteen years he had held a high position in the secret police, testimony to his astonishing powers of survival. He had in fact survived too long and in too high a position for Stalin's comfort, and his downfall was due as much to his longevity as to his pride.

When shortly before his downfall Stalin permitted him to live within the Kremlin and promised that he would become an alternate member of the Politburo at the next meeting of the Party Congress, Yagoda had understandably come to the conclusion that he was being groomed for the succession. It was a dangerous conclusion, and he paid for it with his life.

Within the Politburo there were feelings of dismay when it was learned that Yagoda was about to become an alternate member. Kaganovich in particular seems to have sounded the alarm. Stefan Zweig's *Fouché*, a biography of the famous minister of police who served successively the French Revolution, the Directory, Napoleon and Louis XVIII, had recently appeared in Russian translation, and inevitably a copy of the book had fallen into Stalin's hands. Joseph Fouché, who became Duke of Otranto, was a small, lean, lantern-jawed man with a bloodless face, and Yagoda bore a remarkable physical resemblance to him. 'I have known only one really perfect traitor – Fouché!' said Napoleon at St Helena. Balzac, who was Stalin's favourite author, has described the menacing presence of the minister of police in a brilliant passage of a story called 'Une Ténébreuse Affaire': 'That man of pallid visage, trained in monastic dissimulation, knowing all the secrets of the men of the Mountain to whom he belonged and of the royalists to whom in time he would also belong – this man pursued his slow and silent study of men and things and whatever advantages lay in the political scene; he had divined the secrets of Buonaparte . . . and he had more power over men than Buonaparte . . .'

So Yagoda disappeared from sight, emerging eleven months later in a public trial at which he confessed to having been in secret correspondence with the enemies of the Soviet Union almost since the day he became a member of the Cheka. In prison he had grown small and frail, his hair had turned white, and he trembled convulsively.

There is an apocryphal story that while he was in prison he came to believe in the justice of God. 'From Stalin I deserved nothing but gratitude,' he is supposed to have said, 'and from God I deserved the most extreme punishment. Now look upon me and judge for yourself: Is there a God or not?'

During that sombre year Stalin set about destroying those who had served him most faithfully. The entire party, the entire managerial class, and the entire army was purged as it had never been purged before.

In the summer came the executions of Marshal Tukhachevsky and seven other generals followed by the decimation of the officers of the Red Army. It was as though Stalin were deliberately designing to render the Red Army useless. The shock wave caused by the execution of the eight generals and the subsequent executions in the Red Army could still be felt four years later when Hitler gave the order for attacking the Soviet Union.

There was almost no warning. Quite suddenly on June 11th, 1937, the Moscow radio broadcast a lengthy communication from the Office of the Public Prosecutor announcing the names of the eight generals who had been arrested at various dates by the organs of the NKVD. The broadcast said that they were being tried *in camera* by a special bench of judges appointed by the Supreme Court. On the following day *Izvestiya* announced that all the defendants had been found guilty and summarily executed. The brief announcement read:

Yesterday, June 11, the Supreme Court of the USSR, composed of Comrade Ulrich, presiding judge and chairman of the Military Collegium together with the member judges A. M. Alksnis, Deputy People's Commissar of Defence, S. M. Budyenny, V. K. Blücher, B. M. Shaposhnikov, P. E. Dybenko, N. D. Kashirin, E. M. Goriachev, I. P. Belov examined in closed proceedings under the law of December 1st, 1934, the case of M. N. Tukhachevsky, I. E. Yakir, I. P. Uborevich, A. I. Kork, R. M. Eideman, B. M. Feldman, M. V. Primakov, V. K. Putna.

The above persons were accused of breach of military duty and oath of allegiance, treason to their country, treason against the peoples of the USSR and treason against the Workers' and Peasants' Red Army.

All the defendants were condemned to the extreme penalty, which was duly carried out.

We know now that nearly all these statements were untrue.

There was no trial, and therefore there were no judges, and therefore the invocation of the dreaded law of December 1st, 1934, which was promulgated on the day of Kirov's assassination, was designed merely to give a pretence of legality to a summary order of execution.

For nearly two decades the broadcast on June 11th and the printed announcement on the following day comprised the only information published on the 'trial' in the Soviet press. The official rehabilitation of the dead generals took place slowly and cautiously after Khrushchev's speech at the Twentieth Congress where they are not mentioned by name, though they are evidently included among 'the many military leaders falsely condemned by Stalin during 1937–41' to whom Khrushchev paid belated tribute. By 1958 their names were reinstated in the *Great Soviet Encyclopedia*. On October 27th, 1961, they were officially rehabilitated by Khrushchev in the name of the government. But Soviet sources have remained strangely silent about the complicated chain of circumstances which led to their deaths.

Mikhail Nikolayevich Tukhachevsky was born into a family of the Russian *petite noblesse*, and claimed descent from Baudouin VIII, Count of Flanders. His military career in the First World War was brief, for he was captured by the Germans early in 1915 and imprisoned in the famous Camp IX at Ingolstadt, where one of his fellow prisoners was a young French captain called Charles de Gaulle. He made five attempts to escape. Four times he was caught and severely punished; the fifth attempt in the autumn of 1917 succeeded. He returned to Petrograd to find the city already in the hands of the Bolsheviks.

During the civil war Trotsky gave him important commands. Early in 1920 he showed his devotion to the Bolshevik cause by superintending the massacre of the Kronstadt sailors. He performed the task so well that he was appointed commander in chief of all Soviet forces in the war against Poland. He was then twenty-seven years old. Though the invasion of Poland led to a disastrous defeat, Tukhachevsky's reputation emerged unimpaired. A superb strategist, he was not responsible for the defeat. He continued to receive important military commands. In 1931 he was appointed Vice-Commissar of Defence under Voroshilov. On September 22nd, 1935, he was one of five military leaders raised to the rank of marshal – the others were Voroshilov, Budyenny, Blücher and Yegorov. In

January 1936 he attended the funeral of King George V as the personal representative of Stalin, travelling by way of Poland, Germany and France.

The passage of Marshal Tukhachevsky through Paris had been observed at a distance by General Nikolay Skoblin, a former officer of the Tsarist army, one of the leaders of a White Russian movement to overthrow the Bolsheviks. He was a short, wiry, precise man with a neat moustache who wore his hair in the manner of Hitler. Filled with a mystical belief that he was himself the chosen leader assigned to command the forces of liberation in Russia, he sought for allies among the leaders of the Third Reich. After Marshal Tukhachevsky returned to the Soviet Union, General Skoblin sought out Reinhard Heydrich, the dreaded chief of the Sicherheitsdienst, the Nazi security service, and reported that he had been appointed by Marshal Tukhachevsky to contact the German High Command. According to General Skoblin the Red Army was preparing a *coup d'état* which would bring about the destruction of the Soviet system. He brought forged documents to show that he was indeed what he represented himself to be.

The information given to Heydrich was soon in the hands of Himmler and Hitler, who were neither particularly interested nor unduly alarmed. Hitler's anti-Bolshevik campaign was merely incidental to his compulsive dream to colonize Russia and add its vast territories to the 'Thousand-year Reich', and it was immaterial to him whether Russia was ruled by Stalin or by Tukhachevsky. If the *coup d'état* served to weaken Russia, so much the better. They put little faith in General Skoblin's disclosures; he was a man who could be used if it served their purposes.

Towards the end of 1936, in a manner which has never been made completely clear, General Skoblin became a double agent. While acting as a secret agent for the Germans, he was also sending reports to Moscow. His contact with the NKVD was Mikhail Spiegelglas, the deputy head of the bureau dealing with espionage.

His sympathies however had not changed. His thoughts were directed towards the overthrow of Bolshevism, and he was using his contacts with the NKVD to that end. He seems to have felt a particular hatred for Marshal Tukhachevsky, who had served as an officers of the Semyonovsky Regiment in the First World War and who had sworn an oath of loyalty to the

Tsar, but the destruction of the marshal and as many leaders of the Red Army as possible was merely incidental to the greater plan of destroying the Soviet state. He knew exactly what he was doing, and he very nearly succeeded in accomplishing his purpose.

Already Stalin was beginning to seek a *rapprochement* with Hitler, The Spanish Civil War, following so quickly upon the Italian campaign in Abyssinia, demonstrated the weakness of the democracies. While publicly excoriating the fascist states, he was secretly attempting to arrange a *modus vivendi* with them. He foresaw a war in which France and Great Britain would be overwhelmed by the combined might of Germany and Italy, and the Soviet Union would be compelled to make terms with the victors. He had apparently never read *Mein Kampf* and was not in the least aware of Hitler's real intentions. By the spring of 1937, convinced that time was running out and that desperate measures were needed, he was beginning to think that some important gesture towards Hitler was necessary to establish his good faith.

The NKVD was in possession of substantial files filled with the well-documented fantasies of General Skoblin. These files were already in their possession during the trial of Radek late in January 1937, for Radek was made to speak of mysterious conspiratorial contacts with Marshal Tukhachevsky and General Putna, the former military attaché in London. They were introduced sketchily into his cross-examination, and the tentative scenario was soon abandoned, perhaps because it had not yet been worked out in sufficient detail to convince Stalin that anything could be gained by it. Marshal Tukhachevsky remained Vice-Commissar of Defence. His position however was considerably weakened by Radek's obscure references to a Bonapartist plot, and there was little comfort to be derived from Radek's statement in court that 'Tukhachevsky could never have been connected with counter-revolutionary activity since his attitude to the party and the government is that of an absolutely devoted man'. He was understandably nervous. General Putna was under arrest, other officers had vanished, and there were rumours that a purge of the officers was in the making.

About this time Alexander Barmine, an armament expert attached to the Arms Export Commission of the Supreme Defence Council, paid an official visit to Marshal Tukhachevsky's office. He recalled later:

The Marshal came forward to greet me with that spontaneous courtesy which he always showed to his juniors. He had grown heavier; his hair was greying at the temples. His expression, however, was still young and virile. He had the same air of calm assurance and the same attentive manner of listening and speaking.

During our interview the telephone rang. The Marshal took up the receiver calmly, and then suddenly jumped to his feet, replying in an entirely different, a definitely respectful voice:

'Good morning, Kliment Yefremovich . . . Exactly as you wish, Kliment Yefremovich . . . That will be done, Kliment Yefremovich . . .' This was the way he took orders from Voroshilov.

The incident made a sad impression on me. Seeing a great soldier take orders in just that fashion helped me to understand why it was that all my questions took days to get an answer. Even Tukhachevsky no longer dared to make decisions; he merely carried out commands.

The Tukhachevsky seen by Barmine was not a man capable of leading a Bonapartist coup. He was a man who realized that his life was in danger and that only by the most devoted service to the party could he hope to survive. He did not know he was already doomed.

The strange plot which General Skoblin had set in motion began to come into focus about March 29th, the day on which Stalin's speech against the 'double-crossers' was published. By mid-April most of the forged documents implicating Marshal Tukhachevsky had been prepared, probably in the Gestapo headquarters in the Prinz-Albrechtstrasse in Berlin, and the delays seem to have been caused more by the uncertainty of the political situation than by any lack of skill on the part of the forgers who worked under the supervision of Reinhard Heydrich and Hermann Behrens. The forgeries consisted of a series of letters and plans exchanged between Tukhachevsky and high military officials in Germany. A voluminous portfolio was required. Through Spiegelglas, General Skoblin informed the NKVD that the entire portfolio would be ready about the middle of May, and the question arose about the various methods in which it should be conveyed to Russia.

On April 6th General Yan Gamarnik, chief of the Political Administration of the Soviet armed forces, was summarily dismissed from his post and replaced by Lev Mekhlis, a prominent member of Stalin's secretariat. Gamarnik, who wore a fan-shaped beard, was one of the most popular men of the Red Army. He was an Old Bolshevik, a friend of Lenin, one of the trusted provincial leaders of the October revolution, and his sudden dismissal could only be explained by Stalin's determination to exert absolute authority over the political administration of the Red Army. The dismissal was all the more surprising because Gamarnik was a member of the Central Committee, and believed to be in Stalin's trust. He was a political rather than a military figure, and ranked with Marshal Tukhachevsky, General Alksnis, the head of the Soviet air force, and Admiral Orlov, the head of the Soviet navy, as one of the four Vice-Commissars of Defence under Voroshilov. There were some who believed that the dismissal of Gamarnik heralded the beginning of a purge of the Red Army.

There were however no outward and visible signs of the coming purge. The traditional May Day parade took place in the Red Square, and Tukhachevsky as usual was present at the Lenin mausoleum in full uniform. Some years later General Walter Krivitsky, the chief of the Western Europe section of the NKVD, who later defected, told a curious story of how Marshal Tukhachevsky took his place on the reviewing stand and seemed more solemn and nervous than usual, and after watching one of the parades he abruptly left the reviewing stand and marched out of the Red Square and out of sight. Krivitsky suggests that Tukhachevsky already knew he was doomed, but the official photographs taken at the May Day parade do not reinforce the suggestion. On these photographs we see Stalin, Andreyev, Mikoyan, Molotov, Kalinin and the diminutive Yezhov standing on the topmost terrace of the mausoleum, while immediately below them we see Tukhachevsky, Belov, Voroshilov, Yegorov and Budyenny in that order. Tukhachevsky does not look in the least dispirited.

Four days later it was officially announced that Tukhachevsky would not be attending the coronation of King George VI. His place would be taken by Admiral Orlov.

On May 10th Voroshilov and Mekhlis summoned a convocation of all the commanders of the military districts. Following the convocation Tukhachevsky was appointed military commander of the Volga District, and his place as Vice-Commissar of Defence was taken by Yegorov. General Yakir, military commander of the Kiev District, was appointed to Leningrad. There were a few other changes, none of them surprising. Tukhachevsky spent a few more days in Moscow, and seems to have left Moscow on May 20th, accompanied by a small staff. He was never seen in public again.

There were conflicting reports of what happened after he boarded the train. According to one account, he reached Saratov and was ordered on a direct wire from the Kremlin to return to Moscow. According to another account, his railroad car was uncoupled in the middle of the night at a halt called 'The Bandits', where he was told that he was under arrest and would be escorted under armed guard to Moscow. There is still another account that he never left Moscow and when the order of his arrest was received, he shot the NKVD officer who attempted to arrest him and a pitched battle took place in the Defence Secretariat in which the marshal was severely wounded. Soon afterwards he was carried on a stretcher to the Kremlin to be interrogated by Stalin. There was a dramatic scene, with the dictator and the wounded marshal screaming abuse at one another. This third variant seems to have been coloured by memories of the interrogation of Nikolayev. It would have been more characteristic of Stalin to order him to make a long journey, so giving him a feeling of complete safety and confidence. Then there would come the sudden sharp tug on the reins.

By May 18th the 'proofs' of the generals' conspiracy were in Stalin's hands in the form of a portfolio of photostats prepared by the Gestapo with the assistance of General Skoblin. Lev Mekhlis flew to Berlin, examined the documents, and pronounced on their authenticity. With him were various NKVD experts, among them a certain Rodosz, who survived the purges and was still alive in 1956. In that year he was interrogated by a special commission appointed by Khrushchev. 'We have questioned this Rodosz,' Khrushchev reported, 'and he showed himself to be a moron and a man completely corrupt morally. To think that such men as these could decide the fate of members of the Politburo.' He was executed in April 1956, being the last survivor among the Russians who took part in the plot to destroy the generals.

The plot succeeded beyond all expectations, but its success was measured in different ways by the participants. General Skoblin believed he had brought himself closer to the day when he would lead a victorious army to the gates of Moscow, Heydrich and Himmler believed they had successfully outwitted Stalin and weakened the fighting strength of the Soviet army. Stalin believed that by accepting the spurious evidence supplied by the Gestapo he was demonstrating his willingness to embark on a *rapprochement* with Hitler. He knew, as everyone knew, that a Bonapartist *coup* led by Tukhachevsky could never have taken place. He was perfectly prepared to sacrifice a few generals to prove his good faith. The technique had been worked out by Lenin when he ordered the assassination of the German ambassador in Moscow and then executed leading members of the Left Socialist Revolutionary party, who were publicly blamed for the murder of the German ambassador. In effect there was an 'internal loan', the borrowing taking the form of a liquidation of disposable assets.

In Stalin's mind the death of the generals was of no more importance than the death of a kulak or of a nameless party member. His best generals were expendable, as everyone was expendable. With wide-open eyes Stalin was committing the same crime which he accused 'the Trotskyists and doubledealers' of committing: he was offering hostages to the enemy. The name of this crime is treason.

At this time he was in that delirious mood, born of many years of conspiratorial activity, when it seemed to him that by offering the enemy a small advantage, he would be in a position to reap a far greater advantage. He hated the Trotskyists more than he hated Germany; hated Trotsky more than he hated Hitler. This hatred for Trotsky was personal, deeply engrained, and like some form of grief it increased with the years. His hatred for Hitler was impersonal, and careless; he had no understanding of the working of Hitler's mind. He believed that by offering up the generals as a sacrifice to Soviet-Nazi friendship, the purity of his intentions would be recognized. Hitler was not deluded. He accepted the sacrifice with good grace, but never for a moment forgot his ambition to destroy the Russian people and to populate Russia with Germans. But on one matter the Gestapo officers involved in the plot were deluded. They were deluded in their belief that the forged documents came as a surprise to Stalin. They did not know he had been receiving through General Skoblin weekly, and perhaps daily accounts, of their manufacture. As Hermann Behrens admitted many years later: 'We were the tools of Stalin.'

No one knows how the generals died; all those who took

part in the executions have long since passed away. According to a contemporary account they were executed not in the cellars but in the courtyard of the Lubyanka, not at night but in midmorning. An NKVD general drew a line across the courtyard in chalk, and wrote their names at intervals along the chalk-line. Then the prisoners were led out through a small door, their arms pinioned behind their backs, their insignia and badges of rank ripped off them. Tukhachevsky came first, followed by Putna and Uborevich and the rest. Each general was accompanied by his executioner, who took up a position immediately behind him. At a signal, trucks and automobiles in the courtyard revved up their engines. Marshal Blücher, the hero of many battles in the Far East, was placed in charge of the execution squad. When he whipped out his handkerchief, the NKVD gunmen slowly raised their pistols and shot each general in the back of the head. The bodies were then buried in the ravines of Khodynka Field, where nearly a thousand had died during a tragic stampede at the time of Tsar Nicholas II's coronation in 1894. Such was the contemporary report, but it is more probable that they were simply butchered in the cellars of the Lubyanka. In Stalin's mind no purpose was to be gained by granting them even a faintly ceremonial death. In the cellars they would die in that helpless anonymity which was the only mercy he granted to his victims.

The manner of these executions has been described by an NKVD official, who later defected to the West:

The cellar, which is really the basement of the building, is subdivided into a number of rooms, for the use of the executioners, for changing the prisoners' clothes and so on. Before execution the prisoner changes into white underclothes only; he knows that he has been sentenced and is about to be executed. He is led into the death cell, where he is shot in the back of the head by the executioner, either as he stands facing the wall or just as he walks into the cell. The weapon used is a 'TT' 8-shot automatic pistol. If the first shot does not dispatch the prisoner, the executioner follows it up with others. A doctor certifies death; his certificate is the last paper placed in the victim's file. A tarpaulin is spread on the floor of the cell, and a woman is employed to clean up afterwards. The bodies are taken away and buried immediately in a common grave. The names of important prisoners of state murdered in this way are published, but complete silence surrounds the lesser victims.

We do not know how the generals died, and even the date of their deaths is uncertain. According to a brief announcement which appeared in *Pravda* on June 2nd, General Gamarnik committed suicide the previous day. The announcement read: 'Gamarnik, ex-member of the Central Committee of the Party, fearing that his anti-Soviet machinations would be unmasked, has committed suicide.' Gamarnik, no more than Tukhachevsky, was likely to have committed suicide, and was probably shot. Tukhachevsky and the other generals were probably shot the same day. With two exceptions – Budyenny and Shaposhnikov – the eight generals who are supposed to have sentenced the other eight generals to death were themselves liquidated later, perhaps on the classic assumption that liquidators, real or imagined, must be liquidated in their turn.

The massacre of the generals was only the beginning, for the purge of the Red Army continued unabated. The purge was not confined to the Red Army. It reached down into the lowest strata of the country and into the Politburo itself. In his secret speech in 1956 Khrushchev declared that 'the number of arrests went up ten times between 1936 and 1937', and in the following year they must have gone up another ten times, and the executions in proportion. Stalin seemed determined to do the work of Hitler – to make Russia a desert ripe for German colonization.

In that empire of fear where thousands upon thousands were perishing for no known reason, the execution of the generals was only one incident among many. Insofar as it meant that the lives of a few men had been snuffed out, it was not even a matter of any great importance. But in the eyes of the Russians these generals were not ordinary men. At least three of them had acquired the dimensions of legend. They were the men who had led the revolution to victory. Tukhachevsky, the conqueror of Kolchak, murderer of the Kronstadt sailors and brilliant strategist of the Polish campaign, shared with Trotsky the honour of being one of the two authentic military geniuses thrown up by the civil war. Yakir, an Old Bolshevik, had broken through the iron ring around Odessa in 1919 and led his forces to victory. Uborevich defeated Denikin at Orel in 1920, and went on to defeat the last remaining White forces in the Far East in 1922. These men were the flower of the Red Army, the ablest and most experienced of the Soviet commanders, the men upon whom the defence of the country ultimately rested. Unlike the simple-minded Budyenny, a former sergeant in the Tsarist army, they were men of great personal distinction and courage; and they were not expendable. It mattered very little if commissars perished: the state could survive the loss. But it was another matter whether the state could survive the loss of its best generals.

After the generals had been executed, Stalin exacted from his people vociferous applause, which took the form of countless letters, telegrams, and testimonials. In all government offices, in all trades and industries, people were expected to signify their approval by putting their signatures to messages proclaiming the justice of the executions and the wisdom of Stalin in ordering them. Soviet writers and poets were also ordered to express their approval, and it was made clear to them that silence was dangerous. A testimonial to Stalin was therefore drawn up by the union of Soviet Writers, and a copy of the testimonial was sent to Boris Pasternak, who had a fairly close acquaintance with Tukhachevsky. He could not bring himself to sign it. He knew the risks, and was surprised to discover that he no longer cared. He felt that there was so much blood, so much terror, that it was no longer important whether he survived. He expected to be arrested at any moment. His wife was pregnant, and begged him to sign, but even then he refused. So it happened that the testimonial from the Union of Soviet Writers was sent to the Kremlin without his signature. He was not arrested. It seemed that no one troubled to read the testimonials and no one had dared to report to Stalin that Pasternak had not signed.

In this way the purge sometimes failed to terrify because it numbed the senses and made men almost indifferent to the crimes committed around them. They no longer cared whether they lived or died. For them Stalin played the role of impersonal vengeance, arbitrary and terrible beyond mortal calculation. He was a storm, a force of nature, something that must inevitably pass away, but while he lived there was nothing that anyone could do to prevent him from dealing death as he pleased. He was a name to be mentioned with bated breath, or not at all. No one in Russia wrote against this obscene monster which had grown up in their midst; no one dared to probe his character. Even in those writings which authors called 'literature for the drawer', because it was intended for publication only at some future and perhaps unimaginable time, they took care to write about him indirectly and parenthetically, employing all manner of disguises. So Boris Pasternak, writing about Stalin, disguised him as King Lear:

> There is the wilful, obstinate old man, there are the gatherings in the echoing palace hall, shouts, orders, and afterwards curses and sobs of despair merging with the rolls of thunder and the noises of the wind. But in fact, the only stormy thing in the play is the tempest at night, while the people, huddled in the tent and terrified, speak in whispers.
>
> Only the criminals in *King Lear* wield the notions of duty and honour; they alone are sensible and eloquent, and logic and reason assist them in their frauds, cruelties and murders. All the decent people are either silent to the point of being indistinguishable from each other or make obscure and contradictory statements which lead to misunderstandings. The positive heroes are the fools, the madmen, the dying, and the vanquished.

But in those days in Russia everyone except Stalin belonged to the ranks of the vanquished.

THE TRIAL OF BUKHARIN

THERE IS A SENSE in which the trials which convulsed Russia in the thirties were no more than sacrificial offerings to placate the demons consuming Stalin. There was about all of them a strange compulsive air. They did not belong to history and they did not obey historical laws, any more than an earthquake obeys historical laws. They reflected the passions of Stalin's soul, and they came into existence because his soul, in its despair and loneliness and humiliating sense of inadequacy, cried out for them. He saw enemies where none existed and struck out at them blindly; and as these shadowy and wholly imaginary enemies increased in numbers, proliferating because they were drenched in his own guilt, so he struck out all the more blindly, more violently, and more recklessly. Once he had begun to murder, there was no end to it.

If Stalin had spent the thirties alone in a cell of a madhouse, he would have gone on murdering, at the mercy of his compulsive mania of destruction. If there was nothing else to murder, he would have murdered ants. If there was nothing else living in the cell, he would have drawn the figures of men on the wall and then rubbed them out. His psychosis had reached that stage of murderous and frenzied exaltation which is only a hairbreadth from suicide. The wonder is that he did not kill himself or put on a gigantic show trial in which he became the defendant, the prosecutor and the judge, and finally condemned himself to death as a traitor to the Soviet people and the betrayer of the revolution.

Something of this kind did in fact happen. In the strict sense of the word the trials were not trials at all. There were no judges, no prosecutors, no defendants, no witnesses, no evidence. Nothing was said or done which was not the direct expression of the will of Stalin. He told the prosecutors and the defendants what to say, and he made sure that they followed the scenario he had prepared for them. Each defendant became the mouthpiece of Stalin, parroting the words learned in the torture chamber or in the silence and loneliness of his cell. Stalin took care that no one should speak out of turn. If by some mischance their own authentic voices were heard, they were immediately removed from the courtroom and tortured into admitting their error. There was no resilience in Stalin's mind. It never seemed to have occurred to him that there might be some advantage in staging more convincing trials, with some of the prisoners permitted to argue rationally in their defence. To the very end he remained the puppetmaster playing with his collection of broken dolls, jerking the strings, making them speak with his voice and dance to his tune.

Only a man with absolute power over the state could have brought these trials into existence. They were not necessary, and they were even dangerous to him, but he was not concerned with necessity or danger. They contributed nothing to his own power, for he had already brought the Russian people into a state of humiliating subjection to his will. His real enemies were not to be found among the ranks of the defendants, but in Berlin. He knew this, but chose not to permit this knowledge to override his judgement that Russia needed to be purged of its sins by placatory blood baths. He hardly cared who was punished. He chose his victims at random and threw them into the pit with a casual indifference. He killed the people he had loved and still loved, on whom he depended, and he killed people he had never heard of. He was not pursuing real enemies: he was pursuing ghosts, shadows, the disordered phantoms of his diseased mind. He was at the mercy of forces far stronger than himself, and he could not have stopped the purges or changed them in any way even if he had wanted to.

Trotsky was to claim that all the trials were in effect trials of Trotsky, but this was to misjudge the nature of Stalin's quarrel with the world, his ferocious judgement on himself. Stalin had long ago taken Trotsky's measure. He knew the essential barrenness of Trotsky's mind, his illimitable vanity and intellectual self-indulgence. He had learned from Trotsky how to put a people in chains, and he wanted no other lessons. The continual existence of Trotsky was valuable to him, for he could always blame the purges on non-existent Trotskyist conspiracies, while Trotsky himself, continually writing reckless speeches and conducting himself with the air of a practised conspirator, though the numbers of his co-conspirators never amounted to more than a handful, survived as a pleasant irritant. Trotsky was like those sores which give pleasure when they are scratched. Except during the days when Lenin was fighting for his life after his third stroke, Trotsky had never been a threat to him. He had not only taken Trotsky's measure, but he had outmanoeuvred him. By December 1940 Trotsky's usefulness was over. In a characteristic outburst of wanton destruction, he had Trotsky murdered.

While Trotsky claimed that the purges were directed at himself, others with more reason claimed that they were directed at the considerably more imposing figure of Lenin, long dead, but still capable of directing the course of events from the grave. Those charismatic qualities which he possessed during his life still seemed to radiate from his mausoleum in the Red Square. Almost singlehandedly he had hammered the revolution into shape. His image hung like an icon in every house, almost in every room. He had become the father image, to whom everyone turned in despair, hunting in his works for the appropriate text which would allay a grief. Stalin, too, found comfort in the sacred texts. He repeatedly consulted them and announced that his own chief claim to fame was that 'he followed humbly in the paths opened out by Lenin, the great leader of the world proletariat'. He wrote that only once in several centuries does a leader of Lenin's stature arise. At Lenin's grave he had uttered such a prayer as one normally addresses only to God. Lenin's greatness was undisputable, for the evidence of it lay all around him. But greatness can be irksome. Sometimes the courtiers around the throne find the greatness of the king so burdensome that they feel compelled to kill him. Stalin loved and hated Lenin, and he possessed an unyielding and continuing hatred for all those whom Lenin loved, and in the end destroyed them. He was merciless to Lenin's favourites, finding excuses to punish them not once but over and over again. He would place them on trial, send them into exile, recall them to face another trial where they were confronted with more imaginary evidence, and once again they would be punished with imprisonment and exile, and they were not killed until they had suffered the ultimate degradation and humiliation. Three times Zinoviev and Kamenev faced trial on trumped-up charges. When they were finally executed, Stalin had squeezed out of them every last vestige of their essential humanity: they were no more than empty husks.

Among the many ghosts whom Stalin pursued with relentless fury was the ghost of Lenin.

On March 2nd, 1938, there opened in a Moscow courtroom the third and last of the great trials. At the time no one knew it would be the last, and indeed there was no evidence that Stalin intended to bring them to an end. These trials had become as inevitable as the seasons.

Once again Stalin was absent, but his presence was felt throughout. He stage-managed and orchestrated the trial, supervised the machinery, saw to it that the principles recited their roles until they were word perfect, and did not permit the trial to take place until he was satisfied that the defendants would compromise themselves so completely that the whole world would applaud the inevitable death sentences. He had learned some lessons from the previous trials. This time there would be no mistakes – no one would slip out of the net.

Twenty-one prisoners were on trial. One towered above the rest. This was Bukharin, now fifty years of age. He was a brilliant theoretician, and the successor of Zinoviev as Chairman of the Third International. For twenty years he had been the intimate friend of Lenin, who described him in his Testament as 'not only the most valuable and most important theoretician in the party, but he may also be considered legitimately as the favourite of the entire party'. He stood accused of conspiracy, treason, and espionage. He pleaded guilty.

Once Bukharin had stood in a very special relationship to Stalin. At the time when Stalin was only one member of a triumvirate which included Zinoviev and Kamenev, Bukharin proved to be a useful ally. In Lenin there was combined a theoretician of astonishing daring and a man of action. He invented theories and related his actions to them, being always careful that there should be a theoretical support, however tenuous, for everything he did. At his death the Soviet state was almost completely lacking in theoreticians who commanded respect. Of those who remained Bukharin alone had a popular following and the intellectual skill to improvise theories by the hour. He was a small, good-natured, ebullient man with a high forehead, prominent cheekbones, a prominent nose, a wisp of reddish beard, an engaging and rather sly smile. He was interested in art, in literature and in people, and he was one of the very few Bolshevik leaders who were well-mannered and kindly. It was characteristic of him that when in the early years of the century he encountered Lenin for the first time, he wanted to talk about paintings rather than revolution.

Stalin, determined to rid the world of Zinoviev and Kamenev, looked upon Bukharin as a likely ally. He was the man of action in search of a Machiavelli. He needed an intellectual basis, or at least an intellectual pretext, for his rule, and Bukharin could supply it. Stalin knew Bukharin's strength and limitations, and he was perfectly prepared to divide the rule, giving him some high position in the Politburo, while retaining all effective power for himself. But Bukharin was wary. He despised Stalin, while retaining the intellectual's awed respect for the man of action. Once he was heard muttering that Stalin was nothing more than a new Genghis Khan, who had introduced a new barbarism. Stalin, whose ears were everywhere, attempted to placate him. 'Why are you against me, Kolya?' he asked. 'Why don't you come and take your seat beside me and direct the party and the country? You and I together will rule Soviet Russia. I am alone now, terribly alone, surrounded by a lot of idiots! What is Molotov but an official? And Kalinin? Nothing more than a crafty but unimportant village mayor who would like to end his days drinking tea with four lumps of sugar instead of two! And Voroshilov? A *feldwebel* like his father before him, nothing more nor less. So join with me and help me to set up the young Communists, and let all the others go to the devil! Why do you hate me, Kolya? You and I are the Himalayas!'

So perhaps they were, but Bukharin was never able to quite see himself on those lonely heights. A garrulous man, he made the mistake of telling others what Stalin had said. He told Voroshilov, who immediately ran to Stalin and begged for an explanation. Stalin denied the conversation had ever taken place. 'It is nothing more,' he said, 'than a despicable invention by an enemy of the party.'

Now frail and broken, Bukharin stood in the dock with twenty other prisoners in a high room with light-blue walls and gilded Corinthian columns, one of the ballrooms of the former Nobles' Club, now renamed the House of Trade Unions. Not many yards away, in a vast room known as the Hall of Columns, the body of Lenin had lain in state fourteen years before; and many, seeing Bukharin standing there, must have thought that Lenin had returned from the grave, for they were much alike, both being small, with high-domed foreheads, little goatees and mischievous smiles. But the time for smiling was over. Bukharin seemed to be no more than a shrunken ghost of himself.

Among the other prisoners were most of the surviving Old Bolsheviks who had achieved prominence and world fame. Among them were men whom Lenin admired almost as much as he loved Bukharin.

There was Alexey Rykov, short and squat, with a shock of thick hair and a small beard, a warm-hearted, stubborn, intelligent man, who spoke with a slight stutter. For six years, from 1924 to 1930, he had been Lenin's successor as Chairman of the Council of Commissars. Arkady Rosengoltz was a former Commissar of Foreign Trade and commander in chief of the Soviet Air Force; with his powerful face, large eyes, and small moustache, he had something of the look of a successful businessman. Faisullah Khodjayev, dark-skinned, curly-haired, handsome and clean-shaven, had long been a power in Soviet Central Asia. Nikolay Krestinsky, small, sharp-featured and courageous, usually wearing his steel-rimmed spectacles perched on the end of his nose, had been Vice-Commissar of Foreign Affairs. Christian Rakovsky, slender, wily, formidable in debate, had been Soviet Ambassador to Great Britain and France. Isaac Zelensky had been Chairman of the State Planning Board. Grigory Grinko, Vladimir Ivanov, Mikhail Chernov and Vasily Sharangovich had all been high-ranking commissars. Dr Lev Levin, the senior consultant of the medical department of the Kremlin, was one of the doctors who attended Lenin. Dr Dmitry Pletnev was the outstanding heart specialist in Russia. Benyamin Maximov had been Kuibyshev's secretary, and Pyotr Kryushkov had been the secretary of Gorky. There were also a few mysterious defendants who were perhaps police agents caught in their own web.

By some kind of poetic justice the ranks of the accused included Yagoda, the former pharmaceutical assistant who rose to become chief of the NKVD. Yagoda was listed in third place immediately after Bukharin and Rykov. He, too, was a ghost of himself, pale and shrunken, his hair and toothbrush moustache dead white. His face twitched, his hands trembled, and there were indications that he had been tortured more severely than the rest. Most of the prisoners had spent more than a year in jail.

The judge or president of the court was Ulrich, assisted by two military jurists. Once again Vyshinsky was the prosecutor, dapper in a blue suit and stiff white collar. His moustache was a little greyer than during the previous trial, and his voice a little shriller. He, rather than Ulrich, seemed to be in command of the trial. He was like a conductor supervising a large and varied orchestra, and he would make a little bow when some quick retort or damaging sally earned the applause of the audience, which consisted largely of officials of the secret police. A few diplomats and foreign correspondents were permitted to attend the trial. The audience sat on wooden benches, and one of the foreign observers commented that the ballroom had come to resemble a schoolroom.

The trial lasted for eleven days, interrupted by two days of rest. The official verbatim report, heavily expurgated, runs to eight hundred closely printed pages. It is an unsatisfactory report because the expurgated material, amounting to about a sixth of the trial proceedings, is clearly the most valuable and revealing. There are strange lacunae, sudden alterations of course, and inexplicable *non sequiturs*. Not all of them are due to the editors of the official verbatim report. The trial was many trials, and many layers of deceit were involved.

Sometimes questions remained unanswered because it was inconceivable that any answers could be formulated, because the actors in the drama were hopelessly miscast, or because men who have been tortured and who have learned their lines by rote speak out of turn and say the wrong thing. There were many moments during the trial when it seemed to be bogged down in hopeless confusion.

Stalin had directed the scenario of the first and second trials with the help of Vyshinsky and Yagoda; those three scenarists had sometimes succeeded in giving an air of verisimilitude to the trials, although the fact that only a small portion of the transcript of the trial of Zinoviev was published suggests that they were by no means satisfied with their first effort. The second trial was a more impressive performance with Radek, a highly skilled performer, playing the role assigned to him to perfection. With Yagoda no longer among the scenarists, the machinery began to creak and reveal itself in all its appalling banality and vulgarity. In the third trial the master's hand was lacking, and the puppetmaster himself had become a puppet.

Inevitably the eyes of the foreign correspondents were on Bukharin and Yagoda, the one an analyst of revolution, a professional theoretician whose face in normal times shone with the glow of his thoughts, the other a murderous pygmy with an undeniable talent for murder and conspiracy. Their presence together in the dock seemed almost incomprehensible, yet they were not totally dissimilar. They had both played the game of revolution with a casual indifference to ordinary human values. The gentle Bukharin would speak of 'the annihilation of the bourgeoisie' as though it was nothing more than a mathematical formula. Yagoda carried out the tasks of annihilation with a calm and deliberate intelligence, and it seems never to have occurred to him that a revolution that begins with the annihilation of the bourgeoisie must inevitably end with the annihilation of the annihilators.

Drugged by pain and suffering and the sense of the hopelessness of their position, both Bukharin and Yagoda confessed to crimes that they could never have committed. They confessed to being traitors, spies, Trotskyist wreckers, paid hirelings of intelligence services. Sometimes the effect of the drug would wear away, and they could be heard speaking with their own voices clearly and dramatically. At such times their confessions seemed to recede into the background, be-

coming no more than the vain gestures one makes to conciliate an implacable enemy. When they spoke in their own voices
they were immediately recognizable. They had been too close
to the sources of power to be able to play effectively any
roles except their own.

Others, too, sometimes spoke in their own voices. At almost
the first moments of the trial, after the charges had been read
and Bukharin, Rykov and Yagoda had all pleaded guilty,
Krestinsky jumped up and said: 'I do not admit my guilt!
I am not a Trotskyist! I have never been a member of the
Rightist-Trotskyist bloc, and I know nothing about the existence of such a bloc! I am not guilty of any of the crimes
with which I am charged! I have never had any relations
with the German intelligence service!'

There was stupefaction in the court. The small and nervous
Krestinsky had a powerful voice; his words carried conviction. He had been a former envoy to Germany and Vice-
Commissar of Foreign Affairs, but he had also been a jurist
and in the whole courtroom there was probably no one else
who was so familiar with the due processes of the law. He
knew what he was doing. He knew, among other things, that
unless he had confessed, he would not have been brought to
trial, for Stalin would have simply destroyed him in his prison
cell, as so many others had been destroyed. By denying his
guilt at the opening of the trial he had shown unparalleled
boldness, and he may have known that he would have to pay
for his courage.

An eye-witness at the trial has described how the whole
audience seemed to quiver as though it had been struck.
Vyshinsky tapped the papers in front of him and glanced
sharply at Ulrich, who whispered to his colleagues on the
bench, earnestly inquiring into the reasons for this sudden
volte-face. At last Vyshinsky asked him what he meant by
answering in this way. Krestinsky said: 'Before my arrest I
was a member of the Communist Party, and I am still a member.' This answer was intolerable, and it was now the turn of
Ulrich to elicit a confession of guilt, but Krestinsky was in
no mood to confess. He said: 'I have never belonged to the
Rightist-Trotskyist bloc, and I have never committed any
crime!' Ulrich turned away in disgust. The remaining prisoners were asked whether they pleaded guilty. All answered
that they were guilty, and Zelensky gave a little speech
enumerating his crimes at some length, concluding with the

rather surprising admission that he had been a secret agent of the Tsarist police. After the prisoners had pleaded, the court recessed for twenty minutes, presumably to inform Stalin of the extraordinary behaviour of one of the prisoners.

At this point in the trial nothing could be done to force a retraction from Krestinsky. Sergey Bessonov, a former counsellor at the Soviet Embassy in Berlin, was cross-examined. He testified that Krestinsky and Trotsky had met secretly at Merano in the autumn of 1933, a statement that Krestinsky vociferously denied, saying that he had been in Merano for a holiday with his wife and had seen neither Trotsky nor any of his followers. He asked that a letter written in 1927, in which he had broken off all relations with Trotsky, should be included in the evidence. The letter could not be found. Meanwhile Bessonov continued to describe the details of the Trotskyist conspiracy in which Krestinsky was so deeply involved, and sometimes he would return to the famous meeting at Merano which took place 'at the Hotel Meranhoff – I do not remember the exact name', at a time when 'it was easy for people to travel there and back because it was the grape season, and I fully concede that Trotsky might well have managed this, although it was extremely difficult for him to disappear from France'. Trotsky was depicted as a man seeking the help of the Germans to overthrow the government of the Soviet Union and preparing to deliver up the Ukraine to German hands. But all this was curiously unsatisfactory. Krestinsky could not be shaken from his statement that he had been forced to sign a full confession while being completely innocent, and at the end of the morning session the following exchange took place between Vyshinsky and Krestinsky:

VYSHINSKY: Accused Krestinsky, did you hear this testimony?
KRESTINSKY: I deny it.
VYSHINSKY: You deny it?
KRESTINSKY: I do.
VYSHINSKY: Absolutely?
KRESTINSKY: Absolutely.
VYSHINSKY: Of course.
KRESTINSKY: Of course.

No one supposed that this would be the end of the matter.

During the afternoon Grinko took the stand and confessed to his own participation in a vast conspiracy involving Bukharin, Rykov, Gamarnik, Yakir and others, who were preparing to kill Stalin and Yezhov and seize power. Krestinsky was also involved, and once again he denied having any knowledge of the conspiracy or of having arranged any contacts with the conspirators. There was some significance in the fact that Yezhov should be included among the list of people to be killed off: it testified perhaps to his increasing sense of his own importance, since he was helping to write the scenario. Rykov confessed to having embarked on a programme of wrecking, but when he was asked whether he had discussed overthrowing Stalin with the help of the Rightist-Trotskyist bloc in a conversation with Chernov in 1930, he answered: 'I do not remember having such a conversation with Chernov, but of course the possibility of such a conversation is not precluded.'

'. . . of course the possibility of such a conversation is not precluded' was a theme to be remembered throughout the trial, for many prisoners would say these words as they searched through their memory for the fallible signs of their guilt. The blueprints had been prepared, and they followed as best they could, but there were terrible moments when they could no longer remember the imaginary conversations they were ordered to remember. Sometimes, too, they forgot what positions they had occupied. Chernov could not remember whether in 1930 he had been Vice-Commissar of trade or merely a member of the Trade Commissariat. At various times all the prisoners suffered from memory failure, to the amusement of Vyshinsky, who protested that he could not understand how intelligent men could have risen to such high positions when they suffered from such lapses. 'It's astonishing,' he said. 'You only remember what you want to remember.' But prompted by Vyshinsky they could usually remember the most damning evidence in time to receive one of those ice-cold smiles with which the prosecutor celebrated his triumphs.

His triumphs were considerable, for all the accused except Krestinsky seemed eager to tie the noose tighter round their necks. If they were discussing secret meetings, they remembered the exact place and time and every word that was uttered. They especially remembered passwords and aliases. Ivanov said he went under the alias of 'Samarin' and had a spy number 163 when he was recruited into the Tsarist secret police in 1911, but he could not remember conversations which took place only a year before. 'There were so many conversations,' he said helplessly, 'and you can't remember everything.'

So the trial continued with the well-trained defendants showing themselves as adepts of self-incrimination, while Vyshinsky prompted and jerked the strings and it seemed possible that Krestinsky's refusal to plead guilty would simply be forgotten as the details of vast conspiratorial forces were unfolded. It was not until the evening of the second day of the trial that Vyshinsky turned to settle accounts with Krestinsky. The mysterious letter to Trotsky had been found and was read into the testimony. Dated November 27th, 1927, two weeks after Trotsky was expelled from the party, the letter was a carefully worded rebuttal of Trotsky's claim to be a political force. 'It is absurd to talk of preservation of influence over the masses,' Krestinsky had written. 'Where has it happened in history that a group which has been utterly defeated in the struggle owing to its mistakes has been able to preserve influence over the masses?' He pointed out that Trotsky's tactics had been profoundly erroneous, and the small groups of Trotskyists still at large in Russia, amounting to perhaps two hundred, would soon enough find themselves in prison or exile. It was a fair and legitimate attack on Trotsky and went far to proving that Krestinsky had never been a Trotskyist. Having read the letter into the record, Vyshinsky turned to Krestinsky and asked him what he meant when he refused to confess his guilt, thus performing an act of Trotskyist provocation.

There was a hush in the courtroom, for the reading of the letter had come as a surprise and there was a feeling that more surprises were in store. Then Krestinsky rose slowly and delivered his carefully worded reply:

KRESTINSKY: Yesterday, under the influence of a sharp momentary feeling of false shame, evoked by the atmosphere of the dock and the painful impression caused by the reading of the indictment, aggravated by my poor state of health, I could not bring myself to tell the truth. I could not bring myself to say that I was guilty. And instead of saying, *Yes, I am guilty*, I almost mechanically answered, *No, I am not guilty*.

VYSHINSKY: Mechanically?

KRESTINSKY: Before world opinion I had not the strength to say that I had long carried on a Trotskyist struggle against the Soviet regime. I beg the court to register my declaration that I fully and completely admit that I am guilty of all the gravest charges made against me personally and I admit my complete responsibility for the treason and treachery I have committed.

To foreign observers especially Krestinsky's admission came like a shock on exposed nerves. For the first time the emerging pattern of the trial appeared in all its undivided horror, for the little man with the thick spectacles and high white forehead, almost unknown outside of Russia, had revealed the mystery. From this moment onward it became clear that there was collusion between the prosecution and the defence. Krestinsky had been tortured during the previous night. For hours he had withstood injections and psychological pressure; he had been made to sit facing a battery of bright lights which had the effect of giving him screaming headaches and further injuring his already damaged eyes. Even then he had refused to admit his guilt. Finally he had bargained with his torturers. He would admit his guilt freely on one condition: that the testimony of his innocence should be entered into the record – the letter in which he denounced Trotsky and all his works. In this way, with extraordinary courage, he snatched victory from inevitable defeat.

During the following days Krestinsky played the game that was expected of him. He confessed to a vast number of crimes, described at great length his imaginary conversations with Trotsky at Merano, explained in detail how the government was to be overthrown, and implicated anyone and everyone. According to his testimony the conspirators were especially concerned to kill Molotov and Voroshilov, and to place Tukhachevsky in a position of power. From time to time Vyshinsky would slyly ask him whether he was telling the truth.

Already a great deal of time had been spent in examining minor figures, but the purpose of these examinations was becoming clear. The complex details of the plot were being hammered into some kind of recognizable shape. There were plots within plots, and sometimes one plot would become strangely entangled with another, at a different time and in another country and with different principals. The conspirators showed themselves capable of committing an amazing number of unrelated crimes.

Bukharin was examined for the first time on the fourth day. He looked pale and drawn, uncharacteristically apathetic, as though he scarcely realized where he was. Normally his features glowed with his thoughts and he gave a striking air of health and intelligence. His rosy cheeks had turned grey, his wisp of reddish beard was threaded with silver, there were bluish-purple hollows under his eyes.

Ordered to summarize the reasons why he pleaded guilty, Bukharin answered in a tired voice: 'I plead guilty to the sum total of crimes committed by this counter-revolutionary organization, irrespective of whether or not I knew of, whether or not I took a direct part in, any particular act. Because I am responsible as one of the leaders and not as a cog of this counter-revolutionary organization.'

It was a theme he repeated many times: he was guilty, overwhelmingly guilty, assuming full responsibility for all the criminal acts of his associates, and having made this admission, he went on to point out that it was inconceivable that he was ever in a position to commit these crimes, or wanted to commit them. True, he was the agent of a foreign power, he had agreed to dismember the Soviet Union, he had plotted to destroy Stalin: all these things were true, but only in principle. Each statement, taken in its proper context, was shown to be meaningless. He had always possessed the gift of analysing statements out of existence, giving lessons to Vyshinsky on splitting hairs. Unlike Radek, who incriminated everyone he disliked, Bukharin carefully avoided incriminating people. He was supremely interested in only two things: in elaborating for the last time his political and economic theories, and in throwing confusion and doubt into the enemy's camp. He was the master of amiable confusions. Sometimes the transcript reads like a page from *Alice in Wonderland*. A certain Slepkov had been sent to foment a kulak rebellion, and Bukharin assumed full responsibility for his mission.

VYSHINSKY: Did Slepkov fulfil your instructions?
BUKHARIN: Apparently he did.
VYSHINSKY: Apparently?
BUKHARIN: Yes.

VYSHINSKY: But did he speak to you about it?

BUKHARIN: I say that I met him once.

VYSHINSKY: Did Slepkov tell you how he had fulfilled your commission?

BUKHARIN: I don't remember him having said much.

VYSHINSKY: But why do you say that he did not speak in detail?

BUKHARIN: He spoke in general.

VYSHINSKY: He spoke in general?

BUKHARIN: Yes, in general.

VYSHINSKY: If he spoke in general, then he spoke?

BUKHARIN: If he spoke in general, then he spoke.

VYSHINSKY: But you have only just said that he did not speak.

BUKHARIN: He did not speak in general.

Because it was important that Bukharin should be made to appear an archcriminal rather than a famous theorist, Vyshinsky continually reminded him that he must avoid philosophical words and keep strictly to the point. Bukharin would point out that facts have philosophical implications, and philosophy could not therefore be outlawed from a criminal trial. There were questions, too, of semantics. Vyshinsky was incapable of understanding that there were some questions which could not be answered simply with a 'yes' or a 'no'. Sometimes Vyshinsky would lose patience. Once he exploded: 'Be so kind as not to instruct me how to conduct a preliminary investigation, the more so since you do not understand a thing about it.' Despairing of making Bukharin confess to treason except in the most general terms, Vyshinsky introduced as a witness Faisullah Khodjayev, a former head of the Uzbekistan Soviet, who had confessed during a preliminary examination that he had discussed treasonable affairs with Bukharin. Vyshinsky turned to Bukharin:

VYSHINSKY: Accused Bukharin, were you with Khodjayev at his country place?

BUKHARIN: I was.

VYSHINSKY: Did you carry on a conversation?

BUKHARIN: I carried on a conversation and kept my head on my shoulders all the time, but it does not follow from this that I dealt with the things of which Khodjayev speaks. This was the first conversation ...

VYSHINSKY: It is of no consequence whether it was the first

or not the first. Do you confirm that there was such a conversation?

BUKHARIN: Not such a conversation, but a different one, and also conspiratorial.

VYSHINSKY: I am not asking about conversations in general, but about this conversation.

BUKHARIN: In Hegel's *Logic*, the word *this* is considered to be the most difficult ...

In this way, with boundless effrontery, talking to Vyshinsky as an equal, Bukharin continued to answer the vague accusations with vague replies. He admitted that he had once contemplated arresting Lenin for twenty-four hours in 1918. However, there had been no plan to harm him in any way. He had simply contemplated, and then rejected, the idea of putting Lenin under temporary restraint.

VYSHINSKY: But the atmosphere was ...

BUKHARIN: The atmosphere was the atmosphere.

It was an unequal contest, and Bukharin, though ill, was so far the superior of Vyshinsky that the prosecutor would sometimes find himself tongue-tied, or else he would use threats to silence his formidable opponent.

VYSHINSKY: You are obviously a spy of an intelligence service. So stop pettifogging.

BUKHARIN: I never considered myself a spy, nor do I now.

VYSHINSKY: It would be more correct if you did.

BUKHARIN: That is your opinion, but my opinion is different.

VYSHINSKY: We shall see what the opinion of the court is.

One of the major mysteries about the trial was provided by the prosecution's determined efforts to show that the defendants were spies for the Nazis. Even Yagoda, who had been high in Stalin's councils, was accused of being a notorious spy. In his final plea he answered the charge with satisfying simplicity. He said: 'I am not jesting when I say that if I had been a spy, dozens of countries could have closed down their intelligence services.' On the subject of the murder of Kirov, he said: 'I was an organizer, but not an accomplice,' meaning perhaps that he helped to arrange the murder from the Kremlin, but left his agents in Leningrad to their own resources. In his cross-examination he seemed about to lift a curtain on that mysterious affair, and then fell silent.

VYSHINSKY: Did you personally take any measures to effect the assassination of Sergey Mironovich Kirov?

YAGODA: I personally?

VYSHINSKY: Yes, as a member of the bloc.

YAGODA: I gave instructions ...

VYSHINSKY: To whom?

YAGODA: To Zaporozhets in Leningrad. That is not quite how it was.

VYSHINSKY: We shall speak about that later. What I want now is to elucidate the part played by Rykov and Bukharin in this villainous act.

YAGODA: I gave instructions to Zaporozhets. When Nikolayev was detained ...

VYSHINSKY: The first time?

YAGODA: Yes. Zaporozhets came to Moscow and reported to me that a man had been detained ...

VYSHINSKY: In whose briefcase ...

YAGODA: There was a revolver and a diary. And he released him.

VYSHINSKY: And you approved of this?

YAGODA: I just took note of the fact.

VYSHINSKY: And then you gave instructions not to place obstacles in the way of the murder of Sergey Mironovich Kirov?

YAGODA: Yes, I did ... It was not like that.

VYSHINSKY: In a somewhat different form?

YAGODA: It was not like that, but it is not important.

VYSHINSKY: Did you give instructions?

YAGODA: I have confirmed that.

VYSHINSKY: You have. Be seated.

In this way Vyshinsky silenced Yagoda and put an end to any more revelations about the murder of Kirov. Yagoda had attempted to bring up the matter of Nikolayev's first arrest and inexplicable release, only to be met with an abrupt dismissal from Vyshinsky. Sometimes Yagoda himself would dismiss a subject in mid-passage, holding his head to one side, gaping, so weary that the effort of speaking seemed too much for him. He confessed to murdering Gorky, Kuibyshev, Menzhinsky, and Gorky's son. He spoke about these murders convincingly, with expert knowledge, but since he had arrested and executed millions of people these murders acquired the appearance of carefully planned dramatic scenes designed to give prominence to small and unimportant affairs while the real terror continued in the background.

In his last plea Yagoda begged for mercy. White-faced, in a low voice, he pleaded to be spared from death, and instead sentenced to imprisonment for life. There, behind bars, he would watch the building up of the country he had betrayed.

Bukharin, who knew he was to die, pleaded not for mercy but for his honour as a philosopher who had reached the end of the road, where hope had become an illusion:

> While I was in prison, I made a revaluation of my entire past. For when you ask yourself: 'If you must die, what are you dying for?' – an absolutely black vacuity suddenly rises before you with startling vividness. There was nothing to die for, if one wanted to die unrepentant. And, on the contrary, everything positive that glistens in the Soviet Union acquires new dimensions in a man's mind. This in the end disarmed me completely and led me to bend my knees before the party and the country. And when you ask yourself: 'Very well, suppose you do not die; suppose by some miracle you remain alive, again what for? Isolated from everybody, an enemy of the people, in an inhuman position, completely isolated from everything that constitutes the essence of life ...' And at once the same reply arises. And at such moments, Citizen Judges, everything personal, all the personal incrustation, all the rancour, pride, and a number of other things, fall away and disappear.

On March 13th, 1938, at 4 am, the judges who had retired early in the evening to decide upon their verdict returned to pronounce judgement on the prisoners. All except three were sentenced to death. The executions were carried out the same night.

Many years before – it was in fact twenty years before – Bukharin caught sight of Trotsky in one of the corridors of the Smolny, and ran up to him. The Constituent Assembly had just been smashed, and the Soviet government was solidly in power. Bukharin threw his arms round Trotsky, weeping.

'What are we doing?' he exclaimed. 'We are turning the party into a dungheap!'

THE WARS

The friendship of the peoples of Germany and the Soviet Union, cemented by blood, has every reason to be lasting and firm.

THE STRANGE ALLIANCE

LIKE A SLEEPWALKER Stalin moved from one disaster to another. He was so sure of himself, so certain of his power, that he would say and do things which had no relation to reality. He compiled his endless death lists with careful devotion, and punished minor officials with careless abandon. No one questioned him or warned him or – so far as is known – made any serious plans to kill him. From the pinnacle of absolute power he alone decided what was good for the country and how many men should be killed each year.

The years 1937-38, when Nikolay Yezhov nominally ruled over the secret police, were perhaps the most dreadful in all Russian history. The *Yezhovshchina*, that period of twenty-five months that seemed like a quarter of a century, demonstrated only that the Russians possessed a limitless endurance of suffering. No one was safe, the secret police least of all. In the nineteenth century the Marquis de Custine paid awed tribute to the cruelty of the Russian peasants. 'Murder is designed and executed in an orderly manner,' he said. 'There is no rage, no emotion, no words.' So it was during those years when the murder machine was let loose over Russia.

Even Stalin felt the heavy weight of terror, and at last in December 1938, having mowed down most of his enemies, he decided to take a vacation at Sochi on the Black Sea coast. It was a long vacation, the longest he ever took after he assumed power, for he did not return to Moscow until the following March, in time for the Eighteenth Congress.

During his vacations Stalin was usually accompanied by a large staff, which included two or three commissars. Most of his secretaries were with him. At the head of his secretariat was the imperturbable Alexander Poskrebyshev, small, fat, pock-marked, bald and red-cheeked, who resembled an office clerk in nineteenth-century Russia. There was nothing about Poskrebyshev to suggest that he wielded immense power. He was not only Stalin's secretary. He was the boon companion, the colleague who shared Stalin's amusements, and listened tirelessly to Stalin's occasional monologues. He was remarkable for his silence, and his invisibility.

The revolution threw up an extraordinary number of skilled

mechanics of power, men who left their work benches to become Red Army commanders and commissars. It also threw up a host of clerks and doorkeepers, who behaved exactly like the clerks and doorkeepers of Tsarist Russia. Every commissariat had its secretariat. The secretaries fought for power, connived and intrigued, denounced everyone who threatened their positions. The secretaries attached to Stalin were in particularly favourable positions. Some became commissars, others vice-commissars. Mekhlis, for example, formerly Stalin's secretary in charge of the press, later became Vice-Commissar for Defence. Yezhov, who gave his name to an age of suffering, had also been one of Stalin's personal secretaries. The general fate of the secretaries was to move into positions of power and then to be liquidated. Only Poskrebyshev, staying close to Stalin's side, remained unharmed as long as Stalin lived. He was shot a few hours after Stalin's death.

The trail of Poskrebyshev cannot be followed with any degree of certainty, for it merges into the trail of Stalin. We see him first in 1922 when at the age of thirty he performed 'special duties' for the Central Committee. In the following year he is already in the service of Stalin. In March 1939 he receives the Order of Lenin 'for many years of exemplary self-sacrifice in the apparatus of the leading organs of the Central Committee'. The date is important, for it suggests that about this time Poskrebyshev had emerged as a leading member of the policy-making board which constituted Stalin's brain trust. For many years he had been chief of the Secret Department nominally attached to the Central Committee, but in fact attached to Stalin. His power was vast, reaching out over the length and breadth of Russia, and its extent was incalculable. He decided whom Stalin should see and not see, what documents he should read and not read, what policies should be discussed, and what laws should be enacted. He had become the *éminence grise*, whose every word and gesture affected the destiny of Russia.

Unlike the secretaries who became commissars, Poskrebyshev never acquired the habits of grandeur. He worked eighteen hours a day, lived quietly and modestly, had no vices, and devoted himself to Stalin's service. Wherever Stalin was, Poskrebyshev was always in the next room. His sole recreation was billiards, and he seems to have chosen to play billiards only because this was one of Stalin's favourite recreations. This small, fat, ugly, colourless man, whom no one would ever notice in a crowd, was a figure of pure evil.

In the spring of 1939 Stalin had come to the parting of the ways. The Munich Pact of September 1938, and the Anglo-French guarantees to Poland, Rumania and Turkey in March 1939 had decisively altered the situation. The Spanish Civil War had ended disastrously, and the Popular Front had failed in its objective. Stalin was now prepared for an accommodation with Hitler. For some months secret negotiations had been conducted through the Soviet embassy in Berlin with high Nazi officials, especially with the German generals who in the twenties had shown a remarkable interest in the Red Army. Poskrebyshev was placed in charge of these negotiations, which were always tentative, obscure, and evasive, but which nevertheless opened the way for the more deliberate negotiations which came later.

Stalin's speech at the Eighteenth Congress in March 1939 was one of the most remarkable he ever made. The turgid prose has vanished; he speaks clearly and simply, like a man who has pushed away the last remnants of doubt, and who knows exactly where he is going. In his own eyes the opposition had been crushed, and he was now free to devote himself to vast strategic plans which would affect the destiny of the world for generations to come. 'In the main, socialism has come into being in the USSR,' he declared, and he explained that this was due to the practical implementation of the course embarked upon at the Seventeenth Congress held five years before, when he had called for 'the complete liquidation of the opposition'. The opposition no longer threatened the security of the state. By crushing the opposition, he had strengthened the state and brought it to a position of unparalleled strength. He said:

In 1937 Tukhachevsky, Yakir, Uborevich and other fiends were sentenced to be shot. After that, the elections to the Supreme Soviet of the USSR were held. In these elections 98·6 per cent of the total vote was cast for the Soviet power. At the beginning of 1938 Rosengoltz, Rykov, Bukharin and other fiends were sentenced to be shot. After that, the elections to the Supreme Soviets of the Union Republics were held. In these elections, 99·4 per cent of the total vote was cast for the Soviet power.

Never had there been such unanimity in the Soviet Union! Never had the people of Russia shown such trust and abiding confidence in their government! He laughed at the foreign pressmen who wrote that the purges had 'shaken' the Soviet power and 'demoralized' the people. 'To listen to these foreign drivellers,' he said, 'one would think that if the spies, murderers and wreckers had been left at liberty to work at murder and spying and wrecking without let or hindrance, the Soviet organizations would have been far sounder and stronger.' Paraphrasing a famous statement by Lenin, he explained that 'the humblest Soviet citizen, being free from the fetters of capital, stands head and shoulders above any high-placed foreign bigwig, whose neck wears the yoke of capitalist slavery'.

Lenin had spoken when the Soviet state was still fighting for its life. Now it was another story. The Soviet state, according to Stalin, was now the strongest in the world.

The tone of his speech to the Eighteenth Congress was one of unrelieved triumph. 'We have outstripped the capitalist countries as regards technique of production and rate of industrial growth,' he said, and he supplied figures showing that the volume of industrial output of the Soviet Union equalled the combined volume of industrial output of the United States, Great Britain, France, Italy and Germany.

Volume of Industrial Output Compared with 1929
(1929=100)

	1934	1936	1938
USA	66·4	88·1	72·0
Great Britain	98·8	·115·9	112·0
France	71·0	79·3	70·0
Italy	80·0	87·5	96·0
Germany	79·8	106·3	125·0
USSR	238·3	382·3	477·0

These magnificent figures, whether concocted by the State Economic Planning Board or by Stalin himself in his idle moments, were solemnly presented to the Eighteenth Congress as proof that Russia had outstripped a combination of all the Western capitalist powers. He did not mention that the figures rested on no known statistical evidence, and that at best they were purely relative, and therefore they could not be usefully compared. His resounding verdict was that Russia led the world in industry. With equal satisfaction he pointed out that the visible gold reserves of Germany, Italy and Japan were less than those of Switzerland.

Stalin was in a mood to present statistical evidence to demonstrate the triumph of Soviet society, and there are no fewer than thirteen statistical tables in his speech. Never had so much grain been grown, never had so many railroads been laid down, never had so many tractors been built. He presented the portrait of a society flourishing as never before, while the capitalist countries were sinking helplessly into chaos, one crisis following another.

He reserved his greatest contempt for the British, French, and Americans, who were soon to be his allies. He took care not to attack Germany. 'They' had let Germany invade Austria: 'they' had permitted the march on the Sudetenland and abandoned Czechoslovakia to her fate; 'they' were vociferously calling upon the Germans to march farther east into the Ukraine; 'they' were poisoning the atmosphere and attempting to provoke a conflict between Germany and the Soviet Union without any visible grounds.

As for the Germans, if they were so foolhardy as to attack Russia, let them listen to the story of the gnat and the elephant:

Imagine: The gnat comes to the elephant and says perkily, 'Ah! brother, how sorry I am for you ... Here you are without any landlords, without any capitalists, with no national oppression, without any Fascist bosses. Is that a way to live? ... As I look at you, I can't help thinking that there is no hope for you unless you annex yourself to me. Well, so be it. I allow you to annex your tiny domain to my vast territories ...'

When the laughter subsided, he went on to attack the Western democracies with considerably more venom than he had ever used before. He pointed to their criminal provocations and the inevitable punishment they would receive when the Germans 'refuse to meet their bills and send them to Hell'. As for the Soviet Union, it stood for peaceful relations with all nations and the support of all nations which were the victims of aggression. Germany received a slight tap on the wrists; the Western democracies were condemned as *provocateurs*, imperialists, and worse.

The tone of Stalin's speech could not fail to please Hitler, who thought he detected the long-promised signs of a new orientation in Soviet foreign policy. When Ribbentrop flew to

Moscow in August to sign a non-aggression pact and a secret protocol, he mentioned that Hitler had interpreted the speech favourably as expressing Stalin's desire for a *rapprochement* with Germany. Stalin replied: 'That was exactly my intention,' and then Molotov raised his glass and toasted Stalin, saying: 'It was Stalin himself who, in his speech of March, which was well understood in Germany, brought about this reversal in political relations.'

Stalin's speech was therefore decisive. With his theory that the Western democracies were effete *provocateurs*, loudly provoking the Germans to new conquests, he set the stage for the future wars. His task, as he saw it, was to cut the throats of the *provocateurs*, or at least to render them powerless.

Stalin saw in Hitler a man who resembled himself more than he resembled any other man. They had both risen from obscurity and taken power by arbitrary and savage means; both were utterly indifferent to the social side of life; both were concerned exclusively with the manipulation and growth of power. During World War II Hitler described Stalin as 'a tremendous personality, an ascetic who has taken the whole of that gigantic country firmly in his iron grasp'. On another occasion Hitler said: 'Stalin is half beast, half giant. The people can rot for all he cares.' Neither Hitler nor Stalin was remarkable for any particular concern for the people.

As Hitler and Stalin moved towards one another in the late spring and summer of 1939, they took care not to appear over-eager. The negotiations were conducted in an atmosphere of delicacy and refinement. Great Britain, which had concluded a pact of mutual assistance with Poland on April 6th, increasingly assumed the aspect of a common enemy. While Stalin conducted secret negotiations with Germany, Molotov conducted negotiations with Britain designed to camouflage the progress of his understanding with Germany. When British and French military missions reached Moscow on August 11th, Stalin and Hitler were already sketching out the programme for a non-aggression pact and a war on Poland. Ten days later a trade treaty between Germany and the Soviet Union had been signed, Molotov had drawn up the draft of the non-aggression pact, and Stalin had received a personal message from Hitler asking him to receive Ribbentrop in Moscow for a final discussion on the pact and the inevitable secret protocol. Stalin's reply came in less than twenty-four hours:

To the Chancellor of the German Reich, A. Hitler:

I thank you for the letter. I hope that the German-Soviet Non-aggression Pact will mark a decided turn for the better in the political relations between our countries.

The peoples of our countries need peaceful relations with each other. The assent of the German Government to the conclusion of a Non-aggression Pact provides the foundation for eliminating the political tension and for the re-establishment of peace and collaboration between our countries.

The Soviet Government has authorized me to inform you that they agree to Herr von Ribbentrop's arriving in Moscow on August 23rd.

J. STALIN

When the message was conveyed to Hitler, he gave way to a hysterical outburst of joy. Everything had happened as he desired it, for the non-aggression pact meant, if it meant anything, that Russia would remain neutral during the wars he intended to inflict upon the world. He would crush Poland, then the West, and with an empire extending to the borders of India he would have no difficulty in destroying Russia. One of his intimates has described the scene as Hitler heard the message, turned to the wall and began hammering at it with his fists, all the while uttering inarticulate cries of joy, finally shouting exultantly: 'I have the world in my pocket!' On the following day he summoned his General Staff and ordered them to prepare for the invasion of Poland. 'Close your hearts to pity! Act brutally!' he told them. 'Be steeled against all signs of compassion!'

Ribbentrop flew into Moscow at noon on August 23rd, and after a brief lunch at the German Embassy he drove to the Kremlin. The first meeting with Stalin and Molotov lasted three hours. Ribbentrop was accompanied by Count von der Schulenberg, the German ambassador, and Gustav Hilger, counsellor at the German Embassy. The atmosphere was cordial. Stalin broached the question of giving Russia the Latvian ports of Windau and Libau on the Baltic. Ribbentrop telephoned later in the day to Hitler, who ordered an atlas to be brought to him, glanced at a map of Latvia, and answered promptly: 'Yes, certainly.' If Stalin had asked for Persia or China, he would have agreed just as promptly.

Ribbentrop had dinner at the German Embassy, and then

resumed his talks with Stalin. The discussion ranged over a wide area. Japan, Italy, Turkey, England, France and the Anti-Comintern Pact were discussed. Stalin observed that the Anti-Comintern Pact had frightened principally the City of London and the English shopkeepers. With heavy humour Ribbentrop replied that this was true and he imagined that Stalin was surely less frightened than the English financiers, and he went on to tell Stalin a joke, which had originated among Berliners, who were well-known for their wit and humour, that Stalin would yet join the Anti-Comintern pact himself. Only once did Stalin show any signs that he had his wits about him. Ribbentrop wanted to insert in the preamble of the agreement a paragraph concerning the friendly, not to say affectionate relations existing between Germany and the Soviet Union. Stalin objected that 'the Soviet government could not suddenly present to the public assurances of friendship after they had been covered with pails of manure by the Nazi government for six years.' Ribbentrop good-humouredly accommodated himself to Stalin's wishes.

The macabre spectacle continued until the early hours of the morning. Ribbentrop continued to denounce the enemies of peace (unnamed) and the friendship existing between the two greatest powers on earth (Germany and Russia). 'The Germans,' he said, 'desire peace,' and Stalin repeated the words and paid tribute to Hitler as the guardian of peace. Champagne was brought, and Stalin proposed a toast to the Führer, saying: 'I know how much the German people loves its Führer. I should therefore like to drink to his health.'

Molotov drank to the health of Ribbentrop, and soon there were general toasts to the non-aggression pact, to the new era of German-Soviet relations, and to Germany and the Soviet Union. When the photographers came in about midnight, Stalin and Ribbentrop were both smiling from ear to ear, as though they had performed some act of universal benevolence and rejoiced over their accomplishments.

At one o'clock in the morning the non-aggression pact and the secret protocol were solemnly signed by Ribbentrop and Molotov. The protocol remained unknown in the West until after the war, when men had grown so accustomed to physical horrors that they could scarcely breathe a sigh for horrors committed on paper. The secret protocol was a diabolic document, for it ensured that Poland would be destroyed and that the war would extend across the whole earth:

SECRET ADDITIONAL PROTOCOL

On the occasion of the signature of the Non-aggression Pact between the German Reich and the Soviet Union the undersigned plenipotentiaries discussed in strictly confidential conversations the question of the boundary of their respective spheres of influence in Eastern Europe. These conversations led to the following conclusions:

1. In the event of a territorial or political rearrangement in the areas belonging to the Baltic States (Finland, Estonia, Latvia, Lithuania), the northern boundary of Lithuania shall represent the boundary of the spheres of influence of Germany and the USSR. In this connection the interest of Lithuania in the Vilna area is recognized by each party.

2. In the event of a territorial and political rearrangement of the areas belonging to the Polish State, the spheres of interest of Germany and the USSR shall be bounded approximately by the line of the rivers Narew, Vistula and San.

The question of whether the interests of both parties make desirable the maintenance of an independent Polish State and how such a state should be bounded can only be definitely determined in the course of further political developments.

In any event, both Governments will resolve this question by means of a friendly agreement.

3. With regard to South-eastern Europe attention is called by the Soviet side to its interests in Bessarabia. The German side declares its complete political disinterestedness in these areas.

4. This protocol shall be treated by both parties as strictly secret.

Moscow, August 23rd, 1939

For the German	Plenipotentiary of the
Government	Government of the USSR
VON RIBBENTROP	V. MOLOTOV

Everything about this document was fraudulent, including the date, for it was signed in the early hours of the morning of August 24th. Since it was secret – the German version uses the words *streng geheim* – it could be regarded in the same light

as a document signed by potential murderers on the subject
of the disposal of corpses. Germany and Russia were not in
friendly alliance. Stalin and Hitler were conspirators giving
aid and comfort to one another as they both prepared to
plunge their knives into Poland.

As Ribbentrop was about to leave the Kremlin, Stalin took
him by the arm and said: 'The Soviet government takes the
new pact very seriously.' He added pathetically: 'I can guarantee on my word of honour that the Soviet Union will not
betray its partner.'

His word of honour, as Ribbentrop well knew, was not to
be trusted; nor could Hitler's word of honour be trusted; nor
could the word of honour of any of those who took part in
the negotiations be trusted. At dawn on the first of September
the German armies poured across the Polish frontier, and the
Second World War had begun. Stalin who had not expected
such a rapid attack was nonplussed. Molotov was ordered
to learn through the German ambassador the date when the
German army could be expected to reach the gates of Warsaw; on that date Stalin would hurl the Red Army into
Poland 'in order to protect Soviet interests'. By September
10th the Germans reached Warsaw, and still Stalin hesitated,
fearing, as he told Churchill and Roosevelt at Teheran, 'the
war which was approaching the frontiers of the USSR with
giant strides'. A week later he acted, and on September 17th
the Red Army crossed the frontiers of Poland. The German
and Russian armies met at Brest Litovsk, where twenty-one
years earlier the Germans had dictated peace terms to a Soviet
government which was only a few weeks old.

Great Britain and France had declared war on Germany,
and Russia now assumed the role of a compliant ally of the
Third Reich. Communist agents in Great Britain and France
were ordered to hinder the war effort. The Soviet Union became a base for military supplies pouring into Germany.
Arrangements were made for the building of ships for the
German navy in the dockyards of Leningrad; Soviet oil replenished the German war machine. There still remained the
problem of whether Poland should be allowed to exist in the
form of a small rump state dividing the two powers. Stalin
saw his opportunity; he offered to exchange the imaginary
rump state for a real Lithuania. Hitler regarded the proposal
with equanimity, and sent Ribbentrop to Moscow for the
second time to sign a 'German-Soviet Boundary and Friend-

ship Treaty'. Once more there was a secret protocol. 'The territory of the Lithuanian state,' read the secret protocol, 'falls to the sphere of influence of the USSR, while the province of Lublin and parts of the province of Warsaw fall to the sphere of influence of Germany.' There was a further clause stating that Polish agitators on both sides of the new frontier would be suppressed. Poland was drowned in blood and washed off the map; and the secret police of the Nazis and the Communists co-operated to extinguish Polish agitation wherever it occurred.

The cordial relations between Stalin and Hitler continued through the autumn and winter. In private Hitler confessed to a growing admiration for Stalin. In November he was telling Admiral Raeder that he feared only that Stalin might be replaced by some extremist. A year later he was telling Mussolini that as long as Stalin was alive, the Russians would never take the initiative against Germany. He had judged the man well.

On December 21st, 1939, Stalin celebrated his sixtieth birthday, and Hitler telegraphed his greetings: 'Best wishes for your personal wellbeing as well as for the prosperous future of the peoples of the friendly Soviet Union.' Stalin replied the same day: 'The friendship of the peoples of Germany and the Soviet Union, cemented by blood, has every reason to be lasting and firm.'

Hitler had spoken of friendship, but this was an illusion. Stalin had spoken of blood, but this was not an illusion. The cement was provided by the blood of Poland.

THE WINTER WAR

WHEN THE RED ARMY and the Wehrmacht struck into Poland, Stalin began to look closely at his western defences. The agreements signed by Molotov and Ribbentrop were no more than scraps of paper which depended for their validity on the balance of brute forces; and he was not a man to be enchanted by written agreements of any kind. The balance of forces might change; France might be overrun, Great Britain might make common cause with Germany; he had no way of knowing what direction the war would take, and therefore must prepare against all eventualities. What he wanted – and he wanted it urgently – was security against the massive power of the Wehrmacht if Hitler should decide to throw it against Russia: it was in the hope of delaying that attack indefinitely that he had entered into an alliance with a natural enemy.

Stalin had very little knowledge of military strategy, but his mind moved easily among broad geopolitical concepts. He saw that if he extended the western boundaries of Russia, he would be able to make it all the more difficult for the Germans to launch an attack. By acquiring space he would gain time. Accordingly in September he ordered the Red Army to take up defensive positions in Latvia, Lithuania and Estonia. The countries were too small to offer resistance. It was explained that these were merely garrison troops who would be removed when the emergency was over, and for the moment no effort was made to change the form of government of the Baltic states. Stalin then turned his attention to Finland.

To subdue Finland, or to send troops into the country, or to establish powerful forts along the Finnish coast were not easy matters. Unlike Latvia, Lithuania and Estonia, Finland possessed a powerful army. Throughout its history it has fought ferociously for its independence, so that even under the Tsars it retained the right of self-government under a governor general. During the last days of 1917 the new Bolshevik government declared for the independence of Finland, and ironically it was Stalin himself who was sent to Helsinki to proclaim the independence of the country while simultaneously attempting to overthrow the government. The attempt failed, and thereafter he seems to have retained a considerable respect for the Finns.

In the autumn of 1939 he was still in a mood to deal with Finland leniently. He wanted to transform the Gulf of Finland into a Russian lake and to strengthen the security of Leningrad by moving the frontier northward along the Karelian Isthmus. Leningrad was only twenty miles from the Finnish frontier, within reach of shells from long-range guns, and though the Finns had not set up any long-range guns there was in theory nothing to prevent them. In exchange for the islands in the Gulf of Finland, the lease of the peninsula of Hanko and a small area near Petsamo which threatened the approaches to Murmansk, Stalin was prepared to do some horse-trading by offering the Finns a considerable area of

Soviet Karelia. The new maps had already been drawn up when the Finnish government was invited to send a delegation to Moscow to hear the Russian demands. On October 12th, 1939, the delegation had its first meeting with Stalin.

The delegation was headed by Juho Kutsi Paasikivi, who at the time was minister in Stockholm. He was one of the forgotten men of Finnish history, an elder statesman, a scholar and a man of furious energy – he had been known to throw inkpots at unruly subordinates – and his opinions on Communism were well known. He had helped to smash the Red uprising in 1918, and he was the premier of the government which was established immediately afterwards. He had been deliberately selected in order to demonstrate that the Finns were in no mood to be dictated to. He was sixty-nine years old.

The first meeting was curiously informal. Molotov, who opened the conference, asked whether Finland would agree to a mutual assistance pact similar to those which had been concluded with the Baltic states. Paasikivi replied that this was unthinkable in the light of the traditional neutrality of Finland. The Russians had expected as much, and did not pursue the matter further. When the exploratory skirmishing was concluded, Stalin took over and announced that in order to safeguard Leningrad it had become necessary to take possession of certain islands and territories which he described briefly, and in compensation he was prepared to cede to Finland a district in eastern Karelia twice as large as the districts to be ceded to the Soviet Union. There the matter rested, and the meeting was resumed two days later after the Finnish delegation had received its instructions from Helsinki.

The instructions were brief, and called for the delegates to hold out against the Russian demands, and if possible to limit the discussion to the three islands, Seiskari, Lavansaari, and Peninsaari, which lay closest to the Soviet shore. An instruction paper, drawn up by the Finnish General Staff, sought to show that no peril threatened the Gulf of Finland, and this was read out at the meeting. Stalin was not prepared to listen to theoretical discussions. He said that while no doubt the paper might cause lively debate if printed in a military journal, he refused to take part in such a debate. When Paasikivi pointed out that the new frontier would be quite impossible on economic grounds alone, Stalin replied: 'Soldiers never think in economic terms.'

He saw himself as a soldier, a master strategist, determined to neutralize the enemy by complicated manoeuvres before the battle had begun. Inevitably he found himself thinking back to the time when Yudenich threatened Petrograd during the civil war, and to his own achievements in capturing the forts of Krasnaya Gorka and Seraya Loshad. The capture of these small forts was his solitary claim to military fame. He was immersed in his memories of the civil war, and he thought often about the shadowy naval units flying the British flag which had appeared briefly off Koivisto to support Yudenich before vanishing into the northern mists. For Stalin Russia was especially vulnerable at the Gulf of Finland.

A Finnish secretary attached to the delegation took notes while Stalin was speaking. It was a long speech, and Stalin went into considerable detail to show the reasonableness of his demands. He said:

It is a law of naval strategy that passage into the Gulf of Finland can be blocked by the crossfire of batteries on both shores as far out as the mouth of the Gulf. Your memorandum supposes that the enemy cannot penetrate into the Gulf. But once a hostile fleet is in the Gulf, the Gulf cannot be defended.

You ask which power could attack us – Britain or Germany? With Germany we now have good relations, but everything in this world can change. Yudenich attacked through the Gulf of Finland and later the British did the same. This can happen again. If you are afraid to give us bases on the mainland, we can dig a canal across Hanko Neck, and then our base won't be on Finnish mainland territory. As things stand now, both Britain and Germany are able to send strong naval forces into the Gulf of Finland. I doubt whether you would be able to avoid an incident in that case. Britain is already putting pressure on Sweden for bases. Germany is doing the same. Once the war between these two is over, the fleet of the victor will sail into the Gulf of Finland.

You ask, why do we want Koivisto? I'll tell you why. I asked Ribbentrop why Germany went to war with Poland. He replied, 'We had to move the Polish border farther from Berlin.' Before the war the distance from Posen to Berlin was about 200 kilometres. Now the border has been moved to 300 kilometres farther east. We ask that the distance from Leningrad to the border should be 70 kilometres. This is our

minimum demand, and you must not think we are prepared
to reduce it piece by piece. We can't move Leningrad, so
the border has to move. Regarding Koivisto, you must bear
in mind that if sixteen-inch guns were placed there, they
could entirely prevent the movement of our fleet in the in-
most extremity of the Gulf. We ask for 2,700 square kilometres and offer more than 5,500 in exchange. Would any
other great power do that? No. We are the only ones that
simple.

So, with cajolery and threats, Stalin pursued the argument
in favour of his 'just demands', always emphasizing that they
were dictated by the circumstance of the time. He merely
wanted a little piece of land and was prepared to give a much
larger piece in return. Was there anything wrong in trading
land? Russia had sold Alaska to the United States, Spain had
ceded Gibraltar to England. It was inevitable that there should
be slight border changes from time to time. To these arguments Paasikivi replied by reminding Stalin that Finland
must retain its independence and neutrality at all costs. Thereupon Stalin said that matters had reached a dangerous crisis
– the Finns had already evacuated their cities, mobilized and
sent troops to the border – and the acceptance of his reasonable demands could not be delayed indefinitely. The Finns
were given typewritten copies of the minimum demands and
ordered to report back to Moscow within a week.

Before leaving, Paasikivi pointed out that the surrender of
Hanko with the establishment of a Soviet garrison and naval
base was not likely to be accepted by the Finnish Diet.

PAASIKIVI: The Hanko Neck concession and the concession
   of the area on the Isthmus are exceptionally difficult matters.
STALIN: It's nothing, really. Look at Hitler. The Posen frontier was too close to Berlin for him, and he took an extra
   three hundred kilometres.
PAASIKIVI: We want to remain at peace and keep away from
   all incidents.
STALIN: That's impossible.
PAASIKIVI: How do these proposals of yours agree with your
   famous slogan, 'We do not want a crumb of foreign territory, but neither do we want to cede an inch of our
   territory to anyone.'

STALIN: I'll tell you. In Poland we took no foreign territory.
And now this is a case of exchange. So we will expect you
back on the twentieth or the twenty-first.

MOLOTOV: We'll sign the agreement on the twentieth and give
you a dinner the next day.

PAASIKIVI: When we come back will depend on the government.

In this ominous way the meeting came to an end. The Finns
were under no illusions about what was at stake. They had
received no formal ultimatum. No one had shouted, no inkpots were thrown. Stalin had made his points with bluff good
humour, as when he spoke about cutting a canal across Hanko
Neck so that the Finns would no longer need to regard it as
part of their own territory. Reaching Helsinki on October 16th,
Paasikivi told reporters that he found Stalin a pleasant fellow
with a sense of humour, but that was only part of the
truth. Stalin enjoyed bantering good-humouredly with his
victims.

Confronted by Soviet power, the Finns could only wait on
events and pray that a war could be averted. Sweden, the
traditional ally of Finland, was approached, and it was pointed
out that if Finland accepted the Russian demands it would
mean that Soviet influence would reach to the borders of
Sweden. The Russians were adamant; the Finns were equally
adamant, and frightened. It was decided to send Paasikivi
back to Moscow with instructions to modify as much as possible the Russian demands and to employ delaying tactics.
Sweden had promised 'full diplomatic support'. But something
more than diplomatic support was needed.

This time Paasikivi was accompanied by Väinö Tanner, the
foreign minister, a quieter and gentler man, who had spent
most of his life in the co-operative movement. Tanner was
stubborn, methodical and unassuming. Like Paasikivi, he
could read Russian, but he could not speak it easily.

Stalin seems to have thought they had come fully prepared
to accept his minimum demands. He was in a reminiscent
mood, and talked about the days during the civil war when
the British naval squadron wandered freely through the Gulf
of Finland and sent torpedo boats against Kronstadt. He
mentioned the British fleet several times, but Paasikivi sensed
that he feared the Germans more than the British. Once when
Stalin mentioned Germany as a possible invader, Paasikivi

asked him what there was to fear. Had not Germany and the Soviet Union just concluded a non-aggression pact?

The skirmishing ended abruptly when Stalin asked whether the Finns would accept his minimum demands. Paasikivi answered that they were prepared to make some small adjustments, but the sweeping changes in the Russian memorandum were unacceptable to the Finnish government. Stalin repeated that by minimum demands he meant exactly what he said; there could be no question of whittling away at them. Paasikivi rose from the table and explained that in that case nothing would be gained by any further discussion. Molotov looked astounded. 'Do you want to cause a conflict?' he asked, and Paasikivi replied: 'No, but you seem to.' Then the Finnish delegates stalked out of the room.

Very few people have dared to stalk out of Stalin's presence in a cold rage, and Molotov's look of shocked surprise reflected the novelty of the event. Tanner remembered afterwards that Stalin merely smiled in his enigmatical fashion.

The Finns returned to their legation to discuss the impasse. They were still discussing it when the telephone rang with the news that they were expected to resume the conversations later in the evening. The talks went on as though there had been no interruption, with Stalin as affable as ever. In the interval the demands had been slightly modified. In the original draft the proposed Soviet naval base at Hanko would have a strength of 5,000 men. In the new draft it would have a strength of 4,000 men, who would be withdrawn at the end of the 'Anglo-Franco-German war'. For the Finns, and perhaps also for Stalin, the reduction was cynical and meaningless. They replied that they were powerless to act until they had received the authority of their government; once more there were delays, while the government in Helsinki set about trying to discover some means of retaining the independence of Finland while submitting to as few as possible of the Soviet demands.

Since they could only wait, the delegates decided to remain in Moscow. Paasikivi feigned a head cold and refused to leave his room, but Tanner took this opportunity to see the sights and to attend diplomatic parties. At one of these diplomatic functions Tanner had a conversation with Mikoyan, who seemed surprised that the Finns had not yet bowed to the 'minimal demands'. Mikoyan said that Stalin was acting very circumspectly with regard to Finland only because it was a small nation.

'Consider,' said Mikoyan, 'if there were just Russians in our government, things would be quite different. But Stalin is a Georgian, I'm an Armenian, and many of the rest are minority nationals. We understand the position of a small country very well.' Then he went on to speak of the difference between Lenin and Stalin. 'Lenin was a very gifted man,' he explained, 'but Stalin is a genius.'

On the morning of November 8th a coded telegram arrived from Helsinki, saying that only very minor concessions could be granted. The Finnish government refused outright to abandon Hanko, for a naval base on the peninsula was a threat to the very existence of Finland and also of Sweden. For the third time the negotiations reached a stalemate. Half-heartedly Stalin inquired what islands the Finns were prepared to surrender. Tanner gives an illuminating account of Stalin haggling over islands so small that they scarcely appear on the map.

Stalin pointed out Russarö on the map. 'Could you perhaps let go of this one?'

As our instructions prescribed, we replied in the negative.

'Then it doesn't look as if anything will come of it. Nothing will come of it,' said Stalin.

At length it appeared that neither party had any more to add concerning a base in the neighbourhood of Hanko. All arguments had already been presented.

Next we brought out a chart and said we proposed to offer the southern part of Suursaari.

Stalin replied, 'The island will have two masters. It won't do. What do you offer on the Isthmus?'

'There is nothing new to propose,' we replied. 'We reject your suggested boundary line. We stand on our earlier proposal.'

'You don't even offer Ino?'

'We have not asked our government's opinion on that point.'

Now the opposing negotiators pointed out the narrows opposite Seivasto. Here there had to be a fortress on both shores. Otherwise the aperture was not closed. The islands to be ceded were merely small points. Not much could be done with them. 'We would just be shooting at each other – you at us, and we at you' (on Seivasto).

Next Stalin and Molotov seized upon the question of Ino again, observing that for its protection twenty kilometres of hinterland would be required.

Stalin remarked, 'On that patch of land you offer us we would sit as though on the point of a sharpened pencil' – he indicated the point of his pencil.

I tried to measure the breadth of the area.

Molotov asked, 'How much is it?'

'About eight kilometres,' I answered.

A few weeks earlier Stalin had been busily presiding over the dismemberment of Poland; now he was debating whether to accept peace offerings amounting to only a few acres. As Paasikivi wrote later, he seemed oddly uncertain in his intentions. Did he really want the islands? Did he want all of Finland? Or was he simply following the traditional Russian attitude of regarding Finland in terms of purely strategical concepts, paying little attention to ideological or economic ideas? Was he still fighting the ghosts of Yudenich and the British torpedo boats?

Paasikivi was inclined to think that Stalin would settle for a few islands. The Finnish government believed that Stalin was bluffing. In this they were tragically mistaken.

The negotiations came to an end on November 8th when Tanner suggested that an appropriate formula might be to agree to disagree. Stalin smiled. There were no harsh words, and they parted amicably. Stalin's last words to the Finnish delegates were: 'I wish you all the best!' Molotov, hinting at further negotiations under altered circumstances, said: 'Au revoir.'

For two weeks Finland lived in a fool's paradise. The Finns congratulated themselves on their firmness towards Stalin. The evacuees returned to their apartments, schools reopened, soldiers returned to civilian life, and the strips of paper pasted over windows as a protection against bomb blasts were peeled off. Finland went back to normal, secure in the possession of her islands.

Meanwhile Stalin was discussing with his close advisers and with the leaders of the Finnish Communist Party the best way to accomplish his purpose. On the available evidence a Communist uprising in Finland, heavily backed by the Russians, offered little hope of success. It had been attempted before in January 1918, with disastrous consequences, for seventy thousand Red Guards perished during the Finnish civil war. Under General Baron Karl Mannerheim the Finns put up a ferocious resistance against the Communists, and thereafter they had been left in peace.

In 1918 Stalin gave the orders for the Red uprising, which was put down by Baron Mannerheim. Now once again Stalin and Mannerheim were to become adversaries.

By November 24th Stalin had decided upon a blitzkrieg similar to the one which permitted him to take over eastern Poland. A Communist government headed by Otto Kuusinen, the veteran Finnish Communist, would be set up outside the borders of Finland. A suitable *casus belli* would be invented, and the organs of propaganda would be ordered to go into high gear. Stalin believed that in three weeks Finland would crumble before the massed power of the Red Army.

On the morning of November 26th seven shells fell into the village of Mainila, killing three Red Army soldiers and one non-commissioned officer. The Russians said the shells had been fired as an act of provocation from a Finnish battery. The Finns strenuously denied it. With the firing of those shells the winter war began.

Early in the morning of November 30th the Soviet Union invaded Finland by land, sea and air. Some thirty Russian divisions attacked at eight points along the frontier. At 9:30 am the first bombs fell on the capital, while the Cabinet was discussing a note from Molotov breaking off diplomatic relations. On that day Mannerheim was appointed commander in chief, and Finland was formally declared to be in a state of war.

The winter war lasted for three months. Until the beginning of February the Finns maintained an unexpectedly savage resistance. They had 600,000 men under arms; the invaders were about the same number. The Finns however had the advantage of knowing the difficult terrain, they could manoeuvre more swiftly, and they were adept at camouflage. Finnish ski patrols, camouflaged in white sheets, played havoc with the Soviet columns, falling on them by surprise in the silent forests and on the frozen lakes. Carl Mydans, the American photographer, spoke of it as 'an Arctic winter war, like the showing of endless footage of under-exposed film'. Voroshilov commanded the Soviet forces; an incompetent bungler, he showed that he had learned nothing since the battle of Tsaritsyn. The Soviet losses were tremendous. If the attack on Finland was intended as a demonstration of Soviet power, it failed miserably.

The sympathies of the world went to Finland. France, Great Britain and the United States looked on helplessly, but there was no doubt where their sympathies lay. Even in Fascist Italy there were parades honouring the Finns, and Mussolini was compelled to tell Hitler that the Italians were incensed by the unprovoked aggression of the Red Army. Ribbentrop hurried to Rome to present the case for non-intervention: Hitler needed the supplies that were coming to him from Russia. Speaking with the authority of a man who had met Stalin face to face, Ribbentrop told Mussolini: 'I am firmly convinced that Stalin has renounced the idea of world revolution.' He went on to explain to the Italian dictator that all preconceived ideas about Stalin must now be abandoned. Stalin and Hitler, according to Ribbentrop, were almost brothers in arms. Stalin was imitating Hitler even to the extent of mounting an anti-Jewish campaign; all Jews had been removed from positions of power in the Soviet Union with the exception of Kaganovich, 'who looks more like a Georgian than a Jew'. With his own eyes Ribbentrop had seen a picture of Tsar Alexander hanging in the Kremlin, and there was a notable resemblance between Stalin and the Tsar. Ribbentrop professed to see in the picture of the Tsar the evidence that Russia had reverted to her ancient and perhaps less dangerous ways.

But while the sympathies of the Italians were with the Finns, they were in no position to give any effective help. The French, British and Americans offered token assistance. Finland fought alone. Towards the end of December Finnish troops won a crushing victory at Suomussalmi, but the General Staff sometimes found itself wondering how many victories it could afford to win. Few doubted that the Red Army with its formidable weight of numbers would eventually succeed in overrunning Finland by brute force.

After two months of disastrous fighting, the Russian high command was reorganized. General Boris Shaposhnikov, a former member of the Tsarist Imperial General Staff, assumed the tactical command and ordered a massive attack on the Mannerheim Line, which consisted of a series of small forts spread out in depth along the Karelian Isthmus. These forts were little more than concrete pillboxes, many of them out of date, having been built with the help of British engineers in the early twenties, and as Mannerheim himself declared, the line named after him consisted chiefly of the tenacity and courage of the soldiers manning it. During the first two months of the war the line, though occasionally pierced, was never broken.

On February 2nd some twenty-seven divisions and an uncounted number of guns were brought up against the line. General Semyon Timoshenko assumed operational command on the Karelian front. It was hoped to overwhelm the Finns by concentrated bombardments and by sheer force of numbers.

Even then the Finns held out. They reeled, but the line did not break. The advantages of terrain were now turning in favour of the Russians – the ice was so hard on the lakes that the Russian tanks were able to roll over them. Meanwhile Finnish efforts to obtain aid, or even promises of aid, were proving to be abortive; Sweden, the long and faithful ally, refused to send troops, and Norway refused to permit the passage of British or French troops. Viipuri (Vyborg) remained in Finnish hands, but its fall could not be delayed indefinitely. Finnish manpower was being exhausted, with the gaps in the ranks being filled by schoolboys and men over military age. When at last it was decided to negotiate an armistice, Stalin demanded terms far in excess of those he demanded before the war broke out. The formula was provided by Molotov: 'The blood which has been shed contrary to our hopes and through no fault of our own calls for augmented guarantees to the security of the frontiers of the USSR.' For Stalin the war had its uses. As he told President Roosevelt at Teheran, 'In the Finnish War the Soviet Army showed itself to be very poorly organized and did very badly. As a result the entire Soviet Army was reorganized.' But in fact there was no reorganization of the entire army, only a half-hearted attempt to shore up a ruined house. After the Finnish war the morale of the army was at its lowest ebb.

The Finns paid for their heroic resistance by being forced to surrender the entire Karelian Isthmus. The cities of Viipuri, Kexholm and Sortevala were surrendered to the Russians. From these still-unconquered cities the Finns marched wearily northward. The war was over.

It was a year of many wars and many easy victories. With Poland prostrate and Russia an ally, Hitler could turn his attention to the west. Denmark and Norway were conquered in a day, Holland in five days, Belgium in eighteen, Luxembourg in an hour. Then it was the turn of France which capitulated in six weeks. The blitzkrieg which destroyed Poland moved with increasing speed, well oiled by Russian and Rumanian oil. It was stopped at the English Channel. The British fought on. They had only one ally – the sea.

The savage pace of the war caught Stalin by surprise, but he continued to believe against all the evidence that he had formed a close and enduring friendship with Hitler. His duty, as he saw it, was to maintain the alliance at all costs, since he was wholly unprepared for a war with Germany. When Sir Stafford Cripps, the British ambassador in Moscow, called upon him in July to urge that Germany was striving for the complete domination of Europe and was as potentially dangerous to the Soviet Union as to Great Britain, Stalin turned a deaf ear. He said he knew Germany well – he had spent perhaps two months in the country – and was well acquainted with the German leaders – he had met only Ribbentrop for seven or eight hours. He laughed at the dangers which Cripps earnestly presented, saying that the non-aggression pact was the sheet anchor of Soviet policy, and he was aware of no menacing moves on the part of the Germans. Then he did something which was wholly characteristic of the man. *He instructed Molotov to give a memorandum of his conversation with Cripps to Count von der Schulenberg.* He had become the running-dog of fascism. He feared the Germans, and was prepared to placate them to the utmost of his power.

In fear and torment Stalin watched the growing power of Germany. He had reason to be afraid, for in the following month the German Army High Command ordered ten divisions and two armoured divisions to be transferred to Poland 'with a view to possible swift action for the protection of the Rumanian oil fields'. German moves towards the Russian frontier were continually being reported to him. When news that heavy reinforcements were being poured into Hungary reached the Kremlin, Molotov was instructed to seek an explanation. He was told they were intended to crush the British in Greece, and the Soviet espionage systems must have known there were scarcely any British soldiers in Greece. German forces landed in Finland, without giving advance warning to Moscow, and they were pouring into Rumania, and converting the Balkans into a German province, all this in flagrant violation of the non-aggression pact and the secret protocols.

Ribbentrop, vaguely aware of Stalin's displeasure and acutely aware of the need to affirm the uneasy alliance, so that the preparations of the invasion of Russia could go on unchecked, wrote a rambling letter to Stalin couched in the terms of one dictator talking confidentially to another. The war had been won, Great Britain was on her knees, and it was merely a matter of time before she would be compelled to admit defeat. A German military mission had been dispatched to Rumania at the request of the Rumanian government, with a few instruction units: Ribbentrop carefully omitted to say that the 'instruction units' consisted of three divisions, which would be increased in February 1941 to fifty divisions. Similarly he explained away the tripartite pact which had been signed by Germany, Italy and Japan. He suggested that Molotov should come to Berlin to discuss with Hitler the developing relations between the two countries.

Stalin replied a week later:

MY DEAR MR VON RIBBENTROP:

I have received your letter. I thank you sincerely for your confidence and for the interesting analysis of recent events contained in your letter.

I agree with you that a fresh improvement of the relations between our countries is perfectly possible on the permanent basis of a full delimitation of our mutual interests.

Mr Molotov admits that he is under obligation to pay you a visit in Berlin. He hereby accepts your invitation.

We have still to agree on the date of his arrival in Berlin. The period from the 10th to the 12th November is that which suits Mr Molotov best. If this date is agreeable to the German Government, the question may be regarded as settled.

I welcome with pleasure the desire which you express to come to Moscow again in order to resume the exchange of views begun last year as regards questions of interest to both our countries, and I hope this desire will be realized after Mr Molotov's journey to Berlin.

As regards a common consideration of certain questions in which the Japanese and the Italians would take part, I think, without being opposed to this idea in principle, that it should be subjected to a previous examination.

Very respectfully yours,

J. STALIN

Behind the formal display of interest and the inelegant diplomatic phrases, there can be detected a note of caution, and a pathetic hint of defiance. He must know more, probe more deeply into German intentions. It was time the quivering alliance was taken to pieces and put together again on a more permanent basis. In this hope he sent Molotov to Berlin.

Ribbentrop had lived so long in the shadow of Hitler that he could think only in cloudy generalities. Molotov was precise and factual. Ribbentrop spoke of Great Britain falling to her knees, the imminent dissolution of the British Empire, the stability of East Asia, the need for Russia to turn her eyes towards the Persian Gulf and India. While they were talking in the old Russian Embassy on Unter den Linden, the British, who had got wind of the meeting, staged an air raid over Berlin. There was no air-raid shelter in the Embassy, and the foreign ministers of Russia and Germany took refuge in the nearby Hotel Adlon. They were discussing how the world should be carved up by the four great powers, Germany, Russia, Italy and Japan, when Molotov said: 'What will England say about all this?' Ribbentrop waved England aside. 'England is finished,' he said. 'She is no more use to us as a power.' 'If that is so,' Molotov replied, 'then why are we in this shelter, and whose are those bombs that fall?' Molotov told the story to Stalin, who later told Churchill.

The lessons of the story were lost on Stalin. In spite of the British bombs on Berlin, he still believed that safety lay with Germany, and that an accommodation could be reached with Hitler. The grandiose division of the world among Germany, Russia, Italy and Japan still appealed to him. 'Stalin is clever and cunning,' Hitler told his military command. 'He demands more and more. He is a cold-blooded blackmailer.' The two blackmailers were looking in each other's eyes; neither liked what he saw, but each took comfort from his chosen profession.

Stalin searched for allies, and there occurred to him the unlikely prospect of alliances with Yugoslavia and Japan. On April 6th, 1941, he signed a treaty of friendship with Yugoslavia; on the same day Belgrade was heavily bombed by the Luftwaffe, putting an end to the treaty almost before the ink was dry on the page. Japan, however, was unlikely to be bombed by the Luftwaffe, and when the Japanese foreign minister, Yosuke Matsuoka, was invited to Moscow on his return from a visit to Hitler, Stalin took the opportunity to suggest a pact of neutrality and friendship to be signed immediately. Matsuoka, preparing to attack British and American outposts in the Far East, saw some advantages in having a friendly Russian army in Siberia. 'I am a convinced adherent of the Axis,' Stalin told Matsuoka, 'and an opponent of England and America.' Wearing his heavy military greatcoat, smiling from ear to ear, Stalin accompanied Matsuoka to the railroad station, embraced him, and said: 'We are both Asiatics!' Then he called for Count von der Schulenberg, who was not an Asiatic, and embraced him, saying: 'We must remain friends, and you must do everything to this end.' There were tears of joy in his eyes.

Peace at last! In alliance with Germany and Japan, he could face the future with the knowledge that he had done everything possible to safeguard the Soviet Union. From time to time he would look at the immense globe in his office, and reflect on the large segment which would soon accrue to him. Germany had fulfilled to the letter her agreements with Russia, and though there were large armies on both sides of the Soviet-German frontier, they were there as peaceful agents of two vast imperial powers, and those who said the contrary were liars and *provocateurs*. In this blissful mood he decided to resume his interrupted holiday on the Black Sea coast.

It was the best of all possible worlds.

INVASION

ON JUNE 22nd, 1941, in the early hours of the morning Hitler launched an attack on Russia on a broad front stretching from the Baltic to the Black Sea.

The attack had been planned long before in meticulous detail. To attack and destroy Russia had indeed been Hitler's main objective ever since he rose to political power, and with his secret directive for 'Operation Barbarossa', issued under his signature on December 16th, 1940, he explained the exact scope of the attack. 'The German armed forces must be prepared to crush Soviet Russia in a quick campaign even before the end of the war against England,' he wrote. 'The ultimate objective of the operation is to establish a defensive line against Asiatic Russia from a line running approximately from the Volga river to Archangel.' All preparations were to be made by May 15th, five months after the directive was issued.

Hitler's plans were aimed at the destruction of Russia's industrial potential and the elimination of Russia as a political power. But these were only the more formal and casual aims. His real aims were more terrible, and included the massacre of most of the inhabitants of western Russia with the survivors being permitted to live as slaves for the use of the German *Herrenvolk*, and the annihilation of most of the great Russian cities. Leningrad was to be levelled to the ground, the Kremlin was to be blown up, and Kiev was to become merely a German command post. Russia was to be extinguished like a candle that has blown out. The war was to be a *Vernichtungskampf*, the total annihilation of a nation and its peoples, without any regard for the laws of war.

That a massive attack was being planned had long been suspected by observers in the West, and Stalin had received at least three separate warnings from the British government. Trusting to the good faith of Hitler or his own powers of blackmail, he chose to ignore them. On the morning of June 22nd the German armies were formed into three prongs aimed at Leningrad, Moscow and Kiev, and with their overwhelming superiority in heavy artillery, tanks, airplanes and trained officers there appeared to be nothing to prevent them from reaching their objectives within a few weeks. By the end of October it was expected that Russian resistance would have collapsed.

For many Russians the war came as a welcome relief from the intolerable strain of living under Stalin's rule; the nightmare was exchanged for the waking reality. Among those who welcomed the war was the poet Boris Pasternak, who wrote later: 'When the war broke out, its real horrors were a blessing compared with the inhuman power of the lie. The war came as a relief because it broke the spell of a dead letter.' To Stalin, who was then vacationing in his palatial villa at Gagra on the Georgian coast of the Black Sea, the war did not come as a relief: it came as nemesis.

For this invasion the Russian people were totally unprepared. The fault was Stalin's. For seventeen years he had been a destructive force sapping at their energies, attempting to reduce them to mere automatons obedient to his will. As a result of his own vast ignorance of military affairs and the purges of the officers, which continued with a kind of mechanical precision right up to the invasion of Russia, the country was virtually defenceless. During the purges of 1937–8 the Russian army lost three marshals, 13 army commanders, 57 out of 85 corps commanders, 110 out of 195 divisional commanders, and 220 out of 406 brigade commanders. Of the regimental commanders there remained only 225, and of these only about twenty had taken a full course at the military academy. It was learned later that nearly all the German regimental commanders were veterans of the First World War. None of the Russian regimental commanders had any experience of fighting except in Finland.

Again and again during the twenties and thirties Stalin had proclaimed the necessity of building up the industrial might of Russia in order to prevent an invasion which could come only from Germany. The Russian defence forces had not however been the beneficiaries of the accumulated industrial power. According to German estimates, the 15,000 tanks and 10,000 aeroplanes belonging to the Red Army and Air Force were of obsolete design, transport and supply systems were archaic, while Red strategy and tactics were clumsy, inefficient and wasteful. Along the frontiers there were no reserve echelons to back up front-line troops, because Stalin regarded defence in depth as 'sheer nonsense'. No defensive war plans had been prepared. Supply depots were set up close to the front lines within range of enemy artillery, with the result that vast quantities of arms, ammunition and fuel were captured within the first days of fighting. Rarely has a country ever been so ill-prepared for invasion.

Although Graf von der Schulenburg had called on Molotov at 5.30 am, an hour and a half after the invasion began, to announce that a state of war existed between Germany and Russia, Molotov waited for nearly seven hours before broadcasting the news to the Russian people. In a flat unemotional voice he declared that 'without presenting any claims to the Soviet Union and without a declaration of war' German troops had invaded Russia, and German aeroplanes had already bombed Russian cities. He spoke at length about the non-aggression pact he had signed with Ribbentrop, and seemed more concerned with the fate of the pact than with the fate of the country. 'Our troops have been ordered to repulse the predatory attack and to drive the Germans from the territory of our country,' he declared, but there seemed to be little conviction in his voice. Like the Russians who listened to him on that hot, sunlit day, he was numbed by the disaster that had overtaken the country.

Stalin continued to take his vacation at Gagra. Ivan Maisky, the Soviet Ambassador to London, has described how Stalin, prostrated by news of the invasion, cut himself off completely from Moscow, refused to answer the telephone, gave no orders, and abandoned Russia to its fate. For four days he remained incommunicado, drinking himself into a stupor. When he recovered, he was in no hurry to return to Moscow, for he did not know and could not guess the mood of the country towards him.

Not until July 3rd, eleven days after the German attack, was his voice heard. The voice came from a recording, as he spoke from a prepared script, in slow and faltering tones. The recording was made at Gagra. The speech came on the air at dawn and was repeated at intervals during the day. Three years had passed since he had publicly addressed the Russian people. He began with the words: 'Comrades! Citizens! Brothers and sisters! Men of our army and navy! I am addressing you, my friends!'

These extraordinary opening words – extraordinary only because they came from Stalin – announced the major theme: his affection for the Russian people, and his desperate need of their help. He had never spoken in this way before, nor was he ever to speak like this again.

Nearly everything he said was predictable. He spoke of the Soviet Union as a peace-loving country treacherously attacked by 'fiends and cannibals'. Like Molotov he felt impelled to defend the non-aggression pact with Germany since 'it offered a definite advantage for us and a disadvantage for fascist Germany'. Had he not secured peace for eighteen months, thus permitting the army to rearm and to regroup its forces? Again and again he spoke of the treachery of the enemy, as though it had suddenly been revealed to him in all its enormity.

Predictably, too, he employed phrases and ideas which showed that he was still thinking of a war measurably comparable with the civil war, the only war in which he had had any practical experience. 'The enemy,' he declared, 'is determined to restore the rule of the landlords, to restore Tsarism,' and he went on to speak of the German princes and barons who would employ the Russians as serfs on their vast estates.

With memories of Budyenny's cavalry, he ordered that guerrilla units should be formed, 'mounted and on foot', as though the time for mounted guerrillas had not long since passed.

Predictably, too, he denounced traitors. 'We must wage a ruthless fight against all disorganizers of the rear, deserters, panicmongers, and rumourmongers,' he declared. 'All who by their panicmongering and cowardice hinder the work of defence, no matter who they are, must be immediately hauled before the military tribunal.'

There was however one unexpected note in the speech, when he spoke of the gratitude evoked in the hearts of the Soviet people by 'the historic utterance of the British Prime Minister Churchill regarding aid to the Soviet Union, and the declaration of the United States government signifying its readiness to render aid to our country'. Since he rarely spoke of gratitude, the words came all the more unexpectedly. At the conclusion of the speech he announced that a State Council of Defence had been formed, in whose hands the entire power of the state had been vested.

While Stalin's speech was being heard all over Russia by radio and through loudspeakers set up in the streets, he was still on the train bringing him to Moscow. He seems to have delayed the journey for fear of sabotage on the railroad. He arrived in Moscow on July 4th. Then once again he vanished from sight, to be seen only on rare occasions by special envoys and ambassadors. Two or three times a year during the course of the war he would appear on the platform of Lenin's mausoleum, but always briefly. He spent the war years in one or other of his many villas in the country, in his Kremlin office, or in his bomb shelter.

The bomb shelter was the safest in all Russia. It was 115 feet below ground, and provided with a variety of automatic steel doors, booby traps and warning devices. It had been conceived on a grand scale, and resembled a grandiose version of the underground Avlabar printing plant, with secret tunnels extending in all directions. At the first sound of the air-raid-warning system, he would take his private elevator from his second-floor office to the ground floor, and then make his way to the second elevator, which carried him in a matter of seconds to his suite of underground rooms. There was one large room comfortably furnished with leather armchairs and a green-covered conference table, and in adjoining rooms were the emergency command posts where high military officers sat beside banks of telephones.

Few foreigners were permitted to enter the bomb shelter. One of the few was Admiral William H. Standley, the American ambassador, who described his journey through a maze of connecting corridors. He wrote:

> We stepped out of the elevator into a short arched tunnel about six feet wide and twelve feet high. At the end were a pair of massive steel doors ... My guide took me through four arched compartments about sixteen feet long, lined with steel plates, and two pairs of steel doors at either end of each compartment, which opened automatically at his touch. This tunnel led into an elaborately equipped air-raid shelter, which could also be entered through a tunnel from a nearby station of the Moscow subway ... We came out into a larger compartment, which must have been the emergency War Room. Mr Stalin and his military aides were sitting around a long table. The room was as handsomely furnished as any of the Kremlin offices topside.

In this room, in the early days of the war, some of the most disastrous decisions were taken. Perhaps the most disastrous of all was Stalin's determination to assume supreme command of the armed forces. To Timoshenko, who had shown praiseworthy initiative in fighting the defenceless Finns, went the command of the Central Army protecting Moscow. To Voroshilov went the command of the Northern Army protecting Leningrad, and to Budyenny the command of the Southern Army in the Ukraine. Stalin tended to view the war against Germany in the light of his experiences in Tsaritsyn. Voroshilov and Budyenny were his oldest surviving friends and his constant drinking companions.

So incompetently had Stalin prepared his defences that the German army marched into Russia at an average speed of twenty miles a day. On July 16th it had already progressed two thirds of the way to Moscow, a distance of 440 miles. General Halder, from his high eminence as Chief of Staff of the German Army High Command, thought the war was virtually over in the first two weeks; there would remain only a brief mopping-up campaign. He had left out of account the heroic tenacity of the Russian people.

The Russians retreated, vast numbers of them were killed or captured, their cities were pulverized, but they were in no mood to surrender. The Germans entered Smolensk on July 16th. The loss of Smolensk was a serious one, for the city guarded the approaches to Moscow, only a little more than two hundred miles away. Timoshenko had been able to extricate nearly half a million men during the battle, withdrawing them to a defensive line closer to Moscow. The Germans claimed they captured 185,487 prisoners, 2,030 tanks and 1,918 guns. Already Russia was being bled white.

In despair Stalin wrote to Churchill a lengthy memorandum on July 18th, calling upon the British Army to establish two diversionary fronts, one in the Arctic and the other in northern France. He seemed to be begging for sympathy as he complained of Hitler's unexpected violation of the non-aggression pact; it still rankled that Hitler should have acted so treacherously. He wrote:

> The consequences of the unexpected breach of the non-aggression pact by Hitler, as well as of the sudden attack against the Soviet Union – both facts bringing advantages to the German troops – still remain to be felt by the Soviet armies.
>
> It is easy to imagine that the position of the German forces would have been many times more favourable had the Soviet troops had to face the attack not along the line Kishinev-Lvov-Brest-Byalistok-Kaunas-Viborg, but along the line Odessa-Kamenets-Podolsk-Minsk and the environs of Leningrad.
>
> It seems to me therefore that the military situation of the Soviet Union, as well as of Great Britain, would be considerably improved if there could be established a front against Hitler in the West – Northern France, and in the North – the Arctic.
>
> A front in Northern France could not only divert Hitler's forces from the East, but at the same time would make it impossible for Hitler to invade Great Britain. The establishment of the front just mentioned would be popular with the British Army, as well as with the whole population of Southern England.

Stalin had never possessed to any large degree an understanding of the mood of the inhabitants of Southern England, nor had he shown any particular sympathy for Great Britain during the year in which she was compelled to fight Germany alone. Churchill was understandably puzzled by the letter, and could not forbear to point out in his reply that Great Britain was already fighting on several fronts, notably in the Middle East. He promised what help he could. From time to time Stalin would refer angrily to the absence of a second or a third front, as though these new fronts were the very least that Great Britain could offer in gratitude to the Russians for fighting Germany singlehanded. In September he was asking Churchill to send twenty-five to thirty divisions to Archangel or to Persia, through which they could reach southern Russia. 'In this way,' he wrote, 'there could be established military collaboration between the Soviet and British troops on the territory of the USSR.' He noted that a similar situation had existed during the last war in France, and such an arrangement would constitute a great blow to German aggression.

Churchill could make nothing of this proposal. It alarmed him that the head of the Russian government, surrounded by able lieutenants and competent military experts, could have known so little about the way the British were conducting their shoestring war as to commit himself to such an absurdity. 'It seemed hopeless,' he wrote, 'to argue with a man thinking in terms of utter unreality.'

Throughout their long wartime correspondence Churchill and Stalin maintained a curiously formal relationship. There was no warmth in their letters, only a kind of grudging respect. At intervals Stalin would give way to uncontrollable bursts of anger, flurries of petulance, long-cherished rancours. Churchill concealed his angers and was incapable of rancour. Very early in their correspondence he detected that Stalin had very little real knowledge or experience of military affairs.

Meanwhile help was coming from America and Great Britain. Harry Hopkins, sent to Moscow by President Roosevelt as his personal representative, brought offers of almost unlimited aid. Stalin was affable, considerate, down-to-earth. What he wanted most were 20,000 anti-aircraft guns, vast quantities of aluminium sheeting needed in the construction of aeroplanes, and enormous numbers of machine guns and rifles. He would come back again and again to these four specific requests, sometimes changing the order, occasionally omitting one or two, but always returning to them in the end. Once he said: 'Give us anti-aircraft guns and the aluminium and we can fight for three or four years.' At other times he asked for short-range bombers and aircraft technicians. He wanted Soviet pilots trained in America and admitted that

Soviet losses in aeroplanes had been very heavy: he hinted that there would soon be a shortage of pilots. He said he had no very high impression of German aeroplanes, though he found the Junkers-88 as good or better than anything in the Russian air force.

1) Anti-aircraft guns
   calibre 20 or 25 or 37 mm.
2) Aluminium
3) Machine guns 12·7 mm.
4) Rifles 7·62 mm.

These meetings took place on July 30th and 31st, and at the second meeting Stalin once again spoke of the need for anti-aircraft guns, aluminium, machine guns and rifles. He wrote the words on a slip of paper, and gave it to Hopkins. This appears to have been the only formal document exchanged between them.

But although the atmosphere was informal, the matters under discussion were the gravest possible. Stalin had no illusions about the gravity of the occasion. Hopkins came as personal representative of the President, but he was also on fairly in-

timate terms with Churchill, with whom he had talked only
a few hours before, and therefore he represented in a sense
the entire English-speaking world. A frail man, who lived on
his nervous energy, he gave an impression of absolute direct-
ness and simplicity.

Stalin, too, spoke directly and simply. He had rarely shown
himself to better advantage. He made no attempt to conceal
the precarious position of the Russian armies. He emphasized
that he had no intention of underestimating German power.
The organization of the German army was of the best; they
had large supplies of fuel, food and men; they were perfectly
capable of waging a winter war in Russia. He believed the
Germans were producing 2,500 to 3,000 fighter and bomber
planes a month, while the Russian production of planes
amounted to only 1,800 a month. He went into considerable
detail about the numbers, the performance and the range of
Russian aircraft; and if he could not remember a fact or a
detail he would touch a button and instantly some secretary
would appear with the required answer. He seemed to revel
in figures. For the first time a foreign statesman was being
granted a factual summary of the Russian war potential. Stalin
spoke frankly. His subordinates however dared not speak
frankly, and when Hopkins asked a certain General Yakovlev
the weight of Russia's heaviest tank, the general could only
answer: 'It's a good tank.' Hopkins asked the same question
of Stalin, who said the two heaviest Russian tanks were of
48 and 52 tons respectively, with 75-mm. armour and 85-mm.
guns. He, at least, was not bound to secrecy.

Occasionally, as the conversations proceeded, there came
revealing glimpses into Stalin's mind. The violation of the
non-aggression pact rankled like a wound; it was an act of
treachery so great as to be almost beyond his comprehension.
'There must be a minimum moral standard between all nations,' Stalin said pathetically and went on to complain that
the Germans were a people who had no conception of the
sanctity of treaties; they would tear up a treaty without the
slightest compunction, and then write another one the following day. 'Nations,' he went on, 'must fulfil their treaty
obligations, otherwise international society will be unable to
survive.' It was odd that he should become the apologist of
the minimum moral standard, and there were odder things to
come.

Like all embattled commanders he was compelled to put

the best face on things, and sometimes the best face was a poor simulacrum of reality. He told Hopkins that the early defeats of the Red Army were due to the difficulty of mobilizing troops in time. He said:

Russia had 180 divisions at the outbreak of the war, but many of these were well back of the line of combat, and could not be quickly mobilized, so that when the Germans struck it was impossible to offer adequate resistance. The line which is now held is a far more propitious one than the more advanced line which they might have taken up had their divisions been prepared.

This was to make a virtue of unpreparedness; it was as though he was saying that the loss of large areas of European Russia had resulted in signal benefits since the shortening of the lines placed the Russian army in a more propitious position. Wish fulfilment rode roughshod over facts. In a similar spirit he announced that the German soldiers were already tired and had no stomach for the offensive. It was untrue, and he must have known it was untrue; but the fiction pleased him.

Nevertheless the face he presented to Hopkins was one of mastery and authority. He had recovered from the strange lethargy which afflicted him in the early days of the war. Hopkins was impressed by his quiet self-assurance, his calm answers to hard questions, a certain sardonic humour. 'He was an austere, rugged, determined figure in boots that shone like mirrors, stout baggy trousers, and snug-fitting blouse,' Hopkins wrote. 'He wore no ornament, military or civilian. He's built close to the ground, like a football coach's dream of a tackle.' Margaret Bourke-White, the photographer, who was introduced to Stalin by Hopkins, saw a slightly different figure. To her, he was grey and tired, and he had the look of a man who has been stout but has recently grown thinner. She observed that his hands were deeply wrinkled, and his moustache and hair had 'a kind of chewed-up, strawlike look'. He showed exemplary patience during a photographic session, permitting light bulbs to be exploded within a few inches of his face, smiling frequently, but when the smile ended his face turned blank 'as though a veil had been drawn over his features'.

August was a month of desperate stratagems, as the Germans swung north against Leningrad and south against Odessa, which fell after a heroic two-and-a-half-month siege. The gigantic Dnieper River dam, the pride of Russian industry, was blown up to prevent it from falling into the hands of the advancing Germans. The Red Air Force bombed Berlin, to the consternation of Hitler, who had never expected that Soviet planes would fly so deep into German territory, but the bombing raid was scarcely more than a gesture. The Soviet planes were needed nearer home.

In that delirious month, when the Germans seemed to be spreading all over Russia, Stalin decided he could no longer afford the luxury of assuming command of the army, and while retaining the title of Commissar of Defence, he appointed Marshal Boris Shaposhnikov as Vice-Commissar with almost unlimited powers. Shaposhnikov had been a colonel on the Imperial General Staff at Moghilev in 1917. He came from a well-to-do family of Moscow merchants. A tall man, with iron-grey hair *en brosse*, with courtly manners and an air of studied reserve, he did not in the least resemble the stereotype of a Soviet marshal. He was sixty years old, suffered from angina pectoris, and for many years he had been content to preside over the Military Academy. His book, *The Brains of an Army*, was an almost forgotten classic, and he might have sunk into complete obscurity if he had not been ordered by Stalin to prepare a plan for the destruction of the Mannerheim Line during the war against Finland. The plan succeeded. High honours were showered on him, and Stalin wisely took the former colonel of the Imperial General Staff under his protection.

From August 1941 Marshal Shaposhnikov was in virtual command of the Red Armies. From the Kremlin there came a stream of coded telegrams reading: 'Chief of the General Staff Marshal Comrade Shaposhnikov in the name of the Supreme High Command orders . . .'*

These orders were not always obeyed. Supplies, manpower, armaments were in disarray, and Budyenny's Southern Army

---

* Marshal Shaposhnikov remained Chief of the General Staff until the autumn of the following year, when he was replaced by Marshal Vasilievsky. He is one of the great, but forgotten figures of the war. He died in March 1945. Stalin and Molotov carried his ashes to their resting place in the Kremlin wall.

was already crumbling. Kiev fell on September 19th after a month's siege. By the end of September the Germans and Finns were threatening Leningrad, and had silenced the guns of Kronstadt. The Crimea had been cut off. Soon the rains would come, and then the snow, but for the moment there was no doubt who was winning territory. 'The Soviet Union is in a state of total chaos,' Goebbels declared. 'Already the war against Bolshevism has been decided in Europe's favour.' Many months were to pass before the issue was decided.

At the end of September Averell Harriman and Lord Beaverbrook flew into Moscow to attend a conference on the aid to be sent by Great Britain and the United States to Russia. The conference was largely formal, with only two meetings and a few committee sessions. Most of the work had already been done; it was a conference for tidying up loose ends and putting signatures to the agreement. Aid to Russia was divided into six categories: military, naval, air, transport, raw materials, and medical supplies. Averell Harriman and Lord Beaverbrook accordingly appointed members of their missions to the six committees. Churchill wrote later that the meetings were bleak and the discussions not at all friendly, but this impression, which he derived from Lord Beaverbrook, was probably due to the recognition by the Russians that many weeks and months would roll by before effective aid reached them. The opening stages of the battle for Moscow were only a few days away.

Outwardly the conference proceeded as well as could be expected. Molotov headed the Soviet delegation, but Stalin was the voice of authority. Like Harry Hopkins, Lord Beaverbrook was impressed by Stalin's command of detail. At one point in their discussion he said the engine of the Hurricane fighter plane had 1,350 horsepower. Stalin smiled and said: 'No, it has 1,200 horsepower.' Stalin was right.

Lord Beaverbrook wrote about Stalin on his return to London: 'Is he an easy man to satisfy? Not so. He is an exacting man, even though he does not look it. He is short of stature. Well dressed, very well dressed. There is nothing slovenly about him. He is always ready to laugh, quick to see a joke and willing to make one. His eyes are alert. His face quickly reflects his emotions. Gloom and joy are marked therein. His countenance lights up with pleasure when the word of assent is given. He is a judge of values, and his knowledge of armaments is vast and wide.'

There was the inevitable state dinner attended by Stalin, Molotov, Beria, Voroshilov, and the high dignitaries of the Soviet government. Toasts were drunk, speeches were made, vast quantities of caviar were consumed. Stalin proposed a toast to the President, 'who has the very difficult task of leading a nonbelligerent country which nevertheless desires to do everything it can to help the two great democracies of Europe in their fight against fascism.' It was odd that he should have referred to Great Britain and the Soviet Union as two great democracies of Europe, and perhaps even odder that he should conclude the toast with the words: 'May God help him in his most difficult task!' The American correspondent Quentin Reynolds, who was present, says that when the banqueters rose from the table they were taken to see a film called *The War of the Future*, made three years before, in which the prophetic film director showed the German army invading the Soviet Union, with battle scenes represented by animated models. In this film the two gigantic armies hurled themselves on one another, but the final triumph of the Soviet Union was never left in doubt. Stalin, impersonated by an actor, showed the way to victory.

The War of the Future was a disquieting film because it suggested that the self-glorification of Stalin had reached towering proportions. One could imagine Hitler making a film of this kind, portraying his march of triumph across the Red Square, but it was not the kind of film which would normally be associated with Stalin, the calm, phlegmatic, pipe-smoking dictator believed to be living in a world of realities. Naked paranoia leaped from the screen, while Harriman and Beaverbrook watched in puzzled silence.

What was the purpose of showing the film? Was it to arouse respect for Stalin? Was it to intimidate? To amuse? To instruct? It was being shown at a time when the whole Southern Army was in a state of collapse. Was the film simply a graceful act of prophecy? Or was it designed to satisfy not the needs of the audience but the needs of the man depicted on the screen?

In a film all things are possible. Time can be speeded up, a journey which takes half a year can be performed in a split second. Time can be reversed: the dead on the battlefield rise and are shown marching backward to their appointed stations. All the natural laws which human beings must obey can be dispensed with on film. Night after night Stalin saw films until they must have seemed more real than the world he saw around him every day; and since many of these films described his own accomplishments, immensely magnified and distorted, he had long ago become a prey to delusions of grandeur.

We shall not know how deeply he was immersed in delusions until we know a good deal more about his mental life. There is some evidence that his paranoia, far from being quieted by the shock of war, was inflamed by it, and became more unmanageable and more dangerous. In the *Short Biography* which he wrote later he called himself 'the sublime strategist of all times and nations'. It would seem that *The War of the Future* was not shown as the result of a momentary impulse, but in order to convey to the audience a sense of his proper glory. Many years later Khrushchev said Stalin saw the events taking place in Russia only through films.

Meanwhile there were civilities to be performed, conferences to be attended, a war to be fought. Among the civilities was a letter written to President Roosevelt, thanking him for sending Averell Harriman to Moscow. It is a rather formal letter, lacking in warmth, and gives every indication of having been written by Stalin himself and not by his secretaries. He wrote:

> Soviet of People's Commissars
> 3rd October 1941
> Moscow, Kremlin

DEAR MR ROOSEVELT,

Your letter has been presented to me by Mr Harriman.

I avail myself of the opportunity to express to you the deep gratitude of the Soviet Government for having entrusted the leadership of the American delegation to such an authoritative person as Mr Harriman, whose participation in the proceedings of the Moscow Conference of the Three Powers has been so effective.

I have no doubt that you will do everything to ensure the implementation of the decisions of the Moscow Conference as speedily and completely as possible, particularly in view of the fact that the Hitlerites will inevitably try to use the pre-winter months to exert every possible pressure at the front against the USSR.

Like you, I have no doubt that final victory over Hitler will be won by those countries which are now uniting their efforts to speed up the liquidation of bloody Hitlerism, for

СОЮЗ
СОВЕТСКИХ
СОЦИАЛИСТИЧЕСКИХ
РЕСПУБЛИК

СОВЕТ НАРОДНЫХ КОМИССАРОВ

3 · октября 194 1 г.

МОСКВА, КРЕМЛЬ

Уважаемый г-н Рузвельт,

Ваше письмо мне передано г.Гарриманом.

Пользуюсь случаем, чтобы выразить Вам глубокую благодарность Советского Правительства за то, что Вы поручили руководство американской делегацией столь авторитетному лицу, как г.Гарриман, участие которого в работах московской конференции трех держав было так эффективно.

Я не сомневаюсь, что Вами будет сделано все необходимое для того, чтобы обеспечить реализацию решений московской конференции возможно скоро и полно, особенно ввиду того, что предзимние месяцы гитлеровцы наверняка постараются использовать для всяческого нажима на фронте против СССР.

Как и Вы, я не сомневаюсь в конечной победе над Гитлером стран, которые теперь об'единяют свои усилия для того, чтобы ускорить ликвидацию кровавого гитлеризма, для чего Советский Союз приносит теперь столь большие и тяжелые жертвы.

С искренним уважением И. Сталин

which the Soviet Union is now making so great and so
heavy sacrifices.

Yours sincerely,
J. STALIN

That Averell Harriman should have been called 'authoritative', when so many other adjectives were available, is perhaps
not so remarkable as the reference to 'the pre-winter months',
for winter had almost arrived and the first snows were to fall
on Moscow four days later. On the previous day Hitler had
commanded his troops to enter Moscow.

By October 16th the situation at the front had become so
critical that orders were given for the mass evacuation of
Moscow. Posters appeared all over the city: 'All citizens
whose presence is not needed are hereby ordered to leave.
The enemy is at the gates.' Foreign embassies and all except
the most essential government establishments were evacuated
to Kuibyshev, formerly Samara. Stalin remained in the Kremlin. Since the beginning of the war he had not shown himself
to the people. For many years he had remained a mysterious
figure hidden behind the Kremlin wall, but the very nature
of the war demanded that he should show himself, if only for
a moment.

The moment came on November 6th, the eve of the anniversary of the revolution which brought the Bolsheviks to
power. On that day Stalin slipped out of his bomb shelter in
the Kremlin by way of the underground tunnel that led to
the Mayakovsky subway station, and made one of the best
and longest of his wartime speeches. His main theme was the
justice of the Soviet cause and the inevitable victory of Soviet
arms – 'Our cause is just, and victory will be ours!' – but
inevitably there were other themes, and some of them revealed the way his mind was working. He derided the National
Socialists, who were neither national nor socialist. They were
not national, for they had appropriated the territories of the
Czechs, Slovaks, Poles, Norwegians, Danes, Dutch, Belgians,
Frenchmen, Serbs, Greeks, Belorussians and the Baltic
peoples, and they were not socialist because they had deprived
the peoples of Europe of their elementary democratic liberties. These were dangerous arguments, for he had himself
appropriated the territory of Poland and he had never given
much thought to elementary democratic liberties until this
moment. Having proved that the National Socialists were

neither national nor socialist, he went on to describe them as they were – plunderers, blackguards, rapacious imperialists, and oppressors. 'The Hitler regime,' he said, 'is comparable with the reactionary regime of the Tsars.' He was still fighting the old battle with the Tsars, there in the subway station, with the Germans less than forty miles away.

He went on to speak of his gratitude to Great Britain and America, which had just granted his government a billion-dollar loan. Great Britain had ensured the supply of adequate amounts of aluminium, lead, tin, nickel, and rubber. These glorious countries had been denounced by Hitler as decadent plutocracies. 'It is not true, comrades,' Stalin declared. 'In Great Britain and the United States there are elementary democratic liberties, there are trade unions of workers and employees, there are labour parties, there are parliaments, whereas the Hitlerite regime has abolished all these institutions in Germany.' Such graceful tributes to the democratic liberties of Great Britain and America were never repeated.

He quoted from the writings and speeches of Hitler. One quotation was especially significant because it does not occur anywhere in Hitler's works. It read: 'Man is sinful from the moment of his birth and can be ruled only by force. All methods are permissible in treating him. When politics require it, it is necessary to lie, betray and even kill.'

He seemed to be quoting from some long-forgotten page of his own notebooks.

Towards the end the speech gathers momentum and power, dreams and apologetics giving way to a sense of the realities of war. He said:

> Only Hitlerite fools can fail to understand that not only the European rear but also the German rear represent a volcano ready to erupt and bury the Hitlerite adventurists.
>
> We have now a coalition of the Soviet Union, Great Britain and the United States against the German fascist imperialists. It is a fact that Great Britain, the United States and the Soviet Union have united in a single camp with the avowed purpose of crushing the Hitler imperialists and their armies of conquest. The present war is a war of engines. Whichever side has the overwhelming superiority in the production of engines will win the war. If we combine the output of the engines of the United States, Great Britain and the Soviet Union, we shall have a superiority of at

least three to one as compared with Germany. Herein lies one of the bases of the inevitable doom of Hitler's robber imperialism.

When he spoke in this way he was saying what needed to be said, with power and conviction. He gave a list of German and Russian casualties – the Germans had suffered four and a half million killed, wounded and prisoners, while the Russians had suffered only 350,000 killed and 378,000 missing and 1,020,000 wounded – and these figures, though wholly imaginary, perhaps needed to be stated. Again when he said: 'The German invaders want a war of extermination against the peoples of the Soviet Union – well, if they want this kind of war, they shall have it!' he was saying the right thing at the right time at the right place: in the heart of Moscow, where the German guns could be heard rumbling in the distance. And again:

> The Hitlerites are deprived of honour and conscience, and they have the morals of beasts. They have the audacity to call for the annihilation of the great Russian nation, the nation of Plekhanov and Lenin, Belinsky and Chernyshevsky, Pushkin and Tolstoy, Glinka and Tchaikovsky, Gorky and Chekhov, Sechenov and Pavlov, Repin and Surikov, Suvorov and Kutuzov.

If it was strange that he should place Plekhanov, whom he detested, at the head of the muster roll of heroes, there was nothing in the least strange that he should recite the names of the men who made Russia great. This was what the people wanted, and belatedly he was giving it to them.

On the following day, in another radio speech celebrating the anniversary of the revolution, he offered an even more significant muster roll, this time of the heroes who had led the Russian armies into battle:

> On you the whole world is looking, as the power capable of destroying the brigand hordes of the German invaders.
> On you the enslaved people of Europe, under the yoke of the German invaders, are looking, as their liberators.
> A great mission of liberation has fallen to your lot!
> May you be worthy of this mission!
> The war you are waging is a war of liberation, a war of justice.
> May you be inspired in this war by the heroic figures of our

ancestors – Alexander Nevsky, Dmitry Donskoy, Kuzma
Minin, Dmitry Pozharsky, Alexander Suvorov, Mikhail
Kutuzov.
May the victorious banner of the great Lenin inspire you!*

In this liturgical way, like a voice speaking across centuries
of history, Stalin invoked the ancient heroes. Alexander
Nevsky, Great Prince of Vladimir, had triumphed over the
Teutonic Knights in the thirteenth century. Dmitry Donskoy,
Great Prince of Moscow, had triumphed over the Tatars in
the fourteenth century. Kuzma Minin was a butcher of Nizhni
Novgorod who joined forces with Prince Dmitry Pozharsky
to hurl back the Poles who invaded Moscow in the early
years of the seventeenth century. Prince Suvorov defeated the
French in 1799, and Prince Kutuzov defeated Napoleon in
1812.

The speech with its appeal to the noble and aristocratic
warriors of the Tsars showed that profound changes were
taking place in Stalin's attitude towards the war. He was in
fact beginning to learn what every ten-year-old Russian
schoolboy already knew: that Russia was worth fighting for.
It was another question whether Stalin and the Communist
system were worth fighting for.

Henceforth when he spoke about the war, he would stress
that it was fought by Russians against Germans, not by Communists against National Socialists; and in his office two new
portraits were hung on the walls to accompany the portrait
of the thickly bearded Marx – the delicate features of Prince
Suvorov and the amiable features of Prince Kutuzov hung
side by side.

The speech which was broadcast all over Russia was delivered during the parade of troops on the Red Square held
at eight o'clock in the morning, three hours earlier than the
normal time. Snow had fallen during the previous night, but
the sun shone murkily through the clouds as he took his place
on top of Lenin's mausoleum, wearing his long unadorned
greatcoat and military cap. Cavalry, artillery and tanks crossed
the square, and rumbled straight off to the front. Similar
parades took place in other cities, Voroshilov taking the salute
at Kuibyshev and Timoshenko at Voronezh. But it was the
parade on the Red Square in Moscow which was chiefly

* Stalin used the word *osyenit*, which can also mean 'to bless',
'to sanctify', or 'to make the sign of the cross'.

memorable. In that grey early morning light with a thin mist hovering over the Kremlin walls, something which had been forgotten for nearly a quarter of a century was coming to life again.

Four days later, on November 11th, Stalin signed a decree renaming a tank brigade. 'For heroic conduct and brave fighting on the battlefield against the Germans,' he wrote, 'the Fourteenth Tank Brigade is hereby awarded the title of First Tank Brigade of Guards.'

In this way, at first tentatively, and then in full spate, the ancient traditions were revived. Lenin, dreaming of his people's militia and a vast homogeneous proletarian society, would have been surprised to see the emergence of a new officer class so grandly independent of the other classes that it took to wearing uniforms which rivalled those of the Italians in outward splendour. Soon new and ever more expansive uniforms were being designed, new medals and orders were created, and the officers acquired a status they had never known before under the Communist regime. Until the war was won, Stalin was content to share his rule with his officers.

GENERALISSIMO

WHEN THE SOVIET HISTORIANS began to write the history of the war, they were never able to describe precisely the role played by Stalin. He was like a mist pervading the whole of Russia, silent, invisible, strangely unreal. He did not conform to any pattern set by the heroic warriors of the past. He never rode out to battle, never gazed at the opposing armies through a telescope, never brandished a sword or fired a gun. To the very end of the war he remained a remote and inaccessible figure in the Kremlin.

Sometimes, it is true, he liked to imagine himself as a military leader in direct contact with his troops. From time to time he would encourage the rumour that he was visiting the front. When Admiral Standley, the American ambassador, asked to see Stalin on urgent business, he was told that it was impossible; Stalin, it was explained, was with his soldiers at the front. Apparently he made many visits to the front. He wrote to President Roosevelt on August 8th, 1943:

'I can answer your last letter now that I am back from the front.' At other times he would write: 'I have frequently to go to different sectors of the front and all other matters must be subordinated to the interests of the front', or 'I had no opportunity to leave the front even for one week'. It is possible that on very rare occasions he did go to the front, but no records of these journeys have survived, and they are never mentioned in military histories. So secret and mysterious were these journeys that no one ever observed him in his triumphal progress.*

Even in those strange wartime films which were produced with his assistance, he never appears at the front. Instead, we see him alone in the Kremlin late at night, leaning over an enormous map and smoking his pipe, a calm, meditative figure lost in dreams. Suddenly he traces out a mysterious line on the map with his pipe-stem, lifts a telephone, and calls Zhukov: 'Now Comrade Zhukov, I think the time has come to attack on the right flank.' The scene cuts to Zhukov's headquarters as the order for the attack is given, the guns roar, the Russians advance, and the Germans retire.

During the war Stalin played an astonishingly ambivalent role. He was in total command, but the words 'total' and 'command' can only be loosely defined. He was the supreme authority in the state; indeed, he was the only authority. He ruled by decree, but even more by the power of his legend. If he had died very early in the war leaving behind a few tape-recorded speeches encouraging the Red Army, he might conceivably have had the same effect on his troops. If he had died, it would have been necessary to pretend for weeks and perhaps months that he was still alive. For the Russians during the greater part of the war he was the disembodied voice of authority.

Although it pleased him to imagine that he was continually visiting the front, there is only one reasonably authentic account of a visit to his troops. This was related by his chief secretary, Alexander Poskrebyshev, who wrote that in the autumn of 1941 Stalin visited the Central Military Hospital in Moscow where 'he acquainted himself with the condition

* In an article in *The New York Times*, August 23rd, 1942, Ralph Parker reported that 'Stalin has appeared at the front'. Similar general statements appeared at intervals in the Soviet press.

of the sick and wounded officers and soldiers, and showed an interest in medical supplies'.

Throughout the war Stalin was generous in his appraisal of his own military genius. He claimed to have advanced military science by bold, new innovations. In a remarkable paragraph of his *Short Biography* he summarized his own theoretical contributions to military science in the following way:

> The advanced Soviet science of warfare received further development at Comrade Stalin's hands. Comrade Stalin elaborated the theory of the permanently operating factors that decide the outcome of wars, the theory of active defence and the laws the counter-offensive and of the offensive, of the co-operation of all services and arms in modern warfare, of the role of big tank masses and air forces in modern war, and of the artillery as the most formidable of the armed services. At the various stages of the war Stalin's genius found the correct solutions that took account of all the circumstances of the situation.

The reality, however, was far different. His incursions into the field of military strategy were nearly always disastrous. He knew very little about war, and was constantly surprising his associates with his ignorance. According to Khrushchev, he mapped out his infantile strategies on a large globe in his office, and was too lazy, or too indifferent, to study detailed war maps. He interfered continually with his military staff, promoted and demoted officers at will, gave orders which had to be countermanded, and was a perpetual nuisance to the high command. The high command learned how to satisfy his vanity by giving him the impression that he was in active command when, as sometimes happened, he was conducting military affairs when he was drunk.

He was a man who could not be argued with. Like Hitler he was always demanding full-scale frontal attacks even when the men and the supplies were not available; like Hitler, too, he refused to abandon a cherished plan of campaign even when it was demonstrated to him that the consequences of continuing it would only end in the annihilation of his forces. No commander, except perhaps Hitler, had ever been so wasteful of his resources. He was continually exercising his sovereign right to commit gratuitous errors.

The worst and most suicidal errors were committed in the early stages of the war, when Stalin simply threw down the reins of government, absented himself from military head-quarters, surrendered to despair and drank himself into a stupor. Khrushchev declared that it was a well-known fact that after the first severe disasters and reverses Stalin abandoned all hope, saying at a meeting of the Politburo: 'All that Lenin created we have lost forever.' There was a lengthy period when Stalin took no part in military affairs and ceased to do anything whatsoever. Sometimes, when he returned to work, his lieutenants wished he was still in a drunken stupor.

In his speech at the Twentieth Congress Khrushchev described how Stalin obstinately refused to contemplate a change of plans even when the existing plans inevitably led to defeat. Here Khrushchev describes his efforts to make Stalin see reason:

When there developed an exceptionally serious situation for our army in the Kharkov region in 1942, we correctly decided to drop an operation whose objective was to encircle Kharkov, because the actual situation at that time would have threatened our army with fatal consequences if this operation were continued.

We communicated this to Stalin, stating that the situation demanded changes in operational plans so that the enemy could be prevented from liquidating a sizable concentration of our army.

Contrary to common sense, Stalin rejected our suggestion and issued the order to continue the operation aimed at the encirclement of Kharkov, despite the fact that at this time many army concentrations were themselves actually threatened with extermination and encirclement.

I telephoned to Vasilievsky and begged him, 'Alexander Mikhailovich, take a map, and show Comrade Stalin the situation which has developed.' We should note that Stalin planned operations on a globe. Yes, comrades, he used to take a globe and trace the front line on it. I said to Comrade Vasilievsky, 'Show him the situation on a map; in the present situation we cannot continue the operation which was planned. The old decision must be changed for the good of the cause.'

Vasilievsky replied that Stalin had already studied the problem and that he, Vasilievsky, would not see Stalin further concerning the matter because the latter did not want to hear any arguments on the subject of this operation.

After this talk with Vasilievsky I telephoned to Stalin at his villa. But Stalin did not answer the telephone and Malenkov was at the receiver. I told Comrade Malenkov that I was calling from the front and that I wanted to speak personally to Stalin. Stalin informed me through Malenkov that I should speak with Malenkov. I stated for the second time that I wished to inform Stalin personally about the grave situation which had arisen for us at the front. But Stalin did not consider it convenient to raise the phone and again stated that I should speak to him through Malenkov, although he was only a few steps from the telephone.

After 'listening' in this manner to our plea, Stalin said, 'Let everything remain as it is!'

And what was the result of this? The worst that we had expected. The Germans surrounded our army concentrations, and consequently we lost hundreds of thousands of our soldiers. This is Stalin's military 'genius'; this is what it cost us.

Khrushchev is here describing a single incident which was being continually repeated; there were no holidays from Stalin's incompetence. The debâcle at Kharkov was to have fearful consequences. The official *History of the Great Fatherland War* says sombrely that after this defeat 'the Soviet command decided to go over to the defensive, and the strategical initiative now passed into the hands of the enemy'.

Although Khrushchev is not an altogether reliable witness to Stalin's general incompetence in military matters, for he had much to gain by proving that Stalin continually falsified his own role in the conduct of the war, nevertheless his testimony cannot be lightly dismissed. Khrushchev was one of Stalin's most faithful and loyal adherents.

As one might suspect, Stalin says nothing at all about the defeat at Kharkov in his *Short Biography*.

Stalin believed he could do no wrong. He claimed for himself the credit for organizing the army and planning all its campaigns, and he quite seriously believed that he possessed powers of divination denied to ordinary mortals. He wrote:

Stalin divined the design of the German command. He saw that the idea was to create the impression that the seizure of the oil region of Grozny and Baku was the major and not a subsidiary objective of the German summer offensive. He pointed out that the main objective was to envelop Moscow from the east, to cut it off from the rear, the area of the Volga and the Urals, then to strike at Moscow, and end the war in 1942.

As it happened, Hitler had no intention of attacking Moscow from the rear and after the failure of his offensive against Moscow in November and December 1941 he became supremely disinterested in the fate of the city. He planned at some future date to drown Moscow by damming up the Moskva river. In this way he would save his people the trouble of destroying it stone by stone.

Even at the beginning of the Russian campaign, Hitler showed little interest in Moscow. 'Only completely ossified brains, absorbed in the ideas of past centuries, can see any worth-while objective in taking the city,' Hitler declared, and he went on to explain that the chief purpose of the campaign was the capture of Leningrad and Stalingrad, which for some reason he regarded as the chief breeding grounds of Communism. 'If we destroy these two cities,' he said, 'then Bolshevism is dead.'

Stalin continued to believe that Moscow was Hitler's main objective, and Hitler continued to believe that Leningrad and Stalingrad were the two powerful poles which generated the Communist electricity. They were both labouring under delusions.

Probably Stalin believed that Moscow was Hitler's main objective because he was himself permanently established there. He had excellent reasons for remaining there. It was the hub of Russian rail communications and the headquarters of his highly centralized and streamlined government, now made more manageable by his decision to exile most of his commissars to Kuibyshev. It was 'the third Rome', the Mecca of world Communism, and the words 'Kremlin' and 'Moscow' had long since acquired charismatic qualities giving authority to words spoken from them. In the Kremlin he was on sacred ground. For him to have left Moscow would have been to admit defeat.

Though Stalin regarded himself as the commander in chief, powerfully deciding all military issues, his main service to the Russian cause was a symbolic one. He was the mysterious figurehead, the vengeful and ghostly creator of self-perpetuating legends of invincibility, the source of all power, the oracular and prophetical voice. Simply by remaining hidden behind the Kremlin walls, he conserved his power.

Although Stalin constantly proclaims that he directed the entire war effort of the Russian people, he very rarely offers concrete examples of leadership. He speaks in generalities. Once or twice we are given precise dates of his actions. He tells us, for example, that on October 5th, 1942, he sent an order to the commander of the Stalingrad front, saying: 'I demand that you take all measures for the defence of Stalingrad. Stalingrad must not be surrendered to the enemy.' Then we are told that six weeks later, on November 19th, the Soviet troops at the approaches of Stalingrad passed over to the offensive 'on the orders of Stalin'. He intends us to understand that he, and he alone, decided when the Red Army should pass over to the offensive.

In describing his accomplishments during the war Stalin was careful never to give credit to others. He never mentions the names of generals or soldiers. He never mentions the sufferings undergone by the Russian people. We learn that 'all operations during the Patriotic War were planned by Comrade Stalin and executed under his guidance', but since there were tens of thousands of operations, the claim is a manifest absurdity. He did not write these words. They were written by Marshal Bulganin on the occasion of Stalin's seventieth birthday; Bulganin was merely following the accepted interpretation of events.

In the *Short Biography* Stalin carefully lists under the appropriate dates the medals he received and the titles which were conferred on him in recognition of his services. He was awarded the title of Marshal of the Soviet Union on March 6th, 1943. He received the Order of Suvorov First Class on November 6th, 1943, and the first Moscow Defence Medal on June 20th, 1944. The Order of Victory was conferred on him on July 29th, 1944, and he was invested with the supreme military title of Generalissimo* of the Soviet Union on June 27th, 1945. He evidently felt a compulsive need for such honours and distinctions, but there must have been times when they weighed heavily on him. Once when Churchill complimented him on his new uniform as Marshal of the Soviet

---

* In Russian, *'Generalissimus'*. The title had been granted only once before, to honour the successful campaigns of Field Marshal Prince Alexander Suvorov.

Union, he brushed the compliment aside with the words: 'They said I ought to accept the position of head of the armed forces in order to improve the morale of the troops.' He did not say who 'they' were. The historian need not abide by Stalin's silence. 'They' was Stalin, who enjoyed heaping honours upon himself.

I, and I alone ... All through the *Short Biography* we are made aware of a man kneeling before his own altar, in solemn converse with his own image. We seem to be in a small dimly lit chapel, with a few faded portraits on the wall. From time to time we hear the noise of distant gunfire, and the sound of muttered prayers, and sometimes there comes the full-throated chanting of a strange liturgy. At rare intervals he rises and lights a candle to himself, or offers incense. We see him measuring out the incense with calm precision, with a disturbing intensity, and with a kind of exquisite patience. It is a process that will continue as long as there is any breath left in him.

In August 1942, when Churchill paid his first visit to Moscow, Stalin had been in power for nearly twenty years. He was a man who had forgotten what it was to have his orders disobeyed. He had known defeats and disasters on a scale unprecedented in Russian history, and he was himself responsible for those defeats and disasters, but except for a few days in the early weeks of the war when he simply retired from the war and gave himself up to prolonged drinking bouts, he remained calm and sanguine, certain of eventual victory. Churchill, too, was certain of victory. But they were fighting different wars.

Churchill and Stalin were men so different from one another that they seemed to belong to different species. The aristocratic, ebullient Churchill confronted the slow-moving, cautious descendant of peasant serfs. Churchill had hoped to strangle Communism at its birth. Stalin had hoped to destroy throughout the world the land-owning gentry from whom Churchill descended. They were natural enemies whose alliance in the nature of things could only be temporary. They hated and admired one another in equal proportions.

When Churchill, accompanied by Averell Harriman, flew into Moscow on an American B-24 bomber, he was received with all the honours due to a courageous ally. At the airport the flags of the Soviet Union, Great Britain and the United

States flew together, and the military band played the three national anthems. They arrived on one of those calm summer afternoons when only a few white clouds hang in the pale-blue sky. The sun shone, but there were storms coming.

These storms were inevitable, not only because Stalin and Churchill found themselves so often talking at cross-purposes. They arose from the frustrations of the time. On the Russian front Sevastopol had fallen after an eight-month siege, and the Germans were pushing deep into the Caucasus and beyond the Don elbow to Stalingrad. In the Far East Singapore had fallen, the battle of the Solomons was raging indecisively, and the Japanese had gained a precarious foothold on the Aleutian Islands. Rommel was on the threshold of Alexandria. The Germans were never again to be so strong as they were in the late summer and autumn of 1942.

To a glowering Stalin Churchill explained his reasons for not bringing about a second front in Western Europe – neither the manpower nor the resources were sufficient. Stalin asked whether it would be possible to throw six divisions into France, and Churchill answered that nothing would be gained by sacrificing 150,000 men if no German troops were drawn away from the Russian front. Stalin asked why Churchill was so afraid of the Germans. A man who was not prepared to take risks was hardly likely to win a war. Troops must be bloodied in battle: what good were they doing in England?

He was in an ugly mood, cunning and vituperative, playing, as he thought, on Churchill's weaknesses – his pride, his honour, his aristocratic background. There were long oppressive silences, interrupted by occasional moments of exuberance, as when Churchill enlarged on the bombing of Germany and Stalin indicated his pleasure at these bombing attacks, emphasizing the importance of striking at the morale of the German population. He revived again when Churchill outlined TORCH, the concerted Anglo-American attack on French North Africa. The plans were brought out. Churchill explained the nature of the operations – the British must win in Egypt in September, and in North Africa in the following month. Then it would be time to slice into the soft under-belly. And as he explained how the Anglo-American forces intended to cross the Mediterranean and land on German-occupied territory, he drew a picture of a crocodile and explained how he intended to tear into the soft belly while attacking the hard snout. Stalin, his interest at a high pitch, commended the enterprise, saying: 'May God prosper this undertaking.'

As Churchill tells the story, Stalin saw at once with remarkable precision all the advantages of TORCH. Churchill says he was deeply impressed with Stalin's assessment of the situation. The meeting lasted four hours. Towards the end they gathered round the famous large globe on which Stalin worked out his strategies. He was happier now, for he knew the best and the worst. Churchill, too, was happier, for he had succeeded in breaking through the iron crust. The next day, seeing Molotov, Churchill said: 'Stalin will make a great mistake to treat us roughly when we have come so far.' Molotov replied: 'Stalin is a very wise man. You may be sure that, however he argues, he understands all. I will tell him what you say.'

For once Churchill was able to use Stalin's weapon and turn it against him. He had made a threat.

Yet there was no immediate gain. Stalin's ugly temper returned at their next meeting. Once more there were taunts of cowardice. He wanted six or eight divisions thrown on to Cherbourg, and was in no mood to be rebuffed. In his eyes – it was an opinion that he was to preserve throughout the war – the British and Americans were deliberately stalling in the hope that Russia would bear the brunt of the war. Again and again he brought up the subject of an Allied invasion of France until Churchill lost patience and remarked sweetly that the proposal for a landing on Cherbourg overlooked the existence of the Channel, and then went on to point out that Great Britain had fought alone for a year against Germany and Italy, and there had never been any question of Russian aid to Britain. Stalin said he liked Churchill's tone, but went on grumbling.

When Harriman asked about the plans for flying American aircraft across Siberia, Stalin answered curtly: 'Wars are not won with planes.' It was perhaps his way of showing that he was in command.

There was the inevitable banquet in the Kremlin, with Stalin sitting at the centre of a long table with Churchill on his right and Harriman on his left. Churchill wore his battle dress, blue overalls with a zipper and no tie, to the discomfiture of the Russians who expected formality at their banquets. Churchill and Stalin exchanged small talk. Somehow the subject of Churchill's attempts to strangle the Russian Revolution at birth came up, and the astute Pavlov, translating or mistranslating Stalin's words, said: 'Premier Stalin, he say all that is in the past, and the past belongs to God.'

The menu has been preserved, and reads like a banquet under the Tsars:

Fresh and pressed caviar, white *balik*, salmon, garnished herring, and *shamaya*, a smoked fish from the lower Don.

Cold ham, *pâté de foie gras*, cold game with mayonnaise, cold duck.

Sturgeon prepared with jelly and pickles, tomato salad, vegetable salad, cucumbers, tomatoes, radishes, Caucasian pickles, cheese, butter, toast, fish-stuffed pastry, rolls.

White mushrooms, served hot with sour cream, game minced with herring and potatoes, squash *meunière*.

Cream chicken soup, consommé, and clear beet soup.

Sterlet cooked in champagne.

Turkey, chicken and hazel grouse, spring lamb with potatoes.

Cucumber salad, cauliflower, asparagus.

Ice cream, sherbet, liqueurs, coffee, *petits fours*, and roasted almonds.

There were countless toasts at the banquet, the most curious being one proposed by Stalin to intelligence officers.

'I should like to propose a toast that no one can answer,' he said. 'It is to intelligence officers. They cannot answer, because no one knows who they are, but their work is important.'

He went on to emphasize the importance of intelligence officers by reminding his audience that Churchill had won the Dardanelles campaign in 1915 without knowing it. The Germans and Turks were already retreating, but faulty British intelligence resulted in a withdrawal exactly at the moment when they should have followed up their advantage. It was an oddly insulting toast – Churchill somehow succeeded in convincing himself that it was intended to be complimentary – but it was not clear why Stalin had chosen to be insulting at that moment. The situation was saved by Captain Jack Duncan, the United States naval attaché, who rose and said:

'I can answer that toast to intelligence officers, because I'm one of them. If we make mistakes, it is because we know only what you tell us – and that's not much.'

Stalin laughed, and called down the table: 'If there's anything you want to know, ask me. I'll be your intelligence officer.'

Then he left his seat and walked up to Duncan to drink a personal toast with him. Stalin was so pleased with Duncan that when the dinner broke up, he sought out the American officer and they walked out of the room together, arm in arm.

But although Stalin promised to act as an intelligence officer, he volunteered very little information; and even Marshal Shaposhnikov, still the Chief of Staff, when confronted with Sir Alan Brooke, Chief of the Imperial General Staff, and other high military figures Churchill had brought with him, remained obstinately silent. The Russians, under Stalin's orders, were giving nothing away.

Churchill had decided to leave for Teheran at dawn on August 16th. At seven o'clock the previous evening he went to call on Stalin to say farewell, thinking there would be a brief talk and perhaps a glance at the huge ten-foot-diameter globe in his study and then it would be over. Stalin however was in no hurry to let him go. 'Why should we not go to my house for some drinks?' he asked, and soon they were wandering through many passages and rooms until they came out into a quiet road within the Kremlin walls and some two hundred yards further on they came to the apartment where Stalin lived. It was, Churchill noted, a moderate-sized apartment, simple, dignified, with four rooms – a dining-room, workroom, bedroom and large bathroom. Soon Svetlana, Stalin's red-haired daughter, appeared. She kissed her father dutifully, and then vanished, while he uncorked the bottles. There was another banquet, and more quiet talk, but Stalin could rarely sustain a pleasant mood, and soon enough there came the ugly taunts, the senseless sallies. Most of the ships of an Arctic convoy had been sunk, and Stalin, who knew only that the convoy had failed to bring into Murmansk much needed equipment, said: 'Has the British Navy no sense of glory?'

'You must take it from me that what was done was right,' Churchill replied. 'I really do know a lot about the Navy and sea war.'

'Meaning,' said Stalin, 'that I know nothing?'

'Russia is a land animal,' Churchill answered. 'The British are sea animals.'

There was an uncomfortable silence. So it had been

throughout Churchill's visit to Moscow: the silences were deafening.

Wendell Willkie, who reached Moscow the following month as a special emissary of President Roosevelt, was received more gently. He was, after all, in no such commanding position as Churchill. 'Stalin looked tired,' Willkie reported, 'not sick, but desperately tired.' Willkie was surprised to discover how short he was – five feet four or five. His face looked hard, and the mind behind it was hard and tenacious. 'He asked searching questions, each of them loaded like a revolver,' Willkie said. Among those questions was one which Willkie went to some pains to answer. Stalin asked why the Allies did not simply take over bases in neutral countries, particularly if the neutral countries were unco-operative and unable to defend them.

Inevitably the discussion turned to Stalingrad. Stalin, a realist, had no illusions that the city was impregnable. 'He made no predictions,' Willkie reported, 'as to Russia's ability to hold it, and he was quite definite in his assertion that neither love of homeland nor pure bravery could save it. Battles were won or lost primarily by numbers, skill and materiel.'

On September 22nd the Germans were already fighting in the streets of Stalingrad, but the battle for the city had only just begun. It was in fact one of the longest and most bitterly contested battles on record, for altogether it lasted for 162 days. Nearly 300,000 Germans and Rumanians were killed or taken prisoner in the Stalingrad debacle; and when Field Marshal Friedrich Paulus finally capitulated at the end of January, the Russians celebrated the greatest of all their triumphs during the war. The end came two days later with a dispatch addressed to Stalin by Generals Voronov and Rokossovsky:

Carrying out your orders, the troops of the Don front at 4 pm, February 2nd, completed the rout and annihilation of the encircled enemy troops at Stalingrad.

But even before the dispatch was received, Moscow celebrated the victory with fireworks. For the first time since the beginning of the war it became possible to believe that the Nazi tide could be rolled back.

In his Order of the Day published on February 23rd, 1943, on the occasion of the twenty-fifth anniversary of the founding of the Red Army, Stalin claimed that in twenty months of war the Red Army had disabled nine million German officers and men, of whom four million had been killed on the battlefield, while the Rumanian, Italian and Hungarian armies which were fighting on Russian soil had been completely routed. He paid tribute to the flexibility of the Red Army commanders, who had learned to take advantage of the inflexibility of the German military code: and he warned against complacency. Many more long hard battles would have to be fought before the Germans were finally ousted from Russian soil. Victory was not yet assured.

Inevitably vast changes were taking place in the fabric of the Soviet Union. The life of a Soviet worker, harsh before the war, became harsher. A series of decrees signed by Stalin withdrew from the workers the few rights they had possessed. For being twenty minutes late at work, people were hauled before criminal courts and fined 20 per cent of their wages for six months. Exemplary punishment was meted out to those who did not produce their norms. But while the severity of Communist law was visited on the workers, there were other areas where the laws were relaxed. The relations between Church and state improved, for Stalin was perceptive enough to realize that the Church was useful to the Communist cause. On November 7th, 1942, on the twenty-fifth anniversary of the Bolshevik revolution, Sergey, the acting Patriarch and Metropolitan of Moscow, wrote an extraordinary letter to Stalin:

> In the name of our clergy and all true believers of the Russian Orthodox Church, true children of our Fatherland, I sincerely and prayerfully salute you, who have been chosen by God to lead our military and cultural forces, leading us to victory over the barbarian invaders, to a peaceful flowering of our country and to a bright future for its peoples.
>
> God bless with success and glory your great deed for the sake of the Fatherland.

When this letter was reproduced in the Soviet press, the word 'God' was capitalized for the first time since the October revolution. In the following year the churches were reopened. In September 1943 Stalin signed what amounted to a concordat with the Orthodox Church. While the Church offered its full support to the Soviet war effort, Stalin dissolved the League of the Godless and suspended the *Atheists*

Journal. Ironically, the printing presses of the League of the Godless were turned over to the church authorities, and on these presses Sergey promptly began to publish a monthly *Journal of the Patriarchate.*

These were not superficial changes: they reflected profound changes in men's minds, and in the mind of Stalin. The military was in power and demanded that its power should be recognized. On January 10th, 1943, a decree of the Supreme Soviet ordered the reintroduction of officers' epaulettes.* A decree issued during the battle for Stalingrad subordinated the political commissars to the military. A month later 'socialist competition' was abolished in the army. Saluting became obligatory, and the privileges of the officers' corps were revived with separate messes for junior and senior officers. The hierarchical divisions were intended as temporary measures, but continued after the war.

Stalin's new-found benevolence towards the Red Army was dictated by the nature of the war; so, too, was his new-found benevolence towards the Allies. In that same year he announced the dissolution of the Comintern, the officially sponsored conspiratorial organization with which the Russian communists hoped to overthrow most of the existing governments in the world. Towards the end of the same year he announced that the 'Internationale' was no longer the official anthem of the Soviet Union. In the new anthem *Rus* – the

---

* Gold and silver epaulettes were reserved for the officers, but the soldiers also wore epaulettes distinguishing them by regiments and trades. Among other innovations was the introduction of the battle flag accompanied by a precise ritual of worship. When the banner was presented to the soldiers, all knelt and kissed it three times while the 'Internationale' was sung. The new ritual, evidently modelled on the kissing of the icon in Tsarist times, was ordered in a decree dated December 21st, 1942. As Alexander Werth observed: 'The gold braid of the Red Army emerged from the fires of Stalingrad.'

The Red Army appears to have planned these changes long before the battle of Stalingrad. Alexander Werth reports a curious conversation in January 1943 with General Rodion Manilovsky, who mentioned 'the revolutionary changes which had been carried out in the Red Army in the summer of 1942'. The general did not explain what the changes were, and an attentive reading of the official *History of the Great Fatherland War* fails to elucidate them. Yet it is certain that they involved a vast surrender of political power to the Red Army.

medieval Russian state of Kiev – was rhymed with *Sovietsky Soyuz*, the Soviet Union. In this way he was able to strike a balance between the claims of the present and the past.

The German tide was rolling back, for after Stalingrad the initiative passed into the hands of the Red Army. Victories were being announced almost daily. When November came, with the traditional celebrations in honour of the 1917 revolution, Stalin was able to report that Russian forces had succeeded in liberating nearly a million square kilometres of territory, almost two thirds of the land seized by the enemy, and the Germans were no longer fighting for world domination: they were fighting to keep body and soul together. The Germans announced 'total' mobilization. 'It may prove necessary,' Stalin commented, 'for them to announce still another "total" mobilization. It will not help them. It will only lead to their "total" collapse.'

Such heavy-handed humour was appropriate to the occasion, and he went on in the same vein to enlarge on the penalties of counting on a quick victory.

When they entered the war, the parties in the Hitlerite bloc counted on a speedy victory. They had already allotted among themselves the various rewards and penalties – who would get the buns and the pies, and who would get bumps and black eyes. They naturally meant the bumps and black eyes for their adversaries, and the buns and pies for themselves. Now it is obvious that Germany and her flunkeys will get no buns and pies. They will have to share the bumps and black eyes.

On that day the Germans received one of their worst black eyes – Kiev was recaptured by the Russians, and Moscow celebrated with salvos of artillery and displays of fireworks. Kharkov was recaptured in August and Smolensk in September. As the famous cities returned to their hands, the Russians felt a renewed sense of confidence. No one any longer believed that Hitler would win the war.

In honour of these victories Stalin permitted himself to receive from the aged President Kalinin the newly established Order of Suvorov. Wearing the new order, he appeared before the Moscow Soviet in his marshal's uniform, more resplendent than ever. He wore a white tunic and epaulettes of gold. It was a strange uniform for a revolutionary to wear; one could not imagine Lenin wearing it. Nevertheless it suited the occasion. Another Napoleon had been hurled back from the gates of Moscow; another Prince Suvorov had appeared, ready to lead his armies across Europe.

A few days later Stalin flew to Teheran to meet Roosevelt and Churchill. Between them they would decide the countless issues of the war.

TWO CONFERENCES

FOR MANY MONTHS the Allied leaders had been debating among themselves where they should meet. Stalin preferred a meeting on Soviet soil, and suggested Astrakhan or Archangel. Churchill preferred North Africa or the Middle East, and at various times he favoured meeting places in Cairo, Baghdad, Basra, Khartum and Asmara, the former capital of Eritrea. On the theory that the ideal meeting place would be midway between Moscow and Washington, he sometimes chose sites nearer home – Iceland and Scapa Flow were mentioned. Stalin, however, was adamant. He was determined not to go far from Russia, and he seems to have been dubious about the advantages to be gained by a direct confrontation between the leaders, who had been confronting one another weekly and sometimes daily in their correspondence.

There were, of course, many reasons for his reluctance to travel. Except for his annual prewar holidays on the Black Sea coast, he had forgotten the habit of travel and took no pleasure in finding himself in unfamiliar surroundings. He had not travelled abroad for thirty years, and for fifteen years he had been settled permanently in Moscow. There was some question too about the state of his health, and there was the difficulty of arranging for the transport of his army of security guards. He wanted Roosevelt and Churchill to meet him in Russia, to add lustre to his vast and increasing power, but neither Roosevelt nor Churchill was yet disposed to become a hostage on his own soil. Teheran was chosen because Iran was already occupied by Soviet, British and American troops. They had deposed the pro-German Shah and set his son on the Peacock Throne.

Stalin arrived in Teheran by air two or three days before the others, to set the stage. His movements were shrouded in secrecy, but he is said to have made a short stopover in Stalin-grad and another at Armavir. If his aeroplane landed at Stalingrad, this was his first visit to the city since 1918, and his only known visit during the period when it bore his name. It was rumoured during the battle of Stalingrad that Stalin appeared briefly at field headquarters, but the rumours were never substantiated.

As usual, Stalin's first task at Teheran was to impose his will. It occurred to him, or to Molotov, that something might be gained by inviting President Roosevelt to stay in the large compound of the Soviet embassy on the excuse that he would be safer. There was the possibility of assassination attempts, and these, it was suggested, must be dealt with seriously; and if the President refused to accept Stalin's hospitality, then he, the President would have to accept the entire responsibility in the event that Stalin was assassinated while making his way to the American embassy.

It was an astonishing manoeuvre, and a successful one, for although the President first refused the offer – accommodation had previously been offered to him by the British and by the Shah who offered the use of one of his palaces – he appears to have accepted it only when Stalin insisted that his, Stalin's, life was also at stake. Throughout the greater part of his stay in Teheran the President therefore remained within the Russian embassy, watched over by NKVD guards who made his bed, listened through hidden microphones to his most secret conversations with his aides, and kept close watch on his movements. Without giving himself the time to weigh the consequences of the move, Roosevelt had become Stalin's prisoner.

He had hardly settled in his new quarters when Stalin came to welcome him, wearing a camel's-hair topcoat and a dark-blue uniform with red stripes down the trouser legs. It was the first meeting between the two statesmen, and they sat down to take each other's measure. The meeting lasted for nearly three-quarters of an hour. Stalin began by painting a melancholy picture of the military situation in Russia – Zhito-mir had just fallen to the Germans, Korosten was about to fall, and the Germans were continually bringing up new divisions. Only in the Ukraine was it possible for the Soviet armies to take the initiative and carry out offensive operations. Roosevelt listened sympathetically, and answered that it was precisely in order to discuss the best way to remove 30 or

40 German divisions from the eastern front that the meeting in Teheran had been arranged. They went on to discuss the Chinese army, and Stalin said it fought very badly, but that was the fault of its leaders. He took an equally dim view of the French army, explaining that he had no particular affection for General de Gaulle, 'who acts as though he were the head of a great state, but in fact commands little power'. Then he launched an attack on the French ruling classes who had co-operated with the Germans and should not be entitled to share in any of the benefits of the peace. He seemed to regard the French as enemies and said they must pay for their criminal collaboration with Germany. The President said that after a hundred years of French rule in Indochina, the inhabitants were worse off than they had been before, and it would be better if Indochina were placed under a trusteeship. Stalin agreed. He also agreed when Roosevelt suggested that India would probably have to be reformed 'from the bottom, somewhat on the Soviet line'. He noted that this would mean revolution. On this note the preliminary conference between Stalin and Roosevelt ended, for the first general meeting between the three allied leaders was about to take place.

There were to be three plenary meetings, and a number of protracted discussions. The conversations, which have been reported in great detail in an official publication of the Department of State, make saddening reading. Stalin was in the position of an emperor dealing with kings. He spoke always briefly, and often rudely. Once when the President asked him a question while he was looking at a document, he said without looking up: 'For God's sake allow me to finish my work!' When he realized that the President had asked the question, he showed for the first and last time during the conference some embarrassment, but made no apologies; instead, he simply resumed the reading of the document.

To Roosevelt he usually showed a cautious deference; to Churchill he showed an intermittent contempt. He was industrious in his attacks on Churchill. He evidently enjoyed needling the Prime Minister, and it amused him that Roosevelt rarely came to his defence. Not that Churchill needed defending; he was perfectly capable of answering in the same coin, and did so frequently, but without venom. His incredible buoyancy and serenity saved him from the temptations of bitterness. Stalin's attacks on Churchill sought to present him as a weakling, a secret admirer of Germany and a public enemy of the Soviet Union. On one occasion at a dinner in the British legation, Stalin drank a toast to Roosevelt and Churchill, calling them his 'fighting friends', adding pointedly, 'if it is possible for me to consider Mr Churchill my friend'.

Clearly he did not regard Churchill as a friend. Churchill was a nuisance, tolerated only because he commanded vast military forces. There were moments when Stalin seemed about to order Churchill's execution. At a dinner in the Soviet embassy, following the second plenary meeting, Stalin put forward one of his favourite ideas. He suggested that after the war some 50,000 to 100,000 German officers should be summarily liquidated. Churchill was aghast. This was cold-blooded political murder, and he said so. Stalin taunted him with a secret affection for the Germans. Churchill denied that he had any affection for them, and said: 'I would rather be taken out into the garden here and now and be shot myself than sully my own and my country's honour by such infamy.' Roosevelt, who also enjoyed baiting Churchill, offered a compromise, suggesting that only 49,000 German officers should be shot, so perhaps reducing the argument to ridicule. Churchill records in his memoirs that Elliott Roosevelt, the President's son, presented himself at the banquet and intervened with a speech in which he said he cordially agreed with Marshal Stalin and he was sure the United States Army was also in agreement. A shocked Churchill then rose and made his way to the next room: Achilles brooding in his tent. The room was in semi-darkness. Suddenly out of the gloom Stalin and Molotov appeared, grinning broadly, eagerly explaining that they were only playing when they spoke of liquidation and that no harm was meant. Churchill decided to return to the banquet hall, with an uneasy feeling that no amount of persiflage and good-fellowship would wipe the crime away.

There was not the least doubt that Stalin intended to inaugurate a vast *chistka* among the Germans without bringing them to trial. He spoke of having interviewed German prisoners and asking them why they killed women and children. When he received no satisfactory reply, he ordered them to be shot out of hand. It was one of his minor pleasures. Such interrogations indeed had been the commonplaces of his life. So it had been in Leningrad in 1934, and so it was again during the period of the great purges. He still enjoyed choosing his victims at random.

As the three heads of state gathered round the council table, they sometimes resembled destructive children tearing a sand castle to pieces. They relished discussions about the dismemberment of Germany. Sometimes they would wonder how it could be brought about. 'What is the use of ordering them not to rearm?' Stalin asked bitterly. 'Can you forbid the existence of watchmakers and furniture factories, which make parts of shells?'

'Nothing is final,' Churchill replied. 'The world rolls on. We have now learnt something. Our duty is to make the world safe for at least fifty years by German disarmament, by supervision of German factories, by forbidding all aviation, and by territorial changes of a far-reaching character. It all comes back to the question whether Great Britain, the United States and the Soviet Union can keep a close friendship and supervise Germany in their mutual interest.'

This was indeed the crucial question, but it remained unresolved: they avoided it by mutual consent. They were strangely discursive, jumping from one subject to another, returning at intervals to pick up the threads. They spoke of their towering responsibilities, but their mutual rivalries impeded a consciousness of responsibility to the world. There were a vast number of subjects Stalin refused to talk about, with the result that Churchill and Roosevelt acquired a sixth sense which enabled them delicately to skirt dangerous areas. Stalin was continually asking questions, and they were continually seeking to please him, or at least not to offend him, with their replies. He dominated the conference not so much by force of character as by his angry determination to get what he wanted.

In the end he could do with them what he wanted. Above all, he wanted OVERLORD, the invasion of France across the English Channel, with no Allied adventures in the eastern Mediterranean. Churchill had worked out a sensible formula by which a preponderance of military power would be directed at northern France while smaller forces were retained in Italy and the eastern Mediterranean. Stalin wanted everything thrown at northern France, and laughed at diversionary tactics. 'What do you gain by getting Rhodes?' he asked Churchill, who growled that there was a good deal to be gained by getting Turkey. Stalin let it be known that he regarded Churchill as the expert on diversions; for himself he preferred the mass attack.

A singular and inexplicable incident occurred when Churchill, at the command of King George VI, presented a Sword of Honour to Stalin to commemorate the gallant defence of Stalingrad. The sword was of gilded bronze with a pommel of flawless crystal, encased in a scabbard of scarlet and gold. It was a breathtaking example of the swordmaker's art made by English craftsmen who had been employed in swordmaking for generations. The blade bore the inscription: 'To the steel-hearted citizens of Stalingrad, a gift from King George VI as a token of homage of the British people.' A Russian band played, British and Russian soldiers stood at attention as Churchill solemnly offered the sword to Stalin who lifted it to his lips and kissed the scabbard.

It was a moment of quite extraordinary emotion. The years of strain and horror seemed to vanish in the ceremonial presentation of the sword. The movie camera recorded the solemn scene: a large room, chandeliers blazing, Stalin standing between Voroshilov and Molotov, Churchill a little way away, the sword lying in its sumptuous case, then the presentation and the long kiss. A moment later Stalin turned to Voroshilov, whispered something, and solemnly handed him the sword. The movie cameras follow the scene closely, and for a brief moment we see Voroshilov gazing pensively at the sword, with a faint smile. Suddenly the cameras jerk away, and there is only a confusion of heads craning down at the carpet. Voroshilov has dropped the sword. He seems to have let it fall deliberately.

Some months later Roosevelt, who was present at the ceremony, told Frances Perkins that he had been deeply impressed by Stalin's behaviour during the presentation of the sword. He told her:

It was a magnificent ceremonial sword on a crimson velvet cushion, and Churchill made one of his best brief speeches. Churchill himself was pretty well worked up with emotion as he expressed the admiration of the British people for the Russians' gallant battle and for Stalin's magnificent leadership.

As Stalin rose to accept the sword he flushed with a kind of emotional quality which I knew was very real. He put out his hands and took the sword from the crimson cushion. There were tears in his eyes. I saw them myself. He bowed from the hips swiftly and kissed the sword, a ceremonial gesture of great style which I know was unrehearsed. It was really very magnificent, moving and sincere.

He is a very interesting man. They say he is a peasant from one of the least progressive parts of Russia, but let me tell you he had an elegance of manner which none of the rest of us had.

Roosevelt was fascinated by Stalin and by all things Russian; puzzled and curiously uninformed. He was inclined to give Stalin the benefit of every doubt. Once, during the early part of the war, he received a rude and peremptory letter from Stalin and was dumbfounded. He decided to wait a day before replying. The next morning there came another letter from Stalin; it was couched in amiable terms and made no reference to the previous letter. The change of mood was ascribed by Roosevelt to the waywardness of the Russian character. In this he was almost certainly wrong. Stalin was a long-established devotee of shock treatment, and he knew exactly how to apply it.

Because he was fascinated and puzzled by Stalin, Roosevelt went to great pains to penetrate the mystery. It occurred to him that he could please Stalin by making a laughing-stock of Churchill; in this way Stalin might become more amenable. He told Frances Perkins about the incident:

I talked privately with Stalin. I didn't say anything I hadn't said before, but it appeared quite chummy and confidential, enough so that the other Russians joined in to listen. Still no smile.

Then I said, lifting my hand up to cover a whisper (which of course had to be interpreted) 'Winston is cranky this morning, he got up on the wrong side of the bed.'

A vague smile passed over Stalin's eyes, and I decided I was on the right track. As soon as I sat down at the conference table, I began to tease Churchill about his Britishness, about John Bull, about his cigars, about his habits. It began to register with Stalin. Winston got red and scowled, and the more he did so, the more Stalin smiled. Finally Stalin broke out into a deep, hearty guffaw, and for the first time in three days I saw light. I kept it up and Stalin was laughing with me, and it was then that I called him 'Uncle Joe'. He would have thought me fresh the day before, but that day he laughed and came over and shook my hand.

From that time on our relations were personal, and Stalin himself indulged in an occasional witticism. The ice was broken and we talked like men and brothers.

It was in this mood of banter and contrived gaiety that Roosevelt sought to win Stalin and influence him, and if at times he seemed to succeed there were many occasions when he failed. Months later, when asked what kind of man Stalin was, he shook his head with an expression of bafflement and said: 'Who knows?' Shortly after Teheran he said: 'Stalin is a man hewn out of granite.'

At the end of the conference an official communiqué was prepared and the world was informed that the three leaders had 'shaped and confirmed' a common policy. Some definite decisions had been arrived at, but there was little evidence of a common policy. They decided upon a firm date for the opening of the Second Front, they approved the establishment of the United Nations, and they were in general agreement that the war potential of Germany must be destroyed and that the Curzon Line should be maintained as the eastern boundary of Poland. For the first time Stalin agreed to let the British and American air forces use Russian bases. On other matters they agreed to disagree. Churchill and Roosevelt were continually raising questions which Stalin adamantly refused to discuss; most of these questions involved the territorial aggrandizement of the Soviet Union. When Churchill asked for an exact statement of the territorial interests of the Soviet Union, Stalin answered: 'There is no need to speak at the present time about any Soviet desires, but when the time comes, we will speak.'

Such, indeed, was his common practice: he would make no commitments, while demanding that Churchill and Roosevelt commit themselves to the hilt. He gave nothing away, contented himself with ill-defined promises, and acted in the imperial manner. He spoke from a position of strength, and both Churchill and Roosevelt permitted themselves to be interrogated and found it more agreeable to do little interrogation of their own. Churchill, at one of their meetings, offered the toast of 'Stalin the Great'. In their different ways both Churchill and Roosevelt felt compelled to pay continual homage to Stalin.

Churchill had few illusions about the nature of Stalin's desires. He was, he knew, dealing with a man who had a monstrous appetite. Stalin wanted all he could get, and more. Nevertheless it was necessary to invent the diplomatic fiction that he was fair and scrupulous, and to pretend that there were no grounds for suspicion. Churchill's judgement of the conference was a realistic one: he had to get along as best he could with a tyrant of unparalleled greed in order to dethrone another tyrant of unparalleled greed. He would find honourable excuses for all Stalin's faults. If his armies were being defeated, then he must be excused for his suspicious nature. If his armies were winning, he must be excused for being so domineering. Churchill wrote: 'It would not have been right at Teheran for the Western democracies to found their plans upon suspicions of the Russian attitude in the hour of triumph and when all her dangers were removed.'

The conference ended on a note of apparent cordiality. There were to be two more conferences; at each of them there was an air of outward cordiality, while the suspicions grew stronger, the disagreements became more fearful, and the antagonisms more ominous.

When the three leaders met again in Yalta in February 1945, they already knew that Germany was doomed. Russian, American and British troops had already penetrated German soil. Japan, too, was doomed, for the Americans were already closing in on the islands, Manila was about to fall, and there was fighting on Iwo Jima.

The conference at Yalta was therefore brought about to decide the issues which attended the ending of the war and the beginning of the peace. It should have been, and conceivably might have been, a congress of the victors determined to safeguard the peace from their own rivalries and ambitions, but it succeeded only in exasperating their rivalries and in quickening their ambitions.

From the beginning an air of menace hung over the Yalta conference. Stalin was determined that it should be held on Russian soil, or not at all. At various times Roosevelt and Churchill had discussed other sites, mostly on the shores of the Mediterranean. Jerusalem, Alexandria, Athens, Malta, Rome, Taormina, Cyprus, and the Riviera had been proposed, only to meet with relentless opposition from Stalin. At one time Roosevelt suggested a meeting in Fairbanks, Alaska. Batum was suggested by Stalin, and Churchill backed by Roosevelt put forward the claims of Scotland. Stalin refused

With respect to the post-war period, the Governments of the United States, the U.S.S.R., and the United Kingdom are in accord with the Government of Iran that any economic problems confronting Iran at the close of hostilities should receive full consideration, along with those of other members of the United Nations, by [~~any~~] conferences or international agencies held or created to deal with international economic matters.

The Governments of the United States, the U.S.S.R., and the United Kingdom are at one with the Government of Iran in their desire for the maintenance of the independence, sovereignty and territorial integrity of Iran. They count upon the participation of Iran, together with all other peace-loving nations, in the establishment of international peace, security and prosperity after the war, in accordance with the principles of the Atlantic Charter, to which all four Governments have subscribed.

Winston S. Churchill.

U. G. Stalin.

Franklin D. Roosevelt

to compromise. Pleading ill-health and his intense dislike of travelling by aeroplane – he had suffered an infection of the ears during the return flight from Teheran – he decided that the meeting must be held within easy reach of Moscow. The choice of Yalta was made without any consideration for the comfort of Roosevelt or Churchill; and they accepted the choice with an uneasy sense of being imposed upon.

When Roosevelt reached Yalta, he was a dying man. So, too, was his chief adviser, Harry Hopkins. They had been so ill during the journey that they were unable to read through the voluminous position papers prepared by the State Department, and on many large and small matters they were surprisingly ignorant. Roosevelt still believed that he could charm Stalin into acquiescence, and Churchill, relegated to the position of a junior partner in the enterprise because the military power he commanded was considerably less than that of Russia or America, found that he had to fight for every principle and every inch of territory.

The overwhelming question at the Yalta conference was whether the three powers would be able to work together, or whether they would soon be at each other's throats. Stalin raised the question at an early stage of the conference. He said:

I would like to ask Mr Churchill to name the power which may intend to dominate the world. I am sure Great Britain does not want to dominate the world. So one is removed from suspicion. I am sure the United States does not want to do so, so another is excluded from the powers having intentions to dominate the world.... I know that under the leaders of the three powers represented here we may feel safe. But these leaders may not live forever. In ten years' time we may disappear. A new generation will come which did not experience the horrors of war and may probably forget what we have gone through. We would like to secure the peace for at least fifty years. We have now to build up such a status, such a plan, that we can put as many obstacles as possible to the coming generation quarrelling among themselves. I think that our task is to secure our unity in the future, and, for this purpose, we must agree upon such a covenant as would best serve that purpose. The danger in the future is the possibility of conflicts among ourselves.

Stalin spoke in a mood of irony, but there was no doubting his seriousness of purpose when he came to speak the last sentence. The danger was real and crucial, and it would remain crucial even if the United Nations came swiftly into existence. There was simply no adequate machinery to prevent conflicts between the three great powers. It was no longer a question of the possibility of conflict, but of its eminent probability. In an oblique fashion Stalin discounted, or pretended to discount, the possibility that Great Britain or the United States intended to dominate the world, while remaining silent about the intentions of the Soviet Union. His silence was ominous. So, too, was his unyielding attitude towards Poland.

For Churchill the question of a free and independent Poland was a matter of honour. Stalin replied that for Russia it was a matter of life and death, adding that a weak Poland would always provide a corridor for the German army, and an unfriendly Poland was a perpetual menace. 'It is a question of honour for Russia that we shall have to eliminate many things from the books,' he said, and what he meant by this was that many Poles would have to be eliminated. He spoke menacingly about the Polish government-in-exile in London, accusing it of being vigorously anti-Russian. He preferred the Communist government established in Lublin, which was obedient to him, and said so in terms which were not calculated to make Churchill or Roosevelt less fearful. He said:

Now as a military man I must say what I demand of a country liberated by the Red Army. First there should be peace and quiet in the wake of the army. The men of the Red Army are indifferent as to what kind of government there is in Poland, but they do want one that will maintain order behind the lines. The Lublin Warsaw government fulfils this role not badly. There are agents of the London government connected with the so-called underground. They are called resistance forces. We have had nothing good from them but much evil. So far their agents have killed 212 Russian military men. They have attacked supply bases for arms. It was announced that all wireless stations must be registered, but these forces continued to break all the laws of war and complained of being arrested. If they attack the Red Army any more they will be shot. When I compare the agents of both governments, I find the Lublin ones are useful and the others the contrary. The military must have peace and quiet. The military will support such a government and I cannot do otherwise. Such is the situation.

In reply Churchill said: 'I cannot feel that the Lublin government has any right to represent the Polish nation,' but he was in no position to enforce his views. Stalin was not attending a conference of equals; he was dictating his terms.

Churchill fought helplessly for Poland, knowing that the odds were against him; for France he fought like a tiger. Neither the President nor Stalin showed much affection for France. They had both, they thought, taken the measure of General de Gaulle, and found him wanting. Roosevelt could not forget that the general had once compared himself with Joan of Arc, Stalin could not forget that France had opened the gates to the enemy. Churchill pleaded to let France have a zone of occupation in conquered Germany and a place in the control machinery, and he wanted France to have an army of occupation on German soil all the more keenly when he learned that Roosevelt intended to withdraw all American troops from Europe in two years. Stalin mocked at the French, pointing out that the Lublin Poles had an army of ten divisions, as large as the French army. If the French, he asked, are permitted to take part in the control machinery, then what about the other states? For a moment there hovered around the conference table the idea that Germany might be split into eight or nine zones of occupation, but the moment passed. Three zones of occupation were drawn hurriedly on a map, and Stalin explained that he would raise no objection if France was permitted to have a zone of occupation carved out of the zones already allotted to the British and Americans. The implications of the division of Germany into four zones were never studied; and though the three powers had long since agreed that Berlin should be occupied by them jointly, there was no agreement on how they could avoid the dangerous frictions of joint rule.

There remained the question of Japan, and how soon the Soviet armies could be thrown against the Japanese armies in Manchuria, and on what conditions. It was generally believed that the Japanese would fight for every inch of their homeland. General Marshall had estimated that it would cost a million lives to conquer the Japanese islands, and once the islands were captured there might still be a vast mopping-up campaign in China and Manchuria. Confronted with the nightmare of a Japan doomed to destruction but still fighting, Roosevelt was prepared to pay a high price for Russian intervention. Stalin pledged to take part in the war against Japan two or three months after Germany's surrender at a price so immoderately high that it was felt best to keep it secret. Churchill himself did not dare to inform the Dominion prime ministers until six months later. The secret protocol to the Yalta agreements, when disclosed, showed that Russia was to receive Dairen, Port Arthur, the southern part of the island of Sakhalin, and the Kurile islands, while the Chinese Eastern Railway was to be managed by a Soviet-Chinese commission. It was a strange agreement, for it involved the sacrifice by China, an ally in the war against Japan, of two of her cities. Stalin was adamant. These were his conditions, and though he permitted minor amendments – he was prepared, for example, to allow Dairen to become a free port so long as the special interests of Russia were recognized – he refused to compromise on the essential demands; and he charged the President to secure the concurrence of the Chinese government.

When the war against Japan came to an end, Stalin issued a proclamation claiming that he had now, forty years later, wiped out the defeats suffered in the Russo-Japanese War. The ancient disasters were avenged; the Communists had regained the land lost by the Tsar. Traditional imperialism and revolutionary imperialism went hand in hand.

The secret protocol shocked Churchill. 'I must make it clear,' he wrote in his memoirs, 'that though I joined on behalf of Great Britain in the agreement, neither I nor Eden took any part in making it. We were not consulted, but only asked to approve.' Once again Churchill had been forced to capitulate to the intransigence of his allies.

The Yalta agreements involved the surrender of Eastern Europe to the Soviet Union and the end of any formal democratic rule in the countries invaded by the Red Army. Stalin insisted that where the Red Army penetrated, Communist rule must be acknowledged. He would accept the formula that the liberated peoples should 'form interim governmental authorities broadly representative of all democratic elements in the population and pledged to the earliest possible establishment through free elections of governments responsive to the will of the people', but he understood by these words that only those elements who approved of a Russian dictatorship should be allowed to vote freely. In Poland especially he was determined that there should be a government which took orders from the Kremlin. Poland became the test case; and the last hours of Roosevelt's life were to be clouded by the knowledge that nothing could be done to save Poland for democracy.

Yet the Yalta agreements were not entirely without merit. The United Nations received official sanction, machinery for the government of a dismembered Germany was sketched out and elaborated, Stalin had been induced to take part in the war against Japan. In their time and in their context these were not small matters.

At the end the three leaders toasted each other's health and wearily discussed their triumphs, which seemed even then to be dangerous. They were in a reminiscent mood. Roosevelt remembered that his wife travelling across the United States in 1933 had come to a country schoolroom. She saw a map of the world with the Soviet Union represented only by a blank space, and when she asked why it was left blank, she was told it was a country the schoolteacher was not allowed to mention. Now all that had changed. The Soviet Union was now mentioned with bated breath all over the world.

When the three leaders signed the documents and instruments of the Yalta Conference, they were already exhausted by their interminable discussions, and their signatures were less flamboyant than they had been at the Teheran Conference. Roosevelt's signature shows the tragic signs of failing health.

The Yalta Conference came to an end, and the three leaders returned to their own homes. On his way back to Moscow, Stalin heard the news that Budapest had fallen to the Red Army; and now every day was accompanied by its victories, and with every day his intransigence grew. Within a month the agreements made at Yalta seemed in his eyes to have lost all meaning. Whenever a German army surrendered to the British or the Americans without some high Soviet official being present, he flew into a rage. He believed, almost to the end of the war, that the allies were engaged in a plot to snatch victory from his grasp. Why were the Germans still fighting so strenuously against the Red Army while surrendering *en masse* to the allies? Roosevelt gave Stalin the benefit of every doubt and trusted him as a man of honour, only to discover that he could not be trusted and was determined to do as much injury to his allies as he could. In March a cable was brought to Roosevelt's office in the White House. He read it, grew tense, and suddenly banged his fist on the arm of his chair and said: 'Stalin can't be trusted! He has broken his word on every promise he made to me at Yalta!'

By the beginning of April Stalin had come to believe in the duplicity of Roosevelt as an article of faith. His secret agents in Berne had sent him reports that Field Marshal Alexander and Field Marshal Kesselring were engaged in a conspiracy 'to permit the Anglo-American troops to advance to the east, in return for a promise that the peace terms would be eased'. He accused Roosevelt point-blank of aiding and abetting the conspiracy. Roosevelt sent a long cable expressing his 'bitter resentment towards your informers, whoever they are, for such vile misrepresentations of my actions or those of my trusted subordinates'. He sent the cable on April 5th. Two days later Stalin replied, saying of course he had never doubted the integrity and trustworthiness of Roosevelt or Churchill, but he saw no reason to disbelieve his informants. Facts must be faced. 'It has become evident,' he wrote, 'that our views on what is admissible and what is inadmissible differ as between one ally and another.' In the east the Germans were putting up ferocious resistance against the Russians, defending insignificant places which were no more use to them 'than hot poultices on a corpse', while great and proud cities in the west were falling to the British and Americans like ninepins. There could be only one explanation – collusion. On the same day he wrote another angry message to Roosevelt, saying that the Polish question had reached a dead end, and it was all the fault of the British and American ambassadors in Moscow who had departed from the principle of the Yalta Conference. He was preparing to take the Polish question into his own hands, permitting no interference. He wrote in the tone of a man trumpeting his unchallengeable rights.

With these letters the long exchange of communications between Stalin and Roosevelt came to an end. These communications began with buoyant hopes, and ended in bitterness. In the afternoon of April 12th, four days after receiving Stalin's last cables, the President died at Warm Springs, Georgia, of a massive brain haemorrhage.

It will consist of three representatives - one from the Union
of Soviet Socialist Republics, one from the United Kingdom and
one from the United States of America.

4. With regard to the fixing of the total sum of the
reparation as well as the distribution of it among the countries
which suffered from the German aggression the Soviet and
American delegations agreed as follows:

"The Moscow Reparation Commission should take in its
initial studies as a basis for discussion the suggestion of
the Soviet Government that the total sum of the reparation
in accordance with the points (a) and (b) of the paragraph 2
should be 20 billion dollars and that 50% of it should go
to the Union of Soviet Socialist Republics."

The British delegation was of the opinion that pending
consideration of the reparation question by the Moscow Reparation Commission no figures of reparation should be mentioned.

The above Soviet-American proposal has been passed to
the Moscow Reparation Commission as one of the proposals to
be considered by the Commission.

February 11, 1945

Winston S. Churchill

Franklin D. Roosevelt

I. Stalin

Earlier that day Roosevelt sent his last message to Churchill. 'We must be firm,' he wrote. It was his legacy to the democracies.

THE END OF HITLER

THE NEWS OF ROOSEVELT'S DEATH was received with cries of joy in the underground bunker in Berlin, where Hitler was still going through the motions of commanding the German army. A telephone message was received from Goebbels: 'My Führer, I congratulate you! Roosevelt is dead. It is written in the stars that the second half of April will be the turning point for us!' The leaders of the German government consulted the astrological tables and found comfort in the stars, while Berlin burned and the Allied armies raced across Germany.

By the end of the month the stars were less favourable. On the morning of April 30th the Red Army crossed the river Spree and attacked the Reichstag, no more than a few blocks from the Chancellery, where Hitler was holding his last conference. He heard a sombre report on the military situation, sent out his last telegram – characteristically, it was a plea to Dönitz 'to proceed at once, and mercilessly, against all traitors' and then retired to his private quarters for a leisurely lunch with Eva Braun, the woman he had married a few hours before. At half past three his wife took poison, and about the same time Hitler shot himself through the mouth. Later the bodies were placed in a shallow grave in the Chancellery garden, gasoline was poured over them, and a match was struck. The reign of Hitler was over.

With the death of Hitler the Third Reich came to an end. For a few more days, like a twitching corpse, it presented the semblance of life, as the German generals maintained a half-hearted resistance against the Russians while offering to surrender to the Americans, the British and the French. Their purpose was to divide the Allies, and in this they failed. With the signing of the terms of unconditional surrender at Rheims on May 7th in the presence of American, British, French and Russian representatives, the Third Reich finally ceased to have even the semblance of existence. Hitler had promised that it would endure for a thousand years. It had endured for twelve.

Though Hitler was dead, many mysteries remained unsolved, especially the mystery of how he was able to rise to supreme power. The sources of his strength, the nature of his ultimate beliefs, and the workings of his fatal weaknesses, all these would be debated for many years to come. No final assessment could be made at the time, nor can we reasonably expect to reach a final assessment in our generation. Hitler's verdict on himself was given in the testament he drew up the day before his suicide. It is an astonishing and revealing document. Having sacrificed millions of Germans to his own glory, he claimed that all his actions had proceeded out of love and loyalty to his people. With perfect detachment and single-mindedness he claimed that he had shown the German people the way which destiny had pointed out to them, and it was not his fault that they had proved unworthy of the task. He urged the Germans to continue their struggle for *Lebensraum* in the East. While he was dictating these words, the Russians had encircled Berlin and the Chancellery was being bombarded by Russian guns at close range. Hitler wrote that he chose to die by his own hand rather than submit to 'cowardly abdication or capitulation'. But the most revealing paragraph of his testament referred to his possessions, which he bequeathed to the party, or if the party was no longer in existence to the state. 'Should the state too be destroyed, no further decision on my part is necessary.'

In fact, no decision on his part was necessary concerning any matter whatsoever. He was no longer in a position where decisions had any meaning. In the characteristic manner of a baffled dictator, he issued his final orders, but these orders were meaningless, or rather they possessed significance only among the warring phantoms of his brain. He ordered death to all traitors, but the traitors were everywhere. The whole German nation had committed treachery against him. In much the same way Stalin, and Lenin before him, had urged the merciless destruction of traitors even when none existed. It was a game played according to easily discernible rules: the dictator absolved himself from his own fears by ordering the destruction of all those who could conceivably be counted among his enemies.

The nihilistic strain in Hitler's character is clearly indicated in his disposal of his property to the party, and then to the state, for he was consigning his possessions to institutions which, as he well knew, were about to die; for there was a sense in which he was himself the party and the state, and they could have no existence without him. He went on to request that his relatives and secretaries should be supported modestly in a *klein-bürgerlich* fashion out of the funds he had accumulated; the son of a petty customs official showed himself in the end to have retained the mentality of his father.

There was only one matter on which Hitler wrote with precision: the disposal of his corpse. He asked that it should be 'burned immediately in the place where I have carried out the greater part of my public work in the course of my twelve years' service to my people'. He would kill himself, and immediately afterward, somewhere within the walls of the Chancellery, he would be given to the flames. It was a matter of complete indifference to him what happened to his ashes.

The Allies showed an understandable disinclination to share his indifference. The ashes could become the talisman of a revived National Socialist party. They possessed the magic potency which is always associated with the ashes of great historical figures. If they fell into the possession of one of the Allied nations, then that nation would be able to claim the ultimate physical victory over Hitler. What happened to the ashes is an instructive and illuminating story, which throws considerable light on the character of Stalin.

Through the investigations of Professor Trevor-Roper, a great deal is known about the events in the Chancellery on the afternoon and evening of April 30th. Hitler had asked that his body and that of his wife should be burned immediately, and this was done. By four o'clock the shallow grave had been dug, the bodies had been laid in it, and the gasoline had been poured over them and set alight. There was a sudden huge sheet of flame, followed by a long slow burning. At intervals one of the guards attached to the Chancellery would see the bodies lying together, burning and smouldering. Shells fell and exploded in the garden, but none of them touched the grave. By about ten o'clock preparations were being made to bury the bodies in a shell crater near the emergency exit to the bunker. Accordingly this was worked into a rectangular shape, and what was left of the bodies was placed on three boards and carried to the crater. Hitler's feet had been burned away, but the skull, cranium, upper and lower jaws were still recognizable; the flesh and skin burned black. The burial was ordered by Johann Rattenhuber, the commander of Hitler's detective bodyguard, and carried out by two of his subordinates, Harry Mengershausen and a man called Glanzer.

The Chancellery was stormed by troops of the Eighth Guards Army during the morning of May 2nd. The Russians already knew that Hitler was dead, for during the evening of April 30th General Hans Krebs, a former military attaché in Moscow and Hitler's last Chief of Staff, made his way under a white flag to the Russian headquarters with a letter signed by Bormann and Goebbels, asking for a limited surrender. He talked freely. He spoke Russian well, and was on good terms with many of the Russian officers. Only a few hours before, he was present at one of the ceremonial leave-takings which occupied a large part of Hitler's last hours. He was a man who made it his business to know everything that was happening around him, and he knew that Hitler's body had been placed in a shallow grave in the garden and then set on fire.

With the help of the information gathered from General Hans Krebs, and from prisoners captured in the Chancellery, the troops of the Eighth Guards Army had little difficulty in discovering the body. It lay on a blanket which was still smoking. The face was scorched black, there was a bullet hole in the temple, and though the features were hideously distorted, they were recognizably those of Hitler.

The Russians made no secret of their discovery, but no official announcement was made at this time. It was decided to act cautiously, to prove beyond doubt that this was Hitler, and then too there was the question, which had to be decided carefully, about what should be done with the remains.

Within a few days Johann Rattenhuber and Harry Mergershausen, both captured by the Russians, were cross-examined about the events in the Chancellery garden. Though the bodies had already been removed and were in safekeeping, the prisoners were able to point out the grave. Hitler's dentist had escaped from Berlin, but the dental charts were discovered in the dentist's office. An X-ray photograph of his head, made shortly after the assassination attempt the previous year, was also found. The dental charts and the X-ray confirmed the identity.

Understandably, Stalin attached enormous importance to the discovery of Hitler's remains. Marshal Zhukov, the conqueror of Berlin, was ordered to report directly to Stalin on the investigation, and these orders were confirmed when Beria and Mikoyan arrived in Berlin a few days later. In April Stalin had ordered that the embalmed body of Lenin should be returned from its secret hiding place in Siberia, thirteen hundred miles from Moscow, to the mausoleum in the Red Square. He had deliberately delayed giving the order until the fall of Berlin had become imminent. Now the remains of another dictator occupied his thoughts.

So much importance was attached to the identification of the body that seven senior officials of the NKVD were placed in charge of the investigation. Almost daily reports were sent to Moscow. By the end of the month the investigators had established the identification beyond reasonable doubt, and at the beginning of June the remains, consisting of the head, part of the torso, some arm and leg bones, and the Iron Cross which Hitler had worn at the time of his death, were flown to Moscow.

On May 26th, while the investigations were continuing, Harry Hopkins, Averell Harriman and Charles Bohlen had a meeting with Stalin and Molotov at the Kremlin. The question of Hitler's body was raised. Stalin replied that he did not believe that Hitler was dead; he was hiding somewhere. 'The whole matter is strange,' he said, and perhaps remembering the voluminous reports which had crossed his desk, with the charts showing the shallow grave in the garden and the other grave which had been carved out of a bomb crater, he added : 'All the talk of funerals and burials strike me as very dubious.' When Hopkins mentioned the disappearance of several very large German submarines, Stalin suggested that Hitler might have escaped to Japan by submarine. The official transcript taken at the meeting says:

> Marshal Stalin said he also knew of these submarines which had been running back and forth between Germany and Japan, taking gold and negotiable assets from Germany to Japan. He added that this had been done with the connivance of Switzerland. He said he had ordered his intelligence service to look into the matter of these submarines but so far they had failed to discover any trace and therefore he thought it was possible that Hitler and company had gone in them to Japan.

There was nothing new in the theory that Hitler might have escaped by submarine; what was new was the suggestion that this was done with the connivance of Switzerland, which had no seaports and nothing to gain by assisting Hitler's escape. After the capitulation of Japan, he would say that Hitler was probably in hiding in Argentina or Spain.

Meanwhile the Russian officers in Berlin spoke as though the matter had been already established. Many of them had seen the body, and were convinced that it was Hitler. Marshal Chuikov, who had interviewed General Hans Krebs on the night of Hitler's suicide and was therefore among the very first to hear about it, saw no reason to question the reports of the investigators. That the body of Hitler had fallen into Russian hands was a matter of plain fact. On June 5th, when the Allied commanders in chief met in Berlin, Russian officers talking to members of General Eisenhower's staff said the evidence seemed conclusive. Four days later came the bombshell. The new official version was published to the world by no less an authority than Marshal Zhukov. According to the new doctrine the Russian investigators had failed to identify the body of Hitler, and it was now believed that he had left Berlin at the last moment.

The doctrine was not based on ascertained facts, but on the incalculable moods, prejudices and suspicions of Stalin. He sent Vyshinsky to Berlin to make sure that the doctrine was announced clearly and emphatically. While Zhukov was holding his press conference, Vyshinsky sat beside him, ominously silent. He was Stalin's watchdog, and his function was to make sure that Zhukov spoke the lines which had been written for him.

'The circumstances are very mysterious,' Zhukov told the press. 'We have not identified the body of Hitler. I can say nothing about his fate. He could have flown away from Berlin at the very last moment. The state of the runway would have allowed him to do so.'

On the following day, still accompanied by Vyshinsky, Zhukov travelled to Frankfurt and gave the same message to Eisenhower. At Frankfurt, too, he made a speech calling upon soldiers to offer implicit obedience to their political leaders, and once again Vyshinsky was present. Speaking to Harry Hopkins in Moscow, Stalin had made it abundantly clear that Zhukov would have very little power concerning political affairs in Germany. He was already in disgrace, and only his vast popularity among the Russian soldiers saved him from being recalled.

Towards the middle of June Stalin attended a special screening of Yuri Raizman's film *Berlin*. This was a full-length documentary prepared by army photographers in an astonishingly short space of time. The film begins slowly with the preparations for the assault, follows the progress of the battle and ends with Zhukov confronting General Keitel at the table where the surrender terms were signed. There are brilliant scenes of the bombardment of Berlin by 22,000 guns standing wheel to wheel in the outskirts of the city, and the camera follows the street fighting up to the capture of the Reichstag and the Chancellery. It is Zhukov's film. Consciously or unconsciously the cameramen gave him pride of place. It is not so much that he dominates the film as that his presence can be felt throughout, and he is especially present during the signing of the surrender terms. Keitel signs stiffly, Zhukov signs gaily, cocking his head to one side, gazing down at his signature with a look of amused wonderment, and then smiling warmly at Air Marshal Tedder, the youthful-looking representative of Britain, who was Eisenhower's deputy. Stalin never appears.

Enraged by the film, Stalin ordered that there should be a new ending, and the name and person of Stalin should be made more prominent. The new ending seems to have been a matter of considerable debate, but finally it was agreed that the victory processions on the Red Square should be included: the massed troops, Stalin himself taking the salute from Lenin's mausoleum, and the fireworks blazing over the victorious city. The film, which should properly have ended in the Chancellery, was now provided with a tailpiece glorifying Stalin, who is seen waving languidly to the troops as they march past. He looks very heavy and totally unconcerned with the events happening all round him.

Stalin had made few contributions to the victory of the Red Army. His advice was often disregarded, his rare interventions were usually disastrous. Nevertheless he was the Generalissimo, supreme over all generals, and there seems never to have been a time when the generals seriously contemplated seizing power. The terror of Stalin's name was enough to make generals quail in their boots; a call from Stalin on the direct telephone would make their hair stand on end, and they stammered like children. Zhukov was more popular than Stalin, and he was therefore in grave danger.

Among Zhukov's many duties was to superintend the continuing investigation of Hitler's remains. In theory, though not in fact, he was still in direct charge of the investigation. From time to time witnesses were interrogated or taken to the Chancellery, where they were ordered to re-enact the roles they had played, and sometimes they would be taken repeatedly, day after day, in the hope that some new fact would emerge. By the middle of September the investigators had finished their work. Their final report was never published. Instead, they presented a political document which added little to Stalin's statement to Harry Hopkins four months before. They wrote:

No trace of the bodies of Hitler or Eva Braun has been discovered.

Nor has any trace been found of the grave drenched with gasoline in which, according to some witnesses, the bodies of the Führer and of his companion were burned.

Certain witnesses have now admitted that they took an oath before Hitler, affirming that if they were to fall into enemy hands, they would say they had *seen* the bodies of Hitler and of Eva Braun consumed in a funeral pyre in the garden of the Reich Chancellery.

All witnesses have now admitted to our investigators that they saw neither the funeral pyre nor the bodies of Hitler and of Eva Braun.

It is established that Hitler, by means of false testimony, sought to cover his traces.

Irrefutable proof exists that a small aeroplane left the Tiergarten at dawn on April 30th, flying in the direction of Hamburg. Three men and a woman are known to have been on board.

It has also been established that a large submarine left Hamburg before the arrival of the British forces. Mysterious persons were on board the submarine, among them a woman.

This statement, offered as the considered verdict of a commission of inquiry which had been sitting since early in May, shows signs of having been written by Stalin himself. It betrays its origins by its lack of logic and by its repetitions. It rests on three assumptions: that all those who said they saw the funeral pyre were lying, that a light aeroplane did leave the Tiergarten in the early morning of April 30th, and that a submarine left Hamburg a few hours later. Two of the assumptions are unwarranted. The witnesses were not lying,

as Professor Trevor-Roper was able to show demonstrably
in his book *The Last Days of Hitler*. No aeroplane left the
Tiergarten at dawn on April 30th. A light aeroplane did however leave the Tiergarten at about 2 am on the morning of
April 29th. The pilot was Hannah Reitsch and the passenger
was General Ritter von Greim, who was under orders to
arrest Himmler. The third assumption depended upon statements from a captured shipyard worker in Hamburg who
said he had seen a woman who resembled Eva Braun and
a man with his face half hidden in bandages embarking on a
submarine. The shipyard worker noted that although the man
did not wear a moustache, he had some physical resemblance
to Hitler.

The verdict of the commission of inquiry was no verdict;
totally implausible explanations were being offered to account
for Hitler's disappearance from the scene. 'I accepted the
verdict,' said Zukhov. 'I believe Hitler and Eva Braun are
alive. They could have left Germany in 1945 and reached
some deserted island off an unexplored coast.' He accepted
the verdict because he knew that it would be dangerous not
to accept it.

Nevertheless he knew, as all the other high Soviet officers
in Berlin knew, that the body of Hitler had been found and
subjected to tests that established its identity beyond doubt.
This knowledge however was deliberately concealed, because
Stalin wanted it to be concealed. Even after Stalin's death the
Soviet government retained its official silence; and in the fifth
volume of the massive *History of the Great Fatherland War*,
published in 1963, there is only a brief reference to the capture
of the Chancellery and no reference at all to the fate of Hitler.
Official silence ended only in February 1964, when Marshal
Chuikov's memoirs began to appear in the weekly magazine
Literaturnaya Rossiya. For the first time there came from
Russian sources a clear and unequivocal statement about the
events leading up to the discovery of Hitler's body. Marshal
Chuikov describes how General Hans Krebs came to his headquarters under a flag of truce on the night of April 30th, with
a letter from Bormann and Goebbels. To the letter was
attached a copy of Hitler's testament. That the Russians were
in possession of the testament so early had not previously
been revealed, but it was a matter of some importance, for in
the testament Hitler had ordered that his body should be
burned within the Chancellery walls. The testament therefore

corroborated General Krebs's account of Hitler's suicide and the funeral pyre in the garden. When the Chancellery fell into their hands, the Russians knew where to look.

Marshal Chuikov wrote pityingly of the British investigator who spent months tracking down the details of Hitler's suicide and the burning of the bodies. 'We Soviet forces took Berlin,' he wrote, 'and we were therefore able to see and discover far more than outside observers who, on the day of the storming of Berlin, were far from the scene.' The statement was true, but does not explain why the Russians had to maintain their silence for so long.

The Russians had no difficulty finding the body. 'When the troops of the Eighth Guards Army broke into the courtyard of the Reich Chancellery,' Marshal Chuikov wrote, 'they found in the morning of May 2nd a still-smoking rug, and in it was the scorched body of Hitler.'

It was so simple that it was almost beyond belief. The years of mystification were over; the endless cross-examinations, the interminable rounding-up of witnesses, the voluminous reports, the verdict of the commission of inquiry, all these amounted to nothing, or rather they performed the function of a smoke screen. The investigators had not been investigating; they had been concealing. Russian soldiers had seen the body, and then they were sworn to secrecy.

For Stalin the discovery of Hitler's body by Russian troops was the sweetest of all triumphs. Against Hitler he had waged a strange vendetta which could only end with the death of one of them. Stalin had feared Hitler as he feared no one else. Each recognized in the other an adversary worthy of him, and neither was disposed to offer mercy to the other. Inevitably for Stalin the vendetta took a Georgian form; he would not rest until he had the body of his adversary in his power, until he had insulted it, and until he had left upon it the indelible sign of his victory.

According to the ritual of a Georgian vendetta the body of the dead enemy becomes a trophy, and the victor can do with it whatever he pleases. Usually the skull was kept and fashioned into a drinking cup, while the dismembered body was thrown into a ravine and a dead cat was thrown after it. No one knows what punishment Stalin inflicted on the charred body of Hitler. What is certain is that it came within the circle of his power and that he was able to do with it as he pleased.

THE EMPTY YEARS

The mighty voice of the Great Stalin, defending the peace of the world, has penetrated into all corners of the globe, into the hearts and minds of the working and progressive people of the entire world.

— KLIMENT VOROSHILOV

IVAN THE TERRIBLE

THE WAR AGAINST GERMANY, which had been won at the cost of so many lives and so many ruined hopes, now belonged to history. Men would discuss interminably the details of every offensive and every retreat; blame and praise would be apportioned; and the historians, calmly surveying mountains of documents, would find themselves at a loss where to begin. The war was so vast and so complex and so well documented that no single scholar would ever be able to describe its scope. Armies of scholars would be employed to discover what happened in a single campaign. There were no simple answers to the questions Who won? How did we win? Why?

For Stalin, the master of the simple answer, the war against Germany had been won because he had invented superior strategies and because, as the faithful follower of Lenin, he had immersed himself in the techniques of Marxism. He gave more credit to the Soviet system than to the Russian people. No doubt they had fought well, but all their fighting would have been in vain if they had not learned in the school of Communism. In his more forgiving moods, he would sometimes pay tribute to military commanders in the field or to sections of the population which had displayed unusual bravery, but these occasions were rare. He was continually repeating that the war had been won by Marxist-Leninism, leaving it to be understood that he regarded himself as the incarnation of this abstraction. His pride in his own victory was complete.

On May 24th, 1945, two weeks after final victory, there took place in St George's Hall in the Kremlin an extraordinary celebration in honour of the victorious generals and of those who had made the victory possible. The entire high command was present together with hundreds of scientists, engineers, writers and Stakhanovite workers. As the evening approached its climax Stalin appeared, wearing a white uniform with gold epaulettes, to accept a thunderous ovation. This time he did not speak in terms of abstractions. Neither Marx nor Lenin was mentioned. He admitted that the government had made mistakes, and he even hinted that the mistakes were so serious that the people would have been justified in ridding themselves of their rulers. He claimed that the victory was due to the valour of the Russian people. He said:

> Comrades, permit me to propose one more toast, the last one. I should like to propose a toast to our Soviet people, and in the first place to the Russian people. I drink first of all to the health of the Russian people because it is the most eminent of all the nations belonging to the Soviet Union. I drink to the health of the Russian people because it has earned in this war universal recognition as the leading force of the Soviet Union among all the peoples of our country. I drink to the health of the Russian people not only because it is the leading people, but also because it has a clear intelligence, a firm character and great patience. Our government made quite a few errors, we had moments in 1941-2 when the situation was desperate, when our army was retreating, abandoning our own villages and towns in the Ukraine, Belorussia, Moldavia, the Leningrad province, the Baltic Republics, the Karelian-Finnish Republic – abandoning them because there was no other way. A different people could have said to the Government: 'You have failed to justify our expectations – get out! We shall install another Government which shall make peace with Germany and secure for us quiet lives.' The Russian people, however, did not take this path, because it trusted the correctness of the policy of its Government, and it made sacrifices to ensure the destruction of Germany. And this confidence of the Russian people in the Soviet Government proved to be the decisive force which insured the victory over the historic enemy of mankind – Fascism.
>
> Thanks to the Russian people, for their confidence! To the health of the Russian people!

Stalin's speech at the victory celebration in St George's Hall is more than a revealing comment on the dark days of the war; many subterfuges are concealed within it; and there are moments when it sounds like a sigh of relief. The speech was not written for him; the liturgical incantatory manner, with its repetitions and curious windings, is wholly his own, and for once he is showing some generosity of spirit. The toast to the endurance, character and intelligence of the Russian people was deserved, but it was entirely another matter whether he deserved their confidence.

This speech was addressed to the Russians; the people of the other fifteen Soviet Republics were casually omitted, perhaps for good reason, since few except the Belorussians had shown any wholehearted support to the Russians. In the same speech Stalin paid special tribute to Marshal Zhukov. 'The name of Comrade Zhukhov will remain forever as the symbol of victory,' he said, but these words were carefully omitted from the official transcript. It was not Zhukov, he was to say later, but the leader of the party who had brought victory about, and soon the symbol of victory was assigned to a minor administrative post in Odessa.

It occurred to Stalin that his triumph deserved to be celebrated in some vast and formal manner commensurate with his achievements. It would be no niggardly triumph, but one comparable with the great ceremonial processions which passed through the streets of Rome in honour of the triumphant Caesars. The captured German banners would be flung down at his feet, and the victorious army would salute him as the sole symbol of victory. The triumph was held on June 24th. While Stalin took his place on Lenin's mausoleum, detachments of the Red Army marched across Red Square with bared swords, saluting him as they passed the grey mausoleum. The clouds swung low overhead and the rain fell and the only sound came from the tramp of marching feet. It was one of those dismal days in midsummer which to the people of Moscow are like a foretaste of autumn. The crowning moment of the triumph came at the end when hundreds of brilliantly coloured standards captured from the Germans, with the tassels and the bronze eagles still in place, were solemnly lowered before him and then tossed in an ungainly pile.

Two days later Stalin was awarded the title of Hero of the Soviet Union 'for extraordinary courage in the Fatherland War'.

In the following month came the Potsdam Conference designed to put an end to the remaining problems brought about by the war. Truman had succeeded Roosevelt, but Churchill still represented Great Britain and continued to hold a watching brief for Poland, Greece, and the other countries of Europe which had not yet been occupied by the Red Army. Hopefully he had invented the code name for the conference: Terminal. It was a bleak ending.

The conference was originally to have begun on July 16th,

but Stalin was delayed. He had intended to fly to Berlin, he said, but at the last moment his doctors refused to permit him to fly 'because of a weakness of the lungs'. It was assumed that he had suffered from a slight heart attack. During the previous year he suffered a prolonged attack of cardiac asthma. Yet he looked vigorous and high-spirited, wearing his white uniform with the gold epaulettes and the gold star of Hero of the Soviet Union on his left breast. He showed signs of restlessness and physical discomfort after long debates, but he was a match for the younger heads of government at the conference table.

The conferences were held at the Cecilienhof palace, which had once belonged to Crown Prince William, and was named after the Crown Princess Cecilie. Truman was ill prepared for the tussle with Stalin, for he knew little about the previous conferences and had only a remote conception of the real issues at stake. He had, however, one advantage which was not possessed by his predecessor – he could speak from a position of overwhelming strength. Early in the morning of July 16th, 1945, the first atomic bomb exploded at Alamogordo, New Mexico, and Truman's arrival in Berlin coincided with the arrival of the first secret reports of the explosion. The flash of the explosion had been clearly visible at Albuquerque 120 miles away from the testing ground; the roar of the atomic explosion was heard a hundred miles away; the destructive power of the new bomb was believed to be the equivalent of twenty thousand tons of TNT. Churchill called the bomb 'the second coming of wrath', and there were many beside Churchill who felt that the Day of Judgement was at hand.

The question arose whether to inform Stalin about the bomb, and under what conditions. Among the innumerable problems raised by the existence of the bomb this was by no means the least, for in his attitude towards the Western allies Stalin had already shown himself to be suspicious to the point of believing any insane rumour or deliberate invention of his secret agents. At Yalta he had joined Roosevelt and Churchill in an avowal that the liberated countries of Europe should be permitted to hold free and unfettered elections on the basis of universal suffrage and the secret ballot, and within a month he had shown himself in favour of Communist puppet governments backed by the bayonets of the Red Army. He could not be trusted. He would cheerfully make promises, and just as cheerfully break them. Finally it was decided that he should be told about the new bomb in the most casual manner possible. On July 24th Truman took him aside and spoke briefly of a new type of bomb of unusual destructive power. Stalin showed no special interest. He said he hoped it would be used effectively against Japan, and then passed to other matters. Truman and Churchill, who was also present on that momentous occasion, had the impression that Stalin knew very little, if anything, about the bomb; and they sighed with relief.

At the Potsdam Conference Stalin was more intransigent than he had been at Teheran and Yalta. Poland, Bulgaria, Rumania, Hungary, and large areas of Czechoslovakia, Austria and eastern Germany had fallen to his grasp, and he was in no mood to permit anyone else to stake out any claims. Finland, too, was being occupied by the Red Army. In some of these countries Stalin's puppet governments were already in power, in others they were preparing to seize power. One evening at the beginning of the Potsdam Conference Stalin and Churchill were dining alone except for their interpreters and discussing the violent alterations of power in the wake of the Russian conquests. Churchill drew a line from North Cape to Albania, and named all the capitals east of the line already in Russian hands. It looked, he said, as if Russia were rolling on westward. Were all the capitals to fall one after another? Stalin said he had no intention of marching westward. On the contrary he was withdrawing troops from the west, and within four months two million men would be demobilized and sent home. He would have withdrawn them sooner, he said, but he was confronted with difficulties in railroad transport.

So they talked in an atmosphere of ominous quiet and conviviality, and from time to time they would return to contemplate the map of Europe with its shifting frontiers and its permanent capitals. Once again Stalin spoke of the Germans as sheep and told the story he had related so many times before about the two hundred German Communists who missed a meeting because there was no one to take their tickets at the railroad station; the story seemed to please him and gave him some comfort. He spoke of the terrifying Russian losses – five million men killed or missing: the figures were inaccurate, for the losses vastly exceeded five million. He spoke, too, of the continuity of Soviet policy, and of how he had educated his associates so that good men would be ready to step into his shoes. 'He was thinking thirty years ahead,' Churchill commented, awed by the permanence of Stalin, who was then sixty-six years old.

Though they talked amicably, they were like men who had long ago lost hope of agreement and found contentment in reckless horse trading. Churchill said he wished to see Russian ships sailing across the oceans of the world; too long had Russia resembled a giant with his nostrils pinched by the narrow exits of the Baltic and the Black Sea. The Baltic, the Kiel Canal and the Dardanelles should be opened to the Russian fleet. Warming to the offer, Stalin responded by declaring that in all countries liberated by the Red Army the Russian policy would be to see strong, independent, sovereign states. There would be free elections, and all except fascist parties would participate. This momentary generosity scarcely survived the evening. From time to time he continued to use his power over the countries in Eastern Europe to exact such terms as he pleased from the allies, who sometimes found themselves wondering why he spoke to them as though they represented conquered nations.

When Churchill was defeated at the elections, Clement Attlee, the Labour Prime Minister, took his place. A strange moment, recorded on US Army films, occurred when Truman introduced Attlee to Stalin. Someone, perhaps a photographer, called out that one of the chairs stood in the way, and asked a guard to remove it. Stalin, thinking he was being addressed, darted forward, and with surprising vigour lifted the chair bodily into a new position. Then he stood back to observe what he had done, and at that moment his crooked left arm jerked and dangled helplessly from the shoulder, as though its mechanism had suddenly become out of control. Then that swinging, dangling arm, which appeared to have no connection with him, being held high and at some distance from the body, like the arm of a marionette, gradually resumed its normal position.

Stalin was the victor of Potsdam, and there were times when he looked the part well, sitting back in a gilded chair decorated with cherubs who smiled playfully at him. He sat there with the expression of someone bemused by his own success and by the innocence of his adversaries; and his flamboyant signatures on the documents he signed show him fully aware of his triumph. When he returned to Moscow, he forgot his promises and established puppet governments in all the countries occupied by the Red Army. Sometimes he would permit a more liberal government to rule on a temporary basis, merely in order to see whether it would show common cause with the Western allies; and if it did he destroyed it. Of all the countries of Eastern and Central Europe where the Red Army had penetrated, only Austria survived without being converted into a satellite.

When Stalin looked back on the war, he could tell himself that everything he had done was for the best, and that he alone by the power of his decisions had brought the Allies to victory. History would perhaps record that there had been one brief interval when he had failed, for he confessed to Hopkins that he had been unable to prevent the early disasters of the war when the Germans were in the suburbs of Moscow.

Now, with the benefit of hindsight, he began to reassess the record. He now believed that he had deliberately drawn the Germans into the depths of Russia in order to destroy them all the more effectively. It astonished him that military historians failed to recognize his perspicacity, and he proceeded to remind them that in 1941 he had acted according to an established historical precedent. By a similar manoeuvre the Parthian chieftains defeated the Roman general Crassus. In the military academies students began to study the Parthians.

The opportunity to express his views came early in 1947 during a discussion among the professors at the Frunze and Voroshilov military academies, as they debated the merits of Clausewitz's theories on the art of war. In Lenin's eyes Clausewitz was 'a simply fantastic theoretician', who could do no wrong. Engels, too, admired him this side of idolatry. Stalin, who admired no one, reminded the professors that it was absurd to regard Lenin as a military theorist and equally absurd to rely on the judgement of Engels, who had made the mistake of giving prominence to Barclay de Tolly, who was descended from a Scottish family, rather than to the wholly Russian Kutuzov. Then he went on to explain his doctrine of the counter-offensive, which was to be carefully distinguished from a counter-attack. In a letter addressed to Colonel Razin, one of the professors of military history, Stalin wrote:

In your theses on the war you have failed to include a section on the *counter-offensive*, which is not to be confused with the counter-attack. I am speaking of a counter-offensive which takes place after a successful offensive by the enemy, one however which fails to bring about decisive results, and in the course of which the defending side gathers its forces and goes over to the counteroffensive and administers a decisive defeat on the adversary. I regard a well-organized counter-offensive as a very interesting kind of offensive. To you as an historian it would be appropriate if you interested yourself in these matters. The ancient Parthians knew about this kind of counter-offensive when they drew the Roman general Crassus and his army into the interior of their country and then struck back in a counter-offensive and destroyed them. And our own General Kutuzov, a commander of genius, knew this well when he destroyed Napoleon and his army with the help of a well-prepared counter-offensive.

Stalin's knowledge of military history and even his knowledge of his own wars was never extensive. Until his death Soviet military historians were compelled to pay lip service to the theory of 'the counter-offensive which is not to be confused with the counter-attack', and to repeat at intervals that the counter-offensive was 'a very interesting kind of offensive'. Two years later, on the occasion of Stalin's seventieth birthday, Voroshilov, who bowed to no one in his admiration of Stalin's genius, pointed out the numerous strategical concepts Stalin had invented. Stalin had carefully analysed the transient and the permanently operating factors in war; he had shown the need for massive reserves 'to ensure the transition to the decisive counter-offensive' by which it was possible to strike at 'the entire operational-strategic depth of the enemy'. Stalin had described the conditions for the skilful tactical and operational co-ordination of all arms. Stalin had invented an entirely new Stalinist science of war based on an exhaustive study of all the factors which make for victory; and if there had been no Stalin, there would have been no victory.

So Voroshilov spoke in that confused tribute which sometimes reads as though it was written by Stalin himself in a mood of exalted self-appreciation, but the truth was otherwise. Stalin's chief study was the naked application of power – power in the abstract and power in its most naked and concrete form. For him war was only one of the many aspects of power, and perhaps the least interesting. War was almost an abstraction, a wavering line drawn on the massive globe which stood beside his desk. A bullet or a bombing plane was concrete; spies, informers, subverters, active members of foreign Communist parties were also concrete, for he knew them well and could manipulate them with ease. Slogans and manifestoes were also concrete; they were instruments of power, with precise purposes. The slogan 'Glory to great Stalin' had a precise, calculated effect: it was a weapon to be employed cold-bloodedly, and Stalin was not in the least intimidated by it. When the German author Lion Feuchtwanger asked him why he permitted so much adulation of himself, he said he could excuse the people's 'naïve joy', since they were not cheering him personally, but as the representative of the Soviet state. It was not true. They cheered him whether they liked him or not, because they were ordered to cheer him and the penalties for not cheering were too terrible to contemplate.

But although Stalin had very little appreciation of the complex strategies of war, he recognized the usefulness of weapons of destruction. When Lieutenant Colonel Tokaev came to Moscow from Berlin with reports that the Germans had invented a new kind of rocket plane capable of flying from Moscow to America and back, he was ordered to present himself at the Kremlin. The designs for the rocket plane were drawn up by Professor Sanger in 1944 and shown to Goering and Hitler, too late to be used in the war. The Russians had no rocket planes of any kind, but they knew that the Americans were working on them. On April 17th, 1947, Tokaev attended a meeting of the Council of Ministers held to decide whether to proceed with the construction of the Sanger rocket plane.

Tokaev's description of the meeting is one of the few available documents showing Stalin at grips with naked power. He writes:

At the far right-hand corner, as I entered, stood Stalin's desk. Against the inside wall, on my left Malenkov, Beria, Voznesensky, Mikoyan, Voroshilov, Zhdanov and Molotov were seated at a table. There were vacant chairs at head and foot. Stalin, on his feet, came up close to me and greeted me. I was to sit at the end of the table, in the chair usually taken by Andreyev, who at that moment was away in the Ukraine, together with Khrushchev and Kaganovich. Throughout the sitting Servo *stood* ready at my back ...

I spoke for about three quarters of an hour, standing. Stalin also stood, sucking at his pipe. At moments he came close up to me, and, lips parted, peered into my eyes, as if trying to decipher my inward thoughts. Of course he had been exhaustively informed who I was, what I had been. It was a trial of strength, speaking extempore, without any notes, but I held those renegade eyes. Only Stalin asked me questions; the others sat like schoolboys in their master's presence.

Most of all, at first, I think my reference to our backwardness startled him, but I had considered it my duty to my country to let him know how profoundly German applied science had impressed me. They were at least ten years ahead of us. Speaking quietly, Stalin replied:

'In other words, we shall have to learn from the *Nazis* — is that it?' he asked, striding up and down the room. Then, again coming right up to me, and sucking furiously at his pipe: 'And what's the reason?' he demanded. 'What do *you* think the causes are? ... Well, come on, what's wrong with us? Why have we dropped behind?'

'It's hard for me to say, Comrade Stalin,' I replied. 'Perhaps the Germans have given more thought to war than we have. Perhaps in their history militarism occupied a more fundamental place ...'

For some moments Stalin paced up and down in silence. Then he swung straight into the attack on the Sanger plane. What could I advise? I advised working on it.

'Very good, Comrade Tokaev.' He raised his index finger. 'Without confidence that a thing is indispensable, one would never begin anything. I see you hold that we cannot think of designing this aircraft.'

Again I went over the ground I had covered earlier, and Mikoyan said he was inclined to support me. Beria joined him. What Malenkov and Voznesensky thought I already knew – they wanted the giant bomber. Zhdanov and Molotov remained as cautiously silent as a couple of grumpy hedgehogs. Voroshilov fidgeted with his feet like a schoolboy, every now and then giving me an involuntary little kick. Still Stalin hesitated. When at last he came up to me again, his silent stare lasted a long time, as if he wanted to test my endurance. Then, slowly, he said: 'Hmmm! But if we take up the Sanger suggestion, it will be in order to make a real rocket aeroplane, not just to get abstract scientific information ...' He asked me if I had ever heard of Mr Truman. 'For your information, Comrade Tokaev, that little businessman is more interested in real rockets and aircraft.'

This portrait of Stalin slowly pacing about, in total command of the Council of Ministers, is not a flattering one, but it presents the essential Stalin determinedly seeking after the realities of power. He had no knowledge or understanding of scientific abstractions. What he knew with astonishing completeness was the nature of power.

Ever since he came to power he had acted like an absolute tyrant; he knew power because he was accustomed to it, and it may have saddened him that others knew it less well. He was aware, too, that he had constructed the ideal mask of a tyrant, and to actors portraying him he would explain patiently how they were to go about acquiring that mask. In much the same way Napoleon talked to Talma, saying that his portrayal of Pompey was inaccurate. 'You wave your arms about too much,' Napoleon complained. 'Rulers of empires are not so prodigal with their gestures. They know that the wave of a hand is an order, that a glance means death, and they are therefore sparing in their gestures.'

Over the years Stalin studied the tyrants. He was an especially close student of Ivan the Terrible. To some extent he had modelled himself on the medieval Tsar, while cultivating the fiction that Ivan was a mild tyrant who was more sinned against than sinning. He encouraged the director Sergey Eisenstein and the actor Nikolay Cherkasov to make a full-length film on the life of Ivan, with the result that the director and the actor spent the war years celebrating the Tsar in a film of great violence and beauty, and incredible length. The film was in three parts; and the last part presented insuperable difficulties, since during his last years Ivan had given way to fits of maniacal depression and a series of senseless massacres. Eisenstein presented Ivan as a sympathetic figure, though mad. Stalin was not satisfied, and he called the director and the actor into his office on February 24th, 1947. Cherkasov has left an account of Stalin's views on Ivan the Terrible :

In answer to our questions J. V. Stalin offered a series of unusually interesting and valuable observations relating to the epoch of Ivan the Terrible and the principals of the artistic embodiment of historic forms.

Speaking of the state activity of Ivan the Terrible, Comrade Stalin pointed out that Ivan IV had been a great and wise ruler who protected the country from the infiltration of foreign influence and had tried to bring about the unification of Russia. In particular, talking about the progressive activity of Ivan the Terrible, Comrade Stalin emphasized that Ivan IV had been the first to introduce a foreign trade monopoly in Russia, adding that Lenin had been the only one to have done this after him.

Comrade Stalin also remarked on the progressive role played by the Oprichnina, saying that Malyuta Skuratov, the head of the Oprichnina, was a great Russian general who fell heroically in the war with Livonia.

While referring to Ivan the Terrible's mistakes, Joseph

Vissarionovich remarked that they partly consisted of a failure to liquidate the five remaining great feudal families, and the failure to fight the feudal lords to the end. Had he done this, Russia would have had no Time of Troubles. At this point Joseph Vissarionovich added humorously: 'There God stood in Ivan's way.' Ivan the Terrible would liquidate one feudal family, one boyar clan, and would then repent for a whole year and pray for forgiveness of his 'sins' when instead he should have been acting with increasing determination.

This extraordinary conversation, in which Ivan the Terrible was held up as an example of a great and wise king, continued into the small hours of the morning. Stalin appears to have done most of the talking. Eisenstein, weak from a recent heart attack, seems to have played the role of an attentive listener, taking little part in the discussion. The conversation ranged over a wide field, but always returned to the flawed masterpiece on which both Eisenstein and Cherkasov had spent so large a part of their lives.

Finally Stalin asked how they proposed to end the film, and Cherkasov answered that it would be best if they retained the original ending, fading out on a heroic Ivan gazing pensively across the Baltic and saying: 'We have reached the sea and here we remain!' Stalin smiled. The ending pleased him, and he wished them success in putting the film together. The two friends thereupon bade farewell to the dictator and walked out into the Red Square. 'There,' says Cherkasov, 'we discussed the impression made on us by our unforgettable meeting with Stalin.'

Eisenstein left no record of this meeting with Stalin, but he did write a long *mea culpa* in which Stalin's opinions on Ivan the Terrible are faithfully reproduced. This *mea culpa*, which appeared in the magazine *Culture and Life*, is a painful document, in which Eisenstein confesses that he has wholly misunderstood the great role played by Ivan the Terrible in Russian history. He had depicted a mad, treacherous, infinitely tormented Tsar, haunted by the memory of his crimes, and now he had to confess that he had distorted the true creative elements in Ivan's character. Ivan, according to Stalin, was not mad. He was absolutely sane, the wisest man in all Russia, with a clearly defined policy and the power to enforce it, although he had inexcusably offended against history by not liquidating the five remaining great feudal families. As for the Oprichnina, who were given *carte blanche* to murder, rape and plunder as they pleased, they too were to be regarded as the destined saviours of Russia, the princely servants of a benevolent emperor. Eisenstein had read the wrong history books.

Like the confessions of the political prisoners during the purges of the thirties, the *mea culpa* of Eisenstein must be read on many levels. He confesses his errors, but he also excuses them. He accepts the justice of his accusers, but he also hints at the justice of his own cause. He declares that he has committed a crime against historical law, but there is more than a suspicion that he obeys another historical law. He wrote:

> In the second part of *Ivan the Terrible* we committed a misrepresentation of historical facts which made the film worthless and vicious in an ideological sense.
>
> We know Ivan the Terrible as a man with a strong will and firm character. Does that exclude from the characterization of this Tsar the possibility of the existence of certain doubts? It is difficult to think that a man who did such unheard of and unprecedented things in his time never thought over the choice of means or never had doubts about how to act at one time or another. But could it be that these possible doubts overshadow the historical role of historical Ivan as it was shown on the film? Could it be that the essence of this powerful sixteenth-century figure lies in these doubts and not in his uncompromising fight against them or unending success of his state activity?
>
> Is it not so that the centre of our attention is and must be *Ivan the builder, Ivan the creator of a new, powerful, united Russian power*, Ivan the inexorable destroyer of everything that resisted *his* progressive undertakings? The *sense of historical truth was betrayed by me* in the second part of *Ivan*. The private, unimportant and non-characteristic prevailed over the most important element. The play of doubts crept out in front, and the wilful character of the Tsar and his historically progressive role slipped out of the field of attention. The result was that a false and mistaken impression was created about the image of Ivan.

With this confession Eisenstein put an end to the long love affair with Ivan the Terrible which began in 1940, before Germany attacked the Soviet Union, and absorbed all his creative energies in the intervening years. While making the film, he had no illusions about the daemonic nature of Ivan's character. He wrote in his programme notes that he had no intention of whitewashing the Tsar. He would depict him as he was, ferocious and terrible, because in that age only a man capable of inspiring terror could have ruled over Russia. When Eisenstein died, his masterpiece remained unfinished.

In one of those long, despairing letters which Ivan the Terrible wrote to Prince Andrey Kurbsky inviting him back to the court from which he had escaped in fear of his life, the Tsar wrote: 'If thou considerest thyself just and faithful to the Tsar, so why didst thou not accept sufferings and the crown of death from me, who are thy wicked master?'

GLORY TO GREAT STALIN

AS HE APPROACHED his seventieth birthday Stalin began to think more and more often about the image of himself which would be preserved through the centuries. He knew he was not immortal, and this knowledge seems to have weighed heavily upon him, though he liked to remind himself that Georgian peasants had been known to live to 150. He was in ill health, suffering from heart trouble, sciatica, arthritis, and a number of related diseases. His ankles were swollen, and he still had trouble with his left arm. In spite of these portents he showed no disposition to retire from the scene, groomed no successor, and behaved as though he would continue to rule his Communist empire for another quarter of a century.

In the relentless war they wage against mortality, dictators have few weapons. They can, and do, inflict upon the country countless statues of themselves, and it pleases them to set these statues in high and remote places as well as in the farthest villages; but Stalin had no taste or understanding of sculpture, and the statues produced during his reign had a uniformly leaden look about them. Still, he was determined to set up these statues while he was still living, and in the years following World War II some ten thousand were erected, not only in the Soviet Union, but in the countries conquered by the Red Army. There were statues in plaster, in hammered iron, in bronze and aluminium; some were gilded, others were sprayed with silver paint. Millions of smaller statues were stamped out by machines. Like Ramses II, he would die with the certain knowledge that thousands of years after his death his enduring image would survive, because he had made so many of them.

The time had come to present his complete works to the public. He had worked on them since the end of the war, slowly gathering the chronological material, selecting his speeches and articles according to a judicious plan, omitting those passages which offended his sense of historical justice, and sometimes editing and rewriting them. A good deal of this work was done by his secretariat. Stalin was his own editor in chief, with Poskrebyshev as his chief assistant. Together they went to work to produce the monumental *Collected Works*.

It was a complex and baffling task, for there was always the temptation to edit the articles out of existence or simply to omit them. Since Stalin was by nature lazy, took no pleasure in writing and wrote comparatively little, the editors seem to have accepted from the beginning the fact that the *Collected Works* would never be as imposing as those of Lenin. Lenin wrote voluminously and tirelessly, his complete works amounting in the current edition to some 40,000 pages printed in small type in fifty fat volumes. Since Stalin's *Collected Works* would occupy only about a tenth of this space, it was arranged that they should be printed in large type on thick paper. Originally there were to be sixteen volumes, bringing the story to the end of World War II. Other volumes would of course appear at intervals, but the sixteen formed a satisfactory beginning. The first volume would be concerned with his obscure revolutionary origins, the sixteenth would culminate with his triumphant victories and his emergence as a figure of formidable power on the world's stage.

Anyone who has studied Stalin at any length might reasonably guess that he would pay special attention to two periods in his life above all others. Those two periods were his early years and the years 1928-9 when for the first time he found himself in possession of supreme power. In fact these were the periods he first worked on. So it happened that Volume I and Volume XI were completed and published in 1949. Two years later he completed and published Volumes II, III, IV, and XIII. The first three dealt with the years 1907-20, with about half the pages devoted to the 1917 revolution, while Volume XIII was devoted to the year 1934. There was method in this madness. It was obviously necessary for him to give his final verdict on the 1917 revolution and his own place in it, and this he accomplished to his own satisfaction by bringing out Volumes II, III, and IV. The choice of Volume XIII was slightly more puzzling, and may be explained by the fact that his mood in 1934, on the eve of the great purges, was not very different to his mood in 1950. In 1952 seven more volumes in the familiar ugly chocolate-coloured bindings were published. That he should have brought out these seven volumes in a single year suggests that he was in a hurry to complete his *Collected Works.**

On the eve of his seventieth birthday he seemed to be mellowing. His hair was nearly white, his face was becoming puffy with age, his movements were slow and deliberate. The cleft in his chin was a little more prominent, the eyes were a little more protuberant, and the eyelids more heavily veined. There was something in his manner which suggested that he was becoming more tolerant, almost avuncular. But though he was growing old, he was still murderous, still tyrannical.

To the very end he remained a creature of habit. He still rose late in the morning or early afternoon, and worked far into the night. The occasional diplomats who were invited to see him were granted audiences between nine o'clock in the evening and midnight. He made few speeches, few broadcasts, and rarely met any deputations of workers. Indeed, he had a horror of deputations, and in his last years he saw few people outside his immediate entourage. His holidays on the Black Sea coast grew longer. He still lived in his modest apartments in the Kremlin, but spent more and more time in the four or five luxurious villas he possessed near Moscow. Outwardly simple in his tastes, he possessed the self-indulgence of all dictators. As he grew older, it never occurred to him to step down to make way for a younger man.

Visiting Communist leaders found him as unyielding and

* When Stalin died in 1953, there remained three volumes still to be published. Volume XIV was to cover the period 1934-40, Volume XV was to consist of *History of the Communist Party of the Soviet Union: Short Course,* of which he had written some fragments – it had already appeared, and its absence in the *Collected Works* was no particular loss – and Volume XVI was to have been devoted to the years 1941-5.

demanding as ever. Milovan Djilas, invited to Moscow to discuss a Yugoslav quarrel with Albania, found that nothing had changed. Stalin spoke of nations as though they were toys, which he threw away when he grew tired of them. He had the imperiousness of a child, and sometimes the imperiousness of the mad. He talked about Albania as though it were an apple. 'We agree to Yugoslavia swallowing Albania,' he said, making the gesture of a man lifting food to his mouth and then swallowing it. Djilas protested that it was not a simple question of swallowing Albania, but the far more difficult question of establishing some sort of unification. Stalin smiled, made the swallowing gesture again, and said: 'We agree with you. You ought to swallow Albania – the sooner the better!' A little later he said: 'Write Tito a dispatch about this in the name of the Soviet government and submit it to me by tomorrow.' He expected all foreign Communists to submit to him. At the least hesitation he would break out into a tirade of gutter words, threats and paralysing appeals for Communist solidarity by which he meant simply that everyone would have to agree with him, no matter what decision he made.

He still liked to change the names on maps. Djilas tells the story that when he went to dinner that night in Stalin's villa, he came upon a vast map of the world in the entrance hall. Stalingrad was encircled in blue pencil. The city of Königsberg was about to be renamed Kaliningrad, and Stalin pretended to search for it on the map. Then, observing that there were still some towns near Leningrad – Peterhof, Oranienbaum, and others – which still bore the German names given to them at the time of Catherine the Great, he said curtly: 'Change these names – it is senseless that these places still bear German names!' Zhdanov, who was present, immediately took out his small notebook and recorded Stalin's order with a little pencil.

Stalin said he was on a diet, and Djilas expected a simple meal in keeping with the spartan Communist tradition. The meal was a feast, Stalin eating voraciously, 'as though,' observed Djilas, 'he feared that there would be not enough of the desired food left for him.' Though gluttonous with food, he was abstemious with liquor, carefully measuring out each drop. For Djilas, and probably for the host, the meal took place in an atmosphere of excruciating boredom relieved only by childish games, as when Stalin proposed that everyone should guess how many degrees it was below zero and that the losers should be punished by being made to drink as many glasses of vodka as the number of degrees they guessed wrong; and when they tired of this there would be similar games of estimating the length of the room in feet or of the table in inches. Uncultured and boorish, without inner resources, the lords of the Soviet empire, with power of life and death over hundreds of millions of people, amused themselves like country yokels. From time to time Stalin would fall into a reminiscent mood, recalling incidents from his childhood and his exile in Siberia, losing himself in the recital of anecdotes which seemed pointless and which originated with stories told by others. 'Yes, I remember the same thing ...'

Beria was there with his rimless spectacles, green eyes and faint withdrawn smile. Zhdanov, with his clipped brown moustache and sickly red face, vied with Molotov in being scrupulously attentive to Stalin's moods. The young Voznesensky, Chairman of the State Planning Commission, blond and curly-haired, smiling pleasantly at being in the presence of so many great men, seemed the most at ease, though from time to time he too would be caught up in the sullen rage which simmered below the surface. Malenkov, bulging with fat, the small inner face almost absorbed by the flabby cheeks, took little part in the conversation, happy to be relieved of the task of speaking, though noticing everything.

Djilas, seeing them round the table, was overwhelmed with a feeling of futility. The conversation was drab and sometimes spiteful. They were all encouraging the old man, all applauding his wit, his wisdom, his penetrating insight, laughing ecstatically over his jokes, and only too well aware that he had raised them to their high positions. Stalin in turn kept gazing at them good-humouredly, cunningly and spitefully. The name of Mosa Pijade, the veteran Yugoslav Communist, was mentioned.

'Pijade, short, with glasses?' Stalin recalled. 'Yes, I remember, he visited me. And what is his position?'

'He is a member of the Central Committee, a veteran Communist, the translator of *Das Kapital*,' Djilas explained.

'In our Central Committee there are no Jews,' Stalin laughed, and went on to taunt Djilas for being pro-Jewish.

Wearying of these taunts, Stalin went on to discuss more serious matters. Turning to Voznesensky, Stalin asked whether it might be possible to dig a canal between the Volga and the Don.

'It's a terribly important matter from the military point of view,' he declared. 'In case of war they might drive us out of the Black Sea – our fleet is weak and will go on being weak for a long time. Imagine how valuable the Black Sea Fleet would have been during the battle of Stalingrad if we had had it on the Volga! The canal is of first-class, first-class importance!'

Voznesensky agreed that some means would be found to dig the canal and took out his little notebook and wrote down the order with a little pencil.*

Zhdanov, who looked sickly, was drinking orangeade instead of vodka, and once Djilas turned to him and asked him why he was drinking orangeade.

'I have a bad heart,' Zhdanov replied. 'I might die at any moment, and I might live a very long time.'

Zhdanov, the head of the Leningrad party organization, died a few months later, apparently of poison administered by an agent of Malenkov. Zhdanov and Malenkov were both contenders for the succession.

As Djilas well knew, the cold calculating conspirators sitting round the table lived from day to day, from hour to hour, in mortal fear of the gluttonous tyrant who told senile stories and amused himself by pitting one against the other. They were his tools, his sycophants, his court jesters. They not only lived in fear of Stalin, but they were in fear of one another. They were afraid to speak to Stalin, and still more afraid not to speak. Stalin was slightly deaf, and a perfectly innocuous request might be taken as an affront, or a simple precise statement might become wildly misinterpreted, with dangerous results. To survive, it was necessary to stay on Stalin's level, to be casually boorish, to enjoy vulgarity, and to be indifferent to anything except the exaltation of the dictator. How boorish Stalin could be was shown at the end of the dinner, which Djilas has recorded with a proper solemnity:

Stalin ended the dinner by raising a toast to Lenin's memory: 'Let us all drink to the memory of Vladimir Ilyich, our leader, our teacher – our all!'

* Stalin was obviously playing a game with Djilas. The Volga-Don Canal had been planned long before. Work was begun in 1938, abandoned during the war years, and resumed in 1947, many months before this conversation took place. The canal was finally completed on June 1st, 1952.

We all stood and drank in mute solemnity, which in our drunkenness we soon forgot, but Stalin continued to bear an earnest, grave, and even sombre expression.

We left the table, but before we began to disperse, Stalin turned on a huge automatic record player. He even tried to dance, in the style of his homeland. One could see that he was not without a sense of rhythm. However, he soon stopped, with the resigned explanation: 'Age has crept up on me and I am already an old man!'

But his associates – or, better said, courtiers – began to assure him, 'No, no, nonsense. You look fine. You're holding up marvellously. Yes, indeed, for your age ...'

Then Stalin turned on a record on which the coloratura warbling of a singer was accompanied by the yowling and barking of dogs. He laughed with an exaggerated, immoderate mirth, but on detecting incomprehension and displeasure on my face, he explained, almost as though to excuse himself, 'Well, still it's clever, devilishly clever.'

In this way Stalin amused himself in his free hours, and sometimes it must have seemed to those who knew him that the sound he had been listening to all his life was the mechanical uproar of a coloratura singer accompanied by yowling dogs. It was a sound to chill the heart and blood, and gave him an exquisite pleasure.

He still spoke with considerable authority on music. In the following month came his decree condemning the music of Prokofiev, Shostakovich and Khachaturian.

Of all those who gathered at the table, only one man left a pleasant impression on Djilas. Like the rest he was a sycophant, only too obviously pleased to render his master some service, the notebook and little pencil always within reach, but he possessed qualities which gave him distinction. He had an orderly cultured mind, said little, and when he spoke, made good sense. He could be boorish with the rest, when it served his purpose, but at such times he was obviously acting, while the others were just as obviously serious and determined in their boorishness. Voznesensky was forty-five, and looked younger than his years. He had a fresh complexion, high cheekbones, and a rather high forehead. He looked like a stranger at the feast.

Voznesensky was then at the height of his fame. He had won the Stalin prize for his book with the oddly repetitive title

The Wartime Economy of the USSR in the Period of the Fatherland War. It was a slim book of less than two hundred pages, and attempted to analyse in seventeen brief chapters the vast and intricate complexities of the wartime economy, with copious quotations from the works of Stalin. The book celebrated Stalin as the master planner of all time, the man who had singlehandedly developed the science of war economics. 'Honour and glory, unprecedented in the history of human society, belongs to the party of Lenin-Stalin,' Voznesensky wrote in the introduction, adding: 'The theory of socialist war economics has been created by the labours of our leader – the great Stalin.'

The basic argument of the book was that the concentration of the means of production in the hands of the Soviet state enabled the country to develop its resources to an unparalleled degree. The change-over from a peace economy to a war economy was accomplished with lightning speed, thanks to Stalin who had foreseen the coming of war and planned accordingly. Even when the most valuable and productive territory fell to the Germans, there was only a brief period in January and February 1942 when productive capacity in industry fell from the prewar norms, and then only very slightly. In spite of the evacuation of all the major industries of western Russia to the Urals, the Volga, Kazakhstan, Siberia and Central Asia, Soviet production more than held its own, and in some areas there were phenomenal increases. More aluminium and magnesium, for example, were produced in the Urals and western Siberia in 1943 than in the whole of the USSR in 1940. Voznesensky does not say how much more. He gives precise figures for the increase in the number of mechanics, drillers, lathe operators, tool makers, and ships' engineers during those years, but notes that 'individual consumption decreased somewhat'. The pages are black with figures. We learn that as a result of the German invasion the Soviet Union lost 4,709,000 houses, 216,700 stores and trading enterprises, 98,000 *kolkhozes*, 82,000 primary and secondary schools, 43,000 public libraries, and 31,850 plants and factories. Voznesensky says the Soviet government increased the wages of workers in the coal-mining, iron and steel industries both before the war and during the war, 'unlike the governments of capitalist countries which kept the wages in the iron, steel and coal-mining industries at the lowest level'. Throughout the book he compares the industrial capacity of the Soviet

Union with that of capitalist countries and with that of Tsarist Russia. He observes that anyone who compares real earnings in the Soviet Union and in capitalist countries by comparing the wages received is 'nothing but an illiterate, or better still, a slanderer', since the Soviet worker receives sickness benefits, maternity leaves and free education all paid for by the state.

Throughout Voznesensky is concerned to justify the ways of socialist planning with the haphazard crisis-laden methods of capitalism. Socialist planning itself becomes an economic law, for the Soviet Planning Board is the supreme arbiter of prices which are calculated not according to supply and demand but according to the needs of the state. He discusses incentives, piecework, and bonuses, but very briefly; they are sometimes useful, but they have no deep roots in the economy. He commends the brilliant reorganization of Soviet industry with its fair and equable distribution of consumer goods with the savage practices of monopoly capital. In a passage which may have been inserted by Stalin, for it breaks the flow of the argument and is not written in Voznesensky's customary style, he says:

> After the end of the Second World War the government of the United States of America, fulfilling the will of the rulers of American capital monopolists, has abandoned all attempts at planning production and circulation. Instead of planning, the President of the United States of America began to admonish the monopoly capitalists to lower their excessively high and continually rising commodity prices, which are beyond the means of the American people. When these admonitions were exposed as hypocritical, and when the demagoguery had come to an end, then the rulers of the United States of America started demanding that the people reduce their needs and tighten their belts.

With these fictions Voznesensky's arguments acquire a curious lucidity. The Planning Board, which knows the needs of the state much better than anyone else, must be ensured its continued existence unhampered by the laws of supply and demand. Yet strangely he remains on the defensive. Here and there he implies that all is not well in the Soviet economy, and that it was even worse during the war. There is a long discussion of Sir William Beveridge's plan for social insurance; he half approves of it, and then dismisses it because the workers of the Soviet Union would not be attracted to a plan for the elimination of want as long as it is based on the retention of private ownership of the means of production. Moreover, there is one overwhelming reason why the Soviet Union should seek no change in the Planning Board. Only by retaining the Planning Board could the country prepare itself for the Third World War, which was the inevitable consequence of the predatory policies of the imperialist states. Henceforward the Planning Board would continue to supervise the entire economy of the state, dictating the exact number of houses to be built, the exact number of automobiles to be manufactured, and the exact number of shoe buttons and yards of cloth.

Voznesensky's short book has considerable importance because it accurately reflects Stalin's economic thought at the time. Stalin's ideas were to change. In later years he would laugh to scorn the idea that socialist planning is itself an economic law, but he left no doubt that he regarded the Planning Board as a permanent necessity. The State alone determined production; the iron laws of the State determined how the workers should be rewarded. Voznesensky hints that there may be some advantages in piecework and incentives, but he does not insist on them. Some 750,000 copies of the small book were printed. Some months later, when he was actively engaged in preparing the draft for the new Five Year Plan, he seems to have returned to the question of incentives with more force. He spoke of the need for some relaxation in the overcentralized planning. Stalin accused him of seeking to restore capitalism to Russia. Voznesensky explained that this was far from his mind, but when he left Stalin's presence he hurried to see Khrushchev, Malenkov and Molotov. By accusing him of seeking to restore capitalism, Stalin had shown that he could dispense with the services of Voznesensky.

Khrushchev, speaking in Sofia in the summer of 1955, told what happened to Voznesensky:

The three of us, Malenkov, Molotov and myself, immediately asked for an interview with Stalin, and we were received by him at noon. We stated that we had seen and approved the measures proposed by Voznesensky. Stalin listened to us, and then he said: 'Before you go on, you should know that Voznesensky was shot this morning.'

There you are. What could we do? A man is prepared to be a martyr, but what use is it to die like a dog in the gutter? There was nothing we could do while Stalin lived.

Until Khrushchev gave this account of the fate of Voznesensky, nothing was known except that he had disappeared from sight. He vanished as completely as though he had never existed. There was no trial. A brief paragraph in *Pravda* in March 1949 said he had been deprived of all his posts. The mellowing dictator had shown that he could still solve economic problems simply and expeditiously – by shooting. Voznesensky had survived Zhdanov by only eight months.

On the eve of his seventieth birthday, Stalin still held all the reins in his hands, but for the first time he was aware that he was being challenged by forces over which he had no control. The satellite countries in Eastern Europe were obedient to his will, but further to the west Yugoslavia was demonstrating distressing signs of independence, and in the East Mao Tse-tung was bringing to birth a new Communist empire, which owed nothing to the Russian Communist Party. In April 1949 the Chinese Communists crossed the Yangtze river. In a few months the whole of mainland China would lie at their feet. For Stalin, Mao Tse-tung was both a fearful portent and a menacing presence.

If there was little he could do about Mao Tse-tung, there was a good deal he could do about Marshal Tito, the leader of the Yugoslav Communists, who had consistently defied him. He could invite Tito to the Soviet Union and then arrest him; he could send his agents to infiltrate the Yugoslav secret police; he could send assassins into Yugoslavia; if all these failed, he could solemnly outlaw Yugoslavia from the confederation of Communist nations. On March 27th, 1948, the Soviet ambassador in Belgrade handed Tito a letter so full of menaces that it was obvious that Stalin had decided to terrify Tito into submission. There had come to Stalin's ears, or he had invented, the rumour that leading Yugoslav Communists were saying that the Communist Party of the Soviet Union was degenerate and that great-power chauvinism was rampant in the USSR. He thundered:

> Trotsky also began by saying that the Communist Party of the Soviet Union was degenerate and that it was suffering from the limitations inherent in great-power chauvinism. Naturally he camouflaged himself with leftist slogans about world revolution. But in fact it was Trotsky himself who was degenerate and who, on being found out, sided with the sworn enemies of the Soviet Communist Party and of

the Soviet Union. We think that the political career of Trotsky is not uninstructive.

There was a good deal more of this letter, bristling with menaces and accusations of treasonable conspiracy. Though signed 'V. M. Molotov, J. V. Stalin', there was not the least doubt that Stalin was the sole author, for it betrayed the erratic, repetitious style which Stalin assumed when he was in his more desperate moods. Why, he asked, was a certain Vladko Velebit still retained as first assistant minister in the Ministry of Foreign Affairs, when the whole world knew he was a British spy? Why had the Yugoslav Communists failed to prevent the development of capitalism? Why had they borrowed ideas from Mensheviks, from Bernstein and Bukharin? Why was the Yugoslav Communist Party neither Marxist-Leninist nor Bolshevik in its organization? So he went on, piling accusation upon accusation, as though he hoped that Tito would break under the strain of so much criminal conspiracy. And when he wrote: 'We think that the political career of Trotsky is not uninstructive', he was employing the most naked menace of all, for at his orders Trotsky had been assassinated.

In those days Stalin seemed to be consumed with rage against Tito. He could scarcely believe that a Communist would dare to disobey him. 'Once when I came from Kiev to Moscow,' Khrushchev said in February 1956. 'I was invited to visit Stalin who, pointing to the copy of a letter lately sent Tito, asked me, "Have you read this?" Not waiting for my reply, he answered, "I will shake my little finger – and there will be no more Tito. He will fall!"'

But Tito did not fall. A dictator, he continued to defy a greater dictator. He parried all Stalin's thrusts, replied gracefully to all taunts, and continued to sign his occasional letters to Stalin 'with comradely greetings', so that Stalin became more and more angry and inconsolable. In one of his notes addressed to the Yugoslav government dated August 30th, 1949, Stalin wrote: 'The puppy is feeling so good that he barks at the elephant.'

When Stalin was unable to get his hands on an enemy, he would do the next-best thing: he would arrest, torture and put on trial, or simply liquidate, as many of the enemy's real or imagined associates as possible. A vast Titoist conspiracy evidently existed in Eastern Europe and determined measures were necessary to prevent it from spreading. In Bulgaria and Hungary he accordingly staged show trials on the model of the Moscow trials of 1936-8. The old techniques were restored, and the ghosts of Kamenev, Zinoviev and Radek presided over the courtrooms where once again innocent men confessed to inconceivable follies. Urged on by intimidation, threats and promises, they recited the complex scenarios which they had learned by heart.

Laszlo Rajk, a former Minister of the Interior and Minister of Foreign Affairs in Hungary, was one of those who quietly assented to their own doom. He confessed that throughout his government service he had given information to American intelligence. More recently he had been building up a nest of espionage composed of Tito's secret agents, and plotting the invasion of Hungary by a Yugoslav army dressed in Hungarian uniforms. The invasion would take place at a time when the Soviet Union was deeply involved in an international crisis, and therefore unable to come to the rescue of the Hungarians. The scenario bears the characteristic signs of Stalin's workmanship. Rajk was hanged. Seven years later, following the Communist custom, he was officially rehabilitated. For the same reasons, and following similar scenarios, Traicho Kostov was hanged in Bulgaria and Koci Xoxe in Albania.

Still Tito eluded Stalin. From behind the Carpathians he wrote to the Politburo a series of quiet letters which had the effect of making Stalin all the more enraged. Diplomatic relations between Yugoslavia and the Soviet Union were broken off. Stalin decided upon a military invasion, and then thought better of it. In the last resort he could not rely on the neighbouring Balkan states, and he may have guessed that the direct military use of Soviet troops in a large-scale campaign presented strategic difficulties. Nor did it escape him that Tito had potential allies in the west.

When the name of Tito was mentioned in the Kremlin he would curse and fly into a rage, and then he would grow quiet and remorseful, thinking of the time when Tito had visited Moscow and supped at his table. He could have hanged Tito then. Now it was too late.

A collective hallucination descended on Russia on Stalin's seventieth birthday on December 21st, 1949. The guns blared in salute, the processions marched across the Red Square, and

huge balloons bearing the features of a younger Stalin climbed
into the wintry sky. The official buildings were draped in red,
the colour of happiness. From all over the country there came
gifts of embroidered cloth, tapestries and carpets bearing his
name or his features. Ornamental swords, cutlasses, tankards,
cups, everything that might conceivably please him, were sent
to the Kremlin, and then displayed in the State Museum of
the Revolution on Upper Gorky Street. Poets extolled him
in verses. He was the sun, the splendour, the lord of creation.
The novelist Leonid Leonov, writing a few days earlier in
Pravda, foretold the day when all the peoples of the earth
would celebrate his birthday; the new calendar would begin
with the birth of Stalin rather than with the birth of Christ.
Had he not singlehandedly created the Communist state? Had
he not singlehandedly introduced to the world an era of
happiness and joy?

All the members of the Politburo vied with one another
on his birthday in public worship of the godlike Stalin, and
on his seventieth birthday the entire issue of *Pravda* was
given over to their panegyrics. They acclaimed the good, kind,
wise Stalin, generous in triumph, patient in adversity, calm in
danger.

Malenkov wrote:

> With a feeling of great gratitude, turning their eyes to
> Stalin, the peoples of the Soviet Union, and hundreds and
> millions of peoples in all the countries of the world, and
> all progressive mankind, see in Comrade Stalin their beloved
> leader and teacher, and they believe and know that the
> cause of Lenin and Stalin is invincible.

Beria wrote:

> Millions of fighters for peace and democracy in all coun-
> tries of the world are closing their ranks still firmer around
> Comrade Stalin as their fighting banner. In all languages
> of the peoples of the world, the words of greeting to our
> leader: 'Glory to Comrade Stalin! Forward to new vic-
> tories under the leadership of Great Stalin!' ring out with
> greater force on this memorable day.

Voroshilov wrote:

> The mighty voice of the Great Stalin, defending the peace
> of the world, has penetrated into all corners of the globe,

into the hearts and minds of the working and progressive people of the entire world. They, the ordinary and honest people, know that every word of the Great Stalin sounds the tocsin calling for vigilance and active resistance to the instigators of a new world war; and in answer to Stalin's appeal they are forming mighty columns of fighters for peace, for the liberty and happiness of the peoples.

Mikoyan wrote:

Without Comrade Stalin's especial care, we would never have had a network of meat combines equipped with the latest machinery, canneries and sugar refineries, a fishing industry and everything that has been created and is still being created in our country in the sphere of food industry.

Molotov wrote:

Comrade Stalin took in his hands both the political and economic leadership of the country together with the military leadership, commanding the armed forces of the country, inspiring the army and the entire people to self-sacrificing, heroic struggle. The gigantic Soviet army created during the war was under the direct leadership of Comrade Stalin and built on the basis of the principles of Stalinist military science.

The panegyrics were interchangeable. Molotov, for example, spoke in the authentic voice of Voroshilov, and Voroshilov in turn repeated words which had been spoken by Beria. They had said all these things so many times before that the formulas had lost all meaning and they scarcely knew what they were saying.

The birthday, however, was not an unalloyed pleasure. Five days before, on December 16th, 1949, Mao Tse-tung had arrived in Moscow. At fifty-six, vigorous and determined to give to Communist China a special place in the sun, he represented the kind of Communist that Stalin most abhorred. He owed very little to Stalin and was not prepared to submit to Stalin's will. His armies had conquered China in a single year. Six hundred million people had become the servants of his will. He spoke therefore as an equal, demanded the rights of an equal, and sometimes he would hint that he was even greater than Stalin.

THE FAG END OF THE TRIUMPH

WITH THE CONQUEST OF China by Mao Tse-tung, new and unpredictable forces began to work on the Communist system. From the beginning communism had represented itself to be an international movement, seeking to change not only individual governments but all governments, speaking of a new world order in which the capitalists would be dethroned from their positions of eminence and replaced by the universal proletariat ruling through their chosen leaders. In fact, communist governments were coloured by fiercely nationalistic sentiments, deeply rooted and inescapably present. They did not speak with one voice; they spoke with a multitude of voices. Stalin and Mao Tse-tung were Communist leaders, but they were also intensely nationalistic. Their meeting in Moscow did not put an end to the centuries-old conflict between Russia and China.

They were well matched: the seventy-year-old Stalin, who had spent fifty years of his life in a ruthless quest for domination, and Mao Tse-tung, younger by fourteen years, who had only in this last year acquired a position in which he could exercise his taste for ruthlessness. Stalin had never thought of him as a potential leader. In 1945 he still regarded Mao Tse-tung as a pretentious parvenu, who would never succeed in imposing his will on China. Over the years he had done his best to remove him from any position of authority in the Chinese Communist movement. He had sent a succession of spies, infiltrators, and Moscow-trained Chinese Communists to Yenan in the hope of restoring the Stalinist line. Mao Tse-tung continued along the line he had chosen for himself. The two dictators met, vowed eternal friendship, declared that no ideological differences existed between them, and there could have been scarcely a moment when they were not aware that they were separated by centuries of culture and decades of antagonism.

Mao Tse-tung had intended to spend ten days in Russia: he stayed for two months. He was a hostage in an imperial court. Day after day excuses were made, urging him to remain. From time to time he was taken on a conducted tour of factories, which visibly bored him. He caught a cold. Stalin, too, caught a cold. The tragicomedy of the two-month visit reached its climax when the Sino-Soviet Treaty of Friendship, Alliance and Mutual Aid was finally signed. The mountain produced a molehill. China was promised a loan of $300,000,000 for industrial reconstruction. Implicit in the agreement was the understanding that China would accept Soviet administrative techniques, Soviet industrial blueprints, and Soviet methods of cost accounting. Floods of Soviet engineers would be sent to China, to dominate the industrial reconstruction of China for years to come. Stalin had been incapable of the grand gesture.

The agreement showed evidence of hard bargaining. China was compelled to recognize the independence and sovereignty of the Mongolian People's Republic. The South Manchurian Railway was to be restored to Chinese control, Soviet troops would leave Port Arthur, and Russia would surrender its interests in Dairen, but only after a peace treaty had been concluded with Japan, or, lacking that, at the end of 1952. There were, of course, many secret protocols to the agreement, which are still unpublished. Included among them there must have been an agreement to make a concerted attempt to put an end to American influence in eastern Asia. The seeds of the Korean War were sown. Many other wars were being plotted and planned during their secret meetings at the Kremlin.

The temper of Stalin's mind was hardening with age. He was beginning to believe that there was still time enough for him to crown his life work with the military destruction of the Western democracies, for he felt that only in this way could the world-wide victory of communism be achieved. With Mao Tse-tung in command of China, and all of southeast Asia within the Communist grasp, he believed that within a few years the whole of Asia would be added to the Communist empire, and he began to pay special regard to India. The Red armies, aided by millions of Asian recruits, would walk across Europe at their leisure. Deprived of her markets in Europe and Asia, the United States would shrivel into insignificance, a martyr to 'the inner contradictions of capitalism'. South America would fall like a ripe pear, and then it would be the turn of Africa. If immortality was not granted to him, he would spend the declining years of his life as a world emperor.

For these dreams to materialize he needed absolute control

of Communist movements wherever they existed. In particular he needed to control Mao Tse-tung, who had shown demonstrable signs that he was unwilling to surrender any part of his dictatorship over China. Nevertheless, by making China industrially dependent on the Soviet Union, Stalin was in a position to bring the full weight of his influence on the Chinese dictator. Between them they already shared responsibility for ruling nearly a thousand million people.

While Mao Tse-tung remained in Moscow, Stalin was making strenuous efforts to bring the Communist revolution to India and Japan. The Japanese Communist leader, Sanzo Nosaga, was ordered to abandon his efforts to seize Japan by legal means, and to come out in open rebellion. He refused, maintaining that Communism would eventually win power in Japan by an electoral victory, and nothing was to be gained by a war with the American army in occupation. Once more a local Communist had refused to obey the edict of the master. The Japanese Communist Party was split between the followers of Stalin and the followers of Nosaga. Instead of bringing about a Communist victory of Japan by direct action, Stalin had merely succeeded in seriously weakening the Japanese Communist movement.

In June 1950 the American occupation authorities banned the entire leadership of the Japanese Communist Party from taking any further part in political affairs. The American authorities acted only just in time. Stalin and Mao Tse-tung had together planned the take-over of Korea, to coincide with a Communist revolution in Japan. When the revolution failed, it became clear that the take-over would be a far more lengthy and costly process than either had anticipated.

In January 1950 Stalin ordered the reintroduction of the death penalty in the Soviet Union. In theory the death penalty had been suspended for the preceding three years. It was a charming theory, for it permitted Stalin to represent himself as a man of gentle persuasions while the murders went on as before.

In the same month he ordered Jacob Malik, the Soviet representative in the Security Council of the United Nations, to walk out. These two decisions – the public reintroduction of the death penalty and the withdrawal from the Security Council – arose from the same principles, the same determination to present a ruthless and uncompromising face to the world. But when the summer came he seemed to weary of his ruthlessness, and turned to more cultural pursuits.

The summer of 1950 was enlivened by a series of pronouncements by Stalin in a field in which he had previously shown very little interest – philology. During June and July five letters over his signature appeared in *Pravda*, all of them concerned with the nature of language and the theoretical bases of linguistic theory. Stalin admitted his incompetence to deal with the problem, but nevertheless felt called upon to expound some basic views because there were considerable differences of opinion among Marxists about the role played by language in bourgeois and proletarian states.

The controversy was not new. At various times Marx, Engels and Lenin had discussed the nature of language without however contributing any far-reaching ideas. Marx defined language as 'the direct reality of thought', and he had gone on to declare that 'ideas do not exist divorced from language', and these questionable and not very helpful assertions showed that he had paid very little attention to the problem. What was language? How did it develop? Did the different classes speak different languages? What would happen to language when the world socialist state came into existence? Would all the existing languages vanish and give place to a world language comprehensible to everyone? To this last question Stalin had replied at the Sixteenth Party Congress held in 1930, saying: 'The national languages will flow together into a universal language which of course will be neither Russian nor German, but something altogether new.' But such prophecies remained curiously unconvincing. Noel Coward has one of his characters entering a dark room after a drunken party, and as he fumbles for the light switch he announces that he has at last discovered the secret of the universe. It is a very simple secret – 'Everything merges'. Stalin, making his pronouncement about the final merging of languages into one which is 'neither Russian nor German, but something altogether new' seems to be speaking from the heights of the same exaltation. The pronouncement however throws some light on his thought processes and suggests that he did not expect the complete victory of socialism to come about except in some remote period of the future.

European philology has been concerned with the comparative study of the languages derived from ancient Sanskrit. It is largely a question of tracing phonetic laws according to principles established in the nineteenth century. In Russia, too, there was a general acceptance of the validity of these principles. Occasionally crackpots attempted to confound the authorities. They studied animal noises or the sounds made by the wind in the trees, and wrote learned disquisitions proving that human speech developed when men first imitated the barking of dogs or the whispers of the wind. Among these crackpots was a certain Nikolay Yakovlevich Marr, the son of a Scots father and a Georgian mother, who was brought up in the Caucasus and therefore had ample opportunity to study a variety of languages. He believed that the masses were originally inarticulate, communicating by gestures, and that language emerged from the needs of the privileged ruling class of priest-magicians. Language therefore was a weapon in the class struggle employed by what he termed the 'superstructure' of society. He affirmed that human speech derived from four syllables – sal, ber, yon and rosh. He was never able to explain why these precise sounds and no others were able to produce the infinite variety of words employed in Western speech, but he held doggedly to his beliefs and attached extraordinary importance to them. In time the four 'Japhetic' syllables were incorporated in the language of the exploited class, and the priest-magicians went on to evolve a more complicated language which the exploited were unable to understand. Throughout the history of the class struggle language had remained the weapon of the ruling classes, who immaculately preserved their own speech from the encroachments of the under-privileged, but with every revolution the under-privileged acquired a greater control over the resources of language. Marr believed that all language had developed in the same way, and that the languages of people in the same stage of development had fundamental similarities. In his 'Japhetic studies' he produced voluminous, if inconclusive, evidence to show that the development of language arose in direct conformity with the development of the class struggle.

On these quicksands he built a theory which was especially attractive to dogmatic Marxists, who were free to accept his conclusions because neither Marx nor Engels had said anything to the contrary. Indeed, they would not have understood what Marr was talking about. At meetings of philological societies in Russia Marr's familiar presence was usually the signal for fierce debates and bitter denunciations against the classical philologists. Marr claimed to have married scientific

Marxism to philology, and anyone who derided his theory deserved to be treated as a counter-revolutionary. He was a persuasive speaker, intoxicated by his own discoveries, and with his rumpled hair and shabby clothes he resembled a dedicated professor. He died in December 1934, but his influence was felt on a whole generation of Soviet philologists, who continued to proclaim that all language derived from *sal, ber, yon* and *rosh*.

On May 9th, 1950, *Pravda* published an article filling more than two pages with an outright attack on Marr's theory. His defenders rushed to the rescue, and a heated debate ensued. Every Thursday *Pravda* published a special summary devoted to philological questions arising from the debate. The purpose of the entire inquiry became clear on June 20th when Stalin intervened with a long letter purporting to be an answer to four questions sent to him by a group of young students. In his circuitous way Stalin had provoked the debate in order to put an end to it with an authoritative discussion of the issues going far beyond mere questions of philology.

The four questions were: (1) Is it true that language is a superstructure on a base? (2) Is it true that language always was and is of a class character, that there is no such thing as a non-class language common and uniform to all the people of a society? (3) What are the characteristic features of language? (4) Did *Pravda* act correctly in inaugurating an open discussion on questions of linguistics?

Stalin's answer to these questions assumed the form of an exhaustive attack on Marr's theories. 'The sooner our linguistics is rid of N. Y. Marr's errors,' he wrote, 'the sooner will it be possible to extricate them from our present crisis.' The professors who had taught that language was a product of the class struggle were warned that any further teaching on these lines would result in dismissal. Language was autonomous and self-perpetuating, the product not of classes but of the entire history of society, the gift of all past generations. Far from being the weapon of the ruling classes, it was the common heritage of all men. There were no revolutionary upheavals in language during revolutionary times. After the French and Russian Revolutions a few more words were added to the vocabulary, but these words did not prove that any fundamental alteration had taken place in the nature of language; on the contrary they showed that language could absorb new concepts with the greatest of ease. Stalin wrote:

According to Marxism, the transition of a language from an old quality to a new does not take place by means of an explosion, by the destruction of an existing language and the creation of a new one, but by the gradual accumulation of the elements of the new quality, and hence by the gradual withering away of the elements of the old quality.

In general we should explain to the comrades who are infatuated by sudden upheavals that the law of transition from an old to a new quality by means of a sudden upheaval is not only inapplicable in the history of the development of languages, but it is also not always applicable in other social phenomena, whether of the superstructure or of the base. It is compulsory in the case of a society divided into hostile classes, but it is not at all compulsory in the case of a society where there are no hostile classes. In a period of eight or ten years we effected a transition in the agriculture of our country from the bourgeois-individual-peasant system to the socialist collective-farm system. By this revolution the old bourgeois economic system was eliminated throughout the countryside and a new socialist system was created. But these revolutions did not occur as the result of an explosion, that is, by the overthrowing of the existing power and the creation of a new power, but by the gradual transition from the old bourgeois system of the countryside to a new system. And we succeeded in doing this because it was a revolution from above, because the revolution was accomplished through the initiative of the existing power with the support of the overwhelming mass of the peasantry.

Stalin's talent for rewriting the history of the Soviet Union was never more cogently displayed than in this discussion of philological principles. Marx had demanded the revolt of the masses, and looked forward to the time when the proletariat would take power in their hands. For Marx, the revolutions always began from the base, from below. Now Stalin was openly proclaiming that the great revolutions come from above, from the superstructure, and he gave the example of the forced collectivization of the peasants – a collectivization accomplished by the massive employment of troops and detachments of armed police, but which he described as a 'gradual transition from the old bourgeois system of the countryside to a new system'. This quiet and gentle revolution was guided from above and received 'the support of the over-whelming mass of the peasantry'. It was therefore not true that revolutions arose from the base, or that violent revolutions were necessary or desirable. Marr's theory of violent upheavals – both Stalin and Marr used the explosive word *razryv* for 'upheaval' – could find no support in the Soviet Union, where power streamed not from below but from above, and its effects were felt not in revolutionary explosions but in gradual and peaceful transitions. Through Marr, Stalin was attacking Marx. He was dethroning Marx by turning Marxism upside down, and he was rewriting Russian history and justifying his own dictatorship. The discussion on linguistic theory was a pretext for a discussion on the fundamental bases of the Communist state.

He had found the bridge – from Marr to Marx. In a final letter written on July 28th, he demolished the theory of the withering away of the state after the victory of the socialist revolution. The theory was first advanced by Engels in his *Anti-Dühring*, and it was one of the principal themes of Lenin's work *The State and Revolution* written shortly before Lenin took power. Now, thirty-three years after the revolution, Stalin wrote:

> After the victory of the socialist revolution in our country, the textualists and Talmudists in our party began to demand that the Communist Party should take steps to bring about the speedy withering away of our state, to dissolve state institutions, to give up a permanent army.
>
> But the Soviet Marxists, on the basis of the study of the world situation in our time, came to the conclusion that, under conditions of capitalist encirclement, when the victory of the socialist revolution has taken place in only one country, while capitalism rules in all the other countries, the country of the victorious revolution must not weaken, but in every way strengthen its state, the state institutions, the intelligence agencies, and the army, if this country does not wish to be crushed by the capitalist encirclement. The Russian Marxists came to the conclusion that Engels's formula implies the victory of socialism in all countries or in the majority of countries, that it is inapplicable to the case when socialism triumphs in one particular country, while capitalism rules in all the other countries.

In this final letter Stalin abandoned Marr – there was no

reason any longer to demolish him – but he occasionally reverted to the subject of the world language which would come about when the whole world was ruled by communists.

In the following months he took less and less part in the government, spending more and more time on the Black Sea coast. A vast weariness came over him, as he cultivated his lemon trees and saw that the prospects of becoming world emperor were diminishing. He would fall into long fits of solitary meditation, and one of his former security officers, writing about this time, described him as 'an old horse, grown grey in harness, dreaming motionless, with unseeing eyes, in a corner of the pasture'.

It was not, of course, an accurate picture of the man; on occasion the old horse could be as mettlesome as a foal. He could still strike fear in people's hearts. The ruthlessness, the nihilistic force, the desire to terrorize persisted, but they assumed quieter and more devious forms. Like other men he had periods of activity followed by periods of recuperation. Usually he was more murderous in winter. With the spring thaws, he would grow calm again, too much in love with lethargy to superintend the complicated manoeuvres of mass murder.

Towards the end of the summer of 1950 came the first fruits of his long contemplated 'Great Stalinist Plan for Remaking Nature', which he had announced in October 1948. Suddenly the Soviet press was filled with reports of gigantic construction projects and new agricultural and forestation projects. Soviet citizens were informed that while the Americans massacred women and children in Korea, the Soviet Union was engaged in peaceful pursuits designed to make the earth the servant of man. Rivers would be dammed, new canals would be built, the atomic bomb would be used to level mountains and thus in some mysterious way bring a more temperate climate to northern Russia. Among other construction projects was a seven-hundred-mile canal in Central Asia, which was finally abandoned only after Stalin's death. These projects were not quite so peaceful as the Soviet press claimed, for they employed slave labour on an unprecedented scale. To the end Stalin remained an unrepentant Pharaoh.

After the letters on linguistics Stalin wrote only one more sustained work, a fifty-page summary of the economic laws of socialism called *Economic Problems of Socialism in the USSR*. The dry title conceals an entire *volte-face* in his pre-

viously held beliefs, a summary repudiation of long established socialist principles. Without mentioning Voznesensky,
who had put forward the contrary thesis, Stalin said that
economic laws were absolute, and were the same whether a
country was governed by the dictatorship of the proletariat
or by the dictatorship of capitalists. These laws 'take place
independently of the will of man', and they are therefore not
to be confused with the economic plans drawn up by Soviet
leaders. 'Man,' said Stalin, 'cannot change or create economic
laws.'

For the greater part of his life he had been saying the exact
opposite, but now in old age it pleased him to acquiesce to
the existence of a law even more imperious than his own.
Nature had her own laws; science, too, had its laws; the world
was ruled by laws, and it was man's task to understand them.
Nevertheless, although the laws did not change, their validity
sometimes changed. There were laws which could be dispensed
with because man no longer needed them, or had passed
through a phase where they no longer affected him. For centuries men had believed that devastating floods were the inevitable results of natural law. At a time when men had
learned to curb the destructive forces of nature and to harness
them, this natural law no longer applied. So, too, with economic laws. In the past men had been drowned in the devastating flood of capitalism; under socialism they would remake
nature until she served the interests of man, and there would
be no more floods.

The theme delighted him so much that he repeated it with
variations several times, like a musician warming up to his
main theme, which was the necessity to re-examine all the
basic concepts of socialism in the light of his discovery that
the laws existed, and had always and would always exist
whether or not Communists paid any attention to them. Good
Marxists, following Marx, had introduced into the Soviet
economy concepts of 'necessary' and 'surplus' value, 'necessary' and 'surplus' labour, 'necessary' and 'surplus' production.
These concepts had been 'artificially pasted on' the economy
of the Communist state, although they had long since lost
any meaning they ever possessed. They had been devised,
according to Stalin, 'to arm the working class with an intellectual weapon for the overthrow of capitalism'. They were
no more than propaganda tricks, and the mature Communist
should leave them alone.

In his discovery of the existence of permanent laws, Stalin permitted himself a certain freedom in defining the laws. The law of value was a law, and not a law. It operated under capitalism, while assuming a restricted form under communism. One of the major troubles about communist planners was that they did not realize that even in its restricted form it possessed certain applications. He gave as an example the decision by the State Planning Board to equate the price of a ton of cotton with the price of a ton of grain. Being the absolute masters of price control, they could give whatever value they pleased to a ton of cotton and whatever value they pleased to a ton of grain. For incomprehensible reasons they had decided that there should be parity between grain and cotton. When the preliminary decision was brought to the attention of the Central Committee, someone asked whether cotton sold for the same price as grain on the world market; and since it did not, the price was fixed in line with the world markets, thus saving the cotton growers from ruin.

While scoffing at the arbitrary cost-price relationships of the planners, Stalin reserved the right to scoff at the capitalists. He wrote:

> In spite of the steady and rapid expansion of our socialist production, the law of value in our country does not lead to crises of overproduction, while in the capitalist countries this same law, whose sphere of operation is very wide under capitalism, does lead, in spite of the low rate of expansion of production, to periodical crises of overproduction.

In this way the argument revolves in circles, for value under a communist state is arbitrarily determined by the State Planning Board. The value is no less arbitrary when the planners decide that cotton is more valuable than grain, because it is more valuable on the world market.

For Stalin the law of value was not an absolute law: it would vanish altogether during the second phase of communist society, when, as Lenin predicted, production would be regulated by the requirements of society and the computation of the requirements of society would acquire paramount importance for the planning bodies. For the present, production served the interests of the state; what people wanted and needed was secondary.

So he goes on, playing with ideas of value and the laws of value, watching them disappear only to emerge again, at intervals repeating with a kind of shocked surprise his discovery that laws – some laws – exist and must be obeyed, because they are eternal and beyond the wit of man to change.

Having discussed the laws, he turns his attention to what he calls 'the antitheses' still remaining in communist society. Under capitalist states there is an antithesis between the country and the towns, but this antithesis cannot exist under conditions of communist economy, since the industrial workers and the farm workers are working for the same ends. Yet there remains at least one antithesis in communist society: the antithesis between the workers and the intellectuals. He notes that the problem was never previously discussed in the Marxian classics. 'It is a new problem, one that has been raised practically in our socialist construction,' he says. But having raised the problem and remarked on its profound seriousness, he returns to the contemplation of the antithesis between the town and the country, which does not exist, but is nevertheless annoying. Someone had suggested that there would come a time when all the essential distinctions between industry and agriculture, and between physical and mental labour, would disappear. 'No, comrade,' says Stalin, 'these distinctions will never completely disappear.' He goes on:

> The abolition of the essential distinction between industry and agriculture cannot lead to the abolition of all distinction between them. Some distinction, even if inessential, will certainly remain, owing to the difference between the conditions of work in industry and in agriculture. Even in industry the conditions of labour are not the same in all its branches: the conditions of labour, for example, of coal miners differ from those of the workers of a mechanized shoe factory, and the conditions of labour of ore miners from those of engineering workers. If that is so, then all the more must a certain distinction remain between industry and agriculture.
>
> The same may be said of the distinction between mental and physical labour. The essential distinction between them, the difference in their cultural and technical levels, will certainly disappear. But some distinction, even if inessential, will remain, if only because the conditions of labour of the managerial staffs and those of the workers are not identical.

These discussions, reminiscent of the complex arguments

concerning the withering away of the state, which becomes stronger the more it withers away, belong to the higher lunacy of Communist theory. The statements are delivered with great seriousness, almost as pontifical revelations. On these matters Stalin had long considered himself to be an authority, and indeed he was the only authority, and his voice was the only permissible voice.

Stalin completed his *Economic Problems of Socialism in the USSR* in February 1952. Following his usual custom, copies were distributed among leading Communists for their comments. Sometimes they dared to disagree with his findings, and he would reply at length, bitterly upbraiding them for their heresies; and if they quoted a text of Marx against him, he would quote a better text of Marx against them. They become 'stupid reactionaries', 'makers of mythical formulas', and worse. A certain Comrade Yaroshenko denied the necessity for a single political economy for all social formations, on the grounds that every social formation has its own specific economic laws. Stalin attacks him unmercifully; almost the best he has to say is that Yaroshenko's words fly in the face of the entire body of Marxist theory.

Economic Problems of Socialism in the USSR is a baffling work. Again and again, as though haunted by them, Stalin returns to a few primitive ideas. Man has controlled the floods; he has tamed fire and placed it at his service; the same destructive force which causes electric thunderstorms has been made to serve the peaceful interests of men by becoming the electricity which flows out of generators. Throughout the book he seems to be grappling with thoughts of destruction. When he mentions the natural laws, he continually refers to their destructive effect. He found no comfort in them.

Nor, looking out over the Kremlin wall, did he find much comfort in the world. The Korean War, planned as the brief prologue to the exodus of the United States and Great Britain from the Far East, proved to be a long-drawn and costly adventure. Marshall Aid, which Stalin rejected on behalf of the Communist states of Eastern Europe, saying it was offered only 'to strangle them', had given new life to the Western democracies. Tito was as defiant as ever. Mao Tse-tung showed no signs of surrendering his hard-won independence. Too often the mischievous conspiracies of Communist agents only proved what he already knew: Communist victories were won by armies, not by revolutionaries, and there were large areas of the world where his armies dared not penetrate.

In this dilemma he revived the long-forgotten peace offensive, representing himself as the guardian of peace and the Soviet Union as 'the greatest bulwark of peace'. On May Day in 1952 he made one of his rare appearances on the platform above Lenin's tomb, while a million civilians marched past bearing the slogan 'Stalin is Peace'.

He liked to talk of peace, but the word, as he used it, was a negotiable one and could be changed at will to mean almost anything he desired. He wrote in *Economic Problems of Socialism in the USSR:*

> The object of the present-day peace movement is to rouse the masses of the people to fight for the preservation of peace and for the prevention of another world war. Consequently, the aim of this movement is not to overthrow capitalism and establish socialism – it confines itself to the democratic aim of preserving peace. In this respect the present-day peace movement differs from the movement of the time of the First World War for the conversion of the imperialist war into civil war, since the latter movement went further and pursued socialist aims.

> It is possible that in a definite conjuncture of circumstances the fight for peace will develop here or there into a fight for socialism. But then it will no longer be the present-day peace movement; it will be the movement for the overthrow of capitalism.

By definition therefore the peace movement had nothing to do with peace; and the word 'peace' had nothing to do with peace. Under certain conditions peace meant revolutionary war. Under no condition did it mean peace as peace is understood in the West.

Stalin's desire to present himself as a peacemonger was only equalled by his desire to present the capitalist powers as warmongers. When someone suggested that wars between capitalist countries were no longer inevitable, he observed that such may appear to be the case, but those who are knowledgeable perceive 'the deep forces operating imperceptibly which determine the course of events'. In his view Great Britain and France would inevitably make war against the United States, and there were deep and mysterious forces working to bring such a war about. As for the Soviet Union, it would never under any condition attack a capitalist country, even though the capitalists for their own propaganda purposes were continually bemoaning Soviet aggressiveness.

As he wrote about the eternal laws, about the inevitability of capitalist wars, about the increasing happiness enjoyed under the Communist regime and the interminable misery of people living under capitalist regimes, he was like an old man by the fireside dreaming his life away. In those disjointed chapters fantasies abound, and there is never any feeling that he is attempting to construct a logical programme. He says himself that the book is simply a series of notes intended to guide the authors of a definitive 500- or 600-page study of Soviet economics. Nevertheless he attached a vast importance to the book, for he ordered it to be published a few days before the opening of the Nineteenth Party Congress, the first congress to be held in thirteen years. Inevitably at this congress the book stole the thunder. There was scarcely a speaker who did not go out of his way to praise the great genius who had added such vast new wealth to Marxist-Leninist theory. One after another they acclaimed his resolution of hitherto insoluble problems.

Malenkov, who delivered the long keynote speech, was almost delirious in his praise. Stalin's discovery that there were objective laws which take place independently of the will of man was greeted with special fervour. A new stage in the development of Marxism-Leninism had been opened up; a new era was beginning. The antithesis between the town and the country, the worker and the intellectual was now abolished. Through his theories of epoch-making importance Stalin had set the stage for a new and more perfect form of communism. The ultimate goal of communism was now within reach, Malenkov was saying, if the party remained vigilant enough, if it followed Comrade Stalin's new theories, and if world peace, by which he meant world revolution, could be established.

While the delegates continually interrupted to cheer every mention of Stalin's name, Malenkov read out his long speech, which covers 150 pages of text and took a whole day to deliver. His speech was at once a cry of triumph and a recital of frustrations and disastrous impediments to the onward march of communism. Over Stalin shone the light of triumph; but elsewhere there was only a murky darkness. Malenkov bitterly attacked the members of the Russian Communist Party who were interested only in their own welfare. Did they not know that the great Stalin had, by his genius and single-minded devotion, brought about the new millennium? The veils were about to be lifted; the communist paradise was about to be revealed; then why were so many communists dragging their feet?

Malenkov suggested that the period of frightful cataclysmic struggles between the communists and the capitalists was about to take place. He painted a violent portrait of the United States imperialists who had yoked Great Britain, France, Italy, Western Germany, Japan and Yugoslavia to their chariot. They were giving way to a bacchanalia of militarism. United States armies on foreign soil were acting like punitive police troops, who had given themselves the task of implanting fascism and strangling freedom.

This strange, delirious congress, shouting itself hoarse whenever Stalin's name was mentioned, was not in any real sense a congress. It had been convened for one purpose only – to pay tribute to the undying genius of Stalin. It was Stalin's gift to himself, the last and perhaps the most remarkable of all the gifts he offered himself after World War II.

The hand-picked delegates had been brought to Moscow to listen to the edicts. They heard that the 12-member Politburo was to be transformed into a 25-member Presidium, but the party secretariat, previously run by Malenkov, would be increased to ten members, and would therefore assume many of the functions of the old Politburo. They heard, too, that the Orgburo would be dissolved, and that the name of the party, known since the time of Lenin as the All-Union Communist Party (Bolsheviks) would become more simply the Communist Party of the Soviet Union, perhaps because it had become inconvenient to be reminded of the party of Lenin. They heard interminable speeches. Molotov spoke of the warmongers, and like Malenkov he depicted the President of the United States as the inheritor of the mantle of Adolf Hitler. Beria spoke on the subject of the nationalities, Bulganin on defence, Suslov on ideology, Mikoyan on consumer goods, Vasilievsky on the army, and all at regular intervals mentioned the name of Stalin and waited patiently for the applause to subside.

The Nineteenth Party Congress met from October 5th to October 14th, and on the last day Stalin delivered a brief and perfunctory speech. It was the last he ever made. He spoke of peace, and of the new Communist parties which had emerged in China, Korea, Czechoslovakia and Hungary, and how with their help it had become easier for the party to fight for peace. 'This work,' he said, 'is going on more merrily now.' He paid tribute to the Russian Communists who fought under terrible difficulties under the Tsars. The young Communists of today would never have to live through such difficult times. Then he said something that scarcely anyone could have expected from him, for he gave his blessing to democracy and national independence. Once, the bourgeoisie had upheld democratic liberties, but they had trampled all these liberties in the mud, and now the Communists alone were the spokesmen for equal rights between men and nations. Therefore it was necessary that the Communists should uphold 'the banner of bourgeois democratic freedom' and the banner of 'national independence'. His last words were in his characteristic style:

> You, the communist and democratic parties,
> > will have to raise the banner and carry it forward,
> > if you want to gather around you the masses.
> There is no one else to raise it ...

> You, the communist and democratic parties,
> > will have to raise the banner and carry it forward,
> > if you want to be patriots of your country,
> > if you want to become the leaders of the nation.
> There is no one else to raise it.

This little poem, the last of so many, was received with the inevitable applause, but he received even more applause for his last words: 'Long live peace among nations! Down with the warmongers!'

He had grown fat in those last years, and as he stood quietly accepting the applause, he seemed like a caricature of the earlier Stalin, so stern and unyielding. Now he looked benevolent, his hair white as wool, smiling faintly. Somnolent, slow-moving and heavy, he clapped languidly in answer to the applause, following the Soviet custom by which the performer claps his audience. On his face there was no expression except a cowlike contentment.

He did not know how soon he would be brought to the slaughter-house.

THE SUDDENNESS
OF DEATH

Our peasant is a simple man, but wise. When he sees a wolf, he shoots it. He does not preach morals to the wolf – he shoots it!

ALL THE YEARS OF HIS LIFE Stalin had been aware of
the presence of death. It was, after all, something he knew
well and intimately, for it was never very far from him; and
his familiarity with it never led to contempt. It was a subject
he had studied minutely, learning its uses and purposes, making it his servant by offering it the tribute of many holocausts.
He had a healthy fear of it, and perhaps feared it more than
most men, for he had more to lose. As well as a man can, he
had protected himself from its unchallengeable edict, but
neither processions of armed guards nor the services of the
most skilled physicians offered ultimate assurance against its
inevitable victory. He would fight death as he had fought it
so many times before – by killing off his enemies. With death
so busy, it would have no time to turn its face towards
him.

During the last weeks of his life he was planning a holo-
caust greater than any he had planned before. The *chistka*
had become a ritual like a ceremonial cleansing of a temple
performed every three or four years according to ancient
laws. The first *chistka* had taken place during the early months
of the revolution; it had proved so salutory that periodical
bloodbaths were incorporated in the unwritten laws of the
state. This time there would be a *chistka* to end all *chistkas*,
a purging of the entire body of the state from top to bottom.
No one, not even the highest officials, was to be spared. Molotov, Beria, Mikoyan, Voroshilov, Kaganovich, Khrushchev
and Mekhlis, the men who had been his closest companions
and most willing executioners, would be the first to fall, followed by the leaders of the second rank, then of the third
and fourth, and so right down to the lowest stratum, until
there was no one in the entire country who had not felt the
touch of the healing knife. The plan for the new *chistka* was
entrusted to Poskrebyshev and Ignatiev, who were ordered to
prepare the groundwork. The intricate details of the plan are
unknown, but it would seem that the arrests and executions
were to take place at the beginning of March. For a few
specially selected victims there would be public trials.

Meanwhile Stalin did nothing to allay the growing suspicions of his closest associates. Either because he was careless, being so certain of his authority over them, or because he deliberately wanted to incite them to revolt, he gave them every reason to believe that they were doomed. At a meeting in the Kremlin he accused Voroshilov of being an agent of British intelligence. It was a ludicrous accusation, but no one took such accusations lightly. Voroshilov succeeded in leaving the Kremlin unharmed, but he can scarcely have hoped that this would be the end of the matter. Nor was his long service as an agent of British intelligence the only crime that could be laid at his feet. In Stalin's eyes the Jews presented a mortal danger to his regime, and had not Voroshilov married a woman of Jewish extraction? And not only Voroshilov – there were others among his immediate associates who were tainted with Semitic blood. Kaganovich was a Jew, Molotov had married a Jewess, Beria's mother was half-Jewish, and Khrushchev had permitted his daughter to marry a young Jewish journalist. There was no end to the ramifications of the Jews in the Soviet Union, and now at last he had decided to put an end to this source of corruption. A plan, which had been long maturing in his diseased brain, now seemed ripe for fulfilment. In addition to the giant *chistka* which would cleanse the entire body of the nation, there would be another, relatively milder *chistka* reserved for the Jews who were to be transported to some region far in the north, where they could die quietly of cold and starvation.

He summoned a meeting at the Kremlin and outlined his plans. When Mikoyan and Voroshilov protested vigorously, pointing out that they had fought a war against Hitler and nothing was to be gained by imitating him, Stalin worked himself into a fury. Kaganovich wept and pleaded, but to no avail. He even offered to surrender his party card. The Communist leaders left the meeting with the knowledge that Stalin was mentally deranged, but perfectly capable of carrying out his threats. From that moment they knew – they could not help knowing – that their lives were in danger.

Throughout the winter the strange plot thickened, with only a handful of people knowing what was in store for the country. There was a sense of menace and horror, almost tangible; it was nameless, and sometimes it seemed to gather strength, and at other times it would fade away for a few hours, only to return. The foreign correspondents felt it in their bones; the people of Moscow whispered about it; the press and the censorship reflected its curious workings. Suddenly, on January 13th, 1953, both *Pravda* and *Izvestiya* printed long announcements which showed that the terror was beginning its work.

The ten-paragraph announcement proclaimed that a sinister plot by the Kremlin doctors had been uncovered. The doctors, who were named, were accused of 'using improper techniques to murder their patients', and of having attempted to murder Marshal Vasilievsky, Marshal Koniev, Marshal Govorov, Admiral Levchenko, and General Shtemenko. The doctors were accused of having murdered two former Politburo members, Andrey Zhdanov and Alexander Shcherbakov at the direction of Jewish-American-British intelligence. Six of the doctors were Jews. They had been able to commit their extraordinary crimes through the slackness of the Soviet security organization.

No one reading that long and detailed account could have any doubt that a great purge was on its way, and indeed the announcement brought out the parallel with the failure of the security agencies in the past. Gorky, Kuibyshev and Menzhinsky had all died mysteriously while under the care of the Kremlin doctors. History, said the announcement, was repeating itself.

It was precisely this element – the repetition of history – which was so terrifying. Nearly twenty years had passed since the murder of Kirov introduced a reign of terror unlike any that had ever existed on earth. Was Russia to be decimated again at the will of a dictator? *Pravda* and *Izvestiya* said that nine doctors had been arrested, but in fact several dozen had vanished from their consulting rooms and hospitals. Some were never seen again. Among the nine was Dr Vladimir Vinogradov, one of the most respected figures in Russian medicine. He was seventy-one years old, and his awards included four Orders of Lenin and an Order of the Red Banner of Labour. He had signed the death certificate of President Kalinin in 1946. He was charged with being the leader of the conspiracy, and it was learned later that he was put in chains and beaten until the required confession was extracted from him. He confessed to having been a long-standing spy for British intelligence. He survived his beatings. Two other doctors, Kogan and Etinger, died under torture.

For a week nothing more was heard of the 'doctors' plot'. Then on January 20th the Presidium of the Supreme Soviet of the USSR decorated a certain Lydia Timashuk with the Order of Lenin 'for the help she had given the government in unmasking the murderous doctors'. Three days later *Pravda* published a flattering article on her. She was an elderly woman, a grandmother, working in the Kremlin medical centre as an electrocardiograph specialist. She had apparently been induced to write directly to Stalin, warning him of her suspicions about the murderous doctors. The newspapers, at Stalin's dictation, launched into attacks on officials, lawyers, doctors and philosophers with a vindictiveness which would have been eerie if it had not become commonplace.

It was evident that the strings were being tightened, and that soon enough there would be a series of great public trials to prove that the regime had been honeycombed with spies. Somewhere a vast and comprehensive scenario was being written. The authors were probably Stalin and Poskrebyshev. In those days Beria seemed to be espcially in danger, for the accusations against the inadequacy of the secret police seemed to be aimed at him. But in the newspapers there was no hint of the larger plot which was being engineered behind the Kremlin wall. That it was already being prepared was something that people felt on their nerves. Meanwhile the deathly chill of winter was setting in.

Stalin bided his time. Perhaps he delayed the execution of his plan until he was sure that all the strings were safely in his hands. Of his lieutenants only Mekhlis, who had celebrated his glory in a hundred speeches and built up the legend of the leader who was blessed with divine insight, was ordered to be killed. Fearing for his life, Mekhlis slipped out of Moscow and made his way to Saratov. He did not escape the vigilance of the MVD, whose agents followed him and brought him back to the Lefortovo prison in Moscow. He was already dying and was given a room in the prison infirmary. He was shot after a lengthy interview with Poskrebyshev, who presented him with a 'confession' and ordered him to sign it.

Why Mekhlis alone was killed is something of a mystery. Voroshilov, Mikoyan and Molotov, all of whom were accused of crimes against the state during the January meeting, were better candidates. Molotov's wife was arrested and sent to Siberia, but Molotov himself retained his high position. For the moment Stalin was holding the reins lightly. He seemed to be sorry for his intended victims. 'You're all blind like young kittens,' he told them. 'What will happen without me? The country will perish because you do not know how to recognize enemies.' The death of Mekhlis became known on February 10th. About the same time several secretaries of the new members of the Presidium were arrested, among them Ivan Klyachko, who had been Khrushchev's secretary for some years. These arrests followed a familiar pattern. First, the secretary would be confronted with the evidence of small crimes committed during his tenure of office, and then with the larger crimes he had committed in collusion with his superior. Tortured, he would be forced to sign documents implicating not only his superior but also the heads of other departments. Forged documents would be presented to him; more and more torture would be applied; and soon he was confessing readily to crimes which had never previously occurred to him, and were in fact unthinkable before he fell into the hands of the secret police. Stalin's threat to send all Russian Jews and everyone who was in any way related to the Jews to the frozen north involved half the members of the Presidium. The arrest of the secretaries was an even more direct threat. They had received sufficient warning. The time had come for them to act.

Outwardly Stalin showed no signs that he was riding the storm. He took pains to show that nothing had changed, and he was unusually kind and affable to foreign visitors. On February 8th Leopoldo Bravo, the newly appointed ambassador from Argentina, was granted an audience late at night. The audience lasted forty-five minutes, and Señor Bravo reported that Stalin was in excellent health and more loquacious than he expected. They talked of trivialities. There was some discussion on sending an Argentine football team to Moscow and perhaps the Russian ballet would be sent to Argentina. Stalin was vaguely agreeable. He said: 'This would be very interesting, because when people get to know one another through cultural, scientific and sports affairs they inevitably become friendly.' Señor Bravo offered Stalin the personal greetings of Juan Peron, the head of the Argentine government, and Stalin replied in kind. He wore a plain military tunic, and was unusually gracious and friendly.

Foreign diplomats were a little baffled by the audience accorded to the Argentine ambassador, who had been in Moscow only a month and had received so speedy a summons to the Kremlin. Why was Stalin showing a vivid interest in Argentina, a country for which he had rarely shown any marked affection? Few ambassadors ever saw him. The last ambassadors to be invited to an audience were the American ambassador, Admiral Alan Kirk, in the summer of 1949 and the French ambassador, Louis Joxe, in the summer of 1952. They began to wonder whether Stalin was preparing to see ambassadors more regularly.

The next foreign visitor to be accorded an audience was an Indian, Dr Saiffrudin Kitchliu, the chairman of the All-India Peace League, a fellow traveller and Stalin prize winner. The audience took place on the afternoon of February 17th.

Once again Stalin was gracious and friendly. Dr Kitchliu reported that he was in excellent health and good spirits. This time the conversation had serious political implications. Stalin spoke favourably of General Eisenhower, who had just been elected to the Presidency, and he approved of the American policy of isolation and non-involvement in the affairs of other nations. Eisenhower was better than Truman, who was 'under the thumb of Churchill'. Unfortunately Eisenhower was surrounded by capitalists, and American foreign policy was fairly consistent: it was a capitalist policy. All the Americans were interested in was making profits.

Stalin reserved his greatest scorn for the British, saying that their attitude towards the Russians remained incomprehensible. What chiefly astonished him was their ingratitude, for had not Russia 'saved their hides during the war'? It was an odd remark, for the British had fought on alone when Stalin and Hitler were allies, and they had saved the world from becoming a Nazi empire. Stalin was deliberately playing on Dr Kitchliu's anti-British sympathies.

Warming to the subject, Stalin described the fate of Great Britain if war broke out between America and Russia. Both America and Russia would suffer grievous wounds, but Great Britain would be annihilated. Meanwhile the British were in no position to support America in a war, and he went on to suggest that if they had any sense they would join the Russian camp. 'France and England are going to break – it is bound to happen,' he said.

On the subject of India Stalin was less authoritative. He thought India had more to learn from China than from Russia, and he did not think America could 'buy' India. There was some talk about a future meeting between Stalin and Nehru and about a diplomatic offensive to end the Korean war. Stalin said he did not want war with America, which would jeopardize all the achievements of the Soviet Union during the past thirty-five years.

So much did Dr Kitchliu worship Stalin that he offered to keep secret from both Nehru and the Indian ambassador in Moscow anything that Stalin told him. Stalin was in a truculent mood, now blustering, now threatening, now cooing like a dove. Dr Kitchliu was deeply impressed, and said later that Stalin was 'extremely well-informed, seemed to have all the facts at his finger tips, and spoke most frankly'.

On the same evening Stalin received a more distinguished visitor. This was Mr K. P. S. Menon, the Indian ambassador, a man who combined remarkable honesty with intellectual agility. He was the first Indian ambassador to China, where he was regarded with a kind of awe, since he was one of those who inspire undeviating confidence. Trained in the Indian civil service, a former High Court judge, he had no patience with doctrinaires and was unlikely to be influenced by blandishments or by diatribes against the British. The conversation was long and friendly, and covered a great number of subjects from the nature of the Hindu language to the habits of Russian shepherds.

'Mr Ambassador,' Stalin began, 'I conceive it my duty as Prime Minister to receive the heads of diplomatic missions.'

It occurred to Mr Menon that Stalin had not been overzealous in the discharge of this duty.

There followed the usual exchange of courtesies, and when Mr Menon expressed his gratitude for the prevailing friendliness towards India, Stalin replied by saying it was only natural. 'Even shepherds in Russia are hospitable,' he said, 'and we are no worse than shepherds.' He said that all races and nations are equals, and the Soviet people had no trace of condescension towards any nation on earth. He asked what was the chief language spoken in India – Urdu or Hindi? Did these languages derive from a common stock? How did they differ? What language was spoken by the Gujeratis? Mr Menon answered as best he could, remembering that he was speaking to an authority on the structure of languages, who with a stroke of a pen had settled the perplexing linguistic problem put forward by Marr. Stalin wanted to know whether Pakistan had evolved a language of its own. When Mr Menon explained that Urdu, the language of Pakistan, had developed as a language of the camp, and contained a mixture of Persian and Arabic words, Stalin observed that the language suffered from impurities. 'It cannot be the real national language,' he said.

Mr Menon went on to describe the pacific nature of Indian foreign policy, which was rooted in the teachings of Gandhi. The Indians had been searching for a formula for a settlement in Korea and had offered a resolution to the United Nations, in which they had carefully excluded any phrases branding the Chinese as aggressors. Stalin had apparently not heard of the Indian resolution. For him it was obvious that the Americans were the aggressors. 'In America there are certain people who are bent on widening the conflict because they want more business and greater profits,' he said. 'Not all Americans are like that, but many are. It is no use preaching morals to them, because they are out to accumulate profits even at the price of blood.' A little later he was to use the phrase about the uselessness of preaching morals in a more terrifying context.

Stalin gave the impression of a man at ease, calmly doodling with a blue pencil. He spoke bitterly about the Americans. When Mr Menon remarked that Great Britain and Canada were restraining the Americans, Stalin answered dryly: 'There is no sign of it yet.' And when Mr Menon said that trade between India and Japan was growing, Stalin said with a smile: 'Then Japan will undersell you and flood your markets with cheap goods.'

Stalin was interested in the Indian army, and it occurred to him to ask the Indian ambassador: 'Is your army capable of defending India?' It was an ominous question. The ambassador explained that India had a compact, well-trained and well-disciplined army, with a small air force. Stalin nodded approvingly. 'It is difficult,' he said, 'to defend a country effectively without a powerful air force.'

Then without any warning Stalin said: 'Mr Ambassador, our peasant is a simple man, but wise. When he sees a wolf, he shoots it. He does not preach morals to the wolf – he shoots it! And the wolf knows it, and behaves accordingly.'

Stalin had been doodling throughout the conversation, and now Mr Menon looked over and saw that he had been doodling a number of wolves in different postures, one wolf standing on its hind legs, two more wolves confronting one another, the whole sheet of paper full of wolves. There was not the least doubt of the threat behind the words, but it was so generalized a threat that it was difficult to know to whom it was directed.

The ambassador had trained himself to observe the slightest implications and nuances in the speech of the heads of state to whom he was accredited. Five weeks had passed since the announcement of the 'doctors' plot', and like everyone else in diplomatic circles he was perfectly aware that another *chistka* was being prepared on a scale which would shake the Soviet Union to its foundations. He realized that Stalin was not discussing the habits of the Russian peasantry, but was continuing the long monologue which dictators always hold with themselves. Stalin was himself 'the simple, wise peasant' who knew how to deal with wolves. He was an expert marksman, who would go to any lengths to destroy real or imagined enemies. But what wolves was he talking about? Russian wolves? American wolves? The Soviet press, directed by Stalin, had shown unmistakable signs of hysteria over the election of Eisenhower to the Presidency, even though in private conversations Stalin indicated his approval of the general. Or was he thinking of the wolves in his own cabinet, men like Mekhlis, the former head of the Political Administration of the Red Army, who had been shot only a few days previously? Or was he thinking of that vast Jewish conspiracy which he thought he had uncovered, and which he would soon drown in blood? On February 12th he had broken relations with the government of Israel, though he had been among the first to recognize Israel after she had obtained her independence. The ostensible cause for the break was the bomb thrown into the Soviet consulate in Haifa a few days before, but there were some reasons for believing that the bomb had been thrown by a Soviet agent. Among such a plethora of wolves – Russian, American, Jewish – it was hard to choose. As Stalin doodled more and more blue wolves on a sheet of paper, Menon had the feeling that plans for vast and murderous mischief were brewing in Stalin's mind, but there was no knowing in what direction he would strike. Later in the evening he returned to the Indian Embassy and wrote out a careful report for Nehru. Neither he, nor any foreigner, saw Stalin alive again.

In those haunted weeks the 'doctors' plot' acquired a sinister momentum. All over the Soviet Union people were becoming aware of the preliminary tremors which announce an earthquake. Everywhere there were secret arrests. Some of the members of the Presidium went into hiding, while others took care to increase the number of their armed guards and to inform only their friends of their whereabouts. The doctors themselves – those pathetic heralds of the storm – were continually beaten into insensibility, then revived and beaten again until confessions had been extracted. 'If you do not obtain confessions,' Stalin told Ignatiev, 'we shall see that you are shortened by a head.' The confessions were satisfactory. They pointed to a world-wide Jewish conspiracy. The conspiratorial organization bore the name of 'Joint', implying that it was a federation of many conspiratorial groups financed from many sources, with world-wide ramifications, employing the weapons of subversion, terrorism, and espionage. It was not difficult to discover why Stalin came to believe in the existence of this organization, for it was no more than a mirror image of the organization he had himself created. Not all the doctors, however, confessed to being members of 'Joint'. Three of them confessed to being spies for British intelligence. In this way Stalin paid his last tribute to British intelligence, for which he had always shown a healthy respect.

The last days of February were intensely cold and blustery, with raw winds tearing through the streets of Moscow. Diplomats and correspondents kept close watch on the Kremlin, but though they were obscurely aware that great decisions were being taken, and dreadful events were taking place, they were unable to make out the evolving pattern. They could feel the tremors, but had no means of locating the earthquake's epicentre. What little news came out of the Kremlin was singularly bland. On February 21st, for example, it became known that Marshal Sokolovsky had replaced General Shtemenko as Chief of Staff of the land forces of the Soviet Union. General Shtemenko was one of the high officers whom the doctors had allegedly 'attempted to put out of commission'. No explanation was given why, at this juncture, he should have been relieved of his duties. Such tidbits of news were perhaps designed to put inquirers off the scent. They did nothing to slake the general thirst for information.

In the early hours of March 4th, Moscow Radio broadcast the news that Stalin had been elected to the Moscow City Soviet. The announcement was not altogether unexpected; it was only one more of those bland and unhelpful statements which filled the columns of *Pravda* and the bulletins heard over the radio. Moscow Radio went off the air in a perfectly normal way, to resume broadcasting at 6 am. During the night orders were given to stop the presses of *Pravda*, and when Moscow Radio resumed its broadcasts the usual light music was replaced by a women's choir and a Beethoven concerto. At the end of the concerto Moscow Radio again went off the air; this time there was no closing announcement.

By half past seven most of the workers who had been streaming into the city were at work at their factory benches. Some of them were aware of the failure of Moscow Radio during the early morning, but it was not a matter which particularly alarmed them; there had been failures before. Scarcely one of them could have guessed the news that was in store for them half an hour later.

THE FIRST DEATH

AT EXACTLY 8 AM ON March 4th there came over Moscow Radio, without any preliminary announcement, a long communiqué delivered in trembling tones. The voice belonged to Yuri Levitan, who was the chief announcer, known for his clear and resonant voice, the sense of excitement he could convey in the dullest official communiqué. Now the words dragged, there were curious pauses in the middle of a sentence, and sometimes he seemed to be gasping for air.

The communiqué was dated March 3rd, and took the form of a message to the nation from the Central Committee of the Communist Party and the Council of Ministers representing the entire hierarchy of the Soviet government. The names of Soviet leaders were carefully omitted, thus giving the broadcast an oddly anonymous quality like a message delivered from on high, or from some nameless and faceless officials who had assumed the powers of government during the night. The communiqué showed signs of having been written hastily, after long and nervous argument, by many hands with many diverse motives. This patchwork quilt was almost drowned in the names of doctors.

The communiqué read:

The Central Committee of the Communist Party of the Soviet Union and the Council of Ministers of the USSR announce the misfortune which has overtaken our Party and the people – the serious illness of Comrade J. V. Stalin.

During the night of March 1st–2nd, while in his Moscow apartment, Comrade Stalin suffered a cerebral haemorrhage affecting vital areas of the brain. Comrade Stalin lost consciousness, and paralysis of the right arm and leg set in. Loss of speech followed. There appeared to be serious disturbances in the functioning of the heart and breathing.

The best medical brains have been summoned for Comrade Stalin's treatment:

> Professor-Therapeutist P. E. Lukomsky, permanent member of the Academy of Medical Science of the USSR,
> Professor-Neuropathist N. V. Konovalov,
> Professor-Therapeutist A. L. Miasnikov,
> Professor-Therapeutist E. M. Tarayev,
> Professor-Neuropathist I. N. Filimonov,
> Professor-Neuropathist R. A. Tkachev,
> Professor-Neuropathist I. S. Glazunov,
> Reader-Therapeutist V. I. Ivanov-Neznamov.

Comrade Stalin's treatment is being carried out under the guidance of the Commissar of Health, Dr A. F. Tretyakov, together with L. I. Kuperin, Director of the Medical Health Board of the Kremlin, and under the constant supervision of the Central Committee of the Communist Party of the Soviet Union and the Soviet Government.

In view of the serious condition of Comrade Stalin's health, the Council of Ministers of the USSR have recognized the necessity of publishing medical bulletins on the condition of Joseph Vissarionovich Stalin's health as from today.

The Central Committee and the Council of Ministers, as leaders of the nation, are taking into consideration with all seriousness the circumstances connected with the temporary withdrawal of Comrade Stalin from the leadership of the Government and Party activity.

The Central Committee and the Council of Ministers express their conviction that our Party and the whole Soviet people will in these difficult days display the greatest unity, solidarity, fortitude of spirit and vigilance; that they will redouble their energy for the building of Communism in our country and rally round the Central Committee of the

Communist Party and the Government of the Soviet Union
even more closely than hitherto.

The communiqué was followed by the first bulletin signed
by the eight doctors already mentioned and by Tretyakov
and Kuperin. While the communiqué gave some hope that
the patient might fully recover, the bulletin made it clear that
he was suffering from a mortal sickness. The bulletin read:

During the night of March 1st-2nd, 1953, Joseph Vissarionovich Stalin suffered from a sudden cerebral haemorrhage
affecting vital areas of the brain, as a result of which there
set in paralysis of the right leg and right arm with loss of
consciousness and speech.

In the course of March 2nd-3rd, appropriate medical
measures were taken for the purpose of improving the
affected functions of breathing and blood circulation, which
came to no substantial crisis in the course of the illness. Towards 2 am on March 4th, the condition of J. V. Stalin
remains serious. Considerable disturbance in breathing was
observed, the rate being up to 36 a minute and the rhythm
irregular with periodic long pauses. Pulse has increased up
to 120 times a minute. There was a full arhythmia. Blood
pressure was of a maximum of 220 and a minimum of 120.
Temperature was 38·2 Centigrade. In connection with the
affected breathing and blood circulation a lack of oxygen
was observed. The degree to which the functioning of the
brain is affected is somewhat increased. A number of thera-
peutic measures for the purpose of restoring vital functions
of the organism are being carried out at this moment.

This communiqué together with the medical bulletin were
repeated over Moscow Radio at intervals during the day, and
printed in *Pravda* which appeared four hours late. Attentive
readers, especially doctors, felt that the bulletin was curiously
unconvincing, and there was some question whether it had
been written in good faith. It was almost inconceivable that
a man who had suffered such a massive haemorrhage could
be still alive.

There were other things which readers and listeners found
disturbing. Why were such accurate figures given for respiration, blood pressure and temperature when the time of the
attack was so vague? Presumably the night of March 1st-2nd
could be at any time between eight o'clock in the evening

and five or six o'clock in the morning? Did the doctors know when the attack occurred? Were they present, or were they called only after a long delay? Why was it so important to establish that it happened in his Moscow apartment? Why was there a long list of doctors' names, while the names of the members of the Presidium responsible for the communiqué were not mentioned? The second paragraph of the communiqué, which purported to be a brief preliminary outline of the doctors' findings, included the statement: 'Comrade Stalin lost consciousness, and paralysis of the right arm and leg set in. Loss of speech followed.' It was inconceivable that a trained doctor, especially careful in his choice of words when reporting on so illustrious a patient, would have chosen to write these words. Someone, who was not a doctor, had evidently written these words. Why was it necessary to emphasize that Stalin's medical treatment was being carried out 'under the constant supervision of the Central Committee of the Communist Party ... and the Soviet Government', thus giving the impression that the entire Presidium was gathering round the bed of the dying dictator? Why did they speak of 'the temporary withdrawal of Comrade Stalin from the leadership of the Government and Party activity'? A man suffering from a massive brain haemorrhage is not likely to return to work next week. So many of these statements seemed to be *defensive* in character. The field of argument was overextended: the simple report of a man's near-fatal seizure was buried in irrelevancies.

Even more puzzling was the brevity of the medical information in the communiqué, which gave details about the patient's condition on the night of March 1st-2nd, while omitting any details about his condition on the nights of March 2nd-3rd and 3rd-4th, though these were evidently known at the time of the broadcast. *More than two days passed between the composition of the communiqué and the composition of the bulletin.* Assuming that the cerebral haemorrhage occurred around midnight on March 1st-2nd, then fifty-six hours passed before it was made public. In that time many crimes could have been committed, many subterfuges could have been prepared. No one was ever able to offer a convincing explanation for the delay.

The intention of the communiqué was clear: it was to inform the people after a long silence that Stalin was dying and would soon be dead. Yet, though the intention was clear, the method of carrying it out was ambiguous. At intervals throughout the day came appeals for unity in the face of the threatening disaster, and these appeals would be followed by mournful music. The urgency of the appeals, the contrived nature of the communiqué, the curious anonymity of the broadcasts had the effect, not of reassuring the people, but of making them more frightened, more intimidated. They had known for a long time that there would be a bitter battle for the succession. Now, in this long silence, the battle was being waged, but no one knew who was fighting whom.

The communiqué was signed: 'The Central Committee of the Communist Party of the Soviet Union and the Council of Ministers of the USSR, 3rd March 1953.' Broadcast at 8 am on the following day, it purported to have been written at some time before midnight. Had the commissars met, discussed the situation, and then gone to bed? Why, so suddenly, were they urging the people to display the greatest unity, solidarity, fortitude of spirit and vigilance? Surely these things had been necessary two days before, immediately after the seizure?

To those who studied the bulletin with the memory of the bulletin issued following the death of Lenin in mind, it seemed that something was missing. What was missing was simplicity. The very complexity of the announcement suggested that truth and falsehood were concealed in it.

On that long day Alexis, Patriarch of All Russia, and Solomon Shliffer, the Chief Rabbi, bade the people pray for Stalin's recovery. In the cathedral the Patriarch called on God to spare the dying man in the Kremlin, and offered special prayers for his soul, while the acolytes raised aloft the Scriptures in their gold casing and the candles glowed before the iconostasis. In the synagogue, equally bright with candles, the Chief Rabbi ordered the Jewish community to hold a day of prayer and fasting.

Still there was no news. People clustered around the newspaper kiosks or the newspapers pasted on walls, but they read there only what they already knew. There was no storm of grief, as when Lenin died. People went about their normal affairs, walking, it seemed, a little faster than usual, as though by hurrying they could shake off the ominous news. It had been a brilliant day, with the sun shining. After dark it began to snow.

Not until the afternoon of the next day, March 5th, was a

second bulletin issued. It provided some strange details of the treatment which was being given to the patient, but otherwise added little that was new. It read:

During the past twenty-four hours the state of health of Joseph Vissarionovich Stalin has remained grave.

The haemorrhage of the left hemisphere of the brain, which developed during the night of March 1st-2nd, as the result of hypertonic disease and arteriosclerosis, has, in addition to paralysis of the right extremities and loss of consciousness, affected the *truncus cerebri* of the brain, accompanied by a derangement of the major functions of respiration and blood circulation.

During the night of March 3rd-4th the disturbances of respiration and circulation continued. The greatest changes were observed in the respiratory functions; the intermittent phenomena of the so-called Cheyne-Stokes breathing became more frequent. As a result of this, the state of circulation deteriorated and the extent of lack of oxygen increased. By the systematic administration of oxygen and drugs, to regulate respiration and the action of the heart vessels, there was a gradual slight improvement of the condition, and by the morning of March 4th, the degree of lack of respiration had been somewhat reduced.

Subsequently, during the day of March 4th, the serious respiratory disturbances reappeared. The rate of breathing was 36 per minute. Blood pressure continued high (210 maximum-110 minimum) with a pulse rate of 108/116 a minute, irregular (fluctuating arhythmia). The heart is enlarged to a moderate degree.

During the past twenty-four hours no substantial changes have been observed in the lungs or in the organs of the abdominal cavity. The normal ratio of albumen and red corpuscles was found present in the urine. A blood test showed an increase in the number of white blood corpuscles (17,000). During the morning and afternoon, the temperature was high, reaching 38.6 degrees Centigrade.

Treatment during March 4th consisted of the administration of oxygen and camphor preparations, caffeine, strophanthin and glucose. Blood was drawn off again by leeches.

In view of the high temperature and high leucocytosis, penicillin therapy was intensified. It had been applied for prophylactic purposes from the beginning of the illness.

Late on the evening of March 4th the state of health of Joseph Vissarionovich Stalin remained grave. The patient is in a soporific, deeply unconscious state. The nervous regulation of respiration as well as the cardiac activity remain gravely disturbed.

This bulletin was signed by the doctors mentioned in the first communiqué.

The medical details in their variety and minuteness seemed to be designed to give a total picture of the dying man. Yet doctors were sometimes puzzled by these details. What, for example, was the medical meaning to be attached to the words: 'The normal ratio of albumen and red corpuscles was found present in the urine,' when normally albumen and red corpuscles are not present in the urine? Everyone knew he was dying or already dead, but not everyone was convinced that the bulletin meant what it said.

Meanwhile the battle for the succession was being fought round the deathbed. It would appear to have been a short, sharp battle, with Malenkov as the victor, for *Pravda*'s leading article on March 5th, headed 'The Splendid Unity of Party and People', mentioned only three names – Lenin, Stalin, and Malenkov.

One final bulletin was to be announced to the world, and it told only what everyone was expecting: the end was near. The bulletin was issued at 6.30 pm on March 5th. Like the previous bulletin it was written in the precise, technical language of medicine and seemed to be addressed only to doctors. It read:

During the night and the first half of March 5th the condition of Joseph Vissarionovich Stalin deteriorated. In addition to the cerebral haemorrhage detected earlier, there has now been observed a sharp disturbance of the functions of the heart. On the morning of March 5th phenomena of acute respiratory deficiency were observed, lasting for three hours, which responded only with difficulty to the appropriate therapeutical treatment.

By 8 am symptoms of a sharp deficiency of the blood-pumping system were observed. Blood pressure dropped, the pulse became more rapid, and the patient grew paler. Under the influence of intensified medical treatment these symptoms were removed.

An electrocardiogram taken at 11 am on March 5th showed a sharp disturbance of the blood circulation in the coronary arteries of the heart, accompanied by changes in the sections of the back wall of the heart. An electrocardiogram taken on March 2nd did not establish these changes.

At 11.30 am a second heavy collapse occurred which was overcome with great difficulty by appropriate medical treatment. Later on, the cardiovascular changes eased somewhat, although the general condition of the patient continues to remain grave.

At 4 pm the blood pressure was 160 maximal and 100 minimal, pulse 120 per minute, arhythmic breathing 36 per minute, temperature 37·6 Centigrade, leucocytose 21,000.

At present, treatment is being mainly directed towards combating irregularities in respiration and blood circulation, in particular the coronary zone.

Such was the third and final bulletin recording with great care and exactitude the formidable changes taking place in the body of a dying man. Of the three bulletins it was the only one issued without considerable delay. The people of Russia were being told at 6.30 pm the condition of the patient at 4 pm. His condition was now hopeless, and it was obvious that he could not last through the night.

Officially the patient died at 9.50 pm that same evening, but the announcement was delayed until the early hours of the morning. Around 4 am, after a roll of drums, came the voice of the announcer saying that 'the heart of the comrade-in-arms and continuer of genius of Lenin's cause, of the wise leader and teacher of the Communist Party and the Soviet Union, has ceased to beat'.

A more formal communiqué, covering three closely printed pages and taking half an hour to deliver on the radio, came later in the morning. It was a strangely defensive document, for although Stalin was accorded all the honours due to a dead leader and granted the role of being with Lenin the co-founder of the Communist Party, the greater part of the encomium consisted of a plea to the Russian people to rally to the support of the party and a justification for the party's existence. 'The monolithic cohesion and adamantine unity of the party are the main requisite of the party's strength and power.' Everything the party had done in the past was correct, everyone knew that its only interest was the preservation and consolidation of peace, everyone was aware that the might of the Soviet army, navy and air force was continually being strengthened. In view of all this the working people were encouraged to behave 'in a spirit of lofty political vigilance, in the spirit of irreconcilability and staunchness in the struggle against internal and external enemies'.

That long encomium, written in the style of Malenkov, was both a warning and a reminder that the spirit of Stalin had survived his physical death. There would be no interregnum. The new government was announced the same day. The new leader, the inheritor of great Stalin, was Georgy Malenkov. He was the half-Bashkir son of a small landowner, and he had entered the party at the age of eighteen in 1920. A small, pudgy, dark-eyed man, with no popular appeal, he became one of Stalin's secretaries and climbed to power by remaining close to Stalin, whose wishes he carried out during the purges with exemplary devotion. He was much, much harder than he looked. He was Stalin's deliberate choice as his successor, and the relationship between them was heavily underscored at the Nineteenth Congress in October 1952, when Stalin permitted him to prepare and to read to the delegates the main speech at the opening of the first session. The speech lasted five hours.

The other members of the new government followed the same pattern: they were all men who had been on terms of intimate friendship with Stalin. Voroshilov, Stalin's old drinking companion, became titular President, replacing the colourless Shvernik. Kaganovich became Deputy Premier, and Bulganin became the Commissar for War. With Molotov as Commissar for Foreign Affairs and Beria once more Commissar of Internal Affairs, the six essential positions in the government were filled. All could claim to have been faithful comrades-in-arms of Stalin.

Eleven hours after the first announcement of the death of Stalin, at three o'clock in the afternoon, a blue vanlike vehicle belonging to the Moscow Sanitation Department left the Kremlin by the Spassky Gate and drove to the Hall of Columns, which was already draped in black. There a few minutes later came the new rulers to pay their last respects to the man who had brought them to power.

At this time or perhaps a little later photographs were taken showing them standing beside the coffin in the great Hall of Columns under the chandeliers draped with black ribbons. One of these photographs, the most widely reproduced, is a photomontage with the body of Stalin lying immense in the right foreground, while from another angle altogether we see the new members of the government drawn up in two rows on the left. All except Malenkov and Beria are gazing at the coffin. Malenkov, Beria, Voroshilov, Kaganovich and Molotov stand in order of precedence in the front row. Vasilievsky, Koniev, Sokolovsky, Zhukov, Mikoyan and Khrushchev stand in the second row. Khrushchev, indeed, appears to have been added as an afterthought, for a close examination of the photograph makes it clear that his portrait was not taken at the same time. Of the twelve disciples he is the one furthest away from Stalin.

Like the positions of the leaders when they stand on the mausoleum in the Red Square, the positions of the new members of the government were carefully and precisely ordered according to the protocols of power. Malenkov stood slightly apart from the rest, and he was the closest to Stalin. No one was to be permitted to misunderstand the new role he intended to play. In token of their collective insignificance, they were photographed in such a way that they looked like pygmies beside Stalin.

In a satin-lined coffin, half hidden by banks of waxen flowers, Stalin lay dressed in his Generalissimo's uniform, with the ribbons of his medals sewn on to his right breast. At his feet the original medals were exhibited on small plump red cushions. His hands rested on his thighs, and it was noticeable that one arm was longer than another. He looked quietly restful and at peace; the cheeks were full; there was none of the gauntness to be expected from a man who had fought for three days against a dangerous illness. The pockmarks had vanished.

When Lenin's body lay in state in the same hall twenty-nine years before, the head lay deep in the pillow. In this way the marks left by the saw which cut through the back of the skull so that the brains could be extracted were hidden. With Stalin the whole head was visible except where it touched the pillow. It appeared that no effort had been made to extract the brains.

The mourners who passed beside the coffin in their thousands were permitted only a cursory look at the body; they were hurried on at a relentless pace by the guards. No one was permitted a close look. He looked very waxen and the face seemed to be a little larger than it was in life. The real Stalin – if it was the real Stalin – lay hidden under ample layers of mortician's wax.

The body lay in state for only three days. Some of the violence of Stalin seemed to have been communicated to the crowds which formed mile-long columns outside the Hall of Columns. Winter was not yet over; the raw winds were still blowing through the streets. The poet Evgeny Yevtushenko has written a memorable description of those cruel and impatient crowds:

I was in the crowd in Trubnaya Square. The breath of the tens of thousands of people jammed against one another rose up in a white cloud so thick that on it could be seen the swaying shadows of the bare March trees. It was a terrifying and fantastic sight. New streams poured into this human flood from behind, increasing the pressure. The crowd turned into a monstrous whirlpool. I realized I was being carried straight towards a traffic light. The post was coming relentlessly closer. Suddenly I saw that a young girl was being pushed against the post. Her face was distorted and she was screaming. But her screams were inaudible among all the other cries and groans. A movement of the crowd drove me against the girl; I did not hear but felt with my body the cracking of her brittle bones as they were broken on the traffic light. I closed my eyes in horror, the sight of her insanely bulging, childish blue eyes more than I could bear, and I was swept past. When I looked again the girl was no longer to be seen. The crowd must have sucked her under. Pressed against the traffic light was someone else, his body twisted and his arms outflung as on a cross. At that moment I felt I was treading on something soft. It was a human body. I picked my feet up under me and was carried along by the crowd. For a long time I was afraid to put my feet down again. The crowd closed tighter and tighter. I was saved by my height. Short people were smothered alive, falling and perishing. We were caught between the walls of houses on one side and a row of army trucks on the other.

The army trucks, deliberately brought up to channel the crowd, were chiefly responsible for these deaths, but the fierce impatience of the crowd also contributed to the horror. Some five hundred people choked or were trampled to death or were broken against traffic lights and trucks. Like the old Scythian kings Stalin was dragging his own people with him to the grave.

Not everyone in the crowd was desperate to see Stalin in his coffin. A strange, lighthearted mood had settled on Moscow. The emperor, who had seemed to be a power of nature, eternal as the snows, the winds, and the tempests, proved at last to be mortal; and there was some discreet rejoicing. The theatres remained open. *Boris Godunov* was played at the Moscow Opera House to a crowded, enthusiastic audience which applauded the death of Boris. In the streets boys lit bonfires and played their balalaikas and sang, while waiting to join the procession. No one would have been particularly surprised if the death of Stalin had been accompanied by earthquakes, falling stars and blood-red skies, but when none of these things happened, it was generally assumed that there would be no visitation of avenging angels and that the ordinary affairs of life would continue. Those who stepped out of the Hall of Columns found themselves in the presence of an army soup kitchen: the sweet and sickly smell of death was exchanged for the smell of borsch.

On Monday March 9th came the funeral ceremonies. Khrushchev was appointed chairman of the funeral committee, a position occupied by Stalin at the time of Lenin's death. The coffin, surmounted by the Generalissimo's military cap, was removed from the Hall of Columns on the shoulders of nine men – the eight men who had seized power and Vasily Stalin, who was permitted to take his brief place in the ceremony because he was Stalin's son. His place was immediately behind Malenkov and in front of Molotov. On one side therefore stood Malenkov, Vasily Stalin, Molotov, Bulganin and Kaganovich, and on the other side were Beria, Voroshilov, Mikoyan and Khrushchev. Malenkov and Beria, as the most formidable possessors of power, took the leading places.

There was a chill in the air and all wore heavy fur-lined coats and fur hats. The ceremony of lifting the coffin on to the waiting gun carriage was soon over. Following the gun carriage, the new rulers of Russia walked to the Red Square. The name of Stalin was already inscribed on the mausoleum beneath the name of Lenin.

Only three speeches were made, and in this, too, the funeral of Stalin contrasted strongly with the funeral of Lenin, where a vast number of speeches were delivered throughout a whole day. The speeches were delivered by Malenkov, Beria and Molotov, and followed a predictable pattern. Malenkov repeated what he had said before in the communiqué which accompanied the first announcement of Stalin's death. He spoke in a clear, firm, pleasing voice, with complete self-assurance. His cultured Russian accent gave no clue to his Cossack and Bashkir origins. 'The name of Stalin,' he declared, 'is boundlessly dear to Soviet men and women and to the broad masses of the people all over the world. Boundless is the greatness and significance of Comrade Stalin's work for the Soviet people and for the working people all over the world. His work will live on through all ages and a grateful posterity will pay homage to his name.'

In this strain he continued for nearly twenty minutes, depicting a man who had singlehandedly transformed a backward country into a mighty industrial and collective-farm nation where there were no economic crises and unemployment had become impossible. Concerning the members of the new Politburo he said: 'We are the servants of the people.'

Beria, who spoke Russian with careful precision, predictably concerned himself with the enemies of the state; he warned them that they confronted the monolithic unity of the Soviet Union. 'Anyone who is not blind,' he declared, 'can see that in these melancholy days the party is closing its ranks more firmly, united and steadfast as never before.' He paid a graceful tribute to Malenkov, calling him 'the talented pupil of Lenin and loyal colleague of Stalin'. He described how the Soviet people had responded with unanimous approval to the decisions of the new rulers 'to ensure the uninterrupted and correct leadership of the entire life of the country'.

The final oration was spoken by Molotov, whose voice, usually sharp and metallic, quavered continually; as he spoke, he was sometimes blinded by tears which he had to brush away before he could continue reading. He alone among the commissars was observed to weep. He paid no graceful tribute to Malenkov, perhaps because he had hoped for the succession. 'We can be justly proud,' he said, 'that we have lived and worked for the last thirty years under the leadership of Stalin.' It was the imperial 'we', for he was speaking of his own undeniably great services to the dictator. He made for Stalin the claim which Stalin most enjoyed making for him-

· self. He spoke of the 'gigantic' role he had played during the war:

> Stalin personally guided the formation and organization of the Red Army's glorious battles at the most decisive fronts in the Civil War. As Supreme Commander in the years of the Great Fatherland War, Stalin led our country to victory over fascism, thus decisively changing the situation in Europe and Asia.

There was no truth in the first statement, and little enough in the second. It was as though Molotov were reading from one of the many articles by Voroshilov praising Stalin as the supreme military genius of all times and all nations.

Of the three speeches only Malenkov's fell on Russian ears with any impact, and this chiefly because he promised that the Soviet government would maintain peace and give the people a higher standard of living. He spoke of vigilance and military preparedness, but he also spoke of peaceful coexistence. His words seemed to presage an era of withdrawal from the highhanded, ruthless and intolerant practices of Stalin; and the people were grateful.

At last, just before noon, the coffin, swathed in black and red silk, was carried by the eight men into the Lenin mausoleum, while thirty guns fired salvos. At noon, by concerted design, there began, all over the Russian empire from Vladivostock to East Berlin, a deafening pandemonium of noise. Guns, steam whistles, factory whistles, the sirens of steamships all combined to produce a vast uproar. The people put their hands to their ears and the birds flew crazily in the air, as the machines lamented.

Then the funeral was over, and men went back to resume their accustomed lives.

The classic tailpiece to any account of Stalin's funeral was provided by Harrison E. Salisbury of *The New York Times*, who recounts how he saw half a dozen workmen lowering the two-storey-high portrait of Stalin which had decorated the Hall of Columns. One end of the portrait fell with a crash to the ground. One of the workmen said: 'Careful!' Another replied: 'Never mind. We'll not be needing this one again!'

THE SECOND DEATH

AT REST AT LAST in the mausoleum, in the place he cherished beside Lenin, Stalin, if he could speak, would have said he was well content. He had done far more than he set out to do when he was a young revolutionary in Tiflis and Batum. He had changed the world and bent it to his will. More than Tamerlane or Genghis Khan, more than Napoleon, even more than Lenin, he had convulsed the nations and reduced them to obedience. He had never cared what history would say of him, for he was himself history. No doubt his legend would diminish in time, as the legend of Ramses II has diminished, but he quite confidently expected to be remembered a thousand years after his death.

The claims he made for himself were similar to those made by the ancient emperors of Egypt and Assyria. He was 'the Father of Peoples', not of one people but of all peoples. He was 'the greatest strategist of all times and nations'. He especially enjoyed this description of himself, inserted it in his own *Short Biography*, and permitted Voroshilov to employ the same words in his articles. It was not enough to become *Vozhd* or 'Leader' of the Russian people; he had to become Supreme Commander and Generalissimo. He regarded himself as emperor, war leader, and high priest. Those who refused to accept him in his triple aspect, political, military, and sacerdotal, were lucky if they were not executed.

In seventy-three years of ruthless, cunning and astonishingly varied activity, he preserved the sense of his own mystery. Like the ancient Chinese emperors who spoke only behind curtains, or like the priests of the Orthodox Church chanting behind the iconostasis, he preferred to be heard and not seen. At his rare appearances on the tomb of Lenin in the Red Square, he was seen only by the secret police who manned the buildings opposite the tomb and by the marchers who caught only brief glimpses of him. So it was again at his death: no one was permitted to look for long on his august presence.

He deliberately encouraged the sense of mystery about his person. There was nothing surprising in this, for an absolute dictator cannot wield authority without surrounding himself with mystery. 'There can be no prestige without mystery,' wrote General de Gaulle in his study on political leadership. 'In the design, the demeanour, and the mental operations of a leader, there must always be a "something" which others cannot altogether fathom, which puzzles them, stirs them, and rivets their attention.' But in the modern world such mysteries are luxuries, too costly altogether to be worth the energy employed in creating them. Stalin cultivated his mystery like any charlatan or sorcerer. At last, believing in his own mystery, he came to believe in his own divinity.

It is the characteristic of divine beings that they perform miracles, possess powers denied to mortals, and enjoy the gift of immortality. There is a sense in which Stalin could justifiably point to his successful accomplishment of miracles and to his possession of powers denied to other mortals – had he not changed the face of Russia? – but the gift of immortality had been denied to him. He was well aware of this unhappy defect, and lived in pathological fear of assassination. No dictator ever took so much care to safeguard his person. He drove through the streets of Moscow in armour-plated Packards with two-inch thick windows, placed vast numbers of guards in his Kremlin office and saw to it that no one came into his presence armed with anything more lethal than a fountain pen, and on his annual travels to the Black Sea coast there were always decoy trains in front and behind the train he travelled in. His fears increased with age. He was like the old widow in one of Chekhov's stories who never left her apartment for fear of catching a germ.

Just as he cultivated his self-deification, so he cultivated his fears, and it never seems to have occurred to him that a frightened divinity was a contradiction in terms. What he feared most of all was being murdered. Because he had himself murdered those who were closest and most intimate to him, so he naturally expected that if anyone murdered him, then it would be someone from among the small circle of high officials who owed their exalted positions to his grace and favour. They were the most dangerous, and accordingly they were the ones who were most closely watched. All the members of the Politburo were spied upon. Their hourly comings and goings, the names of the people they met, their private conversations and telephone conversations, all these were reported to him in great detail. There can have been no other government in the world where the private and public lives of the ministers were so faithfully reported to the premier.

Such spying, of course, produces its inevitable counter-reaction. The ministers became excessively careful and circumspect, spoke as little as possible, and tended to withdraw into themselves. Conversations on the telephone were liberally larded with praise of 'the great Stalin', 'the great genius of all time', and so on. On the rare occasions when they were able to meet unseen, it is unlikely that they discussed the beneficence and wisdom of the dictator. Towards the middle of January they all knew that there was scarcely one of them who would not be affected by the mounting anti-Semitism of Stalin, his paranoid determination to introduce a new and even more bloody *chistka*.

In the light of the 'doctors' plot' and the gradual tightening of the net around the Jews, the carefully documented communiqués at the time of Stalin's death acquire a sombre significance. If Stalin was murdered, they are exactly the documents which would have to be produced. So, too, was the official autopsy, which was no more credible than the communiqués. The autopsy, which was published on March 7th, read:

The post-mortem examination of Joseph Vissarionovich Stalin established a large haemorrhage in the sphere of the subcortical nodes of the left hemisphere of the brain. This haemorrhage destroyed vital areas of the brain and caused irreversible disorders of respiration and blood circulation. In addition to the cerebral haemorrhage, there was established considerable hypertrophy of the left cardiac ventricle, numerous haemorrhages of the cardiac muscle, and in the mucous membrane of the stomach and intestines, and arteriosclerotic affection of the vessels, particularly announced in the brain arteries.

These processes resulted from hypertonicity. Post-mortem results fully confirm the diagnosis of the professors and doctors attending J. V. Stalin. The data of the post-mortem examination established the fatal nature of Stalin's illness from the moment the cerebral haemorrhage occurred. Therefore the radical measures of treatment could not have yielded positive results or averted the fatal outcome.

USSR Minister of Public Health, A. F. Tretyakov.

Director of the Medical Health Board of the Kremlin, L. I. Kuperin.

President of the USSR Academy of Medical Sciences, Academician N. N. Anichkov.

Member of the USSR Academy of Medical Sciences, Professor M. A. Skvortsov.

Associate member of the USSR Academy of Medical Sciences, A. I. Strukov.

Associate member of the USSR Academy of Medical Sciences, Professor S. R. Mardashev.

Director of the Pathological-Anatomical Section of the USSR Ministry of Health, Professor B. I. Migunov.

Professor A. V. Rusakov.

Docent B. M. Uskov.

The autopsy report on Stalin raises many problems. In the first place it is not written in the generally accepted style of an autopsy report, which normally begins with a report on the external condition of the corpse, discusses the internal organs and glands at considerable length, and concludes with an anatomical diagnosis and a formal statement of the cause or causes of death. The autopsy report on Lenin, for example, covers four closely printed pages and describes one by one the condition of the brain, the heart, the lungs, spleen, kidneys and pancreas, the stomach and the glands, and goes into lengthy detail. What is missing in the report on Stalin is the detail. It is as though the doctors made only a very cursory examination of the body, announcing their conclusions while offering a minimum of supporting evidence.

The description of the brain haemorrhage is so brief, and stated in such general terms, that it gives rise to the suspicion that the brain was not uncovered and examined, and the doctors merely contented themselves with opening up the body. The shape of Stalin's head as it rested on a pillow in the Hall of Columns would tend to confirm the fact that the brain was not extracted.

There may have been excellent reasons for not examining the brain. Stalin himself may have forbidden it in his testament, knowing that Lenin's brain, cut into 30,000 slices, had become the plaything of the Brain Institute in Moscow. There are, of course, other possibilities. The doctors may have been so awed in the presence of the dead Stalin that they could not and dared not open the skull case. It is possible that the complete autopsy was never published, and the published report merely indicates the doctors' conclusions. Finally, there is the possibility that the autopsy was fraudulent, and that Stalin did not die in the manner indicated.

Some six weeks after the publication of the report the Moscow newspaper *Medical Worker* carried a brief announcement saying that Professor Arseny Vasilyevich Rusakov died suddenly. About the same time Dr Tretyakov and Dr Kuperin were removed from their posts and disappeared from sight. Of the nine doctors who signed the autopsy report a third vanished in six weeks.

Though we may never know exactly how Stalin died, or even the exact date of his death, there are indications that he died long before the evening of March 5th, and it is possible that he died violently.

It is certain that he was alive and well on February 17th, when the Indian ambassador talked with him. The ambassador had not seen him at close quarters before, but there is not the slightest possibility that the man seated across the table from him was anyone but Stalin. The ambassador, an especially sensitive and intelligent man, would have known whether he was speaking to a double. Stalin's ominous reference to wolves, his attacks on America, his sly question about the fighting capacity of the Indian army, all these were so much in character that it is impossible to doubt that this was the authentic Stalin. At around nine o'clock in the evening the ambassador took his leave. No foreigner saw Stalin again.

During the following week the anti-Semitic campaign, the last flare of Stalin's daemonic energy, continued unrelentingly. All over the country Jews were being arrested. Their names would appear briefly in the newspapers, usually in connection with economic crimes or sabotage. It was obvious that these arrests formed part of a careful and systematic plan originating on the highest levels of the government. It was as though the spirit of Hitler had entered into Stalin. On February 24th it was learned that Semyon Ignatiev had been appointed Commissar of State Security. Later developments were to confirm that Ignatiev had been selected for his high post because he was an adept at torture and was completely ruthless in carrying out Stalin's designs. To Ignatiev had gone the order to make the doctors confess. The confessions had reached Stalin's desk and satisfactorily proved the existence of a world-wide conspiracy against him.

For reasons that can only be guessed at, the news that Ignatiev had been appointed to the second-highest post in the government was censored. The news of the appointment did not reach the foreign press until after he was removed from his post.

After February 25th no more arrests of Jews were reported. Quite suddenly, following the appointment of Ignatiev, within a matter of hours the *chistka* collapsed.

Now it is in the nature of things that a *chistka* is irreversible under all conditions save one. A *chistka* feeds on itself, follows its own course, acquires a strange unhallowed strength by the mere repetition of the crimes committed in its name. It can be stopped only when the dictator is stopped. The Terror ends only when Robespierre loses his head.

At some time therefore on February 24th or 25th Stalin became 'incapacitated'. He may have suffered a stroke, and Ignatiev may therefore have felt that it would be unwise and dangerous to pursue a course which was sanctioned by the will of the dictator and possessed no other sanction. He must have known that he had not the least chance of stepping into Stalin's shoes. He held his hand, or others held it for him.

All the available evidence suggests that between February 25th and March 5th there was a vacuum of power. No one ruled, for no one dared to rule. An irresistible force met an immovable object. An apparent silence reigned over the Kremlin, while the people went about their affairs completely ignorant of the fact that no government ruled over them and they were free to organize whatever government they wished; and because they were free, they were kept in ignorance of their freedom.

Eight days later, on March 4th, the silence came to an end with the strange announcement: 'Comrade Stalin suffered a cerebral haemorrhage affecting vital areas of the brain. Comrade Stalin lost consciousness, and paralysis of the right arm and leg set in. Loss of speech followed.' The news of the stroke had been delayed for about fifty-six hours. It could have taken place a hundred hours or a hundred and fifty hours before without the public being any the wiser. If the anonymous authors of the communiqué were able to say that loss of speech followed loss of consciousness, this was evidence enough that the communiqué was composed in great haste. If they were capable of writing statements so obviously meaningless, what other irrelevancies and inaccuracies were they capable of committing? Why was it composed in haste, when the stroke had happened so long before? There was time enough, and to spare, to compose a credible communiqué. Why was the communiqué issued anonymously? Why was the announcement made in the early morning hours of March 4th?

If we assume that Stalin suffered a massive cerebral haemorrhage or was killed on February 25th, then the pattern of events becomes easier to understand. The *chistka* ended, in the only way that a *chistka* can end. Ignatiev, incapable of reaching out for power, simply surrendered what little power he possessed in favour of Beria, for if in theory the Ministry of State Security was the supreme disciplinary body in the country, it had neither the manpower nor the resources of the secret police with its private armies, aeroplanes and prisons, and the vast accumulations of power and wealth which derived from its control of the slave camps. Because Ignatiev could not act, Beria could act, and because Ignatiev was Malenkov's man, owing his rise to Malenkov's influence, Malenkov would inevitably be involved in the conspiracy to keep the death of Stalin secret, for it was of prime importance that it should be kept secret as long as possible not only from the Russian people but from the other members of the Presidium.

In the early hours after Stalin's death, the power, such as it was, reposed chiefly in the hands of Beria and Malenkov. They were not foolhardy men, and they acted cautiously. They were determined to prevent the army from taking over, and they were just as determined to prevent the hatreds and mutual rivalries of the members of the Presidium from breaking out into open conflict. The only way in which they could prevent this was by introducing them one by one into the conspiracy; or else they would have to be killed, for Beria was now in a position to kill them all. That Beria possessed this power, and was perfectly capable of using it, was known to them when they entered the conspiracy of silence.

Above all, time was needed – time to bring MVD troops to Moscow, time to organize, time to conduct an examination in depth of all the eventualities that might occur, time to think. By good fortune the election returns for the local soviets were still coming in, and the people were more concerned with the returns than whether anything was happening in the Kremlin. When in the early morning of March 4th there came the announcement that Stalin had been elected to the Moscow Soviet, the conspirators realized that something had to be done quickly, for he would normally appear on film or in person at the Moscow Soviet to thank the electors. The announcement appears to have caught Beria unawares. There was need for some demonstrative action. Beria could have announced at this point that Stalin had died suddenly, as Lenin died suddenly, but in his overwhelming need for time he postponed the formal announcement for thirty-six hours. The first communiqué was hastily concocted. The following communiqués were prepared more carefully.

When in the early hours of March 6th the formal announcement was made, Beria and Malenkov knew that they had taken all the precautions that can possibly be taken to ensure the swift and peaceful transfer of power. They had not however ensured their own survival, for they had incurred the hatred of all the other members of the Presidium.

Nine days later Beria formally moved Malenkov's nomination as Premier at the Supreme Soviet. Ignatiev had already received his reward, for on March 6th, though deprived of his dangerous post of Minister of State Security, he was given a post of party secretary. On March 21st Malenkov was compelled to resign. Beria remained in power a little longer. He disappeared from sight towards the end of June and was formally arrested on July 10th, charged with crimes against the state, and immediately shot. The chief conspirators had been outmanoeuvred.

If this analysis of the events following February 25th is correct, then much that is puzzling can be explained. The sudden suspension of the *chistka*, the curious manner in which the first communiqué was announced, as though the conspirators had been taken by surprise, the formation of the duumvirate of Malenkov and Beria, and the hatred they inspired, and the high honour paid to Ignatiev, who was never punished for his crimes, receive a sufficient explanation. Years will pass before we learn exactly what happened in the Kremlin during those ferocious and secret days, and there is much that we shall never know. Beria took his secrets to the grave.

While we know comparatively little about the immediate aftermath of Stalin's death, we know even less about the manner of his dying. The medical bulletins are unsatisfactory, and there is no particular reason to believe that he suffered a fatal cerebral haemorrhage in the manner described in the bulletins.

Inevitably highly coloured stories about his death have been published, purportedly written by eyewitnesses. According to one especially highly coloured account the members of the Presidium gathered in Stalin's office and solemnly condemned him to death, Molotov presenting him with a glass of poisoned brandy. The speeches of the Presidium members are quoted verbatim, together with Stalin's final acceptance of their verdict. The story wears the air of an improvisation, and Molotov is an unlikely candidate for Stalin's executioner.

There remain however four separate accounts which must be treated with less reserve. They were written down at different times, they tell different stories with a lesser or greater degree of authenticity, and they share a family likeness. All agree that Stalin was struck down by a cerebral haemorrhage, but not all of them agree that he died as a result of the haemorrhage. All are reported by men accustomed to reproduce accurately what they have heard. All seem to have come directly or indirectly from Nikita Khrushchev who, although he fought and destroyed the Malenkov-Beria coalition, appears to have had his own agents among them. He knew what happened, and may have been present at the moment of death.

These accounts of Stalin's death were written by Averell Harriman, Philippe Ben of *Le Monde*, Georges Kessel of *Paris-Match*, and Joseph C. Harsch of NBC. Taken separately they are not very convincing, but when assembled together they seem to describe a single event seen dimly through a dusty frosted-glass window. We see shadows moving around a dying man, hear muffled voices and prayers, and wait during long silences. Sometimes the shadows tell us what we want to know.

NIKITA KHRUSHCHEV SPEAKING TO AVERELL HARRIMAN

On Monday evening the head of his bodyguard called us and said Stalin was ill.

All of us – Beria, Malenkov, Bulganin, and I – hurried out to the country to see him. He was already unconscious. A blood clot had paralysed an arm, a leg, and his tongue. We stayed with him for three days, and he remained unconscious. Then for a time he came out of his coma and we went into his room. A nurse was feeding him tea with a spoon. He shook us by the hand and tried to joke with us, smiling feebly and waving with his good arm to a picture over his bed of a baby lamb being fed with a spoon by a little girl. Now, he indicated by his gestures, he was just as helpless as the baby lamb.

Some time later he died. I wept. After all, we were all his pupils and owed him everything. Like Peter the Great, Stalin fought barbarism with barbarism, but he was a great man.

The French diplomat, Emmanuel d'Astier, adds some explanatory details about the previous days, saying that he learned them from Harriman. He wrote:

Khrushchev said that on the Saturday Stalin invited us to dinner in his country house at Kuntsevo. He was in good humour, and it was a gay evening. Then we returned to our own homes. On Sunday Stalin was accustomed to telephone all of us to discuss affairs. But on that particular Sunday he did not call us, and this was strange. He did not come to Moscow on Monday. It was on the Monday, in the afternoon, that the head of his bodyguard called us and said Stalin was ill.

As a pendant to this story Emmanuel d'Astier relates what happened to Svetlana, Stalin's daughter, according to some unnamed informants:

On Sunday March 2nd, Svetlana wanted to speak to her father on the telephone. She could not get through. There was always a guard on the line, preventing her from reaching her father. Two days passed, and then in the morning a secretary came to call for her. They had found her father stretched out on the ground, unconscious. In the garden Svetlana was welcomed by Bulganin, Malenkov, and Khrushchev, who was in tears. They took her to the bedside. He had lost the power of speech, but his eyes were full of life. He was actually lying on the sofa in the main room. On the wall there were pictures cut out of newspapers.

March 2nd, 1953, was not a Sunday, but a Monday. The dates are perhaps not a matter of very great importance. What is more important is the sense of time passing, and the emphasis on the speechlessness of the dictator. For three days Khrushchev, Malenkov, Beria and Bulganin remain in the house, keeping the deathwatch. For two days Svetlana is not permitted to come to her father's deathbed. There is no mention of doctors, only of a nurse feeding him tea with a spoon.

Perhaps significantly Beria is not among those who welcome
Svetlana in the garden.

PANTELEIMON PONOMARENKO SPEAKING TO
PHILIPPE BEN

We were about two dozen sitting around the big table
in the Kremlin room. The discussion was lively. Suddenly
Stalin dropped on the floor. We all rushed to him, but he
could not be moved. He was lying motionless, his eyes
closed, obviously dead.

Suddenly Beria jumped into the middle of the room and
began to shout in a jubilant mood: 'Comrades, what a
marvellous moment! Comrades, at last the tyrant is dead!
What a marvellous day. We are free! We can breathe
freely! We are not afraid of being shot the next day!'

We stood motionless, looking at the motionless body of
Stalin. Suddenly we saw that Stalin opened one eye, then
a second one, and though he did not speak a word he was
looking again perfectly normal, perfectly healthy. Beria
did not notice this at first, but when he realized that Stalin
was looking up at him, he ran to the body, fell on his knees,
raised his hands, and began to plead: 'Dear Joseph Vissarionovich, forgive me! Dear Joseph Vissarionovich, you
know how faithful I was to you in the past! Believe me, I
will be faithful again! Forgive me!'

Stalin did not say a word, and slowly one eye closed,
then the other closed.

This story was told to Philippe Ben and other correspondents by Panteleimon Ponomarenko in the Soviet Embassy in
Warsaw early in 1957. He was the Soviet ambassador and a
former member of the Presidium, famous for leading the
Belorussian partisans during the war. According to Philippe
Ben the same story had been told to Polish Communists by
the ambassador on the previous day.

The story is suspect because it seems to have been inspired
deliberately by sources higher than the ambassador and because exactly the same incident of the eyes closing belongs
to the mythology concerning the death of Ivan the Terrible.
The purpose is clear: it is to reduce Beria to absolute insignificance as a craven imbecile, whining for forgiveness after his
delirious outburst. The event is supposed to have occurred in

Moscow, thus agreeing with the statement in the first communiqué that during the night of March 1st-2nd, 'while in his Moscow apartment, Comrade Stalin suffered a cerebral haemorrhage'.

According to a French journalist, Michel Gordey of *France-Soir*, the same story was given by Khrushchev to a high French government official during his state visit to Prague.

NIKITA KHRUSHCHEV TO AN UNKNOWN INFORMANT AS REPEATED TO GEORGES KESSEL

This story appeared in *Paris-Match* on March 30th, 1963, ten years after Stalin's death. It is clearly related to the Harriman story, adds further details, introduces more dramatis personae, and is far more theatrical in the telling. The adventures of Beria in the presence of the dying Stalin are repeated, but with a different ending.

Towards midnight on March 1st-2nd Khrushchev was aroused by a telephone call from the officer in charge of Stalin's private guard summoning him to Stalin's country-estate fifty miles from Moscow. The city was in the iron grip of winter, the roads deep in icy snow, and Khrushchev's car skidded badly as he set out for the estate. On the road to Kachiry he discovered that six other cars were making the same journey; they belonged to Molotov, Beria, Malenkov, Bulganin, Kaganovich and Voroshilov. It took them three hours to make the short journey. When at last they arrived, they learned that Stalin had recently introduced architectural changes in the mansion, adding an entire wing in the rear. This wing was composed of three identical rooms, each containing an iron bed, a wardrobe, and a table with a telephone, a phonograph, and a pile of records. Photographs cut from magazines decorated the walls. The toilet facilities included a washbasin, a jug, and a chamber pot. Each door was reinforced with armour plate, with a window large enough to allow the passage of a tray of food. Four times a day, at 9 am, 1 pm, 7 pm, and 10 pm, food or drink came through the slit in the armour-plated door. Each time Stalin would prepare the guards by telephone, telling them exactly what he wanted brought in.

The captain of the guards told his visitors that Stalin had rung for his dinner at 7 pm, but had failed to ring for his tea at 10 pm. Nothing like this had happened before. When the captain called Stalin on the telephone, there was no answer. Finally he telephoned to the members of the Presidium. He had done nothing in the interval, for he had been ordered never to break into one of the three rooms under pain of death.

Molotov gave the order to break into the rooms. Then it became a question of how they would break down the armour-plated doors. Kaganovich thought of using the ice axes in the cars, and with these they attacked the first door in the corridor. The captain of the guard was the first to enter the room. He froze on his tracks, and Beria brushed past him. Khrushchev then tells this story:

> I was just behind Beria when I saw Stalin in his marshal's uniform stretched out on his back on the wooden floor. My comrades crowded forward, for they too wanted to see what had happened. Suddenly there came the voice of Beria, piercing, strident, triumphant: 'The tyrant is dead, dead, dead!'
>
> I don't know what obscure peasant instinct made me kneel down beside Stalin's head. And then I saw his eyes, wide open, staring at me – not the eyes of a dead man, but the eyes of the living Stalin!
>
> I jumped up and backed away, my arms spread out. The others behind me understood. And then I saw that they too were backing away towards the corridor. I fled with them. Only one man stayed behind. This was Beria, the compatriot of the stricken Stalin, the head of the police organization with its thousands of ramifications. On this organization Stalin had based the terror he inspired. This man, who had dared to cry out with joy, remained in the room.

The direct quotation from Khrushchev ends here, but the story continues.

It had taken about an hour to break down the door. At 4 am Malenkov telephoned the Kremlin doctors, ordering them to come at once. For the next five hours, until the doctors arrived, the members of the Presidium debated what they should do. It was decided not to break the news to the Russian people.

When the doctors had completed their examination, the oldest of them came out, shaking his head. He said: 'If it had been a more clement night, if we had been notified earlier, if we had arrived earlier, we might have been able to

save the great Stalin. Now there is nothing left for us to do.
I have just closed his eyes.'

There was a long silence, and then one by one the members of the Presidium burst into tears, first Khrushchev, then Molotov, then Malenkov. Only Beria did not weep. With icy calm he asked the doctors: 'How did he die?'

'A cerebral haemorrhage,' the doctor replied. 'Paralysis, strangulation.'

Khrushchev had the last word. 'Tonight,' he said, 'the mice have buried the cat.'

NIKITA KHRUSHCHEV TO AN UNKNOWN INFORMANT AS RELATED TO JOSEPH C. HARSCH

Khrushchev's story of the struggle for power, as I heard it reported, began with Stalin lying on his deathbed in the Kremlin. These are the details. Beria was out of town. The other members of the Politburo for the first time were admitted into Stalin's room. They found to their astonishment that there were no doctors in attendance. They asked why, and they were given three reasons. First, that Stalin had had seizures before, and recovered; second, that he was suspicious of doctors; third, that it was difficult to get doctors to come and attend him because on other occasions doctors had come and never returned home afterwards. They did get one of the top doctors of Moscow. He came, looked through the door, refused however to enter the room until he had colleagues with him. They sent for two more doctors, and when they arrived, the three of them went into the room and examined Stalin, and reported to the members of the Presidium that if they had been called two days earlier there might have been something they could do, but then it was too late.

Here, then, are four accounts of Stalin's death, differing widely, but possessing an imaginative logic of their own. The second springs from the first, the third is an elaboration and revision of the second, while the fourth is a kind of coda, a final view of the deathbed seen from an open door. These accounts possess a kind of mythological pattern like the stories of the Greek gods in Robert Graves's *The Greek Myths*. There are three versions of the death of Hercules. They do not differ in essentials: in all the versions we hear of a bloodstained or poisoned shirt, but in one version he does not wear the shirt but instead gives it to Deianira. So in these accounts of the death of Stalin we are made aware of certain recurring patterns: there is a body on the floor, there are pictures on the wall above him, the members of the Presidium are all present, there is the sense of time passing – a door has to be broken down or they stand around waiting for the end, and the doctors never appear until he is already dead or in the last extremity.

When Nikita Khrushchev gave his account of Stalin's death to Averell Harriman, he was not on oath. Nevertheless he was telling a story which he believed to be credible to a man who was a superb diplomat, capable of distinguishing between truth and falsehood. The story therefore would have to be carefully constructed to give an impression of verisimilitude, with just the right amount of embroidery. The appropriate embroidery was provided by the picture of the baby lamb being spoon-fed by a girl. It is not convincing, but at least it is an attempt to convince. In time the picture of the baby lamb becomes cutouts from newspapers and magazines, and we are suddenly introduced into a world which is so far removed from Stalin's world that we find ourselves wondering how such a detail could be invented. There was only one place near Stalin's office where these cutouts could be expected to be found. They would be in the outer office where the female secretaries worked. And since no one was ever allowed to come into his presence armed, there was only one certain way of killing him – by strangling him. If we imagine that he was strangled in the secretaries' office, then some of the events described in the four stories come into focus.

These stories, however improbable, remain our only source for discovering how he died. They have a family likeness, overlap and dovetail into one another, and betray the evidence of a single imagination. The communiqués and bulletins can be dismissed as deliberate inventions, the stories cannot. The communiqués and bulletins record an improbable death, the stories hint at a death more probable and more terrible.

If he was murdered, who were the killers?

Stalin had spent his lifetime making enemies; there was no end to the number of people who wanted to kill him. At the time of his death all the members of the Presidium with the exception of Molotov regarded themselves as under sentence of death. Even Kaganovich, who was always seen at his side, could expect no mercy from him. Going through the list of the members of the Presidium, we find that nearly all of them had Jewish connections: one was married to a Jewess, another had a Jewish secretary, a third had defended the Jews. Those who had no Jewish connections were irksome to the dictator for other reasons. Within the Presidium there can have been no one who did not believe a purge was being prepared. They were not prepared to die, and long before Stalin's death they had begun to put their affairs in order. The Central Committee resolution of June 30th, 1956, revealed the existence of a conspiracy. The relevant passage of the resolution reads: 'The Twentieth Party Congress and the entire Central Committee policy after Stalin's death show clearly that a nucleus of Leninist leaders existed within the Central Committee.' Stalin could not have been a member of the nucleus. Kaganovich, Beria and Malenkov were almost certainly the leading members. If Stalin was murdered, the most likely candidate for murderer would be Beria. He was accustomed to murder.

Of Beria's death some three or four months later there exist two accounts both narrated by Khrushchev in the summer of 1956. They differ in only one essential. In the account told to Senator Pierre Commin, a French Socialist, Beria was shot. In the account told to Eugenio Reale, an Italian Communist, he was strangled. Eugenio Reale had been a member of the Constituent Assembly of the Italian Republic, a Deputy, and ambassador to Warsaw, and was likely therefore to receive a fuller and more accurate version. Here is his account of Beria's death, as told to him by Khrushchev:

The situation after Stalin's death was untenable. We knew that Beria was planning a private *coup d'état*, but there was little or nothing we could do to stop him; the police were too strong and Beria was too clever. For two weeks running we did not budge from our offices: Molotov stayed at the Foreign Ministry, Voroshilov in the Presidium Building, and Malenkov in the Prime Minister's office. I holed up in the Party headquarters. We did not dare go home because we were afraid Beria would have us arrested. We felt safer in the government buildings, protected by our own armed guards.

Then we got the idea of making Beria think we wanted to put an end to the impossible state of affairs and that we believed that he, as Stalin's closest and most loyal collaborator, was the one man who both could and should take up the reins of power. To save the country and the revolution it was necessary to return to Stalin's absolutism, to give the country the only successor capable of continuing Stalin's giant undertaking. That was the line we took as we exchanged telephone calls, knowing that the phones were tapped; as we exchanged letters, knowing that they would be read before they were delivered; as we kept in touch through people who were known to be under surveillance.

Finally we sent Voroshilov as our spokesman to suggest that Beria take our great Stalin's place both as Prime Minister and Party secretary. Beria listened to Voroshilov, asked some questions and finally told him to arrange a joint meeting of the Presidium and the Party Secretariat to which he would come and discuss our proposal. The next day he arrived at the Kremlin surrounded by his customary bodyguard, who accompanied him to the door of the room where we were going to have the meeting. Once inside, he looked about and, seeing Zhukov, Koniev and Moskolenko among the others, asked why the generals were there since he certainly hadn't asked them to come. Molotov answered that because of the exceptional importance of the decision we were to make we had thought it advisable for the major military leaders to be present so as to have their support and in this manner show the world, which would soon learn of this extraordinary event, that the whole country was behind us and unanimously approved our choice.

Apparently reassured, Beria sat down and the meeting began. Malenkov took the floor, but instead of saying what Beria expected, he launched into a brief and violent indictment, accusing Beria of conspiracy and informing him that he would be judged during this very meeting. As soon as he heard this, Beria realized that he had been tricked. He jumped up and reached for the pistol in his pocket, but before he could get at it, those nearest – Koniev, Moskolenko, Mikoyan and Malenkov himself – jumped him, got him by the throat and strangled him.

In the Khrushchev-Commin version, there is added the useful information that at the time of the murder of Beria, they did not have enough evidence of his guilt to put him on trial. 'Nevertheless we could not leave him at liberty, and we felt easier when, some time after his condemnation, we received sufficient and irrefutable evidence of guilt.'

With Stalin there was never any necessity to find evidence of guilt. Russian history for thirty years showed that he deserved to die.

DESCENT INTO HELL

THE DICTATOR WAS DEAD, but his spirit continued to haunt Russia. During his lifetime he had been feared, and after his death he was still feared. To the Russians it seemed almost incomprehensible that a man who had left his mark in every corner of the land, who had murdered on a prodigious scale and sent men into slave camps on an even more prodigious scale, should prove to be mortal after all. Great Stalin, the *Vozhd*, the Father of Peoples, the Eternal Guiding Light of Marxist Leninism, was dead, and there was no comfort to be derived from his waxen corpse lying in the mausoleum in the Red Square. In the amber light, against the black hangings, he looked quiet and peaceful, but was he quiet, and was he peaceful?

For thirty years they had listened to his grave, ugly and halting voice as he announced year after year the new tablets of the law. For thirty years it had been drummed into their heads that he was the sole repository of all faith, wisdom and knowledge, and that no one else was capable of making the great decisions affecting the lives of everyone in Russia and all the Communists outside of Russia. Had he not pushed back the frontiers of the Russian empire to limits undreamed of by Catherine the Great? Had he not given his name to a hundred towns and villages of Russia, and to innumerable streets outside of Russia? Even Paris had a street named after him, to remind the workers of the benefits to be derived from contemplating his name. In one way or another he had touched the lives of nearly everyone living on the earth. His power was so great and his legend so fraught with mysterious consequences that he seemed to tower over other men, as a mountain towers over a plain. The small, taciturn man who rarely left Russian soil and who knew very little about the world beyond the frontiers of Russia had become a familiar figure; if he had entered a room in Patagonia, men would have recognized him. For thirty years the man had been vanishing in the legend, becoming more and more remote the longer he ruled, but the legend was strangely persistent. And being a legend, he seemed more alive than ever now that he was dead.

All over the world the flags went to half staff, and nations went into mourning. Condolences poured into Moscow from the heads of states, who had feared him and regarded him as one of the greatest tyrants of the age. One after another the grief-stricken speeches were delivered at the United Nations. In Peking mournful processions wound through the streets. From the top of the Tien An Men Gate Mao Tse-tung declared: 'We must transform our sorrow into strength.' In East Berlin a catafalque was raised in the street named after him, and in the pelting rain the mourners heaped flowers on the catafalque. In Prague, Budapest and Warsaw solemn services were held at the foot of his statue, as though beside his grave. In New Delhi Premier Jawaharlal Nehru moved the adjournment of Parliament in memory of 'the great lover of peace, a man of giant stature who moulded, as few other men have done, the destinies of his age'. Nehru spoke of the vast number of men who had felt for Stalin an almost brotherly affection, and how with his passing all men everywhere had lost a friend. 'It is right that we should pay our tribute to him,' he said, 'because the occasion is not merely the passing away of a great figure but perhaps the ending of an historic era.'

But while shock and grief were felt all over the world, they were felt most notably in Russia, where the people listened interminably to radios which could tell them no more than that Stalin was dead. It was not that they loved him: it was simply that the flow of life seemed curiously unreal now that he was gone. He was in the air men breathed, he was in the voices coming over the radio, the drone of aeroplanes, the sounds of marching in the streets. Ilya Ehrenburg, almost the sole survivor of a generation of writers murdered by Stalin, composed a long threnody in commemoration of a man who in his lifetime had achieved the stature of a god. He wrote:

In these difficult days we see Stalin in the whole of his stature. We see him walking the roads of the earth and looming high above our harsh and forbidding times. He walks the mountains of his native Georgia, the battlefields between the Don and the Volga. He walks the wide avenues being built in Moscow, and far away he walks the crowded streets of Shanghai, the hills of France, the forests of Brazil, the piazzas of Rome, the villages of India. He walks on the crest of the century.

The mills of Turin stopped working; agricultural labourers of Sicily froze into immobility; dockers of Genoa ceased working. They too followed the bier of Stalin and wept for him. Through the narrow streets of ancient Peking youths, old men and women carrying small children hurried to the square where China lamented her friend.

Among the ruins of Korea mothers who have achieved the extremes of human misery lowered their eyes and grieved for Stalin. The buildings of Warsaw, reduced to ashes and now reborn, donned mourning. In New York upright people, surrounded by police, informers and ruffians, spoke with sadness: 'The friend of peace has died.'

In these difficult days we have seen for the first time perhaps how many friends we possess. Our grief has become the grief of mankind.

In these difficult days the partisans of peace, wherever they may be found and whatever views they hold, realize what they owe to Stalin. It was he who helped the people to prevent a new war, he who protected millions of children, thousands of cities.

When Stalin's heart ceased to beat, the heart of mankind began to beat stronger than ever in sorrow; the common people felt drawn closer to one another. The people realized they were drawn closer together by the memory of Stalin, by Stalin's behests, by the struggle for peace and the happiness of mankind.

The long threnody filled a whole page of *Pravda*. An exaggerated grief was mingled with a fierce hate for America. For some reason Ehrenburg spoke more often about the grief flowering at the ends of the earth – in China, India, Brazil and Argentina – than in the satellite countries conquered by the Red Army. When he spoke of the grief-stricken multitudes in New York, who were surrounded by police, informers and ruffians, he was perhaps reflecting a fear of American power. Over the radio the Soviet people were continually being warned to stand together in this hour of danger. Stalin was

dead, the country was in peril, everyone must be prepared to
fight in defence of the Soviet Union. There were some who
thought these warnings heralded a nuclear attack by the
United States. Where else could danger come from?

Danger was everywhere in those days when Stalin was
dying his many deaths. The mourners lamented the passing of
a leader they had adored and feared in equal proportions.
Three years after Stalin's death, at the Twentieth Congress,
Khrushchev gave a jolting account of the real Stalin who still
loomed high over 'our harsh and forbidding times', but he
was no longer the serene divinity imagined by Ehrenburg. He
had become a spectre of terror, to be spoken about with bated
breath.

Following Khrushchev's speech at the Twentieth Congress,
there were no more sustained attacks on Stalin. The processes
of de-Stalinization continued, but they were slow, laborious,
and often halfhearted. Though the cult of personality was
under attack, the new rulers of the Kremlin were not averse
to cultivating their own personalities in public; anonymity was
never one of the besetting sins of Communist leaders. In fact
very little had changed. The monolithic state remained monolithic, the secret police still operated without any regard for
the laws, and the prisons were still full. Russia under Khrushchev was still a tyranny, and it has remained a tyranny under
his successors.

In the years following the death of Stalin the ruling classes
of the Soviet Union were confronted with urgent problems
of their own, and they were in no need to be reminded of the
decaying corpse of Stalin. In the age of the sputniks and the
race for the moon, Stalin seemed oddly out of date. Khrushchev brushed him under the carpet and hoped he would be
forgotten.

He was not forgotten. His ghost lingered, becoming more
and more vocal the longer he remained in the shadows. The
new rulers of Russia paid him the tribute of imitation; sometimes their speeches read like exact facsimiles of Stalin's
speeches. His name, which had once decorated the pages of
Pravda with a weird persistence, so that it seemed that nothing ever happened in the Soviet Union but he was a part of
it and no sentence was ever written but he was introduced
into it, now rarely appeared. In the Museum of the Revolution
statues, paintings, relics and documents relating to him were
once so numerous that the visitor went away with the feeling

that Stalin must have been at least as important as Lenin in bringing the revolution about, but now they vanished quietly and once more Lenin was left in sole possession. His photographs vanished from the walls, his statues were melted down, the streets and towns named after him quietly assumed new names. Yet the more he was absent, the more he remained.

It was not easy to obliterate a man who for nearly thirty years had affected the lives of everyone in Russia. Like Julius Caesar he was mighty in the grave, and sometimes it seemed that nothing anyone could do would ever make a dent on his legend. One of the greatest battles of world history had been fought around Stalingrad. Stalin perished, but Stalingrad remained for a little while longer. The fame of Stalin was so much greater than the fame of his successors that they came to resemble pygmies playing at the foot of the Himalayas.

In this desperate situation Khrushchev resolved on desperate measures. He may have remembered that in the Middle Ages murderers were buried at the crossroads with stakes driven through their hearts. Throughout history techniques have been developed for punishing the dead. Sorcerers come forward to utter evil spells and curses over their tombs, and in mysterious ways the power of the dead is torn up by the roots. The body may be carved into little pieces and thrown to the winds, or it may be delivered over to the mercy of dogs, or it may be buried in a place where all can trample over it. Essentially there are four methods for destroying the power of a dead ruler: by removing all the vestiges of his rule, by the continual recital of his evil deeds, by the destruction of his mortal remains, and by weaving magic spells. All these methods, or variants of them, were used by Khrushchev at the Twenty-second Party Congress held in October 1961.

In his concluding speech at the Congress Khrushchev spoke as though the decisions of the Twentieth Congress had put an end to the need for a summary judgement on the dead dictator. 'At the Twentieth Congress of the Party,' he declared, 'we denounced the cult of the individual, restored justice, and demanded elimination of the errors that had been committed. The Central Committee of the Party has taken resolute measures to prevent any return to arbitrariness and lawlessness.' He indicated that the anti-Party group representing the Stalinist diehards had been routed. The battle was over, and the Party was safely embarked on the road of sanity and truth.

But the memory of a nightmare persisted, and at intervals throughout the speech Khrushchev found himself discussing sometimes at length, sometimes briefly, and nearly always evasively – for these memories were painful, and he could rarely bring himself to see them in precise focus – the more notorious crimes committed by Stalin. There was, for example, the Tukhachevsky *affaire*, which was of such importance that it demanded a full report or at the very least the publication of the documents which led to the arrest of the generals, many of whom were known personally to Khrushchev. Instead, Khrushchev merely proclaimed their innocence while producing no supporting evidence. He said:

> A rather curious report leaked out in the foreign press to the effect that Hitler, preparing the attack on our country, launched a forged document through his intelligence service stating that Comrades Yakir, Tukhachevsky and others were agents of the German General Staff. This supposedly secret 'document' fell into the hands of Czechoslovakia's President Benes, who, evidently guided by kind intentions, forwarded it to Stalin. Yakir, Tukhachevsky, and other comrades were arrested and then liquidated.

Such was Khrushchev's brief notation on the Tukhachevsky *affaire*, which added nothing to what was already known. No doubt the Central Committee possessed a complete *dossier* concerning the *affaire*, but the time for producing it had not yet come. Khrushchev had known Yakir well, and he was able to add the intriguing detail that just before being executed, Yakir cried out: 'Long live Stalin!' and when Stalin heard of this, he cursed.

As a companion piece to the story about Yakir, Khrushchev told another about Alexey Svanidze, the brother of Stalin's first wife. He was a veteran Bolshevik, a loyal party member, little known among the rank and file, but very close to Stalin – Khrushchev says he was 'Stalin's greatest friend'. Incriminating documents were found in his possession by Beria, and Stalin ordered him to be shot. He was told that if he asked for pardon, it would be granted to him. Svanidze replied: 'Why should I beg for pardon? I have committed no crime.' Khrushchev says that Stalin was enormously pleased with this reply. 'Look how proud he was!' Stalin would say. 'He died, but did not beg for pardon.'

There were not many of these fleeting portraits of Stalin in the speech. For the most part Khrushchev was content to attack Stalin indirectly through his lieutenants. Once Khrushchev asked Molotov, Voroshilov and Kaganovich whether they were in favour of rehabilitating the dead generals. They said: 'Yes, we are in favour.' When Khrushchev confronted them with the unanswerable question: 'But you yourselves executed these men – when did you act in good faith, then or now?' It was the same question with which Vyshinsky had sometimes confronted his prisoners during the trials of the thirties, when they said one thing during the preliminary examination and another in open court.

Khrushchev spoke about the assassination of Kirov, the classical murder which stands at the beginning of the great purges of the thirties. Nearly eight years had passed since the death of Stalin, and nearly twenty-seven since the death of Kirov, but Khrushchev was not yet in a position to reveal exactly how it had been brought about. 'The deeper we study the materials connected with Kirov's death, the more questions arise,' he said, but he mentioned only two of the suspicious circumstances which had come to his attention. The first was the fact that NKVD guards had *twice* arrested Nikolayev *near* the Smolny, and each time arms were found on him, and each time he was released. That Nikolayev had been arrested *once* in possession of arms *inside* the Smolny was already widely known, and the new information only confused the issue. On the subject of Borisov's death Khrushchev was more informative. It will be remembered that Borisov was the chief of Kirov's security guard, and it was generally believed that he was murdered during a carefully staged automobile accident the day following the assassination of Kirov. It was never made clear whether the accident happened before or after Borisov was to be brought up for interrogation: whether in fact the order for killing Borisov came from Stalin or Zaporozhets. Khrushchev was able to add a few important details.

When the chief of Kirov's guard was being taken for questioning – and he was to be questioned by Stalin, Molotov and Voroshilov – the car, as its driver said afterwards, was deliberately involved in an accident by those who were taking the man to those who were to interrogate him. They said that he died as the result of an accident, even though he was actually killed by those who accompanied him.

In this way the man who guarded Kirov was killed. Later, those who killed him were shot. This was no accident, apparently, but a carefully planned crime. Who could have done this? A thorough inquiry is being made now into the circumstances of this complicated case.

It has transpired that the driver of the car in which the chief of Kirov's guard was being taken for questioning is alive. He said that an NKVD operative sat with him in his cabin during the trip. They went in a truck. It is, of course, very strange that a truck was used to take the man for questioning, as if no other car could be found for the purpose. Evidently, everything had been planned in advance, in detail. Two other NKVD operatives were in the back of the truck together with Kirov's chief bodyguard.

The driver continued his story. When they were driving through a street, the man sitting next to him suddenly wrested the steering wheel from his hands and directed the car straight at a house. The driver regained control of the wheel and steered the car so that it hit only the wall of the building sideways. He was told later that Kirov's chief bodyguard had lost his life in this accident.

Why did he lose his life when none of the other people in the car suffered? Why were both officials of the NKVD, who were escorting Kirov's chief bodyguard, shot later? This means that someone had to have them killed in order to cover up all the traces.

Many, very many circumstances of this and other similar cases are still obscure.

But if they were obscure, it could only be because the Soviet government had not pressed its investigation. There was no full, public inquiry. The driver was still alive; the NKVD officer who had sharply turned the steering wheel was still alive; there were witnesses to the accident, and presumably there was a police report concerning the body of Borisov, and there were the hundreds of former prisoners who had been interrogated and sent to Siberia or to isolators in European Russia, and some of these had survived. Stalin was a merciless killer, but there were always a few who escaped the wide sweep of his scythe. Khrushchev published the testimony of the anonymous driver, but the testimonies of hundreds of others who may have known something about the assassination of Kirov were never published. Why?

Perhaps it was because there was already sufficient evidence to damn Stalin. Who killed Kirov? had become merely a rhetorical question in the eyes of the delegates of the Congress. There was scarcely a family in Russia which had not suffered at the hands of the dictator. Even those who thought they were on good terms with him had felt the terror of his presence. 'Stalin would look at a comrade sitting at the same table with him and say: "Your eyes are shifty today." Afterwards it would be taken for granted that the comrade, whose eyes were supposedly shifty, fell under suspicion.' So Khrushchev tells the story, and by his telling of it, it is almost certain that he was himself the victim of Stalin's suspicions. He, too, had been afraid.

Now the time had come to weave the magic spell and to bury Stalin again. The spell was woven by an old woman, frail and white-haired, with immense glowing eyes. Her name was Dora Abramovna Lazurkina. She was an Old Bolshevik, a member of the party since 1902, a friend of Lenin. Arrested in Leningrad in 1937, she had spent seventeen years in prison and concentration camps, always faithful to the memory of the man who had brought the revolution into being. She had been given the task of uttering the final malediction.

The newsreel cameras caught the moment – one of the most fantastic in Soviet history – when she rose to her feet, wearing a simple black dress with a white lace collar, and spoke of how only the previous day she had conversed with the dead Lenin and heard him speaking the words she wanted to hear. The vast audience grew quiet, strained and attentive, as the shrill voice described a ghostly rendezvous with Lenin.

'My heart is always full of Lenin,' she declared. 'Comrades, I could survive the most difficult moments only because I carried Lenin in my heart, and always consulted him on what to do. Yesterday I consulted him. He was standing there before me as if he were alive, and he said: "It is unpleasant to be next to Stalin, who did so much harm to the party."'

This speech had evidently been rehearsed, but it was no less effective for having been rehearsed. Khrushchev led the applause, and read the decree by which Stalin's mortal remains were ordered removed from the mausoleum on the Red Square. The decree read:

The mausoleum on the Red Square at the Kremlin wall, created to make eternal the memory of Vladimir Ilyich Lenin – the deathless founder of the Communist Party and the Soviet State, the leader and teacher of the workers of the whole world – is to be named in the future: The Mausoleum of Vladimir Ilyich Lenin.

The further retention in the mausoleum of the sarcophagus with the bier of J. V. Stalin shall be recognized as inappropriate since the serious violations by Stalin of Lenin's precepts, abuse of power, mass repressions against honourable Soviet people, and other activities in the period of the personality cult make it impossible to leave the bier with his body in the mausoleum of V. I. Lenin.

In this tortuous fashion Stalin was removed from his place of honour, and in the following days a new grave was found for him a short distance away among the minor heroes of the Revolution. His name was removed from the mausoleum, and by a lucky chance the original engraved stone bearing the name of Lenin was found intact and placed in position over the entrance to the mausoleum. There were no ceremonies at the interment, which took place secretly at night. Ironically, his body lay next to that of Kalinin, the peasant who had survived all the massacres only because he was genuinely simple and always anxious to do Stalin's bidding. Stalin had always despised him.

There were many who wondered whether Stalin would remain in his new grave, and whether his restless spirit would rise to take possession of Lenin's mausoleum. There were even some who thought it was not beyond the bounds of possibility that he would once more take possession of Russia. His ghost still haunted the land. Men who had murdered at his orders were still in positions of power. He was larger than life even when dead, and every order from the Kremlin, every word spoken over the radio, every speech by every local block leader, was impregnated with his spirit. In his lifetime he had shown that Communism, as practised in Russia, was a deadly tyranny, and the tyranny continued.

Stalin's heirs, the men who wielded power, were miniature Stalins, who imitated his gestures and long ago acquired the proper sense of inhumanity. They did not ask themselves whether they had a right to their positions of power. They were perfectly aware they had inherited their power from an archcriminal, and that it was tainted at the source. Against these men and against the continuing influence of Stalin there were few who dared raise their voices. One of the few was Evgeny Yevtushenko, who wrote a mordant elegy on Stalin which was also a bitter attack on his successors. In this poem called 'Stalin's Heirs', from which some lines have already been quoted, he describes Stalin as a man who lived in mortal fear of the Russian people and considered that any means whatever could be used to justify his aims.

STALIN'S HEIRS

Silent was the marble,
  and the glass gleamed in silence.
Silent were the guards,
  turning to bronze in the wind.
As they carried him out of the mausoleum,
  there came through the chinks of the coffin
  a small breath of steam.
Slowly the coffin floated by,
  its sides brushing the bayonets,
But the man inside remained silent —
  threateningly silent,
Sullenly clenching his fists,
  those embalmed fists,
While he pressed himself against the chinks,
  pretending to be dead.
He wanted to remember those
  who dared to carry him away,
The new recruits, youngsters
  from Kursk and Ryazan,
And after a little while
  he would gather his strength and break out,
Rising from the earth
  to punish these injudicious men.
While resting in his coffin,
  he was dreaming up a plot.

I appeal to our government,
  and I say to them:
Double or triple the guard
  beside his grave,
So that he will not rise again,
  and with him — the past.

I speak now not of our treasured, heroic past –
  Magnitogorsk, Turksib, the flag over Berlin.
Now when I speak of the past
  I have in mind
Oblivion of people's welfare,
  calumnies, the arrests of the innocent.
In the name of Stalin
  we poured metal honestly,
And in soldierly formations
  we marched honestly to the front,
But he was afraid of us.
  Believing in great goals,
He never considered that the means
  should be worthy of their grandeur.
He merely pretended.
  Being wise in the laws of struggle,
  he left many heirs on the earth.
It seems to me there is a telephone
  installed in his coffin,
And he is still sending instructions
  to Enver Hoxha.
No – Stalin has not thrown in his ticket;
  death, he believes, can be rectified.
We carried him away –
  threw him out of the mausoleum,
But how shall we remove Stalin
  from within Stalin's heirs?
Some of these heirs have retired
  to cultivate roses,
While in their secret hearts they believe
  they have only retired for a little while.
True, there are those who hurl abuse
  at Stalin from the platform,
Who secretly at night
  ponder their former glory.
True, it is not for nothing
  that Stalin's heirs suffer heart attacks.
They were the former pillars:
  with no liking for empty slave camps,
Or halls jammed with people
  where poets recite their verses.
The Party has commanded me
  not to be calm.

> *Let them repeat over and over again:*
>   *Be calm! But I dare not.*
> *As long as the heirs of Stalin*
>   *remain on this earth,*
> *I shall feel Stalin is still there*
>   *in the mausoleum.*

As long as the heirs of Stalin remain on this earth ... But the heirs were installed in the Kremlin, and they alone possessed power. Stalin, consigned to his grave, to become at last no more than mortal dust, was still laughing. In the end it could have mattered little to him whether he was in the mausoleum or in the grave. It was enough that his spirit was still alive on the earth.

Some weeks after he was buried a simple stone of dark polished granite, bearing only his name and the years of his birth and death, was placed over the grave. The titles and dignities he had amassed in the course of a long life were notably absent. The Supreme Commander, the Generalissimo, the Father of Peoples, the faithful Comrade-in-arms of Lenin, the tyrant and massacrer, all these had vanished in the casual anonymity of J. V. STALIN 1879-1953.

The grave lay under the Kremlin wall, half-hidden by yews and fir trees. It was a public place, and people could wander over him at will. No guards came at hourly intervals to guard his bones; no doctors came to impregnate his body with oils to keep it fresh and supple for eternity. In a few years the grass would grow over him. He had written his name in blood across the face of Russia, and soon nothing would be left of him.

In this way Stalin descended into Hell.

THE FORMER COMMANDANT

WHILE THE PHYSICAL BODY of Stalin went down into corruption and decay, his tyranny remained. Though dead, he was still vastly more powerful than those who followed him, for his laws were still being enacted and obeyed. The Russians were still haunted by his physical presence; even when his portraits were taken down from the walls, they seemed still to be present: it was as though the familiar face had been burned into the walls and could not be wiped away.

His lasting monument was the system he had imposed on the Russian people, but he had never shown any aversion to temporary monuments of bronze or iron. His statues were still standing all over Russia. He had given great thought to their construction and design, and shown a general preference for being represented in an attitude of meditation. There were only a few life-size sculptures of Lenin; there were thousands of Stalin. He liked to see himself larger than life. Two years before his death he signed a decree ordering that thirty-three tons of pure copper should be set aside for a statue of him to stand at the entrance of the Volga-Don Canal. The statue was to be a hundred feet high.

Many years passed before the statues came down; it was felt that they belonged to history and should not be disturbed. They portrayed the idealized figure of Stalin in his youthful middle age; there were no pockmarks on the skin, no withered arm. These statues represented an epoch which had passed away and acquired in reminiscence the proportions of legend.

·The first statue to fall was one in Budapest. It was of comparatively modest proportions: twenty-four feet high on a granite base which was itself thirty feet high. Cast in bronze by a Hungarian sculptor, it represented him in an unusually vigorous mood, one arm raised, the other falling to his side. He wore a military coat, knee boots, his legs planted firmly on the ground. Though it was the work of a mediocre sculptor, it was not therefore a work of mediocrity; its very size gave it compelling power. The inscription read: 'To the great Stalin from the grateful Hungarian people.'

On October 23rd, 1956, the first day of the Hungarian revolution, students and workmen streamed from all over Budapest towards the statue, whose very existence in their midst was an offense against humanity. With rope and tackle they intended to hurl it from its pedestal, but they had not counted on its solidity. A lasso was flung round the neck, but although fifty men pulled on the rope they were unable to topple it. So for about half an hour they pulled this way and that way without result, and then they summoned a young workman with an oxyacetylene lamp who climbed up the legs and melted the bronze knees. Then, by pulling on the ropes again, they were able to bring it crashing down on the stone steps at the base of the monument. The head was hacked off from the shoulders, and what was left was hauled through the streets by cheering mobs. Stalin was a sacrificial animal being led to the slaughter, but being headless and legless he lacked the dignity of an animal. On the granite platform there remained two jagged knee boots, each the size of a man.

In this symbolic way, with oxyacetylene flames, pickaxes, hammers and crowbars the tyrant was demolished and for a few days the Hungarians were able to breathe a cleaner air. They had not acted impulsively, but out of a desperate need to lay the stubborn ghost. When the Hungarian revolution came to an end, the Communist rulers of Hungary wisely decided not to re-erect the statue. The knee boots were removed, the top of the platform was levelled off, and military parades continued to be held beside the Stalin memorial, which had lost its reason for existence.

In other countries the sacrifice took longer to perform. In 1956 the Czech Communist Party completed one of the most grandiose of all Stalin memorials. The 18,000-ton monument dominated the city from the Letna hill. The statue of Stalin was 84 feet high. So vast a monument, constructed at so much expense of treasure, could not be lightly removed. Tentative plans were made to hide it, but it could not be hidden; there were attempts to camouflage it, but it could not be camouflaged. It had become part of the skyline of Prague, as firmly rooted as the Hradcany Castle. Finally in October 1962, a year after the body of Stalin had been removed from the Lenin mausoleum, it was decided to have recourse to drastic measures. The entire monument was blown up.

The statue of Stalin at the entrance to the Volga-Don Canal came down; so, too, did the enormous statue which looked down on Tiflis from the top of Mount Mtatsminda. A recent visitor to Georgia found the massive square pedestal still in place, with the inscription: TALIN. Someone had attempted to erase the name, and having obliterated the S he had grown weary of the task.

So it was throughout Russia and all the satellite states. Here and there a few portrait busts survived in dark corners of museums, but his image has vanished from the official *Outline History of the USSR* used as a textbook all over Russia, except for one small snapshot in which he is seen in the company of Lenin and Kalinin, and he received only passing mention in the great five-volume *History of the Great Fatherland War*. History was rewritten to give him no more than a minor place in the building of the Soviet Union, with the result that history became even more distorted than it had been in his lifetime.

In much the same way the Pharaohs erased the monuments of their predecessors, sometimes merely stamping their own names over the previous names, for all Pharaohs resembled one another. There was nothing new in the state which Stalin brought into being; it was as old as the Pyramids. Like the Pharaohs he murdered with shining impartiality and gave men nothing to live by except mindless obedience. Ruthless almost beyond belief, he killed millions, but this was not his greatest crime. His greatest crime was that he poisoned the sources of Russian life for an entire generation, and a hundred years may pass before the wells are purified.

What is strange is that he should have been permitted to live so long and that his murderous hypocrisy and criminality should have been permitted so large a scope. The phenomenon of the absolute tyrant was well known, it had been studied for centuries, and methods of dealing with it had been practised in the past. Aristotle had described the phenomenon at length, and in more than twenty-two centuries the beast had not changed his stripes:

If anyone raises his head too high, then the tyrant must lop it off, and he must destroy all men of spirit, and forbid common meals, clubs, education, and the like, and he must guard against anything which inspires courage and confidence among his subjects. He is bound to prohibit literary assemblies or any other meetings where discussions take place, and he must do his utmost to prevent people from knowing one another (for their acquaintance with one another brings about mutual confidence). He must compel all people staying in the city to appear in public and live at his gates; then he will know what they are doing. If he can keep them underfoot, they will learn humility. In this way he must contrive to be master of those arts which have been learned by the Persians and the barbarians, and for the same end. A tyrant should know what all his subjects are saying and doing, and he should use spies, like the 'female detectives' in Syracuse, and the eavesdroppers sent by Hiero to resorts and meetings, for the fear of informers prevents people from speaking their minds, and if they do, they are more easily discovered. Another art of the tyrant is to sow

quarrels among his subjects; friends should be made to attack friends, the people with the nobility, and the rich with one another. Also he should take care to impoverish his subjects; he thus provides against the maintenance of a guard by the citizens, while the people, kept at their hard labours, are prevented from conspiring against him. The Pyramids of Egypt afford an example of this policy ...
                                                   – *Politics*, V, 11

Again and again through history the phenomenon has been accurately described. Long before Freud, Plato observed 'the terrible, savage and lawless desires which exist in every man' but which especially exist in tyrants. Tyranny is the domination of men for no other purpose than to commit crimes.

There were no dimensions in Stalin's mind; there was only the bottomless desire to dominate. He ruled not with his head but with his withered arm, and corrupted everything he touched. 'I believe in only one thing, the power of the human will,' he told Walter Duranty, and for once he was speaking the truth. He did not believe in Marx or Lenin; he had no belief in the destiny of the people he ruled; he cared only for his own aggrandizement. In the end he walked with the deathly dignity and unapproachability of a man remote from the springs of life, giving orders mechanically, demanding more and more applause, surrounding himself with more and more images of himself, marching through a maze of mirrors with the imperiousness of the mad.

In Franz Kafka's story 'In the Penal Colony', the explorer learns that the Former Commandant is dead, but the penal colony still operates according to the laws he laid down. 'The organization of the colony was so perfect that his successor, even with a thousand new schemes in his head, would find it impossible to alter anything, at least for many years to come.' The executioner explains that he has taken over the government of the colony, but there has never been any need to change the regulations which he regards as his 'most perfect possessions'. Of course there have been some changes. The resources for maintaining the murder machine have been considerably reduced 'under a mild, new doctrine'.

The explorer asks to see the grave of the Former Commandant, and he is told that the priest would not let him be buried in the churchyard. 'Nobody knew where to bury him for a while, but in the end they buried him here.' At last they found the grave in a teahouse. There was an inscription in very small letters, and the explorer bent down to read it. It said:

Here rests the Former Commandant. His adherents, who must now be nameless, have dug this grave and set up this stone. There is a prophecy that after a certain number of years the Commandant will rise again and lead his adherents from this house to recover the colony. Have faith and wait!

APPENDICES

SELECTED BIBLIOGRAPHY

My chief debt is to the thirteen-volume edition of Stalin's *Collected Works* (*J. Stalin: Sochineniya*) published in Moscow between 1949 and 1952, and to the three official lives of Stalin by Henri Barbusse, Lavrenty Beria, and Emelian Yaroslavsky. Neither the *Collected Works* nor the official biographies are themselves reliable documents – on the contrary they are filled with deliberate distortions and errors – but they have the merit of showing Stalin as he saw himself, as he wanted others to see him, or as he thought history might be disposed to judge him. Happily Stalin showed no talent for dissimulation, and there is nearly always a catch in the voice or a sudden change of rhythm when he tells his more outrageous lies.

The *Collected Works* are far from complete. A number of documents included in it are forgeries, and he has sometimes claimed as his own documents written by others, but these are minor sins in a life given over to crime. The major sin is in the concealment and omission of documents known to exist, and in an occasional tampering with the evidence. That Stalin did not live to complete his *Collected Works* is not a matter of regret; and the omissions can be made up from other sources. The errors and distortions are palpable, and arise quite simply from his habit of claiming prophetic gifts far greater than those he actually possessed.

I owe a special debt to Boris Souvarine's pioneer study written when Stalin's career was still in mid-course, and to Trotsky's fragmentary and unfinished *Stalin*, though I differ from their conclusions. Souvarine's grave sense of the tragic workings of history gives him an authority lacking in Trotsky, whose bitterness was too personal to warrant sympathy. Perhaps because he was himself a tragic hero, Trotsky appears to have had little understanding of tragedy; and I found him often unreliable and tendentious, telling lies more glibly than Stalin.

Abramovich, Raphael R. *The Soviet Revolution*. New York, International Universities Press, 1962.

Alexandrov, Victor. *The Kremlin*. New York, St Martin's Press, 1963.

Alexandrova, Vera. *A History of Soviet Literature*. New York, Doubleday, 1963.

Allen, W. E. D. *A History of the Georgian People*. London, Kegan Paul, Trench, Trubner, 1932.

Astier, Emmanuel d'. *–Sur –Staline*. Paris, Librairie Plon, 1960.

Avtorkhanov, Abdurakhman. *Stalin and the Soviet Communist Party*. New York, Frederick A. Praeger, 1959.

Backer, George. *The Deadly Parallel*. New York, Random House, 1950.

Bajanov, Boris. *Avec Staline dans le Kremlin*. Paris, Les Editions de France, n.d.

Barbusse, Henri. *Stalin: A New World Seen through One Man*. New York, The Macmillan Company, 1935.

Barghorn, Frederick C. *Soviet Russian Nationalism*. New York, Oxford University Press, 1956.

Barmine, Alexander. *One Who Survived*. New York, G. P. Putnam's Sons, 1945.

Beck, F., and Godin, W. *The Russian Purge and the Extraction of Confessions*. London, Hurst and Blackett, 1951.

Beria, Lavrenty. *On the History of Bolshevik Organizations in Transcaucasia*. (*Stalin's Early Writings and Activities*.) Moscow, Foreign Languages Publishing House, 1949.

Bobrovskaya, Cecilia. *Twenty Years in Underground Russia*. Moscow, Co-operative Publishing Society of Foreign Workers of the USSR, n.d.

Bourke-White, Margaret. *Shooting the Russian War*. New York, Simon and Schuster, 1942.

Brzezinski, Zbigniew K. *The Permanent Purge*. Cambridge, Harvard University Press, 1956.

Buber, Martin. *Paths in Utopia*. Boston, Beacon Press, 1949.

Bukharin, Nikolay. *Historical Materialism: A System of Sociology*. New York, International Publishers, 1925.

Bullock, Alan. *Hitler, A Study in Tyranny*. New York, Harper and Brothers, 1960.

Bunyan, James, and Fisher, H. H. *The Bolshevik Revolution 1917–1918*. Stanford, Stanford University Press, 1934.

Byrnes, James F. *Speaking Frankly*. New York, Harper and Brothers, 1947.

Cassidy, Henry C. *Moscow Dateline*. Boston, Houghton Mifflin, 1943.

Churchill, Winston S. *The Second World War*, 6 vols. Boston, Houghton Mifflin, 1949–1953.

Coates, W. P. and Z. K. *The Soviet-Finnish Campaign.* London, Eldon Press, 1942.

Collard, Dudley. *Soviet Justice and the Trial of Radek and Others.* London, Victor Gollancz, 1937.

Correspondence between the Chairman of the Council of Ministers of the USSR and the Presidents of the USA and the Prime Ministers of Great Britain. Moscow, Foreign Languages Publishing House, 1957.

Daniels, Robert Vincent. *The Conscience of the Revolution.* Cambridge, Harvard University Press, 1960.

—— *A Documentary History of Communism.* New York, Random House, 1960.

Deane, John R. *The Strange Alliance.* New York, Viking Press, 1947.

Deborin, Grigory. *The Second World War.* Moscow, Progress Publishers, n.d.

Dedijer, Vladimir. *Tito.* New York, Simon and Schuster, 1953.

Delbars, Ives. *The Real Stalin.* London, George Allen and Unwin, 1953.

Deutscher, Isaac. *The Prophet Armed.* New York, Oxford University Press, 1954.

—— *The Prophet Unarmed.* New York, Oxford University Press, 1959.

—— *The Prophet Outcast.* New York, Oxford University Press, 1963.

—— *Stalin: A Political Biography.* New York, Oxford University Press, 1963.

Djilas, Milovan. *Conversations with Stalin.* New York, Harcourt, Brace and World, 1962.

Draper, Theodore. *American Communism and Soviet Russia.* New York, Viking Press, 1960.

Duranty, Walter. *The Kremlin and the People.* London, Hamish Hamilton, 1942.

—— *Stalin and Co.* New York, William Sloane Associates, 1949.

Feis, Herbert. *Between War and Peace: The Potsdam Conference.* Princeton, Princeton University Press, 1960.

—— *Churchill, Roosevelt, Stalin.* Princeton, Princeton University Press, 1957.

Fischer, George. *Soviet Opposition to Stalin.* Cambridge, Harvard University Press, 1952.

Footman, David. *The Civil War in Russia.* London, Faber and Faber, 1961.

Foreign Relations of the United States: The Conferences at Malta and Yalta. Washington, U.S. Government Printing Office, 1955.

Foreign Relations of the United States: The Conferences at Cairo and Teheran. Washington, U.S. Government Printing Office, 1961.

Gorky, Maxim, and others, editors. *Belomor: An Account of the Construction of the New Canal between the White Sea and the Baltic Sea.* New York, Harrison Smith and Robert Haas, 1935.

Goure, Leon. *The Siege of Leningrad.* New York, McGraw-Hill, 1964.

Granovski, Anatoli. *I Was an NKVD Agent.* New York, Devin-Adair, 1962.

Harriman, Averell. *Peace with Russia?* New York, Simon and Schuster, 1959.

Heisler, Francis. *The First Two Moscow Trials.* Chicago, Socialist Party USA, 1937.

Howard, Roy, and Stalin, J. V. *Is War Inevitable?* London, Friends of the Soviet Union, n.d.

Iremaschvili, Joseph. *Stalin und die Tragödie Georgiens.* Berlin, privately printed, 1932.

King, Ernest J., and Whitehill, Walter Muir. *Fleet Admiral King.* New York, W. W. Norton, 1952.

S. M. Kirov: 1866–1934. In Memoriam. Moscow, Co-operative Publishing Society, 1934.

Kournakoff, Sergei N. *Russia's Fighting Forces.* New York, International Publishers, 1942.

Krassin, Lubov. *Leonid Krassin: His Life and Work.* London, Skeffington, 1929.

Krylov, Ivan. *Soviet Staff Officer.* London, Falcon Press, 1951.

Lang, David M. *A Modern History of Soviet Georgia.* New York, Grove Press, 1962.

Lermolo, Elizabeth. *Face of a Victim.* New York, Harper and Brothers, 1955.

Levine, Isaac Don. *I Rediscover Russia.* New York, Duell, Sloan and Pierce, 1964.

—— *Stalin.* New York, Cosmopolitan Book Corporation, 1931.

Liddell Hart, B. H., editor. *The Red Army.* New York, Harcourt, Brace, 1956.

Ludwig, Emil. *Stalin.* New York, G. P. Putnam's Sons, 1942.

MacIlhone, R., editor. *Petrograd, October 1917.* Moscow, Foreign Languages Publishing House, 1957.

Maclean, Fitzroy. *Escape to Adventure*. Boston, Little, Brown, 1951.

—— *The Heretic: The Life and Times of Josip Tito-Broz*. New York, Harper and Brothers, 1957.

Malkov, P. *Reminiscences of a Kremlin Commandant*. Moscow, Progress Publishers, 1964.

Mehnert, Klaus. *Stalin versus Marx*. London, George Allen and Unwin, 1952.

Menon, K. P. S. *The Flying Troika*. London, Oxford University Press, 1963.

Molotov, V. M., and others. *Stalin: On the Occasion of his Sixtieth Birthday*. New York, Workers Library Publishers, 1940.

Montagu, Ivor. *Stalin: A Biographical Sketch*. London, Communist Party Press, 1942.

Murphy, J. T. *Stalin 1879–1944*. London, Bodley Head, 1945.

Nicolaevsky, Boris I., editor. *The Crimes of the Stalin Era*. New York, *The New Leader*, 1962.

Orlov, Alexander. *The Secret History of Stalin's Crimes*. New York, Random House, 1953.

Ouralov, Alexandre. *Staline au pouvoir*. Paris, Les Isles d'Or, n.d.

Pasternak, Boris. *I Remember: Sketch for an Autobiography*. New York, Pantheon, 1959.

Perkins, Frances. *The Roosevelt I Knew*. New York, Viking Press, 1946.

Petrov, Vladimir and Evdokia. *Empire of Fear*. London, André Deutsch, 1956.

Radek, Karl. *The Architect of Socialist Society*. Moscow, Cooperative Publishing Society of Foreign Workers in the USSR, 1934.

Rauch, Georg von. *A History of Soviet Russia*. New York, Frederick A. Praeger, 1957.

Reed, John. *Ten Days that Shook the World*. New York, Random House, 1960.

Report of Court Proceedings in the Case of the Anti-Soviet Bloc of Rights and Trotskyites ... Moscow, People's Commissariat of Justice of the USSR, 1938.

Report of Court Proceedings in the Case of the Anti-Soviet Trotskyite Centre ... Moscow, People's Commissariat of Justice of the USSR, 1937.

Report of Court Proceedings in the Case of the Trotskyite-

Zinovievite Terrorist Centre ... Moscow, People's Commissariat of Justice of the USSR, 1936.

Reshetar, John S. *A Concise History of the Communist Party of the Soviet Union.* New York, Frederick A. Praeger, 1960.

Reynolds, Quentin. *By Quentin Reynolds.* New York, McGraw-Hill, 1963.

Rossi, A. *The Russo-German Alliance.* Boston, Beacon Press, 1951.

Rush, Myron. *The Rise of Khrushchev.* Washington, Public Affairs Press, 1957.

Rusthaveli, Shotha. *The Knight in the Leopard Skin.* Translated by Marjory Scott Wardrop. New York, International Publishers, n.d.

Salisbury, Harrison E. *Moscow Journal.* Chicago, University of Chicago Press, 1961.

Schachtman, Max. *Behind the Moscow Trial.* New York, Pioneer Publishers, 1936.

Schweitzer, Vera. *Stalin during His Turukhansk Exile.* Moscow, Young Guard, 1943.

Serge, Victor. *From Lenin to Stalin.* New York, Pioneer Publishers, 1937.

—— *Memoires d'un revolutionaire.* Paris, Editions du Seuil, 1951.

—— *Russia Twenty Years After.* New York, Hillman-Curl, 1937.

Seton, Marie. *Sergei M. Eisenstein.* New York, A. A. Wyn, n.d.

Sherwood, Robert E. *Roosevelt and Hopkins.* New York, Harper and Brothers, 1948.

Shirer, William L. *The Rise and Fall of the Third Reich.* New York, Simon and Schuster, 1960.

Smith, Walter Bedell. *My Three Years in Moscow.* Philadelphia, J. B. Lippincott Company, 1950.

Souvarine, Boris. *Stalin: A Critical Survey of Bolshevism.* New York, Longmans, Green, 1939.

Stalin, J. V. *The Great Patriotic War of the Soviet Union.* New York, International Publishers, 1945.

—— *Leninism: Selected Writings.* New York, International Publishers, 1942.

—— *Speeches on the American Communist Party.* New York, Workers Library Publishers, n.d.

Standley, William H., and Agerton, Arthur A. *Admiral Ambassador to Russia.* Chicago, Henry Regnery, 1955.

Sukhanov, N. N. *The Russian Revolution 1917*. Translated by Joel Carmichael. New York, Harper and Brothers, 1962.

Tanner, Väinö. *The Winter War*. Stanford, Stanford University Press, 1957.

Tokaev, G. A. *Betrayal of an Ideal*. Bloomington, Indiana University Press, 1955.

—— *Comrade X*. London, Harvill Press, 1956.

—— *Stalin Means War*. London, Weidenfeld and Nicolson, 1951.

Trevor-Roper, H. R. *The Last Days of Hitler*. New York, Macmillan Company, 1947.

Trotsky, Leon. *The History of the Russian Revolution*. Ann Arbor, University of Michigan Press, 1960.

—— *My Life*. New York, Grosset and Dunlop, 1960.

—— *Stalin: An Appraisal of the Man and His Influence*. New York, Harper and Brothers, 1941.

—— *The Stalin School of Falsification*. New York, Pioneer Publishers, 1962.

—— *Terrorism and Communism*. Ann Arbor, University of Michigan Press, 1961.

—— *Trotsky's Diary in Exile 1935*. Cambridge, Harvard University Press, 1958.

—— and others. *The Twentieth Congress and World Trotskyism*. London, New Park Publications, 1957.

Voroshilov, K. E. *Stalin and the Armed Forces of the USSR*. Moscow, Foreign Languages Publishing House, 1951.

Werth, Alexander. *Leningrad*. New York, Alfred Knopf, 1944.

—— *Russia at War*. New York, E. P. Dutton, 1964.

—— *The Year of Stalingrad*. London, Hamish Hamilton, 1946.

Whitney, Thomas P., editor. *Khrushchev Speaks*. Ann Arbor, University of Michigan Press, 1960.

Willkie, Wendell L. *One World*. New York, Simon and Schuster, 1943.

Windecke, Christian. *L'Ascension de Staline*. Paris, Delachaux et Niestlé, 1945.

Wipper, R. *Ivan Grozny*. Moscow, Foreign Languages Publishing House, 1947.

Wolfe, Bertram D. *Khrushchev and Stalin's Ghost*. New York, Frederick A. Praeger, 1957.

—— *Three Who Made a Revolution*. New York, Dial Press, 1955.

Yaroslavsky, E. *Landmarks in the Life of Stalin*. London, Lawrence and Wishart, 1942.

Yevtushenko, Evgeny. *A Precocious Autobiography*. New York, E. P. Dutton, 1963.

Young, Gordon. *Stalin's Heirs*. London, Derek Verschoyle, 1953.

In Russian

Alliluiev, Sergey. *Proidenniye Put*. Moscow, Gosudarstvennoe Izdatelstvo, 1946.

Alliluieva, Anna S. *Vospominaniya*. Moscow, Gosudarstvennoe Izdatelstvo, 1946.

Arkhangorodskaya, N. S., editor. *Velikiy Oktyabr: Sbornik Statei*. Moscow, Izdatelstvo Akademii Nauk SSSR, 1961.

Arkomed, S. T. *Rabocheye Dvizheniye i Sotsial-Demokratiya na Kavkaze*. Moscow, Gosudarstvennoe Izdatelstvo, 1923.

Arsenidze, Razden. *Iz Vospominanii o Staline*. Novy Zhurnal, June 1963.

Cherkasov, N. K. *Zapiski sovyetskovo aktera*. Moscow, Gosudarstvennoe Izdatelstvo, 1953.

Dokumenti o geoicheskoi oborone Tsaritsyna 1918 gody. Moscow, Gospolimizdat, 1942.

Institut Istorii Partii, editor. *Petrogradskiye Bolsheviki v Oktyabskoi Revolutsii*. Leningrad, Lenizdat, 1957.

Kasbeki, Aleksandr. *Izbranniye Proizvedeniya*. Tbilisi, Izdatelstvo Varya Vostoka, 1957.

Koritzin, N. I., editor. *Marshal Tukhachevsky*. Moscow, Voennoe Izdatelstvo, 1965.

Krupskaya, N. K. *O Lenine*. Moscow, Gosudarstvennoe Izdatelstvo, 1960.

Lakoba, N., editor. *Stalin i Khashim*. Sukhum, n.p., 1934.

Oborona Tsaritsyna: Sbornik Statei i dokumentov. Stalingrad, Kraevoe knigoizdatelstvo, 1937.

Pervaya Konnaya. Moscow, Ogiz-Izogiz, 1938.

Pospelov, P. N. and others. ed. *Istoriya Velikoi Otechestvennoi voini Sovyetskovo Soyuza 1941–1945*. Moscow, Voennoe Izdatelstvo, 1961–1963.

——— *Vladimir Ilyich Lenin*. Moscow, Gosudarstvennoe Izdatelstvo, 1960.

Semashko, Nikolai A. *Vospominaniya o Lenine*. Moscow, Partizdat, 1937.

Schweitzer, Vera. *Stalin v Turukhanskom Ssylke*. Moscow, Molodaya Gvardiya, 1940.

Sverdlov, Y. M. *Izbranniye Proizvedeniya*. Moscow, Gosudarstvennoe Izdatelstvo, 1957.

Sverdlova, K. T. *Yakov Mikhailovich Sverdlov*. Moscow, Molodaya Gvardiya, 1960.

Voznesensky, N. *Voennaya Ekonomika SSSR v period otechestvennoi Voini*. Moscow, Gosudarstvennoe Izdatelstvo, 1948.

Yevtushenko, Evgeny. *Nasledniki Stalina*. London, Flegon Press, n.d.

CHAPTER NOTES

INTRODUCTION

P. 13   Evgeny Yevtushenko, *Nasledniki*, p. 4.

THE KNIGHT IN THE LEOPARD SKIN

PP. 24–25   Shotha Rusthaveli, *The Knight in the Leopard Skin*, pp. 53, 58, 116, 118, 165, 168, 218, 219, 233, 243.

THE CHILDHOOD OF JOSEPH DJUGASHVILI

P. 35   Anna Alliluieva, *Vospominaniya*, p. 167.

P. 37   Joseph Iremaschvili, *Stalin und die Tragödie Georgiens*, p. 5.

PP. 38–39   Aleksandr Kasbeki, *Izbranniye Proizvedeniya*, I, 107–279.

PP. 41–42   E. Yaroslavsky, *Landmarks in the Life of Stalin*, p. 9.

SEMINARIAN AND POET

P. 45   Joseph Iremaschvili, *Stalin und die Tragödie Georgiens*, p. 16.

P. 47   The Georgian text of the poem 'Morning' was kindly given to me by Mr George Gamkrelidse.

P. 48   The Georgian text of the poem 'To the Moon' is reproduced from *Iveria*, October 11th, 1895, from the copy in the British Museum.

P. 50   The poem 'Sesia's Thoughts', translated by Venera Ushadze, appears in David M. Lang, *A Modern History of Soviet Georgia*, p. 102.

P. 51   The poem 'To R. Eristavi' is reproduced from a miniature photograph in M. Kelendjeridze, *Stikhy Yunovo Stalina*, in *Razkazy o Velikom Stalinie*, p. 68.

P. 54   E. Yaroslavsky, *Landmarks in the Life of Stalin*, pp. 16, 17.

PP. 55–56   J. Iremaschvili, *Stalin und die Tragödie Georgiens*, p. 19.

P. 57   E. Yaroslavsky, *Landmarks in the Life of Stalin*, p. 16.

PP. 57–58   E. Yaroslavsky, *Landmarks in the Life of Stalin*, p. 17.

THE YOUNG AGITATOR

P. 61   *Sochineniya*, I, 416–17.
P. 64   Henri Barbusse, *Stalin*, pp. 17–18.
PP. 66–67   E. Yaroslavsky, *Landmarks in the Life of Stalin*, p. 27.
PP. 70–71   *Sochineniya*, I, 21–22.
P. 73   *Sochineniya*, I, 27.
P. 74   Sergey Alliluiev, *Proidenniye Put*, p. 81.
PP. 75–76   S. T. Arkomed, *Rabocheye Dvizheniye*, p. 347.

THE CONSPIRATOR

P. 78   N. Lakoba, *Stalin i Khashim*, pp. 25, 27, passim.
P. 80   E. Yaroslavsky, *Landmarks in the Life of Stalin*, p. 30.
P. 80   Police description of arrest appears in photograph of the original document in the Radio Times Hulton Picture Library, London. It is smudged in places, and cannot be reproduced easily.
PP. 81–82   Police report is given in Boris Souvarine, *Stalin*, p. 44.
PP. 82–83   J. Iremaschvili, *Stalin und die Tragödie Georgiens*, p. 28.
PP. 87–88   *Sochineniya*, VI, 52–53.

THE REVOLUTIONARY

P. 96   *Sochineniya*, I, 57–58.
P. 97   *Sochineniya*, I, 60–61.
P. 99   J. Iremaschvili, *Stalin und die Tragödie Georgiens*, pp. 30, 39.
PP. 101–2   R. Arsenidze: *Iz Vospominanii o Staline*, in *Novy Zhurnal*, June 1963, pp. 218–19.
P. 102   L. Beria, *On the History of the Bolshevik Organizations in Transcaucasia*, p. 100. Not included in the *Sochineniya*.
PP. 102–3   L. Beria, *ibid.*, pp. 109–10. Not included in the *Sochineniya*.
PP. 104–5   E. Yaroslavsky, *Landmarks in the Life of Stalin*, pp. 38–39.

P. 108   *Sochineniya*, VI, 52-53.

THE EXPROPRIATOR

P. 112   *Sochineniya*, I, 310.
P. 113   *Sochineniya*, II, 50–52.
P. 120   Emil Ludwig, *Stalin*, p. 42.
P. 120   R. Arsenidze, *Novy Zhurnal*, June 1963, p. 233.
P. 120   Trotsky, *Stalin*, p. 101.
P. 121   J. Iremaschvili, *Stalin und die Tragödie Georg-iens*, p. 37.

THE GREY BLUR

P. 183   Lenin: *Revolution of 1917*, II, 380.
P. 184   *Sochineniya*, III, 38.
P. 186   *Sochineniya*, VIII, 175.
P. 190   *Sochineniya*, III, 100.

THE JULY DAYS

PP. 193–94   *Sochineniya*, III, 166.
P. 196   *Preparing for October*, p. 27.
P. 197   *Preparing for October*, p. 28.
P. 198   (We argued ...) Trotsky, *History of the Russian Revolution*, I, 281.

ON THE EVE

P. 203   *Petrograd, October 1917*, p. 341.
P. 208   *Sochineniya*, III, 381.

COMMISSAR

P. 215   John Reed, *Ten Days that Shook the World*, pp. 87–88.
P. 216   *Petrograd, October 1917*, pp. 343–44.
P. 217   *History of the Civil War in the USSR*, II, 221.
PP. 218–20   J. Bunyan, H. H. Fisher, *The Bolshevik Revolution*, pp. 282–83.
P. 222   *Sochineniya*, IV, 4–5.
PP. 224–25   *Sochineniya*, VI, 63.

TSARITSYN

P. 229   *Sochineniya*, IV, 118.
P. 233   *Sochineniya*, IV, 127.

PP. 234–35   E. Yaroslavsky, *Landmarks in the Life of Stalin,* p. 113.
P. 236   *Sochineniya,* IV, 127.
P. 238   *Sochineniya,* IV, 128.
P. 239   Trotsky, *Stalin,* pp. 288–89.
P. 240   Trotsky, *Stalin,* p. 289.

TROUBLE SHOOTER

P. 242   Lenin: *Sochineniya* XXIX, 515.
PP. 242–43   Trotsky, *Stalin,* p. 293.
P. 243   *Sochineniya,* IV, 186–89.
P. 245   Trotsky, *Stalin,* p. 294.
P. 247   *Sochineniya,* IV, 203–4.
P. 248   *Sochineniya,* IV, 224.
P. 251   *Sochineniya,* IV, 250.

THE CONQUEROR OF KRASNAYA GORKA

P. 254   *Sochineniya,* IV, 261.
PP. 255–56   *Sochineniya,* IV, 263–64.
P. 257   K. Y. Voroshilov, *Stalin and the Armed Forces of the USSR,* pp. 31–32.
P. 258   *Sochineniya,* IV, 272.
PP. 261-62   *Sochineniya,* IV, 275.
PP. 265–66   K. Y. Voroshilov, *Stalin and the Armed Forces of the USSR,* pp. 61–63.
PP. 266–67   *Pervaya Konnaya,* p. 100.
P. 268   *Pervaya Konnaya,* p. 106.

GENERAL SECRETARY

PP. 269–70   *Joseph Stalin, A Political Biography,* p. 45.
PP. 270–71   *Stalin on His Sixtieth Birthday,* pp. 31–32.
P. 274   *Sochineniya,* IV, 366.
P. 276   *Sochineniya,* IV, 393.
P. 277   *Sochineniya,* IV, 410.
PP. 278–79   *Sochineniya,* V, 50.
PP. 282–83   David M. Lang, *A Modern History of Soviet Georgia,* pp. 238–39.
PP. 282–83   *Sochineniya,* V, 95.
PP. 284–85   Lenin: *Sochineniya* XLV, 122.

LENIN GATHERS HIS FORCES

PP. 292–93   Trotsky, *Stalin Falsifies History,* pp. 231–32. See also Lenin: *Sochineniya* XLV, 211–13.

P. 293   Trotsky, *Stalin Falsifies History*, p. 232.
PP. 296–97   Lenin: *Sochineniya* XLV, 458–66.

The Bombshells

PP. 300–1   Lenin: *Sochineniya* XLV, 338.
P. 302   Quoted by Khrushchev at the Twentieth Congress. B. I. Nicolaevsky, *The Crimes of the Stalin Era*, pp. 10–11.
PP. 304–5   Lenin: *Sochineniya* XLV, 344.
PP. 305–6   Lenin: *Sochineniya* XLV, 346.
PP. 308–9   Lenin: *Sochineniya* XLV, 477–78.
PP. 311–13   Lenin: *Sochineniya* XLV, 485–86.
P. 313   B. I. Nicolaevsky, *The Crimes of the Stalin Era*, pp. 11–12.
P. 314   Trotsky, *Stalin*, p. 361. (T. 787)
P. 315   Trotsky, *Stalin*, p. 361 (T. 788)

The Fight for Power

P. 321   (A Georgian ...) Lenin: *Sochineniya* XLV, 360.
P. 321   (Only a moment .,.) *The Twentieth Century and World Trotskyism*, p. 119.
P. 322   *Ibid.*, p. 112.
P. 323   *Ibid.*, p. 120.
P. 324   *Ibid.*, pp. 120–21.
PP. 327–28   Trotsky, *Stalin*, p. 363.
PP. 328–29   *Sochineniya*, V, 232.
PP. 331–32   *Sochineniya*, VII, 387, where the names of Rykov, Trotsky and Bukharin are omitted.

The Death of Lenin

P. 337   (When I read ...) Lenin: *Sochineniya* XLV, 717.
P. 337   Walter Duranty, *I Write as I Please*, pp. 217–18.
P. 338   Krupskaya, *O Lenine: Sbornik Statei*, p. 74.
P. 340   N. Semashko, *Vospominaniya o Lenine*, III, 340–41.
PP. 343–44   Yves Delbars, *The Real Stalin*, pp. 129–30.
PP. 344–45   Ermolo, *Face of a Victim*, pp. 156–57.
P. 345   (Nothing indicated ...) *Izvestiya*, January 24th, 1924.

THE STOLEN TESTAMENT

P. 351   *Sochineniya*, VI, 419.
PP. 351–52   *Sochineniya*, VI, 46–51.
PP. 354–55   Lenin: *Sochineniya* XLV, 594.
P. 355   Boris Bajanov, *Avec Staline dans le Kremlin*, pp. 43–44.
P. 360   (A clairvoyant who divines ...) *Sochineniya*, VI, 61.
P. 361   (indomitable force which ...) *Sochineniya*, VI, 187.
P. 362   *Sochineniya*, VI, 321.

THE MAN WHO NEVER STOOPS

P. 363   (Neither in ...) *Sochineniya*, VI, 329.
P. 365   *Sochineniya*, VII, 15.
P. 367   Vera Alexandrova, *A History of Soviet Literature*, p. 164.
P. 367   (Perhaps it is indeed ...) *Sochineniya*, VII, 250.
PP. 367–68   *Sochineniya*, VII, 44–45.
P. 368   (By means of agreements ...) *Sochineniya*, VII, 177.
P. 368   (Those who think ...) *Sochineniya*, VII, 341.
P. 368   E. H. Carr, *A History of Soviet Russia*, II, p. 138.
P. 369   *Ibid.*, p. 161.
PP. 371–72   *The Last Words of Adolf Joffe*, pp. 1, 4–6.

DIZZY WITH SUCCESS

PP. 377–78   (To choose one's victim ...) Boris Souvarine, *Stalin*, pp. 482–85. Also Victor Serge, *From Lenin to Stalin*, pp. 90–91, and Trotsky, *Diary in Exile*, p. 64.
P. 378   (If the leaders at the top ...) *Sochineniya*, XI, 31.
P. 379   (Let me see you dance ...) *Sochineniya*, XII, 90.
PP. 379–80   *Sochineniya*, XI, 1–4.
P. 382   Winston Churchill, *The Hinge of Fate*, pp. 434–435.
P. 383   See also Frederick L. Schuman, *Russia since 1917*, who gives figures for 1933.
P. 384   *Sochineniya*, XII, 192.

P. 384   Martin Buber, *Paths in Utopia*, p. 127.
P. 386   *Sochineniya*, XII, 140.
P. 387   *Stalin's Speeches on the American Communist Party*, pp. 13, 15.
P. 387   *Ibid.*, p. 20.

A ROOM IN THE KREMLIN

P. 396   Emil Ludwig, *Stalin*, p. 123.
P. 397   *Ibid.*, p. 84.
PP. 398–99   *Ibid.*, p. 175.
P. 400   (Fate is contrary to law ...) Ludwig, *Stalin*, p. 238; *Sochineniya*, XIII, 122.
P. 400   Emil Ludwig, *Stalin*, p. 7.

DEATH AND THE MAIDEN

PP. 405–6   *Sochineniya*, XII, 173.
P. 413   *Sochineniya*, XIII, 142.
P. 414   On the death of Maxim Gorky see especially *Notes of an Old Bolshevik*, p. 53, Orlov, *The Secret History of Stalin's Crimes*, p. 275, and *Stalin: On His Sixtieth Birthday*, p. 154.

DEATH OF NADEZHDA ALLILUIEVA

PP. 421–22   Lermolo, *Face of a Victim*, pp. 227–29.

THE MASSACRES

P. 437   (The method of ...) *Sochineniya*, VII, 380.
P. 438   (To NKVD ...) Petrov, *Empire of Fear*, p. 73.

THE MURDER OF KIROV

PP. 449–50   *S. M. Kirov: In Memoriam*, pp. 10–11.
P. 451   *Ibid.*, p. 3.
P. 453   Lermolo, *Face of a Victim*, p. 12.
PP. 453–54   *Ibid.*, pp. 23–25.
P. 456   K. T. Sverdlova, *Yakov Mikhailovich Sverdlov*, pp. 420–21.

THE RITUALS OF TERROR

P. 460   Bertram D. Wolfe, *Khrushchev and Stalin's Ghost*, p. 191.
P. 462   *Sochineniya*, XIII, 211.

The Trial of Zinoviev and Kamenev

P. 472	*Official Report on Trial of Zinoviev*, p. 81.
P. 473	*Ibid.*, p. 83.
P. 474	*Ibid.*, p. 92.
P. 475	(I became blind ...) *Ibid.*, pp. 147–48.
PP. 477–78	Victor Serge, *From Lenin to Stalin*, pp. 81–82.

The Great Stalin Constitution

P. 480	*Sochineniya*, XIII, 178.
P. 481	Ouralov, *Staline au pouvoir*, p. 39.
PP. 482–83	B. I. Nicolaevsky, *The Crimes of the Stalin Era,* p. 23.
P. 487	*Stalin–Roy Howard Interview*, pp. 12–13.
P. 489	Stalin, *Leninism*, pp. 389–90.
PP. 490–91	Stalin, *Leninism*, p. 391.

The Trial of Radek

PP. 493–94	Karl Radek, *The Architect of Socialist Society*, p. 64.
P. 495	*Official Report on the Radek Trial*, pp. 31–32.
PP. 499–500	*Ibid.*, p. 543.
P. 500	Lenin: *Sochineniya* XXVII, 372.
P. 505	*Pravda*, January 31st, 1937.

The Murder of the General Staff

PP. 507–8	*Pravda*, March 29th, 1937.
P. 514	Alexander Barmine. *One Who Survived*, p. 219.
PP. 518–19	Vladimir Petrov, *Empire of Fear*, p. 73.
P. 521	Boris Pasternak, *I Remember*, p. 147.

The Trial of Bukharin

P. 524	Victor Alexandrov, *The Kremlin*, pp. 290–91.
P. 530	*Official Report of the Bukharin Trial*, p. 66.
PP. 532–33	*Ibid.*, p. 157.
P. 534	(I plead guilty ...) *Ibid.*, p. 370.
PP. 534–35	*Ibid.*, p. 399.
PP. 535–56	*Ibid.*, p. 421.
P. 537	*Ibid.*, p. 376.
P. 538	*Ibid.*, pp. 777–78.
P. 538	Trotsky, *My Life*, p. 383.

THE STRANGE ALLIANCE

P. 543   Stalin, *Report on the Work of the Central Committee to the Eighteenth Congress*, pp. 36–37.
P. 545   *Ibid*, p. 12.
P. 547   William L. Shirer, *The Rise and Fall of the Third Reich*, p. 704.
P. 549   A. Rossi, *The Russo-German Alliance*, pp. 40–41.

THE WINTER WAR

PP. 554–55   Vaino Tanner, *The Winter War*, p. 27.
PP. 555–56   *Ibid.*, p. 30.
PP. 558–59   *Ibid.*, pp. 75–76.
P. 562   *The Conferences at Cairo and Teheran*, p. 553.
P. 564   Yves Delbars, *The Real Stalin*, pp. 265–66.

INVASION

P. 571   William H. Standley, *Admiral Ambassador to Russia*, p. 429.
P. 572   Winston Churchill, *The Grand Alliance*, p. 324.
P. 576   Robert E. Sherwood, *Roosevelt and Hopkins*, p. 333.
P. 578   Ivor Montagu, *Stalin: A Biographical Sketch*, p. 30.
PP. 583–84   *The Great Patriotic War*, pp. 31–32.
P. 584   *Ibid.*, p. 29.
PP. 584–85   *Fatherland War*, II, 254.

GENERALISSIMO

P. 588   *Khrushchev Speaks*, p. 254.
PP. 589–90   *Ibid.*, pp. 240–41.
P. 596   Henry C. Cassidy, *Moscow Deadline*, p. 249.
P. 599   *Ibid.*, pp. 355–56.
P. 601   *The Great Patriotic War*, p. 104.

TWO CONFERENCES

PP. 607–8   Frances Perkins, *The Roosevelt I Knew*, p. 85.
PP. 608–9   *Ibid.*, pp. 84–85.
P. 612   James F. Byrnes, *Speaking Frankly*, pp. 36–37, where part of this speech is given to Churchill. It is clear from Churchill's own account in

Triumph and Tragedy, p. 304, and from the notes of Bohlen and Hiss in *The Conferences at Malta and Yalta*, pp. 661, 675, that the entire speech was spoken by Stalin.

PP. 613–14   *The Conferences at Malta and Yalta*, p. 681.

THE END OF HITLER

P. 623   Robert E. Sherwood, *Roosevelt and Hopkins*, p. 892.

IVAN THE TERRIBLE

P. 632   *The Great Patriotic War*, pp. 241–42.
P. 638   *Voprosy Istorii*, No. 2, 1947, p. 7.
PP. 640–41   G. A. Tokaev, *Comrade X*, pp. 324–26. See also Tokaev, *Stalin Means War*, pp. 112–14.
PP. 642–43   N. K. Cherkasov, *Zapiski sovyetskovo aktera*, p. 380.
P. 644   Marie Seton, *Sergei M. Eisenstein*, p. 462.

GLORY TO GREAT STALIN

PP. 650–51   Milovan Djilas, *Conversations with Stalin*, p. 161.
P. 653   N. Voznesensky, *Voennaya Ekonomika SSSR v period otechestvennoi Voini*, p. 185.
P. 654   *The New Leader*, February 1959 (Richard Lowenthal).
PP. 655–56   Fitzroy Maclean, *The Heretic*, p. 331.

THE FAG END OF THE TRIUMPH

P. 666   Stalin, *Marxism and Linguistics*, pp. 27–28.
P. 667   *Ibid.*, p. 43.
P. 670   Stalin, *Economic Problems of Socialism*, p. 26.
P. 671   *Ibid.*, pp. 33–34.
P. 673   *Ibid.*, p. 41.
P. 676   Stalin, *Speech at the Nineteenth Party Congress*, p. 14.

THE CHILL OF WINTER

PP. 684–85   K. P. S. Menon, *The Flying Troika*, p. 27.

THE FIRST DEATH

P. 699   Evgeny Yevtushenko, *A Precocious Autobiography*, pp. 84–85.

The Second Death

PP. 711–12   Averell Harriman, *Peace with Russia*, pp. 102–3.
P. 712   Emmanuel d'Astier, *Sur Staline*, p. 165.
P. 712   *Ibid.*, pp. 165–66.
P. 715   *Paris Match*, March 30th, 1963.
P. 718–19   *Atlas*, March 1962. The Khrushchev-Commin version is given in Bertram D. Wolfe, *Khrushchev and Stalin's Ghost*, pp. 316–17.

Descent into Hell

PP. 721–22   *Pravda*, March 11th, 1953.
P. 725   *Khrushchev Speaks*, pp. 440–41.
PP. 726–27   *Khrushchev Speaks*, pp. 438–39.
P. 729   *Pravda*, October 31st, 1961.
PP. 730–32   Evgeny Yevtushenko, *Nasledniki Stalina*, pp. 4–5.

CHRONOLOGICAL TABLE

All dates are given in the New Style. Up to February 1918 the Russians customarily employed an archaic system which differed by about thirteen days from the system employed in the West. Hence the occasional references to the February and October revolutions which occurred according to the Western calender in March and November.

1879	December 21	Birth of Joseph Vissarionovich Djugashvili (Stalin).
1894	June	Leaves Gori Parochial School. In autumn enters Theological Seminary at Tiflis.
1895	January	Stalin's first poem is published.
1898	March 13–15	First Congress of Russian Social Democratic Labour Party held at Minsk.
1899	May 29	Stalin expelled from Theological Seminary.
1899	December 28	Stalin employed at Tiflis Observatory.
1900	April 23	Stalin makes first public speech at Salt Lake near Tiflis.
1901	March 21	Stalin's apartment raided by police.
1901	May 5	Stalin takes part in demonstrations at Tiflis.
1901	Autumn	Stalin's first writings appear in *Brdzola*.
1901	December	Stalin leaves Tiflis for Batum.
1902	March 22	Riots in Batum.
1902	April 18	Stalin arrested for the first time.
1903	August 17	Lado Kestkhoveli killed in prison.
1903	July 30– August 23	Second Congress of the Russian Social Democratic Labour Party held in London.
1903	Autumn	Stalin exiled for three years in Siberia.
1904	January 18	Stalin escapes from Novaya Uda, Irkutsk *guberniya*.

1904	June 22?	Stalin marries Ekaterina Svanidze.
1904	December 13–31	Strike of oil workers in Baku.
1905	January 22	Bloody Sunday in St Petersburg.
1905	April 25–May 10	Third Congress of the Russian Social Democratic Labour Party held in London.
1905	June 27	Mutiny on cruiser *Potemkin*.
1905	December 16	Tsarist government arrests St Petersburg Soviet.
1905	December 25–30	Stalin attends Bolshevik Conference in Tammerfors, Finland.
1906	April 15	Stalin arrested and released following raid on Avlabar printing plant.
1906	Winter	Stalin writes *Anarchism or Socialism?*
1907	April 10	Death of Ekaterina Svanidze.
1907	May 13–June 1	Fifth Congress of the Russian Social Democratic Labour Party held in London, the last until the Revolution of 1917. Stalin attends the conference, but takes no part.
1907	June 26	Kamo in charge of the Tiflis expropriation on Erivan Square.
1907	August 28	Murder of Prince Ilya Chavchavadze.
1908	April 7	Stalin arrested in Baku.
1908	May 28	Archbishop Nikon murdered.
1908	November 22	Stalin leaves Bailov prison for exile in Solvychegodsk.
1909	July 6	Stalin escapes from Solvychegodsk.
1910	April 5	Stalin arrested in Baku.
1910	October 6	Stalin again exiled to Solvychegodsk.
1911	July 19	Stalin returns to St Petersburg after the expiration of his term of exile.
1911	September 22	Stalin arrested in St Petersburg.
1911	December 27	Stalin exiled to Vologda for three years.
1912	February	Stalin is co-opted on the Central Committee of the Bolshevik Party.

1912	March 13	He escapes from Vologda.
1912	April	Works on *Pravda*.
1912	May 5	Arrested in St Petersburg.
1912	July 14	Exiled to Narym.
1912	September 13	Escapes from Narym.
1912	November–December	Goes to Cracow to receive instructions from Lenin.
1913	January 10–14	Attends 'February' Conference at Cracow.
1913	January–February	Visits Vienna and works on *Marxism and the Nationalities Question*.
1913	March 7	Stalin arrested for last time.
1913	July 15	He is sentenced to exile for four years in Turukhansk.
1914	August 1	Germany declares war on Russia.
1915	May–June	Defeat of Russian troops in Galicia.
1915	Summer	Kamenev and Bolshevik deputies exiled to Turukhansk. Stalin visits Monastyrskoye.
1916	December	Stalin summoned to Krasnoyarsk to report for military service.
1917	March 8	February Revolution.
1917	March 25	Stalin and Kamenev arrive in St Petersburg.
1917	April 16	Lenin arrives in St Petersburg.
1917	May 17	Trotsky arrives in St Petersburg.
1917	May 18	Formation of the First Coalition Provisional Government.
1917	July 16–17	The July Days.
1917	July 24	Stalin and Sergo Alliluiev help Lenin to escape to Sestroretsk.
1917	October 20	Lenin arrives in Petrograd from Vyborg.
1917	October 23	Lenin, at Sukhanov's apartment, announces that the time for an uprising is 'fully ripe'. Stalin present at the meeting.
1917	November 7	October Revolution.
1917	November 9	Stalin appointed Commissar of Nationalities.
1917	November 15	Decree on Rights of Nationalities signed by Lenin and Stalin.

1917	November 22–23	Lenin negotiates by telegraph with General Dukhonin.
1917	November 27	Stalin in Helsinki.
1917	December 20	Decree organizing the Cheka.
1918	March 10–11	Transfer of Soviet government to Moscow.
1918	March 14–16	Ratification of Brest Litovsk Peace Treaty.
1918	May 31	Stalin placed in charge of grain procurement in the south.
1918	July 10	Stalin appoints Voroshilov to command Tsaritsyn front.
1918	August 30	Assassination of Uritsky in Petrograd; attempted assassination of Lenin in Moscow; beginning of the Red Terror.
1918	October 5	Trotsky insists on Stalin's recall from Tsaritsyn.
1919	January 5	Stalin accompanied by Dzerzhinsky arrives in Vyatka.
1919	March 24	Stalin marries Nadezhda Alliluieva.
1919	June 18	Capture of Krasnaya Gorka.
1919	November	Order of Red Banner awarded to Stalin.
1920	April 26	Polish Army invades Russia.
1920	May 7	Soviet government signs treaty of friendship with Georgia.
1920	August 17	Red Army retreats from Warsaw.
1920	December	Stalin in hospital.
1921	February	Stalin orders invasion of Georgia.
1921	March 18	Kronstadt mutiny suppressed.
1922	May 26	Lenin has first stroke.
1922	December 16	Lenin has second stroke. Zinoviev, Kamenev and Stalin form a triumvirate.
1922	December 25	Lenin dictates his Testament.
1923	March 5–6	Lenin threatens to break off comradely relations with Stalin.
1923	March 6–7	Lenin appeals to Trotsky for help against Stalin.
1923	March 9	Lenin has his third stroke.

1923	April 17–25	Twelfth Party Congress. Stalin emerges as most powerful figure in the Congress.
1923	May 12	Lenin leaves Kremlin and stays permanently at Gorky.
1923	September–October	Kislovodsk Cave Conference.
1924	January 18	Trotsky leaves Moscow for Sukhum.
1924	January 21	Death of Lenin.
1924	January 26	Stalin reads oath of loyalty to the memory of Lenin.
1925	April	Trotsky removed from Commissariat of War, succeeded by Frunze.
1925	April	Tsaritsyn renamed Stalingrad.
1925	April 27–29	Fourteenth Party Congress. Stalin breaks with Zinoviev and Kamenev, and forms alliance with Bukharin and Rykov.
1925	November	Death of Frunze. Voroshilov becomes Commissar of War.
1926	January	Kirov succeeds Zinoviev in Leningrad.
1926	October 23	Kamenev and Trotsky expelled from Politburo, Zinoviev from Third International.
1927	November 7	Parades in Moscow against Stalin.
1927	November 16	Suicide of Adolf Joffe.
1928	January	Stalin tours Siberia.
1928	January 16	Trotsky exiled to Alma-Ata.
1928	July 11	Secret meeting between Kamenev and Bukharin.
1929	January 18	Trotsky banished from the Soviet Union.
1929	July 3	Bukharin expelled from Third International.
1929	December 21	Celebration of Stalin's fiftieth birthday.
1930	February 23	Stalin receives second Order of the Red Banner.
1930	December 20	Molotov becomes Chairman of Council of People's Commissars.

1931	October 11	Stalin and Voroshilov call on Maxim Gorky.
1931	December 13	Stalin interviewed by Emil Ludwig.
1932	November 9	Death of Nadezhda Alliluieva.
1933	June 20	White Sea–Baltic Canal opened.
1934	December 1	Assassination of Kirov.
1935	January 15–16	Trial of Zinoviev, Kamenev and others for complicity in assassination of Kirov. All sentenced to imprisonment.
1935	Spring	Second Kamenev trial held in secret.
1935	August 30–31	Stakhanov cuts 102 tons of coal in 6 hours, becoming the first 'Stakhanovite' worker.
1936	March 1	Roy Howard interview with Stalin.
1936	June 18	Death of Maxim Gorky.
1936	August 19–24	Trial of Zinoviev and Kamenev, who are immediately executed.
1936	September 25	Stalin sends telegram from Sochi appointing Yezhov as Commissar for Internal Affairs.
1936	November 25	Stalin delivers formal speech on Stalin Constitution.
1936	December	Stalin Constitution becomes law.
1937	January 23–30	Trial of Radek.
1937	February 18	Death of Ordjonikidze.
1937	June 2?	Execution of Tukhachevsky and other generals.
1938	March 2–13	Trial of Bukharin, Rykov, Krestinsky and others.
1938	September	Munich Pact.
1938	December	Yezhov dismissed, and replaced by Beria.
1939	March 10	The Eighteenth Congress opens, the last until 1952.
1939	August 23	Ribbentrop in Moscow. Stalin-Hitler Pact.
1939	September 1	German Army marches into Poland.
1939	September 17	Red Army marches into Poland.
1939	November 30– March 12, 1940	Soviet-Finnish War.

1939	December 21	Stalin receives birthday congratulations from Hitler.
1940	August 20	Trotsky assassinated.
1941	June 22	Germany attacks Russia.
1941	July 3	Stalin makes his first public statement on the war.
1941	July 19	Stalin appointed Commissar for Defence and Supreme Commander.
1941	July 30–31	Harry Hopkins in Moscow.
1941	September 20	Germans capture Kiev.
1941	September 28	Averell Harriman and Lord Beaverbrook in Moscow.
1941	October 10	Stalin proclaims state of siege in Moscow.
1941	October–January 1942	Battle of Moscow.
1941	November 6	Stalin speaks in Mayakovsky subway station.
1941	December 7	Pearl Harbour.
1942	July–February 1943	Battle of Stalingrad.
1942	August	Churchill in Moscow.
1942	November 7	Sergey, Patriarch of Moscow, praises Stalin.
1943	March 6	Stalin becomes Marshal of the Soviet Union.
1943	July–August	Battle of Kursk.
1943	October 19–30	Moscow Conference of Foreign Ministers of USSR, Great Britain, and USA.
1943	November 6	Soviet troops liberate Kiev.
1943	November 28–December 1	Teheran Conference.
1944	March 4–May 9	Soviet spring offensive.
1944	June 5	Allied invasion of France.
1944	July 17	March of 57,000 German prisoners through Moscow.
1944	July 29	Stalin awarded Order of Victory.
1944	August 31	Soviet troops enter Budapest.
1945	February 4–12	Yalta Conference.
1945	April 12	Death of President Roosevelt.
1945	April 30	Suicide of Hitler.

1945	May 2	Soviet troops capture Berlin.
1945	May 24	Victory celebrations in St George's Hall in the Kremlin.
1945	June 24	Victory parade in Moscow.
1945	June 26	Stalin awarded the title of Hero of the Soviet Union.
1945	July 16	First atomic explosion at Alamogordo, New Mexico.
1945	July 17– August 2	Potsdam Conference.
1947	September	Constitution of Cominform.
1948	March 27	Tito receives abusive letter from Stalin.
1948	June	Stalin breaks with Tito.
1949	March	Execution of Voznesensky.
1949	December 16	Mao Tse-tung arrives in Moscow.
1950	January	Stalin orders restoration of death penalty.
1950	June 22–July 28	Stalin's letters to *Pravda* on linguistics.
1952	October 5	Nineteenth Party Congress opens.
1953	February 8	Stalin gives interview to Leopoldo Bravo.
1953	February 10?	Death of Mekhlis.
1953	February 12	USSR breaks relations with Israel.
1953	February 17	Stalin gives interviews to Dr Kitchliu and Mr K. P. S. Menon.
1953	March 5	Official date of Stalin's death.
1953	March 9	Funeral of Stalin.
1961	October 31	Reburial of Stalin.

ACKNOWLEDGEMENTS

So many people have helped in the writing of this book that it is scarcely possible to name them all. The generosity of scholars is always heartening, and never more heartening than to the author of a long and laborious work, who must consult them at every turn.

I owe a great debt to Professor Alexis Shcherbatov of Fairleigh Dickinson University, who patiently discussed with me the progress of the work in all its stages, and to Professor George Nakashidze of Columbia University, who gave me the benefit of his knowledge of Georgian culture and civilization, and translated the three poems of Stalin included in the book. I am deeply grateful, too, to Dr David Marshall Lang of the School of Oriental and African Studies, University of London, who helped me to track down the original Georgian texts of the poems, and found for me an edition of Kasbeki's works which includes the story from which Stalin derived his pseudonym of Koba. Mr David Vachnadze rendered important assistance in elucidating some textual problems connected with the poems, and Mr George Gamkrelidse kindly set up two of the poems on his private printing press. This was especially useful because they could not otherwise have been reproduced.

Dr Alexandra Adler and Dr Robert H. Orth gently guided me through a number of medical problems. Dr Adler helped me especially with the medical bulletins and communiqués, and was no less helpful in her suggestions concerning the psychological forces working on Stalin. Dr Orth carefully examined the evidence concerning Stalin's withered arm, and generously gave me the benefit of his long professional experience.

To Mr Joseph Carter, bookman extraordinary and perennial student of Marxism, I am grateful for help in tracking down rare books. I would never have found, or even known about, Stalin's *Speeches on the American Communist Party* without his assistance.

To Dr Alexander Kerensky I owe more than I can say. Many conversations with the youthful giant helped me to feel my way through the year 1917, and as always he was wise and generous in his counsels. As the sole survivor among those who wielded power in that year of many nightmares, he lends grace to our own age of nightmares; and being with him was to know that nightmares can have an end.

Finally I owe a special debt to Mr Michael V. Korda, who perfectly fulfilled the functions of an editor by not changing a word of the text, while in all other matters offering his kindly and unstinted assistance.

INDEX

THE LIFE AND DEATH OF
LENIN
ROBERT PAYNE   15/-

Lenin reached a position of towering eminence
in world history. But does the legend bear
any relation to the man? What was he like as
a young boy, what were his hopes, his loves?
And what of the tragedy of his fall from power?
Robert Payne's book is a searching portrait
and a memorable biography.

'Mr Payne does magnificent work with fascinating
material, the perfect combination.' *Scotsman*

'There is a great deal about Lenin the man—
his bicycle rides, his love affairs, his fondness
for washing up. It all adds up to a vivid and
colourful story.' *Spectator*

KING GEORGE V 15/-
HAROLD NICOLSON

'This is a beautifully written biography, a
limpid, dignified and continually fascinating
account of the life and service to his peoples
of one of the best of Britain's long,
long line of kings.' *Evening News*

'So well proportioned and composed that it
will surely rank as a classic of its kind . . .
in no other country could such a frank,
if sympathetic, record have been published.'
Spectator

'Towers head and shoulders above most
contemporary English biography, as well as
dwarfing all previous efforts in its particular,
royal field . . . *Times Literary Supplement*

VICTORIA R.I. 15/-
ELIZABETH LONGFORD

'A wonderfully vivid portrait, built up with
skill from massive research and
presented with a beguiling artistry.'
C. V. Wedgwood

'Absorbing . . . easily the best life of
Victoria that has yet appeared.'
Dr. J. H. Plumb *of Cambridge University,
writing in the New York Times*

'VICTORIA R.I. is a work of profound
scholarship.'
Robert Pitman, *Sunday Express*

'Scholarly yet racily readable,
witty yet wise.'
James Pope-Hennessy, *Sunday Times*

A SELECTION OF
POPULAR READING IN PAN

**Obtainable from all booksellers and newsagents. If you
have any difficulty, please send purchase price plus 6d.
postage to PO Box 11, Falmouth, Cornwall.**

**I enclose a cheque/postal order for selected titles ticked
above plus 6d. per book to cover packing and postage.**

NAME --

ADDRESS ---
